W9-CMJ-733

A POPE
— *and* —
A PRESIDENT

A POPE
— *and* —
A PRESIDENT

John Paul II, Ronald Reagan, and the
Extraordinary Untold Story of the 20th Century

PAUL KENGOR

Wilmington, Delaware

Second printing, June 2017

Library of Congress Cataloging-in-Publication Data

Names: Kengor, Paul, 1966- author.
Title: A pope and a president : John Paul II, Ronald Reagan, and the extraordinary untold story of the 20th century / Paul Kengor.
Description: Wilmington, Delaware : ISI Books, [2017] | Includes bibliographical references and index.
Identifiers: LCCN 2017011792 | ISBN 9781610171434 (hardcover)
Subjects: LCSH: Reagan, Ronald. | John Paul II, Pope, 1920-2005. | Reagan, Ronald—Political and social views. | John Paul II, Pope, 1920-2005—Political and social views. | Presidents—United States—Biography. | Popes—Biography. | Anti communist movements—History. | United States—Foreign relations—Soviet Union. | Soviet Union—Foreign relations—United States. | World politics—1945-1989. | BISAC: HISTORY / Modern / 20th Century. | POLITICAL SCIENCE / Political Ideologies / Communism & Socialism. | POLITICAL SCIENCE / International Relations / General.
Classification: LCC E877.2 .K47 2017 | DDC 327.73047—dc23 LC record available at https://lccn.loc.gov/2017011792

Published in the United States by

ISI Books
Intercollegiate Studies Institute
3901 Centerville Road
Wilmington, Delaware 19807-1938
www.isibooks.org

Manufactured in the United States of America

To the memory of Bill Clark,
for the greater honor and glory,
and for the "DP"

"Every human being [is] unique and unrepeatable."
—Pope John Paul II, Christmas Day 1978

"There is purpose and worth to each and every life."
—Ronald Reagan, November 4, 1991

Contents

Prologue

MAY 13, 1981

MOSCOW TAKES ITS SHOT

On May 13, 1981, sixty-year-old Pope John Paul II, two and a half years into an already historic papacy, hopped into his open-air vehicle to ride through Saint Peter's Square and greet the ecstatic crowd. Thousands from all over the world had gathered for the pontiff's weekly public audience: American and Italian, Chinese and German, English and African—Turkish and Bulgarian.[1]

It was a beautiful Wednesday in Rome. It was also a special day spiritually. May 13 was the Feast Day of Our Lady of Fátima, harkening back to the day in 1917 that began a series of remarkable events connected to the Virgin Mary, to whom this pope had dedicated his life and papacy.

The fact that this pontiff was Polish had alone made his papacy historic. When Karol Wojtyła was chosen the 264th heir to the chair of Saint Peter in October 1978, the Polish cardinal was the first non-Italian pope in 455 years and the first Slavic pope ever. More powerful still, his native Poland was the heart of the Communist Bloc in Eastern Europe, and the one spot in the Soviet atheistic empire—which the American president would unforgettably call an "Evil Empire"—where the communist war on religion had failed.

"If you choose the example of what we Poles have in our pockets and in our shops... communism has done very little for us," said Lech Wałęsa, the hero of Poland's anti-Soviet Solidarity movement, and one of millions of Poles whose admiration of John Paul II bordered on veneration. "But if you choose the example of what is in our souls, I answer that communism has done very much for us. In fact our souls contain exactly the opposite of what they wanted. They wanted us not to believe in God, and our churches are full."[2] These were powerful words that Wałęsa's favorite American president, Ronald Reagan, would invoke as an indictment of the Moscow menace.[3]

The Poles' fidelity to the Church rather than to Moscow angered communist authorities; the stunning selection of this Polish pope made them even angrier. In the 1970s, under the détente presidencies of Richard Nixon, Gerald Ford, and Jimmy Carter and the *Ostpolitik* papacy of Pope Paul VI, the Soviets picked up nearly a dozen satellite states around the world. These were major Cold War victories.

Then the Vatican conclave chose the Polish pope. The advent of this pontiff threatened the Soviets' global ambitions, particularly when paired with the new leadership that came to Washington under President Reagan two years later. With characteristic vitriol, one Soviet publication in early 1981 denounced John Paul II as "malicious, lowly, perfidious, and backward" and as a "toady of the American militarists" who was seeking to undermine communism with his "overseas accomplices" and "new boss in the White House."[4]

That was Moscow's take on this future saint and his emerging partner in the Oval Office. But these leaders were not "accomplices," and neither was the other's "boss." Their relationship would be a partnership of equals.

Make no mistake: Pope John Paul II and President Ronald Reagan scared the Kremlin. And with good reason. The pope implored his people to choose God's side over what the Protestant Reagan and the Roman Catholic Church both called "godless communism." The Soviets dubbed Reagan "The Crusader."[5]

Soviet officials knew that this Polish pontiff was a grave affront to their existence. They wanted him dead. And now, on May 13, 1981, two and a half years into his papacy, they were ready to take their shot.

CONSPIRATORS

Carrying out this evil plan was a cabal of plotters primarily from Muslim Turkey and communist Bulgaria. Not since the First World War had Turks and Bulgarians found a way to overcome bitter differences and partner for the cause of murder and mayhem. In World War I, the partnership meant unprecedented death, precipitating the appearance of a Lady in Fátima. Back then, too, the Turks and Bulgarians had the support of the Bolsheviks—all of them violently confronted Czarist-Christian Russia. Now there was common ground again: the Bolsheviks, the Bulgarians, and the Turks all violently confronted the Slavic-Christian man in Rome.

Mehmet Ali Agca of Turkey had been commissioned to deliver a fatal blow. Later he would name seven accomplices, all working under a plan conceived by the Bulgarian secret service, one of the communist world's most restrictive intelligence services, and the one most subject to Moscow's control.[6]

At 9 a.m. on May 13, Agca gathered with his collaborators. The driver was a Bulgarian named Zelio Vasilev. He gave instructions to Agca and his Turkish friend Oral Çelik, telling them that Sergei Antonov, another Bulgarian conspirator, would help them escape after they finished their bloody assignment. Antonov, according to the plan, would whisk away the assassins to a large delivery truck concealed as a Bulgarian household-goods company, a front for the communist state's secret service. At 10 a.m., the Bulgarians drove off, leaving the Turks.[7]

The Turks would wait a while. At 3 p.m. Antonov reconnected with Agca and Çelik in the Piazza della Repubblica. He was driving a blue sports car. With him was another Bulgarian, Todor Aivazov. They handed the Turks two packages, one with a 9-millimeter handgun and the other with a panic bomb to scatter the crowd after the shooting and facilitate their escape.[8]

The four men made their way toward the Vatican, arriving at 4 o'clock. Agca and Çelik took their positions among a crowd of faithful seeking repentance and reconciliation. Reports on the precise plan of action vary, but it seems Agca was supposed to fire all or most of the shots, with Çelik perhaps firing if necessary but at the least setting off the panic bomb.[9]

The Polish pontiff came out in his small, white Fiat "Popemobile," waving to the excited gathering, grabbing hands and giving kisses, lifting children in his arms, smiling joyously.

As John Paul II's vehicle moved slowly along, the twenty-three-year-old Agca anxiously clutched his concealed 9-millimeter semiautomatic. It was well after 5 P.M. before the pope finally came within a few yards of Agca. The pope's vehicle passed the ancient obelisk in the center of Saint Peter's Square. Two millennia earlier, Peter himself would have passed the same obelisk on his way to his execution at the hands of the enemies of Christ's Church.[10]

As John Paul II edged closer, the Turkish national lifted his pistol. Loud cracks of gunfire filled the air. Four shots were fired, two of which hit the pope, one in the left hand and another in the abdomen.[11]

It was roughly quarter past the hour, a time that some have pinpointed as 5:13 P.M.—when the numbers on the clock stood in perfect harmony with the numbers on the calendar on this Feast Day of Our Lady of Fátima.[12]

The strong, physically fit pope folded and collapsed, his white figure sinking into the arms of his aides. Cradling his sagging frame were his loyal Polish secretary, Father Stanisław Dziwisz, and his personal assistant, Angelo Gugel.

"Mary, my mother; Mary, my mother," said John Paul II, who had lost his earthly mother as a child. "Hail Mary, full of grace, the Lord is with thee," he prayed, imploring the mother of Christ for her intercession at the heavenly throne of the Lord, the Lord she had watched be murdered by executioners. "Pray for us sinners, now and at the hour of our death. Amen."

"IT WAS YOU!"

After the gunshots were fired, Oral Çelik fled the scene in panic, failing to ignite his diversionary bomb. He would not be seen again.

Gunman Mehmet Ali Agca tried to flee as well. Here was a veteran terrorist who, in the words of the Italian judge who later prosecuted him, harbored "a natural vocation for crime" and was an "exceptionally gifted killer used for exceptional assignments and paid accordingly." But this paid assassin, a menacing and calculating figure, was nabbed—by a nun.

Sister Letizia, a sturdy and resourceful Franciscan nun from the Italian city of Bergamo, grabbed Agca, and a Vatican security official and bystanders soon joined her in subduing the would-be assassin. "Why did you do it?" the nun asked the shooter. Agca lied: "Not me! Not me!" She responded sternly, "Yes, you! It was you!" as Agca struggled to break her grip.[13]

Agca had been apprehended, but he was safer than he realized in the clutch of Sister Letizia. Unbeknownst to Agca, his own life was in as much danger as the pontiff's: his communist friends were intending to murder him as soon as he got away from Saint Peter's Square.[14] It was part of their plan.

It was how communists did things. It was how they valued life.

THE SOVIET CONNECTION, REVEALED

The fallen pope was rushed into an ambulance that sped through the interior of the Vatican to Porta Sant'Anna, the Port of Saint Anne, a side gate named for the mother of the Virgin Mary. From there, the ambulance headed straight for Gemelli Hospital, the teaching hospital of the Catholic University of the Sacred Heart. It was one of Rome's best hospitals, only four miles away, though traffic was almost impassable. Providentially, a Gemelli physician just happened to be nearby and jumped inside the ambulance.

Back in Saint Peter's Square, the shocked faithful listened as the loudspeaker delivered a message in Italian, English, French, Chinese, and several other languages: "The Holy Father has been wounded. We will now offer prayers for him." The assembled did just that, amid tears. The flock sang. A Polish hymn played over the loudspeaker.[15]

John Paul II was barely conscious when he got to the hospital. "How could they do it?" he asked a nurse before losing consciousness.[16] Who he meant by "they" was not specified. But this Polish pontiff, Public Enemy No. 1 to the communist empire, apparently had a hunch.

His first word to Dziwisz, who had lost himself in intense prayer to "the hands of God" and to the intercession of "Our Lady," was a whispered "Thirsty," reminiscent of the suffering Christ's words of agony on the cross. Then the pope added: "Just like Bachelet." This was a reference to Vittorio Bachelet, a Catholic politician murdered by Italian Red Brigade communists the year before.[17]

The pope was badly hurt. He underwent five and a half hours of emergency surgery, hemorrhaging much worse than anyone knew at the time. In this and other ways, he was mirroring what had happened to Ronald Reagan just six weeks earlier, when a gunman tried to take the new president's life. John Paul suffered a severe loss of blood, requiring a transfusion of six pints. Sections of his mangled intestine were removed. He had watched his dearest friends, some of them fellow Polish priests, die from Nazi bullets and Soviet bullets. Was it now his turn, too, for a martyr's death? And who, ultimately, was responsible for the bullet?

At that moment, only Agca's involvement was known. That would remain the case for weeks, even years. In fact, to this day many observers insist that *only* Agca's role can be confirmed.

But at the time and ever since, many suspected that Moscow was behind the assassination attempt. A few years after the shooting, Agca fingered the Bulgarians as his accomplices. Agca's claim only intensified suspicion that Moscow was involved. As the pope's friends in the Reagan White House could eagerly attest, Bulgaria's secret service was a dutiful stooge of the Soviet KGB (political intelligence) and GRU (military intelligence). Bulgaria's loyal party apparatchiks did practically everything with the supreme comradely confidence of the USSR. It is difficult to conceive that they would attempt a major assassination without Moscow's go-ahead, if not full participation.

Early on, Italian investigators began gathering critical information that appeared to trace the crime to the Kremlin. Many eyes looked in the direction of the KGB. Both Bulgaria and Russia adamantly denied any such accusations and condemned the claims of Italian judges.

A quarter century after the assassination attempt, an Italian commission brought us close to the truth. That commission had access to tens of thousands of pages of documents that Italian investigators had collected, plus some twenty-five thousand highly classified Soviet documents that a KGB archivist had smuggled out of Moscow in 1992. All those documents provide vital evidence not available until years after the shooting.

Yet there is one last piece of this puzzle that has never been reported.

This book will affirm what many have suspected: the Soviets ordered the attempted assassination of Pope John Paul II. The crime is traceable to Moscow—but not, it turns out, to the KGB.

What has not been known—until this book—is that the CIA director under Ronald Reagan secretly investigated the case and discovered the Soviet role. William J. Casey suspected Moscow to the point that he ordered an extremely sensitive CIA investigation known only to a few highly trusted individuals, many of whom took to the grave their knowledge of what really happened that May 13. That investigation, conducted by a tight-knit group under Casey's command, concluded that the GRU had ordered the assassination.

Four years after the shooting, President Reagan learned what had transpired in the lead-up to May 13, 1981. He was informed by Casey alone, just the two of them in the room. The information was so explosive that the report and its dramatic conclusion have never been released or even acknowledged. To this day, it remains the most secret report of the Cold War.

Keep in mind the context: Tensions in the Cold War had never run higher. The Soviets had been on the advance in the 1970s, but now President Reagan and his partner in the Vatican were standing up to the threat of Soviet communism. The 1980s intensified fears of World War III between two nuclear-armed superpowers. Now imagine if news broke that the U.S. government had discovered a Soviet-orchestrated assassination attempt on the leader of the world's largest religion, who was a voice for those suffering under Soviet communism.

One source with knowledge of the report told me, "I've never, ever, in all my years, seen anything as secretive as that document." Speaking of those privileged few who had seen it, most of whom are now deceased, the source added jokingly, "This was so classified that they nearly shot the secretary who typed it." Few reports, if any, have been so thoroughly kept from view.

"That report exists," I have been assured. "If someone can find it, you've got the most explosive report of the twentieth century."

I have searched tirelessly for the report, examining numerous archives and pursuing many other avenues. I have not found the document, but I know its conclusion, based on eyewitness accounts that high-level sources gave me. I hope this book compels action that leads to the release of the report.

THE BOND

Over the past quarter century, historians have increasingly given President Ronald Reagan and Pope John Paul II due credit for their roles in ending the Cold War. But despite the fine work of previous chroniclers,[18] few appreciate the depth or significance of the bond between the president and the pope. That bond drove the two men to confront and ultimately defeat what they knew to be the great evil of the twentieth century: Soviet communism.

The bond between Reagan and John Paul II began forming well before they met. In June 1979, candidate Reagan was moved to tears as he watched news footage of the pontiff's first trip to his homeland.[19] The excited Polish crowds thronging the pope spoke not simply to pride in a native son but also to the enduring religious faith and yearning for freedom behind the Soviets' Iron Curtain. Reagan resolved that as president he would reach out to the pope and the Vatican and "make them an ally."[20]

Nothing intensified the bond as much as the assassination attempts, which occurred only six weeks apart in the spring of 1981. Each man was shocked upon receiving news that the other had been shot. Reagan, still recovering from his own wounds, was so stricken by the news of the attempt on the pope's life that every day for weeks he would ask his national security adviser, Richard V. Allen, for updates on John Paul II's health. The president had a message delivered directly to the pontiff, saying that he "happily" joined him in their "dubious distinction" of surviving assassins' bullets.

The Soviets had worried about an anticommunist, anti-Moscow kinship between the president and the pope. Now, in the space of just weeks, these two men suffered assassination attempts and strikingly similar near-death experiences. The experiences—a unique shared suffering and sacrifice—brought them much closer together.

That connection became apparent when Reagan and John Paul II met for the first time, in June 1982. There, in the Vatican, the president and pope confided their conviction that God had spared their lives a year earlier for the divine purpose of defeating the communist empire.

This book will explore that June 1982 meeting and many other aspects of the partnership between Reagan and John Paul II. It is important to understand the character of their relationship. This book does not suggest that the two men were painstakingly coordinating, day in and day out, their tactical efforts to take down an atheistic empire. But their partnership must not be underestimated, either. As this book will show, the two leaders had common goals, visions, and motivations, and they eagerly worked together where and when they could, with much mutual support and respect. The extent of their communications, including telegrams, phone calls, and private meetings, will surprise some readers.

Just as important, the former Hollywood actor and the Polish priest shared rather remarkable similarities. This book will examine another surprising but crucial element of the story: the deep spiritual bond between the Protestant president and the Catholic pope. Inspired by that bond, they worked together toward a grand objective, one that would benefit people of all stripes, religious or not, from East to West: to take down communism.

Reagan's single most trusted aide throughout his political career was William P. Clark, who succeeded Dick Allen as national security adviser in 1982. Clark was Reagan's closest adviser on fighting the Cold War. A devout Catholic, he often discussed spiritual matters with Reagan. The two of them privately spoke of the "DP": the "Divine Plan" to defeat communism.

Reagan and John Paul II saw God's hand not only in their own roles but also in that of Mikhail Gorbachev, who became the Soviet general secretary in 1985. The final Soviet leader consistently perplexed and attracted Reagan and the pope. Gorbachev's political and spiritual journey remains a complicated subject, with details that have eluded public knowledge. It contains more than a few faith-based elements, beginning with Gorbachev's secret baptism in the Stalin era by his Orthodox mother and grandmothers. Reagan and John Paul II hoped and prayed that the new Soviet leader was a "closet Christian" rescuing an officially atheistic state. A Protestant, a Catholic, and perhaps a man of the Orthodox Church—all part of the DP.

Perhaps the most surprising part of this story relates to Reagan's fascination with the "secrets of Fátima," which date to the reported apparitions of the Virgin Mary in Fátima, Portugal, starting on May 13, 1917—sixty-four years to the day before the attempt on John Paul II's life.

It is hardly news that the pope connected the shooting and many of communism's crimes to the events of 1917. What is new is that the Protestant Reagan, who had a fondness and appreciation for the Virgin Mary, developed an intense interest in Mary's appearance at Fátima and the suggested connections to the Soviet Union, the Cold War, and the shooting of the pope. Reagan discussed the matter with close aides and perhaps even with the pope himself, who was devoted to the Blessed Virgin.

And so this story begins not in 1981 but on May 13, 1917.

Part 1

WARNINGS AND BEGINNINGS

1

MAY 13, 1917

AN ECHO

The sounds of the bullets that pierced the afternoon air of Saint Peter's Square on May 13, 1981, were an echo of a message that began resounding sixty-four years earlier, on May 13, 1917. The message was said to have come from Mary, the mother of Christ.

Before we go any further, an explanation is in order. This book is a work of historical investigation, not a religious apologetic. Given that, it may seem odd to examine the role of the Virgin Mary in crucial events of the twentieth century. To some readers it will be off-putting. But I ask you to stick with me, even if you do not believe in the supernatural or are a religious person skeptical of Catholic claims of Marian apparitions. The fact is that many of the figures in this book believed devoutly in what I am about to share. They believed that these forces underlay important political and historical developments. John Paul II, in particular, connected the appearance of the Virgin Mary at Fátima to his attempted assassination and to the crimes of communism. Non-Catholics like Ronald Reagan lent their ear to this account.

And so the Virgin Mary features prominently in this book for the simple reason that key players saw her as being significant to how the long story of communism played out. This book does not seek to convince you of the Marian connection. The point is that you must understand the role the "secrets of Fátima" played in the thought of John Paul II and Ronald Reagan to gain a full understanding of how the special relationship between the pope and the president changed world history.

I am reporting nothing new when I say that John Paul paid special heed to Our Lady of Fátima. He consecrated himself and his papacy to the Virgin Mary, because doing so brought him closer to her divine Son and His will. "Her mediation," John Paul wrote in his classic encyclical on Mary, *Redemptoris Mater*, comes "in the nature of intercession." The pope argued that the Church had "great trust" in Mary, just as God himself, the Eternal Father, had trusted the Virgin of Nazareth, giving her his only begotten Son. That is why Karol Wojtyła entrusted himself to the Virgin Mary, the "God-bearer," for her "special and exceptional mediation."[1] The sainted pontiff's papal motto was "Totus Tuus," which is Latin for "Totally Yours," meaning totally Mary's, and totally Jesus's via Mary. In a 2003 Angelus address, the pope affirmed his commitment to "entrusting everything" to Mary. He stated unhesitatingly that the Blessed Virgin "directs our daily journey on earth" and makes comprehensible "certain events" in "human history." Her hand helped him comprehend events from 1917 to 1981, from his first to his final days on earth.[2]

But if this Marian dedication to Jesus is something we have long known about John Paul II, we have not known the interest Ronald Reagan had in the Virgin Mary. In 2004 I published a bestselling book on the faith of Ronald Reagan without knowing the intriguing Marian element to his thinking. I learned it only later.

The story begins a century ago, in 1917.

THE THREE SECRETS OF FÁTIMA

Between May 13 and October 13, 1917, three children in a tiny Portuguese village called Fátima claimed to have had six encounters with the Virgin Mary—with the actual spiritual-physical presence of the Mother of Christ. Through the centuries innumerable faithful have claimed encounters with Mary, but it is rare for the Roman Catholic Church even to investigate such claims, and far rarer still for the Church to certify them. The Church approaches claims of apparitions with a prudential skepticism that would surprise a Richard Dawkins or the late Christopher Hitchens. Of nearly four hundred serious claims of Marian apparitions in the twentieth century, in less than a dozen instances the Church gingerly concluded that some supernatural character was apparent.[3] Non-Catholics cannot conceive of the frustration many Catholics feel over the Church's delay or rejection of this or that perceived appearance that a large number of Catholics are convinced is genuine.[4]

Fátima is one of the few approved apparitions, having survived the highest level of rigor. The three children who claimed that the Virgin Mary appeared to them faced a barrage of interrogations, often cruel, and sometimes by outright hostile clergy. Thousands of eyewitnesses offered testimony in support of the claims. No less an authority than Cardinal Tarcisio Bertone, who as Vatican secretary of state was the second highest-ranking official, behind only the pope, said that "what happened at Fátima has been studied, microscopically scrutinized, and thoroughly analyzed."[5]

That is why John Paul II and so many others accorded these events the utmost seriousness.

The three children, Lúcia dos Santos and her younger cousins Jacinta and Francisco Marto, said that Mary first appeared to them on May 13, 1917, a Sunday. At the time, May 13 was the Catholic Church's liturgical celebration of Our Lady of the Most Blessed Sacrament—that is, Mother of the ongoing Real Presence of Jesus in the world. Only eight days earlier, on May 5, Pope Benedict XV had made a direct appeal to Mary to intercede in ending the Great War, which would claim some seventeen million lives.

The three children had gone to Mass before taking their flock of sheep to a spot outside the village called the Cova da Iria, which means "Cove of Irene" or "Cove of Peace." They ate their lunches and played. It was a beautiful afternoon, but then they saw a flash of lightning. Turning to head home to escape what they thought was an impending storm, they saw another flash. This time they were shaken by the sudden manifestation of a lady in white, whom Lúcia later described as "more brilliant than the sun," radiating a "clear and intense" light. The most radiant light of all emanated from a crucifix on a rosary the Lady held, a rosary with beads glimmering like stars. Lúcia later estimated the young woman's age to be about seventeen.[6]

Sensing the trepidation among the children, the Lady repeated the words that a startled earthly Mary had received from the Angel Gabriel. "Do not be afraid," she told them.

Lúcia, at age ten the oldest of the three children, was the only one who communicated with the Lady. "Where are you from?" Lúcia asked. The woman answered, "I am from heaven." The girl then asked what she wanted; the Lady replied that she wanted the children to come to the same spot on the thirteenth day of each month for six consecutive months. "Later," she vowed, "I will tell you who I am and what I want."[7]

On that May 13, Mary asked the children whether they were willing to endure the trials that lay ahead, the divine plan that God had in store. Were they willing to suffer as sacrifice and in reparation for the sins of the world that were offending Him? If so, would they provide supplication in a way that would convert sinners? The children gave their assent.

During each of the next five months, typically on the thirteenth day, the Lady returned. On June 13 she told the children something they must have struggled to assimilate: she said that Jesus Christ wanted the world to make special devotion to the Immaculate Heart of Mary, which had pumped blood into His earthly body as it formed in the womb. On July 13 the Blessed Lady gave the children a vision of hell. As she did, the children were allegedly infused with a protective grace that enabled them to observe the vision without being so terrified as to perish at the sight.

More than that, the Lady provided predictions. According to Lúcia, the Blessed Mother delivered three dramatic prophecies:

First, the Lady of Fátima predicted that the earthly hell of the Great War would soon end but would be followed by an even deadlier war.

Second, she warned about the coming eruption of atheistic communism: "Russia will spread its errors throughout the world," said the Lady, "raising up wars and persecutions of the Church" in the century ahead. Russia would be an "instrument of chastisement." She reportedly shared this prophecy on July 13, only three months before the Bolsheviks shocked the world by taking power in Russia. Over the next several decades, Lenin and his disciples fulfilled the warning of "wars and persecutions" and "chastisement."

Thus, this book will explore not only the extraordinary events that Ronald Reagan and John Paul II faced but also the crimes and errors that the communists committed throughout the twentieth century. Communism made victims of priests, cardinals, bishops, reverends, nuns, rabbis,

Buddhist monks, and Muslim imams, and also of leaders like John F. Kennedy, Pope Pius XII, Aleksandr Solzhenitsyn, Lech Wałęsa, and Pope John Paul II. It is crucial to understand this history of communist "persecutions" and "errors" to grasp why both Pope John Paul II and Ronald Reagan saw communism as the great evil of the twentieth century and came together to confront it.

What was the third secret of Fátima? As we shall see, the Vatican sealed that secret in a vault, where it stayed for the remainder of the long century. Some feared it predicted a third world war, or Armageddon. It turns out that it envisioned another communist crime: the assassination, or at least an attempted assassination, of a man robed and hatted in white—that is, a pope.[8]

The Lady also told Lúcia that her two cousins would be leaving this world "soon," whereas Lúcia was to "stay here some time longer." Both Jacinta and Francisco died within three years, victims of the influenza epidemic that followed the war. Lúcia did live longer—to the age of ninety-seven, in fact, long enough to see the three predictions come true. As an adult—by which point she was Sister Lúcia, a Carmelite nun—she would record the three secrets in writing.

THE MIRACLE OF THE CENTURY

The last of the Virgin Mary's six alleged apparitions in Fátima occurred just a week and a half before the outbreak of the Bolshevik Revolution.[9]

What materialized on October 13, 1917, became the most significant Church-approved miracle of the century. Some enthusiasts among the Catholic brethren contend that it was the greatest supernatural feat since the Resurrection.

A miracle, by its nature, is hard to believe; it's a miracle, after all. But it is imperative to recall the rigorous, skeptical approach that the Roman Catholic Church takes to investigating reports of Marian apparitions. And after having "microscopically scrutinized and thoroughly analyzed" the Fátima case (in Cardinal Bertone's words), the Church concluded that something miraculous transpired in that tiny Portuguese village.

On October 13 a crowd of some seventy thousand, pilgrims and skeptics alike, descended on Fátima. Lúcia, Jacinta, and Francisco had told people to expect a miracle, and word had gotten around. Some four thousand people had been present for the July 13 visitation and twenty-five thousand for the September 13 appearance, though only the children could see and communicate with the Lady. Now there were so many more because the Lady had promised a miracle for all to see in October.

It had rained all morning. Throughout the dreary day, the throng was getting antsy, angry. Where was this miracle? Surely this was a hoax. How could these mere children mislead so many?

Then something suddenly changed. The children became locked in, fixated, staring upward. Something was there, communicating to them. Fulfilling her July 13 promise to Lúcia that she would eventually reveal her true identity, the mystical woman told the children, "I am the Lady of the Rosary." Reiterating what she had said earlier, she told them that the current war would end soon, with fathers returning from the frontlines. She urged reparation and penance.

Then came what everyone was waiting for. As Lúcia later described it, the Lady of the Rosary opened her hands and "made them reflect on the sun, and as she ascended, the reflection of her own light continued to be projected on the sun itself." Lúcia cried out to the gathered to look at the sun.

Two unbelievable things happened. The three children watched the Lady vanish "into the immense distance of the firmament" (as Lúcia later explained it), only to behold in the sky Saint Joseph with the Child Jesus aside the Lady robed in white with a blue mantle. It was the Holy Family. The Christ child and His earthly father traced the Sign of the Cross with their elevated hands as if to bless the world.[10]

This was surreal enough, but as the three children were mesmerized, the stunned thousands were felled by another spectacle altogether: they saw the sun do incredible things, beyond scientific explanation.

THE WITNESSES

If the children had been the only witnesses, no one would remember the scene today. But what happened next was backed by the testimonies of those who were there.

Here are merely a few eyewitness accounts among the many collected and published. One witness was Dr. José Maria de Almeida Garrett, a professor in the Faculty of Sciences at the prestigious University of Coimbra, the oldest institution of higher education in Portugal. Dr. Garrett had gone to Fátima a skeptic, but what he witnessed changed his outlook. He recounted:

> It must have been 1:30 P.M.... The sky, which had been overcast all day, suddenly cleared; the rain stopped and it looked as if the sun were about to fill with light the countryside that the wintery morning had made so gloomy.... The sun, a few moments before, had broken through the thick layer of clouds which hid it and now shone clearly and intensely.
>
> Suddenly I heard the uproar of thousands of voices, and I saw the whole multitude spread out in that vast space at my feet...turn their backs to that spot where, until then, all their expectations had been focused, and look at the sun on the other side.

With all spectators shifting their gaze, Dr. Garrett did the same. He was amazed at what he watched unfold:

> I could see the sun, like a very clear disc, with its sharp edge, which gleamed without hurting the sight. It could not be confused with the sun seen through a fog (there was no fog at that moment), for it was neither veiled nor dim.... The most astonishing thing was to be able to stare at the solar disc for a long time, brilliant with light and heat, without hurting the eyes or damaging the retina. The sun's disc did not remain immobile, it had a giddy motion, not like the twinkling of a star in all its brilliance for it spun round upon itself in a mad whirl.
>
> During the solar phenomenon which I have just described, there were also changes of color in the atmosphere. Looking at the sun, I noticed that everything was becoming darkened. I looked first at the nearest objects and then extended my glance further afield as far as the horizon. I saw everything had assumed an amethyst color. Objects around me, the sky and the atmosphere, were of the same color....
>
> Then, suddenly, one heard a clamor, a cry of anguish breaking from all the people. The sun, whirling wildly, seemed all at once to loosen itself from the firmament and, blood red, advance threateningly upon the earth as if to crush us with its huge and fiery weight. The sensation during those moments was truly terrible.

As he recorded his account, the professor knew that he now would be among those that nonwitnesses would forever dismiss or disrespect. In affidavit-like language, he sought to assure future readers that he had not been overcome with madness or hysteria:

> All the phenomena which I have described were observed by me in a calm and serene state of mind without any emotional disturbance. It is for others to interpret and explain them. Finally, I must declare that never, before or after October 13 [1917], have I observed similar atmospheric or solar phenomena.[11]

As this testimony suggests, Garrett was no wailing zealot. He was a refined and respected scholar, the son of a prominent Portuguese family. Even as he witnessed something miraculous, he opted to describe it clinically, in the language of a scientist. Not given to hyperbole, he nonetheless saw and reported precisely what countless others attested.

Another hardened skeptic who offered an eyewitness account was Avelino de Almeida, editor in chief of *O Seculo*, an atheistic, anticlerical newspaper in Lisbon. Almeida had ventured to Fátima with the intent of mocking the wild expectations of the superstitious. He was shocked at what he encountered, which he shared in his newspaper:

> One could see the huge crowd turning toward the sun, which, standing at the zenith unobstructed by clouds, looked like a piece of opaque silver. One could gaze at it without the least difficulty. It could have been an eclipse, but all of a sudden there was a great cry, and the nearby spectators started shouting, "A miracle! A miracle!" Before the stupefied eyes of the people, who anxiously peered into the sky with uncovered heads like the multitudes described in the Bible, the sun trembled and darted this way and that. Its brusque movements, which were truly astonishing to behold, defied every known law of astronomy. The sun "danced," as the people typically put it.

The secular journalist recorded how the people scrambled to assimilate what they had just experienced:

> At that point, the witnesses began to ask one another what they had seen. The overwhelming majority claimed to have seen the sun tremble and dance. Others claimed to have seen the face of the Holy Virgin. Still others swore that the sun had spun on its axis like a giant windmill and that it had plummeted downwards as if to scorch the earth with its rays. A few said that they had seen it change several colors in succession.[12]

Another doubter was the reporter for *O Dia*, who likewise went to Fátima to debunk the mob's fanciful claims. Like *O Seculo*, *O Dia* was an anticlerical newspaper from Lisbon, the organ of choice for the intelligentsia. *O Dia*'s readers prided themselves in not smoking the opium of the masses. And yet here is how a chastened *O Dia* described what was unveiled at Fátima:

> The silver-colored sun... was seen to whirl and wheel about in the circle that had opened up among the clouds. The people all shouted in unison and then fell to their knees on the muddy ground.... The light took on a beautiful blue tint, as it does when it filters through a stained-glass window of a cathedral, and it spread over the people, who were kneeling with outstretched hands. As the blue color slowly faded, the light seemed to sweep across the yellow grass.... The people were weeping and praying with uncovered heads in the presence of the miracle for which they had hoped. Each second was so vivid that it seemed like an hour.[13]

These events lasted several minutes, and they were visible for miles around. The eyewitness testimonies cited here are just a few of many. In fact, as many as seventy-five thousand people witnessed the phenomena of October 13, 1917.[14] This was no mass illusion or group hallucination. The sheer volume of witnesses made such a deception impossible. Those witnesses talked, with their many testimonies captured at the time and available for us to read today.[15]

WHY 1917?

To modern eyes and ears a hundred years later, accounts of what happened at Fátima in 1917 can seem difficult to accept. I understand that. But again, what is important to this story is how these accounts influenced Pope John Paul II and Ronald Reagan and their understanding of the crimes of communism.

When we look at Fátima from that perspective, a few questions arise. First: Why would such a message be delivered at this particular time?

In 1917 the world was three years into the Great War. On June 28, 1914, in Sarajevo, Gavrilo Princip had set this conflict in motion with his shot heard 'round the world, which murdered the pious Austrian archduke and his wife.

On one side of the fight were the Allied Powers, including Russia, Britain, France, Japan, Italy, Belgium, Serbia, Romania, Greece, Portugal, and the United States, the last of which had entered the conflict only a month before the first Marian apparition at Fátima. On the other side were the Central Powers: Germany, Austria-Hungary, the Ottoman Turks, and Bulgaria. How odd it was that Bulgaria and Muslim Turkey, two unlikely allies who had battled one another as recently as the Balkan Wars (1912–13), would team up in this murderous mayhem. It would not be the last time. A Muslim Turk would work with Bulgaria to fire another shot heard 'round the world seven decades later.

The Great War brought with it the horrors of mechanized warfare: tanks, air power, submarines, machine guns with names like "the Devil's paintbrush," and poison gas, the largest-scale use of chemical weapons in history. Winding through this agony were death-strewn trenches: thousands of miles of wet, freezing, disease-ridden, lice- and rat-infested tunnels where men lived an awful existence below the earth. The condemned creatures arose from this pit only to be thrust into "no-man's-land" and enter the human meat grinder.

It was a war that Pope Benedict XV had publicly declared unjust. The pontiff judged that there was no compelling moral justification or imperative dividing the combatants; these countries should not have been on the battlefield.

An atheist-leftist intellectual named Sidney Hook might have best summed up the moral catastrophe when he referred to World War I not as the Great War, or the War to End All Wars, or, in President Woodrow Wilson's line, the war to "make the world safe for democracy," but as something considerably less inspiring: World War I was, said Hook, "the second fall of man."[16]

Yes, religious metaphor captures it best. The historian Michael Hull, who argues that "the horrors of World War I exceeded those of World War II in terms of the sheer futility of squandered lives,"[17] invokes *O Cristo das Trincheiras*, "The Christ of the Trenches," as an appropriate symbol for the millions who gave their lives in the war. This life-size statue of Jesus Christ on the cross was erected on the Western Front; Hull describes it as "soiled, bullet-scarred, its legs blown off by shellfire." Years after the war, the French gave it to the government of Portugal to memorialize the thousands of Portuguese killed at the Battle of Flanders. Today, the Christ of the Trenches looks down on the Tomb of the Portuguese Unknown Soldier at the Priory of Santa Maria da Vitoria (Saint Mary of Victory) in Batalha, Portugal.

This terrible war, this "Great War" in which no great moral issues seemed clear, not only produced millions of dead young men but also led to World War II and the Cold War. The "punitive peace" that the French imposed on the surrendering Germans at the Versailles Conference created the chaotic conditions in Germany that Hitler would exploit in his rise to power. As the British historian A. J. P. Taylor put it, "The first war explains the second and, in fact, caused it, in so far as one event causes another."[18]

The First World War also enabled the fall of Czar Nicholas II in Russia. The reasons for the czar's fall and the takeover by Lenin and his vicious minions are complex, but one thing is certain: it is difficult to imagine the Bolsheviks supplanting the Romanov dynasty if the Russians had not become embroiled in the Great War. The Russian army entered the war with the rest of the Allied Powers in August 1914 but did not finish the fight. Russia experienced more bloodshed than any other combatant, despite withdrawing from the conflict before its conclusion. The Russian economy was devastated, a situation made all the worse by the fact that, having pulled out of the war, Russia would taste no fruits of victory.

More than anything, World War I unleashed death on the twentieth century. Many millions were killed in the Great War, but World War II would dwarf it in deaths, and the Soviet global communist ideology undergirding the Cold War would kill still more.

WHY PORTUGAL?

Another question arises: Why would the Marian apparition occur in Portugal? A few possibilities come to mind.

Portugal was first touched by Christianity some two thousand years ago, as Saint James, one of the original disciples, is said to have traversed its lands.

Many years later, in the eighth century, the Muslim Moors invaded the Iberian Peninsula and subdued the Portuguese and Spanish. Portugal fought back with a decisive victory over the Moors in the 1100s, becoming an independent nation around the year 1143. King Afonso I, Portugal's first king, secured the victory and gave thanks to the Blessed Virgin Mary. In gratitude, he constructed a glorious church and monastery called the Santa Maria de Alcobaça.

The Portuguese again turned to Mary's intercession when Spain came demanding territory. In 1385 they thwarted the Spanish. In gratitude to the Blessed Mother, King John I erected the cathedral at Batalha, Saint Mary of Victory.

These were just two of many times that Portugal turned to the Blessed Mother for her intervention before the throne of God. The country would long be known as the Land of Holy Mary, entrusting itself to her for intercession, intervention, protection, and patronage.

This became an even greater imperative for the Portuguese when they came under siege not from vandals at the gate but from inside. In the early 1900s, militant secularists toppled the Portuguese monarch and installed a repressive government that persecuted the Catholic Church specifically and religious people generally. It was one of the darkest periods in Portugal's long history. The new government implemented a series of anticlerical measures, culminating in the Law of Separation of Church and State in 1911. The architect of that law boasted that "in two generations Catholicism will be completely eliminated in Portugal."[19]

In short order, Pope Pius X, who three years later would anguish over his Church's inability to stop the continent from leaping into the Great War, issued a scathing encyclical condemning Portugal's Law of Separation, blasting it as "heinous," "absurd," and "monstrous," as an "incredible series of excesses and crimes... enacted in Portugal for the oppression of the Church." Why, asked Pius X, had the new government "promulgated measures breathing the most implacable hatred of the Catholic religion? We have seen religious communities evicted from their homes, and most of them driven beyond the Portuguese frontiers. We have seen, arising out of an obstinate determination to secularize every civil organization and to leave no trace of religion in the acts of common life, the deletion of the feast days of the Church from the number of public festivals, the abolition of religious oaths, the hasty establishment of the law of divorce and religious instruction banished from the public schools."[20]

Pope Pius X gave his statement from Saint Peter's Basilica in Rome on May 24, 1911, the Feast of Our Lady Mary. He closed by invoking the intercession of Mary, "the Help of Christians."

The persecution in Portugal was a forerunner of the far more repressive and vile attacks Soviet communism unleashed in October 1917, after the appearances at Fátima. Against those attacks, too, the Church would seek Mary's intercession.

WHY FÁTIMA?

Still, a question remains: Why the tiny village of Fátima, of all places?

The village was given its name during the Moorish occupation. The name is an Islamic one derived from the much-loved princess of the nearby Castle of Ourem. Like many Muslim girls, the princess was named Fátima after the favorite daughter of Muhammad. Born to Muhammad's first wife, Khadijah, she stood at her father's side through his greatest turmoil. Muslims view her as an exemplar. She eventually married Ali ibn Abi Talib, Muhammad's cousin, and became mother to five of his children. Few men were so influential in Islam as Ali, who was a direct successor to Muhammad. Shiites regard him as the vaunted "First Imam." Fátima's spouse and father alone made her extremely influential.

In a quotation that could be apocryphal, Muhammad is alleged to have said of his beloved Fátima, "She has the highest place in heaven after the Virgin Mary."

Muhammad had a deep love for his daughter and the utmost respect for the Virgin Mary. Mary is the only woman mentioned in the Koran. No woman in the Koran is accorded her respect. Quite the contrary, Sura (chapter) 4 in the Koran, titled "Women," states, "Men have authority over women because God has made the one superior to the other" (4:34). It continues, "As for those [women] that you fear disobedience, admonish them, forsake them in beds apart, and beat them." There is no such demeaning language directed at Mary, who occupies her own Sura (19), titled simply "Mary." She is described as a paragon of purity, a holy virgin who gave birth to Jesus, a man portrayed in the Koran as an exalted prophet, an apostle of God, a "holy son" (19:12–28). Mary is the only woman with a Sura named for her in the Koran; the only men accorded such an honor are Muhammad, Abraham, Noah, Jonah, and Joseph (the Joseph of the Old Testament). In fact, the Koran makes more references to Mary than to almost any man, including Jesus. According to John Esposito, editor of the *Oxford Dictionary of Islam*, Jesus is mentioned twenty-five times in the Koran. By contrast, according to the scholar Giancarlo Finazzo, the Koran makes thirty-four direct or indirect references to Mary. Finazzo notes, quite remarkably, that the Catholic dogma of the Immaculate Conception seems to be implicitly recognized in certain verses of the Koran, and that certain elements of Muslim tradition speak of her ultimate ascension into heaven (Catholics call this the Assumption of Mary).[21]

Muslims believe that the Koran is the literal word of God, taken from an eternal book forever coexisting with the Creator. Thus, its words on Mary carry supreme weight. Muslims reject the notion that Jesus is the son of God, and even reject his crucifixion and resurrection. Yet they accept the birth of Jesus as miraculous, the blessed fruit of a virgin mother. The Koran has passages upholding the Nativity and what Catholics call the Annunciation (when the Angel Gabriel announced to Mary that she would conceive and give birth to the Son of God).

One who noticed the Muslim affinity for Mary, and in relation to Fátima specifically, was Bishop Fulton Sheen, the most influential Catholic American of the twentieth century. Sheen titled a chapter "Mary and the Moslems" in his 1952 book, *The World's First Love: Mary, Mother of God*. He wrote:

> The Koran, which is the Bible of the Moslems, has many passages concerning the Blessed Virgin.... Mary, then, is for the Moslems the true *Sayyida*, or Lady. The only possible serious rival to her in their creed would be Fátima, the daughter of Mohammed himself. But after the death of Fátima, Mohammed wrote: "Thou shalt be the most blessed of all women in Paradise, after Mary." In a variant of the text, Fátima is made to say: "I surpass all women, except Mary."
>
> This brings us to our second point, namely, why the Blessed Mother, in this twentieth century, should have revealed herself in the insignificant little village of Fátima, so that to all future generations she would be known as "Our Lady of Fátima." Since nothing ever happens out of heaven except with a finesse of all details, I believe that the Blessed Virgin chose to be known as "Our Lady of Fátima" as a pledge and a sign of hope to the Moslem people, and as an assurance that they, who show her so much respect, will one day accept her Divine Son, too.[22]

As "evidence to support these views," Sheen pointed to the events that occurred during the longtime Muslim occupation of Portugal. He added: "At the time when they were finally driven out, the last Moslem chief had a beautiful daughter by the name of Fátima. A Catholic boy fell in love with her, and for him she not only stayed behind when the Moslems left, but even embraced the faith."

That is, the princess, Fátima, herself converted to Catholicism. She married the Count of Ourem in 1158. This is the onetime Muslim princess for whom the town of Fátima was named—the town where Mary repeatedly appeared in 1917.[23]

As Sheen put it: "The young husband was so much in love with her that he changed the name of the town where he lived to Fátima. Thus the very place where our Lady appeared in 1917 bears a historical connection to Fátima, the daughter of Mohammed."[24]

Fulton Sheen was an incredibly influential priest. His books were huge bestsellers, and his widely watched weekly television show won an Emmy Award. Sheen was giving voice to and helping disseminate a fascinating and important message, one that would ultimately touch portions of the Muslim world.

Father Andrew Apostoli, vice postulator for the cause of the canonization of Fulton Sheen, states: "Archbishop Sheen... saw in our Lady's choice of Fátima a great significance for her message. She did not come down from heaven to the only place in all of Portugal with a Muslim name simply to convert Russia, he said. Unless we have the conversion of hundreds of millions of Muslims, there will never be world peace."[25]

THE LEGACY OF FÁTIMA

The accounts of so many who insisted they saw and were transformed by a miracle at Fátima in 1917 influenced countless other believers in the years and decades ahead. The miracle redounded to Pope John Paul II, certainly.

And the extraordinary events at Fátima attracted the interest of a Protestant president of the United States named Ronald Reagan.

2

OCTOBER 26, 1917

THE DEVILS TAKE OVER

The place: Moscow.

The year: 1922.

The scene: a "courtroom" for the Church Trials—a classic Bolshevik show trial.

The purpose: Christianity in the crosshairs.

The courtroom is actually a Moscow museum, the Polytechnic Museum. It is a fitting choice. Museums are for things of the past. And things such as justice and religion are no longer of use in Moscow, where communism is the new arbiter of "truth." The presiding judge is Comrade Bek. The prosecutors are Comrade Lunin and Comrade Longinov. The man who relates this story decades later, Aleksandr Solzhenitsyn, does not share the first names of this dubious trio of comrades. It does not matter. Their names—and roles and duties—are interchangeable in the Soviet system.[1]

On trial are seventeen defendants from the Russian Orthodox

Church, including the patriarch, archpriests, and laymen, accused of disseminating "propaganda." In reality, the patriarch has disseminated not propaganda but a proclamation. He told his Orthodox Church officials that the state could not compel the Church to surrender relics, icons, and valuables.

It is the Church's atheistic accusers who are employing propaganda: the Leninist machine portrays the Church as hoarding riches better served converted into rubles to feed the starving masses. The Bolsheviks do not acknowledge the fact that the people are starving because of communist central planning. "Carrion has become a delicacy for the starving population," laments Patriarch Tikhon, "but even this 'delicacy' is not to be found. The cries and moans are to be heard on all sides. It has even brought cannibalism." He estimates that thirteen million are suffering.

The Orthodox Church is not hoarding at all; the patriarch offers Church valuables ("rings, chains and bracelets that adorn the holy relics, silver and gold staves") to help feed the dying, so long as believers donate the valuables voluntarily, not under compulsion by the state.[2]

But that is not good enough. The Bolsheviks do not want the consent of the religious. They want to coerce the religious. And most of all they want the Church's "fabulous treasures," as an aide to Soviet leader Vladimir Lenin hungrily describes them. Leon Trotsky agrees, rubbing his hands together and saying, "The booty is enormous."[3]

And so the Church is told that it must give up everything to the state. Right now, without hesitation. The patriarch protests. Such "forced requisition" is "sacrilege," he says. The Church cannot be compelled to surrender holy objects or materials used to dispense the Eucharist. This is "prohibited by the canons of the Universal Church and is punishable as sacrilege, with excommunication for laymen and expulsion from holy orders for priests."[4]

Lenin views Patriarch Tikhon's resistance as an outrage.[5] Seeing Tikhon's position as a challenge to the Bolshevik regime, he sets forth an official party policy to crush the Church. He instructs Trotsky to have the Politburo ensure that all churches are "cleansed," or stripped of their riches. He has already called on the Politburo to "shoot ringleaders" and to levy "the death penalty for priests." Lenin writes: "There is a ninety-nine per cent chance of smashing the enemy on the head with complete success and of guaranteeing positions essential for us for many decades to come." He drools over the prospect of seizing what he estimates to be "several hundred million gold rubles."[6]

And so on May 5—shortly after May Day, the high holy day of

international communism—the esteemed patriarch is called to "testify" to his transgressions. Judge Bek bores in. In a tense moment, he asks whether the patriarch believes the all-powerful Soviet government has "acted incorrectly."

Patriarch Tikhon answers bravely and succinctly: "Yes."

Comrade Bek is astounded, or at least pretends to be: "Do you consider the state's laws obligatory or not?" he barks.

"Yes, I recognize them," answers the Church leader, "to the extent that they do not contradict the rules of piety."

"Which in the last analysis is more important to you," the judge asks, "the laws of the Church or the point of view of the Soviet government?" All know the expected reply, but the patriarch is unyielding. Bek pounces: "So that means that we, the representatives of the Soviet government, are thieves of holy things? So you call the representatives of the Soviet government, the All-Russian Central Executive Committee, thieves?!"

The calm patriarch answers, "I am citing only Church law."

The Soviet "judge" proceeds to lecture the head of the Russian Orthodox Church on a correct understanding of "blasphemy." The patriarch tells his atheistic expert of an incident at Saint Basil the Great of Caesarea when thugs from the Cheka-NKVD (Soviet secret police) smashed an icon that would not fit in their box of booty.

Bek calls the old man a liar. After all, the patriarch was not there to see this particular (one of millions) trampling of sacred things by the apostles of Marxism-Leninism. "Who spread that repulsive slander?" Bek shrieks. He wants a name.

Patriarch Tikhon wisely does not name the priest who witnessed the destruction at Saint Basil the Great.

"That means you have made an unsubstantiated assertion," declares the man with the guns of the totalitarian state behind him.

After several minutes more of this, the "jury" orders criminal charges against the patriarch. He is arrested and removed from office. He is permitted to keep his life, but only because the Bolsheviks find his suffering more useful to their aims. He will not live more than a few years anyway, ultimately succumbing on the feast day of the Annunciation in the Orthodox Church. By that point he is a broken man living under house arrest.[7]

The Soviets deem the lesser-ranking men under the patriarch to be more expendable. On May 7, Judge Bek's tribunal pronounces its sentence: of the seventeen defendants, eleven are to be shot.[8]

There is no need for witnesses.

To be fair to Bek and crew, this is rather mild behavior for the Bolsheviks. Three years earlier, Lenin issued a stern order: to kill anyone who dared to observe Christmas. The man who had declared, "There can be nothing more abominable than religion,"[9] wrote the following on December 25, 1919: "To put up with 'Nikola' [the religious holiday] would be stupid—the entire Cheka must be on the alert to see to it that those who do not show up for work because of 'Nikola' are shot."[10]

No mercy. No exceptions.

In effect, Lenin and his disciples will spend the next seven decades doing just that to the religious: murdering them.

A Lady in Fátima saw it coming.

BAPTISMS AND PERSECUTIONS

At the time of Patriarch Tikhon's persecution in the Moscow Church Trials, Ronald Reagan was an eleven-year-old boy in Dixon, Illinois, one who had just been baptized by total immersion in the fount at the Disciples of Christ church on South Hennepin Avenue. Karol Wojtyła, nine years younger than Reagan, had been recently baptized as well, though by sprinkling, and as an infant. We will pick up those periods in the two men's lives in the next chapter. For now, let us go back to 1917, when the most dismal of the Fátima prophecies was almost immediately realized.

On October 24, 1917,[11] the Bolshevik Revolution began. Two days later the All-Russian Congress of Soviets officially handed power to a Soviet Council of People's Commissars, whose chairman was Vladimir Lenin. Lenin, Trotsky, and other top Bolsheviks assumed their positions in the new governing regime. Now the whole world would see the bruteness of their ideology.

Lenin hated Christianity. Raised by devout Christian parents, he bragged that as a teen he took off the cross that hung around his neck and tossed it in the rubbish. Speaking on behalf of his comrades and their state, Lenin affirmed unequivocally, "We do not believe in God."[12] They made that disbelief abundantly clear.

There would be no greater foe to religion than atheistic communism. As Marxism-Leninism spread around the world, so did religious repression—into Central and Eastern Europe, Asia, Africa, and the Western Hemisphere. The repression continues to this day, in communist countries like China, North Korea, and Cuba, a tragic legacy of a revolution launched a century ago.

"All the biblical descriptions of hell and the pains of Dante's Inferno are nothing in comparison with the tortures in Communist prisons," the Reverend Richard Wurmbrand told the U.S. Senate Internal Security Subcommittee in 1966.[13] Wurmbrand, the author of the international bestseller *Tortured for Christ*, spent years in Romanian prisons, where communist authorities tortured him and screamed at him that they were the devil. His communist captors relished the pain they inflicted.

Wurmbrand's experiences were hardly unique. Communist governments targeted people of all faiths—Protestants, Catholics, Jews, Muslims, Buddhists, whomever.[14] They were equal-opportunity discriminators. For every tortured Richard Wurmbrand in Romania, there was a Cardinal Mindszenty in Hungary, a Cardinal Wyszyński in Poland, a Bishop Bossilkov in Bulgaria, a Cardinal Stepinac in Yugoslavia, a Natan Sharansky or Walter Ciszek in Russia, a Vasyl Velychkovsky or Severian Baranyk or Zenobius Kovalyk in Ukraine, a Moaddedi clan in Afghanistan, a Methodist missionary or follower of the Dalai Lama in China, a jailed nun in Cuba, a Buddhist monk forced to renounce his vows in Pol Pot's Cambodia. Whether the despot was Pol Pot or Fidel Castro or Joseph Stalin, the sentiment was the same: "Religion is poison," as Mao Tse-tung reportedly told the Dalai Lama. Communists quibbled over how to implement Marx's vision, but they were unanimous in one thing: religion was the enemy, and it had to be vanquished.[15]

The roots of this long "war on religion" (as Mikhail Gorbachev would later describe it) reside in the perverse ideology of Marxism-Leninism, and specifically the Bolshevik takeover of Russia. Lenin's coup, in which the Bolsheviks murdered the (very pious) Romanov family, changed history forever.

Karl Marx had dubbed religion the "opiate of the masses" and insisted that "Communism begins where atheism begins."[16] In the *Communist Manifesto*, Marx wrote, "Communism abolishes eternal truths, it abolishes all religion, and all morality."[17]

Lenin went further. "All worship of a divinity is a necrophilia," he said.[18] In a November 1913 letter, the Bolshevik godfather wrote that "any religious idea, any idea of any God at all, any flirtation even with a God is the most inexpressible foulness... the most dangerous foulness, the most shameful 'infection.'" Scholar James Thrower says that with "infection," Lenin was referring to venereal disease.[19]

Under the Bolsheviks, atheism became the official state belief. Lenin and his underlings promoted it relentlessly. They spearheaded the creation of groups like the Society of the Godless, also known as the League of the Militant Godless.[20] They wanted Marxism-Leninism to replace the Russian Orthodox Church and all other conventional faiths; it became the new civil religion.

The Bolsheviks forbade religious instruction to anyone under eighteen years of age, and children were encouraged to turn in parents who taught anything about God. Marriage became a strictly civil, secular ceremony; weddings, baptisms, and funerals were converted into bizarre "communist" ceremonies.[21] The Russian Orthodox Church's long-standing prohibition against divorce was lifted, leading to an explosion in divorce rates and havoc upon the Russian family.[22] Lenin made good on his June 1913 promise to secure an "unconditional annulment of all laws against abortions."[23] By 1920, abortion was legal and free of charge to Russian women. The number of abortions skyrocketed to levels still unmatched in human history.[24]

The new Soviet authority confiscated all of the Russian Orthodox Church's land and buildings, which the Church had owned for centuries. Lenin's cronies destroyed churches or reconstituted them as communist clubs, workshops, storage houses, offices, and atheistic museums.[25] The Church of the Archangel Michael, a beautiful old church crowned with ornate cupolas on the southwest edge of Moscow, was used to store grain.[26] Of the 657 churches that existed in Moscow on the eve of the 1917 revolution, only 100 to 150 remained by 1976, according to official Soviet statistics. Of those, the Moscow Russian Orthodox Patriarchy said only 46 still held services.[27] Full-time, state-employed "church watchers" reported anyone who came to the church to pray.

The USSR was a huge country that spanned twelve time zones. The Orthodox Church alone had more than 40,000 churches and some 150,000 priests, monks, deans, and bishops.[28] Lenin ordered the shootings of an estimated 14,000 to 20,000 clergy and active laymen.[29] Recalcitrant priests and nuns who weren't executed would be carted to Siberia. Nuns were deliberately housed in special sections of the gulag with prostitutes.[30] They were seen as "whores to Christ."

Russian churches held holy relics, gems, icons, statues, and precious stones, all of which carried liturgical and sacramental value. The Bolsheviks saw only a financial value—hence the forced confiscation that Patriarch Tikhon resisted in the Moscow Church Trials. Their total haul from the churches is unknown, but one internal list of what they took prior to November 1, 1922, recorded 1,220 pounds of gold; 828,275 pounds of silver; 35,670 diamonds; 536 pounds of gemstones; 3,115 gold rubles;

19,155 silver rubles; 1,902 "various precious objects"; and 71,762 unspecified valuables.[31]

The Soviets completely destroyed the Catholic Church in their country. Unlike some other churches in the Soviet Union, Catholicism was not permitted to reestablish a central apparatus after World War II, most likely because its leadership (located in Rome) could not be controlled by Moscow. Writing in the mid-1970s, the scholar Gerhard Simon reported that there was not a single Catholic monastery, convent, school, or welfare institution left in the entire USSR.[32]

Imagine, then, how the Soviets felt in October 1978 when the Roman Catholic Church chose the first Slavic pope ever, and a persecuted Pole no less. It is no exaggeration to say that the Soviet leadership was so livid that it wanted the man dead.

EXPORTING COMMUNISM

Karl Marx had called for global revolution, for workers of the world to unite. The Bolsheviks almost immediately set to work exporting their revolution internationally.

In the first week of March 1919, a gathering of the Marxist faithful convened in Moscow. They formed a congress of fifty-two dedicated comrades from Russia, Austria, the Balkans, Britain, China, France, Germany, Hungary, Switzerland, and the United States.[33] The largest delegation, from Bolshevik Russia, included Lenin, Trotsky, Joseph Stalin, Nikolai Bukharin, and Grigori Zinoviev.[34] It was the First Congress of the Communist International, the so-called Comintern.

Lenin welcomed the assembled on March 2, 1919, by saying: "On behalf of the Central Committee of the Russian Communist Party I declare the First Congress of the Communist International open.... Comrades, our gathering has great historic significance."[35] He continued: "The bourgeois are terror-stricken at the growing workers' revolutionary movement. This is understandable if we take into account that the development of events since the imperialist war [World War I] inevitably favors the workers' revolutionary movement, and that the world revolution is beginning and growing in intensity everywhere."

Speaking of the "greatness and significance of the struggle now going on," Lenin spoke glowingly of "the Soviet system with the dictatorship of the proletariat." This is what Marx had envisioned, and Lenin loved the concept. He repeated the phrase for emphasis: "*Dictatorship of the prole-*

tariat—until now these words were Latin to the masses. Thanks to the spread of the Soviets throughout the world this Latin has been translated into all modern languages; a practical form of dictatorship has been found by the working people. The mass of workers now understand it thanks to Soviet power in Russia.... Victory will be ours, the victory of the worldwide Communist revolution is assured."

The international objectives of the Comintern were self-evident from its title. The communists underscored their objective with other names they gave the Comintern: Trotsky, for instance, described it as the "General Staff of the World Revolution."[36]

The Comintern was centralized under Moscow leadership, which was to have "uncontested authority" over the other communist parties that would soon be established all over the world, including in America.[37] By 1919, already impressed with the "dizzying speed" of this movement's advances, Grigori Zinoviev, the first head of the Comintern, confidently predicted that "in a year all Europe shall be communist. And the struggle for communism shall be transferred to America, and perhaps Asia and other parts of the world."[38]

The Comintern made clear that members of foreign communist parties—from Europe to America—who did not obey Moscow, "who reject in principle the conditions and theses put forward by the Communist International, are to be expelled from the party.... Every party which wishes to join the Communist International is obligated to give unconditional support to any Soviet republic in its struggle against counter-revolutionary forces."[39]

Here we see the pattern established early on: members of communist parties around the world, including in the United States, would see themselves as loyal Soviet patriots.

Among these patriots who saluted the red flag were members of the American Communist Party, founded in Chicago in September 1919, only six months after the Comintern was founded. The American Communist Party would ultimately take the name Communist Party USA (CPUSA) and would be the political party for American communists throughout the Cold War.[40] It cannot be emphasized enough that American members of the Communist Party saw themselves as subservient to the Comintern and to Moscow. Herbert Romerstein, a former communist who became one of America's leading authorities on domestic communism, noted that "from 1919, when [CPUSA] was formed, to 1989, when the Soviet Union collapsed, it was under total Soviet control."[41]

Members of Communist Party USA swore a loyalty oath to Moscow, which stated: "I pledge myself to rally the masses to defend the Soviet Union, the land of victorious socialism. I pledge myself to remain at all times a vigilant and firm defender of the Leninist line of the party, the only line that insures the triumph of Soviet Power in the United States." This particular oath was issued in 1935, during Stalin's Great Purge, which annihilated tens of millions.[42]

By the time the Comintern Congress met for a second time, in July 1920, the communists had agitated uprisings in Germany, Finland, Hungary, and Poland. Lenin, Trotsky, Bukharin, and Zinoviev proclaimed that "world Civil War" was the "watchword" and "the order of the day."[43] The Congress stated explicitly, "The Communist International has declared war on the entire bourgeois world."[44]

GERMANY'S COMMUNISTS TAKE THEIR SHOTS

In his welcoming remarks at the First Comintern Congress, Lenin had been especially excited about prospects for communism in Germany, the home of Marx. "In Germany," he cheered, "civil war is a fact." He said: "Comrades, I think that after the events in Russia and the January struggle in Germany, it is especially important to note that in other countries, too, the latest form of the workers' movement is asserting itself and getting the upper hand.... The Soviet system has triumphed not only in backward Russia, but also in the most developed country of Europe—in Germany, and in Britain, the oldest capitalist country."[45]

Emboldened by the success of Comrade Lenin in Russia, Germany's communists in March 1919 attempted to take over the emerging Weimar Republic. On March 3, Germany's communists seized Berlin. On April 4, a communist cabal seized the government in Munich and declared Bavaria a separate Soviet republic, the so-called Bavarian Soviet Republic (or Munich Soviet Republic). These Marxists immediately began expropriating property, factories, businesses, capital, and forming a "Red Army." Under advisement from Lenin, they seized certain useful individuals as hostages; other political elites who stood in their way were summarily executed.

Postwar Germany was in the throes of revolution. The "punitive peace" negotiated at Versailles at the end of World War I had destroyed Germany's industry, agriculture, and economy generally. Mass starvation seemed likely. Extreme factions were emerging: Germany seemed to face the bleak possibility of a fascist future or a communist one.

Caught up in these political currents was a young Italian archbishop named Eugenio Pacelli, who would play a pivotal role in the battle against Marxism-Leninism.

On May 13, 1917—the exact date of the first Marian apparition at Fátima—Pacelli was consecrated as archbishop in the Sistine Chapel with the blessing of Pope Benedict XV. Soon thereafter, Pacelli began a long period as papal nuncio to Germany. Pope Benedict needed a steady diplomatic hand; really, the job required an almost saintly presence, given the tensions. Pacelli was ideal. The British envoy to the Holy See, Sir Henry Howard, called the choice of Pacelli "a dreadful loss for our British mission to the Vatican, for he is the one man who can be trusted implicitly; however, it is also consoling that there should be such an honest man at Munich at present."[46]

It was consoling to everyone but Germany's communists. In December 1918, Pacelli took to the pulpit of a major cathedral in Munich to denounce communism. The archbishop expressed contempt for what he dubbed "the monstrous face of communism."[47]

Pacelli roamed the Bavarian countryside ministering to the poor and homeless. He walked up to barricades manned by armed and desperate men, opened his cloak, and calmly displayed his pectoral cross. They would soften and welcome him. He felt protected by the love and force of the cross.[48]

For this effrontery, Pacelli found himself on the receiving end of a communist smear campaign—the first of many. They spread lies about him to further their agenda, for as Vladimir Lenin had said, the only morality that communists recognized was that which furthered their interests. "We repudiate all morality that proceeds from supernatural ideas that are outside class conceptions," said Lenin, who included Christian morality among those "supernatural ideas" they firmly rejected. "Morality is entirely subordinate to the interests of class war. Everything is moral that is necessary for the annihilation of the old exploiting social order and for uniting the proletariat."[49] (Lenin's words would be quoted often by a future American president named Ronald Reagan, who understood the gravity of their implications.)[50]

The communists also threatened Archbishop Pacelli with physical violence. The threats intensified when communists took over the government in April 1919.[51]

Most diplomats fled Munich once the communists had control, but not Pacelli. He announced that he was staying at his post. For this, the archbishop would be directly targeted.

Returning one day from a visit to a downtrodden section of Munich, Pacelli was shaken to discover that the ground floor of the Nunciature had been riddled with bullets. The windows were shattered and the façade pockmarked by bullets from machine guns. Presumably, these bullets were intended for him.

That afternoon, while sitting in his office, he heard a crash below. He went into the hall to find it filled with an angry mob armed with butcher knives and Luger automatics. The voices went silent as Pacelli, a tall figure dressed in black with a violet sash around his waist and a glistening cross on his chest, very deliberately walked toward them. Speaking in German, the Italian calmly told them: "You must leave here. This house does not belong to the Bavarian government but to the Holy See. It is inviolable under international law."

One voice yelled: "What do we care for the Holy See? We'll leave if you show us your secret store of money and food."

Pacelli told them that he had given all his money and food to the city's poor. "That's a lie!" shouted one of the communists. Others insisted Pacelli was telling the truth.

The Marxist ringleader threw his heavy gun at Pacelli, striking him in the chest. The firearm hit so hard that it dented the jeweled cross that covered his heart. Pacelli put his hand on his chest but stood his ground, gazing upon the snarling faces with sorrow. The silenced mob slowly withdrew.

Pacelli never understood why the man hurled his gun rather than firing it. One biographical account speculated that perhaps the gun was out of ammunition, or perhaps a remnant of grace prohibited the man from killing a priest bedecked in the armor of Christ. Years later Pacelli would lend the cross to Bishop Fulton Sheen.

As soon as the mob left, the nuncio telephoned the "Central Soviet" in Munich to demand the protection that his Nunciature deserved by international law. But communists had no interest in honoring any agreement contrary to their interests. "We are violating the agreement," Lenin once said of the Treaty of Brest-Litovsk. "We've already violated it thirty or forty times." The voice on the receiving end of Pacelli's phone call told him: "You'd better get out of town!"[52]

Pacelli refused to obey communist orders. He would not leave.

The targeting continued. A few days after the incident at the Nunciature, Pacelli went to the Frauenplatz to meet with another archbishop. He traveled by car. Biographers Alden Hatch and Seamus Walshe described in detail what happened after the meeting:

> It was almost twilight when [Pacelli] started home, with a gray mist blowing off the River Isar. The streets were filled with sullen groups of men, glaring at the car. As it turned into the Maximilianstrasse along the embankment of the river, the groups coalesced into a mob, shouting threats and blasphemies. The car came to a dead stop, and the mob pressed against it, shaking it with their fury, threatening to overturn it. Inside, Pacelli said to his driver, "Put down the top."
>
> The man looked at him as though he had gone mad, crying, "*Nein! Nein!*"
>
> "Do as I say. Put it down."
>
> The frightened driver, fumbling with the catches and straps, finally got the top down. The Archbishop stood up in the tonneau and then on the back seat so that even those at the farthest misty fringes of the crowd could see him. In his purple cloak, he was a shining target for any Communist with sufficient courage of his convictions to shoot.
>
> None did. Instead a weird silence fell, and Pacelli's voice, high and clear, spoke to them: "My mission is peace," he said. "The only weapon that I carry is this holy cross. I do no harm to you, but only good things. Why should you harm me?
>
> Then raising his right hand in the immemorial gesture, he bestowed on them his blessing in the name of the Father, and of the Son, and of the Holy Ghost.
>
> There was not a sound from that great crowd as he sat down, and a lane opened magically for his car to pass on.[53]

Pacelli had escaped, but the communists were not finished with him. One day the little-known archbishop who blessed the communists from his attacked car in Munich would be known to the world as Pope Pius XII. The communists had yet more persecution planned for this shepherd of the Church, his flock, and the world. Such persecutions would be part of the long litany of communist "errors" and evils that the Lady at Fátima had predicted.

3

MAY 1920–JUNE 1922

A BIRTH IN POLAND AND A REBIRTH IN THE MIDWEST

As communism was on the rise in Russia and spreading throughout the world, glimmers of hope emerged in the most unlikely places—in tiny, remote towns with names like Wadowice and Dixon, in countries as distant as Poland and America.

There, in these vastly different but in some ways strikingly similar places, two boys were being molded, two who would decades later emerge as happy warriors to battle communism.

They spoke different languages, but they were raised in a common language of sorts, a shared Christian faith, a common understanding of what was right and what was wrong. They were raised to have courage, to have hope, to have conviction, to do the right thing, to be not afraid, and to never compromise with the forces of evil.

A BIRTH IN POLAND

On May 18, 1920, in Wadowice, Poland, in an apartment comprising two rooms and a kitchen in the second floor of a house across the street from Saint Mary's Church, a baby boy named Karol Józef Wojtyła was born to Emilia Kaczorowska Wojtyła and the senior Karol Wojtyła. Known to friends as "Lolek," the helpless infant would one day rise to greatness. He would become known to the world as Saint Pope John Paul II.

According to at least one report, the birth of the future pontiff almost never happened. Karol Wojtyła's mother was in such precarious health that her doctor advised her not to continue her pregnancy. "You have to have an abortion," the doctor told her flatly. The physician warned Emilia that her own life was at stake and that she should save herself rather than her child. Emilia chose otherwise. As the *Vatican Insider* interpreted this account, "Blessed John Paul II was in danger of not being born."[1] The claim is reasonable, at the very least because Emilia's previous child died shortly after birth, and because she herself was often frail and sickly.

Healthy and strong as an ox, the child was baptized on June 20 by Father Franciszek Zak at Saint Mary's Church. In that same church the boy would find his first altar call. The altar boy's proud mother would tell her neighbors, "You'll see, my Lolek will be a great man someday."[2]

Part of that call to greatness would be to redeem an enemy encroaching Poland the year of his birth. That summer, Lenin's Red Army was advancing toward Warsaw. With some five million Russian forces approaching, it appeared that the Bolsheviks were about to establish in Poland a beachhead to support communist revolutions in Germany, Hungary, Romania, and the Baltic states. Remarkably, a much smaller Polish force stopped them. The British general and military historian J. F. C. Fuller ranked the Polish victory at the Battle of Warsaw decisive in halting the spread of communism. His fellow historian A. J. P. Taylor agreed that a Bolshevik victory would have "largely determined the course of European history for the next twenty years or more." Historian Timothy Snyder states that the Polish victory "brought an end to hopes for a European socialist revolution" and limited Bolshevism to a "state ideology" rather than a wider armed revolution that would conquer Europe, as Lenin had so badly desired. As my Grove City College colleague Dr. Robert Clemm puts it, "Were it not for the Polish victory, the Soviet domination of Eastern Europe might have occurred 25 years earlier."[3]

Clemm says that only a "near-miracle defense around Warsaw" had pushed backed the Bolsheviks.[4] Poles called the victory the "Miracle on the Vistula," because the turning point came at the Vistula River on August 15, the Feast Day of the Assumption of the Blessed Virgin Mary. Poles to this day mark August 15 as a special day of victory against the Bolsheviks with the aid of heaven.[5]

Proud Poland repelled the Soviet Comintern. The next time it would not be so lucky. In the late 1940s the nation would fall to the Red Army occupiers and remain under Soviet control for more than forty years. A great man from Poland would someday be the moral counterforce to drive them out.

Emilia was right: Her Lolek would be a great man someday.

A sister who preceded Lolek died in infancy. Some sources list her as Olga, though there are little to no records of her birth or baptism. There was a brother, Edmund, nicknamed Mundek, fourteen years Lolek's senior. Lolek was close to Edmund, admiring the impressive young man—athletic, smart, handsome, charming, popular.

From 1924 to 1929, when Lolek was a boy, Edmund attended Jagiellonian University in Kraków, where he earned a degree in medicine. He practiced as a doctor. Tragically, during an epidemic of scarlet fever in the winter of 1932, he contracted the disease from a patient. He died on December 5. Dr. Edmund Wojtyła was only twenty-six, with a promising life ahead of him. Karol was twelve. The loss staggered him.[6]

Three years earlier, Karol had lost his mother. Emilia passed away on April 13, 1929, from kidney and congestive heart failure. Little Karol was not even nine. He was in school when he learned of her death. She was forty-five years old.

Not much is known about Emilia, including the precise reasons for her decline. John Paul II would say and write little of her. He loved her, and missed her, and would for the remainder of his life keep a small wedding portrait of his mother and father near his bed, including at his papal residence in Castel Gandolfo, but he admitted having few memories of his mother. He said he did not have a "clear awareness of her contribution" to his faith, though he conceded that her input "must have been great."[7]

He was certain about the impact of Emilia's surviving partner. Born July 18, 1879, five years prior to Emilia's birth, the senior Karol was a highly respected captain in the military who gave nearly thirty years of service to his country. He was admired by his underlings for his unimpeachable integrity. By no means wealthy, he retired with a military pension that allowed him and his only remaining family member to live a decent existence (until the war).

Young Karol's father became the boy's pillar of faith. They read Scripture together, prayed together, did the rosary together. And beyond that direct instruction, the son imbibed the image of the father often on his knees silently praying, a "man of constant prayer." Every day of his long life, Karol would recite a prayer he had learned from his dad.[8] The future priest of the universal Church, the leader of every Catholic seminarian, described his father as his "first seminary," and his father's house as "a kind of domestic seminary."[9]

His father did his best to compensate for the hole left by Karol's mother. In her portrait of John Paul II's life, Peggy Noonan writes that the elder Karol would take his son to Marian shrines as if to tell him, "This now is your mother."[10] And so she was.

Father and son were alone now. They moved their beds closer together to make up for a home suddenly less full of life.

Karol made his first Holy Communion at age nine, about the time of Emilia's death. He was very athletic, swimming, hiking, running, playing soccer; he was an especially talented soccer goalie. In playing these games, he had regular contact with Wadowice's large Jewish community. Jews lived in safety and happiness in Catholic Poland, unlike almost anywhere else outside Palestine. School soccer games were sometimes organized between teams of Jews and Catholics, and Karol often played on the Jewish side.

Karol's kinship with the Jewish people lasted a lifetime. Some sources maintain that his first love affair was with a Jewish girl named Ginka Beer, remembered as "slender" with "stupendous dark eyes and jet black hair." Friends recall her being a "superb actress," which would have made her even more attractive to Karol, who loved to act and apparently was quite skilled at it.[11] He considered a career in acting.

Karol had his share of drama in real life, including personal flirtations with death. When he was around fifteen years old, a friend playfully pointed a gun at him, not realizing it was loaded. The gun fired and narrowly missed the future pride of Poland and shepherd of the universal Church.[12] He would escape other near-death incidents.

A Rebirth in the Midwest

Thousands of miles west, in another second-floor apartment, a young American boy rounded out another family of four: mom, dad, older brother. Not long after Karol Wojtyła was baptized, young Ronald

Wilson Reagan became a Christian, and that rebirth would change his life, his plans, and history.

Whereas Wojtyła had been baptized as an infant, Reagan's christening came in 1922, when he was eleven. His christening was the product not of a father strong in the faith but of a father (likewise Catholic) not nearly so.

Jack Reagan was a shoe salesman with a habit of chasing rainbows, and abusing alcohol. The exact contours of that latter "sickness," as his wife charitably described it, is a matter of dispute. Reagan biographers have flatly called Jack a "drunk," an "alcoholic." Official Reagan biographer Edmund Morris characterized Jack as a "binge drinker."[13] Ronald's older brother, Neil, a reliable source on the subject, maintained that Jack was "a drinker," but not "as serious" as people have suggested.[14]

Let us agree it was a weakness. And not Jack's only weakness.

Jack uprooted the family at every turn. Throughout Ronald's childhood, his family never owned a home, always wayfaring to the next barely affordable rental. Ronald would live in thirty-seven different residences throughout his life, with the majority coming before he left home permanently as an adult.[15] Baby Ronald, born February 6, 1911, in an apartment above a bank in Tampico, Illinois, lived in his first home only four months.

In one of these early moves, the Reagans left Chicago for yet another new job for Jack, this time selling shoes at a store in Galesburg, Illinois. Ronald had a kind of epiphany as a five-year old in Galesburg. Wrestling with the loneliness of a little boy who had just moved to a third new town in five years, he ventured alone to the attic. The previous tenant had left behind a large collection of bird's eggs and butterflies enclosed in glass. The curious boy escaped into the attic for hours at a time, "marveling at the rich colors of the eggs and the intricate and fragile wings of the butterflies." "The experience," Reagan remembered, "left me with a reverence for the handiwork of God that never left me." These wonderments were like "gateways." The notion of a Creator was etched into the boy's consciousness.

Reagan many years later thanked that previous tenant as "an anonymous benefactor to whom I owe much." This pivotal rendezvous with the Creator was Jack's inadvertent doing.

Another foible of Jack's may have indirectly contributed to Ronald's turn to God as well. It was a brisk February evening in 1922, shortly after Ronald turned eleven years old. The family was now in Dixon, the latest new town, a warm, welcoming place that, mercifully, would become the

Reagan family's hometown throughout the 1920s. Young Reagan had just strolled up the 800 block of South Hennepin Avenue, returning from a basketball game at the YMCA. He knew that his mother was out on a sewing job, doing her part to alleviate the Reagan family's chronic financial woes. Like Emilia Wojtyła, Nelle Reagan did part-time work as a seamstress to help the family.

The young Reagan expected to come home to an empty house. Instead, he was shaken by the sight of his father passed out on the front porch, flat on his back, freezing, too inebriated to have made it to the door.

"He was drunk," his son later remembered. "Dead to the world."

The boy leaned over and smelled the whiskey escaping his dad's long snores. Jack's hair was soaked with melted snow, matted unevenly against the side of his reddened face. His arms were stretched out, recalled his son, "as if he were crucified—as indeed he was."

He had been taken by the "dark demon in the bottle."

The boy stood over his father, unsure how to react. He wanted simply to let himself in the door, go to bed, and pretend his dad was not there. But the neighbors would see him lying there.

And so Ronald grabbed a fistful of the old man's overcoat and heaved him. He dragged him into the house and to the bedroom, out of the way of the weather's harm and neighbors' attention. It was a sad moment for father and son. The young Reagan felt no anger, no resentment, just grief. This was the man who until that point had always carried *him*.

When this happened, the eleven-year-old was at a crucial time in his spiritual development. Four months later he told his mother that he wanted to be baptized, born again, starting life anew as a child of God, the son of an infinitely more reliable Father.

The lingering thought of his earthly father sprawled spread-eagle in the snow remained in Reagan's mind throughout his life. Seventy years later, in his eighties, after being president of the United States for two intense terms, he still remembered that moment in the snow as if it were yesterday.

JACK AND NELLE'S SON

Ronald Reagan's parents were John Edward Reagan (born July 13, 1883) and Nelle Clyde Wilson Reagan (born July 24, 1883), called Jack and Nelle by their friends and their children (at the parents' request). They were born within eleven days of each other, in the same small town of Fulton, Illinois.

Jack was a first-generation Irish American. His family came to America thanks to the efforts of Michael Reagan, Ronald's great-grandfather and an Irish Catholic. Nelle was a blend of Irish, Scottish, and English. At the age of twenty-one, they were married on a fall day in November 1904 at the Catholic Church of the Immaculate Conception in Fulton.[16] Yes, Ronald Reagan's parents were married in a Catholic church, and one named for the Immaculate Conception of the Blessed Virgin—one of so many Marian profundities that would occur in the long life of their son.

Getting married in a Catholic church was apparently not a big deal to the Protestant Nelle. Her devoutness came later. But when it came, it roared. Nelle would find Jesus at a Christian revival well after her marriage. From there, the spiritual paths of her and Jack departed markedly.

The exact level of Jack's faith is, like his drinking, a matter of dispute. It is also, like his drinking, a frequent subject for disparagement. By most accounts, Jack was a lukewarm or apathetic Catholic. In a typical judgment, Edmund Morris called him a "lapsed Catholic."[17]

For years I have attempted to pin down Jack's faith, asking about it anytime I speak to anyone from Dixon, especially those who might have had family and friends who knew Jack. It is a frustrating subject, though I learned this much:

Jack attended Saint Patrick's Catholic Church at 612 Highland Avenue in Dixon and was a member there. He usually went to Mass with his son Neil, whereas Ronald attended the Disciples of Christ church with his mother. I was also told that Neil, even though he had been baptized with Ronald at the Disciples of Christ church in the summer of 1922, soon converted to the Catholic Church so fully that he took First Communion at Saint Patrick's Church in 1928.[18] Neil would never regret that move, becoming a devout Catholic whose faith only intensified in the decades ahead.

It is hard to imagine that a "lukewarm" Jack would have had no effect on Neil's strong turn to the Catholic Church.[19] I also learned that both Neil and Jack were active together in the Knights of Columbus.[20] In fact, Jack had been involved with the Knights in Tampico, Illinois, the little town where Ronald was born.[21] A member of the Dixon Council of the Knights told me that contemporaneous newspaper accounts confirm Jack's presence at Knights events. As for Neil, the Dixon Council retains records proving that Neil was a formal member and in fact an officer (or "warden").[22] The Dixon Council forwarded my inquiry on Jack to the national office of the Knights of Columbus in New Haven, Connecticut, which told me that it could find no record of Jack's being a formal member.[23]

Regardless of whether he was an official member, Jack was at least involved with the Knights in his local parishes.

Several Dixon sources over the years have described Jack's Mass attendance to me as "irregular," though their sources are word of mouth. Unlike with Nelle, there are no, say, Sunday school classes with extant records showing Jack's attendance at Saint Patrick's.[24] Ronald Reagan himself in his postpresidential memoirs said that his father's "attendance at Catholic Mass was sporadic," whereas his mother "seldom missed Sunday services at the Disciples of Christ church in Dixon."[25]

It is odd that Ronald Reagan, who as president would be surrounded by devout Catholics with whom he tried to change the world, was as a youth surrounded by a father who reportedly displayed a distinct lack of devout Catholicism. That said, the religious split in young Reagan's household taught him something significant that he would retain all the way to the White House: to respect and love both Catholics and Protestants. This would serve him well, including in his meetings many years later with Karol Wojtyła.

"SAINT" NELLE

It was really Nelle Reagan who was the faith leader in the household, which Jack happily accepted (if not delegated).[26] She was a model of Christian virtue. It was only natural that her son Ronald gravitated toward her faith.

Pivotal to young Reagan's formation was the First Christian Church in Dixon. He acquired his faith there, under the nurturing of an exceptional pastor named Ben Cleaver and, most of all, under Nelle.[27]

The ways that Nelle influenced young Reagan are numerous, but chief among them was in instilling the conviction that God guided him along a preordained path that was just and right. This made Reagan confidently optimistic throughout his life. In Reagan's own words, Nelle taught him that "all things were part of God's Plan, even the most disheartening setbacks, and in the end, everything worked out for the best."[28] He never abandoned that belief. For Reagan, this became a consuming "Divine Plan" personal theology. It convinced him, beyond any doubt and despite any setbacks from childhood to adulthood, that God allows bad things to happen so good things can come from them.

Whereas Jack Reagan's involvement in his son's faith may have been unintentional, Nelle's was deliberate. She chose the Disciples of Christ denomination. The group first met in the basement of the town's YMCA until it could raise funds for a building. The new First Christian Church opened at 123 South Hennepin on June 18, 1922.

Nelle became a pillar in the local church. Aside from the minister, she was maybe its most visible face. One of the congregation's fourteen officers, she wore multiple hats, including directing the choir and the missionary society. The vigorous congregation boasted more than a dozen Sunday school classes each week, with Nelle's True Blue class the largest.[29] It was said that if Nelle had had the education, she would have taken the pulpit.[30] Surely in today's era she would have attended seminary.

Nelle's thoughts and works were fixed heavenward. She was a firm believer in the power of prayer. She led prayer meetings at church and was a "leader" with four other women who provided "home prayer services."[31] She often offered a hand to other churches in the area.[32]

"Lemme tell you," one Dixon resident commented, "Nelle was a saint." That was not a rare sentiment. "If there is such a thing as a saint on earth, it is Nelle Reagan," said another. Yet another observer agreed: "Nelle was too good for this world."[33] One member of the congregation called Nelle a "leader" whom "everybody loved."[34]

Some even claimed that Nelle Reagan's connection to God was so close, so unique, that her prayers on several occasions healed people of serious sicknesses.[35] Even the cynical Edmund Morris could not avoid reporting that friends and associates saw Nelle as a living "saint" with "divine powers" capable of "healing the sick." "Nelle," the afflicted would say, "will take care of us."[36]

From his mother, Reagan learned the power of prayer and the desire to seek it at any time, from childhood to adulthood, from a seat at the dinner table to the seat of world power. From Nelle he also acquired his mystical streak, which stayed with him throughout his life, and which his secular critics enjoyed mocking. A fellow mystic who would not have found it laughable was Karol Wojtyła.

In short, Nelle Reagan was a central figure in her church and in her community, and her influence, and her insistence that her son attend church regularly, helped to define Ronald Reagan's spirituality. She gave him a solid foundation in the Christian faith—one that never left him.

MOTHERS

But it almost was not so. In one of so many intriguing parallels in the lives of Ronald Reagan and Karol Wojtyła, both boys' mothers, born a year apart, suffered significant health crises when the boys were eight years old.

In the winter of 1919, in the town of Monmouth, yet another Illinois town where the Reagans lived briefly, something near-tragic happened to Reagan's mom. As World War I drew to a close, the jubilant Illinois town was jolted by the influenza epidemic that was killing tens of millions from Europe to America (including Jacinta and Francisco in Fátima). The young Reagan was frightened by the sight of townspeople donning facial masks and of wreaths with black ribbons adorning doors. Schools, libraries, dance halls, and even churches were closed or quarantined.[37]

This strange flu bug afflicted not the very young and very old, as most viruses do, but perfectly healthy middle-aged people. Nelle Reagan was one of them. She nearly perished. Her husband and sons were sure they were going to lose her. Fortunately, Nelle hung on.

Ronald Reagan might never have become president if his mother had lost her life that winter. Nelle was that much of a formative figure in his development.

Young Karol Wojtyła was not so lucky. Emilia became sick ten years after Nelle Reagan. Her husband and sons watched in horror as they lost her to kidney and congestive heart failure.

Emilia's husband would outlive her. Nelle would outlive her husband. As we shall see, both Catholic fathers to two great future leaders would die just weeks apart at the start of the tumultuous 1940s.

THE WATERS OF THE ROCK RIVER

The church that so influenced young Ronald Reagan was perched along the Rock River, a tributary of the mighty Mississippi. Church members were once baptized in that river.

When Reagan's family arrived in Dixon in 1920, they fell in love with a little beach at Lowell Park, tucked aside the Rock River. The young Ronald loved to swim. Athletic like the young Karol, he was an even better swimmer (though not a better soccer goalie). Reagan was so adept at swimming that he set local records in the YMCA pool and was approached by an Olympic scout. He would turn to swimming throughout his life for exercise, relaxation, and recuperation, including as an adult in the 1980s recovering from a shooting—as would the adult Karol in the 1980s after being shot.[38]

For young Reagan, it was a dream to serve one day as a lifeguard at the Lowell Park beach. He got that job when he was fifteen. Years later he called it "maybe... the best job I ever had."[39] He patrolled as many as a thousand swimmers at a time, all by himself, in dark, murky water, seven days per week, typically 10 A.M. to 9 P.M., for a mere fifteen to sixteen dollars a week.[40] He carried that exhausting but exhilarating schedule for seven summers.

Those are some eye-opening numbers, but few compare to this one: *seventy-seven*. Reagan saved the lives of seventy-seven people in that river during those seven years. It was a number he always held dear. "One of the proudest statistics of my life is 77," he said decades later.[41] Until his dying days, when Alzheimer's disease would rob him of nearly every memory, he clung to the image of the beach and those saved lives.[42]

The young Karol made his saves in front of the goalie's net; the young Reagan made his saves in front of the lifeguard's stand.

These feats shaped Reagan as a person, helping to make him a dutiful, courageous man. Generally, they taught Reagan quite a bit about life. His close friend and adviser Bill Clark, who more than once listened to Reagan reminisce about summer days at the Rock River, believed that lifeguarding instilled in the young man a basic respect for the "sanctity and dignity of human life" (to borrow the language of John Paul II), which later manifested itself in President Reagan's opposition to abortion, abhorrence of the prospect of nuclear war, and empathy for those suffering under communist occupation.[43]

The experiences at the Rock River also instilled a lifesaving attitude that Reagan carried always. He was fully confident that he could play the role of rescuer—and one day would seek to save millions of people from the scourge of atheistic communism.

In that sense, Reagan's immersion in the waters of the Rock River had an effect not terribly different from his immersion in the waters of the baptismal tank inside the First Christian Church. Both were preparations for related missions, anchored in his Christian faith. He was ready for the wider waters of a treacherous world.

Part 2

PERSECUTIONS AND ERRORS

4

1924–1939

THE "SATANIC SCOURGE" OF COMMUNISM

As Ronald Reagan and Karol Wojtyła were coming of age, Bolshevik Russia was "spreading its errors throughout the world," as the Lady of Fátima had predicted.

Vladimir Lenin died on January 21, 1924. He was only fifty-three years old but had suffered three strokes. His death led to an internal power struggle between the odious Leon Trotsky and the barbarous Joseph Stalin. The more ruthless Stalin gained the upper hand.

Stalin hated religion as much as, if not more than, Lenin did. Like Lenin, he was raised a Christian; he even attended seminary. Also like Lenin, he tossed aside his faith as a teen. He came to disdain every aspect of religion.

That scorn is evident today in surviving correspondence from January and February 1930 between Alexander Likhachev, a Soviet official, and Ivan Tovstukha, personal secretary to Stalin. The pair was examining the ongoing "problem" of the ringing of church bells in Russian villages.

Such noise was strictly prohibited. Who were the cretins responsible for this counterrevolutionary activity? The good comrades discussed removing all remaining church bells, melting them down, and recasting them into "useful things" for the atheist regime—a plan they eventually carried out.

Stalin ordered the destruction of the glorious Cathedral of Christ the Savior, which was visible from the Kremlin. Czar Alexander I had dedicated the church in gratitude to Divine Providence for saving Russia from Napoleon. It was the pride of a nation, with Michelangelo-like artwork adorning the towering ceilings. But the Soviet atheists could not tolerate this holy symbol of old Russia. Stalin called for the destruction of the cathedral. In its place, he ordained, the communists would erect a Palace of the Soviets, a giant monument to their secular ideology.

In December 1931, the Soviets dynamited the ornate cathedral. Finding a construction worker willing to push the button was not easy, but the work was done: the cathedral was reduced to rubble. It would take more than a year to cart away all the debris.

Erecting the Palace of the Soviets proved far more problematic. The Soviets held an international design competition for their massive structure, which Stalin insisted be at least as tall as the Eiffel Tower. But the nearby river often flooded the site, and the Soviets repeatedly delayed construction. What was supposed to be a monument to the glories of communism remained nothing but a huge hole in the ground.

The Palace of the Soviets was never built. Two decades later, Moscow converted the site into a huge municipal swimming pool.

Soviet central planners failed to meet their grandiose ambitions. Stalin and his minions proved effective at only one thing: killing.

A VISIT TO THE UNITED STATES

In the 1930s, Karol Wojtyła was an adolescent, getting along without a mom but buoyed by a loving father. Ronald Reagan was a college student at little Eureka College, a northwestern Illinois institution founded by the Disciples of Christ, his mother's denomination. Both were in training for their later life's calling.

One man whose calling had already come was Eugenio Pacelli. By the mid-1930s, two decades after his appointment as papal nuncio to Germany, the Italian had become Cardinal Pacelli, having risen to the prestigious positions of Vatican secretary of state and *camerlengo* (chamberlain).

He was Pope Pius XI's right-hand man. And in the fall of 1936 he became the highest-ranking Catholic official ever to visit the United States.

In 1936 the United States had no formal diplomatic representation with the Holy See, and still would not for another half century, until a president named Reagan sealed the deal with a pope named John Paul II. Pacelli made the trip to ensure a high-level diplomatic interaction.

He had almost landed in America a few years earlier. The Catholic University of America, in Washington, D.C., had asked him to join the faculty. It was an alluring offer, but his immense duties in Europe kept him from accepting. Now, with Europe under siege, with fascists in power in Germany, with communists fanning out from the Soviet Union, and with fascists and communists battling one another in Spain, Pacelli knew he needed to make the trip so the Vatican could forge closer ties with America. An ailing Pius XI gave Pacelli his enthusiastic blessing.

Pacelli observed that America so "nobly" united "a sense of discipline with a well-ordered liberty."[1] It was a shrewd observation of what the American Founders had intended. A contemporary, the Catholic and conservative intellectual Russell Kirk, spoke similarly of the importance in America of "ordered liberty." This was a proper freedom, a freedom that was not license: freedom infused with a sense of noble responsibility rooted in and fostered by faith. Individual Americans needed "inner order," said Kirk, before their country could successfully operate with "outer order." Another contemporary Catholic writer, Thomas Merton, who was trying to survive a toxic communist influence at New York's Columbia University, referred to this as "trained liberty."

Pacelli, and the Vatican generally, also understood the vital importance of American Catholicism to the long-term vigor of the Church. Even Church critics in America were acutely aware of this. The liberal George Seldes acknowledged that "it cannot be denied that the American voice today is loud at the Vatican." Seldes noted British cardinal Henry Edward Manning's prophecy that "the future of Catholicism is in America."[2]

Pacelli sailed for America in early October 1936. His ocean liner arrived in New York Harbor to a teeming crowd and throng of reporters. One photographer maneuvered himself atop a lifeboat, where he could capture Pacelli's head. He yelled out, "Hey, Mister Cardinal! Look this way." The photographer had himself the best picture of the smiling secretary of state's arrival.[3]

The Italian had come to America for a two-week visit. He saw all the sights in New York, including from the Empire State Building. His New

York stay included a meeting with President Franklin Delano Roosevelt in Hyde Park. FDR was impressed, and would later refer to Pacelli as "a good friend and an old friend."[4] Pacelli met with FDR on November 5 for a two-hour lunch. The future pontiff congratulated FDR on his reelection victory the previous day.[5]

It was a pleasant get-together, notwithstanding the "mental sparring contest" (as FDR described it) over the status of communism. Pacelli warned of a "great danger" of communism in America, which FDR naively dismissed. This was no surprise, given that FDR's administration was soiled with communist agents, sympathizers, fellow travelers, and dupes, including his and Eleanor's close pal Harry Hopkins, plus Lauchlin Currie, Alger Hiss, Harry Dexter White, and Joseph Davies, to name just a few. One day FDR would serve up Karol Wojtyła's Poland (and the rest of Eastern Europe) to Stalin's Soviet Union.[6]

FDR was concerned chiefly with fascism. With many liberals, the preferred enemy was to the right, not the left. The president made this clear to Pacelli, saying that he feared America would go fascist, not communist. "No," replied Pacelli. "Yes," countered FDR.[7]

This went back and forth before a frustrated Pacelli finally said, "Mr. President, you simply do not understand the terrible importance of the communist movement!"

FDR indeed did not. He would spend nearly the entirety of World War II accommodating "Uncle Joe" Stalin and believing just about everything the communist despot told him.[8] After all, FDR said of Stalin, "he likes me." "I think that if I give him [Stalin] everything I possibly can and ask nothing from him in return, *noblesse oblige*," said FDR after one of his conferences with Stalin, "he won't try to annex anything and will work with me for a world of democracy and peace."[9]

That was not Pacelli's view of Stalin.

PACELLI AND THE FAMILY OF THE FIRST CATHOLIC PRESIDENT

As we shall see throughout this book, such exchanges have relevance to the great battle of the twentieth century. All relate to confronting those errors that a Lady in Fátima foresaw. To that end, another Pacelli meeting in America was of particular relevance to the crimes ahead.

Among those present at Hyde Park during that FDR-Pacelli lunch was Joseph P. Kennedy, a rising force who would become known as patriarch of the Kennedy dynasty. Kennedy was one Democrat never naive to the communist threat. To the contrary, if Joe Kennedy had an international blind side, it was to European fascism. But on the communist threat, he and the cardinal were kindred spirits.

Joseph Kennedy's wife, Rose, was there for the Hyde Park lunch as well. Thanks to Rose, we have a written account of Pacelli's activities that day. In an undated entry in her diary, which years later she amended with the label "Cardinal Pacelli Now Pope Pius XII visits President Roosevelt," Rose described the meeting.[10]

She remembered a brisk, sunny November day, when she and her husband left the house to meet Pacelli, his Italian secretary, and New York's Bishop Donahue at the "one hundred and twenty fifth street railroad station" to accompany them to Hyde Park. "He immediately impressed us as being very genial," Rose wrote of Pacelli, "probably because he had a ready smile which lighted his face constantly. In repose he had one of the most inspiring faces I have ever seen. It seemed to reflect great nobility of mind and purpose."[11]

They all boarded the train and started the hour-long ride to the Roosevelt abode, with Pacelli and Joe Kennedy talking about what Rose called "general conditions" in America. FDR's secretary greeted them at the Hyde Park station. At FDR's home, they were welcomed by the president's mother, whom Rose described as "about eighty [years old], dignified, handsome and gracious," resembling a European "duchess." The president greeted them in a wheelchair in his large living room. Rose remembered the two men speaking alternately English and French.

At one point, FDR's two grandchildren were brought to Pacelli for what Rose called "a papal blessing." Rose wrote, "The Cardinal was gentle and understanding and the President beamed approvingly." The adults then went to the table for lunch, with Pacelli saying grace. Rose regretted a lunch conversation that went too fast, with talk mainly of languages (Pacelli knew seven or eight of them), geography, and Pacelli's time "in Belgium during the German occupation after the World War." When lunch ended, the visit was essentially over. Mrs. Roosevelt, the matriarch, asked Pacelli to bless the house. After final handshakes, Pacelli and the Kennedys departed together.

As they neared the Hyde Park station again, Mrs. Kennedy recalled, their group was astonished to see "vast throngs of children, accompanied by Sisters, waving American and Italian flags." Apparently, the policeman at the station had notified the local Catholic school that a special guest was in town. The nuns rallied the kids outdoors. Pacelli responded with what Rose called "an endearing gesture." He got out of the car and "walked the last mile to the station on foot" alongside the children and nuns. "I shall never forget that picture," said Rose, "the Cardinal with his red robe flying in the October breeze, passing from the top of the hill down the long lanes of smiling, excited children, waving their flags and blessing themselves simultaneously." She said the nuns' faces were "radiant, overjoyed... as they knelt reverently on the cold stone pavement for his blessing. He graciously bestowed it right and left." By then, other Catholics had arrived at the station to see the future pope.

Once arrived back in New York, Pacelli rode with the Kennedy couple to their house in Bronxville, where the family lived from 1928 to 1938.[12] Very few sources have reported on this intriguing visit, and those that have done so have not provided extensive details, including whether America's future first Catholic president, John F. Kennedy, was present to meet with this first would-be pope in America.[13] John had started college at Harvard that fall, though Bronxville was not too far a ride for him to come home to greet such an esteemed Vatican official. His ambitious father would have wanted him to meet the Holy See's secretary of state.

Rose Kennedy's account suggests that John was not there, though his devout younger brother Bobby was. Bobby was also presidential timber, and an intense anticommunist who would be victimized by communism.

Rose remembered joyously that Pacelli sat on a couch surrounded by her children. The kids asked Pacelli "childish questions about his jewelled cross and about his Cardinal's ring." She said he answered the questions "simply and smilingly." He then "stood outside patiently" for photographs, gave a final benediction to the Kennedys and their servants, and left. "We had a last glimpse of the colorful red robe with the noble endearing face," wrote a touched Rose, "and His Eminence had gone." Mrs. Kennedy did not record details of any religious or political conversation the future pope might have had.

From New York, Pacelli traveled the country. He took in the sights and ideas of the American founding. In Philadelphia, he visited the Liberty Bell. When he went to Washington, he was escorted by motorcade along the Potomac to George Washington's home in Mount Vernon.

While in Washington, he spoke at Catholic University, where he said that "only the fatherly prohibition" of Pope Pius XI had kept him from accepting the professorship offered there years earlier. He also spoke at the National Press Club, where he said that glory does not belong to "those who triumph on the battlefield, but to those who safeguard tranquility and peace." It was a message that Adolf Hitler needed to hear.

Pacelli took in the fullness and diversity of American life. He received honorary degrees at several Catholic universities, including Notre Dame, and traveled eight thousand miles visiting cities like Cleveland, Chicago, Kansas City, and Saint Paul. He even visited the Boulder Dam. While in California, he visited Hollywood—arriving there just before a young man from the Midwest named Ronald Reagan.[14]

The visit to America was time well spent for the future Pope Pius XII, who was destined to become America's first Cold War ally in the chair of Saint Peter. The visit was rich with tragic irony as well, given that many of the figures he visited would be torched by communism's mendacity and errors, from FDR to the Kennedy boys.

In all, Pacelli was being prepared for the clash against atheistic communism. Unlike the young Ronald Reagan and Karol Wojtyła, whose entrances upon the world stage were decades away, Pacelli's grand entry was only three years away.

DIVINE REDEMPTION: ON ATHEISTIC COMMUNISM

Eugenio Pacelli's predecessor in the chair of Saint Peter, Pope Pius XI, had been embroiled in the battle against communism since Lenin consolidated power.

From the beginning of his papacy in February 1922, Pius XI had been a stalwart fighter against communism. He coined some of the most memorable Church statements against communism/socialism, particularly in his classic 1931 encyclical *Quadragesimo Anno*: "Socialism [is]… irreconcilable with true Christianity. Religious socialism, Christian socialism, are contradictory terms; no one can be at the same time a good Catholic and a true socialist."

In 1937, Pius XI's Vatican responded scathingly to the communist threat, officially describing communism as a "collectivistic terrorism" threatening the world, a "savage barbarity," a pernicious "plague" promulgated by Marxist "powers of darkness." Mincing no words, the Catholic Church called communism a "satanic scourge."[15]

These explosive words appeared in a formal Church encyclical, a major statement titled *Divini Redemptoris*, carrying the subtitle "On Atheistic Communism." Its significance was difficult to overstate, as was the state of apoplexy it unleashed in the communist world.

Divini Redemptoris offered an intense examination of atheistic communism, arguably the most damning official declaration ever issued.

Released March 19, 1937—the solemnity of Saint Joseph, patron of the universal Church and the *custos*, the guardian or protector, of the child Jesus—the encyclical was produced during another scourge: the Spanish Civil War, a brutal struggle between two totalitarian extremes, fascism and communism. The civil war was yet another manifestation of the errors of international communism.

In this striking document, Pius XI called communism "Godless," "by its nature anti-religious," "intrinsically wrong," a form of "perversity," "trickery," a "fury," "poison," "violent, deceptive," an "extreme danger," a "deluge which threatens the world," a "collectivistic terrorism... replete with hate," and a "plague" leading to "ruin" and "catastrophe." *Divini Redemptoris* said that his scourge "conceals in itself a false messianic idea" and was a form of "class-warfare which causes rivers of blood to flow," a "savage barbarity" that "has not confined itself to the indiscriminate slaughter of bishops" and destruction of churches and monasteries. The Marxists were orchestrating a battle against "the very idea of Divinity."

"The evil we must combat," asserted the encyclical, "is at its origin primarily an evil of the spiritual order. From this polluted source the monstrous emanations of the communistic system flow with satanic logic."

This strident rhetoric was grounded in Aquinas, in faith and reason, in revelation, and, equally important, in an already rich tradition of Church critiques of Marxist ideology. That tradition dated back to Pope Pius IX's very early condemnation in the encyclical *Qui Pluribus* (On Faith and Religion), released in November 1846, two years before the publication of the *Communist Manifesto*. *Qui Pluribus* denounced "the unspeakable doctrine of Communism, as it is called, a doctrine most opposed to the very natural law." If this doctrine was accepted, the encyclical said, "the complete destruction of everyone's laws, government, property, and even of human society itself would follow." Pius IX predicted severe destruction from communism, which he assessed as among "the most dark designs of men in the clothing of sheep, while inwardly ravening wolves." These men peddled their nostrums "by means of a feigned and deceitful appearance of a purer piety, a stricter virtue and discipline; after taking their captives gently, they mildly bind them, and then kill them in secret. They make men fly in terror from all practice of religion, and they cut down and dismember the sheep of the Lord." The pope blasted the writings of communists, saying these works, "filled with deceit and cunning," "spread pestilential doctrines everywhere and deprave the minds especially of the imprudent, occasioning great losses for religion."

The next line in the 1846 encyclical is especially interesting, particularly the use of the term *errors*, the word Our Lady of Fátima would choose to describe the coming horrors of Soviet communism seven decades later:

> As a result of this filthy medley of errors which creeps in from every side, and as the result of the unbridled license to think, speak and write, We see the following: morals deteriorated, Christ's most holy religion despised, the majesty of divine worship rejected, the power of this Apostolic See plundered, the authority of the Church attacked and reduced to base slavery, the rights of bishops trampled on, the sanctity of marriage infringed, the rule of every government violently shaken and many other losses for both the Christian and the civil commonwealth.

Those errors are precisely what would come to pass under Soviet communism: "the sanctity of marriage" was violated, divorce and abortion rates skyrocketed, and the Church was attacked at every turn.

Pius IX's successor, the great Leo XIII, likewise went after communism in the first year of his pontificate. On April 21, 1878, he released his first encyclical, *Inscrutabili Dei Consilio* (On the Evils of Society), and then three days after Christmas, on December 28, 1878, released the second, *Quod Apostolici Muneris* (On Socialism).

In *Quod Apostolici Muneris*, Pope Leo XIII excoriated communism as "the fatal plague which insinuates itself into the very marrow of human society only to bring about its ruin." This "deadly plague" was "creeping into the very fibers of human society and leading it on to the verge of destruction." These evils, the pontiff admonished, "have so rapidly increased."

Writing of "that sect of men who, under various and almost barbarous names, are called socialists, communists, or nihilists," Leo XIII said: "They leave nothing untouched or whole which by both human and divine laws has been wisely decreed for the health and beauty of life. They refuse obedience to the higher powers, to whom, according to the admonition of the Apostle, every soul ought to be subject, and who derive the right of governing from God."

Leo's papacy ended in 1903, but the Church's battle with atheistic communism was just beginning. More statements followed, in 1924, 1928, 1930, 1931, two in 1932, and 1933, all before *Divini Redemptoris* in 1937.[16] *Divini Redemptoris* accurately stated that the Church had called public attention to the perils of communism "more frequently and more effectively" than "any other public authority on earth."

By delving into communist thought and taking on the philosophy's own claims, the Church made clear that the notion of a "Christian Marxist" was an oxymoron. In the dialectical and historical materialism Marx advocated, "there is no room for the idea of God."

Divini Redemptoris concluded by affirming, "We place the vast campaign of the Church against world communism." The Church called on the assistance of not just clergy in "these troublous times" but also the laity "to fight the battles of the Lord."

Given this long record of papal declarations, it is no secret why communists so reviled the Roman Catholic Church. The Church knew who they were and did not hesitate to blow the whistle.

ON THE GERMAN REICH

Many of the Roman Catholic Church's critics have contended that the Church was tough on communism but soft on fascism. To make this argument is to overlook another powerful encyclical that Pius XI issued just five days before *Divini Redemptoris.*

On March 14, 1937, Passion Sunday, the Vatican released *Mit Brennender Sorge,* a Pius XI encyclical "On the Church and the German Reich." Its chief author under Pius XI was Eugenio Pacelli, the future Pope Pius XII, recent traveler to America and former bishop to Bavaria.

Writing of the situation in Germany, the encyclical noted that the Church had "tried to sow the seed of a sincere peace." Unfortunately, "other men," whom the Church not-so-diplomatically deemed "the enemy of Holy Scripture," had "oversowed the cockle of distrust, unrest, hatred, defamation, of a determined hostility overt or veiled, fed from many sources and wielding many tools, against Christ and His Church. They, and they alone with their accomplices, silent or vociferous, are today responsible, should the storm of religious war, instead of the rainbow of peace, blacken the German skies."

In a statement that repeatedly used words like *dark* and *evil* to describe the prevailing situation under Hitler, the Church warned, "Whoever exalts race, or the people, or the State, or a particular form of State, or the depositories of power,... whoever raises these notions above their standard value and divinizes them to an idolatrous level, distorts and perverts an order of the world planned and created by God." *Mit Brennender Sorge* urged the German faithful to "refuse to yield to this aberration" that established itself as a "rival" to God. In a direct challenge to the ultranationalism of Nazism and fascism generally, the Church said that "none but superficial minds could stumble into concepts of a national God, of a national religion; or attempt to lock within the frontiers of a single people, within the narrow limits of a single race, God, the Creator of the universe, King and Legislator of all nations."

The encyclical thanked those faithful German priests—many of whom would be dispatched to concentration camps and gassed—for persevering "in their Christian duty and in the defense of God's rights in the teeth of an aggressive paganism." It ordered priests to stay faithful to their Church and the Christian faith, above all sacrificing themselves and their own well-being to help and love their persecuted neighbors: "The priest's first loving gift to his neighbors is to serve truth and refute error in any of its forms. Failure on this score would be not only a betrayal of God and your vocation, but also an offense against the real welfare of your people and country. To all those who have kept their promised fidelity to their Bishops on the day of their ordination; to all those who in the exercise of their priestly function are called upon to suffer persecution; to all those imprisoned in jail and concentration camps, the Father of the Christian world sends his words of gratitude and commendation."

Numerous priests, including the Polish Franciscan Maximilian Maria Kolbe and the German Jesuit Alfred Delp, as well as nuns like Edith Stein, would honor this call. They went to their deaths with their Jewish brothers and sisters, side by side, comforting their neighbors in places like Auschwitz.

In *Mit Brennender Sorge*, the Roman Catholic Church urged "young Germans... not to be overcome by evil, but to aim at the triumph of good over evil." It also implored German parents to stay true and raise their children in the faith. Among such parents at the time were those of a German boy named Joseph Ratzinger, the future Pope Benedict XVI, who would assume the name of the pope (Benedict XV) tormented by Europe's descent into World War I.

The encyclical concluded by imploring the German people en masse to "return to religion, bend the knee before Christ, and arming themselves against the enemies of God, again resume the task God has laid upon them."

The "days of tribulation" that the encyclical spoke of would only get worse, reaching unimaginable depths of cruelty.

One knowledgeable observer was especially impressed with the Church's consistent opposition to both totalitarian threats, fascist and communist. A former communist who had spied for the Soviets, this man was now a writer at *Time* magazine. His spectacular case one day would make the front pages of every newspaper and greatly inspire Ronald Reagan. "No matter what critics might say," wrote Whittaker Chambers, "it is scarcely deniable that the Church Apostolic, through the encyclicals and other papal pronouncements, has been fighting against totalitarianism more knowingly, devoutly and authoritatively, and for a longer time, than any other organized power."[17]

Chambers typed those words in a remarkable cover feature on Pope Pius XII for *Time*. He was impressed with the consistency of the Church and its pope.

AMERICA'S BISHOP: FULTON SHEEN

We could not proceed at this point in the narrative without acknowledging another force in the rising crusade against atheistic communism—a dynamic, brilliant American priest named Fulton Sheen.

As noted, in the twentieth century Sheen became the most recognized and influential Catholic in America, later dubbed "America's Bishop" by biographer and historian Thomas Reeves.[18] He was so renowned because he was so gifted. He was a superb communicator, through the spoken word, on radio and then television, and the written word, delivered via a syndicated column and innumerable books and pamphlets.

Sheen was born May 8, 1895, in El Paso, Illinois, a tiny town eighty miles from Ronald Reagan's Dixon—and, not unlike Reagan, born humbly in an apartment over a hardware store.[19] Like Reagan, Sheen never lost that Midwest feel and touch, even as he ascended to heights of popularity on both coasts and every household in between.[20]

The Illinoisan was ordained in the diocese of Peoria in 1919, just as Eugenio Pacelli faced malevolent forces in post–World War I Germany. Today, a drive out of Peoria, directly from the parking lot at Sheen's onetime church, takes motorists along the Ronald Reagan Highway to Eureka College and to the various towns where Reagan lived, such as Galesburg.

(I have been asked over the years whether Reagan and Sheen ever met.[21] Their paths could have easily crossed. Both were natives of northwest Illinois, and it is possible that Jack or Neil or even Ronald attended a Mass in Peoria while Sheen was present. It is more likely that Sheen and Reagan encountered each other in Hollywood, where the priest hosted an annual event and knew Reagan's ex-wife, Jane Wyman. They had hit

TV shows at the same time in the 1950s. Both were vocal anticommunists. I directed the question to Nancy Reagan, who agreed that "it would make sense that they would have met" but said she could not recall their having done so.)[22]

In the 1930s, Sheen had not yet reached his peak of popularity, which would come with the advent of television in the 1950s. But he was still very well known, particularly via the huge reach of his NBC radio program, *The Catholic Hour.* He was also known to Eugenio Pacelli, as well as to the man who had made Pacelli cardinal and secretary of state.

In the summer of 1934, Pope Pius XI named Sheen a papal chamberlain, a member of the papal household, with the title "Monsignor." A year later, he elevated Sheen to domestic prelate, with the title "Right Reverend Monsignor." Sending congratulations to Sheen was Secretary of State Pacelli.[23]

There was no more effective Catholic apologist in America than Fulton Sheen. He taught on every aspect of the faith, from Mary to the Eucharist. But he was especially effective in dissecting atheistic communism, which brought him closer to Pius XI and the future Pius XII.

During a private audience with Sheen in 1934,[24] Pius XI told the American to study Karl Marx and communism and to expose their fallacies when speaking in public. The pontiff advised Sheen to speak on communism "at every opportunity" and to never cease to "warn Americans of its dangers."

Loyal to his pope and his Church, Sheen heeded the request. The American priest dove into an extensive study of Marx, Lenin, communism, Stalin, and the Bolsheviks. The subject became a core element of his mission, message, and outreach. Sheen read and spoke several languages, thus finding in Marx's most obscure writings various untranslated tidbits and introducing them into the English world. Among the more telling quotations from Marx was this one: "Communism begins where atheism begins," which Sheen exhumed from the French original and repeated often.[25]

"Marx was not first a Communist and then an atheist," Sheen wrote. "He was first an atheist, then a Communist. Communism was merely the political expression of his atheism. As he hated God, so would he hate those who would own property."[26]

Sheen added: "In order to understand the Communists' idea of truth, we have to substitute the philosophy of Communism for God; in other words, the ultimate origin of truth is in their Party, which falls heir to the philosophy of Marx and Lenin."[27]

Sheen dramatically forecast that Soviet communists had "put before the world a dilemma," an "apocalyptic" one: "They have thrown down the gauntlet to the world. The voice is either brotherhood in Christ or comradeship in anti-Christ. There is no alternative. If the one does not reign, the other will. They will have chosen the comradeship in anti-Christ—they can devour anything that is not brotherhood in Christ."[28] Communism, he said, was inspired not by the spirit of Christ "but by the spirit of the serpent... the Mystical Body of the Anti-Christ."[29]

In his 1935 Lenten sermon at Saint Patrick's, Sheen stayed true to his pope's request. He called out communism and its lust to "confiscate, disperse, and annihilate." He described communism as a brutish parody of religion, "the ape of Christianity." He predicted that neither "New Deals [n]or fascism" would stop communism because they could not "summon forth sufficient zeal and fervor." They lacked communists' absolute devotion to their "religion."[30]

In the next year's Lenten sermon, March 16, 1936, Sheen referred to communism as a "slave state" and a form of materialism "gone mad." (Interestingly, Ronald Reagan forty years later would refer to communism as a "form of madness.") "Why can't the modern mind see there is nothing new in communism?" he asked. "It is a groan of despair."[31]

A week later, March 23, Sheen called the USSR "the most anti-Christ nation on the face of the earth." He told the assembled that it was fitting that Soviet communism's emblem was "a rotted corpse, the body of Lenin—a perfect symbol of that to which all communism must lead us all, unto dust, unto dissolution, unto death." The priest said that communism had replaced general heresy as the foremost enemy of the Church.[32]

Sheen said that the communists had failed to convince the world that there is no God. Rather, he quipped, they had succeeded only in convincing the world that there *is* a Devil.[33]

In this and much more—including the Nazi threat—Sheen and Eugenio Pacelli were kindred spirits. While Pacelli was secretary of state, the two spent an hour together in Rome discussing the troubled world. Sheen reported that Pacelli was especially concerned about the threat emanating from Germany, noting that the secretary of state spoke "with considerable vehemence against Hitler and Nazism."[34]

Both ideologies, Nazism and Bolshevism, were totalitarian and had the potential to spark larger wars. But communism was worse in one important respect: it had much broader appeal around the world, as the Comintern was organizing and encouraging communist parties in country after country.

The situation was the same in America. Though there were some Nazi sympathizers, the United States had no Nazi Party or publications akin to the Communist Party USA and its organs. As Fulton Sheen understood, Nazism was (at the moment) the greater external threat to America, whereas communism was the longer-term internal threat.[35] Both threats, fascism and communism, Nazism and Bolshevism, were diabolical and dangerous.

Sheen emphasized that the Church had consistently opposed all forms of totalitarianism. "The Church saw the evils of totalitarianism and condemned each in turn," wrote Sheen. "The Church condemned fascism in the encyclical *Non abbiamo bisogno* which was written in Italian because fascism was a national phenomenon; it condemned Nazism in the German language in the encyclical *Mit brennender sorge* because Nazism was a racial phenomenon. It condemned communism in the universal language of Latin in the encyclical *Divini Redemptoris* because communism is an international phenomenon."[36]

In short, the Church had been eminently consistent.

And so, in March 1939, when Eugenio Pacelli became Pope Pius XII, Fulton Sheen was elated. They had already met several times in Rome and America and exchanged letters and publications (those written by Sheen). Now, beginning in 1939, they would meet privately in Rome every year of Pacelli's papacy, with the pope calling Sheen by his first name. Pacelli told Sheen that he was a "prophet of the times" and would one day have a "high place in heaven."[37]

The feeling was mutual. From the moment the papacy began, Sheen extolled Pacelli's virtues. Tapped by NBC for its special broadcast on the coronation, he sang the new pontiff's praises. From the pulpit at Saint Patrick's Cathedral, he said for the first of many times that the new pope was "the only unified moral voice left on earth."[38]

And with another war approaching in Europe, such a moral voice would be needed more than ever.

5

1939–1945

"BLOOD, BLOOD, BLOOD, AND AGAIN BLOOD"

On October 5, 1938, a nun in Kraków, Poland, died of tuberculosis at age thirty-three. Within a year, Hitler and Stalin would be devouring her beloved homeland and starting World War II.

It turned out that this nun could not have been more prophetic about what the world would need as it confronted totalitarian threats. But most of the world would not know her name for another seven decades, when a fellow Kraków mystic, a Polish priest-turned-pope, discovered her, resurrected her vision, and canonized her.

She was born Helena Faustina Kowalska, the third of ten children, in August 1905 in the village of Glogowiec, in the heart of Poland. In 1924, nineteen-year-old Helena and her sister went to a dance in a park in the city of Łódź, which in two decades would be ripped to shreds. While at the dance, the teenage Faustina had a vision of a suffering Jesus. It would not be her last. "How long shall I put up with you," Jesus asked her, "and how long will you keep putting Me off?"[1]

She dashed to the cathedral, where she said Jesus told her to leave for Warsaw right away to join a convent. She immediately packed a small bag and jumped on a train, not getting her parents' permission; they had refused her request to enter religious life, an intense desire she had felt since childhood. Nothing could stop her after what she had just seen and been told. Once in the convent, she devoted her life completely to Jesus Christ. She took the name "Maria."

Faustina's religious life was a mix of suffering, torment, persecution, illness, dedication, obedience, and ecstasy. As to the last, she was every bit the mystic, experiencing terrifying but profound visions and prophecies and often seeing and communicating directly (she claimed) with Christ and with the Blessed Mother. The most stirring vision came on February 22, 1931, while she was in her cell at the convent. She said that Jesus appeared, clothed in white, with his right hand raised as if giving a blessing to the world, while the left hand touched a garment at his breast. From the opening in the garment, exuding from Jesus's sacred heart, were two large rays, one red and the other white, representing blood and water to heal the world of its sins. "In silence I gazed intently at the Lord," said Faustina. "My soul was overwhelmed with fear, but also with great joy."[2]

The Christ figure instructed the nun: "Mankind will not enjoy peace until it turns with confidence to My Mercy."

Jesus asked Faustina to paint this image displayed before her, and to inscribe it with the words "Jesus, I trust in you." Since she was not a painter herself, painters were commissioned. Jesus also called for the universal Church to celebrate an annual Feast of Divine Mercy the first Sunday after Easter. That feast day would eventually be established but only after a long wait. When it was finally accomplished, nearly seventy years after her death, it would be done through the first and only Polish pope.

Among the nun's grimmest prophetic visions was a Fátima-like vision of hell. "I, Sister Faustina Kowalska, by the order of God, have visited the Abysses of Hell so that I might tell souls about it and testify to its existence," she wrote in her diary. "The devils were full of hatred for me, but they had to obey me at the command of God. What I have written is but a pale shadow of the things I saw. But I noticed one thing: That most of the souls there are those who disbelieved that there is a hell." She also saw, Dante-like, special sections reserved for specific agonies earned in this fallen world. "There are caverns and pits of torture where one form of agony differs from another," she recorded. In a situation similar to what the Fátima children reported witnessing, she added, "I would have died at the very sight of these tortures if the omnipotence of God had not supported me."[3]

The world had fallen so far, so deep, that Faustina said it required an "Ocean of Mercy" that Jesus alone could offer. She said this on the eve of a war that would tear apart Europe.

The Polish nun did not live to see the horrors of the war to come. Less than a year after her death, the Nazis invaded her native Poland, and soon thereafter the Soviets followed suit. The Second World War had begun.

SOVIET ATROCITIES IN POLAND

Poland's fate had been sealed during the dark of night August 23–24, 1939, when Hitler's Germany and Stalin's USSR signed a secret pact. It was a marriage made in Hades.

Some of those in Hitler's close circle at his Berghof felt the chill. As they awaited news from Nazi foreign minister Joachim von Ribbentrop of the deal he was working on with his Soviet counterpart, Vyacheslav Molotov, and Stalin himself, they looked up at the high mountain peaks, where they saw a frightening view. "The entire sky was in turmoil," remembered Hitler crony Herbert Döring. "It was blood-red, green sulphur grey, black as the night, a jagged yellow." Döring added: "Everyone was looking [at the sky] horrified—it was intimidating.... Everyone was watching." A woman in the group told Hitler: "My Führer, this augurs nothing good. It means blood, blood, blood, and again blood."

"Hitler was totally shocked," recalled Döring. "He was almost shaking."[4]

Back in Moscow, meanwhile, Joseph Stalin was all smiles, raising his glass to toast his new "lasting friendship with Germany and the great Führer." He asserted to Hitler's foreign minister, "I assure you that the Soviet Union takes this pact very seriously."[5]

One week later, the fascists and communists consummated their marriage by taking the territory between them called Poland. In keeping with the pact, Hitler invaded Poland from the west on September 1. Two and a half weeks later, on September 17, the Red Army invaded Poland from the east.

The atrocities that followed were legion. The Soviets seized thousands of Polish military officers, some of the best of the young Karol Wojtyła's countrymen. Had the elder Karol Wojtyła remained in the military, he might have been one of them. On March 5, 1940, Stalin signed their death warrant, condemning 21,857 of them to "the supreme penalty: shooting."

The officers were taken to three execution sites, the most infamous of which was in the Katyn Forest, twelve miles west of Smolensk, Russia. There, the Polish men were slaughtered like farm animals. The Soviets covered up their crime.

It was hardly a secret that the Soviets had been shipping captured Poles into Russian territory since 1939. The April 15, 1940, edition of the *New York Times* reported, "The Soviet authorities are transporting a large part of the population of Eastern Poland into inner Russia." They were given "only fifteen minutes to leave their homes," added the *Times*, and "even seriously ill persons are forced into the unheated emigration trains."

But what they did to the 21,857 sons of Poland would remain a Kremlin secret for decades.

The gruesome logistics were divulged decades later, after the Cold War, by General Dmitri Tokarev, who was NKVD chief for the Kalinin region during the slaughter.[6] Tokarev explained how in his prison the Soviets carefully lined two rooms with velvet to muffle the sound of gunfire. Poland's finest were handcuffed, escorted in, pushed to their knees to face the wall, and shot in the back of the head.

"The first night they brought three hundred people," Tokarev recalled of the first shipment of captured Polish officers driven to the slaughterhouse. "This was too much. The night was too short and we had to work only at night." So they scaled down to murdering a mere 250 men per night—every single night for a month.

Tokarev chillingly recalled one Soviet henchman, Vasily Blokhin. Blokhin's attire included a leather cap, leather gauntlets, and a brown leather apron. "This made a horrible impression on me," Tokarev confessed fifty years too late. The filmmakers in Ronald Reagan's Hollywood could not have crafted a better executioner. Historians record Blokhin as having personally executed more than seven thousand Polish officers during the Katyn Forest massacre.

Imagine executing 250 men per night. The mopping up of gallons of blood alone must have been a mighty chore. The Walther pistols the Soviets used, which performed so ably for the Nazi police state, were overwhelmed by the sheer volume of incessant murder. The NKVD masters called on whomever was available—junior Soviet officers, guards, drivers—to pull off this mass extermination and keep it secret.

The bloodletting occurred not only in Kalinin but also in two other

Soviet camps, Sarobelsk and Kharkov. After the Soviets murdered the sons of Poland, they stacked the corpses in trucks and drove them to a mass grave in the countryside.[7]

And then, when it was all finished, those responsible for the murders turned their guns around. Unable to cope with their darkness, several shot themselves.[8]

This was the price of serving the night.

What the Soviets cultivated at Katyn was an early and especially insidious display of what another Pole, Pope John Paul II, would call a Culture of Death.

A STUNNED WORLD

The Hitler-Stalin Pact of August 1939 had made this mass bloodletting possible. When news of Stalin's alliance with Hitler hit the communist world, communists everywhere were stunned, especially Jewish communists. They had long despised Nazism. How could they possibly defend this? Defend, though, many of them would. They swore a loyalty oath always to defend Soviet Russia; they had no other option.

Not everyone was surprised that the Nazis and Soviets had teamed up. In March 1939, Fulton Sheen warned of a possible alliance between the two devils, the brown one and the red one. The two could find common ground, said Sheen, in their joint hatred of good and God.[9]

"There is not a vast difference between them," Sheen said again that summer, just before the Hitler-Stalin Pact was finalized. "What class is to Russia, race is to Germany, what the bourgeois are to the Russians, the Jews are to the Germans."[10] Here, Sheen foreshadowed words by fellow Illinois native Ronald Reagan, who would say there wasn't a "dime's worth of difference" between a fascist and a communist.

Both men were exaggerating for effect. They knew there were significant differences between the two ideologies. In fact, those differences had kept the Nazis and Bolsheviks apart and led many (including Nazi-hating American communists) to think the two could never join forces. But Sheen and Reagan recognized the important commonalities between Nazism and Soviet communism—especially that both were, at their essence, about the tyrannical power of an abusive state that controls and kills certain categories of citizens. The Nazis despised and targeted groups based on ethnicity; the Soviets did so based on class.

"As Americans," said Sheen at a huge January 1939 rally hosted by the National Council of Catholic Men, "we are not concerned with whether a dictator has a long moustache or a short moustache; or whether he invades the soul through the myth of race or the myth of the class; we are concerned only with the fact that there has been an invasion and expropriation of the inalienable liberties of man."[11] He said that Hitler and Stalin were "two gangsters."[12] Both were "assassins of justice."[13]

Above all, there was their joint contempt for God. "The anti-God regime is always the anti-human regime," said Sheen. "What more clearly proves it than the Red Fascism of Communism and the Brown Fascism of Nazism which, by denying the spirit of God as the source of human rights, makes the State the source?"[14]

Sheen summed up the two dictators as the modern equivalents of "Pilate and Herod—Christ haters."[15]

Fulton Sheen was not the only Church leader to see the disturbing parallels between the communists and the Nazis. As Sheen was warning of a possible Hitler-Stalin alliance, his man in Rome was elevated to the chair of Saint Peter. On March 2, 1939, his sixty-third birthday, Vatican secretary of state Eugenio Pacelli was chosen pope on the third ballot, the quickest choice of a pontiff in more than three hundred years. One cardinal who watched Pacelli's face as the votes were tabulated later remarked, "I have never seen anyone look so pale and yet continue breathing."[16]

No doubt he was pale from the sense of awesome responsibility awaiting him as his Church and the world confronted the Nazi and Bolshevik beasts.

The newly installed Pope Pius XII sat down with Fulton Sheen for their annual meeting after the Hitler-Stalin Pact had been signed and as the world was slipping into war. The new pope asked Sheen whether he was surprised by the Nazi-Soviet alliance. When Sheen said he was not, Pius responded: "I'm glad you are not surprised. Anyone who knows the philosophy of these movements knew they were bound to unite. I expected it for a long time, but it is a very grave danger to the world."[17]

TWO YOUNG MEN ACTING IN A BURNING WORLD

No one felt that grave danger like young Karol Wojtyła, nineteen years old when the Nazis and Bolsheviks blew up his blessed homeland that September 1939. The future spiritual leader of the universal Church was in a Polish church when German bombers flew overhead. He was at the magnificent Wawel Cathedral in Kraków, where he had come to make his confession to Father Kazimierz Figlewicz and help serve Mass. He walked past the entombed remains of two Polish heroes, Saint Stanisław and King Władysław Jagiełło, namesake of the university Karol was now attending, when he heard the sirens and Luftwaffe.[18]

Peggy Noonan, the Reagan speechwriter who wrote an insightful book on John Paul II, observed, "Young Karol, the future pope, was always at church and usually at Mass when the great historical occurrences of his lifetime took place."[19]

In high school, Karol had joined and become president of the Society of Mary. He finished high school in Wadowice in 1938, and then he and his father moved to Kraków. There, the young Karol enrolled at the great Jagiellonian University, one of the oldest universities in Europe, famed academic home of the astronomer Copernicus more than four hundred years earlier. While studying philosophy and literature, he also took introductory Russian and Old Church Slavonic in addition to private lessons in French. This was the start of a love of languages that would serve him extremely well. He would dabble in as many as twelve languages.[20]

It was during this time that he met his spiritual mentor, Jan Tyranowski, and was introduced to the Carmelite mysticism of Saint John of the Cross. It deeply affected him. He studied Spanish simply to absorb the fullness of John of the Cross in the native tongue.

Of course, young Karol was not yet a priest. His professional interest at the time was like that of the twenty-eight-year-old Ronald Reagan, who was not yet a political leader: acting. At the end of the 1938–39 academic year, Karol played "Sagittarius" in a fable/play titled *The Moonlight Cavalier*, produced by an experimental theater troupe.

As for Ronald Reagan, his acting was much more advanced. He was thriving at Warner Bros.

In 1937, Reagan had traveled to California with the Chicago Cubs, the team for which he did baseball broadcasts for the megastation WHO in Des Moines, Iowa. While on the trip, he had conducted a screen test. It was a one-in-a-million chance, and Reagan figured he would never get a call back. But he impressed the big shots, and the former lifeguard suddenly hit it big. Really big. The boy from Dixon began making movies in Hollywood's Golden Age.

In his first year, Reagan made eight movies.[21] He would ultimately appear in fifty-three films. While some were "B" movies (leading men from Humphrey Bogart to John Wayne did plenty of Bs), Reagan also did many "As," including with the marquee names in the business: Errol Flynn, Olivia de Havilland, Ginger Rogers, Bette Davis, Lionel Barrymore, Doris Day, and Barbara Stanwyck, to name a few. His face was splashed solo on the cover of *Modern Screen* magazine (among others).[22]

"I only recall respect for him as an actor," recalled actress Judith Anderson.[23] Robert Osborne, the face of Turner Classic Movies, states that Reagan was "exceptionally likeable on film" and had won "worldwide recognition" by the late 1930s and early 1940s. He possessed "all the ingredients required of a leading man."[24]

By 1941, Reagan had become one of the top five box-office draws in Hollywood. He received more fan mail than any other actor at Warner Bros. except Errol Flynn.[25] The kid from a poor family in Illinois was earning upward of $3,500 per week, a pile of money in those days—more money than his father, Jack, had ever earned in a year. Reagan was able to take care of his parents, ending their lifelong financial woes. He bought them a brick house near him in Hollywood, the only home Jack ever owned.

Reagan's life was going great, but he could see that the world situation was not.

In 1939, with war exploding, Reagan grew very concerned. He voiced his fears of Hitler to family members and friends and colleagues in Hollywood. A dedicated FDR Democrat who was keenly interested in politics and international events, Reagan never hesitated to share his political opinions. He openly denounced what he called "Fascist bigotry" and eagerly made training and anti-Nazi propaganda films for the War Department.[26]

Karol Wojtyła was worried as well. His writing reflected the trauma of the times and how he grappled with the mystery of suffering. From the combat deaths at the hands of the Nazis and Bolsheviks to the rounding up and "liquidation" of the nation's huge Jewish population, Poland would lose 20 percent of its population during World War II, the highest percentage of any country in the war.

The future John Paul II looked for a silver living amid this agony. "I have lately given much thought to the liberating force of suffering," the nineteen-year-old wrote to his mentor in the theater, Mieczysław Kotlarczyk, on November 2, 1939, as the country was completely controlled by Berlin and Moscow. "It is on suffering that Christ's system rests, beginning with the cross and ending with the smallest human torment."[27]

The young actor-playwright began penning his second drama, called *Job*. (His first had been called *David*.) It was a retelling of the Old Testament saga as seen through modern Poland's trials. In this rendition, the future pope wrote:

In what I say I see one thing...
How souls are struggling with grief
Whether they are righteous or sinful....
I look and see: He is Harmony. I look and see: He balances all.[28]

Amid the trials, this "Witness to Hope," as his biographer would call him, found Hope. It was not unlike Ronald Reagan's "Divine Plan" theology instilled by Nelle: no matter how gloomy a situation was, God had a plan amid the doom. He would work out things for the best. Still, Karol Wojtyła understood that God's Church would suffer in the meantime. He would convey that in his work as a playwright. "Let theater be a church," he declared.[29]

His dedication to the theater and the Church became one and the same, so much so that it was eventually a seamless transition for the actor-playwright to turn forever to the priesthood.

1941: THE LOSS OF TWO EARTHLY FATHERS

Karol Wojtyła's father watched his proud country be destroyed by the Nazis and their new Bolshevik buddies. His heart could bear little more.

On February 18, 1941, the senior Karol, the only remaining family member to his faithful son, succumbed to a heart attack at the age of sixty-one.

The junior Karol had been working in a rock quarry. Heading home for the hour-long walk, he stopped and grabbed some medicine and food for his father. At his side, as usual, was Mary—a girl named Maria Kydrynski. She often helped the two Wojtyła men, warming up their meal for them in their kitchen.

When they entered the apartment, Maria went to the kitchen while Karol went to his father's room, where he found his beloved father dead. Maria rushed to the room and discovered the son in tears, blaming himself for not being there to help his dad. He knelt next to his father's corpse all night. "I'm all alone," he told friends. "At twenty [years old] I've already lost all the people I've loved!" He would say years later, "I never felt so alone."[30]

Karol was not alone in losing a father at that time.

In yet another parallel in the lives of Karol Wojtyła and Ronald Reagan, the latter lost his father at nearly the same time.

As noted, Jack Reagan's failures finally seemed behind him. His cheerful son even gave his dad a job answering his fan mail, which the father accepted with a joyful grace. At last, Jack had a secure job, and an easy one.

Unfortunately, the long-toiling shoe salesman had little time to enjoy this respite from a life of financial calamity. Ronald's dad had a failing heart, too.

On May 18, 1941, exactly three months after the death of the elder Karol Wojtyła, Jack Reagan's life came to an abrupt end. At 1:30 A.M., after waking, standing, and shifting around the end of his bed, perhaps headed for the bathroom, Jack jerked upright, raised his arms as if asking for help, and collapsed to the floor.[31] As was the case with Wojtyła's father, the culprit was coronary disease, and the place was his bedroom. Jack Reagan was only fifty-seven years old.

Jack's son was on the East Coast at a Warner Bros. event in Atlantic City. Nelle reached him by telephone and told him not to hurry back right away. She and Neil would take care of immediate details.[32]

The funeral service was held at nearby Saint Victor Catholic Church in Los Angeles. There, a saddened Reagan found comfort in his mystical side. He said that at the funeral service he felt "desolate and empty" (an echo of young Karol's longing) until he heard his earthly father's voice, calling out to comfort him from the other side: "I'm okay and where I am it's very nice. Please don't be unhappy." The desolation disappeared.

Ronald turned to his mother and assured her, "Jack is okay, and where he is he's very happy."[33]

The suffering Jack, whom his son described as appearing "crucified" when lifted drunk from the snow in Dixon in the winter of 1922, was carried to his final destination at Calvary. Jack was buried in Calvary Cemetery, a Roman Catholic cemetery in the archdiocese of Los Angeles.

Nelle had stood by her spouse so faithfully for years. When Jack drank too much, she told his sons that their dad had a "sickness," and to grant forgiveness and mercy. Ronald and Neil always did just that.

THE SOVIET-NAZI DIVORCE: JUNE 22, 1941

Mercy was nowhere to be found in the new marriage between Adolf Hitler and Joseph Stalin. The only question was, who would betray the other first? Which one was the bigger liar, the greater abuser?

In January 1941, Fulton Sheen warned: "Mark these words: The enemy of the world in the near future is going to be Russia, which is playing democracies against dictators and dictators against democracies, which is using peace when it can and war when it must, and is preparing, when Europe is exhausted from war, to sweep over it like a vulture to drink its blood and make away with the spoils."[34]

It was as if Sheen had a private copy of Stalin's secret speech to the Central Committee on August 19, 1939, four days before his cynical signing of the Hitler-Stalin Pact.[35] That speech, not declassified until a half century later, sheds light on why Stalin would have trusted Hitler's promise of "nonaggression" against the USSR. It was not because the Soviet leader had any special fondness for his totalitarian partner.

"The dictatorship of a Communist Party may be envisaged only as a result of a great war," Stalin told his Central Committee. "We have before us a vast field of action to develop the world Revolution. Comrades! It is in the interests of the USSR—the Fatherland of the Workers—that war should break out between the [German] Reich and the Franco-British capitalist bloc. We must do everything so that the war should last as long as possible with the aim of weakening both sides." The Soviet dictator added, "It is for these reasons that we must give priority to the approval of the conclusion of the pact proposed by Germany, and to work so that this war, which will be declared within a few days, shall last as long as possible."

That was the reason Stalin granted priority to the nonaggression pact. Sure, he did not want war with Hitler. But mainly he wanted Germany to go down with the rest of the West. "In the event of a German defeat," Stalin confidently predicted, "the Sovietization of Germany and the creation of a Communist government will follow inevitably."

Shortly after making this statement, Stalin joined Molotov and Ribbentrop to sign the Hitler-Stalin Pact.

So Stalin was hardly the loyal spouse in his political marriage to Hitler. But it was the Nazi leader who made the great betrayal. On June 22, 1941, less than two years after signing the nonaggression pact, the Nazis invaded the USSR.

Stalin was stunned. The great divorce was official. And with the Nazi invasion, Europe's war spread wider and became deadlier.

AUGUST 14, 1941: THE MARTYRDOM OF MAXIMILIAN KOLBE

As the Nazis invaded Soviet territory, they also ramped up their killing machine in their vast apparatus of concentration camps in Eastern

Europe. The slaughter was especially horrific in Poland, near the home of Karol Wojtyła—where residents could smell the ovens of Auschwitz. The Nazis killed well over a million people at Auschwitz alone. The vast majority of victims were Jews, many of them from Poland. There were also many Christian victims, including three Polish natives: the remarkable Lutheran pastor Dietrich Bonhoeffer, a Jewish convert to Christianity named Edith Stein, and a Franciscan friar named Maximilian Kolbe.

Bonhoeffer and Stein were born in the same city, Breslau, which is now Wrocław, Poland. Once the capital of Silesia, this lovely city of churches and bridges was known as the "Venice of the North." Bonhoeffer was executed in April 1945, mere weeks before the Nazi surrender and Allied liberation. Stein, a brilliant German-Jewish scholar, never made it that far. The Carmelite nun was executed in Auschwitz in August 1942. Many years after her martyrdom, Pope John Paul II would canonize Stein. Today she is known as Saint Teresa Benedicta of the Cross.

The martyrdom of Maximilian Maria Kolbe had an especially lasting impact on Karol Wojtyła.

Kolbe was born in January 1894. His parents, Julius and Maria, had a special devotion to the Virgin Mary, one picked up by their son.

As a twelve-year-old boy, Kolbe received a dramatic image. He had just had a quarrel with his mother, who in exasperation asked what would become of him. The boy went to church in the town of Pabianice, where he reported that, in the presence of the Eucharist, the Blessed Mother appeared to him in a mystical vision.[36] "What will become of me?" he asked her. The woman who watched her holy son accept a crown of thorns before accepting a crown of glory held out two crowns before this twentieth-century son of Mary. "She came to me holding two crowns, one white, the other red," said Kolbe. "She asked if I was willing to accept either of these crowns." The white crown meant he would persevere in purity; the red crown meant he would become a martyr. "I said that I would accept them both," responded Kolbe.[37]

Shortly thereafter, Kolbe became a Franciscan and entered a minor seminary/novitiate in Lwów, one of the beautiful Polish cities raped by the Germans and Soviets. He was given the religious name "Maximilian"; he added the middle name "Maria" when he completed his vows in 1914. He went to Rome, where he earned two doctorates in philosophy and theology from two of the eternal city's most prestigious Pontifical universities.

Kolbe became a pioneer in the movement of entrustment and consecration to the Blessed Mother. In 1917, the year of Fátima, he organized the so-called Militia Immaculata (Army of the Immaculate Virgin) to bring converts to the faith. When he returned home from Rome after World War I, he was overjoyed that his native land had at last been reconstituted as Poland; the nation had disappeared from the map over the previous 120-plus years (from 1795 to 1918). Kolbe's love of Poland was exceeded only by his love for Poland's patron mother, whose intercession he saw as pivotal in the resurrection of the country after the Great War.

Kolbe harnessed new methods of communication, from the best available printing presses to the use of radio—forms of outreach that a fellow Pole known as Pope John Paul II would later describe as the New Evangelization. In Kraków in 1922, Kolbe began a popular, widely circulated monthly publication, the *Knight of the Immaculata*. He would later use these media to criticize the Nazi regime that occupied the country.

In 1927, Kolbe founded a monastery in Teresin, Poland, that he named Niepokalanów, which means City of the Immaculate Mother of God. It soon became the world's largest Franciscan monastery, with upward of eight hundred friars pledged to become soldiers and saints for God under the generalship of the Immaculate Mary. They followed Professor Kolbe's simple mathematical formula: "W + w = S." This meant that Sanctity (S) comes when we unite our small will (w) to God's larger Will (W).[38]

There was a distinctive Marian element to Kolbe's teachings. The friar preached that no one in the history of humanity had known Jesus as intimately as the Blessed Mother. Her DNA and blood and sweat and tears had poured into the Son of God. Throughout Jesus's earthly existence, from the womb to the tomb, no other creature discerned His Will as closely. No one possessed greater knowledge of what He wanted. And so, argued Maximilian Kolbe, when Christ's brothers and sisters unite their wills to Mary's will, imploring her unequaled intercession, then they more perfectly do God's Will. To seek to unite with Mary's will is to unite with God's Will.

"Kolbe recognized that the greatest way to give glory to God is to unite oneself to the creature who glorifies God most perfectly, Mary Immaculate," writes Father Michael Gaitley in his popular book on Marian consecration. "He also realized that the way to give God the greatest glory is not to do so just as one person, but to have a whole army ('Militia') of people who give God the greatest glory. In fact, he wanted the army of the Immaculate ('Militia Immaculata') to eventually get the whole world to give God the greatest glory, through her, as soon as possible."[39]

Kolbe told his fellow Franciscans: "My dear, dear brothers, our dear little, little mother, the Immaculate Mary, can do anything for us. We are her children. Turn to her. She will overcome everything."[40]

This intense notion of Marian entrustment influenced the future pope from Poland. Karol Wojtyła carefully read and heeded Kolbe's words on the Blessed Mother and the power of her intercession and protection. And when Pope John Paul II sought to consecrate Russia to the Blessed Mother, he did so as Our Lady of Fátima requested and as Kolbe would have recommended—that is, not just as one person, but with the assistance of an army of people who give God the greatest glory.

Karol Wojtyła never met Maximilian Kolbe, who was martyred even before the young Pole began to study for the priesthood. Kolbe did whatever he could to resist the Nazi demolition of Poland. He and his huge group of friars, inspired by his Immaculata Movement, sheltered thousands of Jews. Kolbe stayed behind at his Franciscan monastery, where he practiced obedience and poverty "in the spirit of Saint Francis." Priestly vocations exploded in Poland, directly influencing Karol Wojtyła. With the Nazi and Soviet invasions, the monastery was converted into a hospital for the hurt and maimed. On February 17, 1941, the Nazis shut down the monastery/hospital and arrested Kolbe. The Gestapo herded him to Auschwitz, where Kolbe became Prisoner #16670.

The Nazis trashed Kolbe's Franciscan habit in favor of a striped uniform. They ridiculed and beat the friar, worked him to physical exhaustion, and singled him out for persecution and humiliation.

Near the end of July 1941, one of the captives escaped Auschwitz.[41] In response, the German commander ordered ten other prisoners to be rounded up and starved to death in an airless underground cell known as Death Block 13. One of them, a young father named Franciszek (Francis) Gajowniczek, pleaded, "My wife! My children! I shall never see them again!" Kolbe calmly stepped forward and announced that he was a priest and wanted to die in place of the young father.

Over the next two weeks, each time the cell was opened, Kolbe was seen inside on his knees. Throughout the period, he said Mass and led the others in prayers and hymns. After two weeks of complete deprivation of food and water, only Kolbe remained alive among the ten. Needing the bunker for the liquidation of others, the Nazi guards decided to rid themselves of this troublesome priest. They brought in a lethal solution of carbolic acid.

The priest complied with his sacrificial offering, elevating his left arm and stoically accepting his injection and his long-ago prophesied martyrdom. A fellow prisoner assigned to service the death bunker, Bruno Borgowiec, turned away as he saw Kolbe offer his arm to his persecutor. "Unable to watch this I left under the pretext of work to be done," Borgowiec later remembered. "Immediately after the S. S. men with the executioner had left I returned to the cell, where I found Father Kolbe leaning in a sitting position against the back wall with his eyes open and his head drooping sideways. His face was calm and radiant."[42]

Kolbe had donned the red crown the Blessed Mother had offered him years earlier. The next day, the priest's final remains of a life of Marian devotion rose upward, cremated in the flames of Auschwitz, assumed into the heavens. It was August 15, the Feast Day of the Assumption of Mary.

Four decades later, on October 10, 1982, Maximilian Maria Kolbe was canonized by a native son of Poland. There for the canonization was Franciszek Gajowniczek, the young father for whom Kolbe had sacrificed his life. The Polish pontiff declared Kolbe, already known as the Saint of Auschwitz, "The Patron Saint of Our Difficult Century."

"RUSSIA IS ON OUR SIDE IN THE WAR, BUT NOT IN THE REVOLUTION"

Maximilian Kolbe was yet another casualty of totalitarianism, as the Soviet communists had facilitated the Nazis' path into Poland.

By then, of course, the Soviets and Nazis were at war with each other. Joseph Stalin needed a new ally. He got one at the end of 1941, when Hitler's pals in imperial Japan bombed Pearl Harbor. America was forced into the war, prompting the land of Ronald Reagan, Fulton Sheen, and FDR into an unnatural alliance with the Bolshevik slave state.

At least some observers recognized that, even if Stalin became America's and Britain's ally in the fight against Hitler, the United States needed to remain cognizant of the great evil the Soviet Union represented. In October, after the Nazi invasion of the Soviet Union but before Pearl Harbor, Fulton Sheen insisted that the West should give aid to the Soviets only on certain conditions. Speaking to a large audience in Ontario, Canada, Sheen said, "As a condition of aid to Russia, the U.S. should demand a guarantee of religious freedom in the Soviet Union." He also asked that Communist Party USA be suppressed, reminding his audience that the Soviets' devotion to global communist revolution was real.[43]

As early as 1938, Sheen had insisted that the "interests of democracy lie neither in an alliance with fascism or communism."[44] He did not change his tune for the convenience of a democratic-communist alliance against Hitler. Communism was still evil, just as fascism was. In early 1941 Sheen had predicted that "the enemy of the world in the near future is going to be Russia"; now he said, "Russia is on our side in the war, but not in the revolution."[45]

Sheen posed a question that would be uncomfortable for an America at war to consider: "When the democracies of the world summon to their aid an anti-God nation to help them combat an anti-religious nation, thoughtful men must ask themselves the question: 'If the democracies summon red devils to fight brown devils, how can we be sure that democracy is on the side of the angels and fighting the battle of God?' "[46]

"EVIL IDEAS LEAD TO EVIL CONSEQUENCES"

By the time the Second World War finally ended in mid-1945, more than sixty million people had lost their lives. Many also lost their faith, particularly Jewish victims. One Jew who did not was Richard Pipes, who as a child escaped Poland thanks to a resourceful father.

Pipes lamented that the father he loved so dearly lost his faith because of the Holocaust. For Pipes, the Holocaust had the opposite effect. "The Holocaust did not shake my religious feelings," he said. Rather, the mass murders by the Germans and the Soviets demonstrated to him "what happens when people renounce faith in God, deny that human beings were created in His image, and reduce them to soulless and therefore expendable material objects." Pipes was convinced that his life had been spared "to spread a moral message by showing, using examples from history, how evil ideas lead to evil consequences. Since scholars have written enough on the Holocaust, I thought it my mission to demonstrate this truth using the example of communism."[47]

Pipes would devote the rest of his life to illuminating the evils of totalitarianism, and especially Soviet totalitarianism. He did so as professor of Russian history at Harvard for more than fifty years. He would also join Ronald Reagan's National Security Council and crusade to take down Soviet communism.

It was not only many Jews who lost their faith in the wake of the war. Many Europeans raised their children as agnostics and atheists, eventually surrendering a continent to aggressive secularism and a voluntary de-Christianization that future popes such as John Paul II and Benedict XVI (both Nazi survivors) would grapple with.[48] So many of the erstwhile believers and their sons and daughters hopelessly asked "*Where was God?*" A just God, a living God, they insisted, would not have stood by and done nothing.

This was not the thinking, or warning, of Fátima. The Lady there had exhorted peoples of all nationalities to turn to God rather than to wickedness. If not, they would choose not God but war.

It was also not the thinking of Fulton Sheen. "The only time some men . . . ever think of God," said Sheen, "is when they want to find someone to blame for their own sins. Without ever saying so, they assume that man is responsible for everything good and beautiful in the world, but God is responsible for its wickedness and its wars. . . . They ignore the fact that God is like a playwright who wrote a beautiful drama, gave it to men to act with all the directions for acting, and they made a botch of it."[49]

Sheen was more pointed in his 1942 book, *God and War.* He wrote that when the unbeliever asks, "*Where is your God now?*" the believer should respond: "Where are *your* gods now? Where is your god Progress in the face of two world wars within 21 years? Where is your god Science, now that it consecrates its energies to destruction? Where is your god Evolution now that the world is turned backward into one vast slaughterhouse?"[50]

That little nun from Poland, Sister Faustina, had been prophetic. This was a devastated, wretched world in dire need of an Ocean of Mercy. And as Fulton Sheen knew, much of the world was then turning to a new god, the god of utopian communism. Even when the world war ended, the door to the slaughterhouse did not close. Quite the contrary, the communists threw it wide open.

6

1945–1952

THE IRON CURTAIN DESCENDS

Historians haggle over the start date of the Cold War. After all, the Cold War had no Pearl Harbor, no invasion of Poland, no shot heard 'round the world fired by another Gavrilo Princip. Scholars generally point to the year 1947 as marking the beginning of the geopolitical struggle between the United States and the Soviet Union. But already on March 5, 1946, less than a year after V-E Day, Winston Churchill had declared, "From Stettin in the Baltic to Trieste in the Adriatic, an iron curtain has descended across the Continent."

The conditions for the Cold War were in place even before the Second World War ended. At the Yalta Conference in February 1945, FDR, Churchill, and Stalin agreed to a postwar reorganization that enabled the Soviet communists to take over Eastern Europe. Stalin promised the American president and the British prime minister that free elections would be held in the Soviet sphere of influence he demanded. Of course, he broke his promise. FDR and Churchill should have known.

The Yalta agreement was particularly egregious in regard to Karol Wojtyła's Poland. Military adviser Admiral William Leahy told FDR, "Mr. President, this [agreement] is so elastic that the Russians can stretch it all the way from Yalta to Washington without technically breaking it." The president actually agreed with Leahy: "Bill, I know it. But it's the best I can do for Poland at this time."[1]

Roosevelt conveyed a similar message to Adolf Berle, one of his State Department experts: "I didn't say the result [at Yalta] was good. I said it was the best I could do."[2]

The best turned out badly. On March 23, 1945, less than three weeks before he died, FDR told one of his confidantes, Anna Rosenberg: "Averell [Harriman] is right. We can't do business with Stalin. He has broken every one of the promises he made at Yalta."[3]

Of course. Had FDR really thought this mass-killing communist kingpin would do anything else?

He may have, actually.

FDR mused over how much "Uncle Joe" had impressed him in their meetings. The president said that at the 1943 Tehran conference he had been enchanted by "Stalin's magnificent leadership" and "elegance of manner that none of the rest of us had." Roosevelt and Stalin thus "talked like men and brothers."[4]

After Yalta, FDR said he had detected "something else" in Stalin "besides this revolutionist Bolshevist thing." The Episcopalian elder told his cabinet that perhaps it had been the dictator's youthful training for the priesthood. Never mind that Stalin had been expelled from seminary before he began his merciless destruction of religion in the Soviet Union. No, according to FDR, perhaps the seminary experience had communicated something to Stalin about the "way in which a Christian gentleman should behave."[5]

Stalin's carving up of Poland and the rest of Europe did not strike most citizens as notably Christian or gentlemanly. They did not see the Soviet tyrant as "Uncle Joe."

FDR should have listened more attentively to advice he had received in Hyde Park a decade earlier from his esteemed Vatican visitor, Eugenio Pacelli: "Mr. President, you simply do not understand the terrible importance of the communist movement!"

And now, after Yalta, it was too late.

As Fulton Sheen put it, "At Yalta, three men with a stroke of a pen delivered the eastern part of Europe up to a Godless nation."[6]

The Cold War was on. Fulton Sheen's and Ronald Reagan's America would have its hands full, as would Pope Pius XII's Vatican and Karol Wojtyła's Poland.

"INTO THE HANDS OF AMERICA"

In January 1946, less than a year after Yalta, *Collier's Weekly* published a remarkable assessment of the emerging postwar conflict. Written by the leader of the world's Catholics, the article would have a major impact on Catholics and non-Catholics alike.[7]

"War has struck at the heart of human society which is family life and wounded it unto death!" wrote Pope Pius XII. "War has forcibly separated husbands and wives, parents and children.... It has caused the greatest and most tragic migration of peoples in all history. It has created a vast multitude of exiles, deluded, disheartened, desolate.... In these homeless masses is the yeast for revolution and disorder."

Pope Pius was referring to the so-called Displaced Persons, or "DPs"—an estimated 1.5 million people left homeless in Central and Eastern Europe as a result of the war. The DPs included not only survivors of the Holocaust but also non-Jewish victims fleeing the Soviet Red Army. These Europeans had once feared Hitler; now they feared Stalin. As the *New York Times* reported, they would "dare not go back [to their native lands]...because they will not submit to the arbitrary governments which have been imposed on their homelands [by the USSR]."[8]

The American government set up makeshift camps in Europe to shelter DPs, spending at least $100 million annually on these humanitarian centers.[9] Kremlin propagandists accused the United States of setting up imperialistic "concentration camps." It was an absurd charge, and all the more stunning for the fact that, even as they hurled these accusations against the Americans, the Soviets were reconstituting former Nazi concentration camps such as Buchenwald for their own crimes against humanity.

The DPs were high on the agenda of a young liberal Democrat named Ronald Reagan. Growing more politically active, Reagan became president of the influential Screen Actors Guild in the spring of 1947. In that role he took up the cause of the DPs.[10] On May 7, through the New York–based Citizens Committee on Displaced Persons, Reagan released a statement urging Congress to pass legislation permitting 400,000 DPs to enter the United States.[11] To the thirty-six-year-old former lifeguard, these people needed to be saved from the clutches of Soviet communism.

Reagan would have agreed with Pope Pius's warning that "in these homeless masses is the yeast for revolution and disorder." The Democratic president whom Reagan openly campaigned for, a strong anticommunist named Harry Truman, said the same. In pushing for aid to Europe after the war, Truman argued that "the seeds of totalitarian regimes" are nurtured by "misery and want."[12]

In his exclusive for *Collier's*, Pope Pius XII zeroed in on the enemy that survived Nazism. "The Church teaches that a sound democracy is based on the changeless, unchallengeable principles of natural law and revealed truth," wrote the pontiff. "The Church contradicts and condemns various forms of Marxist Socialism and Atheistic Communism as enemies of Christian civilization and world peace. She contradicts and condemns them because it is her right and duty to safeguard men from currents of thought and influences that jeopardize their earthly peace and eternal salvation."

The pope said that the communists' "denial of liberty" could have "only catastrophic consequences," producing a "slavery" that is "disastrous" to Christian civilization.

One wonders if among the readers of this *Collier's* piece was the former prime minister of Britain, Winston Churchill. Two months after this article was published, Churchill spoke in Fulton, Missouri, at the invitation of President Truman. There, in his historic "Iron Curtain" speech, Churchill warned that international communism posed a dire threat to "Christian civilization."

Churchill saw America as the world's beacon of hope in that regard, as did Pope Pius. In his *Collier's* piece, the pope recalled a "transatlantic voyage" he made to America in October 1936, before he assumed the chair of Saint Peter. The trip gave him a "glimpse" of "America, so young, so sturdy, so glorious." He then made a beautiful statement about America and its providential place in the world:

> The American people have a genius for splendid and unselfish action, and into the hands of America, God has placed the destinies of afflicted humanity. May the noble flame of brotherly love be kindled in your hearts. Let it not die quenched by an unworthy, timid caution in the face of the needs of your brethren, let it be not overcome by the dust and dirt of the whirlwind of anti-Christian or non-Christian spirit. Keep alive this flame, increase it, carry it wherever there be a groan of suffering, a lament of misery, a cry of pain, and nourish it evermore with the heat of a love drawn from the

> Heart of the Redeemer. Armed with the arms of spirit and heart, the merciful weapons of peace: wisdom, justice and charity, we must stand united against the wanton weapons of war: tyranny, hatred and greed. Then the griefs of the world's bereaved and the graves of their martyred dead will be sealed with the tranquillity and the glory of God's peace.

Ronald Reagan read that passage in California, and he would never forget it. For Reagan, too, sensed that God had ordained America, where it was and what it was, for a special purpose: as a force of splendid action against a disastrous and catastrophic ideology.

THE "TRIAL" OF ARCHBISHOP STEPINAC

Karol Wojtyła probably did not read that passage at the time, but he later heeded it.

When Pope Pius published his *Collier's* article, Wojtyła was studying for the priesthood. He had entered an "underground" seminary in Kraków in the fall of 1942. With the Nazis occupying Poland, the seminary operated in utmost secrecy. In August 1944, after the Warsaw Uprising, the Gestapo swept the city of Kraków to prevent a similar outbreak. The Germans seized some eight thousand young men. Karol Wojtyła nearly became one of the victims of "Black Sunday." The Gestapo raided his building but somehow failed to search his basement apartment, where he knelt, praying.

Wojtyła was ordained Father Karol in Kraków on November 1, 1946. By that time the Nazis had been replaced by a new occupation army of God haters: communism was on the march. Just twenty-six, Wojtyła had suffered so much in such a short life, from the loss of his family to the loss of his homeland (twice).

The new priest received a much-needed respite when he was called to serve a two-year stint in Rome. There he began intensive studies that would earn him two doctorates. He also was nearer his pope, Pius XII, than the atheistic turmoil engulfing his homeland.

Other priests, however, were falling captive to communism in Eastern Europe. One victim of the communist menace was Croatian archbishop Alojzije ("Aloysius") Stepinac.

Born in May 1898 to a Croatian peasant family of eleven children, Stepinac served the Hapsburgs in the First World War, where he was taken as a prisoner of war. In 1924, with the trenches far behind him, he ventured to Rome to study for the priesthood. Ordained six years later, he eventually headed the Roman Catholic Church in Croatia, which after the war had been lumped into that new, volatile conglomeration of nations and ethnicities labeled "Yugoslavia."

Stepinac unflinchingly opposed the Nazis and then did the same to the totalitarian regime that replaced it, led by the communist strongman Marshal Tito. The dictator, who would make Yugoslavia his personal fiefdom until his death in May 1980, honored the communist commitment to making war on religious believers. In fact, according to the scholar Gerhard Simon, "Attempts to suppress the Church as a social institution in Yugoslavia did not only start earlier than in other Communist-ruled countries but were in some respects even more rigid and ruthless, intensified by national hate, popular resentment against the hierarchy and spontaneous pogroms."[13] The Tito regime fanned the hate and sponsored the pogroms. Many priests were shot without trial, and mobs were organized to beat priests and bishops as the secret police stood by and watched. Tito despised the Church, and he made his contempt painfully clear.[14]

But Aloysius Stepinac stood in his way. So in May 1945, the UBDA, the Yugoslav version of the KGB, arrested Stepinac and brought the priest to Tito. The communist dictator ordered Stepinac to cut the Croatian Church's ties to Rome. The priest refused, and went further. "I insist upon freedom for all of the people," he told Tito. "I am going to resist you on every move in which you disregard the Constitution and the people."[15]

Tito then asked the Vatican to recall Stepinac and replace him with another archbishop. Pope Pius XII refused.

The communist regime was not above murdering priests. In fact, the Vatican calculated that by 1949 some four hundred Yugoslav priests had accepted the martyr's crown.[16] But Stepinac's plight had already gained international media attention. Even for the ruthless communists, the global backlash that would come from killing Archbishop Stepinac would be too much. They had to find another way to handle this priest.

Moscow was watching the Stepinac situation closely. Stalin dispatched Andrei Vyshinsky, who was not only deputy foreign minister but also persecutor of Christians extraordinaire. Born into a Polish Catholic family, Vyshinsky had moved to Moscow and become what one contemporary Catholic source called "the model Marxist man."[17] The good comrade was a seasoned prosecutor dating back to Stalin's 1930s purge of the Russian Orthodox Church.

In September 1946, shortly after Vyshinsky arrived in Zagreb, Tito's secret police seized Stepinac and charged him with various treasonable offenses—six criminal counts. Chief among them was the hideous lie that he had conspired with the Nazis.

The communist "justice" system moved to trial with lightning speed. Stepinac's show trial began on September 30, less than two weeks after his arrest.

The Croatian priest used the trial as a stage to expose and condemn both Nazi and communist crimes. "Archbishop Stepinac lashed out at the Nazi 'master race' idea and condemned the execution of hostages as 'inhuman and anti-Christian,'" reported *Time* magazine. "He was just as fearless in condemning Communist outrages."[18]

Time understood the big picture: "Marshal Tito struck directly at the only organized force left in Yugoslavia with the power to criticize his dictatorship. Into jail he clapped grave, ascetic Dr. Aloysius Stepinac, 48, Roman Catholic Primate of Yugoslavia, and twelve Catholic priests. The charge: crimes against the people."

After a twelve-day sustained mockery of justice, marked by a parade of falsified reports and witnesses, capped by shouting communist disruptors, Stepinac was sentenced to sixteen years of hard labor.

Believers of all stripes and locales were outraged.

In New York City, Jewish community leader Louis Breier organized a protest. Accusing Stepinac of being a Nazi collaborator was a "slander" against a "great man," Breier said. "He has always been a sincere friend of the Jews." Stepinac had defended Jews at great personal risk, "even in times of cruel persecutions under the regime of Hitler and followers." Breier concluded, "Alongside with Pope Pius XII, Archbishop Stepinac was the greatest protector of persecuted Jews in Europe."[19]

In the Vatican, Pius XII denounced the charges and trial. He noted that Stepinac had personally intervened to save thousands of Jews, not to mention Christians and even Muslims.[20]

In Britain, Winston Churchill told the House of Commons: "This trial was prepared in the political sphere. It was for the purpose of dividing the Catholic Church in Croatia from its leadership at the Vatican. Tito has openly expressed this purpose.... The trial was not based on justice, but was an outrage on justice."[21]

Stepinac joined an estimated three hundred other priests imprisoned by the Yugoslavian communist regime; another hundred simply disappeared.[22] His imprisonment confirmed what Stepinac had written in a pastoral letter more than a year earlier: that the "enemies of the Catholic

Church" and the "followers of materialistic communism" had "exterminated with fire and sword priests and the more eminent of the faithful."[23]

PIUS XII'S RECOGNITION

Marshal Tito was initially under Stalin's thumb, but in 1948 he split from the Soviet leader, working free from Moscow's direct control. He managed to stay in power largely because he remained a communist and did not join a formal military alliance with the West: Tito spurned both the Warsaw Pact and NATO.

Ironically, once he parted ways with Stalin and needed some new pals, Tito began reaching out to some of Stepinac's defenders outside Yugoslavia.

In July 1951, Tito even reached out to the despised Vatican, offering to release the archbishop from prison if the Vatican would remove Stepinac from the country. The Vatican refused: "The Holy See would be pleased if Monsignor Stepinac were freed. The Holy See is informed, however, that that Most Excellent Prelate, being convinced of his innocence, prefers to remain near his faithful."[24]

That was precisely Stepinac's wish. "They will never make me leave unless they put me on a plane by force and take me over the frontier," he said. "It is my duty in these difficult times to stay with the people."[25]

The next year, Pope Pius raised the stakes. On November 29, 1952, he elevated Archbishop Stepinac to the cardinalate. Stepinac by that point had been transferred to house arrest, but he did not go to Rome for the ceremony, knowing that if he left Yugoslavia, communist authorities would not let him return to the country. "I shall stay here, if need be, until my death," " he vowed.[26] He was made a cardinal in absentia.

Tito was furious. The same day his communist regime was celebrating its founding with Yugoslavia's Republic Day, he had to suffer this affront from the pope and his new cardinal. Tito's regime cut all diplomatic relations to the Holy See. It also expelled from the country the entire Catholic theology faculty at the University of Zagreb.

A CASE OF THE REDS

Cardinal Stepinac would spend the remainder of his years living in a tiny house near a small church in the Croatian village of Krašić, where he was permitted to say Mass, celebrate Communion, and send and receive mail through government censors.

In his fifties, he contracted a rare blood disease. The painful illness involved an excess of red blood cells, prompting the cardinal to quip that he was ailing from "an excess of reds."[27]

The cardinal died of a pulmonary embolism in February 1960 at age sixty-one. Former Romanian communist spy chief Ion Mihai Pacepa, in his book *Disinformation* (written with Ronald J. Rychlak), maintains that later tests by Vatican officials indicated that Stepinac had been slowly poisoned.[28]

Reds, indeed.

Pacepa cites the Stepinac case as a key moment in the communist war against Christianity, with the pope among the many victims to follow.[29] Tito became one of the worst persecutors of the Church in Central and Eastern Europe, even as he sought independence from Moscow in other ways. That independence appealed to many in the West, who sought out Tito as a man they could work with, particularly as détente in the 1970s dominated the thinking of leaders in America and even in the Vatican.

The communist smear campaigns against Christian servants worked, shaping the views of the noncommunist left for decades to come.[30] Consider that the *New York Times*, that citadel of secular liberalism, later referred to the "controversial" Cardinal Stepinac. The *Times* thereby passed along an old communist canard. In fact, there was nothing controversial about the cardinal. Stepinac had consistently fought the good fight. The only controversy involved the vicious smear effort the communists orchestrated against him.

One person not fooled by the communists' calumnies against Cardinal Stepinac was a fellow Slav, Karol Wojtyła. As Pope John Paul II, Wojtyła—who had been ordained a priest just weeks after Stepinac's trial began—beatified the late cardinal and named him an official martyr of the Church.

7

1956–1963

CRUSHING HUNGARY AND SMEARING PIUS XII

As Cardinal Stepinac's case made clear, an epic clash was shaping up. Some saw the West's will to respond as a test of its very conscience. One who said so explicitly was America's bishop, Fulton Sheen.

By the early 1950s, Sheen's popularity had skyrocketed. His *Catholic Hour* radio show had run for twenty years, and he picked up a television show, *Life Is Worth Living*, that gave him even greater reach and influence. This prime-time program drew more than ten million viewers a week, becoming the most widely viewed religious series in television history. The priest won the 1952 Emmy for Most Outstanding Personality (beating out, among others, Lucille Ball and Edward R. Murrow). A poll of radio and television editors named Sheen TV's Man of the Year.[1] By April 1952, he was on the cover of *Time*. President Eisenhower invited him to the White House.[2]

All this made Sheen a formidable warrior in the battle against atheistic communism. In his first season on TV, he did a show titled "The Philosophy of Communism." The priest observed that "there is considerable confusion in our American life about communism" and "not sufficient reasoning and thinking about it."[3] He resolved to clear up the confusion.

Two of his recent books, 1948's *Communism and the Conscience of the West* and 1949's *Peace of Soul*, took square aim at Marxism-Leninism, which he called "the new barbarism."[4] "The truth on the subject is that communism and atheism are intrinsically related and that one cannot be a good Communist without being an atheist and every atheist is a potential Communist," Sheen wrote in *Communism and the Conscience of the West*. Fátima-like, Sheen dedicated the bestseller to Russia's conversion, and advised that Christians pray daily for Russia: "It is not Christian to wish for the extinction of Communists, though it is most Christian to pray for the evaporation of communism."

Sheen recognized the suffering that occurred under Soviet communism, but he pleaded with Russians not to lose faith. After all, he observed, "Christianity comes to optimism through pessimism; to a resurrection through a passion, and to a crown of glory through a crown of thorns; to the glory of Easter Sunday through the ignominy of a Good Friday." He advised the Russian people to take heart that Christ's tomb is empty, while Lenin's tomb is not.

Sheen closed *Communism and the Conscience of the West* with the message of Our Lady of Fátima: "But in the end my Immaculate Heart will triumph. The Holy Father will consecrate Russia to the Immaculate Heart, and Russia will be converted and an era of peace will be given to the world."[5]

If there was any doubt about the validity of Sheen's concerns regarding communism, the communists did their part to eliminate it. In the 1950s they put their penchant for errors, persecution, and rampant destruction on full display. Perhaps the most notable Soviet-orchestrated horror occurred in Hungary. The incident outraged the world, and especially a priest named Fulton Sheen, a pope named Pius XII, a Hollywood actor named Ronald Reagan, and a Polish clergyman named Karol Wojtyła.

CRUSHING THE HUNGARIAN UPRISING

It was October 23, 1956, Feast Day of Saint John of Capistrano. In the year 1456, this Franciscan friar, the son of a German knight, led a huge crusade force in Hungary against invading Ottoman Turks. Marching at the head of an army of seventy thousand Christian Hungarians, John secured a monumental victory in the great Battle of Belgrade. The seventy-year-old priest died three months later.

Now, on the five hundredth anniversary of the death of Hungary's great national hero, the successors to Saint John faced new invading anti-Christian forces, this time from the Soviet Union.[6]

Soviet tanks rolled in mere hours after hundreds of thousands of Hungarians marched for freedom. In Budapest the demonstrators toppled a massive bronze statue of Stalin—the largest statue of Stalin in the world, at some eight meters high. (Altogether the Stalin monument, with base and tribune, stood twenty-five meters high.) The communists had erected this tribute to their dear leader on the site of Regnum Marianum (Kingdom of Mary), the church they had torn down in August 1951.[7] Now the masses convened to dismantle this rendering of the Marxist egomaniac, who had died in 1953. A huge crowd gathered around the base of the statue, shouting, "Let's take it down! Let's topple it!" At least two dozen trucks showed up. People grabbed cables and rope. As Stalin was noosed, a truck tried to pull him down. People took a blow torch to Stalin's feet. At last, the giant statue crashed to the ground. "It was really hard to bring it down," said one satisfied observer.[8]

But the sweet victory was short-lived. Stalin's successor, Nikita Khrushchev, ordered Soviet forces to crush the Hungarian uprising. Very quickly, thousands of freedom fighters were dead.

The Vatican responded swiftly, with Pope Pius XII issuing a statement, *Datis Nuperrime*, with the pointed subtitle "Encyclical on the Ruthless Use of Force in Hungary." It was issued on November 5 and directed to the "Venerable Brethren, the Patriarchs, Primates, Archbishops, Bishops, and other Local Ordinaries in Peace and Communion with the Apostolic See."

The pontiff said that he and the Holy See had been hopeful about events in Hungary, inspired by the freedom demonstrations on October 23, the Feast Day of Saint John of Capistrano. But the early hopes for "a new day of peace based on justice and liberty" were quickly dashed, as it became clear that throughout Hungary there flowed "the blood of citizens who long with all their hearts for their rightful freedom." The pope compared those responsible for the bloodshed to Cain, the first murderer, who killed his own brother:

> The words which "the Lord said to Cain... 'The voice of thy brother's blood crieth to me from the earth,'" (Gen. 4, 10) are relevant today.

> For so the blood of the Hungarian people cries out to God. And even though God often punishes private individuals for their sins only after death, nonetheless, as history teaches, He occasionally punishes in this mortal life rulers of people and their nations when they have dealt unjustly with others. For He is a just judge.

Pope Pius XII was far from the only international observer to express outrage. An actor in California was notably displeased. Ronald Reagan wanted to do something, and he did not hesitate to use his huge *General Electric Theater* television platform to help.

Like Fulton Sheen, the Illinoisan had picked up his own big-time TV show, and he would use it to combat communist errors. During the broadcast on February 3, 1957, Reagan urged his viewers: "Ladies and gentlemen, about 160,000 Hungarian refugees have reached safety in Austria. More are expected to come. These people need food, clothes, medicine, and shelter. You can help." The future president requested that his fellow Americans send donations to the Red Cross or to the church or synagogue of their choice.[9]

In retrospect, this moment was a major historical marker on Reagan's path. It was the first of the Great Communicator's many uses of television to reach the American people and enlist their support for the cause of freedom behind the Iron Curtain.

In a later *GE Theater* episode, "The Iron Silence," Reagan played a Soviet major named Vasily Kirov. The setting was the Red Army occupation of Budapest. At the end of the episode, Kirov released two Hungarians in his custody. "I never knew what freedom was until I saw you lose yours," he told them.[10]

Reagan may well have written that line, as he often did for *GE Theater* episodes. Not coincidentally, that exact line reappeared a decade and a half later in one of Reagan's self-written 1970s radio broadcasts.[11]

Ronald Reagan would never forget Hungary's freedom fighters. Eleven years after those fighters faced Soviet guns and tanks, Reagan, in a Veterans Day speech in Albany, Oregon, said he was haunted by the "echoes" of those Hungarians of October 1956 who had cried out: "People of the civilized world, in the name of liberty and solidarity, we are asking your help.... Listen to our cry."[12]

As president, Reagan would resolve not to allow the same thing to happen again. So would the first Slavic pope.

THE LONG MARTYRDOM OF CARDINAL MINDSZENTY

It was no coincidence that in 1956, Pope Pius XII issued three encyclicals condemning communism.[13] Three years after the death of Stalin, the Soviet crackdown in Hungary revealed Nikita Khrushchev's talk of peace to be empty.

Hungarians who had tried to break free from Moscow were ground under the wheels of Russian tanks. Likewise, it would not be a time of freedom for a Hungarian priest named Jószef Mindszenty, whom a close associate of Ronald Reagan would later call "the most significant Christian of the twentieth century."[14]

Born Jószef Pehm on March 29, 1892, in a village called Mindszent in the Austro-Hungarian Empire, Cardinal Mindszenty descended from a long line of Roman Catholic Hungarians. Ordained to the priesthood in June 1915, he took the name Mindszenty in 1941, when the Nazis were running roughshod over Europe, a way of patriotically identifying with his homeland.

Mindszenty had seen totalitarians well before Hitler. Twice in 1919 he had been arrested as an enemy of a totalitarian government, with his life in serious jeopardy. Mindszenty faced in Hungary the same menace Eugenio Pacelli confronted in Germany: Soviet-sponsored international communism. The Marxist despot in Hungary was Béla Kun, angry son of a secular Jewish father and former Protestant mother. Kun was fresh from fighting alongside his Bolshevik brethren in the Russian Civil War.

Mindszenty fearlessly opposed Kun's "Hungarian Soviet Republic." The communists told him to cease and desist or he would be hanged. He refused. He was jailed and told to expect a noose. The execution did not come to pass only because Kun's republic quickly collapsed. Kun fled to Moscow to work as a Comintern functionary. He would ultimately be executed in Stalin's Great Purge.

During the Second World War, Mindszenty, like Aloysius Stepinac in Yugoslavia, like Pius XII in the Vatican, fought to save Jews and believers of all kinds. Mindszenty was consecrated bishop in 1944, the year the Nazis occupied Hungary. In November of that year, the Nazis tossed the bishop into prison. They wanted him liquidated, telling him that his life would be spared if he cooperated. He refused, and somehow survived.

When the Nazis fled Hungary in 1945, the Soviet "liberators" took over. They found Mindszenty still in a cell when they got there.

That fall, Pope Pius XII appointed Mindszenty archbishop of

Esztergom, making him head of the Roman Catholic Church in Hungary. Mindszenty knew that he was in for a difficult ride. Upon receiving news that he had been named archbishop of Esztergom, Mindszenty looked above the altar at the portrayal of the first-century martyrdom of Saint Stephen. He decided to choose that as the theme of his first sermon to the Hungarian people, warning them to be ready for the tribulation to come.[15]

Sure enough, things got progressively worse under the communist puppet government the Soviets installed. The leader of the Hungarian Communist Party was Mátyás Rákosi, the fourth son of a Jewish grocer. Like Béla Kun, whom Rákosi had worked with in 1919, Rákosi repudiated all religion. (He would be the one to demolish the Regnum Marianum church.)[16]

Rákosi also repudiated Jószef Mindszenty, with whom he clashed immediately. Mindszenty resisted the communist crackdown on religion, refusing demands to stop prayer and Mass and other basic expressions of faith. He also organized prayer groups and pilgrimages.[17]

The communists were furious. Rákosi even attempted to have the cardinal wiped out in what would look to be an accident, where a convoy of trucks would smash Mindszenty's vehicle. The plot failed. The archbishop was reinvigorated. He vowed: "We are ragged children of the Blessed Mother and of Hungary.... We have no brothers, we have no friends in the world, so we put all our trust in thee, O Virgin."[18]

In the winter of 1946 Mindszenty mustered a pilgrimage to Rome, where, on February 21, Pope Pius XII elevated him to cardinal. "Receive this red hat," Pius told Mindszenty, "by which it is declared that thou shalt show thyself intrepid even unto death by the shedding of thy blood for the exaltation of the Blessed Savior."[19] As he placed the cardinal's hat on Mindszenty's head, Pius prophesied: "Among the thirty-two, you will be the first to suffer the martyrdom whose symbol this red color is."[20]

Upon the new cardinal's return to Hungary, Mindszenty watched the communists forcibly replace the heads of the Hungarian Reformed Church.[21] The Roman Catholic Church did not cave to the communist pressure, however. To encourage the faithful, Pope Pius broadcast a special message to Hungarians and sent a beautiful, ancient image of the Virgin Mary as a special gift.[22] The new cardinal resisted the communists' efforts to secularize Hungarian schools and launch their anti-God indoctrination upon the nation's youth. Communist ringleaders agitated schoolchildren and factory workers to march in the streets; under Marxist direction, the mob chanted, "We will annihilate Mindszentyism!"[23]

Marxism would be the new religion.

On December 26, 1948, just after midnight, the communists arrested Cardinal Mindszenty. It was not only the day after Christmas; December 26 was also the day the Church celebrated the martyrdom of Saint Stephen.

As was the case with the arrest of Stepinac in Yugoslavia, the nation's new communist secret police (in this case, the dreaded AVO) did the dirty deed. Sixteen police descended on the cardinal's house in the dark of night, kicked open the door, and pointed guns at the priest and his mother, who had been quietly celebrating Christmas. Mindszenty dressed, grabbed his breviary, and tried to speak some comforting words to his shaken mother.[24] The communists then drove the cardinal to the secret police headquarters at 60 Andrassy Street.[25]

Once again, Mindszenty was in prison for opposing totalitarianism. The Andrassy Street headquarters became a torture house. For nearly forty days, Mindszenty endured nightly beatings, often into unconsciousness. The police interrogators also drugged his food; they exhaled smoke in his face; they told him dirty jokes; they profaned his presence and his faith, as the cardinal sat dressed in what he later described as a "clown suit."[26] Mindszenty suffered through it all, vowing never to plead guilty to trumped-up charges of treason, conspiracy, and various other criminal activities.

At one point, Mindszenty's inquisitors kept him awake for thirty-five hours as they badgered and bludgeoned him. Another time, they kept him up for eighty-two hours, during which they brought in two nuns and forced him to watch them pounded to a pulp. The priest tried to bring his two hands together to pray for them but could not reconcile the left and the right. When the image of the thrashed nuns did not compel the cardinal's "confession," the communists escorted in two similarly bloodied priests, swollen beyond recognition.[27] The cardinal continued to carry his cross.

Around the world people understood the outrages the communists were perpetrating and praised Mindszenty's bravery. In a 1948 speech to the Holy Name Society, Fulton Sheen praised the "courage of Mindszenty, who knew he was marked for death, but returned willingly to Hungary to be crucified."[28]

During the classic communist show trial that followed, staged the week of February 3, 1949 (just as Ronald Reagan marked his thirty-eighth birthday), Mindszenty, framed by a stack of fabricated documents, reportedly "confessed" before his accusers, a product of sheer mental and physical exhaustion and manipulation. He was convicted of treason. The kangaroo court sentenced him to life in prison.

Among other cooked-up charges, Mindszenty's tormentors convicted him of conspiring to bring to Budapest the ancient Crown of Saint Stephen for the coronation of Otto von Hapsburg, the last crown prince of Austria-Hungary before the dissolution of the empire at the end of World War I. There was no proof of such a conspiracy, other than that Mindszenty—like everyone else in Hungary—wanted the unelected communist despots dethroned.

The Crown of Saint Stephen is one of Hungary's most revered symbols. When Stephen became king of Hungary on Christmas Day in the year 1000, Pope Sylvester II made him a special crown to honor Stephen's intention to elevate Hungary to the status of a Christian kingdom.[29] At the moment of his coronation, Stephen held up the crown and offered it to the Blessed Virgin as a divine contract between her, the wearer of the crown, and the nation and its people.

Stephen was seen as a model Christian king. Prior to his death in 1038, he is believed to have written a letter, known as *The Admonitions*, to his successor son, in which he insisted: "My dearest son, if you desire to honor the royal crown, I advise, I counsel, I urge you above all things to maintain the Catholic and Apostolic faith with such diligence and care that you may be an example for all those placed under you by God, and that all the clergy may rightly call you a man of true Christian profession. Failing to do this, you may be sure that you will not be called a Christian or a son of the Church."

Stephen was canonized in 1083, forty-five years after his death. He became the patron saint of Hungary. Mary is the patroness of Hungary.

Subsequent Hungarian kings through the ages wore the special crown. Their coronation was not considered official or legitimate until they were so crowned. Thus, the "Holy Crown" became a powerful expression of Hungarian pride and patriotism.

The crown was rushed out of Hungary during World War II for protection. After a dramatic series of events, on May 2, 1945, a Hungarian army colonel in Austria gave the crown, hidden in a large black satchel, to an American army colonel for safekeeping. The crown was first sheltered in Wiesbaden, the American zone of occupation after World War II. Later the Americans transferred it to the U.S. Gold Reserve at Fort Knox, Kentucky, a fitting place for a national treasure. As the U.S. embassy in Hungary later explained, "It was not considered as spoils of war; rather, the U.S. Government stored it in hopes of returning it to the Hungarian people one day."[30] Through the careful efforts of the Hungarian people and the later help of the Americans, this Holy Crown remained out of the hands of both the Nazis and the communists, who doubtless would have melted it down and robbed it of its jewels.

MINDSZENTY AND THE 1956 UPRISING

As soon as word of Mindszenty's conviction reached Rome, Pope Pius XII excommunicated all individuals involved in the travesty.

Of the thirty-one communists involved in Mindszenty's arrest, interrogation, torture, and conviction, twenty-six soon thereafter met their deaths. Only two repented and escaped to the West.[31]

Cardinal Mindszenty's fate was little better. He spent the next eight years in solitary confinement, suffering nearly to the point of death. He was released in 1955 because of ill health, but the communist regime kept him under strict surveillance.

The 1956 revolution, however, shook him loose. Rebel forces freed the cardinal. The communists quickly regained control of the government, but Mindszenty again passed on the opportunity to flee. He took residence in the U.S. embassy in Budapest, refusing to leave his country unless the communist government rescinded his conviction. He lived in the embassy for the next fifteen years, offering up his anguish as a living martyr to Christian life under communism.

His suffering did not go unnoticed inside Hungary or outside. In 1957, shortly after the Soviet invasion of Hungary, Fulton Sheen devoted an entire episode of *Life Is Worth Living* to Mindszenty, whom he called "The Dry Martyr of Hungary." "In the twentieth century, there is a new kind of martyrdom," said Sheen. In the past, Christians had been martyred by murder; they were killed, soaked with wet blood. "The old martyrs were wet martyrs," said Sheen. By contrast, Mindszenty was being slowly killed without being bloodied; he was a dry martyr. Sheen said that the communists excelled at producing "dry martyrs, who suffer brainwashing and mental torture for their faith."[32]

Mindszenty was the newest exhibit in the communist crusade against religion. There was a Mindszenty in every nation in Eastern Europe: Cardinal Stefan Wyszyński in Poland, Cardinal Štěpán Trochta and Cardinal Josef Beran in Czechoslovakia, Archbishop Josyf Slipyj in Ukraine, Cardinal Aloysius Stepinac in Yugoslavia, and too many priests and nuns to begin to name.

Ion Mihai Pacepa and Ronald Rychlak, in their critically important work on Soviet/communist disinformation, expose how the Mindszenty attack followed the pattern of the Stepinac attack and foretold more such smear campaigns. Pacepa was involved in these disinformation campaigns in his work with the KGB and Kremlin as head of the Romanian secret police. He recounts the "highly classified manual" of Soviet/communist *dezinformatsiya* (Russian for "disinformation") "that codified my life within the Soviet intelligence community." On the first page of that manual were these words, in capital letters: "IF YOU ARE GOOD AT DISINFORMATION, YOU CAN GET AWAY WITH ANYTHING."[33]

A core element of the Mindszenty campaign was to frame the religious figure as having been a fascist, pro-Nazi, a willing enabler of or collaborator with Hitler—a grand hypocrisy given how the Kremlin had enabled and collaborated with Hitler. Moscow returned to this "tried-and-true method" again and again, Pacepa says, because the cynical smear worked amazingly well, particularly with the secular-progressive left in the West.[34]

Pacepa reports that the KGB manual began by saying that carefully orchestrated framing and manipulation could "neutralize even a saint"—and the "saint" showcased was Cardinal Mindszenty. As Pacepa remembers, the KGB summed up the "Mindszenty case" as one of "our most stupendous, monumental *dezinformatsiya* operations."[35]

The Stepinac case had taught Moscow what Pacepa calls a "methodology of Soviet framing"; the communists perfected the craft with Mindszenty. Many more such smear operations followed.

Watching it all in sadness and horror was the newly ordained bishop of Kraków, Karol Wojtyła. Though communism was on the march, so was he.

THE PERSECUTION OF PIUS XII

Communists went after Mindszenty and Stepinac while the cardinals were alive and within their grasp. Later they employed their well-honed disinformation tactics against an even bigger target, Pope Pius XII. The communists posthumously slandered the man that Church historian H.W. Crocker III called "the leading religious anti-communist crusader in the world"—and the disinformation campaign worked remarkably well.[36]

On February 23, 1963, a play opened by left-wing German playwright Rolf Hochhuth. Titled *The Deputy, a Christian Tragedy*, the play attacked the good reputation of Pope Pius XII, who had died in October 1958. It indicted the pope as, at best, indifferent to the plight of Jews under Hitler and, at worst, complicit in the Holocaust against them. Thus the myth of "Hitler's Pope" was born. The production was pure ideological bilge, vicious disinformation from start to finish.

A loud chorus of Western liberals and Church despisers and dissenters repeated the libelous line against the late pope. Many who picked up the propaganda were simply ill informed, though others were inclined to believe the worst about the pope, the papacy, and the Roman Catholic Church. Even respected authors like James Carroll, Daniel Goldhagen, Robert Katz, and Garry Wills perpetuated the myth. The most influential exponent of the anti-Pius view was John Cornwell; in 1999 Viking Press published his enormously damaging book *Hitler's Pope*.[37]

Given the prominence of the figures taking this line of attack against Pope Pius XII, it would seem difficult to ascribe the campaign to the communist disinformation machine. But Pacepa and Rychlak have followed the evidence more studiously than any previous researchers and found that Moscow was the first to circulate these defamations of the pope. In fact, the Soviets started the smear campaign some two decades before Rolf Hochhuth's play debuted.

In June 1945, Radio Moscow broadcast a vicious attack against the pope, accusing Pius XII's Vatican of a "vigilant policy of protection of Hitler and Mussolini."[38] The broadcast stated: "No atrocity carried out by the Hitlerites stirred the contempt and indignation of the Vatican. The latter was silent when the German death machines were active, when the chimneys of the crematorium ovens spewed smoke, when grenades and projectiles were thrown against the peaceful population of London, when the Hitlerite doctrine of elimination and extermination of nations and peoples was being transformed into a harsh reality."[39]

This was classic Soviet incendiary rhetoric, and it came straight from the Kremlin. The Soviets, of course, fully understood that Pius posed a mortal threat to their ideology, as he despised communism as much as he did Nazism. He had shown his revulsion in Bavaria long before he was pope, which is why communists tried to kill him there in 1919.[40] After World War II, with the Nazis out of the way, the communists set out to destroy the pope, to scandalize his flock, and to outrage people of other faiths. It didn't matter that they were attacking a genuinely holy man who had done all he could (and then some) to help Jews during the war. The disinformation campaign had begun.

The attacks continued. On February 28, 1946, *Pravda*—the official newspaper of the Soviet Communist Party—published an article that declared: "It is irrefutably established that, during the grim war years when mankind fought the sinister forces of Hitlerism, Vatican policy was pro-Nazi. It remains pro-Nazi to this day." Apparently Pius was still "Hitler's Pope," even after the death of the Führer.

This Soviet propaganda piece was picked up internationally, in the most esteemed publications. For example, the *New York Times* covered the *Pravda* article in its March 1 edition. The *New York Times* piece was explosively titled "*Pravda* Alleges Pius-Hitler Pact."[41]

Yes, a *Pius*-Hitler Pact. It was a ridiculous charge from the regime that actually negotiated, signed, and eagerly enacted a *Stalin*-Hitler Pact.

As the *New York Times* summarized the article, *Pravda* claimed that "the Pope made an agreement with Adolf Hitler that permitted him to convert Russian peoples to Roman Catholicism" and that "Roman Catholic missionaries followed Elite Guard troops and Gestapo men into occupied areas."

"We do not wish to start a religious dispute," the *Pravda* piece innocently stated. "Let theologians do so. But we cannot ignore the Vatican's pro-Fascist policy."

The *Pravda* smear appeared only two months after Pius XII's encyclical *Orientales Omnes Ecclesiae*, a December 1945 statement addressed to the Ukrainian Catholic faithful, whom the Soviet communists reviled. Appearing two days before Christmas, the encyclical commemorated the 350th anniversary of the Ukrainian church's union with Rome. The pope noted all the trials and persecutions the Ukrainian faithful had endured through the centuries and acknowledged, "There seems ground for fear that in the near future still greater hardships will befall those who refuse to betray their sacred religious allegiance."

The encyclical could not have been more restrained, never once using the term *communism* or *socialism*.[42] Still, the Kremlin was furious. Stalin responded by arresting six Ukrainian bishops, who were promptly framed as "Nazi collaborators" and then murdered.[43]

On January 19, 1947, the *New York Times* ran an article headlined "Russian Says Pope Shields Fascists." The article reported an "attack on the Vatican" by the Soviet publication the *New Times*, a foreign-policy magazine produced by the KGB and published in English.

The *New Times* piece, published under the byline of a KGB writer named "A. Galin," was the first of a series of articles assailing the Vatican for (as the *New York Times* put it) allegedly "providing refuge" to "prominent fascists" and for "whitewashing those cardinals, bishops and priests discovered helping Hitler and Germany." The Soviet article blasted the "collaboration between the Vatican, its Cardinals and Archbishops . . . with Hitler, Mussolini and Franco." It called out Pope Pius XII, severely criticizing the pontiff's Christmas message in particular, asserting that the pope's statements about "love, forgiveness and mercy veil an ancient reactionary Vatican policy."

As Pacepa and Rychlak told me, these pieces of evidence "indicate that Moscow was at war with Pius XII long before Hochhuth's play *The Deputy* had seen the light at the *Freie Volksbühne* (Free People's Theater), a Communist theater in Berlin, under the direction of lifelong KGB agent Erwin Piscator."[44] Indeed they do.

Joseph Stalin and Nikita Khrushchev could not storm the Vatican and hang the pope from the ceiling of Saint Peter's Basilica. So they used other means to defame him and destabilize his Church—means they had perfected in their earlier campaigns against Cardinals Stepinac and Mindszenty.

REFUTING THE SMEAR CAMPAIGN

In the two decades since John Cornwall's book appeared, many works have debunked the myth of "Hitler's Pope" and shown that Pius XII was in fact a friend and defender of Jews. They include Rabbi David Dalin's *The Myth of Hitler's Pope: How Pope Pius XII Rescued Jews from the Nazis*; Ronald Rychlak's *Hitler, the War, and the Pope* and *Righteous Gentiles: How Pius XII and the Catholic Church Saved Half a Million Jews from the Nazis*; Gordon Thomas's *The Pope's Jews: The Vatican's Secret Plan to Save Jews from the Nazis*; Dan Kurzman's *A Special Mission: Hitler's Secret Plot to Seize the Vatican and Kidnap Pope Pius XII*; Mark Riebling's *Church of Spies: The Pope's Secret War Against Hitler*; and Sister Margherita Marchione's numerous writings. Some have written not only of Pius's attempts to stop Hitler—including an attempt at a long-distance exorcism—but also of the Nazis' plot to kidnap the pontiff, surely an odd thing to do if Pius were the Führer's handy helper.[45] Pacepa has gone so far as to consider whether Stalin might have had a plan to assassinate Pius XII.[46]

One of several rabbis who has looked at the sinister motives of Pius XII's character assassins is Rabbi Daniel Lapin, who has excoriated these "assailants" for the "rashness and folly" of their "attempt posthumously to assassinate Pope Pius XII." Lapin says that the necessary restoration of this "good man's good name is a mitzvah—a Jewish good deed."[47]

Another is Rabbi David Dalin. Dalin begins *The Myth of Hitler's Pope* with Pacelli's birth and upbringing in Rome. He shows that Pacelli's wealthy parents socialized with the biggest Jewish families in Rome. Pacelli had Jewish classmates and happily interacted with Jews throughout his life.[48]

Upon ascending to the chair of Saint Peter, Pius XII was not silent about the Holocaust, despite what the propagandists claim. Rather, Dalin notes, "Pius XII was a persistent, vocal critic of Hitler and Nazism." As Dalin points out, Pius's first encyclical, *Summi Pontificatus*, "begged for peace, expressly rejected Nazism, and expressly mentioned Jews—all of which his modern critics have missed." Heinrich Mueller, the head of the Gestapo, angrily protested: "This encyclical is directed exclusively against Germany, both in ideology and in regard to the German-Polish dispute. How dangerous it is for our foreign relations as well as our domestic affairs is beyond dispute." Dalin says that from 1933 to 1945, throughout Hitler's reign, Eugenio Pacelli was "almost universally recognized, especially by the Nazis themselves, as an unrelenting opponent of the Nazi regime."[49] It is "especially ironic," Dalin adds, that Pius is called "Hitler's Pope" when the Nazis called him "Jew-loving."[50]

"For Jewish leaders of a previous generation," Dalin writes, "the idea that Pope Pius XII could be smeared as 'Hitler's pope' would have been shocking."[51] In a 1967 book, the definitive work on the relationship between Pius and the Jews, the renowned Israeli diplomat and historian Pinchas Lapide calculated that the pope "was instrumental in saving at least 700,000, but probably as many as 860,000 Jews from certain death at Nazi hands."[52]

The Soviet communists and their enablers were responsible for a colossal injustice against Pope Pius XII.

THE WARNINGS OF FÁTIMA

Pius XII himself would not have been surprised by the disinformation campaign against him. He understood communism, and he understood, too, the warnings of Our Lady of Fátima. Pius had read the words of Our Lady as related by Sister Lúcia, and he did two consecrations to Mary on behalf of Russia, in keeping (he hoped) with what the Lady had requested. The most significant of these came on July 7, 1952, the Feast

Day of Saints Cyril and Methodius, leaders of the Slavs, whom Pope John Paul II would make copatron saints of Europe.[53]

Unfortunately, Church officials (including Pope John Paul II) deemed the consecration inadequate because it was done as a private ceremony and not openly in union with the world's bishops, as the Lady had allegedly requested. Proper consecration would come three decades later, with the Marian pope whose papal motto was "Totus Tuus"—who, at this point, was a young priest in totalitarian-occupied Poland.

International communism would continue its errors and persecutions. It would make a victim of another prominent Catholic, a member of an American family Pius XII had met long ago.

8

NOVEMBER 22, 1963

COMMUNISM'S ERRORS REACH DALLAS

For the communist world, the opening performance for the year 1963 was the debut of a theatrical smear of one of the world's most prominent Catholics. Now Marxism readied for an encore. A grand one.

Before the year was over, an epic tragedy would be performed in America. The stage: Dallas, Texas. This dramatic act took aim at America's most politically powerful Catholic.

THE GUNMAN

On November 22, 1963, the president of the United States sat in the backseat of a Lincoln Continental, a limousine with the top down. To his left was his young wife, America's glamorous first lady.

A crowd of about a thousand had gathered along the route to see the president and the first lady. Perched high above was a twenty-four-year-old sharpshooter named Lee Harvey Oswald—former Marine, onetime defector to the Soviet Union, current communist. He sat secluded on the sixth floor of the Texas School Book Depository, where he had taken a part-time job. He stared out the window through a rifle scope. It was around 12:30 in the afternoon.[1]

As the presidential limo passed by below, Oswald fired, and missed. He expertly corrected his second shot, which hit President John F. Kennedy in the back of the neck. Terrible as the blow was, Kennedy might have survived had his body fallen forward and out of the way. Instead, the follow-up shot struck directly in the back of his skull.[2]

America's vigorous president was finished.

A few hours later, Vice President Lyndon Johnson was sworn in as the nation's new president aboard Air Force One. In preparation for the brief ceremony, White House staff scrambled in search of a Bible. Larry O'Brien, one of Kennedy's closest aides, went into the dead president's cabin aboard the plane and found a book bound in calfskin and embossed with a crucifix, which he and others figured was a Bible. It was, they later realized, a Catholic missal Kennedy used. With his wife, Lady Bird Johnson, to his right, and Jackie Kennedy to his left, wearing a coat that covered her bloodied pink suit, Lyndon Johnson placed his right hand on the missal and took the oath.[3]

The presidency was changed. America was changed. And Americans would soon learn that communism had factored into this evil deed.

KENNEDY AND THE POPE

John F. Kennedy was the first Catholic president of the United States. Many have doubted his dedication to his Catholic faith, not least because of his rampant infidelity to his wife. And yet JFK's belief in God and commitment to the Roman Catholic Church was probably fairly stable. He was raised by a devout mother, Rose, who attended daily Mass. She took her children to Mass every Sunday and to holy day services, and she discussed sermons with them, made them recite their Catechism lessons, and had them say grace before meals. She taught them to pray on their knees each night, which John F. Kennedy did at least through prep school. For every source saying that JFK had no "special interest in Catholicism," another claims he was "a man of deep faith" (to quote Boston's Cardinal Richard Cushing, who knew Kennedy well). A source who closely examined Kennedy's faith is Grove City College professor Gary Scott Smith, author of *Faith and the Presidency*. Of all the presidents discussed in his superb volume, Smith concedes that "Kennedy is the most difficult to analyze."[4]

An issue Kennedy's 1960 presidential campaign had to confront was whether a Catholic president would follow direct orders from the pope at the country's expense. The concerns of some voters, misplaced as they may have been, might have been even more pronounced if Americans had known that John F. Kennedy had met Pope Pius XII several times. But even many Kennedy and Pius scholars are unaware of these meetings.

Kennedy's unique ability to meet the pope stemmed from his father's position as an internationally known American Catholic. As noted, it is unclear whether college freshman John F. Kennedy met Eugenio Pacelli when the future Pope Pius XII visited the Kennedy home in Bronxville, New York, in 1936, though Rose's diary suggests he was not present. We do know, however, that JFK met with Pacelli a year later, in August 1937. The twenty-year-old Kennedy was doing an eight-week tour of Europe with a good friend, Lem Billings. His father—aggressively grooming his sons for public life—suggested the trip as a fact-finding tour to help the young man become aware of events stirring in Europe.

Throughout that tour, Kennedy visited cathedrals and attended Mass, including at Notre Dame in Paris. On July 27 he stopped at Lourdes to visit the grotto where the Blessed Mother was said to have appeared to Saint Bernadette, another major Church-approved apparition.[5] From there, Kennedy and Billings crossed the border into Italy.[6] The few sources that have reported on this Kennedy trip are again short on details, but they affirm that Kennedy saw Cardinal Pacelli at least twice (on August 5 and 7) and met with him privately at least once.[7]

"Of course we had introductions to everybody in the Vatican," recalled Lem Billings, "because Cardinal Pacelli was friendly with Mr. and Mrs. Kennedy.... Also, Count Galeazzi, the chief layman for the Catholic Church, was a close friend of the Kennedys. So we had all the entrees to the Vatican that were necessary, and we were treated very well." JFK was very impressed with Pacelli, recording in his diary: "Had a private audience with Cardinal Pacelli...who asked after Mother and Dad. He is really a great man."[8]

The fact that Kennedy had a private meeting with Cardinal Pacelli is remarkable; it certainly resulted from the intervention of his father, who just several months later would be named U.S. ambassador to England. The father's role explains the next time JFK saw Pacelli; it came on

March 12, 1939, when he attended Pacelli's coronation as Pope Pius XII. Kennedy attended with his father, who was sent as the personal representative of President Roosevelt. "Friday I leave for Rome as J.P. [Joseph P. Kennedy] has been appointed to represent Roosevelt at the Pope's coronation," JFK reported at the time. "So far, it's been damn good and feel quite important."[9]

The March 1939 encounter was certainly quite important. Because of the Vatican's dispute with a succession of Italian leaders, there had not been a traditional papal inaugural ceremony in more than a century. Nearly every nation sent an official representative to this ceremony. America sent both its Catholic ambassador to England and his son, the future president. They were the first-ever official U.S. representatives at the coronation of a pope.[10]

The new pope gave the Kennedys a private audience, and he even offered Joe the honorific "papal duke."[11]

The day after the coronation, Pius and Joe Kennedy held a series of meetings. The senior Kennedy, who had infamously poor judgment of the Nazis, expressed alarm at what he called Pius's "subconscious prejudice... that Nazism and Fascism are pro-pagan." The new pontiff was greatly troubled by this "trend of the times," Ambassador Kennedy told the State Department. Kennedy urged the pope to talk to the Nazis and keep his strong opinions private. Pius seemed to reject that advice, saying the Church would do "what it can," even if "the Church can only do so much."[12]

When JFK returned from Rome, he filled in Lem Billings on what happened, and with his usual good humor: "Just got back from Rome where we had a great time. Pacelli is now riding high, so it's good you bowed and groveled like you did when you met him.... Teddy received his first communion from him, the first time that a Pope has ever done this in the last couple hundred years. He gave Dad + I communion with Eunice at the same time at a private mass and all in all it was very impressive."[13]

So John F. Kennedy, the future first Catholic president, received Communion from Pope Pius XII. And Ted Kennedy, the future U.S. senator and presidential candidate, received his First Communion from the pope.[14]

JFK encountered the pontiff again on January 30, 1951, when Kennedy was a congressman.[15] When Kennedy married Jacqueline Bouvier on September 12, 1953, Pope Pius XII sent his personal blessing. On September 19, 1955, by which point JFK was a senator, the two men met privately at the pope's residence at Castel Gandolfo. A surviving photograph shows a weak Kennedy, who long suffered from various ailments, leaning on crutches aside the aging pope.[16]

From Rome, Kennedy headed to the turf of a future pope. He traveled to Poland, where, reported biographer Herb Parmet, he would "make a study of conditions in Communist Poland."[17] No one has ever reported whether the future president bumped into Karol Wojtyła, then a thirty-five-year-old priest, lecturer, and theology professor, fresh from completing his doctoral dissertation in phenomenology. Wojtyła was one man who detested communism as much as, if not more than, Jack Kennedy.

KENNEDY AND LEE HARVEY OSWALD

Lee Harvey Oswald was a Marxist-Leninist foot soldier in the communist campaign of errors. For decades, pundits and biographers have agonized over what motivated Oswald to shoot the president in November 1963. The answer has always been obvious: it was international communism and his devotion to its errors.

Oswald's fateful turn to Marxism came in 1953, shortly after the troubled twelve-year-old and his mother moved to New York, headquarters of the Communist Party USA, the *Daily Worker*, and American communism.[18] An anonymous communist street agitator handed the boy a leaflet asserting the innocence of the Rosenbergs and, conversely, indicting America for being complicit in their supposedly unjust destruction.[19] It was Oswald's political awakening. He dove into Marxist tracts: "I discovered socialist literature," he later reported. "I had to dig for my books in the back dusty shelves of libraries."[20]

Lee Harvey Oswald's ardor for international communism grew steadily from that moment. It manifested itself in September 1959, when he convinced the U.S. Marine Corps to give him an early discharge. He was so obviously head-over-heels for Russia that fellow Marines nicknamed him "Osvaldovich."[21] He ached to move to the USSR and serve the revolution. A month later, in October, he arrived in Moscow. "I am beginning a new life," he wrote his mother and brother. "I do not wish to contact you again."

What happened over the next two years remains a matter of dispute. It is clear, however, that Oswald spent time with the KGB; the only question is whether he did so as a permanent recruit or as someone the Soviets rejected as unstable and unreliable. Much of his time was spent in Minsk, in Belorussia. There, he met and married a Russian woman,

Marina Prusakova. They had a child together. Oswald and his new family returned to America in June 1962, where the young man prepared to kill the president of the United States.[22]

If Oswald's excitement for the Soviet experiment ever waned, his passion for the communist revolution in Cuba surged. Just as he once immersed himself in the Russian language, he dove into Spanish, wanting to serve Fidel Castro's workers' paradise. He sought out Cuban officials in Mexico, hoping to do anything to help the cause. "Fidel Castro was his hero," Marina would tell the Warren Commission, which investigated the Kennedy assassination. "He was a great admirer.... He would be happy to work for Fidel Castro's causes." Vincent Bugliosi, preeminent authority on the Kennedy assassination, said that Oswald's "devotion and ardor for Cuba knew no boundaries."[23]

When Castro took over Cuba in January 1959, he followed the communist script and made war on religion—this in one of the most pious Catholic countries in the Western Hemisphere. The island had been a pilgrimage center. It began with the apparitions of Our Lady of El Cobre in the early seventeenth century. Here was another rare Church-approved Marian apparition, centuries before Fátima.

JFK became committed to liberating Cuba, specifically through his failed Bay of Pigs invasion in April 1961. He and Castro came to loathe each another. During the Cuban Missile Crisis in October 1962, Castro's contempt for Kennedy grew so intense that he actually called on the Kremlin to launch nuclear missiles on the United States—a request that terrified Nikita Khrushchev and convinced him to get his missiles out immediately.[24]

Oswald grew outraged by John F. Kennedy's efforts to overturn Castro's communist regime, and more broadly by the president's strong anticommunism.

Kennedy was an old-school, Cold War Democrat, with a hawkish preference for espionage, covert action, military spending, and intervention. "By the standards of both his time and our own," argues biographer Ira Stoll, Kennedy was "a conservative."[25] As early as his first political campaign, in 1946, Kennedy was described as "almost ultraconservative." In a June 1953 *Saturday Evening Post* article, Kennedy said of his own ideological thinking, "I'd be very happy to tell them I'm not a liberal at all." Kennedy stated flatly, "Socialism is inefficient; I will never believe differently."[26]

Scholars and Kennedy devotees debate the nuances, but one thing no one can deny: John F. Kennedy was an uncompromising anticommunist.

In June 1955, two months before meeting again with Pius XII, Senator Kennedy told Assumption College that the communist had a "fear" of Christianity and allowed "no room for God." In a passage that could have been spoken by President Ronald Reagan thirty years later, Kennedy said that communists sought "to make the worship of the State the ultimate objective of life" and could not "permit a higher loyalty, a faith in God, a belief in a religion that elevates the individual, acknowledges his true value, and teaches him devotion and responsibility to something beyond the here and now."[27]

As president, Kennedy candidly warned America of its "atheistic foe," the "fanaticism and fury" of communism, and the "communist conspiracy" that "represents a final enslavement." "The enemy is the communist system itself—implacable, insatiable, unceasing in its drive for world domination," declared Kennedy. "This [is] a struggle for supremacy between two conflicting ideologies: freedom under God versus ruthless, godless tyranny."[28]

In all of this, Kennedy could not have been more unlike Lee Harvey Oswald. He was anathema to Oswald. America's first Catholic president, a dedicated anticommunist, fell victim to one of communism's gunners.

THE LEFT BLAMES THE RIGHT

But that was not how the American left saw the Kennedy assassination. Immediately after the shooting, American liberals blamed everything and everyone but communism and its disciples.

Liberals blamed the shooting on "right-wing hysteria," on the "conservatism" of the city of Dallas—a "City of Hate." They fingered right-wing "extremism," "paranoia," "kooks," and an assorted list of bogeymen on the right.[29] Some blamed the intensely anticommunist John Birch Society. This was an especially brazen charge given that Oswald in April 1963 had tried to assassinate Edwin Walker, a retired U.S. Army general who headed the Dallas chapter of the Birch Society; in fact, Oswald used the same rifle to shoot Kennedy.[30]

The very afternoon of the assassination, Chief Justice Earl Warren blamed Kennedy's shooting on "the hatred and bitterness that has been injected into the life of our nation by bigots."[31] In his eulogy at Kennedy's funeral, Democratic senator Mike Mansfield attributed the shooting to "bigotry, hatred, and prejudice." Popular columnist Drew Pearson, whose top staffers included David Karr, formerly of the *Daily Worker* and (according to archival information) a KGB source,[32] blamed the shooting on a "hate drive."[33]

On page one the *New York Times* ran James "Scotty" Reston's column lamenting the "violent streak" and "strain of madness" plaguing America, which he placed at the feet of "extremists on the right."[34] Nowhere in the article did the liberal columnist mention Lee Harvey Oswald, or communism, or Cuba, or the Soviet Union.

Ironically, next to Reston's analysis was a *Times* report on Oswald, which laid bare his ardent communism and many Marxist associations.[35] "LEFTIST ACCUSED," read the headline of the *Times* piece, which referred to a "figure in a pro-Castro group" who was being charged with the president's murder. The figure, Lee Harvey Oswald, had "once lived in the Soviet Union."[36]

But two days later, the *Times* editors condemned the "spiral of hate" infecting America, the "spirit of madness and hate that struck down" the young president.[37]

After its exhaustive investigation, the Warren Commission concluded that Oswald's communist motivations "influenced his decision to assassinate President Kennedy." On page 23 of its huge report, the commission cited five factors, the fifth of which was Oswald's "avowed commitment to Marxism and communism."

American leftists did not take heed. They had the narrative they wanted, and pesky facts would not get in the way. Their reaction confirmed the assessment of James Burnham, the conservative intellectual and convert from atheistic communism to Roman Catholicism, who famously stated that "for the Left, the preferred enemy is always to the Right."

THE SOVIET BLAME GAME

With a more-than-receptive audience on the American left, the Soviets wasted no time doing what they did best: concocting disinformation. If the American left was looking for conservative culprits in the Kennedy killing, the Kremlin was more than willing to conjure them up.

Here again, former communist intelligence officials have revealed what happened behind the scenes in Moscow. Oleg Kalugin told the story in his 1994 book, *The First Directorate*. Kalugin spent thirty-two years in the KGB, rising to the rank of major general and chief of foreign counterintelligence. And Ion Mihai Pacepa, the former Romanian spy chief, provided more details in *Disinformation*, the book he cowrote with Ronald Rychlak—the same source that divulged the communist campaign against Pope Pius XII.

Kalugin is the highest-ranking KGB officer to record his story. The Soviet spy infiltrated America in 1958, studying journalism at Columbia University on a Fulbright scholarship. He immediately proved adept at duping liberals at Columbia and at the *New York Times*, which published a glowing profile of the "student" in 1959.[38] By November 1963, Kalugin had made great strides in his cover role as a Soviet journalist, but in reality he was a KGB deputy station chief in Washington. Some of his contacts most receptive to his messages from Moscow included the journalists Edward R. Murrow, Drew Pearson, and I. F. Stone; former first lady Eleanor Roosevelt; and Senator Mike Mansfield.[39]

Kalugin recounts that immediately after Oswald's Soviet connections were disclosed, he and his fellow agents in Washington began receiving "frantic cables from KGB headquarters in Moscow, ordering us to do everything possible to dispel the notion that the Soviet Union was somehow behind the assassination" (which, to Kalugin's knowledge, it was not). The Kremlin, he noted, was "clearly rattled by Oswald's Soviet connection." So how to dispel that notion? Kalugin explained their orders: "We were told to put forward the line that Oswald could have been involved in a conspiracy with American reactionaries displeased with the president's recent efforts to improve relations with Russia." And so, said Kalugin, "I spoke with all my intelligence assets, including Russian correspondents and various U.N. employees, and told them to spread the official Soviet line. In the end, our campaign succeeded."[40]

American liberals swallowed the Soviet line. They reflexively accepted Soviet innocence and pointed the finger at American conservatives.

Like Kalugin, Ion Pacepa says that the KGB ran a disinformation campaign to blame the Kennedy assassination on domestic elements in the United States, from "right-wingers" and anticommunists to the CIA. Pacepa recalls that on November 26, 1963, four days after Kennedy's assassination, the head of KGB foreign intelligence, Soviet general Aleksandr Sakharovsky, landed unannounced in Bucharest. There, Sakharovsky met with Pacepa and other high-level members of Romanian intelligence and leadership. This was his first stop in a "blitz" tour of top KGB sister services in the Communist Bloc. "From him," recalls Pacepa, "we in the DIE [Romanian intelligence] learned that the KGB had already launched a worldwide disinformation operation aimed at diverting public attention away from Moscow in respect to the Kennedy assassination, and at framing the CIA as the culprit." Nikita Khrushchev himself, said Sakharovsky, wanted it made clear to the sister services that "this was by far our first and most important task." It was crucial "to spread our version about the assassination before Washington could spread its own, so that our disinformation machinery could plant the idea on virgin soil that the CIA was responsible for the crime." They also circulated rumors that Vice President Lyndon Johnson and the "military-industrial complex" had been involved.[41]

The effort would be called Operation Dragon. It became, said Pacepa, one of the most successful disinformation operations in recent history. Pacepa points to Hollywood director Oliver Stone's 1991 movie, *JFK*, which blamed the Kennedy assassination on a cabal that included the CIA, Lyndon Johnson, and the military-industrial complex. It was nominated for eight Academy Awards and won two. Pacepa and Rychlak cite a Gallup poll showing that two-thirds to three-quarters of the American people believe there was indeed a CIA conspiracy to kill Kennedy.[42]

Other sources corroborate the claims of Kalugin and Pacepa. Former Russian president and Soviet Politburo member Boris Yeltsin, in his memoir, reveals a November 23, 1963, letter from KGB chairman Vladimir Semichastny to the Soviet Central Committee recommending publishing, in a "progressive paper in one of the Western countries," an article "exposing the attempt by reactionary circles in the USA to remove the responsibility for the murder of Kennedy from the real criminals, [i.e.,] the racists and ultra-right elements guilty of the spread and growth of violence and terror in the United States." The Central Committee approved Semichastny's request.[43]

Even more significant was information disclosed by the Mitrokhin Archive, some twenty-five thousand highly declassified Soviet documents that KGB archivist Colonel Vasili Mitrokhin smuggled out of Moscow in 1992. Mitrokhin published many of these documents in *The Sword and the Shield*, a book he cowrote with British writer Christopher Andrew. Here, too, Ion Pacepa and Ronald Rychlak connected the dots. As they note, the Mitrokhin Archive reveals that this particular KGB campaign employed some of the same agents used in the disinformation campaign against Pope Pius XII. These agents included Carl Marzani, a KGB agent living in New York and working as a publisher; I. F. Stone, the American "progressive" journalist; and Victor Perlo, whom former Soviet spies Elizabeth Bentley and Whittaker Chambers identified as a Soviet agent—a designation later confirmed by the Venona papers.[44]

None of this, write Pacepa and Rychlak, should come as a surprise.

Both operations, against Pius and JFK, revved up in 1963: the vicious anti–Pius XII play *The Deputy* hit the stage in Berlin in February, and Kennedy was shot in November. Marzani published the first major book to blame the CIA for the Kennedy assassination—*Oswald: Assassin or Fall Guy?*, by Joachim Joesten, a former member of the German Communist Party. Victor Perlo wrote the first review of the book, a glowing account published in the *New Times*, a Soviet front publication.[45]

On December 9, 1963, I.F. Stone, who we now know had been a paid Soviet agent at one point,[46] published a long article calling Oswald a "rightist crackpot" and blaming the "warlike Administration" for Kennedy's killing. A few months later, Stone wrote a hit piece on Pius XII as well, praising Hochhuth's *The Deputy*. That same month, Stone's sister, Judy, conducted a friendly interview with Hochhuth for the radical publication *Ramparts*.[47]

"So again," sum up Pacepa and Rychlak, "we see the KGB rounding up the 'usual suspects,' both in order to smear Pius XII as pro-Hitler and to blame the CIA and other American targets for the death of President Kennedy."[48]

But Pacepa goes further. Picking up from his 2007 book, *Programmed to Kill: Lee Harvey Oswald, the Soviet KGB, and the Kennedy Assassination*, Pacepa argues that the Soviets were actually involved in the Kennedy assassination, or at least helped in the early planning stages. He maintains that the KGB recruited Oswald when he first entered the Soviet Union and persuaded him to assassinate Kennedy. But by 1962, when Oswald was settled in Texas, Khrushchev had allegedly changed his mind about killing Kennedy. Consequently, claims Pacepa, "the KGB tried to turn Oswald off." It was too late. Oswald could not be stopped. He killed Kennedy against the wishes of a Kremlin that had a change of heart too late.[49]

For the record, most Kennedy biographers and investigators dispute this theory. The Warren Commission determined "there is no credible evidence that Oswald was an agent of the Soviet government."[50] Peter Savodnik, author of *The Interloper: Lee Harvey Oswald Inside the Soviet Union*, dismisses the claim, concluding that Oswald had "nothing to offer Soviet intelligence.... They had never thought much of him. If he wanted to go [back to America], that was fine. By mid-1962, he was nothing to them but a lazy, whiny American who built television sets in Minsk."[51]

This much we do know: Moscow did its damnedest to direct suspicion elsewhere, especially toward the United States. The Soviet Union blamed the shooting on "racists, the Ku Klux Klan, and Birchists." One Soviet spokesman said that anticommunist conservative Barry Goldwater, in line for the Republican presidential nomination in 1964, and "other extremists on the right" could not escape "moral responsibility."[52]

Pravda claimed that American "reactionaries" were exploiting the death to try to "fan anti-Soviet and anti-Cuban hysteria." As we shall see, Moscow would use the same line in 1981 after another shooting of another prominent Catholic statesman: Pope John Paul II.

"SILLY LITTLE COMMUNIST"

The American left had no reason to blame the shooting of Kennedy on anyone but Lee Harvey Oswald and his warped ideology—the ideology of international communism.

The *Washington Post* had reported as early as November 1959 that an "ex-Marine" named Lee Harvey Oswald had asked the Soviets for citizenship.[53] Four years later, in November 1963, Oswald's loyalties were made known to all. Everyone knew he was no right-wing anticommunist. Everyone knew he was a communist. Jackie Kennedy did. The widow later complained that her husband "didn't even have the satisfaction of being killed for civil rights. It had to be some silly little Communist. It robs his death of meaning."[54]

Silly little communist? No, there was nothing silly about communism. There was something deadly about communism. And John F. Kennedy was its latest high-profile victim. Rather than robbing his death of meaning, the communist connection contained much added meaning. It revealed the depth of the struggle with what a future president would call an "Evil Empire."

Ronald Reagan keenly understood the enemy, and the struggle America and the West faced. He knew that John F. Kennedy had understood this as well.

Years later, as president, Reagan, in a generous move well beyond his duties as president (or as a Republican), went to the home of Senator Ted Kennedy in McLean, Virginia, where he spoke at an endowment fundraiser for the John F. Kennedy Presidential Library. On hand were Jackie and her two grown children. Reagan commended JFK for his shrewdness in recognizing the enemy: "He understood the tension between good and evil in the history of man; understood, indeed, that much of the history of man can be seen in the constant working out of that tension."[55]

Reagan's thought was not unlike a dramatic line in the Catholic Catechism (section 409): "The whole of man's history has been the story of dour combat with the powers of evil, stretching, so our Lord tells us, from the very dawn of history until the last day. Finding himself in the midst of the battlefield man has to struggle to do what is right, and it is at great cost to himself."

Kennedy had engaged in that struggle at great cost to himself.

Reagan went on: "[Kennedy] knew that the United States had adversaries, real adversaries, and they weren't about to be put off by soft reason and good intentions. He tried always to be strong with them and shrewd."

John F. Kennedy's death at the hands of "some silly little Communist" had meaning all right. When Our Lady of Fátima prophesied communism's repeated persecutions throughout the twentieth century, it is hard to imagine that the Kennedy killing was not among them. She had relayed her warnings in 1917, the year of the Bolshevik Revolution, and also the year of the birth of John F. Kennedy, America's first and only Catholic president. Kennedy was born in May 1917, the exact month that Our Lady of Fátima first appeared.

And consistent with her warnings, much blood remained to be spilled.

Part 3

WOJTYŁA AND REAGAN RISING

9

1946–1959

BATTLING COMMUNISTS IN POLAND AND HOLLYWOOD

Karol Wojtyła and Ronald Reagan could not miss international communism's litany of errors, smears, and persecutions. As they watched the evils wrought by Marxist-Leninist ideology through the 1940s, 1950s, and 1960s, they were being drawn inexorably into the great struggle of their time.

To this point in our narrative, we have seen glimpses of where Wojtyła and Reagan stood at various intervals as communists persecuted everyone from European priests to American politicians. Here, in part 3 of the book, we will pick up the stories of these two future partners in the crusade against communism to understand how they found their calling and emerged as world leaders.

A PRIEST-TURNED-BISHOP IN POLAND

In the fall of 1946, as Soviet communism was crushing one priest in Yugoslavia, Aloysius Stepinac, it was inadvertently helping to raise up another in Poland—one who would eventually avenge Stepinac.

On November 1, All Saints' Day, twenty-six-year-old Karol Wojtyła of Wadowice knelt before Cardinal Adam Stefan Sapieha in the archbishop's private chapel in the seventeenth-century episcopal residence at Franciszkańska 3, named for a Polish order of Saint Francis. Sapieha during the war years had bravely defied the Gestapo by carrying on an underground seminary. Now, post-Gestapo, the cardinal continued to defy anti-Christ authorities, this time Red ones. With Poland, like Yugoslavia, suffering heavy religious persecution, Wojtyła was the only priest ordained that day.

As Wojtyła knelt before the cardinal, the young man held a white candle while the seminary officials spoke on his behalf, vouchsafing his worthiness for this unique sacrament of servanthood that few in the Church contemplate, let alone complete. Cardinal Sapieha asked Wojtyła to be "perfect in faith and action" and "well-grounded in virtue." It was a call to a kind of sainthood he would need, and a call he would fulfill in due course.[1]

Having received that charge, Wojtyła laid himself face down on the floor, arms outstretched—cruciform—embodying the cross itself. The brethren chanted the Litany of the Saints, calling upon those at the altar of God in heaven to intervene in the unrepeatable life of this young man fully entering religious life.

When the extended call for the intercession of the saints was finished, this future pope and future saint humbly kneeled before his cardinal. The cardinal laid his hands on the young man's head, continuing an act of apostolic succession that, for the first but hardly the last time, connected Wojtyła back two millennia to the first pope, Saint Peter. The Holy Spirit was thus conferred upon him, and implored never to leave him. The faithful sang "Come, Holy Spirit," in Latin: "Veni, Sancte Spiritus."

The cardinal anointed Wojtyła and blessed him, stating, "The blessing of God Almighty, the Father, the Son, and the Holy Spirit, descend upon you: that you may be blessed in the Priestly Order and may offer propitiatory sacrifices for the sins and offense of the people to Almighty God, to whom belongs glory and honor, world without end." Such sacrifices the young man had already endured in watching friends and loved ones and fellow priests murdered by Nazis. But many more sacrifices were still to come, especially as the errors of international communism closed upon his very person. "Dearly beloved son," said the cardinal, "consider attentively the Order you have taken and the burden laid on your shoulders. Endeavor to lead a holy and godly life, and to please almighty God, that you may obtain His grace, which may He of His mercy be pleased to grant you."[2]

When Cardinal Sapieha finished, Karol Wojtyła solemnly assented with one word: "Amen."

It was a massive burden the young man had just taken upon his shoulders. He could scarcely imagine the weight that would press on him.

Two weeks after his ordination, on November 15, Karol boarded a train leaving Kraków for Paris. It was the young man's first trip outside Poland. The newly ordained priest was not in Paris long, absconding for more hallowed ground: Rome.

On his first Sunday in Rome, Wojtyła and a fellow priest attended Mass at Saint Peter's Square, where they watched an anguished man with the burdens of the world on his shoulders complete a beatification ceremony. It was Karol Wojtyła's first glimpse of Pope Pius XII, whom he would one day follow in the chair of Saint Peter.[3]

Two years later, Wojtyła returned to Poland, where he received his first parish assignment, completed studies for two doctorates, joined the theology faculty at the esteemed Jagiellonian University, and then, in December 1956, was appointed to the Chair of Ethics at the Catholic University of Lublin, where he taught intensive courses in moral theology.

Still in his thirties, Karol Wojtyła was well on his way.

THE HOLLYWOOD FRONT

Meanwhile, in Hollywood, someone else was on his way.

About the time that Karol Wojtyła was being ordained, a thirty-something Ronald Reagan was in a church for his own special moment that would change his life and plans.

With the Second World War completed, Reagan had returned from military service and resumed his film career. He also became a popular after-dinner speaker. Reagan still considered himself an FDR liberal, and his talks were remarkably political and internationally oriented for an actor whose job was to entertain. In his standard talk during this period, Reagan received enthusiastic applause from his audiences of fellow progressives as he denounced fascism, the totalitarian monster of the recent past.[4]

Then a religious figure in his life refocused his attention on a different, and growing, totalitarian threat.

Reagan was asked to speak to the men's group at the Hollywood Beverly Christian Church, his church at the time.[5] After the talk, the pastor, the Reverend Cleveland Kleihauer, approached Reagan. Dr. Kleihauer was an intelligent man, learned, not overly political, a straight shooter known for his good sense.[6] He thanked Reagan for his usual fire and brimstone against Nazism. Then he reminded the self-described "hemophiliac" liberal that the fascist menace had been defeated and that another danger could replace it: Soviet communism. "I think your speech would be even better," Dr. Kleihauer said, "if you also mentioned that if communism ever looked like a threat, you'd be just as opposed to it as you are to fascism."

Reagan conceded to the reverend that, as a good liberal, he had not given much thought to threats from the far left. Nonetheless, Reagan understood his minister's point, and in his next appearance he took Dr. Kleihauer's advice. Reagan addressed a "local citizens' organization," one of the many that Hollywood's closet communists peddled to friends as a "progressive" organization. Giving his standard talk, Reagan torched the fascists America had vanquished in the war. The "progressives" roared their approval. By his own description, Reagan was a smash. But then, following the Reverend Kleihauer's advice, the young actor closed with a new line: "I've talked about the continuing threat of fascism in the postwar world, but there's another 'ism,' communism, and if I ever find evidence that communism represents a threat to all that we believe in and stand for, I'll speak out just as harshly against communism as I have fascism."

The applause stopped. The smiles fell away. A nonplussed Reagan awkwardly exited the stage—to dead silence.

The addition of a single line to his popular speech had turned him into a flop. Reagan had just learned something critically important about the left. The progressive circles he traveled in were happy to denounce Nazism but did not want to hear a bad word about communism. The incident showed Reagan how naive many on the left were about communism. He would soon see how many progressives saw *anti*communists as the real enemy. He would also learn that for at least some progressives, the problem was not simple naïveté: they actually approved of communism.

Decades later, after his presidency, Reagan thanked the Reverend Kleihauer for the "wake-up call." That moment, prompted by a man of God in a house of God, proved to be the beginning of Ronald Reagan's long crusade against communism.

SALUTING A "SOVIET AMERICA"

Reagan was getting a quick tutorial on the hidden forces at work in Hollywood: people who cloaked themselves as compassionate "progressives" but were, in truth, privately conspiring to create a Soviet-directed American state. They were dedicated to what their leader, Communist Party USA general secretary William Z. Foster, called a "Soviet America." The Marxist poet Langston Hughes put it this way: "Put one more 'S' in the USA to make it Soviet. The USA when we take control will be the USSA."[7]

Had Reagan then known a fellow Illinoisan named Fulton Sheen, he might have been forewarned. Communists, said Sheen, were "boring secretly from within." They "are urged to wheel their Trojan Horse into our labor unions, religious organizations, political parties, athletic associations under the guise of a peaceful United Front... so that they may emerge victorious and thus honor their beloved Comrade Stalin."[8]

The American left laughed at Sheen's warnings. In fact, the bishop was spot-on: under the guise of a popular front, communists were penetrating mainstream associations—including unions and organizations in Ronald Reagan's Hollywood.

Reagan would later admit that in this period he was duped repeatedly by communists masquerading as his "progressive" pals. "The communist plan for Hollywood was remarkably simple," an awakened Reagan explained. "It was merely to take over the motion picture business... [as] a grand world-wide propaganda base."[9]

Communists knew that the film industry could be a tremendous source of propaganda. Vladimir Lenin said that "of all the arts, for us the most important is cinema." Grigori Zinoviev, head of the Soviet Comintern, ordered that motion pictures "must become a mighty weapon of communist propaganda and for the enlightening of the widest working masses." In March 1928 the Soviets held their first Party Conference on Cinema.

By the 1940s, noted Reagan, American films dominated 95 percent of the globe's movie screens, with a worldwide audience of "500,000,000 souls." Reagan wrote: "Takeover of this enormous plant and its gradual transformation into a communist gristmill was a grandiose idea. It would have been a magnificent coup for our enemies."[10]

By the end of this period, Reagan was transformed. He would no longer be easily misled by closet Marxist-Leninists who had sworn a loyalty oath to Moscow. "I pledge myself to rally the masses to defend the Soviet Union," they affirmed upon joining Communist Party USA. "I pledge myself to remain at all times a vigilant and firm defender of the Leninist line of the Party, the only line that ensures the triumph of Soviet Power in the United States."

Liberals today portray the so-called Hollywood Ten, a group of blacklisted screenwriters and directors, as innocent victims of delusional McCarthyites. In fact, every single member of the Hollywood Ten was secretly a card-carrying member of the American Communist Party.[11] One of the Hollywood Ten, Dalton Trumbo (card number 47187), declared that "every screenwriter worth his salt wages the battle in his own way—a kind of literary guerrilla warfare." He said that not to employ film for "progressive" purposes was "tantamount to abandoning the struggle altogether."[12] His angry comrade and partner, John Howard Lawson, known as "Hollywood's commissar," instructed his fellow Marxist screenwriters, "As a writer, do not try to write an entire Communist picture,... [but] try to get five minutes of communist doctrine, five minutes of the party line in every script that you write."[13]

Reagan, as head of the largest union in Hollywood, the Screen Actors Guild, knew these people. At one point, he had been used by all of them.

Now he was chastened, aware, unafraid. Reagan soon began supporting Dr. Fred Schwarz's Christian Anti-Communist Crusade, attending rallies and giving speeches.[14] He also began appearing at rallies for the Crusade for Freedom, whose chairman, General Lucius Clay, had advised President Truman to have U.S. tanks crash Stalin's blockade at Berlin. The Crusade for Freedom called less for containment of the Soviet empire than actual "rollback," precisely the objectives Reagan would one day implement as president. At Crusade for Freedom rallies, Reagan said he wanted to free the "captive peoples."[15] The captives included the men and women of Karol Wojtyła's Poland.

Reagan made his ambitions clear in an article he wrote at the end of 1950 for a Hollywood publication called *Fortnight*. The article was titled "How Do You Fight Communism?"[16] He lamented that "many people" talk about resisting communism, but "they put the emphasis on 'try'" while "the doing gets lost." As a result, communists "infiltrate and control certain key industries." It was a message very similar to Fulton Sheen's. "Democracy does guarantee the right of every man to think as he pleases, to speak freely and to advocate his beliefs," Reagan wrote. "Democracy also provides defense against those who would deliver our nation into the hands of a foreign despot. Call them pro-Russian and take away the screen. If we must fight, make the enemy be properly uniformed."

For Ronald Reagan, the fight had started.

JANE AND NANCY

The early 1950s were a pivotal time for Reagan, politically, professionally, and ideologically, and personally.

His personal life had gone through serious turmoil. In 1949 his marriage to actress Jane Wyman ended in a heartbreaking divorce that Reagan did not want. He was devastated.

Wyman had already been divorced before she and Reagan had met in her early twenties, and she would divorce twice more. Reagan was not so cavalier. He saw marriage as a lifelong commitment. He had watched his mother stand by his father all those difficult years.

In 1954 Wyman converted to Catholicism, having been led in that direction by actress Loretta Young, a close personal friend of Bishop Sheen. Jane became friends with Sheen, and every year she attended the annual Sheen breakfast in Hollywood. Her son, Michael, recalls those breakfasts and meeting Sheen, who, he quips, was always the biggest celebrity in the building.[17] "My Mom was brought to the Church through Loretta," Michael told me. "Both, however, were also inspired by Bishop Sheen."[18]

Jane and Michael and daughter Maureen all came into the Catholic Church together on December 8, 1954, the Feast of the Immaculate Conception of the Virgin Mary.[19] Jane and her two children, sans their father, joined the Church of the Good Shepherd in Beverly Hills, under Father John Osborne. Loretta Young's sister, Sally Foster, served as nine-year-old Michael's godmother.[20]

Ronald Reagan was careful to respect Jane's conversion and that of their children. He had long ago learned to honor the wishes of a Catholic parent. Michael today recalls being a Catholic teen and living with Ronald and Nancy Reagan one summer. One Sunday, the Reagans left Michael at home while the rest of the family went to church. Michael was hurt by this. When years later he complained about it to his father, Reagan gently explained, "I didn't want to upset your mother."[21]

Reagan had learned long ago to respect the religious wishes of the mother.

Faith would get Reagan through some tough times in the early 1950s. He was certain that "God had a plan" for him, even as his marriage to Jane and his movie career fell apart. Things might be bad right now, but, as Nelle always said, God had something better on the horizon.

And indeed, his prospects quickly improved. In March 1952, four years after the divorce, he married Nancy Davis, who stood at his side faithfully and unflinchingly for the next fifty-two years. Nancy always had her critics, including among Reagan's most avid supporters, but he could not have found a more dedicated wife. She would never leave him. "Ronnie is my hero," she said. "My life began when I got married. My life began with Ronnie."[22]

Three months after his marriage, Reagan gave a speech that reflected the political transformation he was undergoing. In June 1952 he and his new bride traveled to a tiny little women's college called William Woods College, located in Fulton, Missouri, the town where Winston Churchill six years earlier had given his Iron Curtain speech. Reagan came to deliver the commencement address. His speech received no publicity, but it was a significant bellwether of the battle ahead.

As can be understood now, the speech was classic Reagan, with soaring language about America and God's hand. He titled the talk "America the Beautiful," and in it he declared, "I believe that God in shedding his grace on this country has always in this divine scheme of things kept an eye on our land and guided it as a promised land."[23]

It was an extraordinary statement. Ronald Reagan would return to this point about America's role in God's divine plan again and again over the next thirty-plus years.[24]

America, Reagan told the graduating seniors, was "less of a place than an idea," an idea that resided deep in people's souls "ever since man started his long trail from the swamps." The idea of America "is nothing but the inherent love of freedom in each one of us." That idea is "the basis of this country and of our religion, the idea of the dignity of man, the idea that deep within the heart of each one of us is something so God-like and precious."

Now America was engaged in a "great ideological struggle," Reagan said. This was "not a new struggle," he added. "It's the same old battle. We met it under the name of Hitlerism; we met it under the name of Kaiserism; and we have met it back through the ages in the name of every conqueror that has ever set upon a course of establishing his rule over mankind."

There was a common thread to these threats: evil. Reagan implored the graduates to join him in an epic struggle against "totalitarian darkness."

To illustrate the point, the forty-one-year-old actor conjured up an image. He spoke of a nighttime football game he had recently attended at the Los Angeles Coliseum. Night games were new to football. The stadium announcer asked the 103,000 people in attendance to light matches as the lights were turned off. A "grand glow" illuminated the structure, said Reagan, "light that battled the darkness." Reagan explained how this metaphor related to the battle America faced:

> It was one of the most spectacular sights I have ever seen, just because each one of the people there did what he could to contribute a little light.... You have an opportunity to decide now whether you will strike a match and whether you will help push back the darkness over the stadium of humanity.... With your help I am sure we can come much closer to realizing that this land of ours is the last best hope of man on earth. God bless you.

Reagan closed his address with that challenge, the first of so many times he would issue it. God had a plan for America. God was counting on America, a land established as a refuge and a beacon of freedom, to take on the totalitarian darkness.

GE THEATER HOST—AND ANTICOMMUNIST CRUSADER

In 1954, General Electric, one of America's most successful and best-managed companies, was looking for a host for a major new TV drama series it was launching. Ronald Reagan got the gig.

Reagan had started the year as a vaudeville act at the aptly named Last Frontier hotel in Las Vegas.[25] It was quite a climb down for a man who had been a star at Warner Bros. His new wife, Nancy, was amazed at the humility with which her husband accepted the situation and how he serenely saw it as part of God's plan. "He again got back to the deep belief that everything happens for a reason," said Nancy. "Whatever happened to him, there was a reason."[26]

His patience was rewarded when *GE Theater* called. This was a plum job. A host of a weekly show on one of only three TV networks instantly became a household name with enormous influence. Like Fulton Sheen, Reagan landed a prime-time television program just as that medium was taking off. Two-thirds of American households now had TV sets. *GE Theater* was carried on CBS Sunday evenings at 9:00, attracting millions of viewers every week.

CBS and General Electric executives saw Reagan as the ideal host—clean-cut and quintessentially American.[27] Debuting in September 1954, the show instantly eclipsed the hugely popular *I Love Lucy*.[28] It drew the very best Hollywood talent from the Golden Age of film: Ethel Barrymore, Joseph Cotten, Bette Davis, James Dean, Judy Garland, Greer Garson, Charlton Heston, Kim Hunter, David Janssen, Vincent Price, Alan Ladd, Lee Marvin, Ray Massey, Walter Matthau, Jimmy Stewart, Natalie Wood, and Donna Reed, to name a few.[29]

GE Theater remained one of the top shows on TV until it finished its long run in August 1962. Ronald Reagan appeared on the cover of *TV Guide* twice during that time (November 22, 1958, and May 27, 1961).

This new platform not only extended Reagan's reach as an entertainer but also emboldened him as a crusader against communism.

As head of the Screen Actors Guild, he had learned how disruptive communism was. Now, as he toured GE plants in towns across the country, he saw free enterprise at work and recognized that it was the polar opposite of the destructive communist system.

Reagan was not shy about inserting anticommunist messages into *GE Theater* episodes. In these episodes he stepped outside his usual emcee role to act as well.

On December 13, 1959, for example, *GE Theater* addressed the communist menace in Asia, where China was firmly under Mao's grip and Korea and Vietnam were under assault. In the episode, called "The House of Truth," Reagan played a U.S. intelligence officer in an Asian village ravaged by communists. The communists set fire to an American library that Reagan's character helped reopen.

Other *GE Theater* episodes carried similar themes. A two-part production titled "My Dark Days" was broadcast March 18 and 25, 1962. Based on a true story, the production featured a communist front group called the Alien Protection Committee, which claimed to be a liberal/progressive organization protecting the welfare of foreign-born Americans. It smacked of one of the more notorious communist fronts, the American Committee for Protection of Foreign Born, which the Communist Party USA had founded decades earlier to (as Congress put it) "exploit racial divisions in the United States for its own revolutionary purposes."[30]

Reagan played the husband of a housewife who was sucked into the group. Not unlike Ronald Reagan in the 1940s, the wife character was a liberal who had been duped by communists masquerading as "progressives." But she came to see what was really happening, and she became an FBI informant who penetrated the group.

Screenwriter Richard Collins adapted the script from Marion Miller's acclaimed 1960 autobiography, *I Was a Spy: The Story of a Brave Housewife*.[31] Reagan could relate; he had lived it himself. MSNBC host Chris Matthews recalled that Reagan as emcee told viewers, "This is a program I care a lot about personally."[32]

Reagan cared so much that he battled to get it on the air. In a letter he wrote a few weeks after the episode aired, he told a friend about the major resistance he had faced. "I had to fight right down to the wire to make the Communists villains," Reagan wrote. "When I say 'fight' I really mean that."[33] Liberals on the producing staff, he said, had dismissed communist infiltration as a paranoid fantasy "dreamed up" by "right-wingers." They attempted to kill the script with a thousand cuts. Reagan was particularly bothered when the director and two producers tried to ax the scene where a little girl prayed. "Finally in a near knockdown drag-out," said Reagan, "they admitted their objection was because they were atheists."

Reagan said that although the GE brass supported this "anti-communist story," the Hollywood liberals in his midst were militantly opposed.

"I HAVE A LOT TO TALK ABOUT WITH THE LORD"

One fellow freedom fighter who would have appreciated Reagan's resistance to communism was Karol Wojtyła.

In 1958, the year Reagan appeared on the cover of *TV Guide* for the first time, the thirty-eight-year-old Polish priest became auxiliary bishop of Kraków. On July 4, Pope Pius XII, who had little time left in this world, made Wojtyła the youngest bishop in Poland, evidently sensing the importance of this rising young man in a communist-dominated Catholic country.

Wojtyła happened to be in Warsaw when word of his elevation came through. Cardinal Stefan Wyszyński at the primate's office gave him the news. Struck by the magnitude of the appointment, Wojtyła immediately sought the Lord's presence in quiet isolation. He went straight to a nearby convent, where he knew the Blessed Sacrament would be available for his prayerful submission. The sisters did not know who he was but, recognizing his cassock, allowed him inside, escorting him to their private chapel and leaving him alone to pray.

After a while, the nuns grew concerned when they realized that the young priest had not left. They peeked inside to check on the stranger and saw him lying face down in front of the tabernacle. Hours passed, and the priest still had not left. The nuns were worried. One of the sisters gingerly walked inside and said to the prostrate figure, "Perhaps father would like to come to supper?" The priest answered, "My train doesn't leave for Kraków until after midnight. Please let me stay here. I have a lot to talk about with the Lord."[34]

He did indeed, and the conversation would continue for the next forty-plus years.

10

THE 1960s

A TIME FOR CHOOSING

In the 1960s, Ronald Reagan and Karol Wojtyła continued on their upward trajectories. By the middle of the decade, Reagan was facing his "rendezvous with destiny." The former actor was now a former "hemophiliac liberal." He became a firm anticommunist and conservative Republican. Meanwhile, the fast-rising Polish priest was going head to head with communist authorities.

TELLING OFF KHRUSHCHEV

In the years after his speech at Fulton, Missouri, Ronald Reagan made his opposition to Soviet communism more and more explicit. In 1959, when Nikita Khrushchev came to America, Reagan boycotted a 20th Century Fox banquet for the Soviet leader.[1] By 1961, when an anticommunist

Democrat entered the White House, speaking out against the communist threat had become a passion for Reagan.

In January of that year, Reagan blasted communism in a speech to an audience at a Minnesota high school. He also used the occasion to criticize government/socialized health care and 90-plus percent federal income-tax rates. Reagan's politics were known well enough by this point that the St. Paul Federation of Teachers protested his appearance.[2]

In May 1961, echoing the words of Fulton Sheen, among others, Reagan publicly warned of communist infiltration. He said that the Communist Party had "ordered once again" a major infiltration of the motion-picture industry and television. Communists in Hollywood were "crawling out of the rocks," he added. Reagan vowed to be undeterred. "We in Hollywood broke their power once," he affirmed, "but it was only an isolated battle."[3]

Reagan's rallying cry made its way into the *New York Times*, courtesy of a piece by a UPI correspondent. UPI covered many of Reagan's talks, no doubt sensing his increasing importance.

UPI was there again when Reagan spoke in Pennsylvania in July and issued this warning about Hollywood communists: "They are renewing in the spirit of Lenin's maxim of two steps forward and one backward."[4]

That same month, Reagan wrote a piece for *Human Events*, which, along with *National Review*, was one of the two leading conservative publications. In it he argued that the "ideological struggle with Russia" was the "number one problem in the world." "The inescapable truth," wrote Reagan, "is that we are at war, and we are losing that war simply because we don't or won't realize that we are in it."[5] He continued: "Karl Marx established the cardinal principle that communism and capitalism cannot coexist in the world together. Our way of life, our system, must be totally destroyed; then the world Communist state will be erected on the ruins." Reagan continued:

> In interpreting Marx, Lenin said, "It is inconceivable that the Soviet Republic should continue to exist for a long period side by side with imperialistic states. Ultimately, one or the other must conquer."
>
> Last November, the Communist parties of 81 countries held a convention in Moscow; and on December 6, reaffirmed this principle of war to the death. In a 20,000-word manifesto, they called on Communists in countries where there were non-Communist governments to be traitors and work for the destruction of their own governments by subversion and treason.[6]

Reagan reported that communists were organizing from Asia to Latin America and were "supremely confident of victory."[7]

He repeated these lines often. They were a refrain in a popular speech he gave, titled "A Foot in the Door," in which he warned that communists were surreptitiously subverting institutions like Hollywood. In May he cited the "one or the other must conquer" line that he included in his July *Human Events* article.[8] In September he told the Press Club of Orange County, California: "There can be only one end of the war we are in. It won't go away.... Wars end in victory or defeat."[9]

Ronald Reagan wanted to win.

In a private expression of his anti-Sovietism, Reagan in October sent a letter to a Republican named Donald Bates. He wrote that Americans were "hungry for someone to tell Mr. Khrushchev off."[10]

That was what Reagan had been doing all year.

"WE ARE IN A WAR"

In 1962, the second year of John F. Kennedy's presidency, Reagan continued to deliver the anticommunist message that he was convinced America needed to hear.

In Fargo, North Dakota, on January 26, Reagan charged: "Whether we admit it or not, we are in a war. This war was declared a half century ago by Karl Marx and re-affirmed by Lenin when he said that Communism and Capitalism cannot exist side-by-side."[11]

From North Dakota, Reagan traveled south to Bartlesville, Oklahoma, and then to Dallas and East Texas, where he sounded the same refrain: "We are in a war, whether we admit it or not";[12] "the free world is at war" with communism; and "the war isn't over."[13] He was unfailingly consistent in his message: "The weapons in this war frequently are strange to us, such as subversion, propaganda, and deliberate infiltration of many institutions of our free society.... The enemy has not resorted to the traditional instruments of war, partly because he has been doing so well without them." Reagan warned in the strongest terms: "Communism is a single, world-wide force dedicated to the destruction of our free-enterprise system and the creation of a World Socialist State. Communism is not a political party, it is a quasi-military conspiracy against our government."[14]

It must be understood that Reagan and no one else wrote these speeches; the comments reflected the real Ronald Reagan.

TWO ENDINGS

As Reagan threw himself into anticommunist crusading, his time at *GE Theater* came to an end. In 1962, after a very successful eight-year run, GE executives pulled the plug on the show. The reasons for this decision are not entirely clear. Some sources cite declining ratings, and it is true that the number of viewers had slipped once *GE Theater* went head-to-head with the hit show *Bonanza*. But it continued to draw millions of viewers. Reagan's outspoken politics may have been a factor in GE's decision as well.

Most intriguing, Robert F. Kennedy may have played a role in the cancellation.

According to Michael Reagan, his father learned that Bobby Kennedy had intervened with GE executives to get him fired. The attorney general was reportedly furious that in the 1960 presidential race, Reagan, then still a Democrat, had endorsed Republican Richard Nixon over his brother. Reagan had chaired the Democrats for Nixon committee.

Michael recalls hearing the news about *GE Theater*. "It came as quite a shock one day in 1962 when Dad came home, sat us all down, and explained that he had just been fired by General Electric," Michael says. "The show was canceled. But why? Why would CBS cancel a successful show?"[15]

Michael's father explained that it had not been a network decision. A GE official had told Ronald Reagan that the company was in the midst of negotiating some major new government contracts. As Michael recounts, "Bobby Kennedy, the attorney general of the United States, bluntly informed GE that if the company wished to do business with the U.S. government, it would get rid of *General Electric Theater* and fire the host."[16]

Bobby Kennedy knew that Reagan had been critical of JFK's administration, but he probably did not know about one particular incident when Reagan had helped: A friend of Reagan's at the Republican National Committee had showed him photos of JFK leaving hotel rooms with women other than his wife. Republicans hoped to share the photos with newspapers, but Reagan advised them not to do so, saying this was Kennedy's private business.[17] Those photos would have been politically devastating to Kennedy.

Michael Reagan says that within forty-eight hours of the attorney general's call to General Electric, the show was canceled and Ronald Reagan was out of a job.

The final episode of *GE Theater* aired in June 1962. The next month brought another end that hurt Reagan far more than losing his TV show: he lost his mother.

Nelle Reagan died in Santa Monica, California, on July 25, one day after her seventy-ninth birthday. She was gone from his life, but her influence remained profound.

He explained that influence two decades later, when he was president of the United States. "I know now that she planted that faith very deeply in me," Reagan told a group of Christian women in 1983.[18] That same year, during a radio address, he said that his mother had taught him of "the God who will guide us through life."[19]

And he always remembered the power of prayer she impressed upon him. "Just seeing my mother's faith under trying circumstances over long periods of time," said Reagan, "has enabled me to realize that when Jesus said, 'wherever two or three are gathered in My name, there am I also,' He meant He is with us in every situation and circumstance."[20]

Even when he was president, he felt like his mom was looking down and helping him with her never-ending gift of prayer. "Maybe she's still giving me a hand now and then," the president told a friend.[21]

"A TIME FOR CHOOSING"

Nelle's little boy was now a man poised for big things. Historic things. As his mother had taught him, when God closes one door, another (better) one opens. Losing *GE Theater* opened the door for Reagan to advance his political work. By 1964 he was campaigning for Barry Goldwater's presidential bid, which would launch him toward the California governorship and the presidency of the United States.[22]

In 1962, the year *GE Theater* ended, Reagan switched his party affiliation to Republican. He was fed up with the direction of the Democratic Party, which he judged had abandoned traditional ideas and values in favor of big-government solutions. He believed that the party's liberal wing, by embracing and extending the welfare state, was fostering a "dependency class." Reagan feared a "creeping socialism" and was distressed at liberals' naïveté about the dangers of communism.

The GOP was happy to have him. The Republicans needed all the help they could get in the 1964 presidential race. They were running a bona fide conservative in Goldwater, who faced the immense task of defeating an incumbent who had come into office less than a year earlier after the assassination of a beloved president. They needed help delivering the conservative message, and few could do so with the polish of the former host of *GE Theater.*

And so, on the evening of October 27, 1964, Reagan gave a nationally televised speech on behalf of the Republican presidential nominee.[23] Aired on NBC the Tuesday before the election, the speech did not save Goldwater, who experienced a crushing defeat at the hands of Lyndon Johnson. But it did launch Ronald Reagan as a major political force. *Washington Post* political reporter David Broder later dubbed it "the most successful political debut" since William Jennings Bryan's "Cross of Gold" speech.

This, too, was a speech that Reagan wrote himself. He began by announcing that he had spent most of his life as a Democrat. "I recently have seen fit to follow another course," he explained. "I believe that the issues confronting us cross party lines."[24]

Reagan started with a long presentation on how American prosperity was being strangled by an excessive tax burden, one approaching a third of gross national product. He then moved to peace, war, and foreign policy, including the escalating conflict in Vietnam:

> As for the peace that we would preserve, I wonder who among us would like to approach the wife or mother whose husband or son has died in South Vietnam and ask them if they think this is a peace that should be maintained indefinitely. Do they mean peace, or do they mean we just want to be left in peace?...We're at war with the most dangerous enemy that has ever faced mankind in his long climb from the swamp to the stars, and it's been said if we lose that war, and in so doing lose this way of freedom of ours, history will record with the greatest astonishment that those who had the most to lose did the least to prevent its happening. Well I think it's time we ask ourselves if we still know the freedoms that were intended for us by the Founding Fathers.
>
> Not too long ago, two friends of mine were talking to a Cuban refugee, a businessman who had escaped from Castro, and in the midst of his story one of my friends turned to the other and said, "We don't know how lucky we are." And the Cuban stopped and said, "How lucky you are? I had someplace to escape to."

That "most dangerous enemy" was headquartered in Moscow and advancing throughout the world, including into Southeast Asia and the Western Hemisphere. Note how Reagan had captured the essence of American exceptionalism via the sentiments of the Cuban refugee: if America lost freedom, there would be no place to escape to. America was freedom's last stand.

"You and I are told increasingly we have to choose between a left or right," said Reagan. "Well, I'd like to suggest there is no such thing as a left or right. There's only an up or down—[up] man's [age-old] dream, the ultimate in individual freedom consistent with law and order, or down to the ant heap of totalitarianism."

Reagan attacked the mind-set of what would become known as détente. To Reagan, this accommodationist foreign policy amounted to "a conspiracy of silence" that kept people from opening their mouths "about the millions of people enslaved in the Soviet colonies in the satellite nations." He said:

> Those who would trade our freedom for the soup kitchen of the welfare state have told us they have a utopian solution of peace without victory. They call their policy "accommodation." And they say if we'll only avoid any direct confrontation with the enemy, he'll forget his evil ways and learn to love us. All who oppose them are indicted as warmongers. They say we offer simple answers to complex problems. Well, perhaps there is a simple answer—not an easy answer—but simple: If you and I have the courage to tell our elected officials that we want our national policy based on what we know in our hearts is morally right.

He warned his fellow Americans that they could not gain security and freedom from the threat of the atomic bomb "by committing an immorality so great as saying to a billion human beings now enslaved behind the Iron Curtain, 'Give up your dreams of freedom because to save our own skins, we're willing to make a deal with your slave masters.'" No, said Reagan, quoting Alexander Hamilton: "A nation which can prefer disgrace to danger is prepared for a master, and deserves one."

In stating that accommodating communist despots was flatly immoral, Reagan again presaged his opposition to détente.

Reagan continued: "This is the specter our well-meaning liberal friends refuse to face—that their policy of accommodation is appeasement, and it gives no choice between peace and war, only between fight or surrender."

Using vivid imagery, he laid out the stakes:

> If nothing in life is worth dying for, when did this begin—just in the face of this enemy? Or should Moses have told the children of Israel to live in slavery under the pharaohs? Should Christ have refused the cross? Should the patriots at Concord Bridge have thrown down their guns and refused to fire the shot heard 'round the world? The martyrs of history were not fools, and our honored dead who gave their lives to stop the advance of the Nazis didn't die in vain....
>
> Winston Churchill said, "The destiny of man is not measured by material computations. When great forces are on the move in the world, we learn we're spirits—not animals." And he said, "There's something going on in time and space, and beyond time and space, which, whether we like it or not, spells duty."[25]

Reagan closed the speech by making it clear to his fellow Americans that they faced a stark choice. Invoking a phrase his former hero FDR had used in Philadelphia in 1936, he said: "You and I have a rendezvous with destiny. We'll preserve for our children this, the last best hope of man on earth, or we'll sentence them to take the last step into a thousand years of darkness."

This powerful presentation instantly made Ronald Reagan a serious political player. Just two years later he would be elected governor of the nation's largest state, California.

Reagan's political rise had begun.

A NEW ARCHBISHOP

Less than a week before Ronald Reagan's "Time for Choosing" address, Karol Wojtyła likewise gave a major speech that signaled his rise up the ranks. It was another of the many striking parallels in their lives and careers.

On March 8, 1964, at the age of forty-three, Wojtyła had been installed as archbishop of Kraków. The ceremony occurred about 10 A.M. at the Wawel Cathedral. There he passed the remains of Saint Stanisław, just as he had twenty-five years earlier when he heard the frightening sounds of the German Luftwaffe flying overhead.

On October 21 the new archbishop was in Rome for the historic Second Vatican Council, convened by Pope John XXIII. That day he made a major statement that, like Reagan's, prompted sudden thoughts that he had a big future ahead.

Archbishop Wojtyła spoke on a topic that would be a major theme of his papacy: human freedom.

A day earlier, the council fathers had begun debate on what became known as the Church's "dialogue with the modern world." Wojtyła made significant contributions to the council's debate, and to the statement that eventually emerged: *Pastoral Constitution on the Church in the Modern World*, one of the seminal contemporary documents of the Catholic Church.

Wojtyła's message, then and throughout the council, was that true human freedom comes not in doing whatever one wants but in uniting oneself to the will of God. As biographer George Weigel characterized the message: "The closer human beings come to God, the closer they come to the depth of their humanity and to the truth of the world. Christian faith is not alienating; Christian faith is liberating in the most profound sense of human freedom." Wojtyła believed that it was precisely this view of God and man that the Roman Catholic Church should present to the modern world.[26] It was a view he would present in his first encyclical as pope. And here, at the Second Vatican Council, he proposed it to the shepherds of his Church.

This view of human freedom would also resonate with a Protestant named Ronald Reagan.

POLAND'S JUBILEE

The timing of Wojtyła's ascent up the Church hierarchy was ideal for Poland's purposes. One year after the closing of the Second Vatican Council came a landmark in the life of Christian Poland: 1966 was Poland's Jubilee.

Ronald Reagan's high point in 1966 was his first successful election (as governor); Karol Wojtyła's was his glorious celebration of the millennium of the Polish Church. The occasion included a huge Mass at Saint John's Cathedral, the vaunted fourteenth-century church and official parish of the archdiocese of Warsaw, plus commemorations at the Jasna Góra monastery (a shrine to the Virgin Mary in Częstochowa), Wawel Cathedral, and elsewhere.

As Poland's top Church official, Cardinal Stefan Wyszyński had been determined to celebrate Poland's Christian achievement despite the communist regime's fierce opposition to anything sacred. Back in 1957 he had initiated a nine-year "Great Novena" leading up to the anniversary.

The communists did everything they could to disrupt the festivities. They refused to permit Pope Paul VI to visit the country, and they barred Wyszyński from attending overseas celebrations. "As always, communists wanted to compete with [the] Church," writes Tomasz Pompowski, the Polish historian and journalist. "They would always try to invent secular holidays or redefine [the] religious dimension of any Christian holidays. For instance, on Easter they would talk about 'Green [Agricultural] Holidays,' trying to revive all possible pagan traditions allegedly of Slavic nations." And so in 1966 the Communist Party organized its own simultaneous celebrations.[27]

The Catholic Church's celebrations started in Gniezno on April 14 and continued for weeks. At Jasna Góra, given that the communist government had denied Paul VI entry, Church officials installed a symbolic empty chair for the snubbed pontiff and placed a large framed portrait of him in it. The portrait was second in size only to Our Lady of Częstochowa, a venerated, centuries-old Polish icon of the Virgin Mary known as the Black Madonna. More than a million people gathered for the open-air Mass.[28] This, of course, showed the communists for the repressors that they were, further enraging them. As Saint Thomas More once observed, the devil cannot stand to be mocked.

The communists did all they could to divert Poles' divine devotion throughout the jubilee. They held what Pompowski calls "mega-celebrations" inside the stadium in the town of Katowice. The main event was a soccer match between Poland and Hungary. The Hungarian comrades, under the leadership of tyrant János Kádár, who was detaining Cardinal Jószef Mindszenty, were happy to partake in an Iron Curtain sporting event that pulled people out of churches.

What Pompowski describes as the communists' "massive propaganda offensive" began years before the jubilee for Christianity. In 1960 the Communist Party and ruling regime commanded a celebration of the 550th anniversary of the Grunwald battle, in which Polish knights defeated Germanic Teutonians. In 1963 the party demanded that Poles celebrate the twentieth anniversary of World War II's Battle of Lenino. In 1964 communists ordered Poles to mark twenty years of the PKWN Manifesto, the political manifesto proclaimed by the Soviet-backed Polish Committee of National Liberation.[29] During the jubilee year, the Polish Communist Party commanded that a thousand schools be built to commemorate a thousand years not of the Polish faith but of the Polish state. It would be a secular-communist millennium.

"All of those celebrations were supposed to counterbalance against the Church Millennium," Pompowski writes. He recalls that the Communist Party's primary day of secular celebrations was announced for July 22, 1966. "They were [a] disaster for Party propaganda," he says. "As was predictable, only hard-line communists appeared [at] the celebrations [with] the highest party establishment."[30]

Oddly, there might have been more communists at the Church's jubilee celebration. They attended as hired agitators.

As Archbishop Karol Wojtyła preached during the April celebrations at the cathedral in Poznań, the communists unloaded a twenty-one-gun salute to honor Minister of Defense Marian Spychalski. Wojtyła and his fellow believers waited patiently until the salute ended. The archbishop then continued his sermon.[31]

The following day, the communists held a military parade outside the cathedral, complete with guns and goosesteps, tanks and artillery and missiles. They also brought in busloads of "workers" and communist youth, who all shouted, "Down with Wyszyński!" They looked drunk, and probably were. Władysław Gomułka, Poland's communist leader, graced the faithful with his presence. Surely he could overshadow the cardinal and priests. But "not many people showed up to welcome Gomułka," says Pomposki. "It was another propaganda disaster for the Communist Party."[32]

On May 7 Archbishop Wojtyła spoke at the Wawel Cathedral. The image of the Black Madonna was displayed, and all night long thousands flocked outside and inside. In what one witness called "an unforgettable experience," Wojtyła made a vigorous defense of religious freedom and protested the regime's many restrictions on the life of the Church—and did so in his skillful way that so bothered the communist authorities.[33]

STEADY ADVANCE

The communist persecution continued the next year, but so did the advance of Karol Wojtyła.

On October 14, 1967, Wojtyła broke new ground for the faith at Nowa Huta. This was a major steel town and a symbol of Poland's working class, especially in the eyes of communists, who claimed the working class as their chosen people. The regime managed, planned, and engineered Nowa Huta to be the embodiment of a communist city: with newly constructed apartment complexes and, most important, no church.

Yes, communist authorities insisted that Nowa Huta be a city without God. "It was socialism's answer to Catholic Kraków," said Father Stanisław Dziwisz, later Pope John Paul II's closest aide. "When they [the central planners] built it, they intentionally left no room for a church."[34]

But the people wanted a church. As they would chant to Karol Wojtyła when he returned to Poland as their pope, "We want God!"

So, of course, did Karol Wojtyła, but communist authorities refused his and his flock's repeated requests to build a church—something for which they needed permission from the high priests of Marx and Lenin. In 1967 the communists tore down a giant cross workers had erected at the site where residents intended to build the church.

Picture the scene: The secret police and their armed men ride to the sacred site in their government vehicles. A tractor is backed up to the giant cross. A Marxist henchman fits a thick noose for the head of the crucifix. The noose is tightened. The Communist Party functionary orders the tractor to start pulling. The cross falls to the ground with a loud thud. Communists cheer.

It was a perfect display of communist ideology.

Dziwisz would call this incident Karol Wojtyła's "first test as a young, newly consecrated bishop." Wojtyła skillfully sparred with the state's atheistic masters, insisting that the people's right to have a cross, a church, a faith, was a basic human right that reflected the innate dignity of the human person—rights to religion and conscience that no state could obstruct. He held firm. And on October 14 he won his first victory in the battle when he, the former quarryman, hoisted an ax and a shovel and broke ground for a new church—the Ark of the Lord (i.e., Mary)—to be built where the communists had hauled down the giant cross.[35]

Many more melees were yet to come. It would take years before the church was erected. But this groundbreaking was no small achievement for Karol Wojtyła. Dziwisz described the Nowa Huta victory as "the beginning of a new strategy based on resistance. The resistance had a religious impetus."[36]

And it was a worker-anchored resistance. Really, one could view the victory at Nowa Huta as a precursor to the Solidarity movement's resistance a decade later. The workers were emboldened, with Karol Wojtyła standing beside them.

Wojtyła had been emboldened himself that June, when Pope Paul VI made him a cardinal. It was a daring stroke by a pope accused (often rightly so) of accommodating the communist world. For this, and his generally favorable treatment and mentoring of Wojtyła, Paul VI deserves only praise. The so-called *Ostpolitik* pope's best moves against communism might well have been these quiet gestures advancing Karol Wojtyła.

Thus, in 1967, both Karol Wojtyła and Ronald Reagan started in positions that would be stepping-stones to their ultimate offices, with Wojtyła joining the College of Cardinals and Reagan taking over as governor of California. Communism remained a potent force, but the rise of these two leaders was a sign of better times ahead.

11

MAY 6, 1975

THE DRY MARTYRDOM OF CARDINAL MINDSZENTY

In November 1966 and again in November 1970, as Karol Wojtyła was winning spiritual victories in Poland, Ronald Reagan won political victories in California. He was a very popular governor, a man likable across party lines, who proved capable of winning elections handily—a sign of even larger political triumphs to come.

Throughout this time, Reagan continued his crusade against Soviet communism. Moscow was on the march in the 1970s. Reagan did not like what he was seeing under the détente presidencies of Republicans Richard Nixon and Gerald Ford. He believed that their policies allowed the Soviets to gain the upper hand, which meant that the United States was letting the people of Eastern Europe live under their "slave masters."

In 1975 Reagan ended his governorship after two terms, but he was not about to end his fight against communism. "Totalitarian communism is an absolute enemy of human freedom," he said in March 1975.[1] Two months later he called communism "evil," "vicious," a "disease." "Mankind has survived all manner of evil diseases and plagues," Reagan said, "but can it survive communism?" He added, "Communism is neither an economic or a political system—it is a form of insanity."[2]

Few individuals excoriated communism quite like Ronald Reagan—though one institution did: the Roman Catholic Church. So did a churchman from Hungary, one admired by Reagan and by Wojtyła. In 1974 this churchman planned a visit to Governor Reagan's California.

OSTPOLITIK

As Reagan neared the end of his two-term governorship, another devout anticommunist was nearing the end of his difficult but heroic life.

Ever since the uprising in Hungary in November 1956, Cardinal Jószef Mindszenty had taken refuge in the U.S. embassy in Budapest. For the next fifteen years he was confined to the embassy's grounds. Throughout that time, Mindszenty had steadfastly refused to consent to Moscow's wishes that he leave Hungary, but now Pope Paul VI asked him to depart his beloved country. The loyal cardinal faithfully accepted his pope's request. On September 23, 1971, he left Hungary for Vienna, Austria.

Paul VI was a wise and prophetic pope, particularly on cultural and human-sexuality issues. In regard to the communist threat, however, Paul VI was no Pius XII. Along with Cardinal Agostino Casaroli, a careful diplomat, Paul VI pursued a form of *Ostpolitik*, the Western European version of détente. They reluctantly accepted that the Cold War division of Europe would prevail well into the future and thus concluded that they needed to engage the communist world to work for religious freedom and other human rights.

It is neither uncommon nor totally unfair to classify Paul VI as a Soviet accommodationist. In aiming for diplomacy rather than confrontation, the Vatican at times muted its criticism of communism. But the pontiff's approach stemmed from his belief that the Church could have no influence on the communists—or on the Christians languishing behind the Iron Curtain—if it was barred altogether. Paul VI had seen what happened when he refused to deal with the communists: recall that in the spring of 1966, as Poland celebrated its millennium of Christianity, the communist regime had banned the pope from entering the country.

Pope Paul VI had support in this approach. The architects of American détente, President Richard Nixon and Secretary of State Henry

Kissinger, also urged Cardinal Mindszenty to leave Hungary. The degree to which Paul VI and President Nixon were simpatico in the early 1970s has never been adequately appreciated. The Italian scholar Andrea Di Stefano has done groundbreaking research revealing that the pope and the president had a shared understanding of the Cold War and of how they wanted to deal with Moscow. Di Stefano describes the correspondence between Paul VI and Nixon as "remarkable," two diplomats who saw eye to eye.[3]

John Paul II's biographer George Weigel notes that Cardinal Wojtyła never doubted Paul VI's good intentions in his *Ostpolitik* and understood that the pontiff was "torn between his heart's instinct to defend the persecuted Church and his mind's judgment that he had to pursue the policy of *salvare il salvabile*—which, as he once put it to Archbishop Casaroli, wasn't a 'policy of glory.'"[4] *Salvare il salvabile*—to salvage the salvageable.

In retrospect, was this the right policy for the time? Was it a difficult but necessary setup to the stronger approach of John Paul II, just as the détente of Presidents Nixon, Ford, and Jimmy Carter preceded the firmer position of Ronald Reagan? Perhaps—but it certainly was not a "policy of glory." Maintaining stability and the status quo did nothing for the suffering souls behind the Iron Curtain; it preserved the travesty of Yalta.[5]

Ostpolitik and détente also meant giving in to communist demands on occasion. A case in point: in December 1973 Paul VI stripped the eighty-one-year-old Mindszenty of his titles. The cardinal suddenly found himself retired from his Church posts as archbishop and primate. The pontiff declared the Archdiocese of Esztergom officially vacated.

Communists, of course, were thrilled with Pope Paul VI's effort to improve relations with the communist world. By stripping Mindszenty, Paul VI had shown himself to be a "reasonable" man, a "sophisticated" diplomat. If not as physically painful as all those beatings the secret police had inflicted on Mindszenty in the winter of 1948–49, this lash was, for the communists, even more effective because it came from the cardinal's pope in Rome.

At the end of 1975 Mindszenty published his memoirs, in which he wrote that communism "knows no God" and has "no immortal soul."[6]

"NOT GIVEN HIS DUE"

In June 1974, Hungary's long-suffering victim of international communism was invited to the University of Santa Clara to accept an honorary degree commending him for his "courage and...heroic perseverance in the cause of freedom and justice." Founded by Jesuits, the University of Santa Clara was California's oldest institution of higher learning.

Governor Ronald Reagan was pleased and honored. He dispatched a close friend, his former chief of staff and trusted aide Judge Bill Clark, to head up an official delegation to meet Mindszenty. Clark was a member of California's Supreme Court, appointed by Reagan. He was also a Fulton Sheen protégé who had left the novitiate to study at (among other institutions) the University of Santa Clara. Clark was proud of the institution and grateful to the Jesuit fathers who had taught him there. And now, in 1974, Judge Clark was thrilled by the university's decision to bestow a degree on Cardinal Mindszenty, and by Reagan's request that he represent the delegation.[7]

Clark was upset with how the Vatican had treated the cardinal. Like Reagan, he considered the Vatican's détente-like mind-set to be ill-advised and immoral. "They did not recognize [Mindszenty's] heroic life," said Clark. "He was not given his due."

For Clark and Reagan, this was even more reason to welcome Mindszenty to California.

Unfortunately, the Santa Clara visit would not come to pass. What happened next is not completely clear, but a major controversy erupted over Mindszenty's appearance. In September 1973, eight months after a group of men on the U.S. Supreme Court legalized abortion in *Roe v. Wade*, the University of Santa Clara appointed a "pro-choice" congressman, Democrat Don Edwards, to its Board of Regents. Outraged by Edwards's appointment were pro-life groups, including the St. Louis–based Cardinal Mindszenty Foundation. Abortion opponents and advocates engaged in a war of letters and public statements. Picketers from both sides planned protests at the university during Mindszenty's ceremony.

Troubled by the turmoil that his mere presence might cause, the aging cardinal canceled his appearance. In a letter to the university president, Father Thomas Terry, Mindszenty said only, "I respectfully decline an honorary degree from your university and shall not be present on your campus."[8]

Thirty years later Clark said: "He had heard that there were going to be pickets. So he said he wouldn't go. He didn't want to walk through the line. He was an old man by then, too old to fight."[9]

Governor Reagan and Bill Clark were sorry about the whole episode, even as Clark sympathized with the pro-lifers. Fortunately, the cardinal did not cancel his June 5–10 trip to San Francisco as the guest of Archbishop Joseph McGucken. Clark was there to greet Mindszenty. He spent three meaningful hours with the cardinal.

"To me, Mindszenty was the crime fighter," said Clark. "A quiet, rugged fighter. The foremost clergyman in the fight against communism."

Until his final days, Clark lamented the mistreatment of Mindszenty and the lack of recognition of his suffering at the hands of international communism. "Some martyrs slip through the cracks," Clark said sadly.

Both Bill Clark and Ronald Reagan saw how the communist malignancy wore down Cardinal Mindszenty. In May 1975, the same month Mindszenty's long life came to a close, Reagan described communism as a "disease," the description Fulton Sheen had used in *Communism and the Conscience of the West*.[10]

The death toll from the communist disease was staggering. From 1917 to 1975, communism had felled between 100 million and 140 million people, perhaps double the combined deaths of the two world wars.[11]

This disease of communism had been "hanging on" for a half century or more, said Reagan. He wanted America and the world to know "just how vicious" communism really was.[12]

Cardinal Mindszenty would have agreed with the California governor. He died in Austria on May 6, 1975. He had outlived Béla Kun, Mátyás Rákosi, Hitler, Stalin, and those who arrested him, convicted him, and endeavored to destroy his mind, body, and soul.

Mindszenty was eighty-three years old. The communists refused his corpse entrance to its homeland.

ANOTHER SACRIFICE TO ATHEISTIC COMMUNISM

A meeting held at the Vatican a month after Mindszenty's death provided a fitting capstone to the persecution of the Hungarian cardinal.

In June 1975, Pope Paul VI received Bulgaria's longtime communist tyrant, Todor Zhivkov. It was a much-anticipated moment for détenteniks and for the Holy Father and his chief *Ostpolitik* assistant, Agostino Casaroli.

Paul VI asked Bulgaria's Marxist kingpin about Bishop Eugene Bossilkov, who had met an even crueler fate than Mindszenty. In 1952 Bulgaria's communists had put Bishop Bossilkov on the rack. He was charged with crimes against the state, espionage, counterrevolutionary activity, refusing to accept a law attempting to remove the Bulgarian

Catholic Church from the Vatican's jurisdiction, conspiring to undermine communism in the country, and on and on. After the routine period of imprisonment and mental and physical torture, Bishop Bossilkov was subjected to a communist show trial, where he was said to have *confessed* his guilt. He was summarily executed with several other priests and shoveled into a mass grave outside the jail.

The communists hushed up the execution. To kill bishops created serious PR problems; the communists could gain more through imprisonment than through murder.

Now, twenty-three years later, the Italian pontiff asked the Bulgarian general secretary for the truth about the persecuted bishop. Zhivkov, "always a faithful mouthpiece for the Kremlin" (in the words of Christopher Andrew and Vasili Mitrokhin),[13] appeared to open up to the *Ostpolitik* pope: he said that Bishop Bossilkov had died in prison. It was a half-truth. Yes, Bossilkov had died in custody in a prison—but via a cold-blooded execution.[14]

Nonetheless, Cardinal Casaroli was impressed with the general secretary. He estimated that Zhivkov had demonstrated "courage and esteem towards the Pope for his work in favor of peace and international détente."[15]

Of course, the Bulgarian communists cared nothing for détente other than as a means to hoodwink gullible Westerners and advance their Marxist objectives.

Pope John Paul II would offer a more accurate appraisal, calling Bishop Bossilkov "one of the many victims sacrificed by atheistic communism, in Bulgaria and elsewhere, in its plan to destroy the Church."

That pope himself would be a victim of Bulgarian atheistic communism.

12

SUMMER OF 1976

TWO FREEDOM FIGHTERS IN AMERICA

Karol Wojtyła could not have been pleased with the Mindszenty treatment, despite his respect for Pope Paul VI, to whom he was always loyal. Each man admired the other for his faithfulness, spirituality, learnedness, and dedication to the Church. In a telling display, Paul VI invited the future pontiff to preach the Lenten meditations at the Vatican in the spring of 1976. This was an honor for any cardinal. Wojtyła used the platform to preach on the excesses of secularism and consumerism in the West and atheism and communism in the East. "Persecution," he told his fellow men of the faith, "is the order of the day" for communist states.[1]

This was hardly the first time the Polish cardinal had challenged communist authorities outside of Poland. On April 16, 1974, Wojtyła had traveled to communist Czechoslovakia and spoken at the funeral of another persecuted son of the Church, Cardinal Štěpán Trochta. This was a bold move. The Marxist authorities had locked up Trochta for a decade and tormented him even longer. Trochta's story was basically the Czech version of Mindszenty's.

The Czech secret police stopped Wojtyła and two other cardinals from concelebrating the Mass, but they could not stop the Polish cardinal from speaking over Trochta's casket at the conclusion of the service.[2] Wojtyła's act of defiance made the communists inside the cathedral hiss.

To Wojtyła, if *Ostpolitik* had led communist authorities to banish cardinals of the Roman Catholic Church from celebrating a Mass of a beloved brother who suffered for so long, then *Ostpolitik* had some serious shortcomings. He still loved his pope, but he would do things differently if he were pope.

COMING TO AMERICA

Two years after Czech authorities censored him at Trochta's funeral, Cardinal Wojtyła got a much friendlier reception in a country where his ideas were welcomed: America.

The Polish cardinal arrived in the United States for a six-week visit in the summer of 1976. He came to America that bicentennial summer for the Roman Catholic Church's Forty-First International Eucharistic Congress, held in Philadelphia, where the Continental Congress had declared independence two hundred years earlier. Like Eugenio Pacelli forty years before, Karol Wojtyła traveled throughout the United States, visiting cities big and small. He began his trek in Boston, home of revolutionary patriots like John Adams and Sam Adams. He ventured to Baltimore, Detroit, Los Angeles, San Francisco, and Chicago, where he met with a group of Polish survivors of Auschwitz.[3] He went to Great Falls and Geyser, Montana. He stopped in Orchard Lake, Michigan, and Stevens Point, Wisconsin.[4]

The Eucharistic Congress ran August 1–8. The huge event included a little-known nun named Mother Teresa, whom Wojtyła had met only recently.[5] Wojtyła and Mother Teresa were overshadowed by the presence of names better known at the time: Dorothy Day, Cardinal John Krol, and even President Gerald Ford, who attended Mass in the city's Municipal (JFK) Stadium on August 3.[6]

Wojtyła spoke at that Mass, which was dedicated to "The Eucharist and Man's Hunger for Freedom." The cardinal's speech might as well have had the same title.[7] He gave a powerful statement expressing not merely the goodness of the Body of Christ but also his sense of the forces of evil threatening the world—the forces aligned against freedom, the freedom that man wanted and that God wanted for man. The cardinal from communist-occupied Poland was very much aware that he was speaking in a country that just a month earlier had celebrated the two hundredth anniversary of its own triumph of freedom.

Wojtyła started by quoting from Luke's Gospel: "The Spirit of the Lord is upon me, because he has anointed me; he has sent me to announce good news to the poor, to proclaim release for prisoners, and recovery of sight for the blind; to let the broken victims go free." These, said the cardinal, were the words of a thirty-year-old Christ as He arose in the synagogue of Nazareth facing His fellow countrymen officially for the first time. By those words, He revealed His messianic mission.

That same Christ, said Wojtyła, "today faces us all, the People of the New Covenant, here on American soil, in Philadelphia, the City of Brotherly Love, where the Eucharistic Congress is taking place. And again Jesus defines himself and his mission in the same way, for he had said to his disciples: 'I am with you always, to the end of time.' (Mt 28:20)."[8]

The future pontiff then addressed the "hunger of the human soul, which is no less than the hunger for real freedom." Each of us to some extent knows what this freedom is, said Wojtyła. "It is the principal trait of humanity and the source of human dignity." He quoted from *Gaudium et Spes*, the Second Vatican Council's *Pastoral Constitution on the Church in the Modern World*, affirming that "authentic freedom" is "an exceptional sign of the divine image within man" and that "man's dignity demands that he act according to a conscious and free choice."

Wojtyła continued, sharing words that the Protestants who signed the Declaration of Independence in that city two hundred years earlier would have appreciated: "Freedom is at the same time offered to man and imposed upon him as a task. It is in the first place an attribute of the human person and in this sense it is a gift of the Creator and an endowment of human nature. For this reason it is also the lawful right of man; man has a right to freedom, to self-determination, to the choice of his life career, to acting according to his own convictions. Freedom has been given to man by his Creator in order to be used, and to be used well." Thus, God is the antithesis of the earthly destroyers of freedom—men like the totalitarians in Moscow and other communist capitals. As Fulton Sheen wrote in *Peace of Soul*, "God refuses to be a totalitarian dictator in order to abolish evil by destroying human freedom."

Of course, Cardinal Wojtyła said, we know perfectly well that humanity abuses liberty. Man can do wrong precisely because he is free. That is the risk.

At the same time, that is the beauty of freedom. As Wojtyła noted, the Creator has given man freedom not so that he will commit evil but so he will do good: "God also bestowed upon man understanding and conscience to show him what is good and what ought to be done, what is wrong and what ought to be avoided. God's commandments help our understanding and our conscience on their way. The greatest commandment—that of love—leads the way to the fullest use of liberty. Freedom has been given to man in order to love, to love true good." It is the freedom to do good, for God, and for brother and neighbor. Those who obey this truth, this Gospel, are the "real disciples of Eternal Wisdom," achieving a state of "royal freedom" in service to the true King.

This was an understanding of freedom that Pope John Paul II would underscore again and again. The concept would be central to some of John Paul's greatest encyclicals, including *Veritatis Splendor* (The Splendor of Truth) and *Fides et Ratio* (Faith and Reason).

Expressing an idea that Ronald Reagan often communicated, Wojtyła said that there is a universal aspiration for freedom: "The hunger for freedom passes through the heart of every man.... The hunger for freedom passes also through the history of the human race, through the history of nations and peoples. It reveals their spiritual maturity and at the same time tests it."

Americans had gained that freedom, said Wojtyła, whereas Poles had lost theirs. It was time for freedom to reassert itself. It had done so in America two hundred years earlier, with the help of two of his compatriots, Tadeusz Kościuszko and Kazimierz Pułaski, "heroes of the Polish nation [who] became heroes of American independence."

Now Poland needed help for its own independence—and soon enough an American leader would assist in that cause.

Above all, said Wojtyła, it was the Christian Gospel that housed a "full and fundamental program" for the liberation of man, announced by Christ, the "true prophet of men's freedom and also of the liberty of nations and peoples, of all the oppressed who suffer from hunger for true freedom." The cardinal asked, "Are we not witnesses in our times of the many-sided limitations and even of the deprivation of freedom of whole societies, nations, and states?" There was no question about that. Captive peoples in Poland and the rest of the Communist Bloc were victims of a modern Soviet communist colonialism. "And so the hunger for freedom continues to be unsatisfied," Wojtyła said.

The need for religious freedom was acute, the cardinal added, but this freedom was lacking in much of the world. Wojtyła invoked the timeless wisdom of the Second Vatican Council's *Declaration on Religious Freedom*, which said, "Forms of government still exist under which, even though freedom of religious worship receives constitutional recognition, the powers of the government are engaged in the effort to deter citizens from professing religion and to make life difficult and dangerous for religious communities." This aptly described the communist world, where various "constitutions" spoke of religious liberty but the regimes never honored it. Quite the contrary, they did everything they could to destroy religion.

Cardinal Wojtyła ended his stirring address with these words:

> And so today we bring to this great community of confessors of the Eucharistic Christ, gathered at the Eucharistic Congress in Philadelphia, the whole hunger for freedom which permeates contemporary man and all humanity. In the name of Jesus Christ we have the right and the duty to demand true freedom for men and for peoples. We therefore bring this hunger for real freedom and deposit it on this altar. Not only a man, a priest, a bishop, but Christ himself is at this altar, he who through our ministration offers his unique and eternal sacrifice. It is the sacrifice of all times. It is also the sacrifice of our twentieth century and of its last quarter.

It was a powerful statement. It is particularly powerful in retrospect, for now we know the significant role the archbishop of Kraków would play in demanding, and securing, this "true freedom" in the last quarter of the twentieth century.

Karol Wojtyła understood how faith and freedom reinforced each other. It was a message he would share with Ronald Reagan, who was equally outspoken in this theological thinking. Reagan spoke of the "twin beacons" of faith and freedom.

"THE FINAL CONFRONTATION"

As stirring as Wojtyła's Philadelphia speech was, the cardinal made a particularly dramatic statement in another address during his U.S. tour that summer. According to the *Wall Street Journal*, which published this statement when Wojtyła became pope two years later, the cardinal said the following in September 1976:

> *We are now standing in the face of the greatest historical confrontation humanity has gone through.* I do not think that wide circles of the American society or wide circles of the Christian community realize this fully. *We are now facing the final confrontation between the Church and the anti-Church, of the Gospel versus the anti-Gospel.* This confrontation lies within the plans of divine Providence; it is a trial which the whole Church, and the Polish Church in particular, must take up. It is a trial of not only our nation and the Church, but in a sense a test of 2,000 years of culture and Christian civilization with all of its consequences for human dignity, individual rights, human rights, and the rights of nations [emphasis added].[9]

What was Wojtyła talking about? Did he mean to say that the Cold War battle against atheistic communism was "the greatest historical confrontation" that humanity had undertaken?

Biographer George Weigel casts doubt on that idea. In *Witness to Hope*, Weigel argues, "Wojtyła never would have narrowed this 'confrontation,' which he insisted 'lies within the plans of Divine Providence,' to the clash between democracy and communism."

Still, as Weigel acknowledges, "communism was one particularly threatening expression of the crisis of world civilization in the late twentieth century." Wojtyła "knew that in his bones."[10]

He did indeed. He had lived through communist repression of human freedom. He had seen fellow priests and nuns become martyrs to communism.

Karol Wojtyła had spent years battling atheistic communist authorities in his homeland. Now, as Weigel notes, he "was going back home to face" the communist menace.

And in just two years he would be in a position of global leadership from which to carry on the crusade against Soviet communism.

GOD AND REAGAN IN KANSAS CITY

The year that Karol Wojtyła toured America, his future partner in the crusade against communism was crisscrossing the country himself. Ronald Reagan was campaigning for the Republican presidential nomination in 1976.

In taking to the campaign trail, Reagan violated his "Eleventh Commandment" of politics: *Thou shall not speak ill of any fellow Republican.* In fact, he was challenging the sitting Republican president. It was an audacious move, but Reagan felt he had no choice. Gerald Ford's presidency had been disappointing in many ways, not least in his embrace of détente.

The previous summer, President Ford had mistreated Aleksandr Solzhenitsyn during the great Soviet dissident's much-anticipated visit to America. In a political version of the Vatican's Mindszenty treatment, Ford snubbed Solzhenitsyn because he did not want to anger Soviet authorities.

Solzhenitsyn was in Washington to speak to the AFL-CIO, just down the street from the White House. It was a perfect time for Ford to meet with him. Conservatives, from Republicans like Ronald Reagan, Jack Kemp, and Jesse Helms to anticommunist Democrats like Scoop Jackson, urged the president to do so. Ford refused. He was backed by his right-hand man in foreign policy, Henry Kissinger. The Ford administration dared not offend Leonid Brezhnev's regime by shaking hands with the Kremlin's Public Enemy No. 1. Worse, as the historian Douglas Brinkley recorded, Ford privately called Solzhenitsyn "a goddamn horse's ass."[11]

Even the liberal *New York Times* editorial board and Democrat Jimmy Carter slammed President Ford for refusing to meet with Solzhenitsyn. William F. Buckley Jr.'s conservative *National Review* actually considered endorsing Carter in 1976 in response.[12]

For Reagan, Ford's humiliation of Solzhenitsyn was one of the final straws. He was so rankled that he decided to challenge Ford for the Republican nomination.

Like Karol Wojtyła, Reagan invoked the American Founders throughout the bicentennial year. This was not a temporary move tied to the celebration. As president, Reagan would quote the Founders more richly and more frequently than any of his predecessors or successors.[13]

Wojtyła would have been pleased to know that Reagan also drew inspiration from a line by the late Pope Pius XII. The line appears repeatedly in Reagan's public speeches and personal letters from the 1960s onward, and particularly during the mid-1970s. "Into the hands of America, God has placed an afflicted mankind," said the pontiff in his 1946 *Collier's* article.[14]

Reagan loved this quotation. He used it as the penultimate line of his July 6, 1976, televised speech marking the bicentennial; he followed it with his three-word sign-off: "God bless America."[15] As Reagan noted, the pope had made the remark after the global devastation of World War II, when America stood alone in strength. "The American people have a genius for splendid and unselfish action," said Pius XII. Both men seemed to sense a divine mission for America in rescuing the world from international communism.

Reagan stressed that Americans had not sought the leadership role that Pius XII spoke of; God had thrust it upon them. If Americans would seize that role with the right leadership, they could win the Cold War, and the Soviets could lose.

Reagan wanted to provide that leadership. And so he went to the Republican National Convention in Kansas City with a most improbable upset victory on his mind. How close did he come to pulling it off? Extremely.

The effort didn't start well. Ford won close contests in the Iowa caucus and the New Hampshire primary before winning four straight decisive victories over Reagan. "When are you going to quit?" was the question of the day for Reagan, but the former California governor was defiant: "I'm taking this all the way to the convention in Kansas City, and I'm going even if I lose every damn primary between now and then."[16] He then won North Carolina, got a huge victory in Texas, and followed with victories in Indiana, Georgia, and Alabama. Reagan was surging.[17]

At the last minute, a number of key states at the convention moved into Reagan's column and nearly allowed the former governor to overtake Ford. In the dramatic showdown at Kansas City's Kemper Arena on August 19, Reagan missed the nomination by a little over a hundred votes. He grabbed 47.4 percent of delegates in an 1,187–1,070 contest. Ford and his team let out a huge sigh of relief.

Once the final ballots were in, a gracious Ford waved to Reagan and Nancy in their box in the arena. With all the TV cameras set on the Reagans, before a national audience of tens of millions, Ford invited them to come to the main stage, as the GOP faithful shouted: "Ron! Ron! Ron! . . . Speech! Speech! Speech!"

"Ron, will you come down and bring Nancy?" pleaded Ford.[18] A reluctant Reagan relented, telling Nancy as they were whisked through backstage corridors, "I haven't the foggiest idea what I'm going to say."[19]

Well, Reagan figured out what to say. Stepping to the microphone to thank Ford and everyone who had supported him, he proceeded to give, extemporaneously, one of the finest, most memorable speeches of his life. The crowd was riveted.

As Reagan struggled to think of what to say, a thought hit him, one that (unbeknownst to the crowd) came from a radio broadcast he had written.[20] "If I could just take a moment," he began. "I had an assignment the other day. Someone asked me to write a letter for a time capsule that is going to be opened in Los Angeles a hundred years from now, on our tercentennial. It sounded like an easy assignment. They suggested I write something about the problems and issues of the day and I set out to do so, riding down the coast in an automobile looking at the blue Pacific out on one side and the Santa Ynez mountains on the other, and I couldn't help but wonder if it was going to be that beautiful a hundred years from now as it was on that summer day. And then, as I tried to write. . . ." Here Reagan paused, asking his audience to turn their minds to the same task: what would each of them write "for people a hundred years from now who know all about us[?] We know nothing about them. We don't know what kind of a world they'll be living in."

Reagan then gave his response to the assignment, which related to nuclear war and a civilized world: "We live in a world in which the great powers have poised and aimed at each other horrible missiles of destruction, that can, in a matter of minutes, arrive in each other's country and destroy virtually the civilized world we live in. And suddenly it dawned on me. Those who would read this letter a hundred years from now will know whether those missiles were fired. They will know whether we met our challenge. Whether they have the freedoms that we have known up until now will depend on what we do here." Reagan pondered: "Will they look back with appreciation and say, 'Thank God for those people in 1976 who headed off that loss of freedom, who kept our world from nuclear destruction'? . . . This is our challenge."

Everyone in the room was locked in, completely silent. "The power of the speech was extraordinary," said Edmund Morris. "And you could just feel throughout the auditorium the palpable sense among the delegates that [they had] nominated the wrong guy."[21]

They had indeed. Gerald Ford, their nominee, went on to lose the presidency to Jimmy Carter.

The conventional wisdom was that in 1980 Reagan would be too old for the presidency. Going down in '76, he was down for good.

The loss was traumatic for everyone except Ronald Reagan. His daughter, Maureen, cried for two days. She couldn't stop. She later recalled that each time her father saw her he would ask, "Are you still crying?" Finally, Nelle's son pulled his daughter aside and shared his calming theology. "There's a reason for this," he told Maureen. "Everything happens for a reason. . . . If you just keep doing what you're doing, the path is going to open up and you'll see what it is you're supposed to do."[22]

DUPING THE VATICAN

On November 3, 1976, the day after Election Day in the United States, Vatican diplomat Agostino Casaroli arrived in Sofia, capital of Bulgaria, at the invitation of the minister of foreign affairs, Petar Mladenov. During his weeklong visit the archbishop discussed relations between Bulgaria and the Vatican with Mladenov and President Todor Zhivkov. He also visited the country's Catholic communities.[23] Casaroli encountered a Catholic Church "exhausted, impoverished, deprived of every social consideration, almost despised," he later wrote. The Soviet-dominated communist country had (by Casaroli's reckoning) no more than seventy thousand Catholics out of a population of eight million subjects. It was a severely repressed and depressed place.[24]

Yet Casaroli somehow came away with hope.

The sixty-two-year-old prelate told reporters in Rome that his talks with Zhivkov and the senior communist leadership "could hardly have been more open or cordial." The Catholic press called it a "glowing statement" and celebrated that these "Vatican diplomatic breakthroughs with Bulgaria have been a shot in the arm for Pope Paul's controversial *Ostpolitik*—his policy of trying to improve the situation of Eastern European Catholics through diplomatic dealings with their governments." Casaroli and his comrades had reached "broad agreement" on implementing the human rights and religious freedom elements of the Helsinki Accords—accords that Ronald Reagan and others described as a "sham" and a "farce." Casaroli claimed that the Bulgarian regime had been extremely amicable and hospitable. It had "put no obstacles or limitations on my meetings with all representatives of the Catholic Church in Bulgaria." It even supplied him with a plane to fly around the country and meet with Bulgaria's Catholics.[25]

"There are problems which remain," Casaroli said, "but the religious climate which I found is very beautiful. I don't want to fool myself, but I am returning to Rome with hope."

Agostino Casaroli had been fooled all right. Bulgaria's regime gave him the classic communist Potemkin village treatment. Zhivkov and Mladenov apparently pulled off their attempt to present themselves to Casaroli as reformers battling against crusty old communists to fashion a kinder, gentler Bulgaria. Remarkably, even decades later, Casaroli would state in his memoirs, "I could not but think that the professions of goodwill expressed by President Zhivkov to the Pope and repeated to me by Minister Mladenov would have continued to clash with the narrow mindedness of the old people of the Party."[26] Casaroli said that he sensed "an atmosphere of improvement" in Bulgaria. He left with, as he put it with an exclamation mark, a sense of "hope for the future!"[27]

Cardinal Casaroli said all this of a Bulgarian communist leadership that, less than five years after his visit, would shoot a pope.

13

1977–1978

"WE WIN AND THEY LOSE"

In late January 1977, only days after Democrat Jimmy Carter was inaugurated president, Richard V. Allen hopped on a plane for California to meet with Ronald Reagan.[1] The forty-one-year-old Allen was contemplating a run for governor of New Jersey, and he flew west to ask the former California governor to support his campaign.

But the conversation in the den of Reagan's Los Angeles home soon became much more. By Allen's description, the two ended up "talking and talking and talking" about foreign policy. Allen had impressive credentials in this area. He had earned bachelor's and master's degrees from the University of Notre Dame, where he studied with the political philosopher Gerhart Niemeyer and the political theorist Father Stanley Parry, before going to Germany for doctoral work in Soviet studies and political science. There he studied under another great political philosopher, Eric Voegelin.[2] Allen went on to serve as a key foreign policy adviser to Richard Nixon and Henry Kissinger, and to hold positions at prestigious centers of scholarship such as the Hoover Institution at Stanford, the Center for Strategic and International Studies, and the Council on Foreign Relations.

Allen and Reagan spoke for four hours. It was "the very first [conversation] I had ever had with him alone," Allen recalled.[3] Deep into this discussion, Reagan turned to Allen and uttered these words: "Dick, my idea of American policy toward the Soviet Union is simple, and some would say simplistic. It is this: We win and they lose. What do you think of that?"

Allen's eyes flew wide open. In all his years in foreign policy, serving a détente-minded president and his top officials, he had never encountered such confidence, such a "we can do it" attitude. He had never heard anyone use the word *win* when referring to the Cold War and the Soviet Union. "One had never heard such words from the lips of a major political figure," Allen later remarked. "Until then, we had thought only in terms of 'managing' the relationship with the Soviet Union. Reagan went right to the heart of the matter.... He believed we could outdistance the Soviets and cause them to withdraw from the Cold War, or perhaps even collapse."

Allen was completely taken aback, but he was also taken in. "Governor, do you mean that?" he asked.

Reagan replied: "Of course I do. I just said it, didn't I?"

Allen paused and responded, "Well, governor, I don't know if you ever intend to run again for president of the United States, but if you do, please count me in."[4]

What Reagan asserted, said Allen, "literally changed my life."[5]

"I needed no additional information," he recalled. He resolved to help Reagan find a way to "elevate that thought to the status of national policy." Allen later assessed, "Herein lay the great difference, back in early 1977, between Ronald Reagan and every other politician: He literally believed that we could win, and was prepared to carry this message to the nation as the intellectual foundation of his presidency."[6]

Allen dropped his own bid for the New Jersey governorship and instead joined the former lifeguard in his crusade to save the world from the Moscow menace.

When Reagan said, "We win and they lose," it reflected what he called the "God-given" optimism that his Disciples of Christ mother had instilled in him. Even after the election of Jimmy Carter, and after his own defeat in the summer of 1976—the one that was supposed to end his political career—Reagan remained convinced that God had instilled in America an ability to prevail as a beacon of freedom in the face of "the heart of darkness."

In that sense, he would not have disagreed with the formulation of America's most popular Catholic. In 1977, nearing the end of his life and public ministry, Fulton Sheen published a final edition of his mighty work *Life of Christ*, the product of years of writing and reflection. Sheen hoped that the history of man and of the troubled century would ultimately be redeemed in the eyes of God—exactly as Reagan would later tell a group of Soviet dissidents in Moscow.[7] In his book, Sheen wrote of Christ and the communists, "If He wins, they lose."[8]

If He wins, they lose. We win, they lose.

Either way, *they lose*.

The future president and the famous bishop, both from the flat farms and plains of northwestern Illinois, were again on the same page.

THE CARTER CATASTROPHE

Ronald Reagan was convinced that America could and would prevail over Soviet communism. He would have been forgiven if his optimism had dimmed as Jimmy Carter's presidency unfolded.

Laying out the full extent of the disaster that was the Carter presidency is beyond the scope of this book. I have touched on it in other writings.[9] To say that Carter accommodated the Soviet leadership is insufficient; Carter literally kissed the Soviet leadership. It was a smooch both physical and metaphorical. Communists quickly realized that this was the American president they had long waited for. It was time to get what they wanted.

I will here focus on just a few of the religious–Cold War elements from the Carter years, examples that have been almost completely forgotten, even by the most appalled Carter chroniclers.

The Crown of Saint Stephen

Recall from chapter 7 the hallowed Crown of Saint Stephen, which freedom fighters had rescued from Hungary during World War II to keep the sacred jewel out of the hands of totalitarians. It had been protected in the United States since the 1940s. Hungary's communists wanted their atheistic hands on this prized jewel. And now, with Jimmy Carter in the White House, they shrewdly made a hard push. In short order, they achieved stunning success.

On December 15, 1977, the State Department of Cyrus Vance, a staunch liberal and kindred spirit of President Carter, announced its intention to return the crown during Vance's upcoming visit to Budapest on January 6. Secretary of State Vance, like his president, was interested in "peace" and improved "bilateral" East-West relations.

Even members of Carter's own party were unhappy. Representative Mary Rose Oakar, a liberal congresswoman from Ohio, saw the outrage among her constituents, many of whom had Eastern European roots. Oakar introduced a bill to prevent transfer of the crown without congressional approval. There was bipartisan support to do something. In the Senate, Republican Bob Dole of Kansas filed suit with a U.S. district judge to try to stop the transfer.

In St. Louis, the Cardinal Mindszenty Foundation, two years after their priest's death, filed a lawsuit to stop the Carter people. Noting that "there are still 200,000 Soviet troops in Hungary," Eleanor Schlafly of the Mindszenty Foundation asked whether the Carter administration could at least seek "some conditions placed on the return—remove the Soviet troops, let the people have freedom of religion and the press."

Not a chance. To the Carter administration, such conditions would offend the Hungarian and Soviet communists, who insisted—in the name of détente—that such matters were a "Hungarian internal affair." Despite the protests, the Carter administration was devoted to getting the crown into the hands of the "Hungarian people."

Senator Dole did not give up. He took the issue to the U.S. Supreme Court, but Justice Byron White turned down the case. "There are no more appeals we can make to the courts," said an exasperated Dole. "It now rests solely upon President Carter, who still has time to reconsider his unfortunate decision to return the Crown of Saint Stephen to the communist government of Hungary."

Carter stayed the course. On January 6, 1978, a beaming Secretary of State Cyrus Vance handed over the crown to the Hungarian communist government. At a news conference following the surrender of the crown, Vance hailed the "progressive" nature of the Hungarian totalitarian regime and the "substantial progress" it was making—just as the Vatican's Agostino Casaroli had recently praised the "openness" and "improvement" to be found in communist Bulgaria. President Carter deemed the move "a good step forward" as a way to convince the Warsaw Pact nations that "we are trying to get them to look to us as friends who want peace, who recognize the horrible suffering that they've experienced, and who are building a basis for friendship and trade and mutual exchange."[10]

Hungarian Americans were enraged. Returning the crown did not alleviate the horrible suffering of their brothers and sisters behind the Iron Curtain. In their view, Carter's "good step forward" merely rewarded those responsible for the suffering. In a representative assessment, John Szostak of the Crown of Saint Stephen Protection Committee declared, "January 6, 1978, will go down in the annals of American history as a day of infamy."[11]

Hungary's longtime communist dictator, János Kádár, was not there for the presentation ceremony when Cyrus Vance surrendered the crown. Perhaps the Carter State Department thought Kádár's presence might have been bad PR for détente.

Carter and Poland

Soon after Carter's State Department announced its goodwill gesture to the communist dictatorship in Hungary, the president himself reached out to the communist dictatorship in Poland.

On December 29, 1977, the president began a six-nation tour with a stop in Poland. Speaking from the airport tarmac in Warsaw, Carter told the communist leadership that "old ideological labels have lost their meaning"—a puzzling and even stunning statement that showed just how right Dick Allen was when he said that Ronald Reagan was unique among major political figures of the time in the way he spoke about communism. President Carter said that "the basic goals of friendship, world peace, justice, human rights, and individual freedom loom more important than ever." Polish Communist Party boss Edward Gierek echoed Carter's call for "peace," and particularly echoed Carter's promise of an additional $200 million in U.S. credits to buy food and grain. Carter said that he and Gierek engaged in a "very fruitful discussion."[12]

While Carter met with Gierek, his national security adviser and the first lady met with Cardinal Stefan Wyszyński, leader of the Roman Catholic Church in Poland, who ranked above another cardinal named Karol Wojtyła. Zbigniew Brzezinski and Rosalynn Carter conveyed to the cardinal President Carter's "appreciation for the degree of freedom of worship in the country." It was a statement that Wyszyński (and Wojtyła) must have found puzzling and even stunning.

President Carter offered an equally puzzling assessment of his wife's and national security adviser's meeting. "Rosalynn's and Dr. Brzezinski's visit with Cardinal Wyszyński showed that there's a pluralism in the Polish society that is not frequently acknowledged in an eastern European country," the president told the American press. "It's obvious that as far as the influence on the minds and hearts and future of the Polish people that there's a sharing between a great religious leader and the political leader."[13]

President Carter was impressed with all sorts of "freedoms" that his communist guides showed him during his Potemkin village tour of Warsaw. He was expertly handled and manipulated, taken only where his guides permitted and shielded from the people and things he genuinely needed to see. The president fell for the propaganda again and again.[14]

"I think that our concept of human rights is preserved in Poland," Carter told the press corps. "There is a substantial degree of freedom of the press, exhibited by this [press] conference this afternoon." There was also, Carter claimed, "a substantial degree of freedom of religion demonstrated by the fact that approximately 90 percent of the Polish people profess faith in Christ."[15]

Again, it was a puzzling and even stunning statement. Yes, 90 percent of the Polish people professed a Christian faith, but that was *in spite of* Poland's communist leadership, which hated religion.

Dissident Poles gathered outside the seventeenth-century palace where the communist leadership held a sumptuous state dinner for Carter. They took a serious risk, shouting, "Carter, save us! Carter, save us!" The communist police pounced on the crowd of a hundred, dispersing them with force.[16]

Yes, the Polish people needed saving, but Jimmy Carter was not the man for the job. That task awaited a very different president, one with an early résumé in lifesaving.

President Carter and Comrade Tito

In March 1978, President Carter continued his cozy relationship with Christian-persecuting communist despots when he hosted Yugoslav dictator Marshal Tito.

From the South Lawn of the White House, Carter on March 7 said, "This morning the people of the United States are honored by the presence of a great world leader, President Tito of Yugoslavia."[17] President Carter called Marshal Tito "a truly remarkable leader," a man of "tremendous personal courage," a "patriot," an "inspiration to the people of his own country," and "worthy of admiration." He was the leader of a "modern, prosperous country."

By this point, Tito was into his thirty-third year of unelected reign over the Balkans, a period marked by unbending repression, particularly of the religious, beginning with (among others) Cardinal Stepinac three decades earlier. But Carter, a devout Christian, said Tito "exemplifies the eagerness for freedom, independence, and liberty in Eastern Europe and throughout the world."

It was another puzzling and stunning statement from the president.

Later that evening, at a White House dinner, President Carter gushed even more. Lifting his glass to toast the Balkans tyrant, Carter said, "We here tonight and all the people of the United States are deeply honored by the visit of a great world leader, President Tito of Yugoslavia."[18]

Quoting the liberal *New York Times* columnist James "Scotty" Reston, who routinely excoriated Ronald Reagan, President Carter called Tito "the last political giant of this century" and "a man of eternal strength, of eternal youth, of eternal vigor, and of eternal courage." To underscore Tito's stature, Carter said, "President Tito was a contemporary of great men, Prime Minister Churchill, President Roosevelt, General de Gaulle, and, as you know, many others, particularly Stalin."

Carter had that statement at least partly right: Tito deserved mention in the same breath as Joseph Stalin.

The president praised Marshal Tito as a "vigorous" leader who was "constantly searching for common beliefs and common hopes and common dreams that can unite people who might otherwise be separated by a lack of communication or differences in philosophical or political outlook." He was "a man who believes in human rights," Carter declared.

It seems unbelievable that the president of the United States could say such things about an unelected communist leader who squashed the most basic human rights and confiscated personal property, amassing vast personal wealth while the people languished in poverty.

President Carter concluded his toast by saying: "There is a feeling of personal friendship and warmth and admiration that exists among the people of the United States toward this great leader. On behalf of the American people, I would like to offer a toast to the great and courageous leader, President Tito, and to the independent and proud country which he leads, Yugoslavia."

Two days later, after a ninety-minute closing meeting with the Yugoslav dictator, Carter pledged his support for the "independence, territorial integrity, and unity" of Tito's Socialist Federal Republic of Yugoslavia and even vowed to crack down on anti-Tito malefactors in the United States. He condemned the "violence" directed against Yugoslavia by "terrorists in the United States" and pledged that the U.S. government would "take firm measures to prevent and to prosecute such criminal activity which is against the interests of the United States and of good United States–Yugoslav relations."[19]

Carter's statements during Tito's visit betrayed baffling naïveté, even self-delusion. The president had revealed a key source of this delusion on the first day of the visit, when he celebrated the Yugoslav dictator as "a man who has understood for a long time our nation's commitment to détente and the true significance of this misunderstood word." Carter added, "He realizes and has told me in frequent, personal communications that he understands that détente must be comprehensive, that it must be reciprocal in nature, and it must be a demonstration constantly by the superpowers of mutual restraint and a constant search for peace."[20]

Tito understood détente completely: he knew it enabled the West to accept his dictatorship. So long as détente reigned, the people of Yugoslavia continued to suffer under Tito and his repressive communist regime. Tito understood that détente needed to be "comprehensive" enough to cover his regime. Like other communist leaders through the decades, he "reciprocated" just enough to dupe Western leaders like Carter into allowing their tyrannical rule to continue. In Carter's understanding of a détente-based "peace," West and East were not firing missiles and were engaging in trade and treaties. For the people of the Balkans, it was anything but an ideal lifestyle.

President Jimmy Carter would spend four years in a mystified "search for peace" with communist dictators. The search would fail him and his country completely.

This was the situation that Ronald Reagan wanted to change.

"KNOCK THIS THING DOWN"

While President Carter accommodated communist tyrants, Reagan stepped up his attacks on communism in his nationally syndicated radio commentaries. A particular target of his commentaries was the special hypocrisy in the Soviet attack on religious faith, given that the Soviet leadership treated Marxism-Leninism as a faith itself.

In a February 1978 commentary, Reagan protested what he called "the nativity according to Marx and Lenin." He called attention to an instance in which political commissars in Ukraine stripped a traditional Christmas carol and replaced it with communist language: "believers" were changed to "workers"; the Star of Bethlehem became the Red Star; the time of the season was not December but October, the month of the glorious revolution; and rather than Christ hovering above us, the song exalted "Lenin's glory hovering."[21]

This was no exaggeration. The Soviets replaced the traditional Christmas season with the secular Great Winter Festival, which celebrated the advent of the atheist New Year. The red star replaced the traditional star atop the tree, which was renamed the New Year Tree.[22] This sacrilege riled Reagan, who exposed it again and again. In a July commentary, he decried that in the USSR "Karl Marx is hailed as the messiah."[23]

These widely heard radio broadcasts may have reached a priest nearing the end of his life, who for years had likewise referred to Soviet communism as sacrilege. "It too has a Bible, which is 'Das Kapital' of Karl Marx," Fulton Sheen had said decades earlier. "It has its original sin, which is capitalism; it has its Messianic hope, which is the classless society and the godless race; it has its laws of sacrifice, which is class struggle; and it has its priesthood, which is the high commissariat."[24]

In November 1978, Reagan made his first visit to Berlin. Traveling with Nancy, his close aides and friends Dick Allen and Peter Hannaford, and their wives, Reagan entered East Berlin through Checkpoint Charlie and was aghast at what he saw in the godless empire.[25]

The six Americans went to Alexanderplatz, unaware that the East German secret police, the infamous Stasi, were photographing their every move.[26] Reagan and his companions took in the scene, particularly the stark contrast between the color and vivacity of the West and the gray drabness of the East. Just then, two East German communist police sauntered past and halted a citizen holding shopping bags. It was time once again to assault the freedom, the property, and the dignity of the common citizen. The communist police forced the citizen to show his bags and papers, poking them and their owner with the tip of an AK-47. "This set Ronald Reagan's blood to boiling," Dick Allen remembered. "Reagan was livid, and muttered that this was an outrage."

But the damnedest outrage was still to come, as the six headed to the Berlin Wall.

Ronald Reagan had long called for the Berlin Wall to be taken down. More than a decade earlier, on May 15, 1967, during an internationally televised debate with Robert F. Kennedy, Reagan had said: "I think it would be very admirable if the Berlin Wall...should disappear. I think this would be a step toward peace and toward self-determination for all people, if it were.... A wall that is put up to confine people, and keep them within their own country instead of allowing them the freedom of world travel, has to be somehow wrong."[27]

Now Reagan saw the notorious structure at last, spread out before him. The concrete, the barbed wire, the guards looking only in the direction of their own people, primed to gun down any poor soul who dared to test the field of landmines and make a run for freedom—he studied all of it. Then he uttered these words to his friends: "We have got to find a way to knock this thing down."

Dick Allen would never forget that moment, realizing it was not only a statement of disgust but also a proclamation, a statement of intent. "I believe the encounter with the wall and witnessing the armed harassment of an ordinary citizen seared into the governor's memory the brutality of the communist system," said Allen. It "reinforced his dedication to placing it upon the ash heap of history." Allen added, "It was clear from his reaction that he was determined to one day go about removing such a system."[28]

Reagan needed to seek the presidency again. And this time he needed to win. When he reached the White House, he would have a partner in his quest to confront communist repression: a new pope who had been chosen just a month before Reagan traveled to Berlin.

14

1978–1979

"BE NOT AFRAID"

It was mid-October 1978, and the College of Cardinals was meeting much sooner than anyone had expected. The cardinals had convened just weeks earlier to elect a successor to Pope Paul VI. Karol Wojtyła had been grieved by the death of Paul VI, whom he looked upon as a spiritual father.[1]

In late August, the College of Cardinals had picked Albino Luciani as Paul VI's successor. The new pope took the name "John Paul," generously and creatively drawn from his two most recent predecessors. He died of a heart attack only thirty-three days into his papacy, requiring the cardinals to convene again.

During his short reign, Pope John Paul made some cryptic statements that some have interpreted as prophecies of his brief tenure and maybe even of Karol Wojtyła as his successor. "Another man better than I could have been chosen," he reportedly told Cardinal Jean Villot. "Paul VI already pointed out his successor. He was sitting just in front of me in the Sistine Chapel." Luciani was referring to Wojtyła. "He will come because I will go," Luciani said.[2]

Monsignor John Magee, the pope's secretary, said that when Luciani was asked the name he would take, he replied, strangely, "John Paul the first." When he was reminded that he could not be called "the first" until there had been a second, he responded, "He will come soon enough."[3]

Shortly thereafter, the pope was dead.

The new papal conclave opened on October 14, a Saturday. When the cardinals started voting, two Italian archbishops took the lead, but eventually they seemed to cancel each other out. On October 16, the cardinals began voting again. After two rounds, Karol Wojtyła attracted a good amount of support. There had not been a non-Italian pope in 455 years, but suddenly it seemed that this Polish cardinal might actually get chosen. Wojtyła's tough old superior, Cardinal Wyszyński, privately urged his junior to accept the call if it came: "You must accept. For Poland."[4]

In the eighth round later that day, Wojtyła was elected. He became the first Slavic pope, and, at fifty-eight, the youngest pope in well over a century. He was, say biographers, "deeply affected."[5] He took the name "John Paul II" as a tribute to his short-lived predecessor.

The Soviets were not pleased that the Catholic Church had looked to the heart of the Communist Bloc for its next leader.

For the Soviets, the war on religion was a taller task in Poland than anywhere else.[6] The nation remained a bastion of Catholic faith, despite the communists' best efforts to repress the Church. Poland had a huge number of religious vocations, including tens of thousands of priests, with another 5,300 to come in seminaries.[7] A 1982 KGB analysis would estimate 26,000 priests in Poland.[8] Many of the young men came from educated families. This did not make sense to the communist mind. Intelligent people should not believe in silly superstition.

The Soviets already knew a lot about Karol Wojtyła. Since at least 1971 they had been working with Poland's communists to monitor the cardinal. Poland's prosecutor general, perhaps at Moscow's behest, had considered "prosecuting" Wojtyła for three unacceptable homilies—specifically, those given May 5, 1973, May 12, 1973, and November 24, 1974—which supposedly violated Article 194 of the communist state's Criminal Code. Although Wojtyła did not go to court, the Polish SB (secret police) had stepped up its surveillance activities.[9]

Father Stanisław Dziwisz said that in the mid-1970s Cardinal Wojtyła's entire residence was bugged—"the study, the dining room, the parlor, and even the cardinal's bedroom...the whole place was 'wallpapered' with listening devices. They were in the telephones, of course, but they were also stuck behind the wall coverings, or under the furniture." Dziwisz said that Wojtyła and his fellow priests "knew perfectly well that electronic ears were eavesdropping on us."[10] It wasn't hard to tell. The communist spies were "incompetent," Dziwisz said. A group of "workers" would show up without warning and claim that the telephone was out of order or that the house had some strange problem with the electrical system. "That was their ruse for planting the bugs," said Dziwisz.[11]

Aware of what was happening, Cardinal Wojtyła would sometimes speak in a loud voice to ensure that the listening communists were able to hear what he wanted them to think. But when he needed to discuss something sensitive, he would leave the residence. When foreign bishops came calling, he would take them to the mountains to discuss guarded information.[12]

Here was a high-ranking Church official on whom communist authorities had been spying for years, and with whom they had been battling for even longer. And now he was the head of the Roman Catholic Church. No, the Soviets were not pleased at all.

HOW COULD THIS HAPPEN, COMRADES?

Polish news sources were communist news sources, which meant that they were not free and could not be believed. They represented what Václav Havel called "the communist culture of the lie."

Still, Poles heard the news that one of their own had become pope. The information first entered Soviet Bloc airspace via free media, such as Radio Free Europe, Voice of America, and the BBC. Krzysztof Meissner, a prominent Polish physicist, later talked of waiting and waiting for Polish media to confirm the exciting reports. At last, presumably after getting marching orders from Moscow, the evening news conceded that something had happened that day in Rome. "An announcer came on with a very, very sad face and said a new pope had been elected," recalled Meissner, "and that it was Cardinal Wojtyła. That was it. Nothing else. Then the announcer switched quickly to the harvest figures or whatever, the potato crop. It was absolutely amazing."[13]

Father Dziwisz recalled being in Rome and trying to gather the reaction in Polish cities. He and Wojtyła heard reports of bells ringing, of vigils in churches, of tears of "great joy" among the people. And yet he estimated that for ten days there was absolute silence in the communist empire—no comment, no statement.[14]

This memory of near silence from the usually chest-pounding communists is accurate. A careful review of Soviet media archives today comes up empty. The only reference to Wojtyła's elevation was a three-sentence report released by TASS, the official Soviet news agency, published in *Pravda* on October 17 under the headline "New Head of the Catholic Church." Here is the complete text of that news report:

> Rome, Oct. 16 (TASS)—The election of the new head of the Roman Catholic Church was announced here. He is a Polish Cardinal, Archbishop of Kraków Karol Wojtyła. He took the name John Paul II.[15]

That was it. Nothing more. The thorough *Current Digest of the Soviet Press*, the leading Western source that compiled Soviet media transcripts, hunted for Moscow's reaction to the conclave's choice and came up only with this three-sentence "report." In a pithy editor's note, the *Current Digest* stated, "This is the only mention of the new Pope's election that we have found in the [Soviet] press to date (including *Pravda* and *Izvestia* through Oct. 28)."[16]

While remaining quiet publicly, the communists betrayed their fears privately. Relaying the opinion of his brother communists in Warsaw, Boris Aristov, the Soviet ambassador there, reported to the Politburo that the new pontiff was a "virulent anti-Communist."

Vadim Pavlov, the head of the KGB mission in Warsaw, forwarded to the KGB an SB assessment stating that "Wojtyła holds extreme anti-Communist views."[17] The SB-Pavlov assessment, revealed after the Cold War by Christopher Andrew and Vasily Mitrokhin, listed several examples of Wojtyła's "extremism." The report said that the cardinal had "criticized the way in which the state agencies of the Polish People's Republic have functioned," had made the "accusation" that "the basic human rights of Polish citizens are restricted," had condemned an "unacceptable exploitation of the workers" in Poland, had said that "activities of the Catholic Church are restricted and Catholics treated as second-class citizens," and had claimed that an "extensive campaign is being conducted to convert society to atheism and impose an alien ideology on the people."[18]

Of course, the SB was spot-on in its assessment not only of Wojtyła's views but also of the Communist Party's destructive objectives in Poland.

It was suddenly clear in Warsaw and in Moscow that decades of work on behalf of atheism and repression in Poland had backfired. Karol Wojtyła's election was crushing news for the communists, their ideology, and their plans.

Polish Communist Party leader Stanisław Kania temporarily forgot the party's official atheistic position when he first heard that there was a Polish pope. "Holy Mother of God," Kania said.[19]

Reeling from the shock, KGB head Yuri Andropov telephoned the chief KGB *rezident* in Warsaw and asked, "How could you possibly allow the election of a citizen of a socialist country as pope?"

The chief responded by saying that Andropov should direct his question to officials in Rome rather than in Warsaw. Andropov was not amused.[20]

Monsignor Jarek Cielecki captured the importance of October 16, 1978, when Karol Wojtyła became Pope John Paul II: "There, on Saint Peter's Square, when [Wojtyła] came out on that balcony—that was the end of communism."[21]

Cielecki was not the only one thinking that way.

"Anti-Soviet Gestures"

The day after his election, Pope John Paul II gave his red cardinal's skullcap, or *zucchetto*, to two trusted priests from Kraków and had them deliver it to a church in Vilnius, Lithuania, where Sister Faustina Kowalska had had many of her visions. There it was placed on the altar of the Virgin Mary.[22] The "Totus Tuus" cardinal-turned-pope was giving his hat to the Blessed Mother. It was totally hers.

This gesture enraged the Kremlin, which demanded "Totus Tuus" from its captives across Europe. The only red that Moscow wanted in Lithuania was the red flag, not a Catholic clergyman's red *zucchetto*.

Worse, from the communists' perspective, the new Slavic pope appointed the steadfastly un-Marxist Audrys Backis as one of his closest advisers.

Moscow did not like the direction this new papacy was heading. Just six weeks after Wojtyła's election, Yuri Andropov ordered up what George Weigel characterized as a "massive" KGB analysis on the potential impact of the new chief at the Holy See.[23]

The Soviets also began working with their stooges in the Polish communist regime to line up Polish clergy willing to betray their native son and shepherd. Father Konrad Hejmo was reportedly one who became an informant for the secret services. He remained so close to the papal entourage that he was placed in charge of Polish pilgrims visiting Rome.[24]

OUT WITH *OSTPOLITIK*

Wojtyła himself was unsure how to react to his election. He turned to Father Dziwisz and uttered the abbreviated Italian phrase "*Li possino*..." Dziwisz translated the intended message: "What have they *done*?"[25]

But Wojtyła was not afraid, and he urged others not to be either. On Sunday, October 22, 1978, in his homily for the official installation ceremony for his papacy, he exhorted the faithful: "Be not afraid! Open the doors to Christ, open them wide! Open the borders of states, economic and political systems, the vast domains of culture, civilization, and development—open them to His saving power!"[26]

It was a homily he wrote by hand, and by heart. And it was a message not only to Catholics or Christians broadly. This was a message to atheists, too, particularly the communist ones who had closed the doors and borders and systems and cultures and civilizations under their control—who had tried to close them to Christ's saving power.

In December, mere weeks after his election, John Paul II sent a personal letter to the bishops of Hungary. Since Pope Paul VI and the *Ostpolitik*ers had banished Cardinal Mindszenty, accommodationists had stepped in for the anticommunist hero in Hungary. As Church officials buckled to the dictates of the communist regime in Budapest, the number of practicing Catholics in Hungary waned. The pope wanted to inspire the bishops to stand up to the communists.

Four months later, the pope met with Hungary's primate, Cardinal László Lékai, who had succeeded Mindszenty as archbishop of Esztergom. The new archbishop was the anti-Mindszenty. John Paul II was unimpressed by Lékai. He decided to follow up with a pastoral letter (the first of several) to the Hungarian faithful. The letter included an urgent reminder of the "need to be catechized" and of bishops' responsibility to ensure the faithful's "right to catechesis."[27]

A few years later, John Paul II made clear his frustration with the post-Mindszenty malaise in Hungary when he was asked when he might visit the country. He replied, "The pope will visit Hungary when the cardinal [of Hungary] has learned to bang his fist on the table."[28]

From late 1978 through 1980, the new pope made many changes that infuriated Moscow. He appointed representatives to high-level posts in communist countries without worrying about Moscow's approval. This was, after all, his Church, not the Kremlin's. *Ostpolitik* was gone, and Moscow was steamed.

The new pontiff expanded the broadcasting time of Vatican Radio in Eastern European countries. He asked that programming be translated into Soviet languages. He put special focus on countries with strong Catholic constituencies severely repressed by communism: Byelorussia, Czechoslovakia, Latvia, Lithuania, Ukraine and especially western Ukraine, long a cauldron of anticommunism and anti-Sovietism. Alex Alexiev, a Russia specialist at the Rand Corporation, aptly noted, "It has now become clear that in the person of the Polish Pope the long-suffering Soviet Catholics have found a determined champion."[29]

Emboldened Lithuanian priests organized a group called the Catholic Committee for the Defense of the Rights of Believers. Its central objective was to assist the Church in exposing the state's abuses against believers. The group's first official act was to compose a letter to the new pope affirming unconditional loyalty to him (and, by extension, disloyalty to the state), and asking for his blessing on their cause. In short order, these Lithuanian priests established a secret seminary, a secret lay society, a secret order of nuns, and a secret but prolific printing press that generated at least a half dozen publications.[30] Worse for Moscow, Lithuania maintained its close cultural ties with Poland.

In a significant move missed by much of the West, the new pope declared Saints Cyril and Methodius to be co–patron saints of Europe along with Saint Benedict. In the ninth century, Cyril and his brother Methodius had traveled to Eastern Europe to preach the faith. There they prepared Slavic liturgical texts in what would become known as the Cyrillic alphabet. They spread not only Christianity into Europe but also language and literacy. The communist press in Eastern Europe attacked this papal move as a "factor in the activization of clerical anticommunism,"[31] as if clerics needed this as a reason to suddenly become anticommunist.

This was all bad enough for Moscow. Then the pontiff decided that his first foreign visit would be to his native land, Poland. No pope had ever set foot in a communist country.

JUNE 1979: NINE DAYS IN POLAND

The communists had been worried about the effects of a papal visit to Poland from the beginning. The night of Wojtyła's election, top Polish communist officials had gathered to determine how to respond to this news. The people of Poland were joyously ringing church bells, but to the communist leaders the advent of this Polish pope was disturbing. "What if the new pope decides to visit Poland?" one communist official asked. Another warned about the risk of a huge upsurge in Polish pilgrimages to Rome: "Those trips alone might pose a threat to the stability of Poland."[32]

The regime saw the new pope as a threat to the communist system itself.

John Paul II was thus shrewd to choose Poland as the site of his first foreign visit as pope. All through 1979 the new pope eagerly planned his return home. Meanwhile, communist authorities tried to figure out how to stop him.

From the outset, the Kremlin had vetoed the idea of having Poland's most famous native son come back to his own country. Poland's Communist Party boss, Edward Gierek, tried to tell the Kremlin that stopping such a visit was impossible. "How could I not receive a Polish pope," Gierek pleaded with Leonid Brezhnev, "when the majority of my countrymen are Catholics?"[33]

Communists reflexively went against the majority of their countrymen. Why suddenly violate standard practice? Brezhnev told Gierek to instruct the pontiff to make an excuse: "Tell the Pope—he is a wise man—that he could announce publicly that he cannot come because he has taken ill."

Gierek gently tried to tell his boss that his proposal would not be very effective. Presumably the pope would recover from his "illness," and there would be great demand to reschedule the trip. The Soviet leader barked at his Polish underling, "Gomułka was a better communist [than you]!"[34]

Brezhnev reluctantly gave his consent: "Well, do what you want, so long as you and your Party don't regret it later." He slammed down the telephone.[35]

Of course, Gierek would regret it, as would Brezhnev.

John Paul II originally planned the trip for May 1979 to coincide with the Feast Day to honor the nine hundredth anniversary of the death of Saint Stanisław, another fearless defender of religious freedom. But such a religious event would have conflicted with the high holy day of communism: May 1.[36] May Day was like Christmas Day for the church of Marx and Lenin. Communist censors wouldn't permit this form of Marxist sacrilege. The pope's visit would need to wait a month, until June.

But the communists miscalculated. To mollify the Vatican, the Polish communist regime granted the pontiff nine days in June rather than two days in May. And then the Church merely switched the celebration of Saint Stanisław to June.[37] John Paul II would invoke the saint throughout his nine days in Poland, surely making the Church haters even angrier.

And so, shortly after 10 A.M. on Saturday, June 2, 1979, the pontiff arrived home. He disembarked from his Alitalia 727 and knelt and kissed the ground of his beloved country. As he did, church bells rang throughout the nation.[38]

The nine-day trip included numerous public appearances, touching moments with millions of everyday Poles, and Masses and homilies and speeches and statements—too many to recount here. The official Vatican repository today posts dozens of transcripts of papal remarks from those nine days.[39]

The Holy Father's trip kicked off with his opening Mass in Warsaw's Victory Square, a symbol of withstanding World War II totalitarianism that was now, with Pope John Paul II's presence, a symbol of withstanding Cold War totalitarianism.

"Together with you," the pontiff began, "I wish to sing a hymn of praise to Divine Providence, which enables me to be here as a pilgrim."[40]

John Paul II recalled another "pilgrim pope," Paul VI, who had "ardently desired" to set foot on Polish soil, especially at Jasna Góra, but had been denied entry by the communist leaders. "Today," the new pope said, "it is granted to me to fulfill this desire of the deceased Pope Paul VI."

The Polish pope dug deeper into the mystery of Providence. "Leaving myself aside at this point," he said, "I must nonetheless with all of you ask myself why, precisely in 1978, after so many centuries of a well-established tradition in this field, a son of the Polish nation, of the land of Poland, was called to the chair of Saint Peter." He continued: "Christ demanded of Peter and of the other Apostles that they should be his 'witnesses in Jerusalem and in all Judea and Samaria and to the end of the earth' (Acts 1:8). Have we not the right, with reference to these words of Christ, to think that Poland has become nowadays the land of a particularly responsible witness?"

Throughout the nine-day pilgrimage, John Paul II avoided being explicitly political. Nonetheless, no one failed to connect the dots. When the Polish pontiff who had suffered under Marxism-Leninism invoked the Polish witness and experience, every Pole knew to connect his words to the struggle against atheistic communist ideology.

"To Poland the Church brought Christ, the key to understanding that great and fundamental reality that is man," said the pontiff. "For man cannot be fully understood without Christ. Or rather, man is incapable of understanding himself fully without Christ. He cannot understand who he is, nor what his true dignity is, nor what his vocation is, nor what his final end is. He cannot understand any of this without Christ."

Those were words that communist man needed to understand. So were these: "Christ cannot be kept out of the history of man in any part of the globe, at any longitude or latitude of geography. The exclusion of Christ from the history of man is an act against man."

And then came this significant statement, the pontiff's strongest political affirmation of the entire nine days, marked with an exclamation: "There can be no just Europe without the independence of Poland marked on its map!"

That was a shot heard in Moscow.

The Polish pope followed this proclamation by urging respect for "the rights of man, indelibly inscribed in the inviolable rights of the people."

John Paul II finished dramatically:

> All that I embrace in thought and in my heart during this Eucharist and I include it in this unique most holy Sacrifice of Christ, on Victory Square.
>
> And I cry—I who am a Son of the land of Poland and who am also Pope John Paul II—I cry from all the depths of this Millennium, I cry on the vigil of Pentecost:
>
> Let your Spirit descend.
> Let your Spirit descend.
> and renew the face of the earth,
> the face of this land.
>
> Amen.

It was a blessing in the face of the communist collectivism that had sought to remove the spirit of the Lord from the face of the earth. Observers described the atmosphere at that moment as "almost supernatural."[41] The papal gesture—the genuine feeling that the Holy Spirit had descended—made Poles smile and weep; it made Marxists wince and groan.

Thousands of young Poles marked the end of the pontiff's speech by hoisting in the air thousands of little wooden crosses.[42] They chanted: "We want God! We want God."

That was the Gospel they wanted, not the false faith of Marxism-Leninism.

"QUITE INEXPRESSIBLE"

The next day, June 3, Karol Wojtyła returned to the cathedral at Gniezno, where Comrade Gomułka and his regime had tried to shout down the celebration of Poland's Jubilee in 1966. Back then, the communists could not stop the crowd from leaving Gomułka's diatribe the minute it ended to hear the homily of Cardinal Wyszyński. And this time their efforts failed even more profoundly. "They could not stop everyone who applauded and cheered," wrote Peggy Noonan, "for there weren't enough jail cells."[43]

Of course, they still caused as much trouble as they could. Prior to the trip, the communist regime sent a directive to schoolteachers instructing them how to characterize the papal visit to students. "The Pope is our enemy," the directive said. "Due to his uncommon skills and great sense of humor he is dangerous.... Besides, he goes for cheap gestures in his relations with the crowd, for instance, puts on a highlander's hat, shakes all hands, kisses children.... It is modeled on American presidential campaigns."[44]

Knowing they could not ignore the trip, the communists tried to minimize it. In "news" broadcasts, the state-controlled media narrowed the camera lens to try to diminish the size of the massive crowds the pope generated. Cameramen were ordered never to show young people and children. They were ordered to focus on nuns, priests, old women, handicapped—the slack-jawed and superstitious seeking out their opiate.[45]

But the camera games mattered little, given that the masses ventured out of their homes to see Karol Wojtyła in the flesh rather than on their television sets.

Lech Wałęsa compared the turnout to a miracle of Christ. "[John Paul II] comes to Poland," said Wałęsa, "and the twenty who followed me were suddenly ten million. It was a greater multiplication than the loaves and the fishes."[46]

A crowd of a million people appeared on June 6 when the pope went to the mountain shrine of Our Lady of Jasna Góra in Częstochowa, the country's preeminent shrine. The shouting and cheering by the massive crowd provoked panic among communist authorities, who moved in tanks to cordon off the area. Still, Poles stood strong.

The pope told the crowd of his previous visits to Jasna Góra. One such visit had occurred when he was in high school and he had come with his father and entire native parish of Wadowice. Another occurred when he was a university student, during what he called "the terrible Occupation." Speaking directly to Our Lady of Jasna Góra, the pope said of that visit, "I remember the audience that you granted to me and to my companions when we came here clandestinely, as representatives of the university students of Kraków."[47]

The Holy Father made a heartfelt plea to the Lady: "Today I have come to you, Our Lady of Jasna Góra... to bid you farewell once more and to ask your blessing for my journey." He told her: "The meaning of this pilgrimage is quite inexpressible. I shall not even try to find the words to express what it has been for me and for us all, and what it will never cease to be."

The pontiff closed with a full consecration to Mary, consecrating himself, his country, his Church, the people of the world, and all nations:

> Our Lady of the Bright Mountain, Mother of the Church! Once more I consecrate myself to you in your maternal slavery of love: *Totus tuus!*—I am all yours! I consecrate to you the whole Church—everywhere and to the ends of the earth! I consecrate to you Humanity; I consecrate to you all men and women, my brothers and sisters. All the Peoples and the Nations. I consecrate to you Europe and all the continents. I consecrate to you Rome and Poland, united, through your servant, by a fresh bond of love.
>
> Mother, accept us!
> Mother, do not abandon us!
> Mother, be our guide!

It would be her hand, he would later say, that guided that bullet that should have killed him. And it would be to her, too, that he would look to consecrate Russia, as Our Lady of Fátima had requested.

BACK IN KRAKÓW

Pope John Paul II left Częstochowa on June 6 and headed home, to Kraków and Wadowice. A huge throng awaited him in Kraków in the rain. The crowd cheered and cried. Karol Wojtyła was treated unlike any other native son of this proud country.

"He left here with a bag, a toothbrush, and a couple of rolls to eat," a hotel doorman told a foreign journalist, recalling the days before Wojtyła was pope. "Look at the way he came back."[48]

The Soviets were certainly looking at the way he came back. Moscow's fright was made more acute by the fearlessness of the Polish pope, the people, and the Gospel message. That fearlessness was evident when the pope told a group of university students in Kraków: "Do not be afraid of the toil; be afraid only of thoughtlessness and pusillanimity. From the difficult experience that we call 'Poland' a better future can be drawn, but only on condition that you are honourable, temperate, believing, free in spirit and strong in your convictions."[49]

After arriving in Kraków, the pope visited Auschwitz, just down the road. He walked through the concentration camp slowly, morosely, paying homage to victims, from Jewish brothers and sisters to Maximilian Kolbe. A large cross made of barbed wire stood erect on the platform of the camp. The pontiff referred to the wretched place as the "Golgotha of the contemporary world."[50]

It was a sobering component of an otherwise celebratory trip.

On Sunday, June 10, the pontiff celebrated Mass on the Kraków Commons, where he was joined by a congregation of two to three million, the largest outdoor gathering in the nation's history.[51]

With that triumphant event, the pope's nine-day tour of his homeland came to an end. At Kraków's Balice Airport later that day, he met one last time with journalists. With tears in his eyes, the witness to hope told reporters in a halting voice: "I hope, I hope, I hope to meet you again in this country. I hope..."[52]

Before boarding his plane, the pope offered a brief, poignant farewell statement. He began by thanking his countrymen for their hospitality and all the work that had gone into making his visit possible. Then he acknowledged that "the visit of the pope to Poland is certainly an unprecedented event,...especially as it is the visit of a Polish pope." He continued, "This unprecedented event is undoubtedly an act of courage, both on the part of those who gave the invitation and on the part of the person who was invited." But that was precisely what the age demanded, he added: "In our times, such an act of courage is necessary." He said it was necessary "to have the courage to walk in the direction in which no one has walked before, just as once Simon needed the courage to journey from the lake of Gennesaret in Galilee towards Rome, a place unknown to him."[53]

That first pope's journey to Rome would lead to his martyrdom at Saint Peter's Square.

The Polish pope said that such acts of "witness" were needed to bring "nations and regimes" closer together as an "indispensable condition for peace in the world." In a final, subtle reference to the rigidity of communist systems, he stated, "Our times demand that we should not lock ourselves into the rigid boundaries of systems, but seek all that is necessary for the good of man, who must find everywhere the awareness and certainty of his authentic citizenship."

That authentic citizenship was in the City of God, not the city that headquartered international communism.

And with that, Poland's native son, its conquering hero, stepped away with a closing benediction: "May Almighty God bless you: the Father, the Son, and the Holy Spirit."

MOSCOW'S REACTION

The communists watched this pilgrimage to Poland every step of the way. One scholar closely studying the Soviet reaction at the time was Alex Alexiev. He noted that prior to the June 1979 trip, Soviet reporting on the new pontiff had been "scant and generally restrained." That approach, however, was "promptly discarded" once the pope visited his homeland.

On the opening day of John Paul II's visit, Moscow television informed its captive audience that "certain Church leaders" were using the visit to foment "anti-state purposes." The newscast credited the old Stalinist sage Andrei Gromyko with a particularly creative analogy: the Soviet foreign minister expressed concern that the pontiff's visit to Poland would "have the same effect on the masses as the Ayatollah Khomeini had in Iran."[54]

So the bishop of Rome and the head of Iran's jihadist mullah-ocracy: one and the same.

The communists launched a massive damage-control operation codenamed LATA '79 (meaning SUMMER '79). Some 480 Polish SB agents monitored Karol Wojtyła's every move and tried to generate whatever problems they could. The devious operation included seven moles who infiltrated the pontiff's group, one of them a clergyman, acting in the spirit not of Jesus but of Judas. Yet more clergy from outside Poland, such as the German Benedictine Eugen Brammertz, were part of the effort. The Benedictine betrayer worked with the East German Stasi, which established a special working group to foul up the papal pilgrimage. These troublemakers infiltrated various Catholic groups and organizing committees, tried to manipulate television coverage of the papal visit (from the tone to the amount of coverage), sought to slow or redirect buses shuttling pilgrims attempting to see the pontiff, and generally created what Dziwisz called "a bunch of ridiculous obstacles" put in the way of the people.[55]

For communists, this was standard operating procedure. While tens of millions of Poles readied to be inspired, thousands of communist operatives readied for their usual devilry.

Despite the best efforts of the Kremlin and Poland's communist regime, the pope's trip went off without a hitch, other than a sore throat from his speaking so often to so many massive crowds. How massive? Some twelve million Poles, or one-third of the population, saw John Paul II in person during the trip. And the crowds were orderly. These were nine days of peace.

The communists were rattled. They could think of nothing but to redouble the repression they had practiced for decades. "The solution for the Karol Wojtyła problem," said Ukrainian Communist Party chief Vladimir Shcherbitsky, "must lie in a renewed and more vigorous propaganda in favor of atheism in the Soviet Union and its 'fraternal socialist societies.'"[56] Well, that vigor had not been enough in Poland.

George Weigel called the June 1979 trip "the dramatic pivot" of John Paul II's three-decade-long struggle with communism—"nine days during which the history of the twentieth century turned in a fundamental way." Not given to hyperbole, the papal biographer said that during those days, Pope John Paul II handed his people the key to their own liberation: "the key of aroused consciences."[57]

Weigel was far from alone in that assessment.[58] Another American looked at the pope in Poland and saw him as "the key."

RONALD REAGAN'S REACTION

In a June 5, 1979, editorial, the *New York Times* declared, "As much as the visit of Pope John Paul II to Poland must reinvigorate and re-inspire the Roman Catholic Church in Poland, it does not threaten the political order of the nation or of Eastern Europe."[59]

Time would reveal just how wrong the *Times* was in this pronouncement. One who recognized it in the moment was Ronald Reagan.

The sixty-eight-year-old former governor of California was emotionally affected by the pope's nine-day pilgrimage. And he sensed the larger importance of the visit and of the pope himself.

In early June 1979, Richard V. Allen was again at Reagan's home, just the two of them. Allen became the closest foreign-policy mind, witness, and observer to Reagan in the formative three to four years before he became president. A year earlier, he had accompanied the former governor to the Berlin Wall, where Reagan's reaction was sheer revulsion. This time, Allen watched a Reagan reaction that was sheer inspiration.

Allen and Reagan were having another long discussion when they decided to take a break. Turning on the television in Reagan's study, they watched news footage of the Polish pontiff in his homeland. They glimpsed the massive crowds. Both men were (by Allen's description) "astounded." Reagan became "intensely focused." Said Allen: "Reagan remained silent for the longest time... and then I glanced at him, saw that he was deeply moved, and noticed a tear in the corner of his eye."[60]

Allen said that "only seldom" had he seen tears in Reagan's eyes, but this, he thought, was a tear "of pride, of admiration, perhaps of astonishment at what he was witnessing."[61]

Reagan reached a conclusion. "He said then and there that the pope was the key figure in determining the fate of Poland," Allen stated. "He was overcome by the outpouring of emotion that emanated from the millions who came to see him." For Reagan, this helped solidify a "deep and steadfast conviction that this pope would help change the world."[62]

In short, said Allen, Reagan viewed the pope's visit as an "extraordinary wedge into the very center of the communist domain."[63]

Allen and Reagan spoke few words as they watched. "As always with Reagan, something remained unsaid," Allen remembered. Nonetheless, Reagan's body language was unmistakable. The future president had been "deeply impressed" by the papal visit "and did not need to explain how he felt."[64] Allen said that seeing Reagan so visibly affected by the pope's historic visit "deeply moved" him.

Clearly, Reagan had discerned a kindred spirit in John Paul II, someone willing to speak out against evil.

And speak out Reagan did. He went into the radio studio and recorded several nationally syndicated broadcasts on the pope's trip and on Poland's history of communist persecution. Reagan's handwritten drafts of these broadcasts, found decades later by researcher Kiron Skinner, give insight into how the future president viewed the new pope's visit.[65]

In one broadcast, Reagan described the "communist atheism" that had descended on Poland after World War II. An outraged Reagan remarked, "These young people of Poland [who greeted the pope] had been born and raised and spent their entire lives under communist atheism."[66] In another broadcast, titled "A Tale of Two Cities," Reagan told his audience that Stalin had once dismissed the Vatican by "contemptuously" asking, "How many divisions does the pope have?" Well, said Reagan, that question has been answered by Pope John Paul II:

> It has been a long time since we've seen a leader of such courage and such uncompromising dedication to simple morality—to the belief that right does make might.
>
> On our TV screens we've seen the reaction to this kind of leadership. Wherever he went in his native land the people of Poland came forth in unbelievable numbers. There were crowds of 400,000, 500,000, 1 million, and then 5 million, gathered from miles around, even though they don't have the easy means of transportation we have, and they gathered knowing there was every possibility they were risking their livelihood and even their freedom.
>
> For 40 years the Polish people have lived under 1st the Nazis and then the Soviets. For 40 years they have been ringed by tanks and guns. The voices behind those tanks and guns have told them there is no God. Now with the eyes of all the world on them they have looked past those menacing weapons and listened to the voice of one man who has told them there is a God and it is their inalienable right to freely worship that God. Will the Kremlin ever be the same again? Will any of us for that matter?[67]

Reagan, for one, was never the same. He would use this same passage in a speech delivered in Dallas in August 1980, on the presidential campaign trail.[68] In fact, he would speak up on this vital matter many times, whether behind a radio microphone or a podium.[69]

The former California governor knew that something of immense importance had taken place. He recognized that the pope's visit was a momentous event that threatened communism's hold on Eastern Europe. He had always perceived Poland as special, but now more so.

"He had a preoccupation with Poland," Bill Clark told me. "He had mentioned Yalta as far back as I go with him as being totally unfair and having to be undone someday."[70] Reagan "greatly" sympathized with Poland for a number of reasons—among them, that no other country lost as high a percentage of its population in World War II.[71]

Asked whether Reagan "realized then and there," during John Paul's June 1979 trip, that Poland could be the "splinter to break apart the Soviet empire," Clark went further: "He felt that far before June 1979. He had tremendous interest in Poland and its strategic importance, going back to Yalta and Potsdam, which he felt were terrible days. He knew Poland would be the linchpin in the dissolution of the Soviet empire."[72]

As president, Ronald Reagan would pull on that linchpin with the help of his Polish partner.

OCTOBER 1979: A POLISH POPE IN AMERICA

Mere months later, in October, the new pope visited the United States, the first of his seven visits to America. The only other pope to visit the United States in its two-century-long history had been Pope Paul VI in 1965.[73]

The pontiff met with President Jimmy Carter at the White House on October 6.[74] The meetings and press conferences with Carter were warm, largely dealing with generalities and common concerns—or, as Carter put it, "striving together for a common future of peace and love." The Southern Baptist was gracious with the leader of the Roman Catholic Church, telling a group on the South Lawn, "Regardless of our faith, we look on him as a pastor, and he's come to know us and to talk to us about gentleness, about humility, about forgiveness, and about love." He called the pontiff "our beloved guest," and stated: "You show in your life and in your teachings a particular concern for human dignity. You know that many people are fearful, but that a person with faith need not be afraid. Our religious faith is, indeed, relevant to a modern world."[75]

It was a fine moment, even if Carter had been far more effusive in praising Comrade Tito. But there was no special bond to launch a partnership akin to what the pontiff would establish with Carter's successor.

Later, John Paul II spent several hours at the Vatican residence in Washington with Carter's national security adviser, Zbigniew Brzezinski, the ethnic Pole and staunch anti-Soviet.[76] No doubt it was a more substantive discussion of freedom and repression in Poland.

Beyond Washington, the pope visited Boston, Chicago, New York, Philadelphia, and Des Moines, Iowa, greeted by phenomenal crowds, including a ticker-tape parade in Philadelphia. He held Masses in, among other sites, Yankee Stadium, which was packed with seventy-five thousand people; Chicago's Grant Park, where the crowd approached a half million; and Philadelphia's Logan Circle, where more than a million showed up.[77] To say that the pope was greeted like a "rock star," a common metaphor for such mass outpourings of affection, is not sufficient. Elvis and the Beatles combined did not evoke responses like this.

One excited pilgrim described the jubilation when the pontiff arrived at Boston Common and held a huge outdoor Mass on October 1, his first day on U.S. soil: "There was just an eruption of noise, a scream all at once. The crowd lit up with flashes; cameras were going off at once, illuminating the whole Common. I've never seen or heard anything like it, and I probably never will again."[78]

On October 3 the pope traveled to Philadelphia, where three years earlier he had spoken on man's hunger for freedom. He noted that he had come in 1976 as archbishop of Kraków, but today, "by the grace of God, I come here as Successor of Peter to bring you a message of love and to strengthen you in your faith."[79]

A surprising moment came after Pope John Paul II arrived in the nation's capital. The papal nuncio in Washington held a reception for diplomats and ambassadors, who, one by one, were received by the bishop of Rome. Given his high rank, Soviet ambassador Anatoly Dobrynin entered the room first. He knew that the Polish pope understood Russian well and thus asked whether he preferred to converse in Russian or Polish. The pope, ever the Pole and ever the diplomat, suggested that he speak Polish and Dobrynin speak Russian.

After some conversation came the surprise. Dobrynin recalled, "He asked me rather unexpectedly whether I would mind if he blessed me as the ambassador of a great country, so that he might wish us success in striving for world peace." Dobrynin cautioned that the pope knew that all Soviet ambassadors were required to be Communist Party members "and therefore officially atheists." Nonetheless, the Soviet ambassador said: "I replied that I would be pleased to receive his blessing, especially in the great cause he mentioned. Thus I believe I am the only Soviet ambassador throughout the history of our diplomatic service to have received a blessing from the Pope."[80]

THE DIGNITY OF MAN

One of John Paul II's biggest moments during his 1979 trip to America was his speech to the United Nations, only the second such papal appearance before the stately body, after Paul VI's. It came early in his visit, on October 2. The oration was striking in length alone, traversing 6,700 words of text and requiring a full hour to deliver.[81]

In this speech, the pope reflected on a theme that he had been speaking about for years and that he had addressed in his first encyclical, *Redemptor Hominis*: humanity's inherent dignity. "Every human being living on earth is a member of a civil society, of a nation, many of them represented here," said the pope. "Each one of you, distinguished ladies and gentlemen, represents a particular state, system and political structure, but what you represent above all are individual human beings; you are all representatives of men and women . . . each of them a subject endowed with dignity as a human person."

The pope recalled that the world had just marked the fortieth anniversary of the invasion of Poland and the start of World War II, in which man's dignity was violated so horribly. He noted that during his first papal visit to his homeland, he had visited Auschwitz. "This infamous place is unfortunately only one of the many scattered over the continent of Europe," said the pope. "But the memory of even one should be a warning sign on the path of humanity today, in order that every kind of concentration camp anywhere on earth may once and for all be done away with." He insisted that "everything that is a continuation of those experiences under different forms, namely the various kinds of torture and oppression, either physical or moral, carried out under any system, in any land," should "disappear forever from the lives of nations and states."

This was surely a reference to Soviet communism, with its repressive tactics, police state, and vast system of Gulag forced labor camps. The pope's advisers knew it. So did the Soviets, who reportedly were angry with the remarks.[82]

The pope said that he wanted to draw attention to "a second systematic threat to man in his inalienable rights in the modern world, a threat which constitutes no less a danger than the first to the cause of peace." He referred to "the various forms of injustice in the field of the spirit"—how man can be wounded "in his inner relationship with truth, in his conscience, in his most personal belief, in his view of the world, in his religious faith, and in the sphere of what are known as civil liberties." He was particularly concerned with threats to religious freedom. Quoting from the Second Vatican Council, he said, "In accordance with their dignity, all human beings, because they are persons, that is, beings endowed with reason and free will and therefore bearing personal responsibility, are both impelled by their nature and bound by a moral obligation to seek the truth, especially religious truth."

In what was surely another reference to communist repression, he continued the quotation from the Council's *Dignitatis Humanae*: "The practice of religion of its very nature consists primarily of those voluntary and free internal acts by which a human being directly sets his course towards God. No merely human power can either command or prohibit acts of this kind." The pontiff said that these words related directly to the "confrontation between the religious view of the world and the agnostic or even atheistic view, which is one of the 'signs of the times' of the present age."

The atheists in Moscow and other communist capitals knew that this meant them.

Finally, in emphasizing the need for "respect for the dignity of the human person," Pope John Paul II noted that the United Nations had proclaimed 1979 the Year of the Child. The emerging champion of a "Culture of Life" certainly appreciated this and especially wanted it understood in America only six years after the legalization of abortion in *Roe v. Wade*. He implored the audience to respect life from its earliest stages: "Concern for the child, even before birth, from the first moment of conception and then throughout the years of infancy and youth, is the primary and fundamental test of the relationship of one human being to another."

That was a statement Ronald Reagan must have loved.

It was a strong speech, no question. It never once used the terms *Russia*, *Soviet Union*, *USSR*, *communism*, or *Marxism-Leninism*. But it clearly dealt with those threats to human dignity and human life.

To the Vatican's Cardinal Casaroli, the message was *too* clear. The high priest of *Ostpolitik* had been uncomfortable with some of the alleged anti-Soviet stridency in the text. Reviewing the speech before the pope delivered it, Casaroli tried to edit lines he thought might be "offensive" to the Kremlin and other communists. He deemed even the use of words like *ideology* and *system* (each used once) to be incendiary, and he wanted to eliminate anything that might be interpreted as a criticism of the USSR and its puppets, including some of John Paul II's references to religious freedom and human rights.[83]

In other words, out of fear of disappointing his Soviet friends, Casaroli tried to gut the text of its essence.

In a scene that would become familiar to President Ronald Reagan and his own accommodationist advisers, the speaker smiled, shrugged, and gently reinserted the original language. For the pontiff, like the later president, this game was often played until the very last minute, as the airplane began its descent or as the speaker approached the podium.

John Paul II had not called out an "Evil Empire," but for the apostles of accommodation, he had been belligerent enough. And the ultrasensitive Soviets interpreted what he had said as vile and confrontational.

The Kremlin had to determine how to respond to this dangerous pope.

"PHYSICAL ELIMINATION OF JP II"

When Ambassador Anatoly Dobrynin later recalled his nice moment with the pontiff in Washington, he did not volunteer whether John

Paul II's blessing had much peaceful effect on the Soviet Union's actions. His colleagues were in no mood to receive such a blessing.

On November 13, 1979, just a few weeks after John Paul's high-profile visit to America, nine members of the Soviet state's Secretariat of the Central Committee assembled at their Moscow headquarters. The tenth and highest-ranking member of the group, General Secretary Leonid Brezhnev, was sick as usual and did not attend. But he was not needed for the Soviet ship of state to sail in its natural direction.

What was to be done about the new Polish pope? That was the issue at hand. The pope and his "cult" had made too much progress and were endangering the communist cause. And so, at the close of the meeting, the Soviet leadership issued a chilling edict directed at Karol Wojtyła:

> Use all possibilities available to the Soviet Union to prevent the new course of policies initiated by the Polish pope; if necessary with additional measures beyond disinformation and discreditation.
>
> The order was signed by Mikhail A. Suslov, Andrei P. Kirilenko, Konstantin U. Chernenko, Konstantin V. Rusakov, V. N. Ponomarev, Ivan V. Kapitonov, Mikhail V. Zimianim, Vladimir I. Dolgikh, and Mikhail S. Gorbachev.[84]

Yes, among the signers was a fairly new member of the Central Committee, a young, fast-rising Soviet official named Mikhail Gorbachev.

"In layman's terms, this was an order for assassination," writes John Koehler, the journalist and Cold War researcher who discovered this striking document nearly three decades later.[85]

Koehler obtained what he believed was the partial text of this order during an interview in Rome with a high-ranking Italian official close to his country's security services. The official showed it to Koehler during a discussion years after the attempted assassination of Pope John Paul II. At the bottom of the paper, at the end of the translated text, was a crucial note from SISDE, the Servicio per le Informazioni a la Sicurezza Democratica, the security service for the Italian government. The note asserted, "SISDE says document found in Moscow points to plan for the 'physical elimination of JP II.'"

That is a reasonable interpretation. How else should one read the phrases "all possibilities available" and "if necessary with additional measures beyond disinformation and discreditation"? The Soviets had taken the "additional measure" of murdering innocents millions of times since 1917.

As John Koehler notes, this order was not the only evidence that the Soviet leadership considered assassination to deal with the troublesome Polish pope. A KGB officer who defected to the United States, Major Victor Sheymov, reported that on a visit to Poland in 1979, he discussed with KGB officials a message from Moscow demanding information on how to "get physically close" to the pope.[86]

Sheymov and the others knew exactly what that meant. "In the KGB slang," Sheymov told American reporters after he defected, "it was clearly understood that when you say physically close, there was only one reason to get close: to assassinate him. Words like *murder* or *assassinations* are never used. They have substituted gentler terms."[87]

When Sheymov examined the cable from Moscow, he saw that it did not bear the usual code name; the sender was KGB chairman Yuri Andropov, the future Soviet general secretary.[88]

15

1980–1981

AN ERA OF RENEWAL

In the summer of 1980, another matter of great significance occurred in Moscow's trouble spot, Poland.

The pope's visit to his native land the previous summer had given new impetus to the workers' movement—that is, the legitimate workers' movement, not whatever manipulated group of forced laborers Moscow claimed and controlled.

For decades, communists had faced huge labor problems in Poland, from the Poznań riots in June 1956 through a tense round of worker expression and repression in 1976. From this crucible, a young electrician at the Lenin Shipyard in Gdańsk emerged as one of the top anticommunist union activists. His name was Lech Wałęsa.

A fervent Catholic, Wałęsa once told an Italian journalist:

> If you choose the example of what we Poles have in our pockets and in our shops, then... communism has done very little for us. But if

> you choose the example of what is in our souls, I answer that communism has done very much for us.
>
> In fact our souls contain exactly the opposite of what they wanted. They wanted us not to believe in God, and our churches are full. They wanted us to be materialistic and incapable of sacrifice. They wanted us to be afraid of the tanks, of the guns, and instead we don't fear them at all.[1]

Among those who heard these words was an American anticommunist named Ronald Reagan, who would quote them often.[2] The fear, as Reagan and Wałęsa both knew, was on the communist side. And the fear level rose higher on August 16, 1980, when Wałęsa called on his fellow workers to leave the shipyard in Gdańsk. Shaken by the massive strike, the Polish communist regime met with labor organizers four days later on August 20. The government agreed to the formal creation of the workers' movement, known as Solidarity.

It was a stunning historic achievement. As Arthur Rachwald, a historian of Solidarity, explained, "The idea of an independent labor organization functioning freely is totally incompatible with the Soviet system."[3] Indeed, *Pravda* responded by objecting that the immortal Lenin had insisted on Communist Party control of all trade unions. Thus, when the Polish communist government officially recognized Solidarity, it had committed heresy in the Church of Lenin.[4] The supremacy of the Community Party, directed from Moscow, was in jeopardy. Not surprisingly, Polish prime minister Edward Babiuch, in power only seven months, resigned. Soon thereafter the most powerful man in Poland, Edward Gierek, was forced out as Communist Party secretary.

When a smiling Wałęsa signed the agreement at the Lenin Shipyard, he used a giant souvenir pen graced with an image of a grinning John Paul II, a relic from the June 1979 pilgrimage. That 1979 visit had helped pave the way for this 1980 agreement.[5]

Within about three months of the agreement, the membership of Solidarity exploded from zero to ten million, a number exceeded only by the multitude of Poles who had defied the Church of Marxism-Leninism to come out and see the first Slavic pope.

Ronald Reagan, for one, relished that Solidarity was a disgruntled workers' group "in a so-called workers' state," "a genuine labor movement suppressed by a government of generals who claim to represent the working class."[6] The workers' union, noted Reagan, "was contrary to anything the Soviets would want or the communists would want."[7] As the former head of Hollywood's huge actors union, Reagan felt connected to Solidarity. He told the International Brotherhood of Teamsters, "Those of us who know what it is to belong to a union have a special bond with the workers of Poland."[8]

Reagan also understood Solidarity's uniqueness at a precarious time for the USSR. He noted that nothing like Solidarity had existed in the Soviet Bloc.[9]

Solidarity was not simply a labor union; it became what the Soviets feared most—a massive political and social movement. This anticommunist, pro–Roman Catholic Church movement favored free speech, freedom of religion, free press, and free elections.[10]

Allowing Solidarity's legalization was a risky move for communist authorities. They hoped that doing so would be like releasing a pressure valve. But those hopes soon became regrets, certainly in Moscow. The Kremlin realized that Solidarity needed to be destroyed.

And Reagan, who was again campaigning for president of the United States, privately vowed that if and when he was elected, he would do everything he could to keep Solidarity from being destroyed.

"REAGAN WILL DO IT BETTER"

On November 4, 1980, Americans did something that was verboten in the communist world: they went into voting booths and cast ballots for their next president. They chose Ronald Reagan over the incumbent, President Jimmy Carter, in a landslide. Reagan swept forty-four of fifty states and took the Electoral College by a margin of 489 to 49.

On December 7, Lech Wałęsa, Poland's newest freedom fighter, spoke of the American election as he stood on a windy plain on the outskirts of Gdańsk. Unafraid, he spoke openly of his support for the president-elect whom Moscow and the Polish communist leadership held in contempt. "It was intuition, perhaps," Wałęsa told a group of reporters, Americans among them, "but one year ago I envisioned what would happen. Reagan was the only good candidate in your presidential campaign, and I knew he would win."

The Catholic labor leader spoke prophetically that December day: "Someday the West will wake up and you may find it too late, as Solzhenitsyn has written. Reagan will do it better. He will settle things in a more efficient way. He will make the U.S. strong and make it stand up."[11]

The world was about to change. Lech Wałęsa understood because he understood the man about to move into the White House, just as he understood the man who had moved from Kraków to Saint Peter's Square.

On January 19, 1981, the day before Reagan's inauguration, Wałęsa happened to be in Rome and visited with the Polish pontiff. The Holy Father greeted Wałęsa at the Vatican's Consistory Hall, replete with frescoes on the walls and gilded ceiling. The union worker was accorded the reception of a visiting head of state. He joined the pontiff, journalists, and fellow unionists in singing the patriotic hymn "God Save Poland." Before going into the pope's study for a private twenty-five-minute meeting, the electrician from Gdańsk dropped to one knee in respect and obedience, despite the pontiff's humble attempts to raise him.

Wałęsa and his delegation celebrated Mass with John Paul II in his private chapel. "I want to gather around this altar all working men, and all that their lives contain," said the Holy Father. He placed on the altar "all Polish labor."[12] It seemed a dedication and a sacrifice and a commission.

Perhaps it was a shield as well. Wałęsa didn't know it at the time, but throughout his Rome visit, a hit man was tracking his every move.

As Italian investigators later determined and the hit man himself confessed, a Bulgarian spy ring had tapped this trained assassin to kill the Solidarity leader who was so unnerving communist authorities. The Bulgarians promised him $300,000 for the job. Bulgarian intelligence reported closely to the Soviets.

The hit man knew everything about Wałęsa's time in Rome—every step of his itinerary, every one of his movements, every detail about where he was staying, down to the color of the walls that were being repainted in the Hotel Victoria. He had a bomb in a small suitcase, and he was all set to plant it in the chosen spot, in a car parked near Wałęsa's hotel. At the right moment, he would detonate the bomb by radio.[13]

For reasons still not totally clear, the plot did not pan out. At one point later, the would-be assassin said that the head of the Bulgarian spy ring called off the bombing at the last minute, allegedly because his Italian informants learned that the police had been tipped off.

The hired killer in the Wałęsa case was a twenty-three-year-old Turk named Mehmet Ali Agca. He would get an opportunity to redeem himself in the eyes of his communist bosses when the Bulgarians called on him to take out another, even more important Polish figure four months later—on May 13, 1981, the Feast Day of Our Lady of Fátima.

"LET US BEGIN AN ERA OF NATIONAL RENEWAL"

The next morning, January 20, mercifully did not start with news of the death of the Polish labor leader—destined to become one of the most important figures in the fall of communism. The day was a happy one for Ronald Wilson Reagan. At noon he stood on a platform erected at the West Front of the Capitol in Washington, D.C., to take the oath of office as the fortieth president of the United States of America. Nelle's son had achieved things she and her husband, Jack, could scarcely have imagined. He had come a long way from the second-floor apartment above a grocery store in Tampico.

With Chief Justice Warren Burger swearing him in, Reagan placed his right hand on the Bible—his mother's well-worn Bible. It was opened to 2 Chronicles 7:14, which states, "If my people, who are called by my name, will humble themselves and pray and seek my face and turn from their wicked ways, then I will hear from heaven, and I will forgive their sin and will heal their land." Next to the verse, Nelle had long ago scribbled, "A wonderful verse for the healing of a nation."

That was what Nelle's son prescribed for his nation on this day: healing, renewal.

"We're not, as some would have us believe, doomed to an inevitable decline," said Reagan, rejecting the "malaise" mentality of Jimmy Carter. "Let us begin an era of national renewal." The new president pledged to heal America, to restore its greatness, and he prayed for a spiritual revival for his country. That renewal for his countrymen, Reagan believed, could renew the world.

Renewal would be a recurring theme for Ronald Reagan. One of his favorite quotations was from Thomas Paine during the American Revolution: "We have it in our power to begin the world all over again." Privately, Reagan had a vision for doing just that. His plan was not merely to pull America out of the domestic crisis he had inherited from Carter but also to rescue the world from atheistic communism, the terrible ideology that had advanced under the détente presidencies of Carter, Ford, and Nixon.

REAGAN'S RIGHT HAND

President Reagan began assembling a team to help in the renewal of America and the wider world. Critical to that new team was Bill Clark.

William Patrick Clark was born on October 23, 1931, in Oxnard, California, not far from Reagan's home in Hollywood or his Rancho del Cielo in the Santa Ynez Mountains above Santa Barbara. Clark was born into a California family of ranchers, cowboys, sheriffs, and lawmen.[14] Like Saint Francis, one of his personal patron saints, he connected with nature. Raised a rancher, Clark shepherded livestock in the majestic mountains of central California, territory that in many spots resembles the hills of Italy that a young Francis Bernardone, the future patron saint of Italy, rode on horseback between Assisi and Perugia in the late 1100s. A young Bill and a young Francis would have shared feelings of awe and humility in the shadow of the Creation.

As a teenager, Bill Clark patrolled some sixty thousand acres of land. He galloped horseback through peaks and valleys, always with a dog at his side and a rifle to protect the sheep and calves from coyotes. Like Francis, he slept under the stars, with no roof. Clark and his fellow shepherd, Martin Iriguoin, recited the prayers of Mass on days they felt were probably Sunday, not having the benefit of a calendar, let alone radio, newspaper, or cell phone. He would later describe himself as "a fool for Christ, like Saint Francis."

In 1947, Clark's family left the rural ranching area for educational opportunities. The young Clark enrolled at Villanova Preparatory School in the Ojai Valley. It was a rigorous private institution founded by the Order of Saint Augustine. Bill worked for his tuition in the kitchen. Mass was celebrated every morning. Religious instruction occurred all day long. Clark was introduced to Church encyclicals like *Rerum Novarum* (1891), *Quadragesimo Anno* (1931), and *Divini Redemptoris* (1937), providing him with a healthy appetite for helping the poor and a robust knowledge of the dangers of communism.

Clark graduated salutatorian in 1949 and enrolled in Stanford that fall. At Stanford, he began to seriously consider the priesthood. Reading Thomas Merton's autobiography, *The Seven Storey Mountain*, published in 1948, had a profound effect on Clark. Merton's book recounts his search for meaning and purpose in life, a search that took him from hedonism to communism and ultimately to Catholicism. Merton eventually became a Trappist monk. And Bill Clark, after his freshman year at Stanford, left the university to enter seminary. Though he felt himself a Franciscan, and always would, Clark attended an Augustinian novitiate in New York.

Ultimately, Clark did not choose the priesthood. He went into law and politics, heeding another call: the call to confront godless communism.

Merton's book certainly influenced Clark's perspective, particularly Merton's account of the Marxist indoctrination he had experienced at Columbia University.[15] But just as influential were two books by Fulton Sheen, *Peace of Soul* and *Communism and the Conscience of the West*. Sheen's warnings on communism stirred Clark, and after the young Californian decided not to pursue the priesthood, he chose another kind of public service. Clark heeded the call of *Divini Redemptoris* to be one of the Church's "sons of light" in combating communism's "sons of darkness." He was one of the laity called on "to fight the battles of the Lord."

This path eventually led him to a California celebrity-turned-politician named Ronald Reagan, who was greatly impressed with Clark—his mind, his faith, his loyalty, his sense of good versus evil, his anticommunism.

Governor Ronald Reagan made Bill Clark his chief of staff in 1967. Reagan later appointed him up the ranks of the California court system, all the way to the California Supreme Court. Recall that he delegated Judge Clark to meet with Cardinal Mindszenty. And in early 1981 the nation's new president-elect wanted Clark to leave his central California ranch to help him confront the sons of darkness. Clark did not want to leave his beloved ranch and family, but he was not one to refuse a call. He went to Washington.

Throughout 1981, Clark served dutifully as deputy secretary of state, President Reagan's number two man at the State Department. That would not last long, as soon Reagan tapped Clark to a higher position, to be his head of the National Security Council. In that role, Clark would be the president's right hand in matters of national security and foreign policy, and especially in taking on Soviet communism.

A critical piece of the Reagan team was in place.

BILL CASEY AT THE CIA

For the immensity of the task ahead, Reagan needed just the right person running the Central Intelligence Agency (CIA). The president found that person in another Irish Catholic named Bill—William Joseph Casey.

During World War II, Casey served as chief of secret intelligence for Europe in the Office of Strategic Services (OSS), the precursor to the CIA. After the war he became a partner in a New York City law firm and then amassed a fortune by packaging legal and economic information for corporate clients. He was a successful venture capitalist as well.[16]

Casey ran unsuccessfully for Congress in 1966 but returned to public service during the Nixon administration, when he chaired the Securities and Exchange Commission and served as undersecretary of state for economic affairs.

Casey had joined the Reagan team early in the 1980 primary season, when Reagan's campaign was struggling under the direction of John Sears. Ronald and Nancy Reagan had first asked their old friend Bill Clark to replace Sears as campaign manager, but the three of them together concluded that Clark was needed more on the California Supreme Court, where his conservative vote was crucial. They eventually settled on Bill Casey. Clark reached out to Casey on behalf of the candidate. "I called him at his home on Long Island, got him out of bed," Clark later said. "And grumpy old Bill said, 'Let me think about it. I'll get back to you tomorrow.'"[17] Casey soon agreed, and as campaign manager he played a major role in getting Reagan into the White House.

Moscow's reaction to Bill Casey as CIA director must have confirmed for Reagan that he had made the right choice. The Soviet press smeared Casey as the "Queens Gangster," a "rich lawyer," and the rotten "Wall Street millionaire." He was, as one Soviet headline put it, the "Untouchable Crook."[18]

Casey joined the president and the pope in the distinction of being vilified in the Soviet media.

Casey knew what he was dealing with in Soviet communism. As CIA director, he gave a speech in which he proclaimed that Marxism-Leninism had unleashed the Four Horsemen of the Apocalypse: famine, pestilence, war, and death.[19]

That religious language hints at one of the most important but unappreciated aspects of Casey's approach: like Reagan, and like Pope John Paul II, Bill Casey felt a sense of divine calling to take down the Soviet Union.

Casey's spiritual side was not commonly known in his lifetime, and it remains underreported today. His right-hand man at the CIA, Herbert Meyer, sheds light on this element of the story.[20]

In the 1970s, Casey had read Meyer's trenchant economic analyses when the younger man was a reporter, international specialist, and associate editor for *Fortune* magazine. Meyer was shocked when Casey called him at the start of the Reagan administration. But he did not hesitate to accept a position as special assistant to the director of central intelligence and vice chair of the National Intelligence Council. Meyer became one of a select few—based on shared worldview and trust—intimately involved in the full scope of the Reagan strategy to take down the Soviet empire, particularly through economic warfare. He and Casey grew very close as well.

Meyer says that Casey had effectively retired by 1980. In his late sixties, Casey assumed he was living out his final days. But then Reagan picked him to run the campaign, and then to serve on the transition team, and finally to run the CIA. According to Meyer, Casey, a devout Catholic, believed that God had given him "one final shot" at the USSR.

Like Reagan, Casey understood the importance of Pope John Paul II to this mission. Casey would play an important role in the Reagan administration's outreach to the pope, providing the Vatican with classified intelligence briefings on Soviet movements in Poland and other Eastern Bloc countries. Dick Allen, Reagan's first national security adviser, later said, "Casey would occasionally climb into his specially equipped windowless C-141 jet, painted black. With the president's blessing, he would fly to Rome, be taken undercover to the Vatican."[21]

Herb Meyer recalls walking into Casey's office one day and noticing a huge framed color photograph on the floor, propped up against Casey's desk.

"What's that?" Meyer asked.

"Oh, it's a picture of the pope! I'm going to give it to him as a surprise birthday present when I see him next week."[22]

This "picture of the pope" was in fact a satellite image taken of a stop during John Paul II's visit to Poland in June 1979—one of the largest gatherings in history. The image captured the sea of bodies—and one small white speck that was the Holy Father himself. At the time the technology to capture such an image was not available anywhere else. Casey, as CIA director, ordered a copy of the satellite image for the pope.

With Casey at the CIA, Reagan's team was coming into place. The "DP," or "Divine Plan," as Reagan and Bill Clark would call it, was starting to unfold.

Consider a prophetic memo that Meyer would draft in November 1983. In this forecast, which was read carefully up through the chain of command, Meyer assessed that the USSR was entering a "terminal phase." He emphasized that a cornered Kremlin might lash out, seeking a destructive war, a final apocalypse. On the other hand, wrote Meyer, more optimistically, "If present trends continue, we're going to win the Cold War."[23]

This marked the first time a senior U.S. government official predicted the Soviet collapse. For that, Meyer would receive the National Intelligence Distinguished Service Medal, the intelligence community's highest honor.

Ronald Reagan and his handpicked team, including Bill Clark, Bill Casey, and Herb Meyer, were in place to figure out how to accelerate the Soviets' demise.

THE THIRD SECRET OF FÁTIMA

In November 1980, the month Ronald Reagan was elected, Pope John Paul II met with a group of Catholics in Fulda, Germany. The discussion centered on Our Lady of Fátima, according to a transcript later published in a German magazine.[24]

At the meeting the pontiff was pointedly asked: "What about the Third Secret of Fátima? Should it not have already been published?"

The pope had not seen the Third Secret at that point. It was still sealed in a vault in the Vatican. John Paul II responded: "Given the seriousness of the contents, my predecessors in the Petrine office diplomatically preferred to postpone publication so as not to encourage the world power of Communism to make certain moves." He continued: "Many wish to know simply from curiosity and a taste for the sensational, but they forget that knowledge also implies responsibility. They only seek the satisfaction of their curiosity, and that is dangerous if at the same time they are not disposed to do something, and if they are convinced that it is impossible to do anything against evil."

John Paul II then hoisted his Rosary and insisted: "Here is the remedy against this evil. Pray, pray, and ask for nothing more. Leave everything else to the Mother of God."

The pope was then asked, "What is going to happen to the Church?"

He replied with this remarkable statement: "We must prepare ourselves to suffer great trials before long, such as will demand of us a disposition to give up even life, and a total dedication to Christ and for Christ.... With your and my prayer it is possible to mitigate this tribulation, but it is no longer possible to avert it, because only thus can the Church be effectively renewed. How many times has the renewal of the Church sprung from blood! This time, too, it will not be otherwise. We must be strong and prepared, and trust in Christ and His Mother, and be very, very assiduous in praying the Rosary."

Again, what was needed was renewal.

What all this meant, if it was indeed reported accurately, remains a matter of mystery and dispute.[25] Did the trial occur and end? Did it apply to John Paul II's very person? Did it occur six months later, in May 1981 in Rome? Has it yet to come for all of us?

This much we know: with the new man in the chair of Saint Peter and a like-minded anticommunist in the Oval Office in Washington, the Cold War dynamic had changed dramatically.

Things were about to get very interesting. The world was indeed facing an era of renewal.

Part 4

GAME CHANGERS

16

MARCH 30, 1981

A BULLET FOR A PRESIDENT

March 30, 1981, started as a regular day for Ronald Reagan. In office just over two months by that point, the president was already accustomed to the routine of morning briefings followed by meetings, messages, and announcements of new appointments to the federal bureaucracy. Also on his agenda that day was a speech, listed blandly in his schedule as "Remarks at the National Conference of the Building and Construction Trades Department, AFL-CIO." It was to be a short set of remarks beginning promptly at 2 P.M. at the International Ballroom of the Washington Hilton Hotel, just a mile and a half from the White House.

But what began as routine soon became anything but.

The speech went well; the union audience, which included many Reagan Democrats, responded enthusiastically. At 2:25, the president, his Secret Service detail, and some staffers left the hotel through a side door. Trying to keep a safe distance from the reporters outside, Reagan smiled as he strolled to the presidential limousine. One unsmiling face in the crowd was that of an unstable individual named John Hinckley.

Hinckley was carrying a gun. He was not a trained assassin hired by a Bulgarian spy ring or the Kremlin or anyone else. He was an addled young man with a singular personal goal: to gain the attention of a young actress named Jodie Foster, his all-consuming obsession.

A reporter shouted a question as Reagan headed toward the car door. The president raised his left arm to deflect the question. Then he heard what sounded like firecrackers, followed by screaming and bodies scrambling, ducking, running, falling. His press secretary, James Brady, suddenly was face down on the pavement, bleeding from his skull.

Secret Service agent Jerry Parr thrust Reagan into the backseat of the limo and landed atop the seventy-year-old president's sturdy frame as he yelled directions to the driver to escape the scene. "Jerry, get off," pleaded Reagan. "I think you've broken one of my ribs."

But the pain near Reagan's chest was not from anything Parr had done. It emanated from the bullet Hinckley had fired into him. Parr soon figured as much. He noticed frothy blood bubbles coming from the president's lip. This was a bad sign, the experienced Parr understood, and he ordered the driver to head straight to a hospital. In mere minutes, they reached George Washington University Hospital.

Parr's snap call might have saved Reagan's life. The president was losing a lot of blood under his coat.

Another blessing: the hospital just happened to be holding its monthly meeting of department heads when Reagan's limousine arrived, which meant that George Washington's best and brightest were on hand to treat the president. The hospital's chief thoracic surgeon and chief brain surgeon were both present and rushed to the president's side. Reagan would joke to the superb surgical team, "I hope you're Republicans." The lead surgeon replied, "Today, Mr. President, we're *all* Republicans."[1]

Though it was typical of Reagan to react with humor, he was scared. "My fear was growing," he later wrote in his diary, "because no matter how hard I tried to breathe, it seemed I was getting less & less air."[2]

Reagan also prayed, looking upward to rely on his heavenly father, just as Nelle had always told him to do. He said later:

> I focused on that tiled ceiling and prayed. But I realized I couldn't ask for God's help while at the same time I felt hatred for the mixed up young man who had shot me. Isn't that the meaning of the lost sheep? We are all God's children and therefore equally beloved by

him. I began to pray for his soul and that he would find his way back into the fold.[3]

While Reagan prayed for this one "lost sheep," the president himself needed all the prayer he could get. Once he was spread out on the table, the surgeons could discern the damage Hinckley had done. The "mixed up" young man had used a fairly mild handgun, a .22, which explains the firecracker-like sounds, but he had employed a destructive bullet called the .22 Devastator, manufactured to explode on impact. One bullet had ricocheted off the armored car and sliced into Reagan's body through his left armpit. The injury was so tiny that the surgeon was able to find it only by examining the blood trail on Reagan's clothing. The president would later recall that the feeling in his upper back was "unbelievably painful." With typical Reagan wit, he quipped, "Getting shot hurts."[4]

The surgical team eventually found the bullet in Reagan's lung, mere centimeters from his heart and close to rupturing a valve. Despite reports in the news media that he was not in danger or (as some reported) had not even been hit, Ronald Reagan came perilously close to joining his late mother and father. Only the quick work of the George Washington medical team, in finding and stitching the wound and giving the president a lot of blood, saved Reagan from bleeding to death.

"SHE WOULD HAVE LAID HER LIFE DOWN"

As Reagan slipped into anesthesia, Nancy Reagan was in agony.

Few were close enough to the first lady after the shooting to understand her mind-set, and fewer still talked about what they witnessed. But a quarter century later, the Reverend Louis H. Evans, the longtime pastor of the National Presbyterian Church, which the Reagans had joined when they got to Washington, called me to share what he had witnessed from Nancy Reagan after her husband was shot. Evans had kept the story pretty much to himself for twenty-five years, but when he called me, he wanted to share his account for the historical record. I sensed that Evans felt that he did not have long to live. (He died two years after our last conversation, in 2008.)[5]

Evans happened to be making his regular pastoral hospital calls when he heard about Reagan's shooting on the radio. He headed straight to George Washington University Hospital and scrambled all over the building in search of the president. When he finally got close, he was intercepted by a frazzled, edgy Secret Service. He showed his card but it did not matter.

Just then, Evans was taken aback by a profound thought, which he felt that God had placed on him. The reverend could distinctly hear these words: "Mr. President, God has a plan for your life. And you're going to be healed." At that time, Evans learned only later, Reagan was being operated on by a team of surgeons.

The day after the shooting, Nancy was in need of spiritual counseling. She asked Evans to help her find the Reverend Donn Moomaw, the Reagans' pastor at the Bel Air Presbyterian Church in California (coincidentally, a church Evans had helped organize in the 1950s). The Reagans were very close to Moomaw.

Evans tracked down the California pastor at a conference, and Moomaw hopped on a plane to Washington. Evans picked him up at the airport and brought him to the White House, where Mrs. Reagan greeted them in a room that included a small group of friends: Frank Sinatra and his wife, the Reverend Billy Graham, and a Los Angeles businessman whose name Evans could not recall.[6]

Nancy's words shocked her friends. "I'm really struggling with a feeling of failed responsibility," she confided. "I usually stand at Ronnie's left side. And that's where he took the bullet." A worried Nancy had nagging regrets: if only she had been next to her husband as he strolled to that limousine, positioned between him and John Hinckley's pistol, she could have taken the bullet for her beloved Ronnie.

It was always understood that Nancy was Ronald Reagan's protector, the one who played bad cop and watched his back as he trusted everyone, regardless of their loyalty. Yet Louis Evans's account shows just how deep her commitment ran. She was utterly, completely devoted to her husband, to the extent that she regretted not being there to take a bullet for him that terrible day in March 1981.

The intense spousal respect was mutual, as Reagan demonstrated in his first diary entry after the shooting. "I opened my eyes once to find Nancy there," Reagan wrote of his unnerving moment on the hospital table. "I pray I'll never face a day when she isn't there. Of all the ways God has blessed me giving her to me is the greatest and beyond anything I can ever hope to deserve."[7]

When I shared Evans's account with Bill Clark, the longtime friend and associate of the Reagans, he was not at all surprised. Clark told me: "I agree with the Scripture that she would have laid her life down for her friend—for her best friend. She would have done that for him."

Clark was with Mrs. Reagan in the hospital the day after the shooting, just as they had been together so often in Sacramento.[8] At one point it was just Nancy and Clark with the head surgeon at George Washington University Hospital, who briefed them on Reagan's condition. Clark learned that Reagan's wound was "far graver" than the media had reported. But the doctor did tell him that there was hope, because the surgeons could see that Reagan's lung was a pinkish color, which meant it had not been damaged by smoking and thus could heal quickly.

Reagan's daughter, Patti Davis, visited her father after the shooting. Patti often publicly expressed embarrassment of her parents and caused them notable distress in the 1980s. Many people suspected that she was (like her brother Ron) an atheist or at least an agnostic. But years later she shared this account of her first visit to the hospital:

> He actually didn't look frail; he looked almost ethereal. There was a light in his eyes that made me think, then and still, that he saw something—visited with God, listened to the counsel of an angel—something. My mother has since told me that he woke up at one point after the doctors had operated on him, unable to talk because there was a tube down his throat. He saw figures in white standing around him and scrawled on a piece of paper, "I'm alive, aren't I?" My mother still has the note.
>
> This story has become one that gathers more truth as it is shared with more listeners. When my mother first told it to me, we discussed how logical it is to assume that the figures in white, standing around my father, were the doctors and nurses who were tending to him. But maybe not, we said; maybe he did see angels. We left it with a question mark. Then I repeated it to a friend—a nurse—who pointed out to me that no one in a recovery room or in intensive care is in white; they're all in green scrubs. I phoned my mother and told her, and her reaction was "I didn't even think of that, there was so much that day—but you're right." I give endless prayers of thanks to whatever angels circled my father, because a Devastator bullet, which miraculously had not exploded, was finally found a quarter inch from his heart. Without divine intervention, I don't know if he would have survived.[9]

This was not the take of a hard atheist. Patti was looking upward for an explanation.

"WHATEVER TIME I HAVE LEFT IS FOR HIM"

The Reagans' daughter was not the only who looked heavenward for answers.

Ronald Reagan would share with many intimates his certain sense that God had intervened as part of the Divine Plan. When he came to in the hospital, he told Bill Clark that he believed the Lord had spared his life for a special purpose. He later said the same to his children Maureen and Michael, from his marriage to Jane Wyman. Both were Christians, and Reagan knew they were more devout than his two children to Nancy, Patti and Ron. White House aides including Kenneth Duberstein and Lyn Nofziger spoke of the president's sense of having been saved for a specific purpose.[10]

When Reagan got back home to 1600 Pennsylvania Avenue, he recorded the sentiment in his diary. "I know it's going to be a long recovery," he wrote. "Whatever happens now I owe my life to God and will try to serve him in every way I can."[11]

He would even mention this conviction publicly. At the National Prayer Breakfast less than a year after his shooting, he would say, "I've always believed that we were, each of us, put here for a reason, that there is a plan, somehow a divine plan for all of us."[12]

What was the special purpose for which he believed his life had been spared? In the days after the shooting, Reagan's thoughts turned to the Cold War. Sitting in the White House solarium in robe and pajamas one morning, still awaiting the doctors' go-ahead to resume a full work schedule, he began to wonder how he might jump-start the negotiating process with Moscow. He later recounted the scene in his memoir: "Perhaps having come so close to death made me feel I should do whatever I could in the years God had given me to reduce the threat of nuclear war; perhaps there was a reason I had been spared."[13]

He wrote a four-and-a-half page letter to Soviet general secretary Leonid Brezhnev. As was the custom, it went to the National Security Council staff and to the State Department for review. The letter came back to Reagan completely rewritten. "Well, maybe they know more about this than I do," Reagan said passively as he looked at the new version. Then his longtime aide Michael Deaver reminded Reagan that the American people had elected him, not some anonymous State bureaucrat, to be president. Reagan thanked Deaver for that needed encouragement. "You know, since I've been shot," he told Deaver, "I think I'm going to rely more on my own instincts than other people's. There's a reason I've been saved."[14] Reagan mailed his original letter.[15] The Cold War would never be the same.

On Good Friday, April 17, Deaver could sense that his boss and old friend was feeling the need for some spiritual counseling. He called the diocese of New York. In short order, the president was sitting in his office with New York's Terence Cardinal Cooke. "The hand of God was upon you," Cooke told Reagan. Reagan agreed: "I know." He then told Cooke, "I have decided that whatever time I have left is for Him."[16]

This would be just one of several poignant Reagan encounters with Cardinal Cooke.

Reagan also spoke with the Reverend Billy Graham, with whom he was close. Graham called the president and told him that he knew the family of the shooter. Reagan recorded in his diary, "They are decent, deeply religious people who are completely crushed by the 'sickness' of their son."[17]

Two days later, Ronald and Nancy Reagan celebrated Easter at the White House with their pastor, Louis Evans, and his wife, Colleen. Reagan asked his pastor to please bring Holy Communion to him and Nancy. Evans usually did not serve Communion via house calls, but this time he made an exception. He served Communion to the Reagans in the Yellow Room of the White House. Evans did not speak of the moment with any reporters or historians until he told me more than two decades later.[18]

I spoke with Colleen Evans about that day approximately ten years after her husband had talked to me; by that point, the reverend had passed away. She remained adamant about maintaining pastoral confidentiality with members of her husband's church, even long after they had passed from this world. Nonetheless, I was able to prod her to say a little about Easter Sunday 1981.[19] "He wanted Communion," Mrs. Evans told me. "He really wanted it." When I pressed her as to why, she was unsure and said only: "Well, it was after the assassination attempt, and he hadn't been to church since, and I think he was just really longing for it." She recalled that she and her husband "came in and went out the back way" of the White House to avoid being seen by reporters. She remembers the moment as a sacred one. "It was just very holy. And I was honored to be able to do that."

We know that Ronald Reagan was honored by the gesture. That evening he recorded in his diary that it was a "beautiful Easter." "Rev. Louis Evans & his wife called and brought us communion," he wrote. "They made it a most meaningful day."[20]

After the private Communion service, Evans told Reagan about the "mental image" that he had at George Washington University Hospital that traumatic day, when he had heard the words "Mr. President, God has a plan for your life. And you're going to be healed"—just as Reagan was being operated on. Reagan thanked Evans and said matter-of-factly that he felt the same way. "God has a plan for my life and I want to find it," he told Evans.

Reagan was ready for the Divine Plan to be carried out. As biographer Edmund Morris put it, for Reagan that meant "a coming to terms with Evil. Not the accidental evil…of John Hinckley's assault, but that institutional murder of all liberties known as Soviet Communism."[21]

WHAT "SICK SOCIETY"?

On the night of April 28, 1981, less than a month after his shooting, Reagan addressed a Joint Session of Congress and a huge national television audience.

This speech was a moment of triumph. Reagan was feted like a conquering hero by the bipartisan crowd, receiving a long standing ovation when he entered the House Chamber. He began by conveying his profound gratitude for his reception—"I have no words to express my appreciation for that greeting"—and for all the messages, flowers, "and, most of all,…prayers, not only for me but for those others who fell beside me." The wounded included his press secretary, James Brady, who remained in bad condition, along with police officer Thomas Delahanty and Secret Service agent Tim McCarthy.

The compassion so many had shown, and the courage those public servants had displayed in risking their own lives for his, "provided an answer to those few voices that were raised saying that what happened was evidence that ours is a sick society," Reagan said. The president elaborated on that point:

> Well, sick societies don't produce men like the two who recently returned from outer space [on the first Space Shuttle flight in history]. Sick societies don't produce young men like Secret Service agent Tim McCarthy, who placed his body between mine and the man with the gun simply because he felt that's what his duty called for him to do. Sick societies don't produce dedicated police officers like Tom Delahanty or able and devoted public servants like

Jim Brady. Sick societies don't make people like us so proud to be Americans and so very proud of our fellow citizens.[22]

Those words were hauntingly similar to comments that Governor Ronald Reagan had made thirteen years earlier, in June 1968, after the shooting of Robert F. Kennedy. Reagan spoke at the Indiana State Fairgrounds, and his remarks were published only locally. To my knowledge, other Reagan biographers have not written of the speech. I found his comments only by securing original clippings from the hard-copy archives of Indianapolis newspapers.

Addressing the crowd in Indianapolis, Reagan objected to those who tried to pin the Kennedy assassination not on the extremist ideology of the shooter but on America and its "violence" and "sickness." "I for one find it unacceptable and worse than no answer at all to be told that all of us collectively are to blame and that ours is a sick society," Reagan told the audience.[23]

No, Reagan looked elsewhere, to another society that was genuinely sick: communist society.

Back in 1968, Reagan had recognized a truth that so many refused to acknowledge: Bobby Kennedy's assassin, Sirhan Sirhan, was an anti-American Palestinian Arab who professed a passion for communism. "Long live communism!" Sirhan had repeatedly penned in his diary. "I firmly support the communist cause and its people—whether Russian, Chinese, Albanian, Hungarian or whoever."[24]

The motivations of Reagan's shooter were different, and yet the instinct to lay the blame on America's "sickness" was the same. Ronald Reagan wouldn't allow his countrymen to indulge that instinct. He knew where the true sickness lay, and he wouldn't hesitate to call it out.

"INTO THE HANDS OF AMERICA" ONCE AGAIN

As he recovered from his shooting in the spring of 1981, President Reagan spoke candidly of the Soviet threat and of America's God-given duty to respond. As he did, he again cited Pope Pius XII's remark after World War II: "Into the hands of America, God has placed an afflicted mankind." Reagan invoked the Pius quotation in major addresses in April and May, including a commencement address at the U.S. Military Academy.[25]

The Soviets understood exactly what Reagan meant by this rallying cry. They knew he was convinced that God had chosen the United

States as a beacon for all mankind and as a hope to counter atheistic communism. And that made them angry. In one of the Kremlin's many government-controlled "news" programs, *International Observers Roundtable*, commentator Viktor Nikolayevich Levin bristled at the American president's use of the late pontiff's words, which he said were "very close to Reagan's heart." "It is precisely this [Pius XII] postulate," Levin said of the Protestant president, "that he is attempting to pursue in the realm of practical politics. This is the origin of the problems that we are encountering."[26]

It is hard to imagine which man the Kremlin's aged Stalinists detested more, the late Pope Pius or the new president. The Soviets had smeared Pius's reputation. To have the Protestant president of the United States resurrecting Pius in service of remonstrating against the Soviets must have made Moscow seethe.

Ronald Reagan had survived an assassination attempt, and now he was confronting Soviet communism more aggressively, more pointedly, more urgently than ever. That was bad news for communism.

17

MARCH 29–30, 1981

THE SOVIET INVASION THAT WASN'T

Field Station Berlin was a vital theater in the Cold War. Built on a transported pile of rubble generated by Allied bombing in World War II, this West Berlin facility became the center of U.S. data and information gathering on the Soviet Union's strategic command and control communication system. The U.S. military and intelligence personnel stationed there were the "eyes and ears" of the West. The East German Stasi operated all around the Americans, as did KGB agents and terrorists of all sorts.

On Sunday, March 29, 1981, the situation at Field Station Berlin was particularly tense. The station's intelligence technicians heard an alarming communication between two high-ranking Soviet military officers. The technicians already knew that the Soviets had as many as eighteen divisions arrayed along the Polish border—more troop strength than the entire U.S. Army boasts today. But they did not know the force status of those troops. Now, based on this intercepted communication, the status was clear: the Soviet divisions were going to the "highest state of combat readiness."

Moscow appeared ready to invade Poland. The long-feared crackdown on the Solidarity movement and Pope John Paul II's countrymen seemed at hand.

Field Station Berlin monitored the Soviet chatter closely that day and into the next. The Soviet channels were buzzing with information. And then, almost in an instant... nothing. The chatter stopped.

As we now know, Soviet military forces did not roll into Poland. So what caused the Soviets to pull back so suddenly, just a day after intelligence revealed that their forces along the Polish border were readying for combat?

Something rather surprising may have played a key role: the shooting of Ronald Reagan.

This is a great untold story of the Cold War: when the Cold War nearly became a hot war—and how, quite inadvertently, an assassination attempt on the U.S. president may have kept it from happening.

The story has never been reported until now. The account that follows is based on the eyewitness testimony of a U.S. Army intelligence technician who was working in Field Station Berlin during those tense days at the end of March 1981. This witness, Jack (not his real name), encountered questions and doubts almost as soon as he began passing this provocative intelligence to his superiors. His life would be changed forever.

I have considered Jack's story extensively. I first learned of his account from his closest friend, a good friend of mine and trusted colleague who remains in regular contact with Jack. I have checked Jack's claims and time line against the historical record and can find nothing to contradict his reports. His account is accurate, I believe. With this reporting here, more than three decades later, perhaps Jack will receive a measure of vindication.

"YOU'VE GOT TO HEAR THIS!"

Jack, whose identity I will keep secret, hadn't initially sought out a career in intelligence. Around 1970 he had enlisted in the Army rather than wait to get drafted into Vietnam. He went through a series of standard tests given by the U.S. military, and the Army determined that he had innate language skills it could use. He chose to study Russian and was sent to the intensive Monterey language school in California. He graduated near the top of his class. Someone along the way discovered that Jack also had a natural gift for code breaking. In the words of our mutual friend: "I have never come across anyone who can focus and concentrate like he can. It's almost scary." Jack was thus trained in the art of cryptology.

In the late 1970s, Jack received an important field assignment in West Germany. He went in with a special-ops team to eavesdrop on Soviet communications. He was second in command of his unit of about eight men. This, and other missions, must have impressed his superiors.

In the fall of 1980, Jack was reassigned to Field Station Berlin, the top echelon of U.S. data and information gathering. There he worked less for the U.S. Army than for the CIA and the National Security Agency (NSA). His unit of technicians was responsible for gathering the "raw data" from all the U.S. electronic monitoring equipment and then passing along what seemed most important to the CIA and NSA analysts who operated in the field station. Jack's team recorded live conversations as well as coded electronic communications in real time, every day of the year.

The technicians discarded more than 95 percent of what they gathered, rejecting most of it as common banter of no strategic use. One of Jack's duties was to determine which data to dump and which to retain for further analysis; he also determined where the retained data should be sent. He saw the data before anyone else, before it was compartmentalized by analytical groups. In other words, he had a holistic view of everything.

On March 29, 1981, one of Jack's technicians came running into his office and said, "You've got to hear this!"

The technician reported a verbal stream of communication between two very high-ranking Soviet officers, one inside the Kremlin and the other positioned on the Polish border. Jack immediately sat down and began transcribing the conversation. What he transcribed clearly revealed an increased threat from the Soviet divisions deployed along the Polish border. Those divisions were going to the "highest state of combat readiness," according to the communication that Jack received.

Field Station Berlin already knew that these divisions had been fully fueled, with refueling on standby in the nearby pipeline. The technicians also knew that the troops had been issued full arms and ammunition, with resupply in the wings. They were even aware that the Red Army had quietly established "forward military communication posts" at key points throughout Poland.

Jack immediately passed along the new intelligence to the appropriate NSA analyst. This was absolutely crucial knowledge to send up through the chain of command. He says that NSA analysts at the field station assured him that NSA headquarters received his translation. Jack later learned that the information may have reached CIA director Bill Casey himself. In 1982 Casey would visit Field Station Berlin (whether the visit was unscheduled or routine, I cannot confirm) and specifically asked to see Jack.[1] Casey thanked Jack for his service and contributions at the station.

But Jack's information was not necessarily welcome at Field Station Berlin. Fear permeated the facility. Every officer there knew that in the event of an East-West eruption, Field Station Berlin would almost certainly be a target. Sitting in West Berlin, the field station personnel were 130 miles behind enemy lines—and they knew they probably would not survive if the Cold War turned hot. Early in the Korean War, the North Koreans had wiped out all their brothers in the information-gathering set at the Korean installation.

So information like that in Jack's possession was potentially very dangerous: what if, once passed on, the intelligence triggered a response from the West (perhaps inappropriately) that actually precipitated a Soviet invasion of Poland?

Jack says that friction developed between him and his superior. The Soviet chatter picked up into March 30, but according to Jack, the officer did not want any more information regarding Soviet troops along the Polish border.

Jack was sure that an invasion of Poland was imminent. He says that by March 30 the fear factor at Field Station Berlin was "off the chart." All nonessential personnel were sent away from the facility.

In retrospect, Jack lays out five key factors that could have enabled a Soviet invasion at that point:

First was the case of John Anthony Walker, the spy who worked against the United States and for Moscow for at least a decade. According to Jack, Walker had passed on the codes for the entire U.S. strategic command and control communications during the mid- to late 1970s, meaning that the Soviet military could read all encrypted electronic mail traffic from the American side.

Second, Jack notes that by the late 1970s, during the Carter years, some Soviet generals believed that a first strike against the West was possible and that a NATO response could be more than contained.

Third, the Red Army was leading huge military exercises, known as "Soyuz '81," in and around the Polish borders in this critical late March 1981 time frame. Meanwhile, the Soviets had maneuvered their nuclear submarine fleet to launch positions closer to U.S. shores than usual. (The transcript of the discussion in the White House Situation Room on March 30, 1981, confirms Jack's claim; Bill Clark confirmed it to me as well.)[2] This was a time of stepped-up military activity.

Fourth, according to Jack, the Soviets had withdrawn key Polish military and political personnel from the country for "meetings" inside the Soviet Union during the week prior to March 30.

Finally, Jack notes that the Soviets did not terminate the Soyuz '81 military exercises on any predetermined date but, rather, quietly extended them with no termination date announced. He points out (correctly) that the exercises were not terminated until about April 7.

This was, in sum, a bubbling hot situation. It was ready to boil over on March 30, 1981.

"I AM IN CONTROL HERE"

Here is where the situation gets even more fascinating.

According to Jack, the Soviets were still readying to strike against Solidarity on March 30. The incoming chatter had been "buzzing" all through that day, he says, and then that night it "collapsed," it "practically went dead." He cannot say when, exactly, Moscow made the no-go decision, but he knows the chatter virtually went silent that night.

According to Jack, what called off the Soviet dogs on March 30 was not prudence, charity, or some other Christian virtue permeating the Kremlin. What called them off was the shooting of Ronald Reagan. He observed that the pronounced "drawdown" in Soviet communications on Poland began just after the news of the assassination attempt broke.

Why? Jack suggests that the shooting set in motion a chain of events that gave the Soviets second thoughts about an invasion. Immediately after the assassination attempt, when the shooter's motives were unknown and no one knew whether he was part of a larger plot, top U.S. officials placed the Strategic Air Command on alert and raised defense readiness.[3] According to Jack, seeing the U.S. military go on alert "unhinged" the Soviets and changed Moscow's calculus.

But what really convinced the Soviets to call off the invasion, Jack says, was a statement that the Soviets took to be a display of military strength and resolve—but that, ironically, is ridiculed in the United States to this day. The statement was the famous one by Secretary of State Alexander Haig, who in the aftermath of the shooting told the White House press, "I am in control here."

Haig was well known to the Soviets. A retired four-star general in the U.S. Army, Haig had served as supreme allied commander of NATO forces in Europe as recently as two years earlier. To Moscow, Haig's televised proclamation was a show of American strength.

To repeat: the shooting of Reagan, by total happenstance, halted Moscow's devious plans, according to Jack.

I first heard Jack's claim thirty years after the events of March 1981. There are those who would doubt his story, and even his credibility. From his position at Field Station Berlin, Jack would see another promotion or two, with even more responsibility, as he cracked Soviet codes and was involved in major intercepts. But the stress kept building, and, as in late March 1981, he sometimes faced demands to keep quiet about information he was receiving. His health deteriorated, physically and mentally. In December 1982 he resigned from his command, and a few months later he received his honorable discharge. Jack truly was never the same from what he endured during that intense period, and especially during the scare of late March 1981.

But here is the remarkable thing about Jack's account: my independent research suggests that it is accurate. Here is what I can confirm.

THE REAGAN SHOOTING

President Reagan was shot at 2:25 P.M. ET, and the twenty-five-year-old John Hinckley was immediately apprehended.[4] White House aide David Gergen made the first statement to reporters at 3:37 P.M. The statement was very brief, slightly more than two hundred words. Gergen maintained that Reagan's "condition is stable," which was a highly generous assessment, and that "a decision is now being made whether or not to operate to remove the bullet."[5]

Gergen told the press: "The White House and the vice president are in communication, and the vice president is now en route to Washington. He is expected to arrive in the city this afternoon." The spokesman added, "I would also like to inform you that in the building [the White House] as of the moment are the secretary of state, the secretary of the treasury, the secretary of defense, and the attorney general, as well as other assistants to the president."

Vice President George H.W. Bush was on a plane over Texas and didn't have secure voice communication available to him. That being the case, who was in control at 1600 Pennsylvania Avenue? "I cannot answer that question at this time," Deputy Press Secretary Larry Speakes (filling in for the critically wounded James Brady) told the assembled media.[6] Secretary of State Haig was alarmed when he heard Speakes's response, so he rushed up to the Briefing Room to address the press himself.

Haig's formal statement was even briefer than Gergen's—fewer than a hundred words. At 4:14 P.M. the secretary of state took the podium and said: "Ladies and gentlemen, I just wanted to touch upon a few matters associated with today's tragedy. First, as you know, we are in close touch with the vice president, who is returning to Washington. We have in the Situation Room all of the officials of the cabinet who should be here and ready at this time. We have informed our friends abroad of the situation, the president's condition as we know it—stable, now undergoing surgery. And there are absolutely no alert measures that are necessary at this time or contemplated."[7]

That last statement was mistaken. In the Situation Room, Secretary of Defense Caspar Weinberger had discussed with Haig and other top officials how the military had already raised the alert condition.[8] Otherwise, though, Haig's comments were accurate and reassuring.

In any case, they weren't the comments that drew criticism and mockery. When a reporter asked whether crisis management would go in effect when Vice President Bush arrived, Haig responded, "Crisis management *is* in effect." Another reporter asked, "Who is making decisions for the government right now?" The secretary of state replied: "Constitutionally, gentlemen, you have the president, the vice president, and the secretary of state in that order, and should the president decide he wants to transfer the helm to the vice president, he will do so. He has not done that. As of now, I am in control here, in the White House, pending return of the vice president and in close touch with him. If something came up, I would check with him, of course."

Haig's "I am in control here" has gone down as a monumental gaffe. His critics jumped on him for seeming to misunderstand the line of presidential succession as laid out in the Constitution's Twenty-Fifth Amendment (in which the Speaker of the House and the president pro tempore of the Senate both come before the secretary of state). Even National Security Adviser Dick Allen, who was standing next to Haig while the secretary of state addressed the media, later said, "I was astounded that he would say something so eminently stupid."[9]

Haig always maintained that he was not referring to the line of succession but rather was responding to the specific question he was asked: who was making decisions for the government at that moment? And it is true that, with Vice President Bush in the air and unable to communicate, Haig was the senior executive branch official in the White House.[10]

The media blasted Haig as an egotist, a power-hungry former general eager to seize power. A witness to the events who disputed that account was Bill Clark—the last person in the world who would think of undermining Reagan. "He was not trying to take over the government," Clark said. "That is inaccurate."[11]

At the time, Clark was not yet Reagan's right-hand man at the National Security Council (NSC). He was the president's number two at the State Department—deputy secretary of state to Al Haig. And so he worked this crisis closely with Haig. His goal, like Haig's, was to show strength and command to America's friends and enemies abroad.

Clark and Haig were both at the State Department when word arrived that the president had been shot. They quickly discussed next steps. "I'll go over there [to the White House]," Haig told Clark, "and you man the ship here. Bill, stand by. We'll have to get out a proper statement for the benefit of our allies and 'non-friends,' assuring them that all is well." At the White House, Haig remained in direct communication with Clark by secure phone. Clark later disputed the caricature of an Al Haig gleefully shouting, "I am in control here!" He said that Haig was not trying to take over the presidency but was merely seeking to demonstrate order and stability. "That place was in great confusion and the vice president was in the air," Clark told me. "Al reminded people that as the primary cabinet member he was going to take charge of the meeting, not of the White House. So some of his detractors I think overplayed the meaning of what he said.... What he said was correct...that he's the primary cabinet member. So he did take charge in attempting to get a statement written and in trying to calm the others who were present."[12]

Clark pointed out Haig's experience as White House chief of staff in the last year and a half of the Nixon presidency. "There had been low periods for Nixon during which Haig effectively served as president," said Clark. Thus, on March 30, 1981, Haig knew what to do better than anyone else in that room.

In any case, those who ridicule Haig's comments have no idea that the secretary of state may have kept the Red Army from invading Poland.[13]

In August 2011 I told Bill Clark about Jack's story, and about Jack's theory that Haig's show of stability had had a stabilizing effect. Clark was intrigued but had no direct knowledge that a Soviet invasion was in the works that day. He acknowledged, though, that accounts of an imminent invasion had been "running around for some time, bits and pieces."

Further, he said: "We were concerned about what the Soviets would do. This was only three months into the presidency and we feared the Soviets would be testing the new president and ourselves—as they had [John F.] Kennedy. We had gotten word that they might try to close the Berlin corridor. I had learned/heard that there was Soviet troop movement that was out of the ordinary. We were on careful watch. It was tense at several junctures. But that was pretty much the extent of it. I don't know of more." I asked Clark whether a Soviet invasion of Poland, or even a threatened invasion, might have been the "test" they feared. He replied: "Perhaps, but I don't know. No hard evidence for you."[14]

Agreeing that Jack's scenario seemed plausible, Clark and I both pursued the topic with a myriad of former intelligence sources, ex-NSC staff, some Polish sources, and Vatican sources. We found no smoking gun.

WERE THE SOVIETS PREPARING TO INVADE POLAND?

Jack's scenario is plausible for another reason: we know from various insider accounts, intelligence sources, historical investigations, and declassified documents that over a roughly one-year period from late 1980 through late 1981, the Soviet leadership carefully considered an invasion of Poland, aided by Eastern Bloc allies like Czechoslovakia and East Germany. None of the evidence I found explicitly connects a Soviet cooldown in Poland on March 30, 1981, to the shooting of Ronald Reagan. All of it, however, shows a steady confrontation in the months prior, and most underscores a major Moscow escalation precisely that week, ending in a cooldown.

Mark Kramer, director of the Harvard Project on Cold War Studies, has written of the intense period from the fall of 1980 through September 1981 in a number of papers and bulletins. In the *Cold War International History Project Bulletin*, Kramer wrote of a plan that called for a contingent of fourteen to fifteen Soviet Bloc divisions to help Polish authorities enact martial law.[15]

Polish state television as early as November 1980 broadcast ominous film of joint Polish-Soviet military maneuvers, using what was probably old footage (the trees in the video had leaves, suggesting summertime). The point of these communist broadcasts was to threaten Soviet military intervention against Solidarity.[16] Over the next four weeks, communist newspapers in East Berlin and Prague attacked Polish leader Stanisław

Kania (who succeeded Edward Gierek in September) for being weak. The papers openly compared the situation to that of Prague in the spring of 1968, an analogy that suggested a coming Moscow military intervention.

Arthur Rachwald, in his 1990 study on Poland, Solidarity, and the superpowers, says that November–December 1980, between the U.S. presidential election and Ronald Reagan's inauguration, was the "most ominous" and "most precarious" period because of the "relative vacuum of power in the West." It was a time in which "a military solution of the Polish crisis loomed" and a "gloomy" atmosphere hung over Poland "in expectation of an armed intervention by Soviet, East German, and Czechoslovak units." By early December, reports Rachwald, Moscow had ordered an "unprecedented buildup of its forces along the Polish border," and East Germany had canceled all military leave by current personnel and called up all reserve forces.[17]

Rachwald shows that the Soviets had a massive invasion in mind. "The plan to invade Poland," he writes, "assumed that there would be a full-scale war," one involving upward of a half million troops on each side. Soviet paratroops would be dropped on most of Poland's sixty airfields to secure landing sites for transport planes carrying soldiers, tanks, and armored carriers. A Soviet naval attack would be orchestrated against Polish ports, particularly Gdańsk, the birthplace of Solidarity. Moscow expected Poles to resist, including much of the Polish military. This would be a bloody battle, sure to be fiercer and longer than the Soviet interventions in Czechoslovakia in 1968 and Hungary in 1956.[18]

Among the many documents KGB archivist Vasili Mitrokhin revealed to the West in the 1990s is one reporting on "an extraordinary meeting of Warsaw Pact leaders" in Moscow on December 5, 1980, a month after Jimmy Carter's defeat in the U.S. presidential election. Gathering "to discuss the Polish crisis," the Communist Party leaders "castigate[d] the weakness" of Kania's policies and demanded an "immediate crackdown" on both Solidarity and the Roman Catholic Church. According to the Mitrokhin Archive, Kania's fellow party leaders told the new Polish ruler that if he did not get a grip on things right away, "Warsaw Pact forces would intervene." They emphasized that eighteen divisions were already on Poland's borders and showed Kania plans to occupy Polish cities and towns.

Mitrokhin also reported that Leonid Brezhnev met privately with Kania after the meeting. The Polish leader told the Soviet general secretary that a military intervention would be a disaster not only for Poland but also for the Soviet Union. This was indisputably true. "OK, we don't march into Poland now," Chairman Brezhnev replied, "but if the situation gets any worse we will come."[19]

Brezhnev's precise views have been a matter of debate. Polish historian Tomasz Pompowski told me that Brezhnev "wanted to invade Poland."[20] Other Polish scholars and friends I consulted told me the same, and that Brezhnev merely delayed the decision to invade. On the other hand, some scholars and insiders maintain that the Moscow leadership (at least some of it) never intended to invade precisely because an invasion would have been so calamitous. Vasili Mitrokhin and his coauthor, Christopher Andrew, subscribe to this view, arguing that Brezhnev's threat to Kania was "probably a bluff."[21]

Eduard Shevardnadze, who served as foreign minister under Mikhail Gorbachev, indicated that the Soviet leadership was split over whether to invade Poland. In his 1991 book, *The Future Belongs to Freedom*, Shevardnadze wrote that some Soviet officials insisted on an invasion while others, like Mikhail Suslov, secretary of the Central Committee, asserted, "There is no way that we are going to use force in Poland."[22]

Professor Marek Jan Chodakiewicz, a Polish-born American who holds the Kosciuszko Chair in Polish Studies at the Institute of World Politics, suggests that Moscow was committed to invading in the fall of 1980 but later changed its mind. Pointing to the latest information available from Soviet sources and archives, plus declassified documents at the Hoover Institution, Chodakiewicz argues that the Red Army "was poised to invade Poland" in September 1980. But he says that the Kremlin slowly changed course, as it recognized "an increasingly unfavorable international situation" and also that the Soviet military was caught up in the quagmire of Afghanistan. According to Chodakiewicz, by March 1981, the communist threats of a Soviet invasion had become bluffs—"just propaganda."[23]

It is also possible, however, that the Kremlin understood the costs and risks associated with invading Poland but remained ready to act if the situation reached a certain intolerable point. The extent of the Soviets' concerns about the destabilizing effects of Solidarity, especially after the Polish pope's visit to his homeland, cannot be underestimated.

Within the Carter administration, there was considerable unease over the prospect of a Soviet invasion during this period. And why not? President Carter had been stunned when Brezhnev, whom he had literally kissed at the Geneva Summit a few months earlier, sent the Red Army into Afghanistan during Christmas 1979. If the Soviets would invade Afghanistan, then why not Poland, a Warsaw Pact member and a nation of far higher importance, especially given Moscow's grave concerns about Solidarity?[24]

The Carter White House knew that Soviet troops were amassing along the border. The United States had a mole in Poland named Colonel Ryszard Kukliński, a high-ranking figure in the Polish Defense Ministry who had become a spy for the Americans because he detested what Moscow had done to his homeland. As a liaison between Warsaw and Moscow, Kukliński was responsible for devising preparations for a "hot war" with the West. These plans included an aggressive roundup of Solidarity leaders, who would be seized, given show trials, and executed. In a report he secretly delivered to the United States in December 1980, he outlined the Kremlin's plans to cross the border into Poland with eighteen Soviet, East German, and Czech divisions.[25] In a later report, dated September 15, 1981, he warned that "the first steps have already been taken" toward martial law. The Polish communist regime would impose martial law on December 13.[26]

Jerrold Schecter, a member of Carter's NSC who had previously served as *Time* magazine's Moscow bureau chief, later reported that the Carter administration knew "the Soviet Union was preparing to invade Poland in 1980, under the guise of a 'peaceful exercise,' and crush the Solidarity workers' movement."[27] As was typical under President Carter's leadership, the U.S. government responded to Moscow with... a strongly worded statement. Washington warned Moscow that military intervention in Poland would seriously jeopardize the U.S.-USSR relationship.

The Carter administration's point man in responding to Colonel Kukliński's warnings was Zbigniew Brzezinski, the ethnic Pole and solid anticommunist who ran President Carter's NSC. Brzezinski had established a good relationship with Pope John Paul II and the Vatican. Reagan's first national security adviser, Dick Allen, later commended Brzezinski for having started a "frank and useful dialogue" with the pope, and complimented him as an "extraordinary man—a determined patriot, brilliant thinker, and courageous."[28]

On December 7, 1980, Brzezinski called John Paul II to brief him on the latest learned from Kukliński and other intelligence about Soviet military activity around Poland, and to tell the pope about how the Carter administration had expressed its disapproval to Moscow. This call prompted John Paul II to make an unprecedented direct appeal to Chairman Brezhnev. On December 16, fearing that the Soviets would announce an invasion to "save Poland," the pontiff sent Brezhnev an unusually tough and personal letter. As George Weigel characterized the letter, by referring to Poland's martyrdom at the hands of Nazis in 1939, "John Paul II subtly suggested that he was prepared to use all the moral power at his command to identify Brezhnev and any new invasion of Poland with the 'fascists' who remained a principal boogeyman of the Soviet propaganda machine."

This letter, Weigel said, "undoubtedly underscored to the Soviet leadership the mortal threat posed by this Polish pope who commanded the world's attention, who was determined to support Solidarity, and who would almost certainly be in sympathy with the vigorous anticommunist stance that would be taken by the incoming Reagan administration in the United States."[29]

THEN CAME THE REAGAN ADMINISTRATION

While the Carter White House worried about the situation in Poland, President-elect Ronald Reagan was across the street, at Blair House, receiving security briefings. The threat of a Soviet invasion was a major focus for Reagan and his closest advisers. They were so concerned that after one briefing the president-elect asked about the possibility of using U.S. military force in Poland if the Soviet forces rolled in. His incoming secretary of defense, Caspar Weinberger, later discussed contingency plans for such a response against Red Army and Warsaw Pact troops.

This is stunning to consider: the threat of Moscow military action was so serious that, even before his inauguration, Ronald Reagan was forced to consider the possibility of using U.S. force in Poland—that is, to engage in a ground war with the USSR and Warsaw Pact nations.

I reported this scenario at length in my 2006 book, *The Crusader: Ronald Reagan and the Fall of Communism*.[30] Weinberger recalled the Reagan team's fears: "There was very considerable worry that the Soviets, with [their] divisions inside Poland, that had been there since the end of [World War II], and the constant military exercises and threatening moves around the borders of Poland, that they might very well decide to wander in there without any fear of adverse results or reprisals." Weinberger told me that the president-elect expressed his concern throughout the transition period. Reagan wanted no false signals given to the Kremlin that the United States would tolerate a military invasion. "The president was very firm about that," Weinberger told me.[31]

Ultimately, Reagan and Weinberger rejected the idea of using U.S. military force in Poland. They both knew that such a response would launch World War III. Also, Weinberger reminded Reagan that the United States just didn't have the military strength to repel a Soviet invasion. "Yes, I know that, Cap," Reagan replied. "But we must never again be in this position. We must never again *not* take action that we think is essential because we're not strong enough to do it." Reagan hadn't taken office yet, but a key element of his plan to counter Soviet communism was in place: "peace through strength."

Once Reagan took the oath of office, a member of the president's NSC began to study the Polish situation carefully. The brilliant Soviet scholar Richard Pipes was the NSC's new director of East European and Soviet affairs. A native of Poland who had escaped the country as a boy with his parents just as the Nazis marched in, Dr. Pipes had been Harvard's leading Sovietologist for years. He took a two-year leave from the Ivy League university to join President Reagan's national security team. From his first weeks on the job, Pipes studied pictures that the Pentagon's Defense Intelligence Agency provided him. "Every few days," Pipes told me, a military officer would deliver satellite photos showing Warsaw Pact troop movements along the Polish border. These were the Soyuz '81 military exercises Jack cites in his account. Pipes was alarmed, knowing that the communists could easily convert the exercises into an offensive. Pipes said that whereas he was once skeptical that Moscow would invade Poland, events that transpired in late March convinced him that a Soviet invasion was imminent.[32]

Pipes had shared this with me before, during my research for *The Crusader*.[33] Thus, in August 2011, he was one of the first people I contacted when I heard Jack's account, which was consistent with Pipes's time line. Pipes reaffirmed his fears of an invasion at the time—"an invasion did seem imminent," he told me again—but conceded no knowledge of an attack that was called off the day of the assassination attempt.[34]

In February, General Wojciech Jaruzelski became Poland's prime minister. Jaruzelski remains a debatable figure, with scholars always questioning his intentions. But we do know that, from the outset, he was close to Moscow, someone the Kremlin believed would follow its marching orders. In Mitrokhin and Andrew's description, he was "a sincere friend" of the USSR.

As the new prime minister, Jaruzelski worked closely with the Polish general secretary, Kania. The two were concerned about military action in their homeland. "In spite of the pressure from Moscow, I don't want to use force against the opposition," Kania reportedly told a member of the Polish Politburo, who in turn informed the KGB. "I don't want to go down in history as the butcher of the Polish people." On March 4 the Kremlin summoned both Kania and Jaruzelski to Moscow and gave them a tongue-lashing.[35]

Under increasing pressure, on March 27 Jaruzelski and Kania signed an ominous document, "The Central Concept of Introducing Martial Law in the Territory of the Polish People's Republic," which established a "legal" rationale for an all-out Soviet Bloc invasion to "liquidate Solidarity."[36]

This leads right to that critical period in late March when, according to Jack, tensions reached a boiling point and then suddenly cooled off. Why would the situation grow so intense as to put the Soviets on the verge of invading? The answer relates to Solidarity's time line.

On March 27 the labor movement staged a nationwide four-hour strike to protest the communist regime's beating of Solidarity members. It was Poland's largest strike since World War II; millions of Poles left work at once, bringing the nation to a halt. This sharp act of defiance was also a warning: if the communist regime did not meet the union's demands, Solidarity announced, the workers would begin an unlimited general strike on March 31.

A number of books suggest that in this narrow period a Soviet military intervention seemed almost certain. None makes mention of the Reagan shooting on March 30; the sources hazard no connection between that event and the immediate fizzling out of military action. All of them, however, support Jack's claim that tensions reached a crescendo March 29–30.

A number of books could serve to illustrate this March 30 climax and then cooldown, but here I will note just two.

One is the late Claire Sterling's *The Time of the Assassins*, the best early investigation into potential Soviet complicity in the shooting of Pope John Paul II. The veteran journalist rattled off four key events, one per day for March 26, 27, 29, and 30, pointing to an imminent Soviet attack on the pope's homeland.[37] She devoted only a sentence or two to each. Here I will present her time line and supplement it with important information.

On March 26, Sterling noted, a spokesman for the Reagan White House pointed to "indications that Polish authorities may be preparing to use force." The White House added, "We are similarly concerned that the Soviet Union may intend to undertake repressive actions in Poland."

This was one of several alerts the Reagan administration sent to Moscow and Warsaw indicating that the United States knew the Soviets were ready to use military force. These alerts made front-page news. The March 27 edition of the *New York Times* carried the headline "U.S. Warns Russians and Poles on Force Against the Unions." The *Times* piece opened, "The White House expressed 'growing concern' today over signs that the Polish authorities might crack down on the labor movement or that the Soviet Union might 'undertake repressive action in Poland.'" In what the *Times* called the (young) Reagan administration's "most serious statement about the situation" to date, the White House declared, "Any external intervention in Poland, or any measures aimed at suppressing the Polish people, would necessarily cause deep concern to all those interested in the peaceful development of Poland, and could have a grave effect on the whole course of East-West relations." The *Times* noted that the White House issued the statement after President Reagan met with the NSC and that the statement "reflected his [Reagan's] views."

When reporters asked how serious the situation appeared, Reagan replied, "Very serious." Asked specifically whether he thought there might be a "military intervention by the Soviet Union," the new president said, "That we don't know, but it is a very tense situation."

The *Times* also quoted a State Department official who said that "all signs are bad" in Poland. The official, speaking on March 26, noted that Solidarity's four-hour strike scheduled for the next day could trigger a communist military action, which he called "a scenario for major trouble."[38]

As Sterling noted in her succinct time line, Solidarity did stage the four-hour strike on March 27. The *New York Times* wrote, "Millions of Polish workers held a four-hour nationwide strike today, the largest organized protest since Communism came to Poland 36 years ago." The *Times* also reported Solidarity's plans for a much larger strike if the labor union did not get what it wanted in negotiations with the communist regime: "Western diplomats believe that if talks fail and the strike goes ahead on March 31, the Polish government will declare a state of emergency."[39]

With the crisis escalating, the Warsaw Pact armies extended their Soyuz '81 military maneuvers in and around Poland.

Sterling's time line then moved to March 29, when TASS, the official Soviet news agency, claimed that Solidarity was launching a full-scale putsch. TASS falsely reported that the labor union was blocking highways and occupying telephone exchanges, and had seized a television transmitter. This disinformation could have been a pretext for a Moscow military intervention.

Finally, Sterling noted that on March 30, Lech Wałęsa reached an eleventh-hour compromise with the Polish communist government, agreeing to call off the impending general strike. His followers, however, disagreed and reacted so violently in some cases that he offered to resign. "Even if he'd want to pull back [from the compromise]," wrote Sterling, "retreat was now cut off."[40]

Poland's communist leadership was divided as well. Leading right up to the compromise agreement, the Polish Central Committee had a marathon eighteen-hour session in which the comrades bitterly debated how to handle Solidarity. Hard-liners wanted to crack down on what one called "creeping counterrevolution," while others pushed for accommodation. By the end of the turbulent session, the moderate faction had prevailed; some hard-liners even offered to resign. The Central Committee rebuked Poland's Communist Party leadership for its handling of the crisis.[41]

Though Poland had averted the strike, Moscow could not have had confidence in Warsaw's leaders to handle the Solidarity problem. Perhaps, as Jack suggests, another factor—the shooting of the American president—helped convince the Soviets to pull back. According to Jack, news of the Reagan shooting broke—and the sudden collapse of Soviet chatter on Poland began—*before* word spread of the Warsaw regime's last-minute compromise with Solidarity.

Seventeen years after Claire Sterling's book, Douglas J. MacEachin, the CIA's former deputy director of intelligence, published a much more thorough account of the tense situation in late March 1981. In *U.S. Intelligence and the Confrontation in Poland, 1980–1981*, MacEachin likewise reveals a crescendo in tensions in the days leading to the Reagan shooting.[42]

MacEachin's key chapter, aptly titled "A Setup for Military Crackdown," opens with the Soyuz '81 exercises, which "began in the third week of March" and ended the first week of April.[43] MacEachin's time line starts with March 24, when Solidarity's National Coordinating Commission announced the four-hour nationwide strike to be held March 27, and the unlimited general strike to begin on March 31. Back on March 22, MacEachin points out, two key leaders of the Polish Politburo had invoked the prospect of declaring martial law.[44]

Some moderates within the Polish Communist Party believed that the Party's hard-liners were trying to provoke Solidarity in a way that would justify the use of military force. MacEachin quotes a March 23 "open letter" from the chairman of the party-controlled Polish Journalists Association. "Our hard-liners stand for no program except the concept of confrontation and disinformation," the chairman said, adding:

"They are trying to involve the whole Party leadership and government in a clash with the entire society. With incalculable consequences, they are trying to provoke society to behavior justifying the use of force."[45] This bold claim again pointed to a coming military intervention.

MacEachin takes the reader to a boiling point in the March 30–31 time frame. He quotes a knowledgeable source, "probably from the Polish military attaché mission," who confirmed that most Warsaw Pact military liaison officers believed "a military suppression was imminent, and that some Soviet military contacts reportedly were saying that they expected their forces to be called upon to actively support the Polish effort." The same U.S. intelligence that cited this source also quoted a "Warsaw Pact military representative," who had accurately dismissed U.S. warnings of a Soviet invasion in December 1980, as now maintaining that a military crackdown "is coming and is coming fast."[46]

Again, note the flair-up in tensions, the all-troops-ready-to-go atmosphere.

But just as suddenly, MacEachin's account fizzles on March 30. The author makes no mention of the shooting of Reagan that day but cites another event from nearly the same time: "On the evening of 30 March, Polish television broadcast a joint announcement by the government and the union that an agreement had been reached and that the threatened strike had been suspended." And then this: "The U.S. government's immediate reaction seemed to signal that it believed the crisis had passed. A State Department spokesman was quoted on 31 March as saying that the fresh Warsaw Pact troops whose deployment in the exercise had earlier prompted a note of alarm did not appear to be moving to the Polish border, and that the U.S. expected tensions to ease. The next day an administration spokesman said the Soviets were not expected to enter Poland."[47]

And just like that, the crisis was over. The headline in the March 31 *New York Times* was suddenly optimistic: "U.S. Expects Tensions in Poland to Ease."[48]

MacEachin reports that by early April, as the Soviets announced the termination of the Soyuz '81 exercises, U.S. and NATO concerns about a possible military intervention "were abating."[49] But the crisis in Poland never fully subsided.[50] It lasted until Poland's communist regime declared martial law on December 13, 1981. Martial law, terrible as it was, at least was not a full-scale military invasion of Pope John Paul II's homeland.

THE REAGAN LIBRARY: THE PRIMARY-SOURCE RECORD

To vet Jack's story as carefully as possible, I also reviewed declassified documents from the Ronald Reagan Library. Many of these documents were declassified through Freedom of Information Act (FOIA) requests that I filed beginning in 2001. Some that I photocopied were photocopied for the first time.[51]

One set of memos pertinent to this episode seems benign on first inspection but suggests how quickly tensions escalated through March 1981. On March 3, L. Paul Bremer III, executive secretary at the State Department (who two decades later would play a major role during the war in Iraq), wrote a memo to National Security Adviser Dick Allen titled "Request That the First Lady Host a Tea for the Wife of the Polish President." Poland's first lady, Madame Jadwiga Jablonska, happened to be planning a visit to the United States to meet with her daughter, who had just given birth to a son. State advised that Mrs. Reagan should meet with Madame Jablonska to "underline the strong human ties existing between our peoples" and to "help signal to the Soviets our interest in Poland."

Two days later, a March 5 NSC memo from Richard Pipes showed that Allen concurred with the recommendation and was passing it along through the proper channels. On March 9, apparently receiving positive feedback on the idea, Allen wrote a memo to Mrs. Reagan recommending the meeting. Movement toward the tea was proceeding swimmingly.

Then, however, progress stopped. No further documents on the subject appear in the file until an April 7 memo from NSC member Charles P. Tyson to staffer Paula Dobriansky. Tyson, after meeting with Allen, recommended delaying the possible meeting "in light of the current conditions in Poland."

Yes, stormy conditions from Moscow to Warsaw to Washington had rained out the tea party.

A second, more important set of documents from this period concerns a potential meeting between Vice President George H.W. Bush and Polish first deputy prime minister Mieczysław Jagielski. According to these memos, Jagielski held a rank "equivalent" to "Vice President in the Polish government." There was no question that Jagielski was worthy of a meeting with America's vice president. The first such memo that I found at the Reagan Library was a March 16, 1981, "Decision Memorandum" from Roger D. Severance, acting deputy assistant of the U.S.

Department of Commerce. It recommended an April 3 meeting between the two "vice presidents" for purposes of strengthening Polish-American relations and "yielding useful new information on Poland's current economic and political situation."

From this memo followed a March 24 NSC memo from Richard Pipes to Dick Allen and, in response, a March 25 memo from Allen to the White House endorsing the meeting. March 26 brought no less than three memos, from the NSC, the White House, and the Office of the Vice President, scheduling a Bush-Jagielski meeting for Friday, April 3, at Bush's office in the West Wing. Those memos were followed by a March 30 NSC memo, an April 1 memo to Vice President Bush from Secretary of State Al Haig, and an April 2 memo to Bush from Dick Allen.

Notably, the meeting was not cancelled, despite the chaos in Poland and with the shooting of President Reagan. Actually, the meeting was moved up to Thursday, April 2. The details of what was said at that meeting are not available to me, but the language in one of the memos is revealing. The Allen memo of April 2, two pages long, was by far the most substantive and least filled with standard bureaucratic talking points. It opened by setting the dangerous context: "Poland, of course, is in a condition of deep crisis." It then listed three U.S. objectives, quoted here in full:

- "To prevent a Soviet invasion and occupation."
- "To stabilize the situation in Poland, politically and economically."
- "To help Poland strike a middle way between East and West—a regime not intolerable to the Russians and yet capable of further development toward democracy."

These were bold objectives. Clearly, the Reagan NSC knew the stakes. The idea of the Red Army's invading Poland was not inconceivable; to the contrary, the NSC made preventing such an invasion the chief U.S. objective.

THE DP STRIKES AGAIN?

What should we conclude from all of this? Does Jack's account pass scrutiny?

Again, I found nothing to contradict Jack's time line or claims in the course of my extensive research, which included reviewing declassified documents, insider accounts, and scholarly and journalistic investigations, as well as interviews with scholars, intelligence sources, and former government officials.

More than that, Jack tells of a Field Station Berlin, and perhaps other parts of the intelligence community, anxious about the implications of the intelligence he passed along. His account jibes with what we know of the concern within the Carter administration and then among President Reagan and his foreign policy advisers about a Soviet invasion. Recall that fears of Soviet military action were so intense that Carter's national security adviser reached out to the Polish pope, who in turn made a direct appeal to the Soviet leader. And as president-elect, Reagan was so focused on the Polish situation that he was forced to consider the possibility of using U.S. military force—a possibility he ultimately rejected. Recall, too, that as tensions mounted in late March 1981, President Reagan's national security adviser laid out a clear primary objective for a meeting with a high-level Polish government official: "To prevent a Soviet invasion and occupation."

The stakes could not have been higher. Jack's account suggests the impact that this incredible tension could have had on the U.S. intelligence community.

Many sources also corroborate Jack's claim that Soviet forces were at a state of high readiness to invade Poland right into March 30 and then suddenly backed down.

Of course, to the world there has been a simple explanation for why crisis was averted on March 30, 1981: Solidarity and the Polish communist government reached a last-minute agreement to avoid the massive strike that Warsaw and Moscow feared.

That may be the case. Or it may be only *part* of the explanation. Jack's account suggests an unreported reason why the Soviets backed down: the shooting of Reagan, which led to heightened U.S. military readiness and to retired four-star general Alexander Haig's announcement that he was "in control" at the White House.

Only further evidence from Moscow could definitively resolve whether the Soviets decided against an invasion because of the Reagan shooting. My hope is that publishing Jack's account might prompt a source from the Soviet side to come forward at last with a yea or a nay.

Ronald Reagan always believed that bad things happen for a good purpose. Could it be that his near-death experience averted geopolitical catastrophe? Reagan and Bill Clark together frequently prayed the "Peace Prayer" of Saint Francis, requesting, "Lord, make me an instrument of your peace." Was Reagan here an unwitting "instrument of peace"?

Given that close Reagan advisers have said they did not have any precise knowledge that the shooting of the president may have halted a Soviet invasion, it seems unlikely that Reagan ever knew of what Jack reports. But if he had known, he would not have hesitated to see the hand of God in it—the Divine Plan acted out again.

All part of the DP? Perhaps so.

18

MAY 13, 1981

A (SOVIET) BULLET FOR A POPE

That final week of March 1981 was a tumultuous one, for reasons that we can only now begin to fully comprehend. The Soviets, it seemed, were losing it. They were ready to invade Poland. They detested the new team in Washington. And they despised the Polish pope at the Vatican.

The communist press was full of vitriol directed at the pontiff. On March 26 a Ukraine paper accused the Vatican of "malicious anti-Soviet and anti-communist propaganda" being pushed by "dyed-in-the-wool anti-Soviets and Nazi remnants."[1] Here we see the vicious old communist canard resurrected once again: the man in the chair of Saint Peter and his priestly pals were Nazis. Karol Wojtyła, survivor of the Nazis, was somehow a "Nazi remnant."

That language was tame compared with an outburst in the Soviet journal *Polimya* the same month. The journal excoriated the "militantly anti-communist" Pope John Paul II as a "cunning and dangerous ideological enemy." Then it accused of him having acquiesced to a secret Nazi-Vatican plan during World War II to exterminate the Polish people, including not only Jews but also clergy.

Sure, it was ludicrous, but such outrageous charges managed to stick to Pope Pius XII, who had saved more than 700,000 Jews, and whom the Nazis had wanted to kidnap.

The *Polimya* writer continued the attack by calling John Paul II "malicious, lowly, perfidious, and backward." According to this article, the pontiff was a "toady of the American militarists" who was battling socialism with his "overseas accomplices" and his "new boss in the White House."[2]

John Paul II's "new boss in the White House" was, of course, Ronald Wilson Reagan.

Such overheated claims betrayed Moscow's mood. The Soviets had been concerned about John Paul II ever since the College of Cardinals picked the Polish pope. There could not have been a worse time for the Vatican to reach into Poland for its first non-Italian pope in more than four centuries and its first Slavic pope ever. They understood, as did Ronald Reagan, that Poland was the linchpin in the Soviet Bloc. Moscow's trepidation had grown as the pontiff made his defiant visit to his homeland. The millions of Poles who came out to celebrate and worship with their native son brought international attention to a fact that discomfited the Kremlin: staunchly Catholic Poland was the only nation within the Soviet empire that had survived the atheistic-communist assault on religion. Then the pope took the unprecedented step of appealing directly to the Soviet general secretary about how Moscow should deal with its Warsaw Pact puppets.

And now this troublesome pope looked ready to partner with the new anticommunist American president. The Soviets were not merely concerned; they were *terrified.*

Their contempt for and fear of John Paul II were palpable. In a matter of weeks, they would show just how deep their contempt and fear ran.

ANOTHER NEAR-DEATH EXPERIENCE

On May 13, 1981, a bullet fired by a Turk named Mehmet Ali Agca pierced the flesh of the Polish pope. The pontiff's body collapsed, sinking into the arms of his aides. "At the very moment I fell," he said later, "I had this vivid presentiment that I should be saved."[3]

Not everyone was so sure.

"Where?" Father Stanisław Dziwisz asked his fallen friend.

"In the stomach," the pope replied.

"Does it hurt?"

"It does."[4]

The pontiff alarmed his immediate caretakers with his heavy bleeding. They removed him from his vehicle and stretched him out in search of the source of the blood. "It was only then that we realized how much blood he was losing from the first bullet wound," Father Dziwisz recalled. "The pope was fading." Quietly groaning, his voice getting weaker, praying, John Paul II said, "Jesus, Mother Mary."[5]

The pope's personal physician immediately decided to get John Paul II to Gemelli Hospital, where the Holy Father slipped into unconsciousness. "What happened at the hospital," he said later, "I do not remember."[6]

On the hospital's ninth floor, he was prepped for emergency surgery. On the doctor's recommendation, Dziwisz administered the Church's last rites to its leader, anointing the silent pontiff.[7] "I did it immediately," Dziwisz recalled, "but I was completely torn up inside."[8]

"I was already practically on the other side," said the Holy Father later. He had almost passed over to his Heavenly Father.[9]

One of Gemelli Hospital's three chief surgeons, Dr. Francesco Crucitti, had been across town at another hospital on the Via Aurelia when he heard about the shooting. He hopped in his car and sped down the wrong side of a two-way street; he convinced a policeman with a submachine gun to let him pass. When Dr. Crucitti ran into the hospital, he was thrilled to find that some "unknown genius" had called all the elevators to the lobby so the surgeon could make his way to the ninth floor without delay. Dr. Crucitti scrubbed up and dashed into the operating room to find a patient whose blood pressure was plummeting.

With the leader of the world's largest church derobed and laid open before him, Dr. Crucitti looked inside his patient and saw "blood everywhere." He and his team began suctioning up the mess and stanching the bleeding so transfusions could begin. That vital first step steadied the blood pressure and pulse. The patient was not safe yet, however. He had multiple wounds in the colon, small intestine, and abdomen. The intestine was so damaged that nearly two feet of it had to be removed.[10]

A long, intricate procedure followed that secured the pontiff's life.

The parallels between the shooting of John Paul II and that of Ronald Reagan six weeks earlier are striking. Both nearly died from their wounds—and yet no one outside the operating room understood the severity of the situation.[11] In each case, the initial media reports downplayed the leader's wounds. Some reports said that Reagan had not even been hit. Vatican Radio reported that John Paul II was "not in serious condition," but in truth the pope's physicians were still listing his condition as "critical" ten days after surgery.[12]

Both the president and the pope lost a lot of blood. Reagan required a transfusion of eight pints, though early reports said that Reagan had lost five pints of blood. John Paul II ended up receiving six pints of blood through transfusions, contrary to reports that he received only one pint during the operation. After the pope's body rejected the first transfusion, doctors in the hospital donated their own blood to the Holy Father.[13]

For both the president and the pope, survival was a matter of mere centimeters: John Hinckley's bullet just missed Reagan's heart, and Mehmet Ali Agca's bullet just missed John Paul II's main abdominal artery.[14] Had the bullets not missed, both men probably would have bled to death in their vehicles speeding to their respective hospitals.[15] "A few more minutes, some [traffic] obstruction along the way," recalled Father Dziwisz, "and it would have been fatal." Any hesitation on the part of the caretakers on the scene would have proven fatal as well. Fortunately, Reagan's Secret Service agent and the pope's personal physician made the snap decision to get their charge to a nearby hospital that would provide excellent care.

Then, too, both Reagan and John Paul II felt a powerful impulse to forgive their attackers. Lying on the operating table, the president began to pray for the soul of the "mixed up young man" who had shot him. Still conscious on the ride to Gemelli Hospital, the pope looked at Father Dziwisz and told him explicitly that he had forgiven his assailant.[16]

A FINAL GOODBYE

It would be three months before Pope John Paul II made it through all his extended hospitalizations and procedures. On August 14, the day before the Feast of the Assumption of Mary, he was at last released from the hospital for good.[17] It was forty years to the day since his Polish Marian mentor, Maximilian Maria Kolbe, was released from the earthly hell of Auschwitz to be with his Maker.

The pontiff was physically in anguish after the shooting. For the first three days he suffered terribly, and prayed continually. His pain was made worse by the realization that the great Polish cardinal Stefan Wyszyński, his friend and mentor, was on his deathbed.

The two shared a final conversation by phone. "We're united in suffering," said Wyszyński, who knew that their suffering also united them to their Savior, "but you're okay." He humbly said to his former underling, "Holy Father, give me your blessing." Knowing the blessing was their last goodbye, Karol Wojtyła told his elder priest: "Yes, of course. I bless your mouth.... I bless your hands."

Father Dziwisz later wrote that when the dying Wyszyński had learned of the trauma to his junior cardinal-turned-pope, he forced himself to hold on to life until he felt sure that Karol Wojtyła would live. "He closed his eyes for the last time only after receiving confirmation that the Pope was out of danger," said Father Dziwisz.[18]

Cardinal Stefan Wyszyński died on May 28, 1981, two weeks after the shooting of Pope John Paul II. The historic Polish prelate who had led his flock through the worst years of atheistic communism was seventy-nine years old.

"AGCA DID NOT ACT ALONE"

The motives of John Paul II's shooter have been long disputed. The pope's would-be assassin was circumspect, but many, including John Paul II himself, suspected that communists were behind the assassination.

These suspicions were hardly unjustified. Pummeling Christians, and Catholics in particular, was standard communist sport. Recall that in 1919 communists in Bavaria had tried to kill an apostolic nuncio by the name of Eugenio Pacelli—the future Pope Pius XII. The few reports on the incident suggest that it might have taken place in May 1919.[19] The exact date remains unclear; one wonders if perhaps it was May 13, 1919. We do know that on May 13, 1917—the exact date Our Lady of Fátima first appeared to Lúcia, Jacinta, and Francisco in Portugal—Pope Benedict XV consecrated Pacelli as archbishop, a sacred stop on his way to the papacy.

The communists failed to assassinate Pius XII in 1919, but later, when they turned to character assassination, they were successful.

Now an even more dangerous anticommunist pope had raised Soviet fears to new levels. Karol Wojtyła's appointment shocked Moscow. When the pope returned to Poland and implored his countrymen to "be not afraid," the Soviet leadership was terrified. There was no question: he had to go.

So, after shots rang out in Saint Peter's Square on another May 13, it did not take long for people to ask: did Mehmet Ali Agca try to kill the Polish pontiff on behalf of communists?

Mainstream news sources in the United States were not among those pursuing the question. The *New York Times*, in its May 15 edition, was quick to report that Agca acted alone, much as it had been quick to editorialize in October 1978 that the election of the Polish pontiff did not threaten communist stability in Eastern Europe. "The police have arrested no one else," reported the *Times*. "They are convinced, according to [Italian] Government sources, that Mr. Agca acted alone—in the sense that he had no accomplices with him in St. Peter's Square and none, in all probability, elsewhere in Rome or in Italy."[20]

The *Times* accepted at face value a note found in Agca's possession after the shooting: "A rough draft of a leaflet found in the young Turk's pocket was signed not by any organization but by Mr. Agca. It began, 'I, Agca, have killed the Pope so that the world may know of the thousands of victims of imperialism.'"

The Italian press was much less credulous. The same day the *Times* published this article, a piece in the Turin-based *La Stampa* reported that Italian attorney general Achille Gallucci had signed an order of arrest accusing Agca of "an attempt on the life of a head of state . . . in concourse with other persons who remain unknown." The attorney general insisted that these words were "not just a precaution; it is more than that."[21]

How much more? Judge Luciano Infelisi, the examining magistrate who signed the arrest warrant, said explicitly, "For us, there is documentary proof that Mehmet Ali Agca did not act alone."[22]

This was a precursor of things to come. All along, the Italians were ahead of others in investigating the shooting and not being cowed by the denials and threats coming from the Soviets and their communist puppets. Especially important were several Italian judges who did excellent work on the case. Italian journalists undertook important investigations, too, including those at *L'Osservatore Romano*, the Vatican newspaper. Even Cardinal Casaroli (not exactly a hard-liner) sensed a plot with many players. In midsummer 1981, Casaroli said, "A heart (or are they hearts?), a hostile heart, has armed the enemy hand to strike, through the pope—and this pope!—at the heart of the Church."[23]

Others grasped the gravity of the allegation. As evidence mounted against communist involvement,[24] William Safire, the savvy *New York Times* columnist who stood apart from the paper's editors, stated that if courts could show communist involvement in the assassination attempt—

particularly fingerprints that led all the way to Moscow—it would constitute "The Crime of the Century." Safire was no naïf when it came to the Kremlin.

The pope himself suspected a Soviet role. Remember that in the hospital, his thoughts had turned to the communists, when he whispered to Father Dziwisz, "Just like Bachelet," comparing himself to a Catholic politician who had been murdered by the Red Brigades, a communist terrorist group. Father Dziwisz later wrote that to the Holy Father "it seemed objectively impossible" that Ali Agca could have acted alone. A process of logical "deduction" pointed to Agca as a "perfect killer" who had been "sent by someone who thought the Pope was dangerous and inconvenient," by someone "who'd been frightened, seriously frightened, as soon as they'd heard that a Polish Pope had been elected." Thus, it was only natural to look to the communist world and wonder whether "the KGB was behind whoever made the immediate decision."[25]

It is unclear when John Paul II began to give serious consideration to a Soviet role in the shooting. But as early as December 1982, *Time* magazine reported that "the Pope believes the KGB ordered the assassination attempt."[26]

"TWO THIRTEENTHS OF MAY!"

The fact that the assassination attempt occurred on the Memorial Day of Our Lady of Fátima—sixty-four years to the day after the Lady had first appeared in the tiny Portuguese village—came to influence the pope's thinking profoundly.

Karol Wojtyła had long ago dedicated his life, priesthood, and papacy to Mary; his native country of Poland and his hometown of Kraków venerated the Blessed Mother as well. Now, as his thoughts turned from the Virgin Mary to suspicions of communist involvement in his shooting, the pope recalled the prophecies the Blessed Mother had made in Portugal sixty-four years earlier.

The Holy Father made the connection while recovering in the hospital during the summer of 1981. Father Dziwisz later reported: "He [John Paul II] started reflecting on what was, to say the least, an extraordinary coincidence. Two thirteenths of May! One in 1917, when the Virgin of Fátima appeared for the first time, and one in 1981, when they tried to kill him. After pondering it for a while, the Pope finally requested to see the Third Secret."[27]

John Paul II had to request the Third Secret of Fátima because it remained sealed in the archives of the Congregation for the Doctrine of the Faith. On July 18, 1981, the prefect for the congregation, Cardinal Franjo Šeper, delivered two envelopes—a white one containing Sister Lúcia's original Portuguese text, and an orange one with the Italian translation. Cardinal Šeper brought the envelopes to the Vatican's deputy secretary of state, Archbishop Eduardo Martínez Somalo, who took them to the pope on the ninth floor of Gemelli Hospital.[28]

It was there that the Holy Father read the secret. "When he was finished," said Dziwisz, "all his remaining doubts were gone." In Sister Lúcia's vision, "he recognized his own destiny." He became convinced that his life had been spared thanks to the intervention of Our Lady.[29]

As Sister Lúcia described it, the Third Secret of Fátima involved a "bishop dressed in white," whom the three children understood to be the Holy Father. In this vision, they saw the Holy Father "killed by a group of soldiers who fired bullets and arrows at him."

Of course, Pope John Paul II was not killed. Father Dziwisz did not see this as an inconsistency, or as a reason to believe the third secret had not been fulfilled: "So? Couldn't that have been the real point of the vision? Couldn't it have been trying to tell us that the paths of history, of human existence, are not necessarily fixed in advance? And that there is a Providence, a 'motherly hand,' which can intervene and cause a shooter, who is certain of hitting his target, to miss?"[30] If anyone could be said to be "certain of hitting his target," it was Mehmet Ali Agca, a trained assassin firing at point-blank range.

Just after the shooting, Polish faithful who had been in Saint Peter's Square to glimpse their hero put a copy of Poland's revered Black Madonna in the empty chair where the pope was to have spoken. Days earlier, they had inscribed on the back of the copy, "May Our Lady protect the Holy Father from evil."[31]

After reading the Third Secret of Fátima, the Holy Father concluded that she had protected him in that terrible moment. He believed that the Blessed Mother, guided by the Trinity, had interceded to deflect the bullet enough to save him.

"One hand shot," John Paul II said, "and another guided the bullet."[32]

Five months after the attack, the Holy Father reconvened with the faithful in Saint Peter's Square to acknowledge his debt to the Blessed Mother and all of the patron saints. There he said, "Could I forget that the event [shooting] in Saint Peter's Square took place at the date and at the hour when the first appearance of the Mother of Christ to the poor little peasants has been remembered for over sixty years at Fátima in Portugal?"[33] He continued, "For, in everything that happened to me on that very day, I felt that extraordinary motherly protection and care, which turned out to be stronger than the deadly bullet."[34]

John Paul II knew the prophecy. In his mind, it all seemed connected. Indeed, if the Soviets were behind the shooting, then it would connect the first and third secrets of Fátima: the attempted assassination of the leader of the world's largest Christian denomination was, apparently, among the "errors" and "persecutions" of atheistic-communist Russia.

Now it was up to the rest of the world to put the pieces together, to connect the dots from Saint Peter's Square to Moscow. The process would take decades, outliving both John Paul II and the USSR.

WHO WAS AGCA?

Any attempt to investigate the assassination attempt, to put the pieces together, must begin with the shooter. So who was Mehmet Ali Agca?

His identity is many things to many people. Agca has often been described as a terrorist, which he was. But some sources call him a Muslim; others say he was nonreligious. Some say he was interested in global politics; others say he was apolitical. Some call him a conspirator; others, a loner. Some call him a brilliant schemer; others, a mentally deranged madman. Some say he was paranoid; others insist he was psychologically sound. Some say he kept changing his stories; others say he was consistent all along. Some call him a servant of international communism; others call him pro-fascist. To this day some people insist he was anything but a conspirator working with communists. At the time of this writing, the Wikipedia entry[35] on Agca describes him as a "far right" "ultranationalist," mainly because of his association with the Turkish extremist group the Grey Wolves.

So what is the truth? Who was he?

Born January 9, 1958, Mehmet Ali Agca came from a poor peasant village on the outskirts of the city of Malatya in the Anatolian plains of Turkey. Malatya had been a peaceful and harmonious city until Islamic terror began ravaging it during Agca's adolescence.

Claire Sterling, the excellent investigative journalist whose work I will cite often in the pages ahead, traveled to the ancient village to find and interview the Agca family. She was intrigued by what she discovered. Although Agca was raised in a Sunni Muslim family (the vast majority of the world's Muslims are Sunni), she estimated that religion had not played a "decisive part" in his upbringing or aspirations.[36] (I cannot confirm this alleged lack of religious influence.)

Agca's father was a drunk who beat his wife regularly and walked out on her and their three children. One source described him as "an enormous drinker"; although people said the father was killed in a traffic accident, in reality he died of cirrhosis of the liver, according to the source.

Sterling described the young Agca as a "silent, sober child." Teachers characterized him as "very kind, very quiet, and thoughtful," as "very bright and conscientious," though haunted by his personal problems. They remembered a loner who usually kept separate from the crowd and from girls. Agca later talked of how he went everywhere alone—to the movies, to the library, to soccer games. He seemed intent on making up for his broken household by accomplishing something big someday. "He always said he'd be famous someday," his teacher told Sterling.

Agca read everything, all the time. "All he cared about was reading," his mother said. He read "every kind" of book—"whatever he could get his hands on, rightist, leftist, poetry, newspapers, comic books."

The mother called her son a "good Muslim" and could not conceive why he would have shot the pope. "He was so loyal, so respectful," she said, adding that the whole family would have felt "very sorry" if the pope had died.

The mother said that her son took a dangerous turn when he left for college in 1976. He attended university first in Ankara and then in Istanbul. There, "those villains got him," his mother said. The influences there, Sterling found, were not from the right but from "left-wing Turks" and the "Marxist-Leninist side."

As the mother spoke to Sterling, Agca's younger brother watched warily, unsure of the intentions and sincerity of their American visitor. So did his sister, who served cups of Turkish coffee. The sister appeared guarded, "painfully timid."

Incidentally, the sister's name was reported in the international press as "Fatma," a Romanized version of a colloquial Arabic pronunciation better rendered as "Fátima."

DISGUISED AS A DISCIPLE OF JESUS CHRIST

By the late 1970s, Mehmet Ali Agca had broken away from his family and village. He began to serve Turkish extremists from both the right and left, though mostly from the left, including several from the Middle Eastern Marxist-Leninist left. Agca received training in terrorist camps from Damascus to Beirut, and possibly even in the Ayatollah's Iran.[37] The Soviets were extremely active in these areas of the Middle East. They were fastidious recruiters, eager sponsors and trainers, fomenters of rebellion and chaos, and architects of propaganda and disinformation against the West and America and Israel and Christianity.[38]

Was Agca pro-communist or pro-fascist? At times he helped both extremes—which was ideal for Moscow's disinformation apparatus: even the slightest connection to the right could be amplified to frame the young man as a "right winger." In a sense, Agca's connections to both the right and the left reflected exactly what John Paul II and Ronald Reagan and Fulton Sheen and Pope Pius XII and the institutional Roman Catholic Church had remonstrated against for decades: the parallel evils of fascism and communism. Both forces infected Agca.

Agca's ties, and his willingness to kill and kill well, eventually brought him into the Communist Bloc, where such misbegotten talents were considered great virtues. He spent much of the summer of 1980 in Bulgaria, arriving in early July and staying for fifty days. There, in the Bulgarian capital of Sofia, Agca purchased from a Syrian contact a Browning 9-millimeter handgun, which he would put to use in Rome at a choice moment.

Agca spent the next nine months traveling through Europe. He spent much of his time in Italy, bouncing among Rome, Milan, Naples, Palermo, Perugia, and Genoa. On May 11 he checked in at Rome's Pensione Isa, where, according to the Italian court's official Statement of Motivation, his room was reserved by someone who spoke fluent Italian.[39]

Agca had plans to stay longer, if need be. A note found in his pocket when he was apprehended contained self-instructions written in Turkish. Among them were the pope's public appearances on May 13 ("Wednesday, appearance in the Square"), on May 17 ("Sunday, perhaps appearance on the balcony"), and on May 20 ("Wednesday, Square *without fail*"). He also reminded himself to "choose a shoulder bag carefully," that "hair dye is essential," and "if necessary, wear a cross." Yes, a cross: the betrayer would be disguised as a disciple of Jesus Christ.[40]

Agca's notes also said to wear "tennis shoes," no doubt to help him flee the scene.[41]

He was ready to go. All he needed now was his gun, bullets, just the right position, and Pope John Paul II.

About a quarter past 5 P.M. on May 13, 1981, Mehmet Ali Agca got his opportunity in Saint Peter's Square. He had his target in sight. He pulled the trigger.

A SHARED "DUBIOUS DISTINCTION"

Across the Atlantic, the president of the United States absorbed the news about the shooting with horror. Six weeks earlier, after the assassination attempt on Reagan, the pope had sent his prayers and best wishes for a full recovery. The president responded by saying that he and Nancy were "deeply touched by your kind expression of concern" and "very much appreciate that you are thinking of us." The president also made a promise: "My administration will continue to advance the goals which we both share. Please be assured of that."[42]

Now, on May 13, the recovered president fired off a cable to the American embassy in Rome to be delivered to John Paul II.[43] It was brief:

> May 13, 1981
>
> Your Holiness:
>
> I have just received the shocking news of the attack on you. All Americans join me in hopes and prayers for your speedy recovery from the injuries you have suffered in the attack. Our prayers are with you.
>
> Ronald Reagan

Now it was time for the president to pray for the pope's recovery. The two had created the world's most exclusive mutual prayer society.

To say that Ronald Reagan was concerned about his partner is not sufficient. National Security Adviser Dick Allen, who met with the president daily for their national security briefing, remembered that Reagan "asked me every day for weeks thereafter about the pontiff's recovery." Allen said that "the president's affection for the pope was greatly magnified" by the shooting.[44] The Soviets had worried about a kinship between the anticommunist president and pope. Now they had to worry much more: the shootings were bringing the two leaders closer together.

Karol Wojtyła's sixty-first birthday fell only days later, on May 18. Reagan sent more best wishes to the pontiff, this time in a formal note on his official Oval Office letterhead. The president asked the respected Italian-American congressman Peter Rodino, a New Jersey Democrat, to deliver the message personally to the pontiff.[45] In the letter, Reagan expressed "my relief and my delight in the encouraging news of your recovery" amid these "troubled times." Reagan then shared his unique form of identification with the pontiff:

> Happily, few leaders in the world today have the dubious distinction of knowing with some precision the kind of event you have just experienced. Fewer still can appreciate, as can I, the depth of courage and commitment on which you must have called, not only to survive that horrible event but to do so with such grace, nobility, and forgiveness.
>
> Your heroism, and the universal outpouring of love and concern which it evoked, is proof that a single irrational act cannot prevail against the basic human decency which continues to inspire most people in most places. The qualities you exemplify remain a precious asset as we confront the growing dangers of the moment—confront them with confidence and faith....
>
> My prayers, and those of all Americans, are with you as your recovery progresses and as you resume the passionate leadership which has given so many parts of the world a spirit of optimistic renewal.

The word *happily* that begins this passage is a choice one. Ronald Reagan was "happy" to join Pope John Paul II in this "dubious distinction," in experiencing such a "horrible" event. It was as if each man had to start their historic journey together with a severe personal sacrifice. It was as if they had to be made worthy of the historical-spiritual mission ahead. And why would anything so significant not include suffering?

"O my Lord, when I think of the many ways you suffered and how you deserved none of these sufferings," wrote Saint Teresa of Avila, "I don't know what to say about myself, nor do I know where my common sense was when I didn't want to suffer, nor where I am when I excuse myself."[46]

John Paul II and Ronald Reagan would have both understood Saint Teresa's sentiment. It would have been common sense to the president. It would have made theological sense to the pope, who understood mortification of the flesh.

EYES ON THE SOVIETS

On the morning of May 14, as the first order of business after the shooting in Rome, Bill Casey, Ronald Reagan's CIA director, gathered the National Foreign Intelligence Board together at its headquarters on F Street in Washington. Ever since taking the helm of the CIA in January, the faithful Roman Catholic had been awaiting a formal CIA National Intelligence Estimate analyzing the Soviets' role in international terrorism and assassinations. Since then, his pope and his president had both been shot. His president almost died, and his pope was in critical condition. What was going on?

"There was no evidence to suggest that the two events were related," Bob Woodward wrote in his bestselling 1987 exposé on Casey and the CIA, *Veil*. "Or that the Soviets had a role in either. But something was fishy and he [Casey] wanted to make sure intelligence was all over the possibilities. Every lead or possible connection was to be followed up, and he was to be informed at once." Said Woodward, "Casey wanted to know whether the Soviets were up to something."[47]

Over at 1600 Pennsylvania Avenue, Ronald Reagan was also wondering what was going on.

19

MAY–SEPTEMBER 1981

COMMENCEMENT

President Reagan's diary entry for Wednesday, May 13, needed little elaboration: "Word brought to us of the shooting of the Pope. Called Cardinal Cooke & Cardinal [Krol]—sent message to Vatican & prayed."[1]

There was not much more to do. In moments like this, he had learned well from Nelle, you pray.

How sad it was. What a potential setback it was. Ronald Reagan had such high hopes for renewal, not just for his country but for the wider world as well. He had great ambitions to turn back the march of atheistic communism. And Pope John Paul II was a big part of that plan.

Would the Holy Father survive? Would good prevail?

GOING TO NOTRE DAME

Ronald Reagan's first major public appearance after the shooting of Pope John Paul II just happened to be an address at Notre Dame, a Catholic university named after its patroness, the Virgin Mary—the same Virgin Mary who was the patroness of John Paul II, and whom the Holy Father believed had spared his life. A Catholic screenwriter could not have written a better script for the actor-turned-president.

On May 17, President Reagan traveled to Notre Dame to give the commencement address. Fittingly, a commencement is not an end but a beginning, for in this speech Reagan publicly commenced his presidential crusade against atheistic communism.

Reagan laid out America's Cold War challenge: "The years ahead are great ones for this country, for the cause of freedom and the spread of civilization. The West won't contain communism, it will transcend communism.... It will dismiss it as some bizarre chapter in human history whose last pages are even now being written."

No one else was making such audacious predictions at the time. Critics would scoff at the president's claim.

The Notre Dame speech was distinctively Ronald Reagan, bearing his personal imprint throughout. Although speechwriter Tony Dolan wrote the original draft, Reagan rewrote the entire address. "Though the archives don't show it," Dolan told me, "the Gipper did a complete rewrite of my draft on this one. And then called me to apologize. Geez."[2]

This highly personal speech drove home Reagan's notion that Americans were part of a larger cause set forth by a higher authority. He drew on remarks Winston Churchill had made during the most ominous days of the Battle of Britain: "When great causes are on the move in the world, we learn we are spirits, not animals, and that something is going on in space and time, and beyond space and time, which, whether we like it or not, spells duty." Recall that Reagan had used this quotation way back in October 1964, in his historic "Time for Choosing" speech. He cited it again at Notre Dame to suggest that Americans had a duty to fight expansionist Soviet communism.

Reagan followed the Churchill passage with a story from his experience filming the movie *Knute Rockne, All American*, about the legendary Notre Dame football coach. Reagan said that Rockne had had an "almost mystical" influence on him when he was growing up in Illinois, so that when the young actor was cast in a film about the coach, it was more than just a movie for him. Reagan played one of Rockne's top players,

George Gipp, who on his deathbed told the coach, "Sometime when the team is up against it and the breaks are beating the boys, ask 'em to go in there with all they've got and win just one for the Gipper." At the movie's climax, Rockne tells his team the story to rally them for a dramatic come-from-behind victory.

Speaking at Notre Dame in 1981, Reagan asked his audience to "look at the significance of that story":

> Rockne could have used Gipp's dying words to win a game any time. But eight years went by following the death of George Gipp before Rock revealed those dying words, his deathbed wish.
>
> And then he told the story at halftime to a team that was losing, and one of the only teams he had ever coached that was torn by dissension and jealousy and factionalism. [None of] the seniors on that team... had known George Gipp. They were children when he played for Notre Dame. It was to this team that Rockne told the story and so inspired them that they rose above their personal animosities. For someone they had never known, they joined together in a common cause and attained the unattainable.

Reagan then told the audience of a dramatic line that one of the real-life Notre Dame players had spoken during the game. The screenwriter and producer and actors knew about the line but were afraid to include it:

> The man who carried the ball over for the winning touchdown was actually injured on the play. We were told that as he was lifted on the stretcher and carried off the field he was heard to say, "That's the last one I can get for you, Gipper."
>
> Now, it's only a game. And maybe to hear it now, afterward—and this is what we feared—it might sound maudlin and not the way it was intended. But is there anything wrong with young people having an experience, feeling something so deeply, thinking of someone else to the point that they can give so completely of themselves? There will come times in the lives of all of us when we'll be faced with causes bigger than ourselves, and they won't be on a playing field.

Just as Coach Rockne rallied a team torn by "dissension and jealousy and factionalism," Coach Reagan seemed to be rallying his audience—and the broader American public—to "attain the unattainable."

Later in the speech, Reagan made clear the stakes:

> When it's written, the history of our time won't dwell long on the hardships of the recent past. But history will ask—and our answer [will] determine the fate of freedom for a thousand years—Did a nation born of hope lose hope? Did a people forged by courage find courage wanting? Did a generation steeled by hard war and a harsh peace forsake honor at the moment of great climactic struggle for the human spirit?... The answers are to be found in the heritage left by generations of Americans before us. They stand in silent witness to what the world will soon know and history someday record: that in its third century, the American Nation came of age, affirmed its leadership of free men and women serving selflessly a vision of man with God, government for people, and humanity at peace.

It is important to place these remarks in context: just a few weeks had passed since Reagan's brush with death, and his pledge to Cardinal Cooke that "whatever time I have left is left for Him."

And, of course, John Paul II had nearly been killed only four days earlier. Reagan did not neglect that fact. Speaking of compassion, sacrifice, and endurance, the president noted the irony that "one who exemplifies [those traits] so well, Pope John Paul II, a man of peace and goodness, an inspiration to the world, would be struck by a bullet from a man towards whom he could only feel compassion and love." Reagan went on: "It was John Paul II who warned in last year's encyclical on mercy and justice [*Dives in Misericordia*] against certain economic theories that use the rhetoric of class struggle to justify injustice." He quoted the Holy Father: "In the name of an alleged justice... the neighbor is sometimes destroyed, killed, deprived of liberty, or stripped of fundamental human rights."

Here, Reagan (like the pope in his encyclical) did not use the word *communism* or *socialism* or *Marxism*. But there was no doubt about what he meant by "certain economic theories" that deprive people of basic rights and even kill to achieve their ends.

In retrospect, this was a telling insight into Ronald Reagan's thinking on the assassination attempt. He seems to have linked John Paul II's shooter to international communism. This oblique but potentially explosive suggestion somehow escaped notice at the time.

Interestingly, the passage on John Paul II does not appear in any of the multiple drafts of the Notre Dame speech on file at the Reagan Library today.[3] None of Tony Dolan's drafts at the library include this paragraph. Thus it is possible, even likely, that Reagan wrote the passage into his text shortly before delivering the speech, which would not have been unusual for him. Given the subject matter and the fact that, as Dolan attested, Reagan did "a complete rewrite," the speech clearly had significant meaning to the president.[4]

Ronald Reagan's attention was fixed on Moscow. Seven years later, when he returned to Notre Dame, he recalled the 1981 speech as "one of the first major addresses of my presidency." He also remembered that his prediction that the West would transcend communism "was treated very skeptically in Washington." That was putting it mildly. But ridicule never bothered Reagan. He didn't back off from his prediction. In fact, at a press conference just a couple of weeks after his 1981 Notre Dame address, he doubled down. When a reporter asked, "Do the events of the last ten months in Poland constitute the beginning of the end of Soviet domination of Eastern Europe?" Reagan answered:

> Well, what I meant then in my remarks at Notre Dame and what I believe now about what we're seeing tie together. I just think it is impossible—and history reveals this—for any form of government to completely deny freedom to people and have that go on interminably. There eventually comes an end to it. And I think the things we're seeing, not only in Poland but the reports that are coming out of Russia itself about the younger generation and its resistance to long-time government controls, is an indication that communism is an aberration. It's not a normal way of living for human beings, and I think we are seeing the first, beginning cracks, the beginning of the end.[5]

THE LADY FROM CALCUTTA

A small but formidable woman from Calcutta had watched the shootings of Reagan and John Paul II with intense concern. Three weeks after the attempt on the pope's life, Mother Teresa visited the White House, where she jolted President Reagan by affirming the sense of divine calling he had felt after the shooting.

On June 4, 1981, the president and first lady sat down for a private meal with the nun and a few selected guests. No cameras, no media. The servant to Calcutta's destitute made an immediate impact on the host. Mother Teresa said: "Mr. President Reagan, do you know that we stayed up for two straight nights praying for you after you were shot? We prayed very hard for you to live."[6]

Humbled, Reagan thanked her, but she wasn't finished. She looked at the president pointedly and said: "You have suffered the passion of the cross and have received grace. There is a purpose to this. Because of your suffering and pain you will now understand the suffering and pain of the world." She added, "This has happened to you at this time because your country and the world need you."

Nancy Reagan dissolved into tears. Her husband, the great communicator, was at a loss for words.

The White House did not hold a press conference or photo op with Mother Teresa. The administration did not do much to document the encounter either.[7] Mother Teresa departed that afternoon as quietly as she came. But the sparse record we have suggests that the lady from Calcutta had made a profound impression on the president.

The official *Public Papers of the President of the United States*, which are silent on the lunch itself, register a short press exchange with the president just as the nun left:

> JOURNALIST (UNIDENTIFIED): How was your visit, Mr. President?
>
> REAGAN: Just wonderful. You can't be in the presence of someone like that without feeling better about the world.
>
> JOURNALIST: What do you think about the tax plan?
>
> REAGAN: Well, I can't talk about that now.
>
> JOURNALIST: What did you talk about with Mother Teresa?
>
> REAGAN: Her work, what she's doing. And just as I said, really, here is someone who's so optimistic about all of us, mankind, and what she's trying to do is very inspiring.
>
> JOURNALIST: What impressed you most about her, sir?
>
> REAGAN: I guess she's just the soul of kindness and great humility, because in all of her work and all that she's done, she expresses thanks for having had the opportunity to do it.
>
> JOURNALIST: Thank you, sir.[8]

It was a brief exchange, not even 150 words. Reagan was in no frame of mind to talk tax cuts. He had been touched in an altogether different way. Reagan might have had in mind his words from the Notre Dame speech two and a half weeks earlier: at moments like this, we learn we are spirits, not animals, and that something is happening in space and time and beyond space and time that spells duty.[9]

THE LADY FROM MEDJUGORJE

Much else was indeed happening in space and time and beyond space and time.

Just three weeks after this meeting between a president and a special lady, amid the shootings and chaos, and, perhaps most important, amid all the prayer, something extraordinary reportedly materialized in the communist world. It smacked of the Fátima apparitions sixty-four years earlier, though the official Roman Catholic Church to this day has not affirmed it.

On June 24, 1981, six young people living in communist Yugoslavia, which had suffered decades of tyrannical rule under the recently deceased Marshal Tito, reported that the Virgin Mary appeared to them on a hillside in the mountain village of Medjugorje (pronounced "Med-jew-gore-yah").[10] It was no minor claim. It would draw countless pilgrims and once again rock the communist world.

The lady allegedly appeared in a valley that lies in the shadow of the fifteen-ton, thirty-six-foot-high concrete cross that rugged villagers had erected on the highest peak nearly fifty years earlier, before the ravages of Hitler and then Soviet communism. The diocese had built the massive cross to commemorate the 1,900th anniversary of Christ's crucifixion. The peak was originally named Mount Sipovac, but locals rechristened it Mount Križevac, which means "Mount of the Cross."[11]

On June 24, 1981, sixteen-year-old Mirjana Dragicevic and fourteen-year-old Ivanka Ivankovic finished their chores and went for a walk when they were thunderstruck by a marvelous glistening figure on the hillside.[12] They fled in fright and fetched four friends, who returned to the hill with them and also observed the image. They all fell to their knees. Some cried, some prayed. They did not know exactly what to do, but they believed the figure, a woman, was the Virgin Mary, the "*Gospa*," or "Our Lady." The lady proceeded to identify herself as just that, "The Blessed Virgin Mary." "I have come here," she reportedly said, "because there are many devout believers here. I have come to tell you that God exists, and He loves you. Let the others who do not see me, believe as you do."[13]

Like the Fátima children, these older children (all teenagers but one) devoutly believed. Also like the Fátima children, they were doubted, denounced, and mocked by friends, family, and even clergy. And yet, like the Fátima children, they remained unshakable. What they saw so convinced them that they could not deny it no matter the pressures around them.

As for the lady, just like the lady at Fátima, she came pointing to her son. These new visionaries even claimed that they saw her standing with the baby Jesus in her arms.[14] She came with the same message of Fátima: peace, conversion, fasting, reconciliation, repentance, penance, reparation, and prayer—but above all, *peace*, peace in the world, especially the communist world.

After June 24,[15] the Blessed Mother allegedly appeared daily in Medjugorje. These became the most acclaimed and popular professions of Marian apparitions since Fátima. Millions of pilgrims worldwide would ultimately flock there, angering the communist authorities, who reacted with force, hate, and repression. The throng became so strong, and the news so widespread, that it eventually attracted the attention of Pope John Paul II and even a Protestant named Ronald Reagan, whose interest at the time was unknown to all but a handful of individuals.

There was much more yet to come. Like "Fátima," the unusual word "Medjugorje" soon spread far and wide, as did its message.

A "VILE CONCOCTION"

Meanwhile, the communists were going to great lengths to deny any role in the shooting of the head of the Roman Catholic Church.

On May 14, the day after the shooting, TASS, the Soviet news agency, released a terse statement: "According to a statement by a Vatican spokesman, Pope John Paul II remains in stable condition after undergoing five hours of surgery. The Pope was hit by three of the four bullets that the terrorist fired."[16]

This was not accurate. Of course, Soviet press statements rarely were. The pope had been hit twice. Moscow was overly hopeful.

On May 15 came *Pravda*'s first published response to the shooting, the tone of which ought to have raised red flags to anyone familiar with Soviet propaganda. "The terrorist who yesterday tried to kill Pope John Paul II is a Turkish citizen," the article started. "He is Mehmet Ali Agca, who in the past has had close ties with Turkey's neofascist National Movement Party, whose leadership is currently on trial before a military tribunal for subversive activities in the country." The brief article (213 words in English) made no mention of Agca's connections to Moscow's puppet regime in Bulgaria. It referred to Agca as a "neofascist" twice, a "terrorist" three times, a "murderer" and "criminal" and "killer" once each. Trying to cast Agca as a right-wing extremist, *Pravda* added that the perpetrator had killed a "liberal" Turkish newspaper editor. The terms *Turkey*, *Turkish*, and *Turkish citizen* appeared no less than seven times in the short article.[17]

Turk, Turk, Turk—Turk, Turk, Turk, Turk.

The Kremlin then went quiet until September, when a piece in the respected leftist British publication *The Guardian*, quoting unnamed Western sources, speculated on whether Moscow might have been involved in the shooting. A September 8 response in *Izvestia*, titled "Red Herring," blasted *The Guardian*'s "ravings," "nonsense," and "vile concoction"—typical Soviet language. *Izvestia* tried to put the focus back on Agca:

> On May 13, it will be recalled, there was an assassination attempt against the Pope in St. Peter's Square. The Turk Mehmet Ali Agca who shot the Pope was arrested and put on trial. A great deal was written about this criminal action, and the would-be assassin was shown on television. It was established that he is a fascist and the murderer of a liberal Turkish journalist. He had been sentenced to death but escaped from jail under mysterious circumstances. Ali Agca had found powerful benefactors who had provided him with virtually unlimited funds, making it possible for him to travel freely in many countries. Naturally, it never occurred to anyone to portray this piece of scum as a "communist agent."
>
> But now *The Guardian* (or whoever gives the orders as to what is to be printed) has decided that this must be rectified without delay, and "rectified," moreover, in such a way as to make people ashamed of the British paper's ravings.

"Whoever gives the orders"? *The Guardian* most assuredly did not take orders from its government. No, that was the mode of operations in Moscow.

"It's not hard to guess what these ravings are, or what their purpose is," *Izvestia* continued. "Ali Agca's shot was said to be the result of a plot—not a simple plot but an international one, organized by 'countries of the Eastern bloc'!" The exclamation point conveyed just how *preposterous* such an allegation was. *Izvestia* said *The Guardian* ran this "nonsense," based on unnamed sources, simply "to sow the seeds of doubt, mislead the public and serve the imperialist forces that are continuing to step up the anti-Soviet campaign, using it as a cover for their adventurist policies, giving further impetus to the arms race and aggravating the international situation."

The committed leftists at *The Guardian* would have had a good chuckle seeing themselves accused of being imperialists and adventurists stoking the arms race for Ronald Reagan and Margaret Thatcher.

"The conclusion is obvious," *Izvestia* wrote. "This new anti-Soviet concoction is as groundless as all the others. It's being spread solely as a 'red herring.'"[18]

From what my research reveals, this was the longest piece on the shooting of John Paul II to appear in the Soviet press up until that point. And it came in response to charges of Moscow complicity. That was probably not a coincidence.

The Kremlin propaganda machine attacked anyone who dared to accuse the communists of malfeasance, including Claire Sterling, the leading journalist investigating the Bulgarian connection. In September 1982, Bulgaria's communist regime would release a 178-page "report" taking aim at Sterling. This communist diatribe was titled *Dossier on the Anatomy of a Calumny*.[19]

It did not take long before both the Bulgarians and Soviets were contending that the CIA had tried to kill the pope. Yes, *the CIA*. Truly, nothing was beyond the communist propagandists.

20

DECEMBER 13, 1981

MARTIAL LAW

In the dark of night on December 13, 1981, all hell finally broke loose in Poland. In Warsaw, in Kraków, in Gdańsk, in industrial areas and mining areas, gunshots rang out, tanks rolled in, sirens wailed, police trucks raced down streets, and Solidarity members were arrested. Thousands of union leaders, dissidents, and intellectuals were shipped off to internment camps.[1]

The long-threatened communist crackdown on the good people of Poland had arrived, just two weeks before Christmas in the already historic year of 1981.

By this point, Solidarity represented upward of ten million Polish workers. Given that many of these workers had families, the ten million actually represented the vast majority of the population (which was then thirty-six million). As one Polish official put it, Solidarity accounted for "pretty much the whole nation."[2] That was too much for the communists. They had had enough.

The communist regime cut off Lech Wałęsa and other Solidarity figures in Gdańsk from headquarters, severing all phone lines. Those lines not cut were monitored. The Polish communists detained Wałęsa in an undisclosed location. They confiscated all of Solidarity's funds. They detained more than a thousand members in the first sweeps and ultimately seized at least five thousand (and perhaps tens of thousands) without trial. They tore down any sign or poster bearing the word *Solidarnosc*. Hundreds of fatalities were reported.[3]

It was a Sunday, the Lord's day. Such was how communism treated the things of the Lord.

The communist regime placed the entire country under curfew and set up army checkpoints everywhere. Military men replaced the governors of four provinces.[4] All flights in and out of the country were banned, unless Soviet planes were involved.[5] All citizens were ordered to carry identification cards.[6]

This was a comprehensive purge. The communists were smashing the proletariat. They were suppressing the workers. Under orders from the Kremlin, the Polish communist regime had imposed martial law.

"It was a real shock," recalled Father Dziwisz, who shared the Holy Father's horror at what was unfolding in their homeland. "Obviously, we were already frightened. And there had been growing concern about a possible invasion in the days leading up to the declaration.... On top of that, we knew that the Warsaw Pact forces already stationed in Poland were heading toward the capital. But no one could believe that they would resort to martial law." The Holy Father was "anguished and surprised."[7] "It was a profound humiliation for Poland," said Dziwisz. "After all that it had suffered throughout its history, Poland didn't deserve this new martyrdom. It didn't deserve to be punished so severely."[8]

Ronald Reagan was likewise anguished. He described the situation in his diary: "Word received that Poland has moved on Solidarity. Leaders have been arrested, union meetings & publications banned, martial law declared. Our intelligence is that it was engineered & ordered by the Soviet[s]. If so, and I believe it is, the situation is really grave."[9]

Prime Minister Wojciech Jaruzelski appeared on television to announce a state of emergency. He explained that Poland would be governed by a committee of fifteen generals and five colonels under the Orwellian name the Military Council of National Salvation.[10]

Four months earlier, in early August, Jaruzelski and Polish general secretary Stanisław Kania had gone to the Kremlin to brief Leonid Brezhnev on the latest developments. Scholar Arthur Rachwald speculates that the decision to impose martial law was made there: "A military solution to the Polish crisis was agreed upon; under the approved plan the blood was to be let by Poles while the Soviet leaders pretended that their hands were clean."[11]

That is probably accurate. As noted, the American mole Colonel Ryszard Kukliński had informed his U.S. handlers in a prophetic September 1981 report that Poland was on its way to martial law. According to that report, the Communist Party in Warsaw held an "extraordinary session" at which—under Soviet pressure—it made the decision to impose martial law. "In brief, martial law will be introduced at night, either between Friday and a work-free Saturday or between Saturday and Sunday, when industrial plants will be closed," Kukliński disclosed. "Arrests will begin around midnight, six hours before an announcement of martial law is broadcast over the radio and television."[12]

Jaruzelski would be Moscow's man to carry out martial law. Marek Jan Chodakiewicz of the Institute of World Politics argues that Jaruzelski had long been "the Kremlin's absolute choice from late August 1980," when Solidarity was first legalized. It merely "took some time to elevate" him properly through the Polish Communist Party ranks in a way that seemed more palatable.[13]

Jaruzelski's precise mind-set remains difficult to determine. But most have argued that the prime minister believed a Soviet-led invasion would produce mass bloodshed and thus persuaded Moscow to allow him to take care of business internally. He saw much greater instability if Soviet soldiers were used rather than Polish ones. Moscow, desiring deniability, allegedly went with his advice.[14] Eduard Shevardnadze would later assert that Jaruzelski probably spared his country an invasion.[15] Some scholars disagree, taking a less positive view of Jaruzelski.[16]

Whatever Jaruzelski's motives, he and his communist cronies were indisputably wielding state power in December 1981. "I am speaking to all Poles," Jaruzelski said on national television. "Our country is threatened by mortal danger." The danger, he said, was not international communism but "forces hostile to socialism" that had pushed the Polish people to the "brink of civil war." The Military Council of National Salvation needed to prevent "the fall of the state."[17]

Moscow backed Jaruzelski immediately. "All these steps taken in Poland are, of course, its internal affair," the Kremlin claimed with feigned innocence. The Soviet leadership added, "It is no accident that the enemies of independent Socialist Poland inside the country had the support of certain external circles in the West."[18] That was actually true.

These "enemies" (read: Solidarity, the Church) had the support of the United States.

Solidarity responded by issuing a plea to its friends around the world, from the White House to the Vatican: "We appeal to you: help us in our struggle by mass protests and moral support. Do not watch passively the attempts to strangle the beginnings of democracy in the heart of Europe. Be with us in these difficult moments." The appeal concluded: "Solidarity with Solidarity. Poland is not yet lost."[19]

"WE NEED TO HIT THEM HARD"

No, Poland was not lost. In a way, ironically, this crackdown would help Poland find its way to freedom faster—with the help of "certain external circles in the West." Ronald Reagan was chief among them.

"The president was absolutely livid" when the Poles imposed martial law, remembered Richard Pipes, who observed Reagan closely from his seat at the NSC. He quoted Reagan's reaction: "Something must be done. We need to hit them hard, and save Solidarity." Said Pipes, "The president was gung ho and ready to go."[20]

Reagan was gung ho to do something he had longed for since he sat with Richard Allen watching news footage of John Paul II's June 1979 visit to Poland. Back then he had excitedly told Allen that the pope was "the key." Now he saw that Solidarity was key as well, for in Poland he saw an opportunity to take down the whole Soviet Bloc. Reagan, as Allen put it, "thought of Poland as a means to the disintegration and collapse of the main danger, the main adversary, the Soviet Union."[21]

One of Reagan's first reactions to martial law was to telephone John Paul II at the Vatican. He made his disapproval clear by telling the Polish pope that "our sympathies are with the people, not with the government." He tried to uplift the pontiff, saying: "Our country was inspired when you visited Poland, and to see their commitment to religion and belief in God. It was an inspiration.... All of us were very thrilled."[22]

The president told the pope that he looked forward to a moment when the two men could meet in person. The pope no doubt felt the same way. Just six months later, Reagan and John Paul II would be sitting down together at the Vatican.

On December 15, the day after speaking with the pope, Reagan met with Cardinal Agostino Casaroli, the Vatican secretary of state. The meeting had been scheduled well before the communists imposed martial law in Poland. The original purpose of the session was to discuss issues of nuclear war, the Reagan arms buildup, and disarmament. The pope had sent a November 25 letter to the president, delivered to the White House via Cardinal Pio Laghi, the Holy See's apostolic nuncio in residence in Washington. Cardinal Casaroli had delivered the same letter to the Soviet ambassador in Italy, to be given to Brezhnev. We do not know what the letter said, other than that it generally expressed John Paul II's concerns about the dangers of nuclear war. We know of it because of a recently declassified four-page cable from the White House Situation Room, dated December 7, 1981, and designated "SECRET." The cable stated that the Vatican "does not intend to release the texts of the Pope's letters." That secrecy has held. When I received the cable in June 2009, for which I had filed a FOIA request with the U.S. government, the entire text of the pope's letter remained redacted.

Casaroli had been scheduled to meet with Reagan on May 15, but that visit had to be called off after John Paul II was shot.[23] The May 15 meeting was to be merely a ten-minute friendly conversation with the president. But now, two days after the crackdown in Poland, the meeting at the White House took on added significance.[24]

Three Vatican officials—Cardinal Casaroli, Cardinal Laghi, and Monsignor Audrys Backis—met for an hour and a half with the president of the United States, Secretary of State Al Haig, Vice President George H.W. Bush, Chief of Staff Jim Baker, and several other top administration officials.

The official White House memo on the conversation, dated December 21, 1981, and prepared by James W. Nance, acting assistant to the president for national security affairs, was not declassified for nearly three decades. The cover letter to the six-page record of conversation insists that the distribution of the document "be limited to those whose duties require them to know its contents."[25] Portions of the document were first published in 2009 in Martin and Annelise Anderson's book *Reagan's Secret War*. It shows that Reagan and Casaroli did most of the talking during this lunch meeting—so much so that the Andersons quipped that it was difficult to see how they ate anything.[26]

According to the record of the meeting, Casaroli agreed with President Reagan that Jaruzelski had acted under Soviet pressure but also said that the Polish general had imposed martial law to prevent the Soviets from intervening.[27] One of Reagan's main takeaways from the meeting, as he wrote in his diary that day, was that the decision to impose martial law "was no sudden reaction as the Communist Govt. would have us believe. The operation is so smooth it must have taken weeks for planning."[28]

When the president argued that "the Vatican and the Pope had a key role to play in events in Poland, and elsewhere in Eastern Europe," Casaroli tossed cold water on Reagan's optimism: "The time [is] not yet ripe for major change in Eastern Europe," the *Ostpolitik* secretary insisted.[29]

As George Weigel noted, the classified memorandum revealed that Reagan and Casaroli had "strikingly divergent views" on the prospects for change in Central and Eastern Europe. Their approaches differed as well. The cardinal counseled a "quiet diplomacy" rather than a "public campaign" underscoring human-rights abuses in the communist countries. This was precisely the opposite of the approach that Reagan would pursue with great success. The Soviet Union was running an evil empire, and Reagan was now more convinced than ever to call it such.[30]

As Weigel put it, the long conversation provided further evidence "that President Reagan was rather more attuned to John Paul II's way of reading and conducting world politics than Cardinal Casaroli."[31]

For all of Cardinal Casaroli's pessimism and caution, he noted America's special position of leadership. His comments may have reminded Reagan of his favorite statement by the late Pope Pius XII, that God had placed a wounded world "into the hands of America." In the words of the note taker, Casaroli "stated that he and others considered the United States 'the sanctuary' for the future of the world. It was a big responsibility for the President, but he should know that the world relied on his good judgment and wisdom."

Reagan, no doubt moved, humbly replied that he hoped he could live up to the challenge.[32]

KEEPING HOPE ALIVE IN POLAND

In addition to this face-to-face contact with the Holy See's chief liaisons, Reagan often communicated with Pope John Paul II directly during this period. His first cable, sent shortly after martial law was imposed, reflected the air of intensity. Sent from the White House Situation Room and designated "SECRET," it went to the American embassy in Rome and was directed to the "Vatican Office." The subject read, "PRESIDENTIAL MESSAGE TO THE POPE ON THE POLISH SITUATION," and the cable carried this explicit order: "YOU SHOULD DELIVER THE FOLLOWING MESSAGE FROM THE PRESIDENT TO POPE JOHN PAUL II THROUGH HIS SECRETARY,

FATHER DZIWISZ IMMEDIATELY. ALTHOUGH FATHER DZIWISZ MAY NOT BE YOUR NORMAL CHANNEL FOR MESSAGES TO THE POPE, IT MUST, REPEAT MUST BE THE CHANNEL FOR THIS MESSAGE [all grammar original]." Dziwisz was trusted.

Reagan began the brief message to "Your Holiness" (I'll hereafter quote the cable in conventional upper and lower case) by stating: "I am following the fate of your countrymen in Poland with mounting concern. We must, I believe, explore every possibility which offers the slightest hope for bringing an end to the current crisis brought on by the declaration of martial law and the accompanying massive arrests of the leadership and advisors of Solidarity." The president told the pontiff that he knew of his call for "dialogue" in Poland and "fully support it." "In that regard," said Reagan, "I strongly urge Your Holiness to draw on the great authority that you and the Church command in Poland to urge General Jaruzelski to agree to a conference involving himself, Archbishop Glemp, and Lech Wałęsa."[33]

The two-page cable finished with Reagan stating, "The United States is prepared to support the search for peace in Poland in any way it can." He signed off, "With deep respect and high regards. Ronald Reagan."

In a follow-up cable on December 29, Reagan continued to lament the "tragedy in Poland, which has saddened us both [i.e., Reagan and the pope] so intensely." He told the pope, "In all likelihood, the Soviets will prefer to intensify the repression, for that is their historic response to those who challenge their hegemony." Reagan added, firmly, "The United States will not let the Soviet Union dictate Poland's future with impunity."

The president informed John Paul II of the countermeasures his administration was taking against the USSR and asked him to use his influence with the Polish Church to lift martial law, to secure the release of Solidarity detainees, and perhaps to resume a dialogue with Solidarity. More than that, he asked the Holy Father to help him press other Western countries—using his influence, his authority, his "own suasion"—to join the United States in working against Moscow's designs. "If we are to keep alive the hope for freedom in Poland," said the president, "it lies in this direction."[34]

This was a tough cable that showed Reagan's resolve and his clear-eyed appraisal of the situation in Poland ("those who urge only patience and understanding for the Jaruzelski regime condemn the Polish people to a military dictatorship"). But it also showed that the president was not the warmonger some of his critics made him out to be. Reagan made clear to the pope that "those who call for drastic unilateral action by the United States endanger Western unity and undermine what incentives there may be for the Russians to draw back from their crime."

John Paul II responded to President Reagan with an illuminating letter of his own, dated January 4 but signed January 5. Archbishop Achille Silvestrini, a Vatican diplomat, handed the letter to the U.S. "Vatican office" in Rome. The entire letter remains redacted to this day. We know of its existence from a partially redacted White House Situation Room cable that was declassified in July 2010, which I obtained from the Reagan Library via a FOIA request. In the cable, the U.S. Vatican office conveyed Silvestrini's explanation of some of the letter's contents. Silvestrini explained that there had been reports "suggesting that the Holy See disapproved of the U.S. actions imposing sanctions against the Soviet Union and Poland." There had indeed been such reports. However, "Silvestrini noted that these reports were false."

Silvestrini said the Vatican understood "that the U.S. is a great power with global responsibilities" and that "the United States must operate on the political plane and the Holy See does not comment on the political positions taken by governments. It is up to each government to decide its political policies. The Holy See for its part operates on the moral plane."

Then came this striking conclusion: "The two planes (politics and morality) can be complementary when they have the same objective. In this case they are complementary because both the Holy See and the United States have the same objective—the restoration of liberty in Poland."

This was a remarkable message. Pope John Paul II was affirming that he saw the Reagan administration and the Vatican as partners with the shared objective of resisting Soviet communism, especially in his homeland. The president and the pope were on the same team; the political plane and the moral plane had come together.

"I TREMBLE TO THINK OF GOD'S VERDICT"

Underscoring the importance of the growing partnership, the record from this period reveals a cascade of correspondence between Reagan and John Paul II: letters, cables, diplomatic pouches, liaisons, telephone calls.[35] Much of this correspondence remains classified, even after the death of the pope, the president, and the USSR; it will probably stay that way for another several decades. For instance, the letters from the pope, which are typically embedded within White House Situation Room cables initially labeled "SECRET," remain totally redacted. One batch of documents that I received from the Reagan Library in June 2009, in response to a bevy of FOIA requests, included four letters from the Vatican and/or pope sent in January 1982 alone—and all remain completely blacked out.

Martin and Annelise Anderson, in their careful research of the declassified material from this period, estimate that by the end of 1981 Reagan and John Paul II had exchanged "a dozen or so" letters. Some were sent by cable, others delivered directly. "The letters from the Vatican," the Andersons write, "were beautifully written on thick embossed paper; Reagan's letters were not quite as elegant, but just as clear and direct as the Pope's in spelling out his intentions." The Andersons note the significance of this rich correspondence: "By early 1982, many months before Reagan would meet the Pope in person, the tone of their relations had been set by these letters."[36]

Some Reagan advisers expressed concern that there might be *too much* correspondence. In a memo dated December 29, 1981 (marked "Confidential" and declassified in July 2000), the NSC's Jim Rentschler wrote to James Nance of the White House, "We seem to be overloading the Vatican circuits of late." Nance, in an undated response typed on White House letterhead, said he agreed that a risk of overloading existed but nonetheless felt the need to continue this "special consultation with the Holy See," which, he noted, "is warranted by the Church's unique role in the present crisis."[37]

At the start of January 1982, Reagan made Bill Clark, his old California friend and adviser, his national security adviser, replacing Dick Allen as head of the crucial NSC. Clark got to work right away, as declassified memos reveal. On January 5 the NSC's Dennis Blair sent Clark a memo noting that "messages have been flying back and forth between the White House and the Holy See on Poland." Clark, in his January 8 response, agreed that "we have been exchanging frequent messages with the Pope on the events in Poland" but, like Nance, saw the need to continue correspondence. These were crucial matters that required the attention and interaction of both sides.

Also among the correspondence from this time is an undated draft of a January–February letter from Reagan to John Paul II typed (and annotated) on the president's formal White House stationery. Not declassified until July 2000, this eye-opening missive communicated nothing about policy; rather, it showed that the two men were expressing their mutual passion for Poland and outrage at the Soviet Union.

Reagan began by acknowledging a January 4 letter in which the pope recounted (in Reagan's description) "the tragic history of the Polish people" and their "unquenchable thirst for liberty and national integrity."

Most intriguing is the second paragraph of the letter, in which Reagan mourned the "terrible crimes and unspeakable affliction so courageously borne through the years" by the Polish people. The typed paragraph referred to "History's verdict on those who acquiesced in these deeds, as well as those who perpetrated them." In the draft on file at the Reagan Library, the word *History's* is scratched out with a pencil and replaced with the handwritten phrase "I tremble to think of God's." Thus, the new, edited line read, "I tremble to think of God's verdict on those who acquiesced in these deeds, as well as those who perpetrated them."

This was a strong assertion. Neither I nor various sources I consulted have been able to confirm whose handwriting is on the document. Did Reagan write the line? If not, did he ultimately approve the bolstered language? The record does not tell us. There is a strong possibility that Bill Clark wrote the line.[38]

Whatever the case, it is an impassioned statement—one in keeping with the bold remarks President Reagan had made at Notre Dame several months earlier.

"MOUNTING FURY"

In between Reagan's December 17 and 29 cables to John Paul II, the president's anger at Moscow spiked. According to Richard Pipes, the NSC meetings of December 19, 21, 22, and 23 were emotionally charged—"inspired largely by Reagan's mounting fury at the communists." Pipes said that Reagan compared the Soviet assault against Poland to the Nazi and Japanese aggression of the 1930s, when the democracies failed to stop the onslaught. At the December 21 meeting, said Pipes, Reagan "spoke eloquently and in great anger" about the egregious aggression in Poland.[39]

The official minutes (now declassified) of the NSC meeting from that day bear out Pipes's recollection. They show an assertive Reagan taking command of a situation. He had assembled key advisers: Vice President Bush, Secretary of State Haig, Bill Clark, CIA director Bill Casey, Defense Secretary Caspar Weinberger, Pipes, United Nations ambassador Jeane Kirkpatrick, Counselor to the President Edwin Meese, Deputy Defense Secretary Frank Carlucci, and Treasury Secretary Donald Regan. "This is the first time in 60 years that we have had this kind of opportunity," Reagan told them, according to the minutes. "There may not be another opportunity in our lifetime." He raised his voice: "Can we afford not to go all out? I'm talking about a total quarantine of the Soviet Union. No détente! We know—and the world knows—that they are behind this. We have backed away so many times! After World War II we offered Poland the Marshall Plan, they accepted, but the Soviets said no."[40]

Reagan refused to allow his country to abandon Poland again. This would not be a repeat of FDR and Yalta. This time around, it would be the Soviets who would lose.

Reagan saw Poland's freedom fighters as inseparable from America's own at the time of the American Revolution—the highest form of praise from this patriotic president. "It is like the opening lines in our own Declaration of Independence: 'When in the course of human events,'" Reagan insisted to his principals. "This is exactly what they [the Poles] are doing now." He reiterated, "There may never be another chance!" Poland needed to be supported and saved now.

A few others around the table spoke up, including Vice President Bush, who agreed with Reagan that "a real turning point" was before them. Reagan jumped in again:

> Let me tell you what I have in mind.
>
> We are the leaders of the Western world. We haven't been for years, several years, except in name, but we accept that role now.
>
> I am talking about action that addresses the Allies, and solicits—not begs—them to join in a complete quarantine of the Soviet Union. Cancel all licenses. Tell the Allies that if they don't go along with us, we let them know, but not in a threatening fashion, that we may have to review our Alliances....
>
> But if not, then we invoke sanctions (against the Soviet Union) and those (of our allies) who do not go along with us will be boycotted, too, and will be considered to be against us.[41]

Despite saying that he did not want to deliver this message to allies "in a threatening fashion," Reagan was in fact proposing threatening action against allies who did not want to turn the screws against Moscow as hard and tight as he did. Secretary of State Haig understood the threat and registered his objections, as did Treasury Secretary Regan, who did not want to impede trade. Reagan brushed off their concerns, saying, "That doesn't bother me at all." The leader of the free world pushed, "If we don't take action now, three or four years from now we'll have another situation and we wonder, why didn't we go for it?" Reagan said he was "tired of looking backward."

If Poles, including the one sitting in the chair of Saint Peter, could have witnessed Ronald Reagan's leadership at this moment, his going to bat for them, they would have been immensely pleased. It was because of such moments that Poles view Ronald Reagan as a hero.

In his diary entry for that day, Reagan wrote: "I took a stand that this may be the last chance in our lifetime to see a change in the Soviet Empire's colonial policy re Eastern Europe. We should take a stand & tell them unless & until martial law is lifted in Poland, the prisoners released and negotiations resumed between Wałesa (Solidarity) & the Polish govt. we would quarantine the Soviets & Poland with no trade, or communications across their borders. Also tell our NATO allies & others to join us in such sanctions or risk an estrangement from us. A TV speech is in the works."[42]

The next day, at the December 22 NSC meeting, Reagan continued his aggressive posture. He declared to his staff that the West faced "the last chance of a lifetime to go against this damned force."[43]

That "damned force" was Soviet-led international communism. Ronald Reagan rarely swore, even with milder invectives, but that is how passionately he felt about communist perfidy.

"We can't let this revolution against Communism fail without our offering a hand," Reagan that night wrote in his diary. He added, once again, "We may never have an opportunity like this in our lifetime."[44] That entry represents the fourth documented occasion of Reagan's offering this urgent warning during those two days of December 21–22, 1981.[45]

There was no question whatsoever: Ronald Reagan saw this moment as pivotal. It had to be seized.

The next day, Reagan cabled Soviet leader Leonid Brezhnev over the Washington–Moscow hotline known in the White House as the "Molink."[46] In a forceful, three-page letter, Reagan condemned the USSR's role in the Polish crackdown:

> The recent events in Poland clearly are not an "internal matter" and in writing to you, as the head of the Soviet government, I am not misaddressing my communication. Your country has repeatedly intervened in Polish affairs during the months preceding the recent tragic events. No clearer proof of such intervention is needed than

> the letter of June 5, 1981, from the Central Committee of the CPSU [Communist Party of the Soviet Union] to the Polish leadership which warned the Poles that the Soviet Union could not tolerate developments there. There were numerous other communications of this nature which placed pressure on the Polish government and depicted the reform movement as a threat to the "vital interests" of all socialist countries. These communications, accompanied by a steady barrage of media assaults as well as military exercises along Poland's borders, were coupled with warnings of intervention unless the Polish government sharply restricted the liberties and rights which it was granting its citizens.

This was stern language. The president of the United States wanted the general secretary of the Soviet Union to know that he held the USSR responsible for martial law in Poland. Reagan continued:

> Our two countries have had moments of accord and moments of disagreement. But since Afghanistan nothing has so outraged our public opinion as the pressures and threats which your government has exerted on Poland to stifle the stirrings of freedom. Attempts to suppress the Polish people—either by the Polish army or police acting under Soviet pressure, or through even more direct use of Soviet military force—certainly will not bring about long-term stability in Poland and could unleash a process which neither you nor we could fully control....
>
> The consequences of each of these courses for our relationship should be clear.

Reagan excoriated the Soviet leader, saying that the USSR bore "heavy responsibility" for the situation in Poland, a situation marked by "political terror, mass arrests and bloodshed." Echoing a comment he had made to John Paul II, he declared that "representatives of the spiritual, political and social forces in Poland need to be promptly released from detention."

A POLE IN ROME

Pope John Paul II had some stern messages of his own. He directed them to Poland's communist leadership.

The pontiff had learned of the imposition of martial law immediately. The Polish ambassador to Italy called him at 1 A.M. that Sunday, December 13. The pope could not, in turn, telephone anyone in his homeland because the communists had cut the phone lines in Poland.

The pope's countrymen were under siege, but he was free in Rome. He used that freedom. In his Sunday Angelus address, he uttered the word *Solidarity* six times—the word that was now banned in Poland.

After the address, the pope did something that was typical of him: he turned to the Blessed Mother. His aide Father Dziwisz described the scene: "Turning to Our Lady, he 'explained' to her—as if she, and not the Kremlin, were his interlocutor—various aspects of the Church's teaching regarding justice." That Lady had come to Fátima and presumably foreseen incidents just like this one unfolding in Poland.

Turning to Our Lady that day, said Dziwisz, was the "origin of the idea" of praying to the Virgin of Częstochowa at the end of each Wednesday general audience thereafter. To the pontiff, the prayer was an opportunity to insist on "the right" of his countrymen to live their lives and resolve their internal problems according to their own beliefs.

After dinner that Sunday evening, John Paul II told his aides: "Let's pray. Let's pray very calmly. And let's wait for a sign from on High." According to Dziwisz, this meant entrusting himself completely to God's Divine Providence.[47]

That was an action at the spiritual level. At the practical level, John Paul II pursued what avenues he could. He knew that he could not go to Poland. So he fired off a missive to Poland's appointed political leader, General Jaruzelski, making a direct and personal appeal "to your conscience, General," to cease "the shedding of Polish blood."[48]

"TRAITOR"

John Paul II was not the only Pole in anguish over the communist crackdown. Less than a week after the Polish regime declared martial law, Poland's ambassador to the United States, Romuald Spasowski, defected to America. His story says much about this tempestuous December 1981.

Ambassador Spasowski defected on December 19. Three days later, he and his wife, Wanda, a lifelong Catholic, were sitting in the Oval Office with the president and the vice president of the United States.

It was morning. Reagan and the ambassador sat next to each other in leather wingback chairs. The ambassador's wife and Vice President

Bush sat together on a couch across from them. Reagan aide Michael Deaver (one of the only witnesses) recalled that Wanda Spasowski, overwhelmed by the events of the past few days, kept her head in her hands the entire time, while Bush put his arm around her to comfort her. Her husband humbly said, "It is unbelievable to me that I am sitting in the office of the president of the United States." He pleaded with Reagan to maintain America's outreach to Poland, and specifically pointed to Radio Free Europe. "You have no idea," he told Reagan. "Please, sir, do not ever underestimate how many millions of people still listen to that channel behind the Iron Curtain."[49]

After a tearful conversation, the ambassador made a special request: "May I ask you a favor, Mr. President? Would you light a candle and put it in the window tonight, for the people of Poland?"

The request was simple but carried spiritual and political significance. Christmas was just three days away, and martial law was nine days old.

"Right then," recalled Deaver, the president stood up, went to the second floor of the White House, lit a candle, and put it in the window of the dining room. The two Polish guests must have been blown away by Reagan's reaction.

After this "emotional meeting," as Reagan remembered it,[50] he led his guests through the walkway out the circular drive on the South Lawn. The president walked them to their car in a persistent rain, hoisting an umbrella above Wanda's head as she wept on his shoulder.[51]

The president and Polish couple said virtually nothing to the press. Reagan told the media only that he was "very proud that he's [Spasowski] here in this office. I think we're in the presence of a very courageous man and woman who have acted on the highest of principle. And I think the people of Poland are probably very proud of them also."[52]

The next evening, December 23, President Reagan gave a nationally televised speech concerning the situation in Poland.[53] Since Solidarity members and their families accounted for the "overwhelming majority" of the Polish population, the president explained, "by persecuting Solidarity" the communist regime was waging "war against its own people."[54]

Christmas was only two days away, Reagan noted. He connected the spirit of the season to Poland's tribulation: "For a thousand years, Christmas has been celebrated in Poland, a land of deep religious faith, but this Christmas brings little joy to the courageous Polish people. They have been betrayed by their own government." Betrayed by communists, by anti-Christians, by a "tyranny" that employed "terror tactics."[55]

Was there hope? At Christmas, yes, of course. As a sign of that hope, the president of the United States repeated for millions of fellow Americans the request that Ambassador Spasowski had made of him personally. He asked them to light a candle for freedom in Poland.

Millions surely did. And the communist world responded with rage.

"What honey-tongued speeches are now being made by figures in the American administration concerning God and His servants on earth!" fulminated a correspondent from the Soviet newspaper *Novoye Vremya*. "What verbal inventiveness they display in flattering the Catholic Church in Poland. Does true piety lie behind this?"[56]

From Moscow, Kremlin propagandist Valentin Zorin went before the communist-controlled media to blast this "rather doubtful Christmas gift" that the president had just provided his countrymen. Reagan had "flagrantly distorted" events in Poland, Zorin said.[57]

A blistering response appeared in *Zolnierz Wolnosci*, the daily newspaper of the Polish military, the yes men who executed the crackdown for the Kremlin. Like the Polish military itself, the newspaper was an arm of Moscow. The article decried Reagan's speech as "blatant interference in the internal affairs of independent and sovereign Poland." It also objected to the Christmas candle and treated Ambassador Spasowski viciously.

TASS circulated the article throughout the Soviet empire and added some incendiary rhetoric of its own. The Soviet news service excoriated "traitor Spasowski" and his "impudent slanderous verbiage" to the American media. This "verbiage," TASS declared, "testifies to that man's moral degradation."[58]

Spasowski, for the record, would later be baptized by Cardinal John Krol of Philadelphia, a good friend and loyal supporter of President Reagan. Krol was among several Catholic bishops and cardinals that Reagan communicated with throughout his presidency.[59] According to the archdiocese of Philadelphia, the Polish-American cardinal met with Reagan "many times" and was "among those who briefed Reagan and the National Security Council" on the evolving situation in Poland.[60] At Reagan's invitation, Krol gave the invocation at the Republican National Convention in Dallas in August 1984, and he appeared with Reagan at a campaign rally at the National Shrine of Our Lady of Częstochowa in Doylestown, Pennsylvania.[61]

All that would be more reason for Moscow to despise Spasowski. Not only did he become a Christian, but he was also baptized by a personal friend of the anticommunist Reagan, a Polish priest no less. This was sheer blasphemy. Why did the communist authorities react with horror at the simple lighting of a candle? They must have known what a powerful symbol, such a light of hope, it would be to Poles trapped under martial law. "When he [Reagan] did this, it was quite a special moment for Poland," one Polish woman told me years later. "This was a wonderful symbol that Reagan was going to help us until we could be free like the United States. He was going to end this."[62]

Another Pole, Jan Pompowski, told me: "Most of us Catholics saw the future with hope. We prayed for Reagan, that God would give him wisdom." The lighting of the candle further convinced Pompowski and his countrymen that Reagan was "a man of truth, who acted according to his beliefs, which were the same as ours. We knew he would not betray us."[63]

Over at the Vatican, another Pole felt the same way. And at 6 P.M. on Christmas Eve, he heeded the request of Reagan and Spasowski. Pope John Paul II lit a candle for Solidarity and placed it on the windowsill of the papal apartment overlooking Saint Peter's Square.[64]

HATE AND HOPE

December 1981 was an extraordinary month, one full of hate and hope. Grim as it was, Ronald Reagan, the eternal optimist, found a bright possibility amid the gloom.

On December 29 the president expressed that optimism when challenged by a reporter. "There is reason for optimism," said Reagan, "because I think there must be an awful lot of people in the Iron Curtain countries that feel the same way [as the Poles]. In other words, the failure of communism to provide that workers' utopia that they have talked about for so long has been made evident in Poland." Then Reagan publicly announced what he had said repeatedly in NSC meetings and his diary that month: "Our job now is to do everything we can to see that [the reform movement] doesn't die aborning. We may never get another chance like this in our lifetime."[65]

21

JANUARY–JUNE 1982

FACE TO FACE IN THE VATICAN

At the end of the tumultuous year of 1981, Ronald Reagan was not just angry at the Soviets for the crackdown in Poland. He also recognized an opportunity that America and the West could not afford to miss. Reagan conveyed his sense of urgency with the line that became his mantra that December: *We may never get another chance like this in our lifetime.* He was taking a stand against the Soviets, and he rallied his closest advisers, other Western leaders, and the American people to join him.

As 1982 began, Reagan brought to his side one of his closest confidants, a friend and adviser since the Sacramento days: Judge William P. Clark.

Bill Clark spent the first year of the administration as deputy secretary of state but, as we have seen, became Reagan's national security adviser in January 1982. He succeeded Richard V. Allen, who had been Reagan's adviser on foreign policy since 1977. Allen saw eye to eye with

Reagan on how to approach the Soviet Union—after all, he had set aside his own political ambitions to join Reagan as soon as he heard the former California governor describe his Soviet policy as "We win and they lose." But Allen had come under fire in the media for an alleged indiscretion. Although the White House Counsel's office cleared the national security adviser of misconduct, Reagan knew that "the press is not going to let up if he's in that job."[1] So on January 4, 1982, Dick Allen resigned.

In stepped Clark. He and Reagan, fellow California ranchers and horsemen, were kindred souls—some said like brothers. One seemed to know intuitively what the other was thinking.

The president and his new national security adviser certainly shared a common sensibility when it came to Soviet communism. "Sophisticated" observers of the time criticized President Reagan for a seemingly simplistic view of the Cold War. But Bill Clark understood that Reagan spoke frankly of truths about the Soviet empire that so many other Western leaders, in their desperate search for "common hopes and common dreams," shied away from acknowledging—starting with international communism's utter disregard for the rights and dignity of human beings. Clark, the former Catholic seminarian who had been influenced by Fulton Sheen's *Communism and the Conscience of the West*, wished and prayed for what Sheen called "the evaporation of communism." And as national security adviser, Clark would become a vital part of the Reagan team that accelerated the evaporation process.

Any student of the Reagan administration knows that the major drivers of the president's Soviet policy went into effect in 1982 and 1983, the two transformational years when Clark headed the NSC. As national security adviser, Clark oversaw the development of the most consequential National Security Decision Directives (NSDDs), the formal documents that created official Reagan administration policy. The goal of many such directives—especially NSDDs-32, 54, 66, and 75—was nothing short of revolutionary: to liberate Eastern Europe from the Soviet grip, and even to bring "political pluralism" (as one NSDD put it) to the Soviet Union. These were objectives that almost no one but Reagan and Clark thought possible at the time.[2] Other milestones came during the same period: the president initiated the Strategic Defense Initiative and gave his landmark Evil Empire speech, in which he voiced for the world convictions that he had held for years—and that he and Clark often discussed privately.

Reagan and Clark grew confident that they had a plan in place to defeat an atheistic communist empire. They had laid the groundwork.

The DP—the "Divine Plan" the two men so often referred to—was ready to prevail.

A central player in the DP would be the devout Clark's pope and Reagan's emerging partner, John Paul II.

"WE ARE STARTING OUR MISSION TOGETHER"

Ronald Reagan had long ago become convinced that "this pope would help change the world" (in Dick Allen's phrase). He began reaching out to the Vatican even before he was inaugurated. In December 1980, Pope John Paul II named Archbishop Pio Laghi his papal representative in the United States. The United States did not have formal diplomatic relations with the Vatican (it would take President Reagan to make that happen), but still, Laghi later reported, "Governor Reagan" sent him a "nice telegram" from California welcoming him to Washington. "He had known that I had been appointed to the United States and he sent me a telegram," recalled Laghi. "I was surprised. He said in the telegram, 'It seems we are starting our mission together—me as president and you as apostolic delegate.' So I answered and thanked him very much. Then we established a very good relationship, I would call it even friendly."[3]

Reagan was not even in the Oval Office and he was already kindling a relationship with the Holy See. Note the language used to describe their endeavor: *mission*. That sense of mission would only increase.

The Reagan administration made contact with the Vatican from the beginning. Dick Allen, the national security adviser throughout 1981, said that "we did indeed brief the Holy Father regularly." CIA director Bill Casey met with Archbishop Laghi in Washington and on occasion flew to Rome, secretly, to show the pope satellite photographs and other evidence of Soviet troop movements and missile installations in Eastern Europe. Another key to the administration's Vatican relations was roving ambassador Vernon A. Walters, a retired Army lieutenant general and the former deputy director of the CIA. Reagan appointed one of his most trusted friends, William A. Wilson, as his personal representative to the Vatican (and eventually the U.S. ambassador to the Holy See, once the administration established formal diplomatic relations with the Vatican).[4]

Reagan "frequently would ask about the pope, expressing the desire to meet with him," Allen remembered. Although Reagan's first-year agenda items, especially working with Congress to implement his economic program, made overseas travel impossible, both Poland and the pope were "very much" on the new president's mind, Allen said. On "several occasions" that first year, Reagan received Philadelphia's Cardinal Krol at the White House. The Polish-American Krol was close to the pontiff and perhaps was one of Reagan's first channels to the Holy Father.[5]

The president first reached out to the pope even before the assassination attempts. In February 1981, John Paul II, well on his way to becoming the most traveled pontiff in history, took a nine-day trip to Asia, stopping in Anchorage, Alaska, for a three-hour layover on his return to Rome. Reagan sent a message welcoming the pope to American territory, adding, "I only regret that your stay must be so brief that you will be unable to visit parts of the country that you have yet to see." (The NSC, in a February 25 note, recommended that Reagan telephone the pope upon his arrival. It is not clear whether that call was made.)[6] For his part, the pontiff cabled a message to the president as his plane approached Anchorage. "I send you my cordial greetings," he said to Reagan, "and assure you of my prayers to God for you and all your fellow citizens."[7]

Since their shootings, and especially since the communists declared martial law in Poland, Reagan and John Paul II had begun a rich correspondence that signaled their growing partnership. Bill Clark wanted to advance that partnership. He made it a priority to secure a meeting between his president and his pope.

"It was always assumed the president would meet with the Holy Father as soon as feasible," Clark remembered, "especially after they both took shots in the chest only a few weeks apart.... Because of their mutual interests... the two men would come together and form some sort of collaboration."[8] So Clark and the White House team worked closely with the Vatican to arrange a meeting, seeking areas of collaboration against Soviet communism in Europe, and especially in Poland.

The White House found the perfect opportunity to get the president to Rome: Reagan was scheduled to make his first trip to Europe as president during the first week of June 1982. And so, on June 7, Pope John Paul II and Ronald Reagan would meet at last.

In the weeks leading up to this meeting, Reagan and his team were preparing for what the president envisioned as a final collision course with Soviet communism. He believed that Moscow's days were numbered, as long as forces in the West, from Washington to Rome, had the courage and the right policy to confront the Soviets. Scarcely any leader had thought this possible. Ronald Reagan believed it could be done.

And he said so publicly as he readied for his Vatican meeting. In April and May he gave significant speeches in which he predicted the coming triumph of freedom over communism. Addressing the AFL-CIO on April 5, Reagan declared: "Poland's government says it will crush democratic freedoms. Well, let us tell them, 'You can imprison your people. You can close their schools. You can take away their books, harass their priests, and smash their unions. You can never destroy the love of God and freedom that burns in their hearts. They will triumph over you.'"[9]

Reagan addressed his alma mater, Eureka College, on May 9. During that speech the president said that the "course" Soviet leaders had chosen would "undermine the foundations of the Soviet system." He said this at a time when most leading experts, especially academic Sovietologists, thought the Soviet system was *not* faltering. Reagan added that the Soviet elite held power so tightly because, "as we have seen in Poland," they "fear what might happen if even the smallest amount of control slips from their grasp. They fear the infectiousness of even a little freedom."[10] In John Paul II's Poland, he sensed the opportunity for freedom to flourish and spread through the Soviet Bloc.

On the strategy side, Clark as NSC head oversaw the completion of a crucial directive. Titled "U.S. National Security Strategy," NSDD-32 included this audacious objective on its first page: "To contain and reverse the expansion of Soviet control and military presence throughout the world."[11] The Reagan White House, as the document reiterated, was seeking a *reversal* of Soviet "influence" on a "*worldwide*" scale. In other words, NSDD-32 wanted not merely to contain the Soviet Union but actually to roll back Soviet-controlled positions and territory. And thus, in a major move, NSDD-32 officially authorized clandestine support for Poland's Solidarity movement. It called for secret financial, intelligence, and logistical support to ensure the survival of the independent trade union as an explosive force within the Soviet empire.

The U.S. support for Solidarity included clandestine CIA aid. Writing decades later, Allen said, "Even now, Lech Wałęsa seems to think that there was no CIA assistance, but indeed there was." The national security adviser would have known. He says that CIA assistance began under his predecessor, Zbigniew Brzezinski, who briefed him on those efforts during the presidential transition in late 1980. The Reagan administration "authorized the acceleration of the assistance he [Brzezinski] had begun." Did Bill Casey brief John Paul II on this CIA support for Solidarity? Given the detailed intelligence about Poland he was sharing with the Vatican, it seems difficult to imagine that the CIA director did *not* pass along this information. Allen matter-of-factly states, "The pope knew that our CIA was clandestinely assisting the Solidarity movement in Poland."[12]

One Reagan-Clark adviser at the NSC, Tom Reed, would later call NSDD-32 "the plan to prevail" and "the roadmap for winning the Cold War." The "bottom line" of NSDD-32, said Reed plainly, was "to seek the dissolution of the Soviet empire."[13] And the Soviets knew it.[14]

Reagan had done his prep work for his first meeting with the pope. John Paul II, for his part, had a trip he needed to make before he met with President Reagan. He had to go to Fátima, to thank his Lady for interceding to spare his life.

"A SPECIAL CALL"

John Paul II left Rome in time to ensure he was in that famous village in Portugal on May 13, 1982, exactly one year after he was shot.[15]

Just after he left Rome, Lúcia, the lone survivor of the Fátima children, wrote him a letter. Sister Lúcia—for many years she had been a nun in a convent—appeared to connect the Third Secret of Fátima to his shooting: "The third part of the Secret refers to Our Lady's words: 'If not [Russia] will spread her errors throughout the world, causing wars and persecutions of the Church. The good will be martyred; the Holy Father will have much to suffer.'" Lúcia said, "We see that it has been fulfilled, Russia has invaded the world with her errors."[16]

That was Lúcia's interpretation. It was the Holy Father's as well.

The pope celebrated Mass at the Fátima shrine on May 13. He opened his homily with a verse from John (19:27) that struck at the heart of his idea of Marian entrustment: "And from that hour the disciple took her to his own home."[17] These were the concluding words of the Gospel for that day's liturgy. From the Cross, the pope noted, Christ had looked at his beloved disciple John and his mother; Jesus said to his mother, "Woman, behold, your son," and then to John, "Behold, your mother." John Paul II said: "This was a wonderful testament. As he left this world, Christ gave to his Mother a man, a human being, to be like a son for her: John. He entrusted him to her. And, as a consequence of this giving and entrusting, Mary became the mother of John. The Mother of God 'became the Mother of man.'" From that hour in which John "took her to his own home," every human being was destined to become Mary's child.

John Paul II proceeded to offer one of the richest explications of his Marian theology in his twenty-seven-year papacy.

He said this of Fátima specifically:

> And so I come here today because on this very day last year, in Saint Peter's Square in Rome, the attempt on the Pope's life was made, in mysterious coincidence with the anniversary of the first apparition at Fátima, which occurred on 13 May 1917. I seemed to recognize in the coincidence of the dates a special call to come to this place. And so, today I am here. I have come in order to thank Divine Providence in this place which the Mother of God seems to have chosen in a particular way....
>
> In the light of the mystery of Mary's spiritual motherhood, let us seek to understand the extraordinary message which began on 13 May 1917 to resound throughout the world from Fátima, continuing for five months until 13 October of the same year....
>
> The message of Fátima is, in its basic nucleus, a call to conversion and repentance, as in the Gospel. This call was uttered at the beginning of the twentieth century, and it was thus addressed particularly to this present century. The Lady of the message seems to have read with special insight the "signs of the times," the signs of our time.

The Lady of Fátima's call to repentance was "a motherly one" but at the same time was "strong and decisive," the pope said. Her message, "addressed to every human being," reflected a fundamental truth: "The greatest obstacle to man's journey towards God is sin, perseverance in sin, and, finally, denial of God. The deliberate blotting out of God."[18]

At the conclusion of the homily, the former actor and playwright offered the perfect dramatic touch. He approached the altar and the statue of Our Lady of Fátima and placed a bullet in her crown.

Yes, a bullet. Mehmet Ali Agca's bullet. His bullet.

The next week, when greeting a group of English-speaking pilgrims at his first general audience in Rome since returning, he flatly said that he had gone to Fátima "in order to give thanks that the mercy of God and the protection of the Mother of Christ had saved my life last year." He also emphasized to the faithful that the Fátima message was "a call to conversion and penance." He was no doubt thinking of Soviet communism, among other sins of the world, when he added that this call "is more urgent than ever, when evil is threatening us through errors based on the denial of God."[19]

TWO PATHS CONVERGE

By the time John Paul II returned to Rome, his first one-on-one with Ronald Reagan was only a few weeks away. The pope's staff would have briefed him thoroughly on the background and thinking of the new president. John Paul II might already have noticed certain Catholic sympathies in the Protestant Reagan. In his brief on Reagan, the pontiff would have learned that the fortieth president had a Catholic father, and might even have learned that Reagan's only sibling, Neil, had remained Catholic and in fact had become devout.

The Holy Father surely was aware also that Reagan had surrounded himself with Catholics on his staff, some of whom were fundamental to his growing efforts against the Soviet Union: Bill Casey, Bill Clark, and Clark's predecessor at the NSC, Dick Allen. Secretary of State Al Haig was Catholic (Haig's brother was a Jesuit priest). Reagan's chief speechwriter, Tony Dolan, was Catholic, a student of Latin and Aquinas.[20] Dick Allen jokes that Secretary of Defense Cap Weinberger, who was high Episcopalian, was "maybe even more Catholic than we all were."[21]

Both John Paul II and Reagan were well aware of one preeminent commonality: their shared "dubious distinction" of having suffered, and survived, assassination attempts. We have already noted the many parallels between their near-death experiences. When the two men sat down one on one, they would find that the experiences shaped them in strikingly similar ways.

The shootings revealed, among many others things, an important similarity between Reagan and John Paul II: each man placed much stock in forgiveness. Lying in the hospital, holding on for his life, Reagan had prayed for forgiveness for his would-be assassin, John Hinckley; John Paul II did the same for Mehmet Ali Agca, and in late 1983 he would even visit Agca in prison to express his forgiveness.

A careful examination of the lives of John Paul II and Ronald Reagan reveals many other commonalities—a surprising number, given the obvious differences between their upbringings and chosen paths. Consider some basic biographical parallels. Each came from a family of four, with a brother, a mother, and a father. Both lost their beloved fathers about the same time, only weeks apart in the spring of 1941. Karol Wojtyła lost his mother when he was eight years old; Ronald Reagan quite nearly lost his mother when he was the same age.

In the mid-1940s, both young men suffered physical traumas that nearly took their lives. In March 1944 a German truck struck the young

Karol, and he spent weeks hospitalized. Three years later, in June 1947, a virulent strain of pneumonia wiped out Reagan for weeks.[22] Both bedridden, they spent considerable time convalescing, thinking hard about whether they would recover and what they should ultimately do with their lives. For each, this was a time to discern the big picture, the call. These were moments that Bill Clark, who experienced such an epiphany himself (though later in life), referred to as a "wake-up call."[23]

Both men took unconventional routes to positions of eminence, positions that, as George Weigel notes, "the conventional wisdom assumed they would never hold."[24] Both had been actors, had done some writing, and had even dabbled in poetry since their youth (Karol Wojtyła wrote and published some fine poetry into adulthood). Both gave up acting reluctantly, but later found their acting skills helpful as they occupied public platforms. Father Timothy Radcliffe, OP, former master general of the Dominicans, writes of Wojtyła, "As John Paul II, his theater skills found a fulfillment he could never have anticipated."[25] That was true for Reagan as well. Weigel notes that their backgrounds in acting helped both men understand the power of words, which made them brilliant communicators.[26] Moreover, each man was notably telegenic and photogenic, which helped as they operated constantly in front of the cameras.[27]

As leaders, John Paul II and Ronald Reagan had major appeal among young people. In 1984 Reagan won a huge majority (61 percent) of voters ages eighteen to twenty-four.[28] Nearly thirty years later, a poll conducted shortly after Barack Obama's second inaugural asked Americans whom they would vote for in a presidential contest between Reagan and Obama. Reagan won in a landslide, taking 58 percent of the vote, and even defeated Obama among voters ages eighteen to thirty-four, the powerful youth segment that swept Obama into the White House.[29] Similarly, John Paul II drew vast numbers of youngsters to the World Youth Day gatherings that he created. He inspired a sizable number of young men and women into religious life. Just as we speak of a "Reagan generation" in American politics, Catholics speak of a "JPII generation."[30]

The similarities between the two men were not lost on Nancy Reagan, who saw John Paul II as a great man. Once, when reviewing old photos of various leaders, Mrs. Reagan gasped and smiled when she came across a picture of her and her husband with John Paul II. "Oh, my favorite!" she said warmly of the pontiff. (I must here add that Mrs. Reagan's favorite picture of her husband and John Paul II "is the one of the two of them in chairs sitting close to one another, with Ronnie speaking very earnestly and the pope listening very carefully."[31] That photo graces the cover of this book.) When asked what she liked so much about the pontiff, Mrs. Reagan pointed to traits that she felt he shared with her husband: both had been actors, were outdoorsmen, were athletic, and were "charming, kind, gentle, and sincere."[32]

Of course, the similarities ran even deeper than that. John Paul II and Ronald Reagan shared some important core convictions, principles that stemmed from their religious faiths. Weigel wrote that John Paul II understood human wickedness and the enduring power of evil in history, and how these could be overcome by the power of truth and by a shrewd sense of how the "children of light" could work to bend events in a more humane direction.[33] Bill Clark said much the same about Ronald Reagan. The president and the pope, Clark observed, saw atheistic communism as an evil. Both men came to understand this evil very early, when others did not—John Paul II when he was a student, and Reagan during his acting days. Weigel adds that both men were "*positive* anticommunists" (his emphasis) who sought to counter communism with a positive alternative of human rights and freedom. Their fierce anticommunism did not prevent them from being nuclear abolitionists. (Only now do scholars recognize this aspect of Reagan's perspective; at the time, few appreciated that Reagan abhorred nuclear weapons.)[34]

In part because of their unconventional paths to leadership, "both men were initially underestimated," said Clark. "Observers did not at first perceive their strength of intellect, courage, and vision." And yet, he added, both persevered in translating their personal vision into an underlying policy and strategy to defeat Soviet oppression and aggression. Weigel suggests that they were successful because they were creative and dynamic in their approach, not locked in to the standard "conceptual categories" of realpolitik or, for that matter, *Ostpolitik* and détente. Weigel adds that "both were unafraid" to challenge the conventional wisdom of their diplomats and bureaucracies.[35]

Reagan and John Paul II believed in God's will and had a faith-based optimism about the future. The pope, in his own words, held a self-professed "conviction that the destiny of all nations lies in the hands of a merciful Providence." Reagan had the same conviction. Moreover, said Clark, they shared a view that each had been given a "spiritual mission—a special role in the divine plan of life."[36]

This shared conviction would become abundantly clear during their first meeting, in June 1982.

Frank Shakespeare, whom Reagan would appoint ambassador to the Vatican, and who briefed both the president and the pope, observed the two leaders keenly and points out that "both men were mystics."[37] That is something perhaps more expected of a Catholic, but those who knew Reagan and who observed his faith side would quickly agree that he had a mystical sense. Reagan wasn't shy about commenting on things like ghosts at the White House or the sudden appearances of rainbows or hearing his late father's voice at his funeral.

Beyond their faith-based understanding of the evils of communism and their belief in a merciful Providence, John Paul II and Reagan embraced other principles in common.[38] For example, they insisted on the reinforcing relationship between faith and freedom; they unapologetically supported the sanctity and dignity of human life; they championed the singular importance of the individual over the state; and they both adhered to what in Catholic social thought is called subsidiarity, which holds that small or local organizations, rather than large, centralized authorities, should handle public functions that they can perform effectively. This last principle animated Reagan's passionate belief in limited government.

To understand the philosophical kinship that Reagan and John Paul II must have felt well beyond their anticommunism, consider just two of those categories. The first is faith and freedom. Ronald Reagan's understanding of freedom was not a libertarian one. One of the many leading philosophical spokesmen for conservatism whom Reagan knew and read was Russell Kirk. It was in his 1974 classic, *The Roots of American Order*, that Kirk wrote of the need for "ordered liberty," for ordering ourselves *internally* so as to secure the nation's *external* order. George Washington made the point in his First Inaugural Address, when he said that "the foundations of our National policy will be laid in the pure and immutable principles of private morality."[39] In other words, self-government requires just that: *self*-government.

To Reagan—and to John Paul II—genuine freedom was not mere license. Freedom carried responsibilities rooted in faith. This is the Christian conception of freedom. In the New Testament, Galatians 5:13–14 states: "For you were called for freedom, brothers. But do not use your freedom as opportunities for the flesh; rather, serve one another through love. For the whole law is fulfilled in one statement, namely, 'You shall love your neighbor as yourself.'" Without the rock and rudder of faith, John Paul II said, freedom can become confused, perverse, and can even lead to the destruction of freedom for others.[40] John Paul II's successor, Pope Benedict XVI, said that the West suffers from a "confused ideology of freedom," one that has unleashed a modern "dictatorship of relativism."[41]

A second area of philosophical harmony centered on the sanctity of human life.[42] Like John Paul II, Reagan believed that the right to life is the first and most fundamental of all human freedoms, without which other human freedoms cannot exist. "My administration is dedicated to the preservation of America as a free land," he stated. "And there is no cause more important for preserving that freedom than affirming the transcendent right to life of all human beings, the right without which no other rights have any meaning." That statement is essentially identical to John Paul II's affirmation in his encyclical *Evangelium Vitae*, which referred to "the right to life" as "the first of the fundamental rights."[43] Both the president and the pope called the right to life "God's greatest gift."[44]

Really, on no other matter did Ronald Reagan and John Paul II agree as closely as they did on the paramount right to life of *all* individuals, from the womb to the tomb. Both men heralded the profundity of the American Founding Fathers' understanding of inalienable rights and how those rights reflected the sanctity of the individual made in God's image. To that end, Reagan quoted Father Theodore Hesburgh of Notre Dame, who said that America's inalienable rights are "corollaries of the great proposition, at the heart of Western civilization, that every... person is a *ressacra*, a sacred reality, and as such is entitled to the opportunity of fulfilling those great human potentials with which God has endowed man."[45] Similarly, Pope John Paul II said that every human being is special, precious, "a unique and unrepeatable gift of God."[46]

This core conviction about the inherent dignity of human life, more than any other, led both John Paul II and Ronald Reagan to oppose international communism so passionately. They did not (as so many dupes during the Cold War did) see the Soviet Union as a different but still "legitimate" political entity; they viewed atheistic Soviet communism as a monstrosity, primarily because it trampled on the first and most fundamental of all human rights. No other system was such an affront to the beliefs they held sacred.

It was evil, and they would not shy away from calling it such.

MR. REAGAN GOES TO THE VATICAN

And so, late in the morning on June 7, 1982, these two kindred spirits finally met at the Vatican. For Reagan, this visit was the long-awaited fulfillment of his desire to reach out to the pope and the Vatican and "make them an ally," a desire he had nurtured ever since he watched television footage of John Paul II's return to Poland three years earlier.

Through all their communications over the past year, the president and the pope had been building to this moment. John Paul II acknowledged as much as he greeted Reagan before the press: "Mr. President, I am particularly pleased to welcome you today to the Vatican. Although we have already had many contacts, it is the first time that we have met personally."

The pope and the president retired to the Vatican Library, where for fifty minutes they talked, just the two of them—no translators, no aides. While the two principals spoke, their advisers met in a separate room: Secretary of State Haig and National Security Adviser Clark from the Reagan administration and Cardinal Casaroli and Archbishop Silvestrini from the Vatican.[47]

Soon after Reagan and John Paul II sat down together, they raised the painful subject of the shootings the year before. Both agreed that a hand from heaven spared them. "Look how the evil forces were put in our way and how Providence intervened," Reagan told the pope, according to Archbishop Laghi. John Paul II agreed with Reagan's interpretation. Bill Clark said the two discussed the "miraculous" fact that they had survived.[48] Ironically, the assassination attempts that could have kept them from ever collaborating actually (as Clark put it) "brought them closer together."[49]

Clark added that the Protestant president easily connected with the head of the Roman Catholic Church because Reagan "understood more about [the Catholic] Church than most Catholics I know."[50] In a 1999 interview with *Catholic World Report*, Clark said that the two men "discussed the unity of their spiritual views." He reported that they huddled at the Vatican "to pray together and talk about life."[51] Yes, the pope and the Protestant president *prayed* together.

Because of his window into Reagan's soul, Clark was probably better equipped than anyone else to analyze the spiritual aspect of the president's relationship with John Paul II. "Both are deeply prayerful—in Reagan's case, without public display," Clark said. The spiritual bond came to the fore in this first face-to-face meeting. Sitting in the Vatican Library that day, each leader shared his conviction that they had been given "a spiritual mission—a special role in the divine plan of life." Both men, said Clark, considered the assassination attempts to be "wake-up calls" of a sort, "driving them onward even more forcefully in their respective leadership roles."[52]

What did their special leadership roles entail? Their conversation quickly turned to "their concern [for] the terrible oppression of atheistic communism." According to Clark, the two men shared a "vision on the Soviet empire"—namely, "that right or correctness would ultimately prevail in the divine plan." Both agreed that "atheistic communism lived a lie that, when fully understood, must ultimately fail."[53] It would be "part of the DP," said Clark.[54] They saw that each played a role in what Clark called "the war of good against evil," and each was inspired by the other's "increasing courage and action" in that war.

More than twenty-five years later, Clark remembered June 7, 1982, as a "wonderful day" and a transformative one. That day "gave the president and pope the ability to form a very personal relationship from then on."

Just as important, the meeting led to real action. Ronald Reagan and John Paul II translated their lofty divine mission into a practical policy mission to sustain the Solidarity movement in Poland as the potential wedge that could split the USSR's empire. As Clark put it, "Each was successful in translating a personal vision into an underlying policy, and implementing the strategy to defeat Soviet aggression and oppression."[55]

Carl Bernstein, probably the first major journalist to investigate this Vatican meeting in depth, corroborates these details. In 1992 Bernstein wrote a cover story for *Time* magazine headlined "The Holy Alliance."[56] He reported that Reagan and the pope then and there, that June 7, quietly joined forces not only to shore up Solidarity and pressure Warsaw "but to free all of Eastern Europe" as well. In that first meeting, wrote Bernstein, they consented to undertake a clandestine campaign "to hasten the dissolution of the communist empire." The two men "were convinced that Poland could be broken out of the Soviet orbit if the Vatican and the U.S. committed the resources to destabilizing the Polish government and keeping the outlawed Solidarity movement alive after the declaration of martial law in 1981." Reagan told the pope: "Hope remains in Poland. We, working together, can keep it alive."[57]

Both leaders were convinced that a free, noncommunist Poland would be, in Bernstein's words, "a dagger to the heart of the Soviet empire." They were certain that if Poland became democratic, other Eastern European states would follow.[58]

Looking back on that 1982 meeting a decade later, one of John Paul II's closest aides said: "Nobody believed the collapse of communism would happen this fast or on this timetable. But in their first meeting, the Holy Father and the president committed themselves and the institutions of the Church and America to such a goal. And from that day, the focus was to bring it about in Poland."[59]

Bear in mind that this meeting occurred only two and a half weeks after NSDD-32, the Clark-led directive that had formally established such aims and committed to seeking such alliances.

To be sure, the Washington-Vatican alliance would involve more than Poland. Soon after Reagan returned to Washington, for example, he received a classified cable from the pontiff on the turmoil in Lebanon. The June 26, 1982, cable (the text of the pope's letter to this day remains fully redacted) prompted a June 30 response from Reagan dealing entirely with Lebanon.[60] Clearly, the Vatican meeting had established a special relationship between the pope and the president.

The leaders gave some hint of that relationship in the remarks they shared with the press right after their meeting. Typically such remarks are pro forma, replete with safe diplomatic speak. The comments of the president and the pope went beyond the usual platitudes to suggest a true meeting of minds.

In his remarks, Reagan acknowledged the "values of freedom" he and the pope shared and said he was leaving their meeting "with a renewed sense of hope and dedication." He said. "One cannot meet a man like Your Holiness without feeling that a world that can produce such courage and vision out of adversity and oppression is capable, with God's help, of building a better future." Reagan also referred to "certain common experiences" that he and the pope "shared in our different walks of life," as well as "the warm correspondence we've carried on." These, said the president, "gave our meeting a special meaning for me."

Reagan spoke of John Paul II's pontificate and the Holy See generally as "one of the world's greatest moral and spiritual forces" in a "troubled world... still stalked by the forces of evil." Here, Reagan pointed to "another special area of mutual concern": namely, "the martyred nation of Poland—your own homeland," which the president called "a brave bastion of faith and freedom in the hearts of her courageous people, if not in those who rule her." He added, "We seek a process of reconciliation and reform that will lead to a new dawn of hope for the people of Poland, and we'll continue to call for an end to martial law, for the freeing of all political prisoners." Reagan asserted that the Solidarity movement "speaks for the vast majority of Poles."

The Protestant president concluded by quoting the great Dante: "The infinite goodness has such wide arms that it takes whatever turns to it." With that, Reagan said: "We ask your prayers, Holy Father, that God will guide us in our efforts for peace on this journey and in the years ahead and that the wide arms of faith and forgiveness can someday embrace a world at peace, with justice and compassion for all mankind."

The pope then spoke. He said: "Throughout the course of their history, and especially in difficult times, the American people have repeatedly risen to challenges presented to them.... At this present moment in the history of the world, the United States is called, above all, to fulfill its mission in the service of world peace." In a Pope Pius XII–like sentiment, he added: "America is in a splendid position to help all humanity enjoy what she herself is intent on possessing. With faith in God and belief in universal human solidarity may America step forward in this crucial moment in history to consolidate her rightful place at the service of world peace."

The special relationship cemented on June 7, 1982, would have far-reaching consequences.

THE WESTMINSTER ADDRESS

If Ronald Reagan had been building up to his audience with the pope in his speeches during the weeks before, he left the Vatican prepared to engage the powers of darkness more directly than ever. The very next day, he traveled to London and gave arguably the most prophetic anticommunist speech of his presidency.

Addressing the British Parliament, Reagan said:

> In an ironic sense Karl Marx was right. We are witnessing today a great revolutionary crisis, a crisis where the demands of the economic order are conflicting directly with those of the political order. But the crisis is happening not in the free, non-Marxist West, but in the home of Marxist-Leninism, the Soviet Union. It is the Soviet Union that runs against the tide of history by denying human freedom and human dignity to its citizens.[61]

Reagan signaled a change when he said, "I have discussed on other occasions...the elements of Western policies toward the Soviet Union to safeguard our interests and protect the peace." This time he was laying out something different: "What I am describing now is a plan and a hope for the long term—the march of freedom and democracy which will leave Marxism-Leninism on the ash-heap of history as it has left other tyrannies which stifle the freedom and muzzle the self-expression of the people."

The president emphasized that policy alone would not determine the outcome. He highlighted the spiritual component—a topic on which he surely spoke with even greater confidence after his meeting at the Vatican. "For the ultimate determinant in the struggle now going on for the world," Reagan said, "will not be bombs and rockets, but a test of wills and ideas—a trial of spiritual resolve, the values we hold, the beliefs we cherish, the ideals to which we are dedicated."

He continued:

> Let us ask ourselves, "What kind of people do we think we are?" And let us answer, "Free people, worthy of freedom and determined not only to remain so, but to help others gain their freedom as well."... Let us now begin a major effort to secure the best—a crusade for freedom that will engage the faith and fortitude of the next generation. For the sake of peace and justice, let us move toward a world in which all people are at last free to determine their own destiny.

Note Reagan's belief that a people "worthy of freedom" should help others gain freedom. They should be willing to embark on a "major effort," on a "crusade for freedom," to help "*all* people" secure their "own destiny" of freedom. This was an exhortation.

John Paul II would not shirk the responsibility.

With the help of the pope, Ronald Reagan was going to try to make the crusade for freedom happen. Poland would be core to that effort. With his speech to Parliament, his so-called Westminster Address, Reagan had laid out the goal for all the world to see: Marxism-Leninism would be tossed on the ash-heap of history.

THE REACTION

The Westminster Address proved to be Reagan's most "farsighted" speech, in the words of biographer Lou Cannon, "predictive of the events that would occur in Eastern Europe." But not many observers at the time hailed the speech for its insight. As Cannon pointed out, most of the Western press derided the Westminster Address as "wishful thinking, bordering on delusional."[62]

Moscow was predictably apoplectic over the Westminster Address.

The Soviets hurled invective at Reagan from government-controlled organs like *Pravda* and *Izvestia* and from their staged TV news broadcasts.[63]

Interestingly, however, the outraged apparatchiks said little about the historic meeting between the American president and the Polish pope, Moscow's two nemeses. Looking back in media archives, I found virtually nothing in the Soviet press about the Vatican meeting. A week and a half after the event, TASS released, and *Pravda* published (on page 5), a tiny article saying only that "certain details" of "Reagan's recent meeting with John Paul II in the Vatican have been learned here." Moscow was not very forthcoming with such details. The article said only that the president "pressed the head of the Catholic Church to take a tougher stand on Poland and to step up pressure on the country's leadership by taking advantage of the possibilities of the clergy and its contact with various antigovernment groups." TASS/*Pravda* portrayed Reagan as the bad guy, an aggressive American president manipulating an apolitical pope to advance his imperialist designs against peaceful Poland.[64]

The Soviet piece added, "According to the same reliable information, R. Reagan expressed a readiness to increase financial support for the opposition circles in Poland, especially through church channels." The Soviets got that one right. How did they know? Was it via a Soviet mole inside the Vatican? That is possible. It is also possible that Moscow simply deduced what many expected had been discussed.

In any case, the brevity of the reporting on the event, and the fact the *Pravda* buried it on page 5, suggests that Moscow hoped to downplay the significance of the meeting.

CAPPUCCINO DIPLOMACY

The Soviets may have wanted to downplay the Reagan–John Paul II meeting, but the face-to-face led to even closer ties between the Reagan administration and the Vatican. The president and the pope remained in contact, as we will see. Just as important, Reagan officials like Bill Clark and Bill Casey began to meet regularly with Archbishop Pio Laghi and other Vatican representatives. Moreover, U.S. diplomats like Vernon Walters, William Wilson, and Frank Shakespeare held hundreds of meetings with Vatican officials. All told, the Reagan administration had extensive contact with the Holy See under Pope John Paul II.[65]

Casey's son-in-law, Owen Smith, told me that Casey and Ambassador Walters went to the Vatican so frequently that it seemed as if "they took turns going over there."[66] "They made a lot more visits there than records indicate," said Smith, "and very often met with the Holy Father privately." Smith says that Casey and Walters did not talk about these meetings, and that they took no notes. (For the record, Smith was told that the pope had note takers present for these discussions, and that those records must exist, though the Vatican has never released them.)[67]

The June 1982 meeting led to something that Bill Clark called "cappuccino diplomacy." Carl Bernstein quoted Clark as saying: "Casey and I dropped into his [Laghi's] residence early mornings during critical times to gather his comments and counsel. We'd have breakfast and coffee and discuss what was being done in Poland. I'd speak to him frequently on the phone, and he would be in touch with the Pope."[68] That coffee, Clark told me with a smile, was the good stuff—genuine Italian cappuccino, which was a rare commodity in Washington in the 1980s. In fact, the coffee became a code. Knowing that their phone lines might be bugged, Clark and Casey, when they felt they needed to touch base with the Vatican, would say, "Would you like to have some cappuccino?" That meant it was time to consult the archbishop.

This colorful trio would exchange views on the happenings in the world, always with special attention to Poland. Clark and/or Casey shared intelligence with Laghi and briefed him on the administration's position on certain issues; Laghi would do the same regarding the Vatican's views. Clark's Vatican contacts provided vital information about what was happening in Poland—a topic that Reagan almost always asked about at morning briefings. The Reagan administration's information was often culled from high-tech intelligence gathering, whereas the Vatican's typically came from sources on the ground. Frank Shakespeare said that the Vatican got a lot of useful information from what people behind the Iron Curtain told priests in the confessional about Soviet communism. These were things that the priests could not discuss in public but that went beyond matters of the soul and into the politics of the earthly realm. Said Shakespeare, "John Paul II got some of the best intel from the confessional."[69] Malachi Martin, in his book *The Keys of This Blood*, quotes Shakespeare as saying that "the Vatican is unrivaled as a listening post."[70] It certainly was during the 1980s.

Sometimes the conversations at Laghi's Connecticut Avenue residence led to meetings at the White House, including with the president himself. Bernstein reported at least six occasions when Laghi came to the White House to meet with Clark or Reagan or both. Each time, the archbishop discreetly entered through the southwest gate, doing his best to avoid the press.[71] (After the Reagan administration extended formal diplomatic recognition to the Holy See, in early 1984, Laghi would enter the White House through the main door.)[72]

Clark emphasized secrecy to me as well, saying that the conversations with Laghi were "back channel." They were not done in the open, in public, or for the media or official note takers. Clark said he and Casey kept the project "in total darkness," limiting knowledge of the meetings to a coterie of trusted officials, outside of normal channels—especially State Department channels.[73] It "had to be that way," said Clark in a 2008 interview with EWTN's Raymond Arroyo. "Had it got to the State Department, it typically would have been leaked to the *Washington Post*."[74] Such leaking would have been catastrophic to the project, not to mention the higher DP.

Edwin Meese, then counselor to the president, knew about Clark's link to the Vatican and confirmed Clark's account of his dealings with Laghi. "Clark would brief Laghi on items that the Reagan team thought the pope would like to know and on matters of mutual interest," Meese told me. "Laghi, in turn, would do the same from his end." Meese had been a close friend of both Clark and Reagan since the Sacramento years, when Meese replaced Clark as Reagan's chief of staff. He told me that he was part of what he called the "core group" of administration officials who knew of Clark's line to the Vatican. That group included Reagan, Casey, Weinberger, Jeane Kirkpatrick, himself, and "a few others," Meese said. These were Reagan's kindred ideological souls, those who embraced the president's vision and merely wanted to "let Reagan be Reagan." Certain White House "moderates" and "pragmatists" were not always in comportment with that will, and they were the ones who often leaked to the media. These leakers were kept unaware of the Laghi connection.[75]

In most cases, Clark told me, he met with Archbishop Laghi alone, without Casey. He and Laghi honored a rule to ensure secrecy: "no notes." Thus Clark had no record of the content of his conversations or even of the dates when they occurred.[76] He did tell me, however, that he and the papal nuncio met "sometimes weekly and sometimes more," depending on the issue. He said the same to Arroyo: "We would meet, in one or another way, every week, usually off-the-record.'"[77]

With their historic meeting in the Vatican, Ronald Reagan and John Paul II had indeed cemented a partnership between the White House and the Vatican. That partnership would prove essential as tensions with the Soviets escalated.

22

JULY–DECEMBER 1982

MOSCOW UNDER SUSPICION

After the assassination attempt on John Paul II, Moscow pulled back from demonizing the pope in the communist press—for a little while, anyway. But the Kremlin could not restrain its impulses for long. Soon enough, the attacks began again—as Rand Corporation Soviet specialist Alex Alexiev later put it, "The media offensive against the Pontiff was resumed again once it became evident that he would survive the attack."[1] The Soviets may not have had much to say about the Reagan–John Paul II meeting at the Vatican, but their inflammatory language betrayed how horrified they were to see the anticommunist president and pope coming together.

For Moscow, there was another big problem. Investigators were finding evidence that the pope's shooter hadn't acted alone. The trail led to the Soviet Bloc. Moscow and its puppet regimes scrambled to deny and distract from the accusations.

POPE JOHN PAUL II: SUBVERSIVE

By late 1982, Moscow's propaganda campaign against the pope was well under way. Typically, as Alexiev noted in his media analysis, Moscow would have "particularly slanderous attacks published first in the press of its Eastern European clients," which would then be "widely reprinted and disseminated by the Soviet propaganda machine."[2]

The communists portrayed John Paul II as a puppet if not actual agent of the Reagan White House. They also portrayed him as a political agitator—not only the driving force behind but even the organizer of the Solidarity movement. The labor union could not have been born of worker discontent, the communist press insisted (workers could never be disgruntled in their "workers' paradise"); instead, troublemakers in Karol Wojtyła's Catholic Church started the movement. A December 1982 TASS release said precisely that, claiming that "the notorious" Solidarity movement "was born not in the wave of the disorders that swept the country in the summer of 1980, but in the Catholic Church."[3]

That same month, December 1982, a Soviet publication condemned the "subversive activities of the Vatican," which, it claimed, were directed not only at Poland but "against all socialist countries and first and foremost against the Soviet people." The article blamed the Vatican for organizing what Alexiev called "anti-Soviet centers" (churches, perhaps?) that were working to "train and send propaganda specialists" and smuggle "subversive literature" (Bibles?) into communist countries.[4] The Soviets were especially displeased with "anti-communist forces of Polish clericalism" (i.e., priests) who "activate destabilizing forces in the other socialist countries."[5]

Shortly after these articles appeared, the KGB followed up with concrete action, rearresting Father Alfonsas Svarinskas, founder of the Catholic Committee for the Defense of Believers' Rights and the most prominent religious dissident in Lithuania. Svarinskas had already spent nearly a quarter century in the gulag. Now the Kremlin's party publication in Vilnius peddled charges of priestly "criminal connections" with Nazis during World War II. Practically every Lithuanian priest could be framed as a closet Gestapo member. Meanwhile, in Ukraine, the Soviets seized another prominent Catholic dissident, Yosif Terelya.[6]

John Paul II was undeterred. Neither the seditious propaganda nor the bullets stopped him from defending the faith and the truth. The Polish pope appointed four new cardinals from inside the Soviet empire: Józef Glemp of Poland, Franjo Kuharić of Yugoslavia, Joachim Meisner of Berlin (representing both West and East Berlin), and Julijans Vaivods of Latvia, a onetime inhabitant of Siberia prison camps. The choice of the Latvian bishop was a particularly bold statement: the eighty-seven-year-old Vaivods was Latvia's first cardinal, and in fact the first Roman Catholic cardinal living in the Soviet Union. "Moscow, evidently, was neither consulted nor informed ahead of time of the pope's choice," Alexiev wryly noted.[7]

DISINFORMATION, FORGERIES, AND LIES

While smearing the pope, the Kremlin's propagandists would have to organize another massive attack and disinformation campaign. The cause? A major piece of investigative journalism charged that the Soviet Union had been involved in the attempt on the pope's life.

In August, *Reader's Digest* published "The Plot to Murder the Pope," the result of journalist Claire Sterling's four-month investigation into the shooting.[8] Sterling showed that Mehmet Ali Agca did not operate alone and was not a "right-wing" assassin either, contrary to popular narratives at the time (narratives the Kremlin had pushed). Her investigation revealed that Agca was part of a Turkish ring controlled by the Bulgarian secret service. The Bulgarian connection may have been even more direct: the fact that Agca spent fifty days in Bulgaria, where he received a counterfeit Turkish passport with a valid Bulgarian entry stamp, suggested that the terrorist had patrons in the communist state.

Nor did Sterling stop with the Bulgarians. An expert on European terrorism, she wrote that Bulgaria's communist regime was "one of Moscow's principal surrogates for terrorism and subversion." Quite simply, the Bulgarians "do what the Russians want them to do," she stated. Many Western European officials Sterling interviewed told her they believed the Soviets were behind the killing.

Reader's Digest had extraordinary reach in those days. It was published in sixteen languages and had 100 million readers worldwide.[9] The communists could not ignore these charges.

This is when Bulgaria's communist regime went on the attack, releasing its 178-page smear against Sterling, *Dossier on the Anatomy of a Calumny*. And that was just the beginning. Herbert Romerstein, a former communist who was arguably America's top expert on everything communist, was a key member of a group the Reagan team created within the United States Information Agency (USIA) to monitor and respond to Soviet "active measures"—that is, covert operations intended to sway public opinion in targeted countries.[10] Testifying before the U.S. Senate two years later, Romerstein would report that Sterling and other journalists hot on the Soviet-Bulgarian trail, including Paul Henze and Michael Ledeen, were subjected to "incredible smear campaigns in the [Soviet-controlled] Bulgarian press which is then replayed in other parts of the world."[11]

Moscow's problem got worse in September 1982, when NBC News aired a documentary on Agca, *The Man Who Shot the Pope: A Study in Terrorism*, which later won a Peabody Award.[12] NBC's investigation reached conclusions similar to Sterling's: specifically, that Agca and his fellow conspirators developed the plot "with the knowledge, and perhaps assistance," of both the "Bulgarian secret service and the Soviet KGB."

The Kremlin propagandists lashed out. On October 4, *Izvestia* ran an article slamming the NBC documentary. In this rant, Moscow made two extraordinary claims. First, it said that the Reagan administration was somehow behind NBC's accusations—a power of persuasion with the liberal American media that Reagan conservatives could only dream of. Second, it pointed the finger at the CIA, marking the first time (according to my findings) that Soviet officials charged U.S. intelligence with shooting the Holy Father.

Izvestia made no pretense of objectivity:

> Having declared a "crusade" against communism, the Reagan Administration is going all out. It is proceeding from a tried and true principle: A lie should be monstrous. A recent example is the fuss over a so-called "Moscow plot" against the Pope. This time the role of strike force was assigned to NBC Television. In recent days it has been mounting a publicity campaign for a television film under the pretentious title "A Study in Terrorism." The falsification's main purpose is to suggest to the average person that the terrorist Mehmet Ali Agca, who attempted to assassinate the head of the Roman Catholic Church in May 1981, supposedly had ties with Moscow!
>
> However, the makers of the false film build all their "proof" on sand. First and foremost, it should be recalled that the US Central Intelligence Agency, in conjunction with certain other NATO intelligence services, actively arms and directs fascist elements in Turkey for the commission of acts of terrorism against democratic and progressive forces both inside and outside the country. Back in 1979, Mehmet Ali Agca, an inveterate fascist and member of the

> Gray Wolves underground terrorist organization, murdered A. Ipekci, the editor of the liberal bourgeois Turkish newspaper *Milliyet*, who had exposed the neofascists' subversive activities.

Moscow was working feverishly to establish links from the CIA to Turkey to Agca to the Gray Wolves, suggesting a right-wing junta organized to shoot the bishop of Rome. Why Bill Casey's and Ronald Reagan's CIA would want this pope dead was beyond anyone's imagination, but there it was.

The *Izvestia* article concluded by alleging that the CIA was planting fabrications and smears of Moscow in Western publications: "A Rome court sentenced Agca to life imprisonment. However, his sponsors simply will not let the matter rest. First they planted their rotten wares on the pages of the *Guardian*, *Le Figaro-L'Aurore* and certain other newspapers. Now the authors of these gross fabrications are pinning their hopes on NBC.... No films concocted with dirty hands will enable political speculators to turn white into black."[13]

Turning black into white was precisely what the Kremlin was trying to do.

Moscow's stunts continued. In November 1982 one of Agca's accomplices, Sergei Antonov, was arrested in Rome under charges of collaboration. TASS submitted Moscow's protest against the seizure of this mere "representative of Bulgaria's Balkan Airlines." Instructively, Moscow spoke with and for the Bulgarian regime in this statement.

The TASS piece, printed in *Izvestia* on December 1, backed the Bulgarian Telegraph Agency in denouncing Antonov's arrest as "an impermissible provocation against the People's Republic of Bulgaria," as "a totally illegal, arbitrary and absolutely unwarranted hostile act," and as an attempt to "further a preposterous and absurd campaign of slander and sensational fabrications in order to damage the traditionally good relations between the People's Republic of Bulgaria and the Italian Republic and present Bulgaria in a bad light where public opinion is concerned." Besides, insisted TASS, "Logic proves that the charge made against the Bulgarian citizen is completely groundless.... The illegally arrested Bulgarian citizen does not and could not have any connection whatsoever with this criminal act. There are no grounds for using such measures against him, since he has done absolutely nothing to violate Italian laws." Speaking on behalf of its Bulgarian lackeys, Moscow stated: "The Bulgarian side expresses the most resolute protest against the totally unwarranted arrest of a Bulgarian citizen and insists on his immediate release.

Legality, justice and international law, as well as the good relations that exist between the People's Republic of Bulgaria and the Italian Republic, demand it."[14]

The Soviet vitriol kept flowing that month. *Pravda* and *Izvestia* published at least five inflammatory articles between December 14 and 30, railing against the "absurd claims" of "Western propaganda," the "widespread campaign to falsify the facts and lull the public," the "sensational" reports "without any verification and with maximum publicity," the "slanderers," the "right-wing forces" that allegedly controlled Western media, the "provocation" and "vile hints that the Soviet Union was implicated" in the papal shooting, and the "immoral antics" of Western forces that ought to "evoke revulsion in every honest person." TASS declared, in a statement published in both *Pravda* and *Izvestia*, that the "imperialist" forces were smearing the USSR "to divert attention from the militaristic psychosis that accompanies the West's military preparations."[15]

In all, proclaimed *Izvestia*, this was a "propaganda uproar of unequaled intensity and scope," on behalf of "the extreme right-wing Turkish terrorist Agca," that "sets a new record for lies and slander, sleazy sensationalism and political provocation." It was sad, the Soviets insisted, that the West was using this "anti-Bulgarian slander" to hurt religious people, especially Catholics. America and its allies had undertaken a "tendentious campaign" that allowed them "to set Catholics against socialist countries and undermine the mutual understanding among supporters of peace—believers and nonbelievers; and finally, to sow discord in relations between Poland and other socialist countries—above all Bulgaria. It goes without saying that this story is very convenient for the US special services."[16]

It hurt the Kremlin to see Catholics hurt. And after all those decades of goodwill that Soviet regimes had shown toward Eastern European Catholics.

These fevered claims set a pattern that would continue well into the following year. Moscow kept up an unceasing barrage of attacks against its accusers. At every opportunity, the communist press blamed Reagan and his CIA for spreading their "concoctions" about Soviet complicity in the John Paul II assassination attempt.[17]

Moscow's leading propagator of the CIA-shot-the-pope slur was Yona (a.k.a. Iona) Andronov, a veteran of KGB campaigns.[18] Andronov wrote articles, pamphlets, and small books that incorporated the "fascists" and "right wing" into CIA plots, thus linking Langley with Ali Agca's Gray Wolves. Moscow ensured that these writings were translated and reprinted into every necessary language, including English, and then fed to sympathetic sources in the West, often using third and fourth parties to obscure the origins of the information.

Such efforts often worked. The Senate would later issue a formal report that listed several examples of how Soviet claims of U.S. involvement in the pope's shooting made its way into Western publications. For instance, a French author, Christian Roulette, reprinted large sections of Andronov's writings, often without attribution or mention of Andronov as the source. This author, it turns out, was a member of the French Communist Party.[19]

Roulette went so far as to publish KGB forgeries. Forgeries were common elements of the Soviets' "active measures." For instance, as retribution for the American boycott of the 1980 Moscow Olympics, the Soviets forged threatening, racist leaflets in the name of the Ku Klux Klan and sent them to Olympians from African and Asian nations before the 1984 Olympics in Los Angeles, hoping to encourage the rest of the world to join the Soviet boycott.[20] Not surprisingly, then, forgeries played an important role in the Soviet disinformation campaign on the John Paul II shooting. During his Senate testimony, Herb Romerstein would produce two Soviet forgeries of USIA cables: one showing the USIA orchestrating a press campaign in Italy alleging that Moscow was behind Agca's bullets, and the second showing USIA officials congratulating themselves for hoodwinking the Italians.[21]

The left-wing, Rome-based newspaper *Pace e Guerra* (*Peace and War*) published these two forgeries in full.[22] The Soviets must have been delighted.

A NEW MAN IN THE KREMLIN

Leonid Brezhnev had been Soviet general secretary since 1964, having succeeded Nikita Khrushchev. But for the past couple of years—essentially, throughout Ronald Reagan's presidency—poor health had rendered Brezhnev little more than a figurehead. Then, in November 1982, the general secretary died, reportedly after suffering a heart attack.

He was succeeded by Yuri Andropov, who had run the KGB since 1967, becoming its longest-serving head by far. When Andropov took the reins at KGB headquarters, he ordered a systematic reorganization of its directorates and duties. This included an upswing in surveillance activities on and control of religious groups, which became the responsibility of a newly created Fifth Directorate. The Vatican was of special interest to Andropov. In 1969 he ordered an intensification of espionage operations against the Holy See, as the journalist and former U.S. Army intelligence officer John Koehler documented in his 2009 book, *Spies in the Vatican*. "Besides the prime target, the pope, he [Andropov] was particularly interested in the activities of Archbishop Agostino Casaroli," wrote Koehler. "Eventually, every department of the Church had been infiltrated."[23] Andropov's infiltration of the Vatican occurred during the leadership of Pope Paul VI. So much for the olive branch that Pope Paul had extended to Moscow.

Andropov, of course, had been in charge of the KGB, and the most influential intelligence official in Moscow, at the time of the assassination attempt on Pope John Paul II.

THINKING THE UNTHINKABLE

Just weeks after Andropov became the Soviet leader, an article appeared in the Italian newspaper *Il Giornale Nuovo* claiming, "The news reaching London is that the Reagan Administration's Sovietologists continue to be skeptical about the whole thing, maintaining that it is virtually unthinkable that the Soviet Union could have acted with such reckless imprudence."[24] That is, it was virtually unthinkable that the Soviets would have been involved in the shooting of the pontiff.

Who were these Sovietologists? No one seemed to know, or bothered to ask. The only "Reagan Administration Sovietologist" that comes to mind is Dr. Richard Pipes, the Harvard Sovietologist on loan to the NSC for 1981 and 1982.

Some three decades after this report, I asked Pipes whether the newspaper was referring to him. He responded with a firm no. "I certainly was not skeptical about Moscow's role in the attempt on the life of John Paul II while working in the White House in 1981," he told me in an e-mail. "I believed then and believe now that the assassination attempt was initiated and organized by the USSR. So the Italian paper was not referring to me in this connection."[25]

These alleged "Reagan Administration Sovietologists" were more likely in the CIA or the State Department. The professional bureaucracy Reagan encountered was rarely distrustful of Moscow.

But Pipes understood that such "reckless imprudence" from Moscow was entirely "thinkable." It was within Moscow's very nature.

In this sense, Pipes was of the same mind as his president, his director of the NSC, and the CIA director. Ronald Reagan, Bill Clark, and Bill Casey—the three men who would play the most crucial roles in the Reagan administration's attempt to take down the Soviet empire—all strongly suspected a Soviet role in the assassination. Just how deep their suspicions ran has never been reported until this book.

"THEY WANTED TO GET HIM OUT OF THE WAY"

The Reagan administration was discreet in its suspicions that Moscow was behind the shooting of the pope, keeping conversations behind closed doors and at the highest levels only.

By late 1982, with high-profile investigations (mainly by Italian officials) pointing the finger at Moscow, reporters had begun asking President Reagan his thoughts on a possible Soviet role. Reagan was extremely careful in his responses.

On December 18 a reporter asked: "Mr. President, there are reports that the Bulgarian Secret Service and perhaps even the Soviet KGB were involved in the attempt to assassinate Pope John Paul last year. Do you believe that's possible?" Reagan replied: "Well, I don't think I should express a personal belief on this now. I do think that since an investigation [by the Italian government] is going forward on this, I think it's a little delicate for a head of state to give an opinion one way or the other." The reporter pressed: "You would rule it out? Or you don't rule it out?" Reagan responded, "No, I just say I'm going to wait and see what the investigation brings."[26] The president's comments suggested that Reagan had a "personal belief" that he was not expressing.

A few weeks later, on January 5, 1983, Reagan received the same question and gave a similar response, though this time he gave a strong vote of confidence to the Italians: "I know that the Italians are investigating. . . . I have great confidence in their abilities." The reporter pressed: "If it turned out that the Bulgarians and the Russians were behind it, what impact would that have on Soviet-American relations?" Reagan's reply revealed his discomfort. He abruptly ended his response by calling on another reporter: "Well, I think that it certainly would have an effect. I think it would have an effect worldwide, and I'd meet that problem when we got to it. But until we do, I'll—well—Bob Thompson?"

It certainly would have an effect worldwide. Liberal columnists such as the *New York Times*'s Flora Lewis noticed Reagan's "remarkable caution," particularly for a man capable of eviscerating Moscow. Here was a man, noted Lewis, who soon after taking office had accused the Russians of reserving unto themselves "the right to commit any crime, to lie, to cheat," but now was "ducking the question" of possible Kremlin complicity in this most egregious of crimes.

Lewis understood why: "That is obviously because it is so dreadful to contemplate the consequences if more damaging facts do emerge." Lewis maintained that what happened in Saint Peter's Square could be "comparable to Sarajevo" in 1914. It was a bracing analogy: if the Soviets had indeed been behind the shooting, could it be another shot heard 'round the world, capable of unleashing a world war?[27]

Privately, Reagan was considerably more candid in his suspicions. Bill Clark recalled that in this period, the winter of 1982–83, he and Reagan several times discussed the shooting of the Holy Father, though only behind closed doors. According to Clark, Reagan believed that the Bulgarians were involved, which meant the Soviets were involved, because "just about everything Bulgaria did was at the behest of the KGB." Clark added: "The Bulgarians had no incentive or motive to do this on their own. And it was the typical pattern of the Soviets to always get someone else to do their dirty work." Reagan shared his thinking with Clark and with Casey as well.

"The president and Casey were both convinced of the Soviet-KGB connection," Clark told me more than twenty years later. "However, we didn't want to reveal our thinking at the time because doing so would have accomplished nothing. People already suspected or assumed it. If it was proven, or if we said we were certain about it, what could we do? Bomb Moscow over it? Of course, not."[28]

Clark did not pin down a precise time when they became convinced. But he said: "Casey felt he had proof. I saw the intel at the time. Ronald Reagan believed it as well. Knowing their [the Soviets'] propensities and how they felt about the Holy Father and how they wanted to get him out of the way... it's almost too crude to want to believe that they would want to assassinate him, but that's how they operated."[29]

Casey was increasingly convinced, but not from the conclusions of the careerists in his own agency. To the contrary, the CIA's investigation of the matter was laughable, as we will see later in this book. Rather, Casey at this point was getting his information from Italian intelligence. Clark remembered, "Casey told me that he had it from his Italian contacts that it [the assassination] was Bulgarian with roots in Soviet sources."[30]

Among Clark's NSC staff, suspicions also ran deep. One of his (and Reagan's) most impressive lieutenants was Roger W. Robinson, who ran the powerful economic-warfare portfolio intended to undermine the Soviet economy. "Although I didn't have direct, memorable conversations with the president, Bill Casey, or Bill Clark on the matter," says Robinson, "it was the belief of most of my NSC colleagues that the Bulgarian security or intelligence services were involved in the assassination attempt. It was likewise believed to be unlikely or even implausible that the Soviets would be 'out of the loop' on an operation of this magnitude."[31]

John Lenczowski, the NSC's director of Soviet and European affairs, likewise sensed Moscow's hand. He told me that he eventually concluded "that Moscow was indeed behind the assassination attempt," since he believed that the Italian investigation "did find a credible link with the Bulgarians." "It was always clear that the Soviets did most of their dirtiest work through proxies," said Lenczowski, "and that these proxies did not act independently without Moscow's permission."[32]

Another NSC staffer, Kenneth deGraffenreid, told me: "I had already come to the conclusion of Soviet involvement early on. Put me on the list with the others. Knowing something of the awful Soviet history of assassinations, Bill Casey and Bill Clark certainly saw the Soviet hand behind this attempt." DeGraffenreid added that Casey and Clark "of course had knowledge in parallel with the pope and the Church, which was unknown to almost everyone else in the USG [U.S. government]."

DeGraffenreid observed closely the resistance of the institutional CIA (the CIA "establishment") to the idea of a Soviet hand in the shooting. He had a special seat to the spectacle: "At Bill Clark's insistence (and over the objections of CIA) I had the privilege of being a (silent) observer at the weekly Thursday evening meetings between Casey and Clark in the Judge's [Clark's] office," deGraffenreid told me in an e-mail. These meetings usually included the CIA's deputy director, John McMahon, as well as the deputy national security adviser, Robert "Bud" McFarlane or, later, John Poindexter. "The most sensitive issues would be discussed," deGraffenreid remembered. Clark had a rule of "no notes," and the "sanitized" memoranda deGraffenreid wrote up remain classified. DeGraffenreid would not discuss their contents with me, but he did say, "I distinctly remember possible Soviet involvement in the attempt on the pope's life being discussed at many of these meetings." He also remembered that McMahon in particular opposed the possibility, and that "the institutional CIA" in general "strongly resisted the very idea that the Soviets could be involved and openly treated our inquiries as crackpot lunacy (just as they did with the notion of Soviet support to terrorist groups)." He added: "The shooting of the pope was just one of the many serious issues [in which] we struggled with the institutional CIA over regarding Soviet intelligence activities, and their larger strategic meaning and the shortcomings in our own counterintelligence response. These were very nasty, no-holds-barred battles."[33]

Thus, despite their suspicions, Bill Clark and the dedicated members of his NSC staff had to keep their thinking to themselves. Besides, they had no conclusive evidence of Soviet culpability at that time.

Likewise, Bill Casey could not openly express his suspicions. He was extremely careful in speaking about the incident. In addition to speaking privately to Bill Clark, he shared his sense of Soviet complicity with Owen Smith, who was very close to him professionally and personally, first as an employee and then as his son-in-law. A former law professor who went on to run the Casey Foundation, Smith in December 2005 told me this of Casey's suspicions: "Yes, I can confirm that he did feel that way. He was convinced that the Soviets were involved."[34]

Smith's wife, Bernadette, who was Casey's daughter, recalled her father's referencing a book that postulated the Soviet theory: "My dad thought that book was right on."[35]

This piece of information is crucial. The book to which Bernadette was referring was Claire Sterling's *The Time of the Assassins: The Inside Story of the Plot to Kill the Pope*, which grew out of her blockbuster *Reader's Digest* article. In that book, Sterling concluded that Bulgarian intelligence, and, by implication and extension, the Soviet Union, had indeed ordered the attempted assassination of Pope John Paul II.

SILENCE FROM THE REAGAN TEAM

Owen Smith offered an intriguing answer for why the Reagan team, including Casey, kept silent about its suspicions: according to Smith, word had come from Rome to keep the issue quiet, to not pursue it; the Holy Father did want this issue to start World War III.[36] I have not located documents on either the Reagan or the Vatican side to confirm this claim, though I believe it is probably accurate.[37]

Reagan, Casey, and Clark agreed that raising the matter publicly could only be harmful. Said Clark: "We discussed it, but we didn't want to rattle the cage. We wanted to act prudently. We had too much going on with the Soviets, which Ronald Reagan did not want to derail. Besides, if the Soviets were involved, what could we do? What was done was done."

This means that Reagan, despite the perception of him as a verbal bomb thrower, showed great restraint in what he said publicly about the USSR. Yes, he could be scathing toward the Soviet Union when doing so advanced positive objectives, but he bit his tongue when he knew certain words could be imprudent and damaging.

Clark's sense of the potential public outcry to any confirmation of a Soviet role was evident in a private memo he wrote to Reagan. Dated August 5, 1983, the six-page memo covered a variety of topics relating to a potential summit with the USSR. In a paragraph on page 4, Clark warned Reagan of a troubling possibility if the president were ever to sit next to the Soviet leader: "We would want to be sure that the trial of the Pope's would-be assassin in Italy is unlikely to produce persuasive evidence of a 'Bulgarian connection,' since you will not want to sit down with a man whom the public believes—rightly or wrongly—to have taken out a contract on the Pope."[38]

In other words, if the trial of the pope's would-be assassin revealed that the Bulgarians were behind the assassination attempt, and thus, by implication, the Kremlin, Reagan might not want to shake hands with and sit across the table from Yuri Andropov, the hard-line former KGB head now running the USSR. This was, for the record, a concern the State Department shared.[39]

In sum, Reagan officials at the top levels were suspicious—if not convinced—of a Soviet role in the attempted assassination of Pope John Paul II. As we shall see in the pages ahead, their suspicions would be confirmed.

23

1983

DEALING WITH AN "EVIL EMPIRE"

The year 1983 would be a hot one in the Cold War.

The year began with one of the great unappreciated forms of outreach during Ronald Reagan's presidency: Radio Free Europe (RFE) and Voice of America (VOA). This work was striking in its ambition and influence. It included an unprecedented effort to broadcast religious programming behind the Iron Curtain.

Recall Romuald Spasowski's plea to the president when the former Polish ambassador defected to the United States: "Do not ever underestimate how many millions of people still listen to that channel [RFE] behind the Iron Curtain." Reagan didn't, and in fact the RFE and VOA efforts quietly became one of the Great Communicator's favorite projects, overseen by his good friend Charlie Wick, whom he appointed to run the U.S. Information Agency (USIA).

Another important but under-the-radar figure behind these efforts was the Reverend John Boyles, associate pastor at the National

Presbyterian Church in Washington, the church that Reagan joined after being inaugurated. Reagan was present at the National Presbyterian Church in October 1981 when Boyles gave a sermon titled "Preserve, Protect, Defend," in which the pastor spoke of the Church in Poland and mocked Stalin's line "How many divisions has the pope?" This was precisely the line Reagan had mocked in his 1979 radio address in response to John Paul II's first trip to Poland.[1] That sermon triggered Reagan to ask Boyles to join USIA/VOA.[2]

In January 1983, VOA, under Reagan's initiative, broadcast for the first time a religious service worldwide—namely, Christmas Eve from the National Presbyterian Church. "It was the first English-language service, Christmas Eve service, or worship service that was actually broadcast into the Soviet Union," Boyles recalled. The reverend pointed out that the service was broadcast from Reagan's own church, which was just one of many unappreciated ways that Reagan (contrary to public perception) was "intensely involved in his own local parish church."[3] This was indeed true, even after Reagan's regular attendance declined after and because of the March 1981 assassination attempt.[4]

The millions of people behind the Iron Curtain were not allowed to have religion. But now VOA was piping an actual Christmas Eve service into Poland, into Czechoslovakia, into Bulgaria and East Germany and Albania and Yugoslavia and Hungary and Romania, into the Soviet Union. This was remarkable.

Reagan displayed obvious pride in this achievement in a speech that January to the National Religious Broadcasters: "Now, these broadcasts are not popular with governments of totalitarian powers," said Reagan with a wink. "But make no mistake, we have a duty to broadcast."[5]

That word—*duty*—is revealing. To what, or whom, did the president of the United States have this duty? Certainly not the federal government. Reagan must have been talking of a higher duty—to God and to the "captive peoples" behind the Iron Curtain.

Reagan seemed to glory in this rebellion against communist authorities. Echoing the message he had delivered to the AFL-CIO back in April 1982, the president said: "To those who would crush religious freedom, our message is plain: You may jail your believers. You may close their churches, confiscate their Bibles, and harass their rabbis and priests, but you will never destroy the love of God and freedom that burns in their hearts. They will triumph over you." He then took this shot at his communist adversaries: "Think of it," he told the National Religious Broadcasters. "The most awesome military machine in history [the USSR], but it is no match for that one, single man, hero, strong yet tender, Prince of Peace."

Reagan was convinced, from discussions and correspondence with John Paul II and Vatican sources and with figures ranging from Malcolm Muggeridge to the Reverend Billy Graham, that an undercurrent of Christian faith was swirling in Eastern Europe.[6] Thus Reagan unleashed VOA literally to spread the Word.

Not long after the Christmas Eve broadcast, President Reagan took action to rescue a family of persecuted Russian Pentecostals who had taken refuge in the U.S. embassy in Moscow and had spent *five years* in a basement storeroom there. "If they attempted to set foot off the embassy grounds, they would be arrested," Reagan later wrote. "Their crime: belief in their religion and belief in God."[7] Reagan biographer Bob Morrison, an expert on Russia who speaks Russian, points out: "The Russian word for the U.S. embassy is Spaso House.... *Spaso* is the Russian word for salvation. So this family, they sought an opportunity to be saved, to have their faith respected. That's what America represented in their hearts, in their minds."[8]

The Reverend Boyles noted that President Reagan "took a very intensely personal interest in this family and in trying to get them out." In fact, in the early summer of 1982, in an episode that never received press attention, Reagan sent the reverend "to pay a pastoral visit directly to this family," Boyles recalled. "So I was sent to Moscow."

Boyles stood in Red Square sporting a jacket concealing a large belt buckle. It was a wooden belt buckle that came apart: when disassembled, it formed a cross. Boyles explains the significance:

> If you went into the Soviet Union in those days, the Soviet guards at customs would be confiscating all religious artifacts: Bibles, devotional books, crosses, icons, whatever. Anything religious would disappear from your luggage or from your person. And so, as a symbol of our concern and the president's concern for the family, we basically smuggled in a cross.[9]

Boyles gave that cross to the Pentecostal family. President Reagan, says Boyles, knew all about this scheme. The cross was "a personal gift, a symbolic gift, and a gift of faith."[10]

Several months later, in February 1983, Reagan had a crucial meeting with Soviet ambassador Anatoly Dobrynin, his first one-on-one meeting with a high-level Soviet official. It came about almost accidentally. At dinner with the Reagans one evening, Secretary of State George Shultz commented on the usefulness of his private meetings with Dobrynin, which some in the administration had opposed. Shultz informed the president that in a couple of days Dobrynin would be dropping by his office again and asked whether Reagan would like to surprise the ambassador by joining in. "The president said, 'Great,'" remembered the secretary of state. "He was itching to engage these people [the Soviets]." Shultz figured the meeting would take ten minutes. It lasted more than an hour.[11]

Reagan carried the conversation, raising a number of topics. He zeroed in on Soviet persecution of the Pentecostals. Reagan, said Shultz, "came down very hard on human rights," particularly religious rights. He told the ambassador that some positive act by the Soviet leadership might make it easier to resume overall U.S.-USSR negotiations. He suggested the Pentecostals as that token.[12] Reagan told Dobrynin that if the Soviet leadership did something about the Pentecostals, he would be delighted and would not embarrass the USSR "by undue publicity, by claims of credit for ourselves, or by 'crowing.'" They cut a deal, and the Pentecostals were set free. Reagan kept his word: he did not publicly celebrate the deal, even though it could have scored him political points at a time when the nuclear-freeze movement and much of the political left were demonizing him as a nuclear-weapons-craving warmonger.[13]

Shultz underscored two lessons from the meeting. One, the Soviets learned that Reagan cared deeply about human rights. Second, they learned that he was a man who kept his word. Both were crucial to future negotiations and summits.[14]

Later that summer, a second group of Pentecostals was permitted to leave. Reagan recalled this gesture in his memoirs: "In the overall scheme of U.S.-Soviet relations, allowing a handful of Christian believers to leave the Soviet Union was a small event. But in the context of the time I thought it was a hope-giving development."[15]

This entire episode is enlightening. In Reagan's first meeting with a high-level Soviet official, he made a matter of Christian belief the priority issue. His first agreement with the USSR was to secure freedom for a group of persecuted Russian believers.[16]

Such persecuted Soviets were always on his mind. Frank Carlucci, who served Reagan as deputy defense secretary, national security adviser, and ultimately defense secretary, recalled that the president "would walk around with lists in his pocket of people who were in prison in the Soviet Union." Each time the secretary of state prepared to travel to the USSR,

Reagan pulled out the names and said, "I want you to raise these names with the Soviets." And sure enough, said Carlucci, "George [Shultz] would raise them and one by one they would be released or allowed to leave."[17]

"AN ASSAULT ON MAN AND GOD"

On February 18, 1983, Reagan addressed one of his favorite venues: the annual Conservative Political Action Conference (CPAC). Speaking at 9 P.M. in a packed ballroom at the Sheraton Washington Hotel, Reagan spoke forcefully of the shooting of Pope John Paul II two years earlier, and of his support of efforts to get to the full truth of what had happened. Tellingly, that passage in a long speech came immediately after a catalogue of crimes Reagan had highlighted by "totalitarian, militaristic regimes":

> Now, it would be also unconscionable during any discussion of the need for candor in our foreign policy not to mention here the tragic event that last year [*sic*] shocked the world—the attack on His Holiness, Pope John Paul II—an act of unspeakable evil, an assault on man and God. It was an international outrage and merits the fullest possible investigation. Tonight, I want to take this opportunity to applaud the courage and resourcefulness of the Government of Italy in bringing this matter to the attention of the world. And, contrary to what some have suggested, you can depend on it, there is no one on our side that is acting embarrassed or feeling embarrassed because they're going ahead with that investigation. We mean to help them.[18]

That pledge "to help" the Italians may have carried more detail than his audience could know, given that he knew Bill Casey was on the case.

Reagan's conservative audience, Catholics and Protestants alike, responded with a standing ovation. Chief speechwriter Tony Dolan remembers that reaction, and also remembers how outside that ballroom Reagan "got quite a bit of opposition" for daring to articulate the "need for candor" about this callous act.[19]

Almost as if on cue, the communists stepped up with more callous acts against His Holiness.

For some time, Karol Wojtyła had been victimized by a plot known as Operation TRIANGOLO, spearheaded by well-trained disinformation masters: the SB, Poland's secret police. The SB had a specific group in charge of antireligious work, and in February 1983 this group came up with a new smear against the nation's most revered citizen.

The SB fabricated a personal diary ostensibly written by a female journalist named Irina Kinaszewska. She was dead, which, for communists, meant she was in a perfect position for exploitation. ("Death solves all problems," said Stalin. "No man, no problem.") Kinaszewska had been friendly with John Paul II, and before she died her husband had abandoned her. The communists forged a personal "journal" in which Kinaszewska claimed she and Wojtyła had been lovers. Not only might this be delicious material to blackmail the Bishop of Rome before the entire universal Church—or, as one Polish historian put it, to "shake the Catholic Church worldwide"[20]—but it would also be handy for discrediting the pope prior to his June 1983 trip to Poland, which the God haters were dreading.

And so, one cold night in February, four SB officers, led by Captain Grzegorz Piotrowski, planted the diary in the apartment of a priest, Father Andrzej Bardecki. The plan was to have the diary magically "discovered" during one of the customary state-ordered raids.[21]

But after hiding the diary, Piotrowski went out with one of his secret-police buddies and got drunk. He left the bar and crashed his car; the police arrested him. The intoxicated communist could not control his mouth and began boasting of his cleverness earlier that evening. The police talked among themselves and to other police, and word got out. Father Bardecki, in the meantime, found the "diary" prematurely and took it to the Kraków curia, which quickly figured out what was happening. The plot unraveled.[22]

Sadly, however, this was not the end of Piotrowski's escapades. All of Poland would soon know of Captain Grzegorz Piotrowski.

"THE FOCUS OF EVIL IN THE MODERN WORLD"

Ronald Reagan expected this kind of evil from the communist world, and on March 8, 1983, he made those expectations clear to the whole world.

It was in Orlando, Florida, at the Citrus Crown Ballroom at the Sheraton Twin Towers Hotel, that the fortieth president hit the dais at 3:04 P.M. and began speaking to an assembly of excited Christian faithful. He was armed with a text that Tony Dolan had originally drafted but that Reagan edited and added to so much he was, beyond doubt, a full coauthor.[23]

Reagan started with a gentle exhortation about the power of prayer and how it was essential to the presidency. He even addressed major current social-cultural issues such as school prayer, drugs, adultery, teen sex, pornography, birth control, abortion on demand, parental notification of abortion, and the Hyde Amendment prohibiting taxpayer funding of abortion. Only after all of that did Reagan begin shifting toward his ultimate focus in the speech: sin.

In a forgotten and downplayed condemnation (forgotten and downplayed by the media), Reagan looked inward, rebuking racism, bigotry, anti-Semitism, slavery, and America's own litany of evils. All this sin and evil prompted him to invoke an esoteric term that would have been familiar to Pope John Paul II: "We know that living in this world means dealing with what philosophers would call the phenomenology of evil or, as theologians would put it, the doctrine of sin."

"There is sin and evil in the world," said Reagan, "and we're enjoined by Scripture and the Lord Jesus to oppose it with all our might." And that brought Reagan to his final point. He recalled his first presidential press conference,[24] saying: "I pointed out that, as good Marxist-Leninists, the Soviet leaders have openly and publicly declared that the only morality they recognize is that which will further their cause, which is world revolution." He added: "I think I should point out I was only quoting Lenin, their guiding spirit, who said in 1920 that they repudiate all morality that proceeds from supernatural ideas—that's their name for religion—or ideas that are outside class conceptions. Morality is entirely subordinate to the interests of class war. And everything is moral that is necessary for the annihilation of the old, exploiting social order and for uniting the proletariat."

Reagan lamented "the refusal of many influential people to accept this elementary fact of Soviet doctrine." It was a refusal "to see totalitarian powers for what they are." "We saw this phenomenon in the 1930s," with the rise of Hitler, Reagan said. "We see it too often today."

Reagan shared a provocative anecdote from his Hollywood days (the friend he mentioned was actor/singer Pat Boone):

> A number of years ago, I heard a young father, a very prominent young man in the entertainment world, addressing a tremendous gathering in California. It was during the time of the cold war, and communism and our own way of life were very much on people's

> minds. And he was speaking to that subject. And suddenly, though, I heard him saying, "I love my little girls more than anything—" And I said to myself, "Oh, no, don't. You can't—don't say that." But I had underestimated him. He went on: "I would rather see my little girls die now, still believing in God, than have them grow up under communism and one day die no longer believing in God."
>
> There were thousands of young people in that audience. They came to their feet with shouts of joy. They had instantly recognized the profound truth in what he had said, with regard to the physical and the soul and what was truly important.

This was the crux of the malevolence of Soviet communism. It denied the soul. To Reagan, what was truly important was the soul, which far outweighed the state. States come and go, but souls are eternal. The Soviet suppression of speech and press and farms and factories was nothing compared to the unrivaled iniquity of trying to suppress souls.

Reagan continued: "Let us pray for the salvation of all of those who live in that totalitarian darkness—pray they will discover the joy of knowing God.[25] But until they do, let us be aware that while they preach the supremacy of the state, declare its omnipotence over individual man, and predict its eventual domination of all peoples on the Earth, they are the focus of evil in the modern world."

They are the focus of evil in the modern world. For Reagan, not to speak out against this evil was itself an evil. Quoting C. S. Lewis in *The Screwtape Letters*, Reagan averred that "the greatest evil" was done less in concentration camps and labor camps than "in clear, carpeted, warmed, and well-lighted offices, by quiet men with white collars and cut fingernails and smooth-shaven cheeks who do not need to raise their voice." Because these "quiet men" do not "raise their voices," said the president, evil is allowed to advance. Reagan asserted:

> You know, I've always believed that old Screwtape reserved his best efforts for those of you in the church. So, in your discussions of the nuclear freeze proposals, I urge you to beware the temptation of pride—the temptation of blithely declaring yourselves above it all and label both sides equally at fault, to ignore the facts of history and the aggressive impulses of an evil empire, to simply call the arms race a giant misunderstanding and thereby remove yourself from the struggle between right and wrong and good and evil.

Reagan refused to be a quiet man. It was time to call the Soviet Union what it was: an Evil Empire.

The president finished by quoting Whittaker Chambers, whose book *Witness* had so inspired him:

> Whittaker Chambers [said that] Marxism-Leninism is actually the second oldest faith, first proclaimed in the Garden of Eden with the words of temptation, "Ye shall be as gods." The Western World can answer this challenge, he wrote, "but only provided that its faith in God and the freedom He enjoins is as great as communism's faith in Man."
>
> I believe we shall rise to the challenge. I believe that communism is another sad, bizarre chapter in human history whose last pages even now are being written. I believe this because the source of our strength in the quest for human freedom is not material, but spiritual. And because it knows no limitation, it must terrify and ultimately triumph over those who would enslave their fellow man.

This was no mere battle of bombs and bullets; it was a battle of moral will and faith, of right versus wrong, of good versus evil. It was up to the West to save the world from this godless force.

"IS THE SYSTEM THAT ALLOWED THIS NOT EVIL?"

It did not take long for the "Evil Empire" speech to make waves outside Orlando. Fittingly, it was those who subscribed to moral equivalency between the United States and the USSR who took greatest offense at Reagan's speech. Anthony Lewis of the *New York Times*, a citadel of moral equivalency, denounced the speech as "outrageous" and "simplistic" before ultimately concluding that it was "primitive—the only word for it."[26] In the *Washington Post*, Richard Cohen asked: "Question: What does Ronald Reagan have in common with my grandmother? Answer: They are both religious bigots."[27]

Another nasty shot at Reagan came from the historian Henry Steele Commager of Columbia University, longtime hotbed of communist penetration. "It was the worst presidential speech in American history," opined Commager, "and I've read them all." This was because of its "gross appeal to religious prejudice."[28] To Commager and his pro-communist pals at Columbia, Reagan's unpardonable sin was his strident anticommunism.

The New Republic, leading voice of the American left, published a sarcastic editorial titled "Reverend Reagan." Reagan's rhetoric was "deeply divisive," said the *New Republic.* He had employed "very poor history." The editors complained that Reagan had given not a speech but a sermon, and protested, "We elected a president, not a priest."[29]

Later, in his memoirs, Reagan wrote: "Although a lot of liberal pundits jumped on my speech at Orlando and said it showed I was a rhetorical hip-shooter who was recklessly and unconsciously provoking the Soviets into war, I made the 'Evil Empire' speech and others like it with malice aforethought."[30] Reagan's chief motivation was laid bare in the speech itself. Reagan believed he had no choice, morally or spiritually, but to condemn the Soviet system because it was evil, and both Scripture and Jesus Christ command Christians to oppose evil with all their might. He would be remiss in his Christian duty if he did *not* denounce and oppose the Soviet Union.

After the presidency, he would explain: "For too long our leaders were unable to describe the Soviet Union as it actually was. The keepers of our foreign-policy knowledge...found it illiberal and provocative to be so honest. I've always believed, however, that it's important to define differences, because there are choices and decisions to be made in life and history." He went on: "The Soviet system over the years has purposely starved, murdered, and brutalized its own people. Millions were killed; it's all right there in the history books. It put other citizens it disagreed with into psychiatric hospitals, sometimes drugging them into oblivion. Is the system that allowed this not evil? Then why shouldn't we say so?"[31] To suggest that the two sides in the Cold War were moral equals was "rubbish," said Reagan.

Reagan believed that honesty was necessary to eliminate illusions. "We were always too worried we would offend the Soviets if we struck at anything so basic," he said. "Well, so what? Marxist-Leninist thought is an empty cupboard. Everyone knew it by the 1980s, but no one was saying it."[32] After a decade of détente, in which both Republican and Democratic presidents had urged Americans to accept their differences with the Soviet Union and allow the USSR to pursue its self-interests, Reagan was seeking to remoralize the conflict. He wanted to make the case to the public that the Cold War with the USSR was not a "giant misunderstanding" but a just war.

This hints at perhaps the most unappreciated aspect of Reagan's rhetoric: though he could not and would not fire weapons at the adversary, he understood that words could be extremely effective in a confrontation in which the core issue came down to good versus evil. Such rhetorical cruise missiles would not knock down buildings, but, Reagan hoped, they might be lethal to the Soviet system in the long term.

Indeed, Reagan's "primitive" speech had an uplifting effect on many trapped inside the Soviet Union. At the time, Anatoly (Natan) Sharansky was an inmate of Permanent Labor Camp 35, confined to a tiny prison cell on the border of Siberia. One of his jailers let him read a copy of *Pravda* that condemned Reagan's remarks. Sharansky immediately recognized the significance of the American president's statement. He began tapping the good news in Morse code to his fellow gulag residents. The word spread quickly through the prison. "We dissidents were ecstatic," said Sharansky. "Finally, the leader of the free world had spoken the truth—a truth that burned inside the heart of each and every one of us."[33]

Remembering the event years later, Sharansky said he learned how much criticism Reagan came under for casting the Cold War as a clash of good and evil. "Well," he wrote, "Reagan was right and his critics were wrong."

POLAND'S PROMOTER

While Reagan excoriated an Evil Empire headquartered in Moscow, he encouraged and even elevated a people suffering within that empire: Karol Wojtyła's people in Poland.

By this time, U.S. aid to the Solidarity underground was covertly flowing, launched via NSDD-32 and directed with Bill Clark's strong push from the NSC. Likewise flowing Poland's way was a steady stream of words of support from the Oval Office.[34] There were so many such words that the final index to Ronald Reagan's official *Public Papers* lists 216 page references to Poland or Solidarity, with multiple references on most pages. Most other countries have far fewer references.

This vocal support for Poland's "freedom fighters" (as Reagan called them) started early and in all sorts of novel ways. In April 1981, while still recovering from John Hinckley's bullet, President Reagan was readying to acknowledge the 190th anniversary of the Polish Constitution, which had been achieved on May 3, 1791. This might seem a stretch: The Polish Constitution? For its 190th anniversary? That was an odd marker. It was not a bicentennial. But that was not the point.

As Polish native Richard Pipes noted in an April 27, 1981, NSC memo to Dick Allen, this document was "of great importance in the history of constitutional and parliamentary government." Professor Pipes added that the constitution had been "issued under conditions which very much resemble those of today, namely direct Russian pressure which the Poles sought to overcome... by democratic internal reforms." Pipes thus recommended that President Reagan issue a proclamation honoring both this historic event and those Poles seeking to restore freedom. The Reagan White House did just that, issuing a formal proclamation commemorating Polish Constitution Day.[35]

Reagan always sought teachable moments to promote Poland. This continued throughout 1983.

On June 23, for instance, Reagan spoke to Polish Americans in Chicago, where he said that Americans were bound to Poles and would "never, never forget the brave people of Poland and their courageous struggle." Martial law would not crush the Polish will, said Reagan: "No one can crush the spirit of the Polish people."[36]

Four weeks later, on July 19, Reagan observed Captive Nations Week by heralding the notion of a free Poland and denouncing Moscow's enslavement of Poles. He quoted his Polish friend in the Vatican: "As Pope John Paul [II] told his beloved Poles, we are blessed by divine heritage. We are children of God and we cannot be slaves."[37] Reagan would use that papal line often in service of fighting for Poles.

Reagan spoke up for Poles so often that a casual observer might have thought that the president was an ethnic Pole himself.[38] The Kremlin felt that way. "One has the impression that it will not take much more for Reagan to start speaking fluent Polish!" complained a writer at *Izvestia*. This writer/propagandist, Alexander Bovin, fulminated that Reagan "does not give a damn about Polish workers' rights." Reagan's words on behalf of Poles were mere "hypocritical sympathy," a "cynical, dishonest, shameless farce and nothing more."[39]

The president's public support for Poland warmed Polish hearts from Gdańsk to the Vatican. Is it any surprise that Karol Wojtyła and Reagan struck such a kinship?

DEALING WITH THE AMERICAN BISHOPS

If only Reagan could have struck such an easy kinship with the pope's officials in his own country—that is, with the bishops in America.

Ronald Reagan and his closest advisers found themselves in an extended and often contentious discussion with the American bishops over nuclear weapons. This battle had gone on since 1981 and reached a peak in 1983.[40]

For a flashpoint of how soon the frictions began, consider this assessment by Bishop Thomas Gumbleton of Detroit shortly after Reagan's election. In November 1980, Gumbleton told the National Conference of Catholic Bishops that Reagan's election and thinking on nuclear weapons meant that "we are getting ever more closer [*sic*] to the day when we will wage that nuclear war and it will be the war that will end the world as we know it. We are at a point of urgent crisis. We have to face this question and face it very clearly."[41]

Gumbleton had been president of Pax Christi, the Catholic peace organization, and was a well-known antiwar activist and member of the religious left. He had openly endorsed George McGovern's presidential bid. Gumbleton became a key figure in the nuclear-freeze movement, a left-wing movement that rose up around the country and world, mobilized by opposition to Reagan's defense and nuclear programs, including the president's plans for the Pershing II missile, the MX missile, and the B-1 bomber. This movement jolted the Reagan administration with its ability to generate massive protests throughout America and Western Europe, including a crowd of close to a million in New York's Central Park.[42] Many or most of those in the movement were genuine peaceniks, but others were from the farthest reaches of the anti-American, pro-Soviet left. Moscow was thrilled with the movement. There remains debate over whether the KGB provided it with any funding.[43] In a way, the point is moot, since the movement did Moscow's bidding against the Reagan administration regardless.

Bishop Gumbleton and other nuclear-freeze activists did not understand that Reagan's tough rhetoric toward the Soviets and plans for an arms buildup were intended not to provoke Moscow to war but, quite the contrary, to bring the Soviets to the negotiating table to cut arsenals. That was the essence of Reagan's philosophy of "peace through strength."[44]

Ronald Reagan was, in truth, a nuclear abolitionist. Unlike his immediate White House predecessors, Democrat and Republican alike, Reagan wanted to reduce rather than merely limit the growth of nuclear weapons. He estimated that the Kremlin would join him in that endeavor only if it had incentive. America needed to build up before it and the USSR could build down. President Reagan, and Bill Clark, grew frustrated by the administration's apparent inability to make this thinking clear to Gumbleton and many other left-leaning bishops (early on, at least).

One representative of this school was Bishop Raymond Lucker, a fellow member of Pax Christi. Lucker complained to the press that the Reagan administration was pushing an arms buildup rather than disarmament.[45] His statement revealed his poor misunderstanding of the Reagan administration's thinking: yes, the administration was pushing an arms buildup, but it was doing so for the *purpose* of achieving disarmament.

The National Conference of Catholic Bishops decided to take up the issue. The bishops formed an Ad Hoc Committee on War and Peace that would ultimately produce a sixty-four-page "pastoral letter" titled *The Challenge of Peace: God's Promise and Our Response.* Gumbleton was included on the committee, as was his polar opposite in the debate, Bishop John O'Connor of the Military Vicariate, and other bishops in between.

The ad hoc committee held its first meeting in Washington on July 26, 1981. On May 13, 1982, it met with several Reagan administration officials, including with Defense Secretary Caspar Weinberger, the State Department's Lawrence Eagleburger, and veteran diplomat Eugene Rostow. Despite the efforts of the president and his staff, however, the bishops never met with Reagan himself. This refusal frustrated Reagan, who had enormous confidence not only in his ideas but also in his personal ability to bring people to his side of an argument, especially when his views were provided directly, without a filter. He later wrote of his frustration in a private letter to Bishop Mark Hurley of Santa Rosa, California: "I can't help but feel if we had an opportunity to talk together we might find there were fewer differences between us than at times seem to be."[46]

The bishops' first draft report appeared in August 1982, under the title "God's Hope in a Time of Fear." It was the first of many contested iterations. As the scholar Jared McBrady notes in his excellent analysis, the draft "embrace[d] the language of the nuclear freeze movement in calling for an immediate end to further development, production, and deployment of nuclear weapons and delivery systems, as well as for a reduction in the number of existing nuclear weapons."[47]

The Kremlin applauded the clergymen for their open-mindedness and dedication to "peace"—that is, to the Soviet position against Reagan. Certain bishops were proving themselves splendid dupes for political exploitation and propaganda.

Of course, many priests were disappointed in the bishops' spectacle. A Catholic priest from Chicago named John Kmech, a former prisoner of a Siberian concentration camp, wrote to President Reagan: "I know how deceitful the Soviet government is. They propose peace to the world while they build-up their war machinery." He typed in capital letters for emphasis: "DO NOT BELIEVE THEM! DO NOT TRUST THEM!!" Kmech encouraged Reagan: "I back you 100%, and I apologize for the silly ramblings of the American bishops.... Forgive them for they know not what they do."

Reagan wrote back to Kmech, "I can't tell you how much your letter...meant to me and how grateful I am." He continued, "If only more people and, yes, if the Bishops could hear and heed the words of someone like yourself who knows firsthand the Godless tyranny of Soviet totalitarianism." Kmech was not the only priest who wrote to Reagan pledging support.[48]

Bill Clark became Reagan's front man in responding to the bishops.[49] Clark wrote the Reagan administration's formal response to the first draft of their report, the text of which was reprinted in many newspapers. As each draft of the bishops' report appeared, Clark would send another lengthy letter to the head of the ad hoc committee, Archbishop Joseph Bernardin. One seven-page missive was part of a package that also featured detailed letters from Weinberger, Eagleburger, and Rostow, laying out in minute detail where and how the bishops simply had their facts wrong.

Aside from Clark's interventions, the most important attempts to talk sense to the bishops came from the Vatican, including Archbishop Pio Laghi; Cardinal Casaroli; Cardinal Joseph Ratzinger (the future Pope Benedict XVI), the prefect for the Vatican's Congregation for the Doctrine of the Faith; and Father Jan Schotte of the Holy See's Pontifical Justice and Peace Commission. Also keenly interested was Pope John Paul II himself.[50]

The Vatican offered thoughtful objections to the pastoral letter. Ratzinger wanted to know more from the American bishops on the morality of deterrence. He asked them to consider whether a country's possession of nuclear weapons for the purpose of promoting disarmament was something that could be judged morally acceptable. Had this been considered? The Holy See also wanted the bishops to be clear about the level of teaching and moral authority of their letter for their flock. This is always a common matter for clarity in Catholicism: to what degree is a certain statement binding upon the laity? In particular, the Vatican seemed bothered that the U.S. bishops were stepping far outside their area of expertise in addressing specific forms of American weaponry and programs.[51]

Father Jan Schotte objected that the bishops seemed to be proposing a new "double Catholic tradition" of just-war theory and pacifism, when, in fact, only the former was a Catholic tradition (dating back 1,600 years to the writings of Saint Augustine). Moreover, Schotte and the others did not appreciate that the bishops appeared to gloss over the horrors of Soviet communism and neglected even to mention the USSR while sharply criticizing the United States.[52] This was no doubt a point that John Paul II agreed with.

Schotte's report was released in January 1983. A few weeks later, on February 2, Archbishop Bernardin met with Pope John Paul II at the Vatican. Of this hour-long lunch, McBrady writes: "The pope did not ask for specific changes [to the pastoral letter], but he warned that the Church must not be seen as pacifist or as calling for unilateral U.S. disarmament. The Soviet Union, the pope said, did not subscribe to the same moral principles as the Church. Finally, the pope gave Bernardin specific responsibility for the pastoral."[53]

Bernardin clearly took the pontiff's counsel to heart. Yet not everyone on the ad hoc committee was satisfied with Schotte's synthesis. At one point, Bishop Gumbleton threatened to quit the committee if certain points were not dropped.[54]

Around this same time, January–February 1983, Clark and Weinberger initiated a key round of letters to Bernardin. Clark intended to drive home Reagan's "peace through strength" approach. This time, Bernardin responded very positively. In fact, the archbishop told the *New York Times* that Clark had "clarified" the administration's position in a way that the bishops had initially "misunderstood." That was a significant admission.[55]

By the time the third draft of the pastoral letter appeared, the tone and content had changed. The *New York Times* headline read, "Bishops Rethink the Unthinkable."[56] The State Department said that the bishops' report had been "substantially improved." For his part, Clark commended the "important and reasonable contribution" of the bishops while acknowledging that the administration did not accept all of their judgments.

More than twenty years later, when he could be more candid in speaking of the affair, Clark told me: "The bishops had to retract some of their statements because they had them wrong. They simply had their facts incorrect."

The bishops' conference approved the final draft of *The Challenge of Peace* on May 3, 1983, by a vote of 238–9. McBrady concludes, "The final text, although no endorsement of Reagan's nuclear policies, was more favorable to the president than earlier drafts had been, and it was much less critical of the administration's policies than the nuclear freeze movement and many U.S. bishops actually desired."[57] Also, as Schotte had requested, the report strengthened criticisms of Soviet behavior, which in some cases it described as "reprehensible."

McBrady underscores the impact of the Reagan–John Paul II relationship: "The nature of cooperation between the Reagan administration and the Vatican, and the shared goals and level of trust that existed between the president and the pope, certainly colored the way *The Challenge of Peace* was revised."[58]

Later that month, on May 25, Congress approved funding for a modified version of the MX missile program. This and other programs, especially the Pershing IIs, would prod the Soviets to the negotiating table, just as Reagan predicted. Within just four years, the Soviet general secretary would be sitting next to Reagan in Washington signing the greatest nuclear-missile-reduction treaty in history. The liberal bishops could not have been more wrong about Reagan and his intentions.

KAROL WOJTYŁA RETURNS TO POLAND

Six weeks after the American bishops approved *The Challenge of Peace*, Pope John Paul II made a second return to his homeland. The trip, which began June 16, has been overshadowed historically by his June 1979 visit. But it is a mistake to overlook this second trip, which was consequential it its own right.

Devoted Poles were again ready, heading to their churches, grabbing their rosaries.

And devoted communists were likewise again ready, heading to their barricades, grabbing their weaponry.

Vadim Pavlov, the head of the KGB mission in Warsaw, sounded the alarm in the Kremlin. It was Pavlov, recall, who, the day after Karol Wojtyła's election as pope, had sent Moscow an assessment by the Polish SB warning of the new pontiff's "extreme anti-Communist views." Now Pavlov forwarded to KGB chairman Viktor Chebrikov a request from General Czesław Kiszczak, chief of Poland's military intelligence, asking for "material and technical assistance in connection with the Pope's visit." This included 20 armed personnel carriers, 150 rifles for firing rubber bullets, 200 army tents, 300 cars to transport plainclothes intelligence officials and their surveillance equipment, and various medical supplies.[59]

According to Pavlov, Kiszczak was in a panic, unsure of what moral-spiritual ammo the pope himself might unload on the communist edifice. The communist general's mind seemed to turn to that near-miss of May 13, 1981. "At the present time," said Kiszczak wistfully, "we can only dream of the possibility that God will recall him to his bosom as soon as possible."[60]

Ah, yes, they could dream: a dead John Paul II.

To Kiszczak and friends, it seemed more than just a dream. As Christopher Andrew and Vasili Mitrokhin later found, both the Polish SB and its ugly twin sister, the Hungarian AVH, sent Moscow reports that the pontiff was suffering from leukemia or perhaps cancer of the spinal column.[61] Sadly for the communists, the reports were wrong. And the pope was coming back to Poland.

WHEN COMMUNISTS SHAKE AND TREMBLE

On June 16, to begin the second papal pilgrimage, John Paul II met with General Wojciech Jaruzelski, the Polish prime minister. The meeting was held at Warsaw's ornate presidential palace, a setting that should have given the Polish political leader a sense of confidence over the Polish spiritual leader. Quite the opposite was true. "My legs were trembling and my knees were knocking together," said Jaruzelski later. "The Pope, this figure in white, it all affected me emotionally." This was a feeling, the atheist conceded, that was "beyond all reason."[62]

From that initial meeting, John Paul II embarked on an intense schedule that would have exhausted a man half his age. Just as four years earlier, millions poured out to see their native son, their shepherd, their hero. The pope held Mass in Warsaw's sports stadium, visited Maximilian Kolbe's Niepokalanów, beatified a nun in Poznań, consecrated a church at Nowa Huta, and beatified a priest and monk in Kraków. He visited the late Cardinal Wyszyński's tomb, where he thanked the Lord for sparing his late friend the agony of observing martial law in Poland. This statement somehow did not make the communist press.[63]

The pope again visited Częstochowa, where he presided over a Mass during which there was a crowning of four images of the Blessed Mother in Jasna Góra, gathered from four different shrines. Before a crowd of two million, the pontiff in his homily stated that Poland should be a sovereign country with basic civil liberties.[64] In his homily, he used the word *dignity* four times, *independence* four times, and *free* or *freedom* twenty times.[65] The pope spoke of the "evangelization of freedom in Jasna Góra." He said that that unique evangelization had a special dimension—"it is the dimension of the freedom of the nation," of a "free country," of restoring the "dignity of a sovereign state." How would this look in practice? The Polish pope had an answer: "This entails among other things the creation of appropriate conditions for development in the field of culture, economy and other life areas of social community. The sovereignty of the state is deeply linked to its ability to promote freedom of the nation." And all of this, Poland's native son stated explicitly, should be "witnessed," as it had over the preceding centuries, by the "special presence of the Mother of God in the history of our nation." This "Queen of Poland," he averred, had been given "for the defense of the Polish nation."

The pope lamented the long period (1795–1918) when the homeland was wiped off the map of Europe. But he said that the Polish nation would perish only if its people allowed it to do so, because "no external force is able to destroy it." Acknowledging Poland's terrible history and political misfortune, he said, "The painful experiences of history stimulated our sensitivity in the field of fundamental rights of man and of the nation: in particular, the right to freedom, to be sovereign, to respect for freedom of conscience and religion, the rights of human work."

In all, it was probably John Paul II's strongest political speech in Poland since he had assumed the chair of Saint Peter. His call for freedom and independence and his invoking of Poland's sovereignty exceeded anything he had said in his historic June 1979 visit.

No wonder the communist authorities reacted as they did.

The Polish Politburo did not like what the pontiff was saying in his homilies and demanded that Bronisław Dąbrowski, secretary of the Polish Bishops' Conference, get a message to John Paul II: *tone it down*. Dąbrowski conveyed the message, but the pope, in no mood to compromise with these devils, insisted that he would say what he wanted or else he would fly back to Rome.[66]

The pope proceeded to Poznań, where, three decades earlier, the communists had killed the workers. Here, he explicitly mentioned the forbidden word *Solidarity* for the first time on the trip. In the city of Katowice, he insisted that workers had a right to form unions without government obtrusion.[67]

In Kraków he addressed another crowd of two million. When the ceremony was over, members of the crowd unfurled Solidarity banners.

The communist authorities responded by unleashing helicopters overhead to try to frighten the masses. It is a wonder that revolution did not break out at that very moment. But the pontiff wanted peace that day, and he got it. The crowd was orderly.[68]

He must have known a deeper truth: a revolution was already under way.

After this event, the Polish government unexpectedly requested a second meeting between the pontiff and Jaruzelski. According to Father Dziwisz, the regime intended this meeting to try to "calm things down a bit." The pope was sympathetic to Jaruzelski's difficult position. Dziwisz said that John Paul II viewed the general as a patriotic and even cultured and intelligent man, but one who was always inclined (by force, of course) to look to Moscow for "every possible outcome." The ninety-minute meeting must have been an uneasy one.[69]

Given the long shadow cast by the pope's June 1979 visit, it is easy for historians to ignore the import of June 1983. But consider Dziwisz's assessment: the June 1983 trip "decided the future of Poland."[70]

The real turning point in this trip, on which the future of Poland—and thus the Cold War—pivoted, was the pope's meeting with Lech Wałęsa.

In fact, the pope had decided to return to Poland in no small part because of how the communist authorities had treated Wałęsa. The mere utterance of the Solidarity leader's name was verboten, airbrushed from photos, from news, from history. The communists did everything short of killing the man, and not for a lack of trying. If there was martial law on the nation, on Solidarity, there was above all martial law on Lech Wałęsa. "This is exactly why the Pope made it known that he would go to Poland only on the condition that he could meet with Wałęsa," Father Dziwisz later said. The pope would brook no compromise. When he got off the plane in Warsaw on June 16 and heard that the communists might not allow his meeting with Wałęsa, the pontiff fumed: "If I can't see him, then I'm going back to Rome!"[71]

Now, on June 23, the meeting finally transpired. It had been kept from public knowledge thus far, but no longer.

That morning, Wałęsa, his wife, and their four children were flown by helicopter to a remote mountain retreat near the village of Zakopane. The entire place had more cameras and listening devices than probably all of KGB headquarters. The Polish SB replaced the usual waiters with their own trained suits. "The whole thing was so obviously rigged," recalled Dziwisz, "though the Holy Father immediately realized what was going on."[72]

The pope walked Wałęsa into the hallway to speak on a bench, which he also knew was bugged. It really did not matter. As Dziwisz put it, the point was not what the two men were saying but simply the fact that they were meeting: "The important thing was that John Paul II was there with Wałęsa." The pope told Wałęsa that he prayed for him every day, and that he prayed for all the men and women in Solidarity every day.[73]

"By meeting with Wałęsa," said Dziwisz, "the pope showed the whole world, starting with the Communist bosses, that the movement was alive and that the story was by no means over."[74]

One month later, General Jaruzelski lifted martial law and began letting Solidarity members leave their prison cells.[75]

Without a doubt, the situation was still bad. The communists had more holy people to wage war against, and one particularly holy priest to send to God's bosom. The battle was not over. As the revised *Catechism* of John Paul II's papacy affirmed, the whole of man's history is one of "dour combat" between the forces of good and the forces of evil.[76]

Nonetheless, as this June 1983 visit to Poland revealed, the March of Freedom was slowly but steadily on the go.

THE DOWNING OF KAL 007

Another instance of dour combat arrived at summer's end.

September 1, 1983, brought yet more Soviet horror. On that day, Russia's manifest errors materialized in the explosion of a Korean passenger airliner, flight 007, which left New York City for Seoul via Alaska. Soviets pilots blasted it into smithereens in midflight. Just as quickly, the Kremlin vehemently denied any involvement, disparaging anyone who dared to accuse Moscow. It was the usual pattern.

Among the 269 passengers killed were 61 Americans.

Ronald Reagan was at his ranch in the Santa Ynez Mountains when he received the news via telephone from Bill Clark. "I told him Bill Casey just relayed an unsubstantiated report that the Soviets may have shot down an airliner, possibly Korean," Clark told me two decades later. Clark never forgot Reagan's reply: "Bill," said Reagan, "let's pray it's not true."

They prayed, but unfortunately it was true.

Clark called Reagan the next morning to confirm the details. Reagan was livid. Secret Service agent John Barletta heard the president shout: "Those were innocent people, those damned Russians. They knew that was a civilian aircraft."[77]

The "Evil Empire" tag seemed to fit more and more each day.

Clark told the press that he personally expected the Soviets to perpetuate the "big lie" technique. He said he would not be surprised if the Russians claimed that the commercial airliner was on an American espionage mission. (An article in *Pravda* the next year would claim just that.)[78]

Reagan immediately helicoptered to Point Mugu Naval Air Station in California to board Air Force One for Washington. From the tarmac, he spoke to the press, where he excoriated Moscow for committing a "brutal," "callous," and "heinous act"—a "barbaric act," a "terrorist act." It was all made worse, he said, by the fact that the Russians "so flagrantly lie."[79]

Arriving in Washington, Reagan immediately met with Clark and the NSC. In the coming days he lit up the Soviets with more public statements, including a radio address on September 3 and a nationally televised Oval Office speech on September 5, in which he repeatedly denounced Moscow's "crime" and "massacre."[80]

Bill Clark also spoke forcefully. In a speech on September 15 to the Air Force Association, Clark accused Moscow of "mass murder" and a "twisted mentality." "The sickening display of Soviet barbarism in the Korean Air Lines massacre shocked all of us," Clark said. "But at the same time, this dramatically brutal act must be deemed consistent with the behavior of a Soviet government that continues to terrorize and murder the Afghan people, using chemical weapons on Afghan villages; a Soviet government that sponsors the repression of the entire Polish nation."

Clark's words had been preapproved; indeed, the White House press office distributed the text of his remarks as an expression of administration policy. The media did not miss the message. "Clark Accuses Soviets of 'Mass Murder,'" read the headline in the *Washington Post*.

Although Reagan was steamed, he did not want to go beyond a war of words. As soon as he heard the first report on the downing of KAL 007, he told Clark flatly: "Let's be careful not to overreact to this. We have too much going on with the Soviets. . . . We've got to protect against overreaction."[81] A military response was out of the question, and the president did not want to respond with yet more sanctions—not when the United States was already taking an economic sledgehammer to the Soviets, and not after he had recently announced the Strategic Defense Initiative. The president did not want to derail the progress they had made toward cutting nuclear arsenals.

So Reagan once again employed a weapon he knew how to use so well: rhetoric. He torched the Soviets throughout September 1983, even when delivering speeches on other topics.

Most notable among these, particularly given the interests of this book, were Reagan's remarks in New York City at the annual Pulaski Day Banquet on September 25. There, addressing a group of Polish Americans, he linked the KAL 007 "crime" to the same Soviet totalitarian evil responsible for the World War II butchery of Polish military officers in the Katyn Forest. "You know that downing a passenger airliner is totally consistent with a government that murdered fifteen thousand Polish officers in the Katyn Forest," he insisted. "We cannot let the world forget that crime, and we will not."

Reagan went further. He affirmed for his audience—"tonight, in your presence"—his "commitment to a free and democratic Poland." Those were significant words. Until then, Reagan had publicly used vague language like desiring "renewal" and "reconciliation" for Poland. Now, however, he was openly calling for a free and democratic Poland, just as John Paul II had done in Poland in June.

This rattled cages at the Kremlin. Three days after Reagan's Pulaski speech, an ailing Yuri Andropov growled from his sickbed that Reagan had "proclaimed a crusade against socialism as a social system" and that "attempts are being made to persuade people that in general there is no room for socialism in the world."[82]

Reagan closed his remarks at the Pulaski banquet with some especially poignant words: "Poland has suffered so much throughout her history, but she's given so much more to the world. And today, the world is grateful that Poland has given us a man whose courage and faith inspires us all and gives us hope when it would be so easy to despair."

Reagan then made a remarkable public gesture, asking those assembled: "I say to you in all sincerity, thank God for Pope John Paul and all that he is doing. And may we all pray that his life be protected."[83]

Onlookers might have wondered if Reagan and his friend Cardinal Terence Cooke had prayed for the life of the Holy Father when they met in New York earlier that day. They had prayed together on Good Friday in April 1981, in the White House, as Reagan was recovering from his shooting. They had agreed then that God had a special purpose for the president. Today, on September 25, 1983, Reagan had gone to the archdiocese residence behind Saint Patrick's Cathedral to meet with Cooke, who was ailing from leukemia and nearing the end of his life.

The White House did not release what they said to each other.[84] Reagan did, however, give a small glimpse in his diary. Reagan recorded that he and Mrs. Reagan had attended a "brief prayer ceremony" that had been scheduled in Cooke's private chapel for the "dying" cardinal—

"without him of course." Then Reagan and Nancy went to Cooke's bedroom and "concluded the final prayer with him." Cooke, Reagan wrote, was "a brave & good man," one who had been "most supportive of what we're doing."[85]

Amid their prayer together, perhaps the president and cardinal did pray for the pontiff's life.

According to a friend of the cardinal and of Bill Clark, Father Benedict Groeschel, Cardinal Cooke was shocked and humbled to see the president of the United States walk into the room. "Mr. President," he whispered weakly, "you didn't need to come here. You're a busy man." Reagan responded by reminding the cardinal that he had been there when Reagan needed him—namely, that special Good Friday. He now wanted to be there for the cardinal.[86]

Cardinal Cooke died not long after, on October 6, 1983. President Reagan, who had had other meetings and communications with the cardinal after their Good Friday meeting in 1981, posthumously awarded him the Presidential Medal of Freedom.[87]

THE POPE MEETS HIS SHOOTER

As Cardinal Cooke reconciled himself to his Heavenly Father, the would-be assassin of John Paul II reconciled himself to the Holy Father. Indeed, a hot and volatile 1983 ended with an instance of calm and reconciliation. On December 27, 1983, Mehmet Ali Agca met face-to-face in his prison cell with Pope John Paul II, the man he had tried to kill two and a half years earlier.

"Agca is my brother," said the forgiving Holy Father afterward, "whom I have sincerely forgiven." The pope asked the world to pray for his shooter. Agca kissed the pope's ring.

"We spoke at length," John Paul II recalled many years later, in a book not published until 2005, the year of his death. "Ali Agca, as everyone knows, was a professional assassin. This means that the attack was not his own initiative, it was someone else's idea; someone else had commissioned him to carry it out."[88]

The Holy Father clearly had concluded that Agca had not acted alone.[89]

John Paul II divulged more from the meeting. "In the course of our conversation it became clear that Ali Agca was still wondering how the attempted assassination could possibly have failed," said the pontiff. "He had planned it meticulously, attending to every tiny detail. And yet his intended victim had escaped death. How could this have happened?"[90]

Interestingly, this "perplexity" led Agca to what John Paul II called "the religious question": "He wanted to know about the secret of Fátima, and what the secret actually was. This was his principal concern; more than anything else, he wanted to know this."

This remains the most fascinating thing about the encounter between the pope and his would-be killer. The pope recounted: "Perhaps those insistent questions showed that he had grasped something really important. Ali Agca had probably sensed that over and above his own power, over and above the power of shooting and killing, there was a higher power. He began to look for it."[91]

In a sense, Fátima was almost haunting Agca. It scared him, but it also sent him searching. Father Dziwisz recounts how the Holy Father tilted his head and ear closer to Agca's lips, almost as a confessor to penitent, the better to hear the prisoner as he pleaded in bafflement, "So why aren't you dead?" The shooter was incredulous: "I know I was aiming right. I know that the bullet was a killer. So why aren't you dead?"[92]

Dziwisz, standing a few yards away from the conversation, sensed that Agca was "terrified by the fact that there were forces bigger than he was." The Muslim had found out that there was not just one Fátima—that is, Muhammad's favorite daughter—but also another one, whom he called the "goddess of Fátima." According to Dziwisz, Agca, who thought in terms of divine retribution, told John Paul II that he was afraid that this powerful "goddess" would avenge herself on him and "get rid of" him.[93]

The entire meeting, said Dziwisz, ended up revolving around this Fátima fascination. That no doubt impressed John Paul II, but Agca's singular focus on Fátima meant that the pope never once heard the words "forgive me."[94] That saddened this pope who was, at heart, a priest. He visited Agca in prison, shook his hand, and performed an act of forgiveness. But Agca was not interested in asking the pope for mercy. Said Dziwisz: "From Ali Agca himself, nothing. All he cared about were the revelations of Fátima. The only thing that interested him was figuring out who had prevented him from killing the pope."[95]

Who was this powerful Lady from Fátima?

24

MARCH 25, 1984

THE CONSECRATION OF RUSSIA

March 25, 1984, was a Sunday. The day was tranquil for Ronald Reagan. The official *Presidential Papers* for the Reagan presidency record not a single happening in the administration that day. By contrast, the next day, Monday, March 26, the president would sign an executive order, send a message to Congress on the raging budget battle, appoint four members to the National Institute of Justice, make a statement on the National Fish and Wildlife Foundation Establishment Act, lead the presentation ceremony for recipients of the Presidential Medal of Freedom, attend an NSC briefing, hold a meeting with Cabinet members, call Federal Reserve chairman Paul Volcker, and discuss everything from cattle to energy policy to El Salvador.[1]

But again, nothing on March 25. Ronald Reagan's normally active diary reflected that. "Quiet day," he jotted down.[2]

In retrospect, that quietude was fully in keeping with the profound solemnity of what was transpiring at the Vatican.

RECTIFYING ERRORS

On March 25, 1984, Pope John Paul II, the "totally yours" Marian pope, endeavored finally to accomplish what Our Lady of Fátima had requested seven decades earlier. He set out to consecrate communist Russia to her Immaculate Heart, the promised step to turning the Soviet state away from its wicked ways.

Consecrations had been attempted before, by Pius XII on October 31, 1942, and July 7, 1952, and even by John Paul II in his May 13, 1982, homily at Fátima. There the Polish pope publicly repeated an Act of Entrustment to the Blessed Mother he had composed on June 7, 1981, less than a month after the assassination attempt.[3] But the Lady in Fátima in 1917 had called for the consecration of Russia to be done in full communion and coordination with the world's bishops. Lúcia herself noted that that failure made the attempted consecrations "incomplete."[4]

Now, on March 25, 1984, John Paul II attempted to rectify all errors. Four months earlier, on December 8, 1983, the Feast of the Immaculate Conception, the pontiff had sent a letter to all bishops of the world, both Roman Catholic and Orthodox, asking them to join him on the Feast of the Annunciation for an Act of Entrustment to the Immaculate Heart of Mary. The four months' advance notice allowed the bishops plenty of time for prayer and reflection.[5]

The pontiff gathered up the previous texts of consecration and consulted Sister Lúcia. He wanted to know where they went wrong and what he needed to do this time to get it right. "Never before in the history of the Catholic Church had any pope gone so far to fulfill the requests made by heaven through a private revelation," states Father Andrew Apostoli.[6]

The site of the consecration would be Saint Peter's Square, resting place of the bones of the first pope, who, during his earthly life, personally stood aside the Blessed Mother in many acts of worship. The current pope would perform the Act of Entrustment in front of a statue of Our Lady brought from Fátima. The statue stood to the side of the altar. The act of consecration would occur outside, in the open air, with the Holy Father kneeling nearest the altar and other priests kneeling nearby. Many cardinals and bishops came, joined by some 200,000 faithful gathered in and around the square. Bishops not present kneeled in their home dioceses around the world. It was this "collegial union" that had been lacking in Pope Pius XII's attempted consecrations.[7]

That union extended even to the Kremlin.

CONSECRATION AT THE KREMLIN

Just before John Paul II led the world's bishops from Saint Peter's Square, a brave bishop from the Communist Bloc, Pavel Hnilica of Czechoslovakia, clandestinely performed the rite inside the Kremlin itself.[8]

Persecuted by the Czech communist regime, Hnilica was forced to live in exile in Rome. He was close to John Paul II, a fellow Slav, and to Sister Lúcia and Mother Teresa as well. The bishop had recently met with Mother Teresa and her translator, confessor, and spiritual adviser, Monsignor Leo Maasburg, who had been ordained in Fátima. Knowing that Hnilica and Maasburg would soon travel to the Soviet Union, Mother Teresa asked the two men to bring with them a bag of Miraculous Medals of the Blessed Mother to "plant" in Russian territory. For the nun, these medals served as a special kind of prayer and act of faith, to be placed in confident hope that God's fruits would one day be produced in the USSR. She armed Hnilica and Maasburg with the medals and commissioned them as lieutenants in "Our Lady's army at work," as Maasburg put it.[9]

Hnilica and Maasburg arrived in Moscow carrying not only Mother Teresa's medals but also Pope John Paul II's prayer of consecration. The pope had asked every bishop, all over the world, to perform the consecration to Russia with him. But who would do this in Russia itself, where there was no Catholic bishop? Hnilica was the answer.

Hnilica and Maasburg encountered their first obstacle as soon as they landed in Moscow. Religious articles were strictly forbidden in the USSR, and they had hundreds of Miraculous Medals with Mary's image, the bishop's sizable pectoral cross, several coins from the Vatican, and more. They needed to get these materials through customs, luggage check, and other inspections. Somehow the men got their wares through, sometimes by bribing the customs agents and inspectors with the Miraculous Medals, which seemed to hold a strange appeal to the Soviet officers.

The biggest break of the trip came on March 24, the vigil of the Feast of the Annunciation. Staff members at an embassy invited the two clergymen—"coincidentally," as Maasburg put it in quotation marks—to join a group of diplomats on a tour of churches on the Kremlin grounds. A security official at the entrance tried to confiscate the small leather case Hnilica carried in his pocket, but once again, the offer of a Miraculous Medal worked its charm. This official, like the one at airport customs, looked around nervously and then took the medal, letting Hnilica pass with the leather case.

Why did the case matter? Because it contained the liturgical material to celebrate Mass—smack in the core of Soviet power. Once on Kremlin grounds, the priests proceeded to the Church of the Annunciation—that is, the church dedicated to the Annunciation of the Virgin Mary. There they celebrated the Mass, somehow failing to escape the attention of the tourists in the church. The priests used a copy of *Pravda* to screen the text of the consecration prayer. "Pravda" means "Truth" in Russian.

Hnilica and Maasburg had pulled off the consecration in harmony with the Polish pope while inside the devil's den itself.

"After we had performed the consecration," Maasburg recalled, "I remembered the assignment that Mother Teresa had given me: to plant medals in the heart of Moscow." And so, while no one was looking, Maasburg tossed one of the medals behind a large sarcophagus containing the corpse of a long-deceased Russian czar. The "clink-clink-clink" of the medal hitting the floor was loud enough to attract the attention of five security guards, who swarmed to the area. The priest played innocent. The guards looked for several minutes but found nothing and moved along.

The medal remains there to this day.

Hnilica and Maasburg flew back to Rome early the next morning, March 25. Given the time difference, they managed to arrive at Saint Peter's Square (as Maasburg remembers it) "at precisely that moment the Pope began the prayer of the consecration: 'Under thy protection we seek refuge, Holy Mother of God...'"

After the ceremony, Bishop Hnilica told the Holy Father of his secret consecration at the Kremlin and what happened with the Miraculous Medals. As Maasburg put it, the pontiff was "deeply moved by these divine coincidences" inside Russia, viewing them as "confirmation" from the Blessed Mother that the consecration had been in keeping with her request at Fátima.

Oh, and today Mother Teresa's Missionaries of Charity have blossomed on Russian soil, where they are active and providing great fruit, right on the soil where those Miraculous Medals were planted.

THE CONSECRATION AT SAINT PETER'S SQUARE

The occasion for the consecration in Saint Peter's Square that Hnilica and Maasburg arrived in time to witness was the Holy Year Mass for Families. Before starting the Mass, John Paul II gave an introduction, which he repeated in English: "In remembrance of the '*Fiat*' uttered by her at the moment of the Annunciation, I will today entrust to her Immaculate Heart—in spiritual union with all the bishops of the world—all individuals and peoples, repeating in substance the act that I made at Fátima on May 13, 1982." Then, at the conclusion of the Mass, the pontiff proceeded with the act of consecration, using a roughly thousand-word text revised from his original entrustment text.[10] He began:

> "We have recourse to your protection, holy Mother of God."
>
> As we utter the words of this antiphon with which the Church of Christ has prayed for centuries, we find ourselves today before you, Mother, in the Jubilee Year of the Redemption.
>
> We find ourselves united with all the pastors of the Church in a particular.... O Mother of individuals and peoples, you who know all their sufferings and their hopes, you who have a mother's awareness of all the struggles between good and evil, between light and darkness, which afflict the modern world, accept the cry which we, moved by the Holy Spirit, address directly to your Heart. Embrace, with the love of the Mother and Handmaid of the Lord, this human world of ours, which we entrust and consecrate to you, for we are full of concern for the earthly and eternal destiny of individuals and peoples.
>
> In a special way we entrust and consecrate to you those individuals *and nations* [emphasis original] which particularly need to be thus entrusted and consecrated.
>
> "We have recourse to your protection, holy Mother of God": despise not our petitions in our necessities.

This was section one of a three-part text. The second part was likewise for all times, all peoples, and all nations:

> Behold, as we stand before you, Mother of Christ, before your Immaculate Heart, we desire, together with the whole Church, to unite ourselves with the consecration which, for love of us, your Son made of himself to the Father: "For their sake," he said, "I consecrate myself that they also may be consecrated in the truth" (Jn 17:19). We wish to unite ourselves with our Redeemer in this his consecration for the world and for the human race, which, in his divine Heart, has the power to obtain pardon and to secure reparation.
>
> The power of this consecration lasts for all time and embraces all individuals, peoples and nations. It overcomes every evil that the

> spirit of darkness is able to awaken, and has in fact awakened in our times, in the heart of man and in his history.

After a few more words in section two, Pope John Paul II went into the third and final part of the consecration:

> In entrusting to you, oh Mother, the world, all individuals and peoples, we also entrust to you this very consecration of the world, placing it in your motherly Heart.
>
> Immaculate Heart! Help us to conquer the menace of evil, which so easily takes root in the hearts of the people of today, and whose immeasurable effects already weigh down upon our modern world and seem to block the paths towards the future!...
>
> Accept, Oh Mother of Christ, this cry laden with the sufferings of all individual human beings, laden with the sufferings of whole societies. Help us with the power of the Holy Spirit to conquer all sin: individual sin and the "sin of the world," in all its manifestations.
>
> Let there be revealed, once more, in the history of the world the infinite saving power of the Redemption: the power of merciful Love! May it put a stop to evil! May it transform consciences! May your Immaculate Heart reveal for all the light of Hope!

And with that, it was finished. This was, the pope hoped, what the Blessed Mother had asked for decades earlier, beginning with three little children in the village of Fátima. Would peace now prevail? Would an Evil Empire now become a better place? Was the Cold War and a century of errors and persecutions by communist Russia now on its way out?

"ALL INDIVIDUALS AND NATIONS"

One will notice in this consecration no direct reference to Russia, to the Soviet Union, to the USSR, to Bolshevism. For diplomatic reasons, John Paul II, like Pius XII, decided not to cite explicitly the country that was the object of the consecration. I do not know which Vatican official/diplomat, or set of officials/diplomats, made that case to the pontiff, but the decision would lead to major controversy, confusion, and problems.

Perhaps out of fear of offending Moscow—*Ostpolitik* still had its exponents within the Vatican—the Holy See did not follow the lead of

Ronald Reagan in forthrightly calling out the Soviet Union. This is not to say that the pontiff should have pronounced the USSR an "Evil Empire" in a solemn proclamation. But refraining from even mentioning "Russia" seems odd given that the Lady in Fátima had spoken openly of "Russia" and had said the performance of this act of consecration would lead to the end of Russia's errors and would bring peace.

As Father Stanisław Dziwisz observed, this particular line "alluded clearly" to Russia: "In a special way we entrust and consecrate to you those individuals and nations which particularly need to be entrusted and consecrated." He used the word *all* several times—"for the world and for the human race... for all time and... all individuals, peoples and nations." *All*, of course, included Russia first and foremost. The pontiff paused several times during the consecration, and during those moments, as Father Andrew Apostoli and others have noted, he no doubt further uttered "Russia" in the silence of his heart.[11]

Countless faithful Catholics and Fátima devotees would take umbrage at the lack of a direct reference to Russia, insisting that the omission meant another unaccomplished gesture of consecration. To this day, many are convinced that the consecration was not successful.

One respected source who did not consider the consecration valid was Gabriele Amorth, renowned worldwide as the chief exorcist of Rome, who knew evil as well as anyone. He was there as an eyewitness, positioned (in his words) only "a few feet away" from the pontiff. The pope performed the consecration "quite timidly," Amorth said. This was because of the prevailing consensus among the "politicians" (certain Church officials) "all around" the pope who insisted "you can't name Russia." "Whoever thinks the prophetic mission of Fátima has been concluded," said Amorth, "deceives himself."[12]

But many others assure the faithful that the consecration was legitimate. Informed observers who take this position include Cardinal Tarcisio Bertone, Father Andrew Apostoli, Timothy Tindal-Robertson, David Carollo, Donal Foley, and Mike Daley, many of them leaders in the World Apostolate of Fátima.[13] Bertone addresses the dispute at length in his seminal book on Fátima, and Apostoli does even more so, with a twelve-page appendix in his book focused on answering objections over the consecration.[14] Likewise, Timothy Tindal-Robertson devotes many pages to the controversies.[15]

For them, the issue is settled. They argue that the spectacular and peaceful fall of communism in Russia and throughout the Communist Bloc is proof that the consecration took place, was valid, and worked.

And yet the best source for affirming the legitimacy of the act was Sister Lúcia herself.

Sister Lúcia confirmed the consecration's authenticity in writing, including in letters dated August 29, 1989, July 3, 1990, and November 21, 1999. In the 1989 letter, addressed to Sister Mary of Bethlehem, Lúcia stated that John Paul II "made the consecration in the way in which the Blessed Virgin had wished that it should be made. Afterward people asked me if it was made in the way our Lady wanted, and I replied: 'Yes.' From that time, it is made!" In Lúcia's 1990 letter, to Father Robert J. Fox, she said:

> I come to answer your question, "If the consecration made by Pope John Paul II on March 25, 1984 in union with all the bishops of the world, accomplished the conditions for the consecration of Russia according to the request of Our Lady in Tuy on June 13 of 1929?"[16] Yes, it was accomplished, and since then I have said that it was made. And I say that no other person responds for me, it is I who receive and open all letters and respond to them.[17]

This was the entire text of her succinct letter. It was emphatic.

Lúcia also verbally affirmed the authenticity, specifically to Cardinal Bertone, who spent much time with Lúcia discussing the matter. In 2008, as the Vatican secretary of state and highest-ranking Church official, he put everything on the record in his crucial book, *The Last Secret of Fátima*. He said there, "The Act of Entrustment was entirely in accord with what the Blessed Mother had asked for." He pointed to a specific statement John Paul II made: "Mother of the Church!... Enlighten especially the peoples whose consecration and entrustment by us you are awaiting." Bertone said of this, "The reference to Russia is implicit, but it is there." He pointed to Lúcia's affirmation: "Sister Lúcia personally confirmed that this solemn consecration of the whole world satisfied Mary's wishes." He quoted her directly in Portuguese, with English translation: "Yes, it has been performed, as Our Lady requested, on March 25, 1984." She told him "the consecration Our Lady wished for was performed in 1984.... It was accepted by Heaven." He further attested: "Lúcia confirmed Mary's satisfaction in a letter she sent to the pope on November 8, 1989."[18] Coincidentally, that date was the eve of the fall of the Berlin Wall.

The Vatican secretary of state reported some fascinating things about Lúcia's sense of certainty. He was personally "convinced," based on his conversations with her and more, that she continued to have some form of contact with Mary, including during a "whole sequence of dates between 1985 and 1989." These interactions fell somewhere within the categories of conversations, apparitions, visions, inner locutions, "whatever you want to call them." Bertone estimated that "it was as if she had been trying to discover from her heavenly interlocutor whether the Act of Entrustment was in accord with God's will." He said that Lúcia generally waited until she was absolutely sure of something—perhaps in consultation with Our Lady—before confirming it in writing. If she harbored the slightest doubt, she preferred to remain silent. Moreover, she was "evasive" about these "continuing conversations" with Mary, changing the subject when they were brought up. Her community of nuns and the prioress observed her behavior at close range, and they concluded that such visions were not a rare occurrence for the grown woman from Fátima. Bertone observed, "The cell of a Carmelite nun holds secrets that the rest of us will discover only in heaven."[19]

Thus, Bertone insisted, "Any debate about the validity of the Act of Entrustment, or agitation for further acts of consecration, has no leg to stand on." He added that it is true, as some have noted, that John Paul II performed another Act of Entrustment in the year 2000, but this was "a prolongation" of the one made in 1984. The pope's intention that time "was simply to throw the mantle of Mary's maternal protection over the beginning of the new millennium."[20]

Finally, Father Dziwisz, John Paul II's personal secretary for so many years, stated unequivocally: "The Pope carried out Our Lady's wish."[21]

And so the consecration was completed. Time would tell whether it worked.

25

MAY 1984

TOGETHER AGAIN

John Paul II's March 1984 consecration came between two significant steps forward in relations between his Vatican and the Reagan administration. In January, just a few weeks prior to the consecration, the Reagan White House made a historic move: it became the first presidential administration to recognize the Vatican formally. It happened at 10 A.M. on January 10, 1984, as the U.S. State Department announced the establishment of diplomatic relations with the Holy See. At the same time, the White House announced the nomination of William Wilson as U.S. ambassador to the Vatican.[1]

Reagan said that one of his earliest goals as president had been to reach out to the Vatican and its head and "make them an ally."[2] He had already made them such via his personal diplomacy. Now it was formal.

This was a major accomplishment, long elusive in the annals of American diplomatic history. Other presidents had wanted to make this move but had never found it politically feasible. Reagan faced opposition as well. The keenest opposition came not so much from secularists, or atheists, or groups long hostile to religion like the American Civil Liberties Union (ACLU), as from fundamentalist and conservative Protestants. Only because of their strong affection for Ronald Reagan was the move even possible. Even then, they were uneasy about their president's overture, and not quiet about telling him so.

The Reagan Library today holds many letters from Protestant churchmen protesting the administration's recognition of the Vatican. Although Catholics and conservative Protestants today are allies in the battle against secularism and relativism, in 1984 the common ground in the culture war was not settled. Interestingly, to protest Reagan's diplomacy with the Vatican, many Protestant critics invoked claims of "church-state separation" that conservative Protestants had long resented when secular liberals levied them against religious people.

On July 29, 1981, Joseph P. Folds, director of missions for the South Florida Baptist Association, wrote President Reagan a letter referencing an article in that month's issue of *Church and State* magazine reporting that the Reagan administration had used $78,000 in public funds to send a delegation to Alaska to meet with Pope John Paul II. Folds said he was "very anxious" and "terribly upset," telling Reagan that this was "absolutely wrong" and "immediately violates the spirit of the First Amendment." "If the officials of the Roman Catholic Church wanted to meet their Pope," he wrote, "that would be their business."[3]

This kind of opposition would continue well after Vatican recognition. In May 1986, when Bill Wilson announced that he was stepping down as U.S. ambassador, conservative Protestants such as Robert P. Dugan Jr., director of the Reagan-friendly National Association of Evangelicals (which had hosted Reagan's Evil Empire speech), and B.E. Pitts Jr. of the Southern Baptist Convention wrote letters urging their president "in the strongest terms" to "not fill the vacancy" (Dugan's words). Oddly, Dugan and Pitts stood on the same side as leaders of left-wing secularist groups, such as Dr. Robert L. Maddox, executive director of Americans United for Separation of Church and State, and John V. Stevens of the Church State Council.[4]

The Reagan White House and John Paul II's Vatican proceeded with recognition nonetheless. It merely formalized a relationship that the president and the pope, and their advisers, had done so much to build.

As diplomatic relations were being formalized, Reagan and John Paul II were communicating regularly via letter, cable, phone call, and liaison, almost always under the radar. The documents to that effect from the

Vatican files remain sealed, and will continue to be for decades to come. White House Situation Room cables carrying papal messages from Rome, initially listed as "SECRET" or "CONFIDENTIAL," remain fully redacted at the Reagan Library. For instance, the files show multipage redacted letters from (among others) October 27, 1983, and February 7, 1984.[5]

The second of these letters, coming not long after formal U.S. recognition of the Vatican, cryptically related an urgent message from John Paul II. That February 7 cable, sent from the Vatican embassy to the State Department, reports that the pope unsuccessfully tried to telephone President Reagan earlier that afternoon and asked that the specific message in paragraph three of the letter "be conveyed to the president immediately." We have no idea what that paragraph said, as the accompanying letter is completely redacted. We know only that it was urgent, because, as the document records, a "charge was called to the Vatican at 2340 hours local time February 7 to receive a personal message for transmission from Pope John Paul II to President Reagan." In other words, the pope called someone to the Vatican at almost midnight to pick up the message for the president.

Just what was so urgent will remain a mystery until the redactions are dropped.

CROSSING PATHS

Soon enough, the pope would be talking directly to the president. Their staffs had noticed that the leaders' whirlwind international travels would allow them to cross paths in remote Fairbanks, Alaska, at the beginning of May. And so their second face-to-face meeting was set.[6]

The pope was stopping in Alaska to refuel on his way to Seoul, South Korea, to commemorate the two hundredth anniversary of Catholicism on the Korean peninsula—the beginning of a trip that would see him traverse twenty-five thousand miles of airspace in eleven days.[7] Meanwhile, Reagan was closing out his own swing through Asia. When the White House learned that the pontiff would be jetting through Alaska not long after the president's own refueling stop, Reagan decided to stay over to ensure that he could see John Paul II.[8]

Given that this was their first opportunity to meet since Reagan had recognized the Vatican, the president and the pope wanted to seize the moment. There was a "mutual desire by the administration and the Vatican" to arrange the meeting, said White House spokesman Bob Sims.[9]

The liberal press, however, did not accept that. Several newspapers tried to frame Reagan's desire to meet with the pontiff as a shameless bid for the Catholic vote. "It's another phase of [Reagan's] election-year strategy," the *New York Times* religion editor told a reporter for the Fairbanks newspaper.[10]

Reagan would go on to win forty-nine out of fifty states in the 1984 election. One doubts that this brief meeting with the pontiff accounted for the victory.

"FREEDOM TO WORSHIP GOD"

Reagan arrived in Alaska having just delivered a message of religious freedom in communist China. At Fudan University on April 30, 1984, the president gave an extraordinary speech that went oddly unremarked upon at the time and has escaped the attention of most Reagan scholars and aficionados since.

Reagan offered this message to the students at Fudan:

> We believe in the dignity of each man, woman, and child. Our entire system is founded on an appreciation of the special genius of each individual, and of his special right to make his own decisions and lead his own life.
>
> We believe—and we believe it so deeply that Americans know these words by heart—we believe "that all men are created equal, that they are endowed by their Creator with certain unalienable Rights, that among those are Life, Liberty and the pursuit of Happiness." . . . They are from the document by which we created our nation, the Declaration of Independence.
>
> We elect our government by the vote of the people. That is how we choose our Congress and our President. We say of our country, "Here the People Rule," and it is so.

This was political sustenance to a people that since 1949 had been shackled by Marxist leaders that Reagan (in a private letter) once described as "a bunch of murdering bums."[11] Although some things had improved in China, others had gotten worse, including the right to reproduce, as communists had imposed a one-child policy on the nation's women.

Religious persecution remained in full force as well. That context provides for the most revelatory passage of Reagan's speech:

> There is one other part of our national character I wish to speak of. Religion and faith are very important to us. We're a nation of many religions. But most Americans derive their religious belief from the Bible of Moses, who delivered a people from slavery; the Bible of Jesus Christ, who told us to love thy neighbor as thyself, to do unto your neighbor as you would have him do unto you.
>
> And this, too, has formed us. It's why we wish well for others. It's why it grieves us when we hear of people who cannot live up to their full potential and who cannot live in peace.

This was spiritual sustenance, and quite bold at that. Reagan had dared to utter the words *Jesus Christ*, *Moses*, and *the Bible* in a nation that banned them. He was committing blasphemy in the Church of Mao Tse-tung. More powerfully still, his remarks were being carried live on Chinese television.

Three days earlier, on April 27, he had stood aside leaders in Beijing and explained before the state-run TV cameras that "America was founded by people who sought freedom to worship God and to trust in Him to guide them in their daily lives."

Did this annoy the Chinese leadership? It sure did, but Reagan was undeterred.

The president surely was excited to share news of his Chinese adventure with Pope John Paul II in Alaska.

"ENORMOUS RESPECT AND AFFECTION"

Reagan's plane touched down in Fairbanks at 3:20 A.M. on May 1.[12] From there, he went to the private residence of Senator Frank Murkowski. After getting some rest, he spoke to the press. When asked what he had said to the Chinese, Reagan stated, "I tried to explain what America is and who we are—to explain to them our faith in God and our love, our true love, for freedom."[13]

At 1:49 P.M. the president spoke at a luncheon with community leaders in the William Wood Student Center at the University of Alaska. "Tomorrow I am meeting with Pope John Paul II, a man and spiritual leader for whom I have enormous respect and affection," Reagan told the crowd, before yet again invoking favored words of an earlier pope. "Pope Pius XII, Eugenio Pacelli," said Reagan, using Pius's birth name for the first time, "noted the burdens that we Americans carry. He was the Pope at the time of World War II. And right after that war, he said of us, 'The American people have a genius for splendid and unselfish action.' And he added, 'Into the hands of America God has placed an afflicted mankind.'"[14]

They were words Reagan had long ago taken to heart and soul. He had them memorized.

"Well," the president told Alaskans, "we're proving to the world that the American spirit is alive and well. Together we'll keep America the land of freedom and opportunity that God intended it to be."

The next morning, thousands descended on Fairbanks International Airport to greet the president and the pope. People began arriving at the airport at 5 A.M. on this rainy day. At 10:09 A.M., Reagan read welcoming remarks to the pontiff. "I want to welcome Your Holiness to the United States and, on behalf of the American people, say how pleased and privileged we are to have you among us," the president began. "We're just returning from a mission of peace, and I can think of no more fitting close to this journey than to be here in the presence of Your Holiness, who has worked so diligently for recognition of the rights and dignity of the individual and for peace among nations."[15]

This was a reference to Reagan's work in China, where he had without question diligently pressed for the rights and dignity of the individual.

"I can assure you, Your Holiness," Reagan continued, "the American people seek to act as a force for peace in the world and to further the cause of human freedom and dignity. Indeed, an appreciation for the unalienable rights of every human being is the very concept that gave birth to this nation." These were thoughts that Karol Wojtyła himself had expressed in Philadelphia a few years earlier. "Few have understood better than our nation's Founding Fathers that claims of human dignity transcend the claims of any government," said Reagan, "and that this transcendent right itself has a transcendent source. Our Declaration of Independence four times acknowledges our country's dependence on a Supreme Being, and its principal author and one of our greatest Presidents, Thomas Jefferson, put it simply: 'The God who gave us life, gave us liberty at the same time.'"

Here was an affirmation of what both Reagan and John Paul II understood as the first and most fundamental of all freedoms: the right to life.

The president added: "But no one knows better than Your Holiness that the quest for human rights and world peace is a difficult, often disheartening task.... To us, Your Holiness, the Holy See and your pastorate represent one of humanity's greatest moral and spiritual forces." This was quite a statement by the president of the United States.

Reagan next made reference to the recent establishment of diplomatic relations: "For over a century we maintained warm and fruitful, but informal relations. Now we have exchanged Ambassadors, and we hope to build on this new relationship to our mutual benefit and to the benefit of peace-loving people everywhere."

The president then commended the pope personally:

> In a violent world, Your Holiness, you have been a minister of peace and love. Your words, your prayers, your example have made you—for those who suffer oppression or the violence of war—a source of solace, inspiration, and hope. For this historic ministry the American people are grateful to you, and we wish you every encouragement in your journeys for peace and understanding in the world. I also want to say how grateful I am for this opportunity to meet personally with you to discuss matters of vital concern to the Holy See and to the United States. We deeply value your counsel and support and express our solidarity with you.

The pope went next, beginning with the words "Praised be Jesus Christ." He thanked Reagan and the people of Alaska. "Openness to others begins in the heart," John Paul II said. "As I stated at the beginning of this year in my message for the World Day of Peace, if men and women hope to transform society, they must begin by changing their own hearts first. Only with a new heart can one rediscover clear sightedness and impartiality with freedom of spirit, the sense of justice with respect to the rights of man."[16]

When he finished, he and the president headed for the airport terminal, where they greeted a group of handicapped children. After that, they and their staffs went inside.

THE MEETING

The meeting inside was not a long one. The two men met privately for what one source reported was only thirty minutes. Afterward their staffs joined them for a larger meeting.[17]

The White House did not say much about the meeting. The official *Presidential Papers* from the Reagan White House list merely the president's welcoming remarks at the airport and this bland 121-word statement from the president's press office:

> In his meeting today with Pope John Paul II, the President discussed his trip to China and the Holy Father's forthcoming visit to Korea. The two engaged in an exchange of views on arms control, East-West relations, regional and humanitarian issues. The President offered to send a Presidential mission to Rome to discuss economic development and humanitarian assistance with Vatican officials. The mission would explain U.S. foreign assistance and economic and humanitarian programs. In turn, the Vatican would brief the mission on its development and humanitarian activities throughout the world. The goal of the Presidential mission would be to begin a dialog that could lead to U.S.-Vatican cooperation in the effort to alleviate hunger and disease and to promote peace worldwide.[18]

Even now, three decades later, the Reagan Library contains next to nothing on the meeting. Unlike the later Reagan-Gorbachev summits, there were no "memcons" (memoranda of conversation) or formal record of the discussion. This is odd for Reagan Library records. One archivist at the library speculated to me that the lack of documentation probably meant that the meeting was of a "more personal nature" and thus no aide was tasked to document the conversation.[19] Bill Clark, who was present that day, took no notes either. "To have not recorded the details, in some way, of the meetings with the Holy Father was shortsighted," he told me twenty years later. "But the world was moving so fast. And I didn't have a full-time note taker to follow me around with pencil and paper, recording all of this for the sake of history."

Very little has been written about this Alaska meeting. In his two lengthy and superb biographies of John Paul II, George Weigel does not mention the meeting at all.[20] Reagan biographers do no better.

Still, it would be a mistake to dismiss this meeting as insignificant. The very fact that Reagan reworked his busy schedule, staying over an extra day in Alaska, simply to have some time with the pope speaks to the importance of the relationship. The U.S. government and the Vatican now had, for the first time ever, formal diplomatic relations. The president and the pope, by coming together again to shake hands, to brief each other, to share common views and visions and goals, were reaffirming a crucial partnership in a tumultuous time.

The photographic record suggests the rapport Reagan and John

Paul II had established. A picture published in the Thursday, May 3, Fairbanks *Daily News-Miner* shows the president and pontiff sitting next to each other in a conference room at the airport. A talkative, animated Reagan, dressed in a dark business suit, appears half out of his seat, his mouth open, eager to make a point. The smiling, serene pontiff listens attentively, with his left pointer finger resting on his temple. A crucifix rests on the wall behind the men.

In most photos, Reagan's mouth is open, as he speaks with a satisfied smile but with force, conviction; the pope listens attentively, pensively, equally at ease. Each man seems almost amused by the other, while simultaneously exhibiting respect and fondness.

At the same time, Reagan did not display the sort of awe that this pope often engendered in Catholics. Jerry Olsavsky, a former linebacker with the National Football League's Pittsburgh Steelers, and a Polish American, recalled meeting John Paul II in Rome during the Jubilee Year of 2000. The pope approached a small group of Polish pilgrims at the Grotto of Our Lady of Lourdes. The pope, said Olsavsky, was "just trying to talk" to them, approaching them in a down-to-earth way, being "just human." To the pope's visible dismay, the Poles were so overcome that they could not even converse with him. "They [were] going absolutely nuts," said Olsavsky, "and he [was] trying to calm them down... telling them, 'Calm down, calm down.' But they wouldn't calm down." Finally, the pope shrugged, shook his head, and walked away in frustration. As Olsavsky colorfully put it, it was as if John Paul II said, "Whoa, you people are crazy, I'm getting out of here."[21]

John Paul II had that effect on many people, but not on Ronald Reagan. Not being Catholic, Reagan never took his admiration of the pope anywhere near that level. The pope seemed to appreciate that. They talked as peers who greatly respected each other. This dynamic was evident in their meetings—captured in the surviving photographic record, including that from Fairbanks.

Note, too, that the White House's short statement, news reports on the meeting, and the pope himself all made reference to Reagan's China trip.[22] One could probably bet that when Reagan was half out of his seat speaking to the pope, it was because he was sharing details of his piercing words on religious freedom and human dignity to China's communist atheists.

Fittingly, the group photo from the Alaska meeting shows Bill Clark sitting to Reagan's immediate right. Reagan's longtime right-hand man had left the NSC in late 1983 to head up the Department of the Interior.[23]

Though no longer part of Reagan's daily national-security circle, Clark just happened to be nearby on a fact-finding trip in Prudhoe Bay for Interior work (or someone so arranged it). Secretary of State George Shultz was there, too, though his countenance was not visible in the photo that ran in the newspapers. Also present were the current national security adviser, Bud McFarlane, and Chief of Staff Jim Baker. It was the interior secretary, of all people, who was positioned closest to President Reagan—an arrangement that makes sense only if one understands the Clark-Reagan (and Clark-Vatican) relationship.

MORE VICTIMS OF COMMUNISM

After the meeting, Ronald Reagan hopped on Air Force One and headed for Andrews Air Force Base, while the pope stayed for a prayer service and other activities with many of the fifteen thousand Roman Catholics in the diocese of Fairbanks.

When John Paul II boarded his plane and took off for South Korea, he offered a special commemorative prayer for the 269 people the Soviets had killed on Korean Air Lines Flight 007 the previous September.[24]

It was not the last time that year that the pope would grieve for someone murdered by international communism.

26

OCTOBER 19, 1984

THE MARTYRDOM OF FATHER JERZY POPIEŁUSZKO

The year 1984 held many positives for Pope John Paul II and Ronald Reagan in their battle against atheistic communism. Tragically, however, that pernicious ideology was about to claim another victim in its long war on religion.

For four years, a mild-mannered Polish priest by the name of Father Jerzy Popiełuszko had served his country, his flock, and his Solidarity. His style and discernible holiness had attracted countless Poles and repelled the country's communists. The Warsaw regime, with perhaps more than a little prodding from Moscow, ultimately decided that it had to wipe out this priest.

John Paul II and Reagan would not be surprised, but they would still be aghast.

FORMATION

Jerzy Popiełuszko was born in the small village of Okopy, Poland, on a street without a name, carrying only a number, 17. He came into the world on September 14, 1947, the Feast Day of the Exaltation of the Holy Cross.

In the spring prior to his birth, his mother, Marianna, pregnant with her fourth child, attended a one-week mission provided by traveling monks at the Church of Saints Peter and Paul in a nearby town. She listened intently to their heavenly assurances amid this trying time of communist persecution. As she said her rosary, a concept formed along with the child in her womb: she promised God that one of her children would become a priest.[1]

When the boy was born, she named him Alfons, after his late uncle, later to become Alek and known as Jerzy. He was so sickly that Marianna and her husband, Władysław, took him to be baptized two days later, fearing his premature death. Jerzy persevered, though throughout his life he would be small and weak. What he lacked in physical strength he made up in courage, will, and spiritual stamina.

At age seven he would trek two miles every morning to serve as an altar boy at 6:30 Mass at the Church of Saints Peter and Paul. The boy became a fixture at morning Mass, visible and punctual. By age thirteen it had become clear to him, his mother, and others that he was destined to be a priest. He told his sister: "Everything's fine. If I die, it won't be for nothing, it will be for the faith. Not for being a hooligan, and not for committing a crime, only for faith."[2]

The young Popiełuszko was well aware that such had been the course of one of his heroes, Maximilian Kolbe. In the spring of 1964, the soft-spoken boy informed his mother that he was going to visit Niepokalanów, the Franciscan monastery that Kolbe had founded. In the first of many ways, he was following Kolbe's footsteps. After visiting Niepokalanów, Popiełuszko was hooked. He applied to and was accepted by the seminary named for another martyr, Saint John the Baptist, in Warsaw. It was there that he changed his first name to Jerzy.

In seminary, Popiełuszko had his first opportunity to rub shoulders with the hierarchy of the Polish Church, including the primate himself, Cardinal Stefan Wyszyński, and a young archbishop named Karol Wojtyła. In May 1966, Popiełuszko observed yet another fiasco that communists created at what should have been a glorious celebration of the millennium of the Church in Poland. During a huge Mass at Saint

John's Cathedral, which included Wojtyła and Wyszyński, young Jerzy witnessed communist thuggery firsthand. Popiełuszko and another seminarian helped guide the bishops to safety, some of them so elderly that they needed assistance up and down stairs.[3]

Popiełuszko was ordained May 28, 1972. The twenty-four-year-old wore his scapular medal proclaiming his special devotion to Christ's mother. Cardinal Wyszyński presided over the ordination. As they were for the Solidarity movement and Cardinal Wojtyła, the 1970s were a time of formation for Jerzy Popiełuszko, readying him for his ultimate calling.

CHAPLAIN TO SOLIDARITY

By the 1980s, Father Jerzy was rising to prominence as a respected priest in Poland. Although he had been diagnosed with Addison's disease, the same affliction that had hobbled John F. Kennedy, it was never enough to slow him from his service to his countrymen. And in the summer of 1980, when he was thirty-three, both the Church and the workers asked him to serve as chaplain to the Solidarity movement. He said yes, becoming, in the words of one Polish priest, "one of the spiritual founders of the movement."[4]

It was an honor, but also an extraordinary challenge. From then on, Father Jerzy was a marked man. He would be under increasing stress as a faithful priest in a country governed by faithless communism. According to biographers Roger Boyes and John Moody, who were working as journalists in Poland at the time, the communist regime added Popiełuszko's name to the list of some five thousand "enemies of the state."[5]

When the Polish regime imposed martial law, the situation became even more acute for the priest. On December 13, 1981, after Sunday Mass, four men from the Polish secret police arrived at the chapel looking for Popiełuszko.[6] His slow martyrdom had begun. He would be under constant surveillance. But he did not back down from the communists. Quite the contrary.

VOICE OF THE FATHERLAND

In early 1982, shortly after the declaration of martial law, Father Jerzy started celebrating a monthly "Mass for the Fatherland" that would change his life and the life of his country. These Sunday Masses, held at Saint Stanisław Kostka Church in Warsaw's Żoliborz district, were a throwback to World War II, when Poles prayed for their nation.

On January 17 he celebrated Mass for those who had been arrested and did not hesitate to say why: "Because martial law has taken from us free speech so, listening to our hearts and minds, let us think of our sisters and brothers who have been deprived of their freedom."[7] On February 28, Father Jerzy offered this opening intention: "The Church always stands on the side of truth. The Church is always on the side of those who are harmed. Today, the Church stands on the side of those who have been deprived of freedom, whose consciences are being attacked."[8]

This became a recurring theme for the monthly Fatherland Masses. In April, Popiełuszko offered an intention for peace and the well-being of "those deprived of their liberty, for persons arrested, interned, condemned, and the intentions of their families." "Almighty God! Lord of our fathers!" he prayed. "We stand before your altar begging for freedom, freedom in our country. We are here in the fifth month of martial law and on the 134th day of our country's anguish."[9] Popiełuszko also prayed for the "evildoers" and "those who destroy human minds," as he did for those who had "the courage to oppose lies" and to reject "falsehood as truth." "You forgive us all our faults," the priest said. "And deliver us all from evil. Show our country the way out of this difficult time. Hear, Oh Lord, the cry of your people."[10]

In no time, atheist communists were attending the services in their official capacity as "church watchers." It was easy for Popiełuszko and the faithful to know these spies: when the priest asked people to kneel in prayer, the communist hired hands were last to react.

The next month's Mass occurred on May 30, which closed the month of Mary in the Polish Church. It did not escape Father Jerzy's attention that John Paul II, Poland's famous native son, believed that the intercession of Mary had foiled the attempt on his life one year earlier. "We gather at Christ's altar in this month of May," Popiełuszko said. "This place dedicated to the Blessed Mother by our nation, has experienced a wave of hate." In his homily, he implored: "Virgin Mother, hear us mother of God. You stood by the cross and suffered when your son Jesus Christ was dying. There, by the cross, Christ made you our Mother and made us your children, so You are our Mother." He launched into a long litany prayer asking Mary's intercession:

> Mother of those who hope in Solidarity, pray for us.
>
> Mother of the deceived, pray for us.

Mother of those arrested in the night, pray for us.
Mother of prisoners, pray for us.
Queen of suffering Poland, pray for us.
Queen of fighting Poland, pray for us.
Queen of independent Poland, pray for us.
Queen of always faithful Poland, pray for us.
We beseech You, Mother, who is the hope of millions, let us all live in freedom, truth and ever faithful to You and Your Son. Amen.[11]

Father Jerzy rattled off more than thirty specific lines of petition asking for the Blessed Mother's intercession. The communist church watchers could not have been pleased.

Popiełuszko delivered messages like these month after month at Saint Stanisław Kostka Church. On September 26, Father Jerzy stood with crucifix in hand to identify with those "who suffer injustice in our land." Only through the cross, said the priest, did all of this make any sense—the "cross of our lives, the cross of our nation." "How like Christ bleeding on the cross is the suffering of our nation today!" said Popiełuszko. Martial law, he insisted, had erected for Poles "an endless number of crosses."[12]

On October 31, Father Jerzy stood at the altar and faced a portrait of Maximilian Kolbe that was displayed for each Fatherland Mass. He referred to Kolbe as "Patron of Poland Persecuted." "We need you so very much, Saint Maximilian," pleaded the priest, "as an example of a man who does not give in to fear, who is not afraid."[13]

Who is not afraid. Here, Popiełuszko invoked words similar to those John Paul II had used to reassure his countrymen. The truth was that Father Jerzy had a right to be afraid. His Fatherland Masses were exposing too much truth. The persecutors were now seeking to stop him, and even to destroy him.

"HATE SÉANCES"

The communist-run media derided these Masses as "hate séances."[14] But far from spreading a message of hate, Father Jerzy preached nonviolent resistance. He said, in a clear reference to communism, that "an idea which needs rifles to survive will die of its own accord." And when Marxist rifles sought to silence the Christian faithful, even unto death, the faithful only grew stronger. As the early Christian author Tertullian said, the blood of the martyrs is the seed of the Church.

Even when speaking frankly about communist oppression, Father Jerzy was sending a message not of hate but of love. "[He] didn't even use the word 'communist,'" recalls Janusz Kotański, a dissident writer who, at the time, was agnostic but was impressed by the priest. "He was talking about sin.... [Here was] a priest stating, 'Don't be afraid, love your enemies—but stick to Solidarity.'" Popiełuszko called for love even for communists.

None of this satisfied the communist watchers, especially as the crowds for Father Jerzy's Masses became so huge that they spilled into and down the street outside.[15] The Polish SB's Department Four, the church-monitoring department within the communist secret police, increased its surveillance of the priest and his counterrevolutionary activities. Overseen by Warsaw's Ministry of Internal Affairs, these communist agents also stepped up their harassment of Popiełuszko. He had to be stopped.

Father Jerzy could feel the mounting pressure. "I was told that they had given me many, many warnings," he confided to his diary in November 1982, "and that if my behavior did not change then they would act according to the martial law decrees. But how can my behavior change? I can't stop serving the people." He knew what the communists could do: "I am aware that they can intern me, arrest me, fabricate a scandal, but I can't stop my activity which is a service to the Church and the fatherland."[16] Popiełuszko would not give in. "I am only saying aloud what people are thinking privately," he said.[17]

The communist harassment took many forms. On the first anniversary of martial law, on December 13, 1982, as the young priest was in his room wrapping Christmas presents, the communists lobbed into his building a miniature bomb strapped to a brick. They failed to kill him—this time.[18]

Friends of the priests and Solidarity members set up round-the-clock guards outside his office. They began traveling with him at all times. They did their best to ensure that he was not alone and unprotected.

On December 28, two weeks after the bomb-throwing incident, the communist police spent three hours, from 1 A.M. to 4 A.M., driving in circles around the priest's house, blowing their horns, shouting, revving their engines. The Solidarity guards on patrol could do little but take pictures of them. As it turned out, the cameras' flashes caused the communists to flee. They were "allergic to bright light," said a Solidarity guard.[19]

The next year and a half was a wearisome period of nonstop surveillance, harassment, arrests, and confrontations. In their superb biography, *Messenger of the Truth*, Boyes and Moody write that Popiełuszko "was stalked like a game animal in the last years of his life, hunted by agents...who knew that the priest had to be silenced."[20] Just around Christmas 1983, the communists tried to frame the priest as having a sexual affair with a faithful female friend who served him and the Church. They made a display of handcuffing the poor girl, broadcasting her seizure on state-run television. Though disgusted, Father Jerzy was impressed by her faith under fire. "She was very brave," he wrote in his diary. "The previous evening she fell asleep with a rosary in her hand."[21]

It was a familiar communist trick. Recall that just months earlier the secret police had tried to concoct an illicit affair involving Poland's even more famous priest: Pope John Paul II.

On the second anniversary of martial law, Father Jerzy sensed the Devil in life under communism in Poland. "One should never negotiate with the Devil," he recorded in his diary after communist authorities broke another promise, this time not to interrogate him more than two hours.[22]

By January 1984, Father Jerzy's Fatherland Masses were attracting congregations of more than twenty thousand people (and lots of riot police). Worse for the Polish regime, Popiełuszko's sermons were being printed and rebroadcast by Radio Free Europe, Voice of America, the BBC, and other sources.[23]

The communists no doubt knew, or at least suspected, that their most hated Polish priest inside Poland was communicating with their most hated Polish priest outside Poland. The editor of the Polish edition of *L'Osservatore Romano*, the Vatican newspaper, carried messages from Pope John Paul II to Popiełuszko. The editor spent several hours with Popiełuszko after Christmas 1983, where he delivered the Holy Father's simple advice: stay strong.[24]

Perhaps not coincidentally, Father Jerzy sounded a message of strength, courage, and resilience in the Fatherland Mass the next month. He quoted from Isaiah 35: "Strengthen the hands that are feeble, make firm the knees that are weak. Say to those whose hearts are frightened: Be strong! Fear not!" He urged his brothers and sisters: "Courage! Do not be afraid!" He quoted Pope Pius IX, the first great anticommunist pope, regarding Romuald Traugutt, a nineteenth-century Polish patriot the Russians executed for fighting for Polish freedom: "Moscow understands that it will not overcome Catholic Poland and that is why it now imposes its greatest fury on our spiritual shepherds."[25]

The communist attacks on Popiełuszko took the form of phony letters mailed to the priest and incendiary articles in the media. One typical letter to Father Jerzy included the line "You hideous Nazi!"[26] On September 9, 1984, Popiełuszko's name appeared for the first time in the Soviet press. *Izvestia* ran a piece ominously titled "A Lesson Not Understood" in the "Letter from Warsaw" section. The "correspondent," Leonid Toporkov, was one of the trained state vulgarians who masqueraded as real journalists. Toporkov's article attacked the priest as "impudent," "militant," "cunning," and "destructive," and charged Popiełuszko with the ultimate sin: "hatred of socialism." *Izvestia* accused the priest and other "clergymen" of cooperating with "hard-core counterrevolutionaries."[27]

Right on cue, the Polish regime's in-house propagandists delivered their own smears. The government spokesman Jerzy Urban wrote a piece for the weekly organ *Tu i teraz* (*Here and Now*) under the pseudonym "Jan Rem" in which he accused Popiełuszko of holding "black masses." He said the "politically rabid" priest was guilty of "political hatred" and referred to him as a "modern-day Rasputin."[28]

Father Jerzy, the new mad monk.

"NOW WE ARE MURDERERS"

For the communists, smears and intimidation were not enough. The "politically rabid" priest had to go.

On October 13 they tried to stone Popiełuszko's car. When that failed, they came up with another plot: on October 19 the secret police kidnapped him as he made his way back from performing duties at the Polish Brother Martyrs Church.

The SB thugs began pummeling Father Jerzy. They bound and gagged him and stuffed him into the trunk of their cream-colored Fiat 125 automobile. They roamed the countryside trying to decide where to dispatch him.[29]

The ringleader this October day was Captain Grzegorz Piotrowski, who headed the secret subgroup within Department Four in charge of the Popiełuszko portfolio. Captain Piotrowski had developed a special hatred for the priest who consumed so much of his work time. It was Piotrowski who had spearheaded the Operation TRIANGOLO effort to plant a phony diary alleging a sexual affair between Karol Wojtyła and a deceased woman. Piotrowski had failed to bring down Pope John Paul II; he would not fail to bring down Jerzy Popiełuszko.

Piotrowski was raised in an atheist household, which was an aberration in this pious Roman Catholic country. The disregard for God and morality made Piotrowski an ideal man for the grisly task ahead, which he assumed with a channeled viciousness.

Piotrowski's first beating that evening was so severe it should have killed Father Jerzy. The small man afflicted with Addison's disease had been recently hospitalized for other infirmities, including stress and anxiety. But somehow the horribly beaten priest managed to survive in the dark trunk of the Fiat. In fact, somehow he unloosened the ropes that knotted him and extricated himself from the car as it slowed. He began to run, shouting to anyone who could hear: "Help! Save my life!"

Piotrowski ran him down. "I caught up with him and hit him on the head several times with the stick," the SB captain later confessed. "I hit him near or on the head. He fell limp again. I think he must have been unconscious. And then I became—never mind, it doesn't matter."

Piotrowski seemed overtaken by another force. As Boyes and Moody recorded, "so wild were the blows" that Piotrowski's accomplices thought their comrade had gone mad. Dr. Maria Byrdy, the pathologist who later performed the autopsy, would testify that Father Jerzy could have easily perished from the beatings.

After another round of thrashing, Piotrowski and his two fellow tormentors grabbed a roll of thick adhesive tape and ran it around the priest's mouth, nose, and head, tossing him back in the vehicle.

Though he could barely breathe or move, Father Jerzy somehow pried open the trunk again. This sent Piotrowski into a rage. He stopped the vehicle, got out, and told the priest that if he made one more sound, Piotrowski would strangle him with his bare hands and shoot him. Boyes and Moody report what happened next: "He [Piotrowski] replaced the gun and lifted [his] club. It came down on the priest's nose, but instead of the sound of cartilage breaking, there was a plop, like a stick hitting the surface of a puddle."

It was the final, deadly blow.

The killers drove to a spot at the Vistula River, tied two heavy bags of stones to the priest's ankles, and dropped the body into the water. It was ten minutes before midnight, October 19, 1984. "Popiełuszko is dead," announced Lieutenant Leszek Pękala to his collaborators. The third helper, Lieutenant Waldemar Chmielewski, affirmed, "That's right."

They drove away, downing a bottle of vodka to try to numb what they had done. Pękala thought to himself as he drank, "Now we are murderers."

When Father Jerzy did not show for 7 A.M. Mass the next day, his parishioners became alarmed. A search for his whereabouts commenced. It became a national sensation. Lech Wałęsa came to Father Jerzy's church, where Masses were said every hour, and pleaded with Poles not to react with violence. It was the priest's message of nonviolent resistance—the only form available in a tyranny where the state held all power and all guns.

Finally, after eleven days, on Tuesday, October 30, the corpse of the fallen priest was retrieved from the mud of the Vistula. It was so decayed and mutilated that it would have been unrecognizable if not adorned by its priestly garments.

The communist police who inspected the body enjoyed a good laugh as they surveyed the victim's identity card. It listed his date of birth and then his profession as a priest. "Priest?" one of the police said. "That's a profession?" The boys howled at that one.

A MOSCOW CONNECTION?

The three SB thugs, Piotrowski, Pękala, and Chmielewski, along with a higher-ranking Polish officer, Colonel Adam Pietruszka, would ultimately be convicted for their roles in the murder of Father Jerzy Popiełuszko. But debate has endured: how involved was Moscow in the killing?

Boyes and Moody, whose excellent work I have benefited from, have been criticized for not directly indicting the Kremlin in Popiełuszko's murder. One Polish source told me that Boyes and Moody mistakenly relied on "the old version of murder imposed on Poles by the chief of the communist secret police." That version "is a lie," the source said.

The Polish journalist Piotr Litka, who made a documentary on Popiełuszko's death, gave an interview in October 2016 in which he suggested that the communist regime staged the trial of the four SB officers to conceal evidence that many more communist officials were involved in the plot. "The trial was set up from the start," Litka told his interviewer. "Some true, verified information was given, but it was carefully rationed. There were a lot of facts and evidence concealed or ignored in the investigation and during the trial."[30]

Tomasz Pompowski, an indefatigable Cold War researcher, insists that "the true version is slowly being uncovered." Pompowski believes that Father Jerzy's agony was worse than previously known. He points to findings that Poland's Institute of National Remembrance (IPN) released in

2008; the IPN, custodian of the communist secret police archives, found evidence suggesting that the priest may have been turned over for further torture at a Soviet military base in Poland and may not have been killed for several more days.[31] Pompowski believes that the Soviet GRU was involved in Father Jerzy's death.[32] As I will address later in this book, the GRU's fingerprints were on the attempted assassination of John Paul II.

When it came to the murder of Father Jerzy Popiełuszko, Pope John Paul II understood that whether the SB, or the GRU, or some other organization carried out the killing, ultimately the same old enemy was responsible. It was yet another error and persecution.

The pope was sickened by the death of his fellow Polish priest, who had become, in the words of George Weigel, "the voice of John Paul II" in their native land.[33] On October 24, even before Father Jerzy's body was discovered, the pope called the seizure of Popiełuszko an "inhuman act" and a "heinous act" in violation of "the dignity of the human person."[34]

In June 1987, when John Paul II made his third papal visit to Poland, the Holy Father went to the churchyard of Saint Stanisław Kostka and prayed at and kissed the tomb of the fallen priest.[35]

"THE WORLD'S CONSCIENCE WILL NOT REST"

President Reagan was outraged as well. Like John Paul II, he condemned the communists' "heinous" crime. The president released this statement:

> All America shares the grief of the Polish people at the news of the tragic death of Father Jerzy Popiełuszko. Father Popiełuszko was a champion of Christian values and a courageous spokesman for the cause of liberty. His life exemplified the highest ideals of human dignity; his death strengthens the resolve of all freedom loving peoples to stand firm in their convictions. Father Popiełuszko's spirit lives on. The world's conscience will not be at rest until the perpetrators of this heinous crime have been brought to justice.[36]

This was a powerful statement of solidarity with the Polish people. It was the kind of thing that forever earned Reagan a warm spot in the hearts of Poles.

Four years later, in a July 1988 statement marking Captive Nations Week, Reagan remembered Father Jerzy for having given his life "in the imperishable cause of liberty."[37]

MARTYR

In the end, the murder of Father Jerzy Popiełuszko backfired. The priest's sacrifice yet again laid bare what communism was all about. Father Jerzy had fought evil with truth, hatred with courage, fear with bravery, the grimness of death with the promise of eternal life.

Jerzy Popiełuszko's torment at the hands of devils was not forgotten. Some 400,000 of his countrymen paid their respects at his funeral. Millions more poured into churches to pay him homage.

Thirty years later, Monsignor Teofil Bogucki, pastor at Saint Stanisław Kostka Church, where Father Jerzy had given the Fatherland Masses, remembered Popiełuszko:

> He was... simple and good. He was not seeking greatness, did not pretend to be a hero, did not like applause. He was ordinary, like all of us. Very friendly and warm. He was obedient with respect to Church authority, ready to do anything.... He was very delicate, never offended anyone, never bore a grudge.... He was brave and unafraid.... He was uncompromising about fighting evil and persevering about doing good.... He lived till the end with a Rosary in his hand. He could repeat after Christ: "It is accomplished."[38]

It was indeed accomplished. The communists could not extinguish Poles' desire for freedom, for the Church, for God. Neither Father Jerzy nor his countrymen nor the communist rulers could have imagined it in late 1984, but communism's death grip on the nation wouldn't last another five years.

Father Jerzy Popiełuszko was one of many martyrs at the hands of atheistic communism. But his service and death were not wasted.

The blood of the martyrs is the seed of the Church.

27

MARCH 1985

A NEW KIND OF SOVIET LEADER

On November 6, 1984, Ronald Reagan was reelected in a landslide. One of his regrets from his first term was, as he later put it, "my delay in getting started in dealings with the Soviet Union." The problem came down to a simple fact: Soviet leaders "kept dying on me," Reagan said.[1]

It was true. Leonid Brezhnev had died in November 1982, and well before his death he had been so sick that he could not function as head of state. Brezhnev's successor, longtime KGB chief and disinformation master Yuri Andropov, experienced kidney failure just a few months after taking office.[2] Andropov was dead by February 1984. Konstantin Chernenko became the third Soviet general secretary in fifteen months—and he, too, was in terrible health. The heavy smoker, suffering from emphysema, could hardly be understood while delivering the eulogy at Andropov's funeral, and he couldn't lift his arm above his shoulder to salute the departed leader.[3] Chernenko died on March 10, 1985, after barely a year in office.

After this succession of ailing leaders, the Kremlin finally went in a different direction: fifty-four-year-old Mikhail Gorbachev became the new general secretary of the Soviet Union. Ronald Reagan would come to view Gorbachev as a new kind of Soviet leader. Gorbachev's relative youth was not the only difference. "I'd finally met a Soviet leader I could talk to," Reagan would later write in his memoirs, describing Gorbachev as "the first Soviet leader I knew of" who did not support "the old Marxist-Leninist goal of a one-world Communist state."[4] He would tell the press that no previous Soviet leader was "comparable to this man."[5]

The previous spring, John Paul II had consecrated Russia to the sacred heart of Mary, just as Our Lady of Fátima had requested long ago. Now he and his partner in Washington would see major changes in Moscow.

BAPTISM

Mikhail Gorbachev's upbringing made him different from many other Soviet leaders. Born March 2, 1931, he had a mother, two grandmothers, and a grandfather who were committed Christians. His sole grandparent who was not a believer, his grandfather, was a "veteran communist" who nonetheless "considered it a personal obligation to respect believers," Gorbachev later said. "My grandfather respected the religious faith of my grandmother, and despite the fact that at that time the Communists were supposed to resent religious faith, he never in any way was disrespectful to my grandmother's faith. And I saw all that." It was a peaceful coexistence. His grandparents had a table that displayed both his grandmother's religious icons and his grandfather's portraits of Lenin and Stalin.[6]

Even if Mikhail Gorbachev would one day deny the faith, he would embrace the respect and tolerance for religion his communist grandfather evinced. "I believe and recognize the quality of human beings," he would say many years later, in March 2009, when asked about his faith. "I am against any and all discrimination."[7]

Oxford professor Archie Brown, the preeminent biographer of Gorbachev, records that Gorbachev's mother, Maria, acceded to the wishes of his two Christian grandmothers and had him secretly baptized as an infant—a risky move in Stalin's Soviet Union. Professor Brown even reports, citing the account of a Russian journalist who worked under Gorbachev in party positions and wrote a book on Gorbachev's childhood years, that the priest who baptized the future Soviet leader actually gave him the name "Mikhail."[8]

"Mikhail" is Russian for "Michael," a word derived from Hebrew. Michael is the archangel identified in Scripture. Michael the Archangel is a saint in both the Russian Orthodox and Roman Catholic Churches, chosen as a patron saint of Russia in the fourteenth century. He is the leader of heaven's armies, patron saint of soldiers battling the forces of evil. A popular Roman Catholic prayer written by Pope Leo XIII, who claimed to see a vision of hell, says: "Saint Michael the Archangel, defend us in battle. Be our protection against the wickedness and snares of the Devil. May God rebuke him, we humbly pray. And do thou, O Prince of the heavenly hosts, by the power of God, thrust into hell Satan and all the evil spirits who prowl about the world seeking the ruin of souls."

The priest who baptized Gorbachev would have had a motivation for choosing the name. The Bolsheviks had shut down the glorious Cathedral of the Archangel Michael, on the southwest edge of Moscow; by 1931, the cathedral was used to store grain. It was another symbol of the communist assault on religion.

Ronald Reagan would affectionately call his Moscow counterpart "Mike," and would often ponder whether this Russian "Michael" was a closet Christian.

RISING STAR

The young Mikhail had a meteoric rise up the ranks of the Soviet leadership. In November 1978, not even fifty years old, he became a senior secretary of the Central Committee—one of the leading fourteen members of a committee that typically had two hundred to three hundred members in this period. Being part of the Secretariat put Gorbachev at the pinnacle of Communist Party leadership. The Secretariat included the general secretary, Leonid Brezhnev, as well as the two who would succeed him, Yuri Andropov and Konstantin Chernenko. It also featured big shots such as Boris Ponomarev (International Department), Dmitri Ustinov (Ministry of Defense), and Mikhail Suslov (keeper of the ideological flame). Gorbachev was a protégé of Suslov and Andropov, who had plucked him from the North Caucasus, where he was a regional party boss, and promoted him through the ranks. This background would normally suggest a hard-liner rather than a soft-liner, a moderate, a reformer.[9]

Another mentor was Andrei Gromyko, the devoted communist and Stalinist. The grim Gromyko famously presented Gorbachev by saying, "Comrades, this man has a nice smile, but he has iron teeth."[10]

Gromyko's statement was telling. Ronald Reagan and John Paul II would need to bear it in mind as they tried to read the new Soviet leader. Western liberals often accepted whatever spin came from the Kremlin, but Reagan and John Paul II knew to be cautious. They were not prone to being duped. Reagan had been too often duped by closet communists as a young man in Hollywood, when he was a "hemophiliac liberal." Now he was a chastened anticommunist, and he knew that, because he was president of the United States and leader of the free world, the stakes were much higher. He needed to be judicious in dealing with the new man in the Kremlin.

Reading Gorbachev would be no easy task. The Soviet leader's intentions were never entirely clear, and some of his actions proved confounding.[11] To be sure, Gorbachev was no Stalinist. He actually described himself as a Leninist, but he saw Lenin as a benevolent, almost saintly figure, probably because of the indoctrination about the "good Lenin" he had received in Soviet universities during the Khrushchev era.[12] He clearly wanted to reform the Soviet Union, making it a kinder, gentler, non-Stalinist state. He also said that he did want not the USSR to fall, but the noble freedoms that he ushered in—including religious freedom—eventually led to the collapse of the Soviet Union.

From the Central Committee, Gorbachev made the jump to the even more selective Politburo. He was promoted to full membership in the Politburo on October 21, 1980, two weeks before Ronald Reagan was elected president of the United States. At fifty, Gorbachev was by far the youngest member of the Politburo.[13]

Even before becoming general secretary, Gorbachev gave some indications of what kind of leader he would be. Anatoly Dobrynin, Moscow's ambassador to six American presidents, including Ronald Reagan, reported in his 1995 memoir: "From the summer of 1984, the Politburo was increasingly dominated by Mikhail Gorbachev, who often chaired its meetings because of the illness of Chernenko. Without much publicity it [the Politburo under Gorbachev's leadership] took two important decisions, first to renew the disarmament dialogue with the American administration (which was broken off by Andropov later as a protest against Reagan's anti-Soviet behavior), and second to move toward a summit with Reagan."[14] These were crucial peace overtures.

Some Soviets recognized the promise Gorbachev represented. On June 18, 1984, Anatoly Chernyaev, the historian who would become a top foreign-policy adviser to Gorbachev, recorded in his journal a conversation with Georgi Arbatov, the Soviet propagandist whose specialty was the Western media. "Arbatov stopped by," wrote Chernyaev. "He said that Gorbachev is our most popular figure in the West. Their press calls him the 'crown prince' and a 'most interesting person with a big future.' I replied that then there's still hope for Russia."[15]

On January 18, 1986, after Gorbachev had become general secretary, Chernyaev wrote in his diary: "My God! What luck that there was a man in the Politburo (Andropov) who showed the wisdom of a true 'tsar,' finding Gorbachev and dragging him out of the provinces—and in a country which has ninety-five different such regions! If Andropov hadn't discovered him and forced him upon Brezhnev, who would we be stuck with today? Especially after the 'Chuchka.'"[16] The "Chuchka" was Chernenko.

"A WHOLESALE WAR ON RELIGION"

Not long after Gorbachev became general secretary, he introduced *perestroika* and *glasnost*, his two signature initiatives for reforming an Evil Empire. With both initiatives he sought to preserve the USSR—a point Gorbachev reiterated again and again, and a position he maintains to this day. But his USSR would not be Stalin's USSR.

Gorbachev's *perestroika* endeavored to create some manner of economic "restructuring." Frankly, what he had in mind and pursued was much more convoluted than his Western admirers understood. His *glasnost*, on the other hand, was more identifiable; it referred to a new form of political "openness" that sought vast improvements in what Americans would understand as First Amendment freedoms: freedom of press, speech, assembly, and religion.

As to the last of those, Gorbachev later candidly admitted that communists had carried out a "war on religion."[17] "Just like religious orders who zealously convert 'heretics' to their own faith," said Gorbachev in his memoirs, written after he left office, "our [communist] ideologues carried out a wholesale war on religion."[18] He lamented that his Bolshevik forebears, even after their brutal civil war ended in the early 1920s, had "continued to tear down churches, arrest clergymen, and destroy them. This was no longer understandable or justifiable. Atheism took rather savage forms in our country at that time."[19]

Gorbachev would call off the savagery. Atheism would take a new, more tolerant form under his government.

28

MAY 1985

A PRESIDENT IN PORTUGAL

As Moscow's new man settled in at the Kremlin, America's president headed for Europe.

On May 1, 1985, Ronald Reagan embarked on a ten-day European tour. Starting in West Germany, he traveled to Spain, France, and Portugal.[1] This is not the place to revisit all of Reagan's stops and speeches and the drama surrounding them, which could fill a separate book. Reagan's visit to the Bergen-Belsen concentration camp and a German military cemetery outside Bitburg generated considerable blowback, as historians and biographers have noted.[2] By comparison, Reagan's speeches in Strasbourg, France, and Lisbon, Portugal, have gone essentially unnoticed. That has been history's loss. Like many events, they make more sense now, decades later, with the benefit of greater perspective.

"THE TOTALITARIAN TEMPTATION"

On May 8, Reagan spoke in Strasbourg to a special session of the European Parliament, the legislature that houses what today is the European Union. He stressed a theme he carried throughout his visit: Europe needed to be "a Europe democratic, a Europe united east and west, a Europe at long last completely free."[3] In other words, Europe needed to be freed from communist totalitarianism just as it had been freed forty years earlier from Nazi totalitarianism.

May 8 marked the fortieth anniversary of V-E Day—the liberation of Europe that ended World War II. Reagan shared anecdotes and personal memories with his European audience:

> On that day 40 years ago, I was at my post in an Army Air Corps installation in Culver City, California. Passing a radio, I heard the words, "Ladies and gentlemen, the war in Europe is over." I felt a chill, as if a gust of cold wind had just swept past, and even though for America there was still a war in the Pacific front, I realized I would never forget that moment. . . .
>
> A few weeks ago in California, an old soldier with tears in his eyes said: "It was such a different world then. It's almost impossible to describe it to someone who wasn't there. But when they finally turned the lights on in the cities again, it was like being reborn."
>
> If it is hard to communicate the happiness of those days, it is even harder to communicate, to those who did not share it, the depth of Europe's agony. So much of it lay in ruins. Whole cities had been destroyed. Children played in the rubble and begged for food. . . .
>
> Hannah Arendt spoke of the "banality of evil"—the banality of the little men who did the terrible deeds. We know they were totalitarians who used the state, which they had elevated to the level of a god, to inflict war on peaceful nations and genocide on innocent peoples.[4]

Reagan paused to commend Europe's different political parties, from the left and the right, for having worked together to create a better Europe:

> Your nations did not become the breeding ground for new extremist philosophies. You resisted the totalitarian temptation. Your people embraced democracy, the dream the Fascists could not kill. They chose freedom.

> And today we celebrate the leaders who led the way—Churchill and Monnet, Adenauer and Schuman, De Gasperi and Spaak, Truman and Marshall. And we celebrate, too, the free political parties that contributed their share of greatness—the Liberals and the Christian Democrats, the Social Democrats and Labour and the Conservatives. Together they tugged at the same oar, and the great and mighty ship of Europe moved on.
>
> If any doubt their success, let them look at you. In this room are those who fought on opposite sides 40 years ago and their sons and daughters. Now you work together to lead Europe democratically; you buried animosity and hatred in the rubble. There is no greater testament to reconciliation and to the peaceful unity of Europe than the men and women in this chamber.

But this tribute to cooperation across the political aisle was quickly forgotten. The problem was that Reagan dared to condemn *communist* totalitarianism in addition to fascist totalitarianism: "The question before us today is... can we undertake a stable and peaceful relationship with the Soviet Union based upon effective deterrence and the reduction of tensions. I believe we can. I believe we've learned that fruitful cooperation with the Soviet Union must be accompanied by successful competition in areas, particularly Third World areas where the Soviets are not yet prepared to act with restraint."

At this mild rebuke of Soviet behavior, some thirty members of the European Parliament, mostly from the British Labour Party, walked out on the president. This was the same Labour Party that Reagan moments earlier had thanked for burying political animosity and seeking reconciliation, unity, and peace. As soon as the American president accused Moscow of not acting with "restraint"—which was a colossal understatement—these British leftists stormed out of the chamber.

The protest prompted Reagan to quip: "You know, I've learned something useful. Maybe if I talk long enough in my own Congress, some of those will walk out." Many of the remaining members of the Parliament loudly applauded.[5]

Other leftists who remained in the chamber heckled the president. One interrupted Reagan by shouting "Nicaragua! Nicaragua!" in support of unelected dictator Daniel Ortega's communist regime in Central America. Reagan again defused the situation with some levity. "Is there an echo in here?" he asked, to laughter.

Reagan concluded his remarks with these ad-libbed comments: "I would like to just conclude with one line, if I could, and say we've seen evidence here of your faith in democracy, in the ability of some to speak up freely as they preferred to speak. And yet I can't help but remind all of us that some who take advantage of that right of democracy seem unaware that if the government that they would advocate became reality, no one would have that freedom to speak up again. Thank you all for your graciousness on this great day. Thank you, and God bless you all. Thank you."[6]

In truth, the audience had not displayed a lot of graciousness. The Associated Press estimated that "a third of the European Parliament jeered, waved protest signs or walked out." Leftist parliamentarians hammered their desks with their fists, pounded their feet, shouted, held up placards, and stomped out of the room.[7]

Reagan was about to experience more of the same in Lisbon.

THE PRESIDENT GOES TO PORTUGAL

From Strasbourg, Reagan headed for Portugal, the land where Our Lady of Fátima had come sixty-eight years earlier to warn of communism's errors and persecutions. Reagan in May 1985 came to do the same.

The American president spoke to the Assembly of the Republic of Portugal on May 9 at 12:30 P.M. This legislature in the land of Our Lady of Fátima had some 44 communist members out of a body of 250 members, an astonishingly high number for an elected Western legislative body. Portugal had even more socialists, including the country's prime minister.

Before Reagan began, most of the Assembly's elected Communist Party members walked out in protest. Their hearts and minds were even more closed to hearing the president than those of the British leftists in Strasbourg had been. And their behavior was worse. In fact, Reagan would receive more hospitable treatment in Moscow when he spoke in front of a statue of Lenin three years later.

The Portuguese people who elected those communist and socialist representatives likewise spurned Reagan's anticommunist message. When he reached Lisbon, the president encountered several small demonstrations and a considerable amount of graffiti that implored, "Reagan Go Home."[8]

In addition to the thirty-five elected communists who filed out of the chamber as President Reagan prepared to speak, nine other communists and their allies had boycotted the session altogether. A member of the socialist Green Party left a caged white dove in his seat. As far as they were concerned, the doves resided in the Kremlin, not in the White House. In a written statement, Portugal's Marxist-Leninists offered a reason why they were protesting Reagan: his resistance to the communist dictatorship in Nicaragua.[9]

This was hardly the only reason. We now know that Portugal's communists were so loyal to Moscow that they received an annual subsidy from the Kremlin's International Department, the successor to the Comintern. The $800,000 per year that the Kremlin handed to Portugal's Communist Party (a huge figure in a country as small as Portugal) was its fourth largest payout, behind only subsidies to Communist Parties in the United States, France, and Finland.[10]

Just two years earlier, Yuri Andropov had tapped these parties as part of a covert campaign to stop the Reagan administration's plan to deploy the Pershing II/Euromissile in Western Europe. These communists would manipulate the wider left—socialists, liberals, peaceniks, dupes—in the nuclear-freeze movement. For this campaign, notes historian Robert Service, "abundant funding was made available from Moscow."[11] Portugal's communists, doing the bidding of their masters in Moscow, were bent on undermining the very Reagan policy that the president believed would lead to nuclear disarmament (and did, in fact, lead to disarmament, as we will see).

Little wonder, then, that Portugal's communists walked out on Reagan.

Reagan began his speech in Lisbon just as he had finished his address in Strasbourg: with an extemporaneous comment. Glancing at the exiting communists, he joked, "I'm sorry that some of the chairs on the left seem to be uncomfortable."

The remainder of the tense assembly laughed, and Reagan proceeded with his prepared remarks. "I'm deeply honored to be with you distinguished ladies and gentlemen here in this assembly that is so rich in history," said the president, "where the voice of the Portuguese people is heard." Here, too, Reagan spoke of peace, freedom, hope, and the "cruelty of totalitarian rule." He praised Portugal's "old and glorious heritage" and expressed his "humble gratitude and admiration for all the achievements of your people." He encouraged them in their battles against "totalitarian ideology," and even ventured a prediction: "Future historians will recognize in Portugal's journey the journey of our time, the journey of our century. For you, the people of Portugal, have chosen freedom. You have elected to embark on a great adventure in democracy."

To say that future historians would recognize in *Portugal's* journey "the journey of our time, the journey of our century," was a powerful statement, even an odd one. Portugal was not a major or even minor world power. It had a tiny economy. It was nowhere on the international radar.

So what did the president mean? Could he have had Our Lady of Fátima in mind? Was he referring to *that* unique journey that began in a small Portuguese village early in the twentieth century?

It is possible. At the least, the speechwriter thought that way. The person who drafted this speech was Reagan's chief speechwriter, Tony Dolan, a devout Roman Catholic with a passion for Mary, for Fátima, and for Marian apparitions and miracles. Dolan knew all about Fátima. When I discussed this particular speech with Dolan three decades later, I asked whether Reagan had any prior knowledge of Fátima. "He knew what Fátima was at that point," Dolan told me. "I'm sure of it. Fátima was long a part of the anticommunist movement. The Fátima movement was something he would've known about. And he had this strong mystical side as well."[12] Moreover, Fátima was well known generally in American culture; it was even the subject of a major motion picture made when Reagan was in Hollywood.[13]

As we will see later in this book, at least one adviser would review Fátima in depth with Reagan. That briefing, by the U.S. ambassador to the Vatican, Frank Shakespeare, would occur when Reagan was en route to Rome in June 1987 for his second Vatican visit with Pope John Paul II.

But Reagan probably learned about Fátima well before that—well before his address in Lisbon, in fact. Tomasz Pompowski, an excellent historian, told me that Bill Clark had talked to Reagan about the Fátima message twice in "longer talks" and again in "shorter" conversations "usually in the morning at the White House."[14] This information jolted me, not because I found the claim to be unbelievable—on the contrary, this was exactly the kind of subject Clark and Reagan would have discussed—but because I somehow never asked Clark whether he had discussed Fátima with Reagan, despite our countless conversations. How did I not ask this? Pompowski, however, did ask.

Pompowski told me that Pope John Paul II actually gave Reagan a "book of interviews" on Fátima from the Vatican Library. The Polish historian claims that the book reached Reagan via Archbishop Pio Laghi and Bill Clark while Clark ran the NSC. Clark was national security adviser from January 1982 through October 1983. Such a book exchange probably would have happened after—and was perhaps prompted by—the June 1982 meeting at the Vatican between John Paul II and Reagan.

It is possible, then, that the pope and the president discussed Fátima as early as June 1982. That would not be a big surprise. We know that at their first meeting the two men discussed surviving assassination attempts and that both said they believed their lives had been spared via divine intervention. For John Paul II, that meant a Marian role. After explaining the Blessed Mother and Fátima to Reagan, the Holy Father may well have sent the president a book on the subject.

I found no record of such a book on the shelves at the Reagan Ranch. I asked the Reagan Library whether Reagan had a Fátima book at his home in Los Angeles, in his office in Century City, or elsewhere. Conversations and e-mails with the Reagan Library revealed that the library today houses three Fátima books, at least one of which we know Reagan saw. They include a small book/pamphlet from 1992, with no inscription and apparently gifted to the library from someone in the public. The library staff believes that Reagan never saw this pamphlet. A second book that Reagan is not known to have seen was the prominent 1954 book *Our Lady of Fátima* by William Thomas Walsh, which was endorsed by Cardinal Francis Spellman. The Reagan Library copy bears an inscription to Nancy Reagan from a donor named Ethel Becker, who gave the book as a gift in 1981.

The third item is a Fátima book that Reagan would have seen: Francis Johnson's *Fátima: The Great Sign*, published in 1980 by TAN Books. This respected work, published in several languages, was not a "book of interviews" (Pompowski's description) but rather a book of contributions from Church authorities on Fátima; most notably, it included an introductory "Commendation" by the bishop of Leiria-Fátima. The back cover featured a photo of John Paul II himself holding the book and peering inside—quite an endorsement. Thus, if the pontiff recommended a Fátima book to Reagan, this probably would have been it. As one Reagan Library staffer told me, this book "could be it."

Did the book come to Reagan via Laghi and Bill Clark? Possibly, or at least with their assistance. It also appears, however, that the book might have come to Reagan later via Tony Dolan and/or Frank Shakespeare. Details are elusive, but the Reagan Library has on file a one-page memo from Dolan to Reagan summarizing the book and delineating how the Fátima story related to the president's views on communism.

In short, Reagan would have seen this book. How exactly he received it, and whether he read it, remains a mystery.

For the record, I am able to confirm that John Paul II sent Reagan other books. In March 1983, for instance, the pope sent Reagan (via Pio

Laghi) a "handsomely bound" (Reagan's description) copy of the Vatican's 1983 *Annuario Pontificio*. On March 18 Reagan wrote John Paul II to thank the pontiff for the gift Laghi had delivered: "I deeply appreciate your kindness, and I shall treasure this 1983 edition as a remembrance of your warm friendship."[15]

To reiterate a key point, if the Polish pope did pass along a Fátima book to Reagan via Archbishop Laghi, that probably happened after the June 1982 Vatican meeting, which suggests that Reagan and John Paul II might have had a Fátima discussion at that first one-on-one.

Whatever the case, we have further evidence to suggest that Reagan knew about Fátima by the time of his May 1985 Portugal speech, as Tony Dolan insisted.

And actually, Reagan showed plainly in his speech before Portugal's Assembly that he knew the Fátima story. He made a striking statement as he shared thoughts on John Paul II:

> This belief in human dignity suggests the final truth upon which democracy is based—a belief that human beings are not just another part of the material universe, not just mere bundles of atoms. We believe in another dimension—a spiritual side to man. We find a transcendent source for our claims to human freedom, our suggestion that inalienable rights come from one greater than ourselves.
>
> No one has done more to remind the world of the truth of human dignity, as well as the truth that peace and justice begins with each of us, than the special man who came to Portugal a few years ago after a terrible attempt on his life. He came here to Fátima, the site of your great religious shrine, to fulfill his special devotion to Mary, to plead for forgiveness and compassion among men, to pray for peace and the recognition of human dignity throughout the world.
>
> When I met Pope John Paul II a year ago in Alaska, I thanked him for his life and his apostolate. And I dared to suggest to him [that in] the example of men like himself and in the prayers of simple people everywhere, simple people like the children of Fátima, there resides more power than in all the great armies and statesmen of the world.

Yes, Ronald Reagan had invoked Fátima. For the first and final time (publicly, that is) of his presidency, Reagan mentioned Mary and the children of Fátima. He said he had told the pope that in the prayers of those children there resided "more power" than in all the world's armies and statesmen. (One might read into this passage that Reagan in Alaska had mentioned the Fátima children to John Paul II, but I think that would be an inaccurate reading.) He knew that after the assassination attempt in Saint Peter's Square, John Paul II had visited Fátima, that "great religious shrine," where he fulfilled "his special devotion to Mary," where he prayed for forgiveness, compassion, and peace.

Clearly, Ronald Reagan knew of Fátima. Note that Reagan carefully reviewed every speech ahead of time. "That was a daring line," said Tony Dolan three decades later. "He [Reagan] could've passed on it, but he didn't. That [speech draft] went through a lot of iterations to be proofed."[16]

Reagan's staff carefully reviewed every speech as well, which makes it remarkable that even an oblique reference to the miracle of Fátima made its way into a presidential address. Reagan's staff included ultra-cautious pragmatists who were aggressive in excising anything they considered remotely odd, unconventional, or potentially controversial. Many lines in Reagan speeches caused a ruckus among his advisers. Any Reagan speechwriter can recall examples, from well-known phrases like "Mr. Gorbachev, tear down this wall" and "Evil Empire" to pro-life statements that Reagan staffers such as James Baker and Richard Darman pounced on.[17] Such lines could tangle up a speech draft for weeks, even months. But this time, somehow, a line concerning three shepherd children and their claims of visits from the mother of Christ slipped through, apparently with no opposition.

As President Reagan uttered the word *Fátima* to the Assembly, a pause followed as the Portuguese legislators awaited the translation for confirmation of what they thought they just heard. When the corresponding words came through in their language, vigorous clapping ensued.[18] This was not what they had expected from a head of state addressing them in formal session, and especially from an American Protestant president.

Saying what he said no doubt gave Reagan joy. He relished these moments when a powerful statement of truth left his lips. "I knew he would love it and use it," Dolan said of the line he inserted for his boss. "Just knew. Very, very daring."[19]

Ronald Reagan finished the 3,400-word oration with a "Thank you, and God bless you all." A standing ovation followed. The communists had failed to spoil his message.

Indeed, the *New York Times* noted that the boycott/walkout "appeared to have limited effect as the remaining four-fifths of the members interrupted Mr. Reagan's speech eight times with applause and stood in ovation at the end." The *Times* reported that the seventy-four-year-old president was "buoyant" after the speech, "skipping up stairs and swapping grins with Secretary of State George P. Shultz."[20] This was the last day of a long European trip, but Reagan seemed as fresh as the instant he had landed in West Germany on May 1.

The *New York Times* was one of the few American sources to cover Reagan's speech in Portugal. Most Western media had spent their press coverage in Bitburg. The *Times* piece seized on perhaps the president's most poignant comments of the entire ten-day swing through Europe. Well before his words on the children of Fátima, and well after his statement on Portugal's journey being "the journey of our time, the journey of our century," Reagan had stated: "I've seen in these past days reminders of the tragedy and the grandeur of our time. I've heard the voice of the 20th century; it is humanity's voice, heard in every century, every time. And the words are unmistakable. They call out to us in anguish, but also in hope: Let the nations live in peace among themselves. Let all peoples abide in the fellowship that God intends." He spoke of the God-given rights of individuals, "the right to speak, to assemble, to publish, and to vote, even to walk out—that is the meaning of democracy."

The *Times* reporter zeroed in on that passage: "President Reagan told the Portuguese Parliament today that he had 'heard the voice of the 20th century' on his visit to Europe and that Communism was losing out to democracy."[21]

Though neither Reagan nor (apparently) Dolan had intended it as such—this passage is not near the section on Fátima—we might read it as an almost unwitting reference to the voice of Fátima, the voice of the twentieth century.

THE CRUSADE

Ronald Reagan returned home on May 10. Perhaps in his stack of briefing papers the next day was a May 11 report from TASS published in *Pravda* under the headline "What the U.S. President's Visit to Europe Showed." The piece declared that Reagan's "aim" in Europe "was to rally his West European partners in the 'crusade' against communism proclaimed by the head of the present U.S. Administration." His objective was nothing less than "overturning" the "postwar structure in Europe."[22]

This was a rare occasion when *Pravda* got it right.

The Kremlin especially appreciated the European leftists who had stormed out of Reagan's Strasbourg speech with shouts of "Down with the 'Star Wars' program" and "Hands off Nicaragua!" These members of the European Parliament had (intentionally or not) helped Moscow's propaganda efforts.

Just as Portugal's communists were protesting America's anticommunist president, one of Reagan's top lieutenants, Bill Casey, was watching closely as two of his CIA analysts were on the verge of confirming something that Our Lady of Fátima had predicted long ago: it was communists who ordered the killing of Pope John Paul II.

29

MAY 1985

"THE RUSSIANS DID IT"

On May 16, 1985, less than a week after returning from Europe, President Reagan met with CIA director Bill Casey in the Oval Office. The president and the CIA director also came together that day for a Cabinet meeting, which some twenty-seven people attended. But this appointment was private.[1]

What did Reagan and Casey talk about? The official record doesn't tell us. I dug into all available materials at the Reagan Library and filed FOIA requests for the release of records for April and May 1985—phone-call transcripts, logs of phone calls made and received, letters, correspondence, memos between Reagan and Casey, and memos between Casey and other members of the Reagan administration. I also requested, for those same two months, the release of any documents by the CIA, the NSC, and other groups of interest.[2] Nothing refers to the content of the Reagan-Casey conversation on May 16.

Reagan did mention the meeting in his private diary. In his entry for that day he wrote that "Bill Casey came in" to discuss a *Washington Post* story on the March car bombing in Beirut that killed more than eighty people. But as published in *The Reagan Diaries*, the entry ends with a bracketed ellipsis ("[. . .]"), which reflects an omission in the cleared and approved published account. In other words, here we run into another redaction. The editor of *The Reagan Diaries*, the historian Douglas Brinkley, writes in his introduction, "The National Security Council read all five diary volumes and redacted only about six pages of material for national security reasons." So Reagan's account of this May 16, 1985, meeting with the CIA director appears to be one of the exceedingly rare instances when the NSC held back material "for national security reasons."[3]

What was happening at this time that could be so sensitive? By May 1985, investigators looking into the shooting of Pope John Paul II were tightening the noose around the Bulgarian communist regime and the Soviets. Claire Sterling and other journalists had already cast suspicion on the communists with their investigative reporting. Italian prosecutors, meanwhile, had been painstakingly assembling a case. In November 1982 the Italians had arrested the Bulgarian Sergei Antonov, former station chief of the Balkan Air office in Rome, in connection with the assassination attempt. Now, in the spring of 1985, Antonov and other accused conspirators were about to go on trial.

And the Soviets were coming unhinged. A year earlier, as Italy's judicial authorities built their case against Antonov, *Pravda* had published a TASS statement headlined "Lies to Order." The *Pravda* piece, published May 10, 1984, charged that the Italians were "clearly acting on orders from reactionary circles in the West" and were "doing their utmost to whip up an anticommunist campaign and to charge Bulgaria with complicity in the attempted assassination in May 1981 of Pope John Paul II." Moscow's propagandists called the Italian case against Antonov an "utterly groundless provocation" and tried to turn the attention back to Mehmet Ali Agca, insisting that the Turk acted alone. Moscow offered a conspiracy theory to explain away the fact that Agca had identified Antonov and two other Bulgarian conspirators: Agca had been "thoroughly worked over by Western secret services," *Pravda* reported. "During his stay in Ascoli Piceno Prison, Agca was repeatedly visited by agents of the Italian secret services, on orders from the U.S. Central Intelligence Agency."[4]

The Soviets kept pushing this line in the months ahead. In October 1984 *Izvestia* ran a piece titled "Outrage Against Truth," which referred to the "Turkish terrorist" Agca as a "piece of scum" who had falsely accused others. The *Izvestia* article declared that "reactionary imperialist circles both within Italy and abroad, particularly in the US," were pursuing this "trumped-up 'case' against Antonov." Why? *Izvestia* explained: "For the simple reason that the large-scale anti-Bulgarian, antisocialist campaign that anticommunist 'psychological warfare' centers launched in the West over the assassination attempt in Rome is intended to be a long-term attack, and its fire, which is barely smoldering at this point, needs constant stoking with new pieces of slanderous 'kindling.'"[5]

According to *Izvestia*, these Western forces were carefully orchestrating "a conspiracy to conceal a conspiracy." This was "the crudest sort of provocation," Moscow said, intended to "conceal the real culprits and organizers of the terrorist act against the Pope, divert suspicion from them, delude public opinion and keep the true criminals from being exposed and punished."

And who were the true criminals? They were the "agents" of "international imperialism," who resided within Washington's Beltway.

Despite the accusations coming from Moscow, Bill Casey didn't meet with Reagan on May 16 to discuss a CIA cover-up of U.S. involvement in the pope's shooting.

No, the truth was that Casey had undertaken his own, secret investigation into the assassination attempt. He had taken an active interest in the case years earlier and was not satisfied with the approach that careerists within the CIA took to the investigation: they tended to dismiss out of hand any suggestion that the Soviet Bloc might have been involved. The published reports by Claire Sterling, a journalist he respected, had stirred the CIA director to investigate the assassination attempt further.

And now, in the spring of 1985, Casey was ready to report the findings to his president. Rational observers have long suspected that the Soviets were behind the shooting of John Paul II. Here I can reveal that certain researchers within the CIA under Bill Casey concluded that Moscow was in fact complicit in the plot to kill the pope.

Through a series of interviews with various sources over the past decade, combined with a thorough search of the documentary record (especially through FOIA requests and archival research), I have pieced together how the CIA's extraordinarily secret investigation came about and what it found. No one has ever published the secret CIA report that resulted. After years of research, I have not been able to find the report or anyone who knows where it is located or how it is labeled and filed.

But I do know what it concludes. As one of the few people who ever saw the report put it to me, the findings can be summarized simply: "The Russians did it."

One source described the report and its extreme secrecy to me: "About thirty pages [in length]. Eyes only. Really, really tight. Only one or two copies.... This was so classified that they practically took the eyeballs out of the corpses [of those who read it].... I don't know where it is today.... That document has never come out. People don't know it, but that's what they really want. That has the answer."

The source added, "The document that I'm referring to answers the question [of who planned the shooting of the pope]." It was "the single most secret document" that this source ever saw.

Here is the story of how it came about.

"HE DID NOT ACT ALONE"

By the time Ronald Reagan and Bill Casey sat down on May 16, 1985, four years had passed since the pope had been shot. Casey had suspected a Soviet role early on, but it was really the work of Claire Sterling that prompted him to commission an independent CIA investigation.

Sterling's first major piece on the subject, her long *Reader's Digest* article, had appeared in the summer of 1982. Her seminal book *The Time of the Assassins* was published in January 1984. Recall that Bill Casey's daughter, Bernadette, told me that her father "thought that book was right on."[6] Then, on June 10, 1984, the *New York Times* ran on the front page a lengthy exclusive by Sterling (who was not even a *Times* reporter) that began, "An Italian State Prosecutor has filed a report in court saying that the Bulgarian secret services recruited the man who shot Pope John Paul II in 1981 in a plot to weaken the Solidarity movement in Poland."[7]

Casey was especially intrigued because Sterling reported material that the CIA did not have, and that, frankly, many in the CIA did not *want* to have. Early in *The Time of the Assassins*, Sterling declared: "He [Agca] did not act alone. We know that now, since he has said so himself and the Italian judiciary has confirmed it. If not for Agca's testimony, no amount of fragmentary evidence would have convinced the world that the Bulgarian secret service, acting on behalf of the Soviet Union's KGB, conspired to murder the head of the Roman Catholic Church." She added: "Much of the world still refuses to believe it."[8]

Sterling was convinced that the CIA establishment and the careerists in other Western intelligence services refused to believe it. In one of the first paragraphs of her book, she quoted the CIA's deputy station chief in Rome telling the Italian interior minister "you have no proof" of Agca's participation in a wider conspiracy.[9] That was the CIA's position from the start, and the agency's careerists refused to budge from that appraisal—or to search for any evidence that might challenge their assumptions.

The situation wasn't much different in West Germany's intelligence service. Sterling quoted one "ranking functionary" as telling her: "Come, now. Whatever makes you believe there was any such thing as an international plot? Our police in Germany really don't see the attack on the pope as the big operation you seem to think it was."[10]

The West Germans said the same to *Time* magazine. "I cannot believe that the KGB would do anything so slipshod and unprofessional," said a West German intelligence official. "Why would the KGB be so stupid as to leave Bulgarians who were closely involved in the thing hanging around Rome, waiting to be arrested?"[11]

A British intelligence official agreed. "I think the Russians have become too sophisticated to try this sort of thing," he sniffed.[12]

Note that these analyses measured Moscow only by its level of professionalism, not by its motives or by its proven capacity for sinister acts.

It did not help that the Italians were at the head of the investigation. The international intelligence community, not to mention the political community, tended to view the Italians as Keystone Kops chasing American women around Rome. In this case, however, the Italians, left to do the investigating virtually alone, did exceptional work.

The French were also subject to negative stereotypes, but French intelligence had a more realistic appraisal of the communist role in the pope's shooting than did the CIA or the West Germans. One French official told *Time* that Communist Bloc subversion was a "permanent threat" that must always be taken seriously.[13] This French realism reflected the anticommunist views of Alexandre de Marenches, who ran France's external intelligence agency, SDECE. De Marenches would title his memoirs *The Evil Empire*.[14] He had no problem imagining the Soviets involved in shooting a pope. In fact, a December 1982 report in a French newspaper claimed that on April 20, 1981, de Marenches had sent "a general and a colonel" to the Vatican to warn the pope of an impending attack.[15]

By contrast, the more "sophisticated" Western intelligence services did little to look into the assassination attempt. Almost two years after the shooting, an anonymous senior CIA official told the *New York Times* that the issue was "not a matter of intense scrutiny." The official said, "It is an Italian matter, and it would be inappropriate for us to intrude."[16]

But as Sterling reported, the CIA *did* intrude, by repeatedly "taking the Bulgarian line."[17]

In December 1982, soon after the arrest of Sergei Antonov, *New York Times* columnist William Safire reported that the CIA's deputy chief of station in Rome "did his best to convey to the Italian Government a high degree of skepticism" about Bulgarian involvement. This was the same CIA official Sterling quoted as saying, "You have no proof." Safire attributed this "shameful American reluctance to urge the Italians on" to a desire to "bring back détente." "That is why," Safire concluded, "after facts are presented which compel common sense to lay the crime at the Kremlin door, we will hear the faceless officials complain, 'You have no proof.'"[18]

Two days after Safire's op-ed piece ran, the *New York Times* published a news story that cited "many professional political and intelligence analysts"—all unnamed—who doubted "that the Soviet Union, which they consider cautious in international affairs, would have taken so great a risk as plotting a political assassination of Shakespearean magnitude."[19]

The Soviet Union a "cautious actor in international affairs"? The statement was absurd.

In January 1983 an "unnamed CIA spokesman" told the *Los Angeles Times* that Agca was "a known crazy" who was "too unstable to be included in an assassination plot, let alone be trusted to do the shooting."[20]

The next month the *New York Times* reported, "Senior agency officials in Washington say they are highly skeptical about any Bulgarian and Soviet links to Mehmet Ali Agca, the Turk convicted of shooting the Pope in St. Peter's Square."[21]

Senator Alfonse D'Amato, a New York Republican, was one of a number of senators alarmed by the CIA's failure to look into the mounting evidence of communist involvement.[22] D'Amato called the CIA's efforts on the pope shooting "shockingly inept." The senator traveled to Italy to meet with Italian and American officials in his capacity as a member of the U.S. government's Commission on Security and Cooperation in Europe (better known as the Helsinki Commission). After meeting with Ilario Martella, the Italian magistrate investigating the shooting, D'Amato said, "The Bulgarian connection is well-grounded in fact, and they [the Italians] have information in their possession which establishes it." He added that a senior CIA official at the U.S. Embassy in Rome had told him, "Not one person has been assigned to follow developments in the case." D'Amato also charged that the CIA (in the *Times*'s words) "had tried to discourage investigation into possible Bulgarian and Soviet involvement in the shooting."[23]

When D'Amato returned from his fact-finding trip to Italy, he headed straight for the Reagan White House to meet with Bill Clark.[24] D'Amato's briefing influenced Clark, which in turn influenced Reagan.

Right after D'Amato called on Clark, Reagan publicly condemned what he now called "an international crime" that merited "the deepest possible investigation." The president also commended "the courage of the Italian government in bringing the problem to world attention."[25]

As the *New York Times*'s Philip Taubman reported on February 19, the leading Republican and Democrat on the Senate Intelligence Committee, Barry Goldwater of Arizona and Daniel Patrick Moynihan of New York, respectively, believed that the CIA was dragging its feet. Some of these CIA critics complained to Clark, who responded by scheduling a meeting with Casey to discuss the status of the agency's investigation. According to Taubman's report, Casey reassured Clark that the CIA was not impeding any investigations.[26] What the *Times* did not report, because it did not know, was that Casey and Clark privately agreed that not only a Bulgarian connection but also a Soviet connection was likely.

The next month, Nicholas Gage of the *New York Times* filed a story stating, "Authorities in Western Europe have information that supports testimony given to them by a Turkish assassin, Mehmet Ali Agca, that when he tried to kill the Pope... he was acting at the behest of Bulgarian intelligence agents."[27] That particular story hit on a disastrous day for Moscow: March 23, 1983. It was the same day that Reagan announced his Strategic Defense Initiative, and two weeks after he had denounced the Soviet Union as an "Evil Empire."

But the CIA establishment tossed the Kremlin a lifeline. An agency source attacked the article as "third-rate hearsay." The CIA had an ally in condemning claims of Bulgarian involvement: the Bulgarian Telegraph Agency, the official press mouthpiece of the communist government.[28]

Such reports were good for Moscow's PR position and detrimental to the Italian investigation. The *New York Times*'s reports usually ended up in the Italian press. A few weeks after the *Times* said that intelligence officials doubted whether the "cautious" Soviets would have risked an assassination attempt, Italy's leftist *La Repubblica* ran a headline trumpeting, "CIA Does Not Believe the Bulgarians Wanted to Kill Pope Wojtyła."[29] If the CIA wasn't suspicious of the Kremlin, then why were Italy's investigators? They must be *reactionaries*.

Erminio Pennacchini of the Italian parliament said: "My impression is that the CIA has attempted to becloud the results of our investigation, and diminish their significance. We got no help from them."[30]

AGCA TALKS

Then the Italians got some unexpected help from a choice witness: Mehmet Ali Agca.

On July 8, 1983, Italian police escorted Agca to an armored car for questioning about a possible deal to exchange him for a kidnapped girl, thus purchasing his "freedom." The girl was the fifteen-year-old daughter of a Vatican employee. A man who telephoned had claimed to be the abductor and demanded that Agca be released by July 20. He did not say what would happen to the girl if Agca was not freed.

Agca was frightened. He wanted no part of any such deal. He knew that the communist definition of freedom was a rotten one.

"I am with the innocent girl," Agca shouted to reporters. "I am with Italy. I am with the Vatican. I am doing very well in Italian jails. I thank Italian justice and the Italian state.... I am repentant for the attack on the Pope. I admire the Pope and I thank the Italian justice."

This was the first time that Agca had spoken to the press since the May 13, 1981, shooting. The Italian journalists seized the moment. "Was it the Bulgarians who sent you to Italy?" a reporter yelled to Agca. His response: "Yes, the Bulgarians." He continued: "I have been several times in Bulgaria and in Syria—and in the attack against the Pope even the KGB took part." He clarified: "*Yes, the KGB.*"

The trained assassin kept going: "I have been trained in Bulgaria. I have been in Bulgaria, I stayed several times. I have been trained by special experts in international terrorism." Asked where, he reiterated, "In Syria, in Bulgaria I have stayed several times."[31]

Mehmet Ali Agca had finally spoken to the press—and he had directly implicated Bulgaria's communists and the Kremlin's.

DUPED AT LANGLEY

Members of the CIA's establishment didn't ignore this information. They couldn't. Instead, they claimed that Agca was lying to protect himself. Moscow and Sofia were still innocent.

Claire Sterling would not have been surprised by this response. She had written at length about the institutional CIA's naive assumptions and arrogant refusal to explore leads.

Inside the CIA, the establishmentarians were doing their best to discredit Sterling, whose high-profile reporting had essentially shown them up. One source told me about an internal CIA review of Sterling's book: "They just trashed it. A nasty review—very vicious. It was amazing." This source told me of a moment when one of the establishment's chief deniers cornered him and said, "I know all about wet operations [i.e., assassinations], and this wasn't one of them." The source explained that the denier, red in the face, "was really mad" and "tried to intimidate me." Such intimidation tactics were no small matter in a CIA veteran, as the source told me: "These veteran guys know how to physically intimidate you and make you uncomfortable. They won't actually assault you, or hit you. They know better. But they know how to use their body."

Another source who observed this establishmentarian and others told me: "They considered the Reagan people a bunch of right-wing crazies. They would disagree with Casey as much as they could get away with." This source added in a follow-up discussion: "Bill Casey had his hands full, and Bill Clark worked hard to keep Casey's spirits up and his eye on the ball—Ronald Reagan's policies."

Still another source, a veteran of the intelligence community on both the intelligence and defense side, told me in great frustration: "The assassination attempt on John Paul II and the way it was handled by our intelligence brahmans is a very sorry and disturbing tale." This source, who was "heavily involved in chasing down Soviet connections to international terrorism," said that the CIA "fought us every inch of the way." The source added that there were "some good agency people with integrity, but they had to operate below the radar." The "brahmans," as the source called the CIA establishment, took pains "to exculpate the Politburo."

But this source stressed another important point: "The DCI [Bill Casey] was of a different mind."

BILL CASEY'S PURSUIT

Casey was from a different mold, as were many of the people he brought in to the CIA. He understood that the Soviets were capable of practically anything. Soviet acts of evil never surprised him. He also understood the institutional hurdles he faced within the CIA.

Claire Sterling already had earned Casey's respect. In 1981 she had published an important book, *The Terror Network*, in which she argued that the Soviets were actively engaged in international terrorism, usually by proxy forces. The *New York Times Magazine* excerpted the book in a cover story on March 1, 1981, just weeks into the Reagan administration—

and only weeks before the attempted assassinations on Reagan and John Paul II. Sterling's reporting did not astound Casey, or Reagan, or Secretary of State Al Haig, or Haig's deputy at State, Bill Clark, or many other Reagan hard-liners. It did, however, send the establishmentarians spinning into fits of denial.

"Read Claire Sterling's book," Casey scolded the deniers, who were busy crafting formal National Intelligence Estimates that could not conceive any Soviet evil, "and forget this mush." Casey dismissed their thinking as "bullshit." He snapped, "I paid $13.95 for this [Sterling's book] and it told me more than you bastards whom I pay $50,000 a year."[32]

So when Sterling started publishing on the plot to kill the pope, Casey and certain aides took her work seriously, at least enough to check her claims.

One source gave an example of the kind of detail in Sterling's reporting that impressed Casey and compelled him to seek her out: "Claire had in her book that Agca spent twelve or fourteen days—or something like that—in this certain hotel. It was an impressive find. So we asked, 'Well, is this true or not?'" Casey requested an internal check, and the resulting CIA report "trashed [her claims] on the number of days," the source said. The CIA analysts estimated that Sterling was off "by a couple of days" and seized on this minor discrepancy as a basis for dismissing her entire report. "She was off by a couple of days," the source told me. "But so what?" Sterling had the essential point right, that Agca stayed in this particular hotel for about two weeks, which was a "crucial" and "really striking" finding, the source added. "Why in the world would this Turk have been there for twelve days? Why? That was quite a find.... The fact that she [Sterling] was off by a day or two didn't matter. It was laughable that they would dismiss the claim for that reason. They didn't want to hear it."

Sensing that his own agency was unwilling to investigate certain claims about the Soviets, Casey began seeking information wherever he could get it. In fact, unbeknownst to the careerists, he sought out Sterling herself. The two of them met in private in New York. Only Casey, Sterling, and the person who arranged the meeting knew what Casey was doing in New York at that moment.

I have no details of the meeting. Its mere existence is reported here for the first time. Both Casey and Sterling have long since passed away. But Sterling was surely pleased and a little surprised: in *The Time of the Assassins* she had been somewhat critical of Casey, Bill Clark, and President Reagan.[33] The fact that Casey reached out must have shown her that, unlike the establishmentarians, the CIA director was not deluding himself.

The CIA deniers faced a more difficult challenge when Sterling published her book and former CIA official Paul Henze published *The Plot to Kill the Pope*, which reached similar conclusions about Bulgarian complicity.[34] The challenge became even harder when the *New York Times* ran Sterling's long (5,691-word) front-page story on June 10, 1984. Relying extensively on the report by Italian state prosecutor Antonio Albano, which was based on some twenty-five thousand pages of documentation Judge Ilario Martella had gathered, Sterling wrote, "The Bulgarian services contracted with the Turkish terrorists [Mehmet Ali] Agca and Oral Çelik for the organization and execution of the plan." The story strongly suggested a Soviet hand as well, though it provided no direct evidence of a Moscow link.[35]

To read such material in Sterling's book was one thing, but to find it on the front page of the *New York Times* was something else. The careerists at Langley were stunned and irate.

So was the Kremlin. TASS responded to Sterling's article by denouncing Agca as a serial distorter of facts. Actually, TASS resorted to referring to Agca simply as "the criminal." The Italian prosecutor's report, said TASS, "totally disregards the numerous distortions of the facts and controversial statements made by the criminal." How sad it was, said the official Soviet press agency, that "reactionary forces are now feverishly pressing ahead for the opening of a trial of a Bulgarian citizen."[36]

Bill Casey was pressing ahead. People close to the CIA director told me he believed that the Sterling article in the *Times* seemed "pretty accurate." Sterling readily cited her main sources: Italian intelligence. Some of those close to Casey had made inquiries with Italian intelligence and knew she was on to something.

On October 26, 1984, Judge Martella ordered three Bulgarians and three Turks (all alleged Agca accomplices) to stand trial for conspiring to assassinate Pope John Paul II.[37] Martella produced a prodigious 1,243-page report based on those tens of thousands of pages of evidence he had assembled.[38] Foremost among the findings that would have caught Bill Casey's eye was the judge's conclusion that Agca and his accomplices had carried out a crime "conceived" by the Bulgarian secret service. Casey knew what that meant: the Soviet Union was involved or at least had foreknowledge.

BULGARIA'S SOVIET STOOGES

Casey knew how tight Sofia was with Moscow. Bulgaria's dictator, Todor Zhivkov, who just a handful of years earlier had charmed Cardinal Casaroli and Pope Paul VI, had begun his stint as Bulgarian Communist Party chief in 1954. He would remain the longest-serving dictator of any communist nation in the history of the Soviet Bloc, lasting until the communist collapse in 1989. He and his secret service, the ruthless DS, were notorious for complete submission to the USSR.

It was said that Zhivkov had pledged allegiance to Moscow "in life and in death."[39] Neither Zhivkov nor his intelligence officials nor his ministries sought the slightest autonomy from the Kremlin.

KGB general Oleg Kalugin, who rose to chief of foreign counterintelligence, wrote that Bulgaria was "so firmly bound" to the USSR that people in both countries referred to it as "the sixteenth Soviet republic." He said that the Bulgarian Interior Ministry was "little more than a branch of the KGB" and that the USSR's longtime station chief in Sofia, General Ivan Savchenko, "virtually ran" Bulgaria's secret services. "No general in Bulgarian Intelligence or in the Interior Ministry dared do anything of consequence without first picking up the telephone and checking with Savchenko," said Kalugin.[40]

The Bulgarian stooges' desire to please their Moscow masters reached absurd proportions. Kalugin remembered that he was always "treated like a pasha" when he visited Bulgaria, being escorted around in limousines, treated to enormous feasts, and invited on hunts. During one bird shoot with officers from the Interior Ministry, a Bulgarian gamekeeper walked up to Kalugin's hunting party carrying a large sack. He opened the bag and dumped a dozen "barely fledged" pheasants on the ground. The frightened birds scampered a few yards away. "Go ahead, shoot!" the eager-to-please Interior Ministry host said to Kalugin with a proud smile. Kalugin felt embarrassed for his sycophantic hosts and saddened for the helpless young birds. Not wanting to offend his obsequious hosts, Kalugin reluctantly pulled the trigger. "The Bulgarians seemed relieved," said the KGB major general.[41]

Bulgaria's communist toadies were also known for their willingness to carry out the ugliest and bloodiest jobs for Moscow, including kidnappings, terrorism, training of kidnappers, training of terrorists, recruitment of seasoned killers, and, naturally, assassination.

Everyone in the intelligence world knew this. Bill Casey certainly knew it.

And so, when material on Bulgaria began coming to light in the media, Casey and a few trusted advisers started digging, investigating what the CIA's old guard would not. Thus began what one source called "the nastiest fight inside the agency" he had ever seen.

Agency bureaucrats would regularly leak to the *Washington Post* and other media outlets to spread the charge that Casey and his advisers were "politicizing" the intelligence process, looking for a predetermined conclusion based on their biases. Of course, Casey and crew did have biases. Everyone has a bias. The key is not letting the bias interfere with your willingness to investigate fairly.

That was the problem with the establishmentarians: they let their bias—the perception that the Soviets could not and would not do such an unconscionable thing to the leader of the world's largest group of Christians—keep them from investigating thoroughly, and so their biases dictated their "conclusions." One source told me: "They stopped time and again from investigating this stuff because of those perceptions. This happened all the time, across the board, over and over on issues relating to the Soviet Union. Another was the question of whether the Soviets ever supported terrorism.... They were afraid of concluding these things on the Russians. The [establishment] CIA would never give a conservative president like Reagan the ammo he needed [against the Soviet Union]."

In other words, those leveling the charges of a politicized intelligence process were *themselves* politicizing the process.

As for those open to the possibility of a Soviet role, they simply took what they felt was a significant claim with some basis and began looking into it, rather than averting their eyes. As the principal agency in charge of information collection, the CIA had a duty to investigate such claims.

"THE MOST EXPLOSIVE REPORT OF THE TWENTIETH CENTURY"

And so, unbeknownst even to Claire Sterling, Bill Casey authorized a special group within his own circle to look into the shooting of the pope. This was a select investigative group not within the Directorate of Operations (DO) but within the Directorate of Intelligence (DI). The DO, known as the clandestine service, might have seemed a more logical choice, but it generally fought any suspicion of the Soviets. The CIA's deputy director, John McMahon, was an establishmentarian who had run the DO before the Reagan administration came in. So Casey, as he had done in setting up a plan to exploit Soviet economic vulnerabilities,[42] set up a CIA within the CIA, or at least a smaller team within the CIA that he could trust.

Driving the group's research were, in the words of one source, "two young women who were really bright and did great work on [the investigation and subsequent report]. They were fabulous, ran circles around DO. Two women—they did 80 percent of the work. . . . One was probably late twenties, early thirties; the other probably forties."

Only a select few would be permitted to see the resulting report. Why such secrecy? Consider this thought: if the Casey-ordered report had concluded that the Soviets were *not* involved in the attempted assassination—which many in the CIA insisted, and which many in the media and Congress and elsewhere were pushing the administration and the agency to affirm for them—then one can assume that this report would have been released and promoted, to end any suspicions.

When I posed that line of logic to a source who saw the report, he chuckled and said simply, "Well, sure." He also confirmed that the report did come to a conclusive answer on the Soviet role, without telling me whether it was a "yes" or "no."

At that point, I told the source something that he did not know I knew. I had spoken previously to a separate source very close to Bill Casey, who had told me that Casey went to his grave agreeing with Claire Sterling's conclusions. I said this meant that the CIA report Casey commissioned must have affirmed Sterling's conclusion of Soviet involvement.

My source on the report was struck by this, not expecting that I had had that confirmation on Casey. He said simply, "Hmm," with a slight grin and nod that I took as a tacit acknowledgment. He could not and would not say anything else.

So even though my source on the secret CIA investigation would not divulge the report's conclusion, he agreed that a report exonerating the Soviets would not have remained secret, and he was surprised I had independent confirmation that Casey was convinced the Soviets were involved. In other words, I could piece together that Casey reached this conclusion based not only on his reading of Sterling's book, as another source had told me, but also on an actual CIA investigation, which this separate source now told me about.

The second source seemed essentially to agree with this conclusion, but he noted: "The problem is that even if I tell you what it [the report] says, what it concluded, I have no way to prove it—and neither do you—because I don't have the report. But that report exists. If someone can find it, you've got the most explosive report of the twentieth century. Without that report, it would be, 'He said, she said.'"

If someone can find it, you've got the most explosive report of the twentieth century. Here again, logic holds that the report would not be "explosive" if it exonerated the Soviets.

THE CIA WITHIN THE CIA: "THE RUSSIANS DID IT"

Despite years of hunting in archives and probing sources, I have not been able to locate that secret CIA report. But I did interview sources who saw the report or spoke to people who saw the report, and from their accounts I have ascertained that the report concluded that the Soviets, not just the Bulgarians, were behind the attempt to assassinate Pope John Paul II.

Even more intriguing is where the CIA found the smoking gun. According to my information, it was not where everyone was looking. The excavators, including Claire Sterling, were digging around KGB headquarters. Mehmet Ali Agca had fingered the KGB in his July 1983 comments to the press. Even Reagan administration sources I interviewed years later said that their suspicions centered on the KGB.

They were all looking in the wrong place. It was not the KGB that was behind the shooting. It was the GRU—Soviet military intelligence.

That was how and why so many investigators of this crime of the century came up empty. As Casey's two crack female researchers figured out, the GRU carried out the attempted assassination of Pope John Paul II. Moreover, I was told that although it was the GRU, not the KGB, the GRU did it under direct order from KGB chief Yuri Andropov, soon to become the Soviet general secretary. The Soviets involved kept the rest of the KGB out of the loop, reportedly.

In their seminal 1999 work, *The Sword and the Shield*, so named for the symbol of the KGB, Christopher Andrew and Vasili Mitrokhin, the latter the namesake of the revelatory Mitrokhin Archive, reported, "There is no evidence in any of the [KGB] files examined by Mitrokhin that it was involved in the attempt on his [the pope's] life."[43] Mitrokhin would have found nothing in the KGB files because the KGB did not commandeer the operation.

"That's what threw off everyone," one source told me, "because everyone looking into whether the Soviets did it looked at the KGB, and pinged their KGB contacts for information, but found nothing. In fact, the KGB knew nothing because it wasn't involved."

The GRU's hand may help explain why all of this, including the CIA's full report, is still so sensitive to this day: even with all the changes in Russia after the collapse of the Soviet Union, and after all the splits in Moscow intelligence, including within the KGB itself, only the GRU has never changed names or subordination. It remains a rock.[44]

Today, more than thirty years later, that report, located somewhere, remains classified. One source told me, "I've never, ever, in all my years, seen anything as secretive as that document." As a joke, he added, "This was so classified that they nearly shot the secretary who typed it."

Since I began this investigation, other sources—including two excellent ones from former Soviet Bloc countries[45]—have insisted to me that the GRU ordered the hit on Pope John Paul II. I will consider their conclusions, as well as similar ones by the Italian parliament, later in this book.

CASEY BRIEFS REAGAN—AND THE COMPLEX CASE OF ROBERT GATES

One of those who saw the secret CIA report was Ronald Reagan. Bill Casey delivered it to the president in 1985.

I learned that Casey personally briefed the president on the report. Casey sat across from Reagan with the package of political dynamite in his hands and began running through the conclusions. Intensely interested in what he was hearing, ready to leap out of his seat, Reagan finally pointed to the report and said to Casey, "Can I have that?"

This made the CIA director laugh. It was as if the president of the United States was asking, "Do I have the clearance to see that?"

Casey replied, "Of course you can!"

Where might copies of this "eyes only" document be located today? Not many copies of the report were made. Was the copy that Casey shared with Reagan a copy for the president to keep? If so, what did Reagan do with it? Might the copy—or at least some acknowledgment of the copy—be located in the Reagan Library? I have found no such report at the Reagan Library.

And what was the exact date of the report?

In investigating these questions, I found some clues in Robert Gates's 1996 book, *From the Shadows*. In the early 1980s, Gates was one of Casey's top CIA lieutenants, having spent a long career mostly with the agency but also with the NSC. In April 1986 he would replace John

McMahon as deputy director of central intelligence, and in 1991 President George H.W. Bush would name him CIA director. Gates later became secretary of defense under President George W. Bush and continued in the role under President Barack Obama.

Gates was always a moderate, not a Cold War hawk. In his service to Bill Casey in the 1980s, he could be alternately brilliant and maddening. His work on the case of the attempted assassination of Pope John Paul II is a case in point.[46]

I checked *From the Shadows* after my initial conversations with my sources on Casey's investigation. What I found helped clear up certain things but also blurred bigger questions.

In a section titled "The Attempt to Assassinate the Pope," Gates wrote, "We may never know whether the Soviet or Bulgarian intelligence services were involved or at least knew in advance." He recounted the positions of opposing camps on the question. "Those who believe the Soviets were involved," Gates wrote, "make the case that the Pope was, in substantial measure, the primary cause of the Soviets' trouble in Eastern Europe and especially in Poland." The "danger" that the pope posed "to Soviet hegemony, the argument went, would justify such a drastic step as trying to eliminate the Pope."[47]

Gates then covered the contrary view, which, he noted, prevailed within the CIA establishment: "The contrary view, and the dominant one among most experts in CIA in 1981–1982, was that the Soviets saw the Pope as a stabilizing element." Yes, somehow the CIA's best and brightest argued that the Soviets saw John Paul II as a force of stability for them. According to this view, the pope would want to "reduce tensions" for communists in his homeland—despite the fact that Karol Wojtyła had seen communists make victims of so many of his fellow countrymen and clergymen, and that, before and after becoming pope, Wojtyła had spoken out against communism's crimes. This view dominant "among most experts" in the CIA at the time was stunningly naive; it speaks volumes about what Casey and Reagan were up against from the establishmentarians.[48]

After looking at these diametrically opposed arguments, Gates noted that as the Italians began investigating the assassination attempt, "policymakers and members of Congress" repeatedly asked the CIA to determine who had been involved. In 1981 and 1982, Gates acknowledged, the CIA "really didn't know very much... apart from what we were picking up from the Italians." The situation, including charges that the CIA was not looking closely enough, "would dog CIA for years," Gates wrote.[49]

Gates returned to the topic later in his book, under a second subhead, "Terrorism: The Soviets and the Pope." That section is a complicated read. But it clearly confirmed that, as my sources emphasized, the CIA endured much "internal discord" over whether the Soviets could have been involved in the shooting. Some within the agency, Gates said, were reluctant to consider the "seamy" side of Soviet policy and "what the Soviets were up to around the world."[50]

Most important, Gates acknowledged the existence of a CIA report on the assassination attempt. He wrote that, after the clandestine service received new intelligence from a source in Bulgaria "in the winter of 1984–1985," he had personally suggested that the CIA write a "paper" assessing "the possible Soviet role in the attempted assassination." Gates even gave a title and a date for the report: "Agca's Attempt to Kill the Pope: The Case for Soviet Involvement," May 1985. He listed only seven people outside the CIA who read the report: President Reagan, Vice President Bush, Secretary of State George Shultz, Secretary of Defense Caspar Weinberger, Joint Chiefs of Staff Chairman John Vessey, National Security Adviser Robert McFarlane, and Anne Armstrong, the chair of the President's Foreign Intelligence Advisory Board.[51]

The "draft paper," Gates said, "drew together all of the strands suggesting Soviet involvement." He wrote that the report "was a compelling study, though clearly identifying the tenuous nature of our sources, gaps in information, and the circumstantial nature of much of the information."

Gates said that when the study was circulated "more widely" inside the CIA, it "elicited a very negative reaction from some analysts who had not been involved in its preparation." One of the analysts in the "Soviet office," said Gates, wrote a critique of the report, which he fired off to Gates on May 20. Gates made clear that this individual was symptomatic of larger problems in the Soviet office that he did not fully appreciate at the time. The author of the critique, he added, disagreed with Casey on the broader matter of "the Soviet role in terrorism." Gates stated explicitly that Casey from the outset had been "convinced the Soviets were behind the assassination attempt."[52]

Gates concluded:

> The paper on the assassination attempt against the Pope published in May 1985 was CIA's last major analytical assessment of that awful event. We never would get additional information from our sources, even after the collapse of the Soviet Union. As a result, the question of whether the Soviets were involved in or knew about

> the assassination attempt remains unanswered and one of the great remaining secrets of the Cold War.[53]

I discussed Gates's account with my sources, who found it frustrating. One source said that Gates had "managed" the investigation into the shooting that Bill Casey had ordered. "Bob was terrific on the pope thing," said the source. "He did great work on it." Yet this source said that Gates's account in *From the Shadows* was "weak and incomplete." The source continued: "I'm assuming—and it's just an assumption—that when Bob wrote this book he was very careful not to write anything the CIA wouldn't clear for publication. And if he told the entire story, that would have glitched." When the source said "glitched," he meant that the government would not have given clearance to publish the account. Even if a CIA review does not remove certain passages outright, the vetting process can require layers of revisions by editors and bureaucrats that obscure the author's original meaning.

The same source told me: "Look, I know what happened with the pope. So does Bob Gates. He knows, too." But perhaps Gates could not write about what he knew as freely as this source spoke. Indeed, if Gates was describing a report that remained classified, he would have been able to write about it only cautiously, with calculated ambiguity.[54]

SANITIZED DOCUMENTS?

All of this raises a question: is the "paper" that Gates mentioned—the one titled "Agca's Attempt to Kill the Pope: The Case for Soviet Involvement"—the same extremely secret report my sources disclosed?

On one hand, it might make sense that the reports were the same. My sources indicated that Casey tasked Gates to manage the investigation, and Gates wrote that he "suggested" it. Moreover, Gates's time line corresponds with what we would expect from Casey's investigation, especially since Claire Sterling's book and her major *New York Times* story, both published in 1984, apparently spurred the CIA director to dig deeper.

On the other hand, Gates in his book described a document that went to President Reagan and six other high-level administration officials, and that was circulated "more widely" within the CIA. Does that distribution align with a report that one source characterized to me as the most secretive document he had seen in his entire career? Moreover,

Gates described a "paper" that merely "drew together" what the CIA knew about a possible Soviet role in the assassination attempt. According to my sources, the Casey report reached a definitive conclusion and even provided evidence that the GRU, not the KGB, sponsored the shooting.

More information came to light in October 1991, when Bob Gates was nominated to be CIA director. The Senate Intelligence Committee released a sheaf of declassified CIA documents as part of its hearings on Gates's nomination. There was some reporting on these documents at the time. On October 2, 1991, for example, the *New York Times* published excerpts from the documents released. According to that story, "Agca's Attempt to Kill the Pope: The Case for Soviet Involvement" was not among the documents made public—but internal CIA critiques of the report were released.[55]

Five days later, *Times* columnist Anthony Lewis zeroed in on the CIA report about Soviet involvement in the papal assassination attempt. During the Reagan administration, Lewis had been an outspoken critic of Reagan's Soviet policy—he called the Evil Empire speech "primitive"—and a reliable mouthpiece for the Soviets-are-not-a-serious-threat perspective.[56] In this October 7, 1991, column, Lewis quoted a couple of lines from "Agca's Attempt to Kill the Pope: The Case for Soviet Involvement," despite the fact that the Senate had not made the report public. As Lewis put it, the report was "still officially secret." (That "officially" might have suggested that part of the document had been leaked to him.)[57]

Researching the subject nearly twenty years later, I needed to get my hands on what the Senate released during Gates's hearings. After probing many sources and experts, in August 2009 I received a package of documents (thirty-six pages in total) from one of the nation's top Cold War archival authorities. In his cover letter, this source wrote, "Some of these things are not complete copies, but that was what was released."

That incompleteness was immediately evident in the package. What followed was a hodgepodge of documents difficult to reconcile. The first document was an undated, single-page cover letter written by Bob Gates, who signed it as deputy director of intelligence, addressed to "The Vice President." It was a "memorandum," with the subject listed as "Attempted Assassination of Pope John Paul II." The opening line stated, "Attached is CIA's first comprehensive examination of who was behind the attempted assassination of Pope John Paul II in May 1981." It went on to state, "While questions remain—and probably always will, we have worked this problem intensively and now feel able to present our findings with some confidence."

Scribbled on the upper-right portion of the memo was (presumably) an acknowledgment from Vice President Bush to Casey that read: "Bill, read with interest, 2-25-85. Nobody else saw it. Thanks."[58] That date, indicating February 25, 1985, seems too early for the time line Gates laid out in *From the Shadows*. Sure enough, a separate pen (in what appears a later correction of Bush's dating) slightly crossed out the "2" and replaced it with a "4," representing the month of April. Apparently, Vice President Bush had misdated the month.

The *New York Times* in October 1991 reported that "Agca's Attempt to Kill the Pope: The Case for Soviet Involvement" was "not among the documents made public." But the package from my source next included what appeared to be the cover page of that report; the title was the same as Gates had rendered it in *From the Shadows*, except an extra word (or something) was redacted. The date of the report, printed in small size in the bottom right corner, was April 1985.

That cover page was it, however. The very next page in the package showed a letter dated April 23, 1985, from the CIA's Richard Kerr to Bill Casey. Kerr's letter noted the existence of the "paper" and the numbered copies that would be delivered to the president, vice president, secretaries of state and defense, and national security adviser. These would be delivered the next morning, a Wednesday. After that, "seven days later, the remaining fifteen copies for external release will be delivered," Kerr wrote.

There followed in the package three partial pages of what looked like an executive summary of the actual report on Soviet involvement in the papal assassination attempt. The first of the three partial pages contained in the upper right the names Kay Oliver and Mary Desjeans—presumably the two women who wrote the report. Without stating that Moscow ordered the shooting, the summary noted that "the Soviets had a strong incentive to move against the Pope," that "the Soviet attitude toward political assassination is essentially opportunistic, pragmatic, and not constrained by moral considerations," and that "the Soviets have demonstrated a willingness to assassinate political opponents when they judge the circumstances propitious." The authors also noted, however, that the Soviets had "disincentives" to do the job against the pope and that in recent years they had rarely attempted assassinations. Unfortunately, this is the totality of what was released—a mere three pages.

The package also included a twenty-two-page memo dated July 12, 1985. The memo was addressed to the "Deputy Director for Intelligence" (unnamed) from something called the "Papal Task Force," signed by three people, Ross Cowey, John McLaughlin, and Christine Williams. Titled

"Review of DI Production on the Attempted Assassination of Pope John Paul II," the memo—in the Senate package, incomplete and at times redacted—criticized the "Case for Soviet Involvement" report for "some serious shortcomings." But the portions of the review the Senate released avoided divulging the exact conclusions of that earlier report. This memo was very much the standard Washington-bureaucratic-insider document, focusing on how "the DI could have improved its performance on the Papal assassination case."

Finally, the package included a May 20, 1985, "MEMORANDUM FOR THE RECORD," with the subject "Agca's Attempt to Kill the Pope: The Case *Against* Soviet Involvement [emphasis added]." This memo was signed by John G. Hibbits, "Chief, Foreign Activities Branch, Regional Issues Group, Third World Activities Division." Five pages in length and broken down into thirteen points, it was a barbed rebuke of the main report on Soviet involvement.

This May 20 memo is useful in that it suggests that the main report implicated the Soviets. The memo began by stating that the earlier report "sets forth primarily arguments which are intended to lead to a conclusion of Soviet collusion in the assassination attempt." It continued, "Evidence and analysis that contradicts this judgment are relegated to the tail end of the main text and are absent from the Key Judgments and Summary."

The May 20 memo is also useful in revealing the perspective of the CIA establishment. It tried to shoot down the case for Soviet involvement by relying on the sort of ridiculously flawed arguments establishmentarians had long embraced. Amusingly, the memo conceded, "The Soviets probably viewed Pope John Paul II's activities as one of the causal factors for the crisis in Poland in 1980–81." "*Probably*"? The memo's main point was that there was not "conclusive support" of a "Soviet-Bulgarian conspiracy." In point 5 the memo dismissed "the unlikely event that the KGB instructed the DS to kill the Pope." Again, there is the fatal flaw: the intelligence community was looking to the KGB when, in reality, the GRU was the culprit.

A few weeks after receiving and reviewing this package of documents, I shared it with my original source on the CIA report about the Soviets' role in the papal shooting. The source said that this package most definitely did *not* include the blockbuster report he had seen. To the contrary, he said it was "excruciating" to read such agency documents again: "Everything is 'on the one hand, on the other hand,' and it's excruciating.... In reading through all this now, after so many years, I'm once again struck by the realization that the CIA's analysts simply didn't understand the nature of the Soviet threat, or the nature of the Soviet leadership." He did agree that the fact that two women were listed as apparent authors was consistent with his memory, though he could not recall (more than two decades after the incident) whether the names printed there were those of the two women he remembered working on the report. Nonetheless, he said, this was not the document he had seen.

Another possibility suggests itself: during Bob Gates's 1991 confirmation, the CIA could have done a sanitized document dump—that is, it could have released a carefully excerpted and redacted assemblage of inconclusive documents. Such would not be unusual for the intelligence world, where misinformation, distortion, and "black ops" are common. The Soviets, of course, were the masters of disinformation. But the United States played the game as well. I reported in a previous book, *The Crusader*, that the Pentagon in June 1984 appears to have faked a missile-defense test to mislead Moscow into believing that the Strategic Defense Initiative was much farther along than the Soviets feared.[59]

Why would the CIA release misleading documents in 1991? Remember that in the 1980s the agency had faced insistent demands from all corners, right and left, from the *New York Times* to Capitol Hill to the State Department, to look into the shooting of the pope.[60] Facing such demands, the CIA would be under pressure to produce a report of some kind. And yet any report that implicated Moscow would have been the closest thing to a missile fired at the Kremlin from Washington. John Paul II himself feared that, figuring that the Soviets were to blame but keeping mum on the subject because he feared igniting a war. And so, when the CIA concluded that the GRU had ordered Mehmet Ali Agca's shot heard 'round the world, Bill Casey and others perhaps decided—maybe with the blessing of the president (and perhaps also the blessing of the pope, as I will note later)—that the report was too much of a bombshell to release.

Keep in mind, too, what was happening in 1991. Yes, the Berlin Wall had fallen, and in just a couple of months the Soviet Union would officially dissolve. But in late August, hard-line Stalinists had attempted a coup d'état in the Soviet Union. The future of Russia, and thus of U.S.-Russia relations, remained very much in doubt. At such an uncertain time, it would have been an inflammatory action to release an explosive report accusing the Kremlin of attempting to kill the pope. Thus, at the time of Gates's confirmation hearings, perhaps the CIA decided to release a watered-down assemblage of documents that—in the finest Langley bureaucratese—did not call out the Kremlin.

I cannot confirm that this was the strategy. It is strictly my speculation. It might, however, make sense of an otherwise puzzling situation.

MAY 16

Bob Gates's account, for all its confusing elements, provided a useful time line of events. Recall that Gates gave May 1985 as the date of the report "Agca's Attempt to Kill the Pope: The Case for Soviet Involvement." Some of the materials in the confusing package of declassified documents the Senate released in 1991 were dated late April 1985. Gates also gave the date of a CIA analyst's critique of the report: May 20. The 1991 Senate documents likewise show a May 20 memo critiquing a report alleging Soviet involvement in the attempt on the pope's life.

Those dates prompted me to try to pinpoint when, in April or May, Bill Casey briefed President Reagan on the findings about Soviet complicity. As noted, I delved into primary sources from the Reagan Library, filed FOIA requests for White House records, examined my own files, and pursued other leads to try to determine when Casey met with Reagan and the president asked of the report, "Can I have that?"

Again, Reagan's diary entry for May 16, 1985, was a tip-off. The president said that he met privately with Casey that day, but the published entry indicates that the government redacted some of what Reagan wrote. My primary-source research led me to the President's Daily Schedule. According to those official White House records, as well as the published *Reagan Diaries*, the May 16 meeting was the only private session Reagan had with Casey in either April or May.[61] Reagan's formal preschedule for that day listed a meeting between him and Casey at 11 A.M., scheduled to last no more than fifteen minutes. The final schedule for the day, handwritten over the typed preschedule, shows the actual time frame for the meeting as "11:02–11:17."[62]

Given the evidence, and especially the lack of other private Reagan-Casey meetings in April and May 1985, I believe that May 16, 1985, was the day Bill Casey presented to Ronald Reagan the finding that the Soviets had ordered the shooting of Pope John Paul II. No other date in this time period is as likely.[63]

To complete the investigation, I checked the Presidential Phone Logs at the Reagan Library for a record of a phone call from President Reagan to the Vatican during one of those days. If Reagan learned from his CIA director that the Soviets were behind the shooting of the pope, would he have communicated this information to John Paul II himself? After a thorough search, my research assistant and I found no such evidence of a phone call made from the White House in the immediate days after May 16.[64] Of course, Reagan could have telephoned from his personal quarters or communicated the finding to the pontiff via a high-level, trusted liaison—or during a later meeting between the two men.

As for locating the CIA report itself, I came up empty-handed. That blockbuster document is buried somewhere. My sincere hope is that these findings will lead to the release of the full report.

BILL CLARK'S SUSPICIONS

Insights I gained from my discussions with, and research into the papers of, Bill Clark form a coda to the entire question of Soviet complicity in the attempt to assassinate Pope John Paul II.

By the spring of 1985, of course, Clark was no longer national security adviser. (In fact, in February he had concluded his tenure as secretary of the interior and returned to his beloved California.) But like so many other close Reagan advisers, Clark harbored suspicions about Soviet involvement.

The taciturn Clark almost never expressed his thinking publicly, but one sultry day in July 2006, as I examined files in the stuffy tack barn at his ranch in central California, I discovered a rare public statement that suggested how strongly he suspected the Soviets. The item I found was the draft of a speech Secretary Clark gave in Las Vegas on August 18, 1984, to a reunion of fellow veterans of the Army Counter-Intelligence Corps. It was an intimate, fairly small gathering, but a public event nonetheless. Perhaps the lack of press in attendance, along with the sense of camaraderie, prompted Clark to open up.

This was a foreign-policy speech, and a strong one, featuring a number of shots at the USSR: over the downing of KAL 007, the Berlin Wall, the Berlin Blockade, Nicaragua, and more. Page 15 of the speech draft included this typed line: "It wouldn't be at all surprising if a similar [disinformation] campaign was now under way to discredit the Italian investigation into the attempted murder of Pope John Paul II." In fact, just such a campaign was well under way; Clark's hunch was spot-on. The draft also revealed a significant addition that Clark himself penciled in: at the end of the line, he replaced the period with a comma and wrote, "which suggests a Bulgarian and therefore Soviet connection."

This was a bold statement. It may be the only example of a Reagan official publicly discussing the possibility that the Bulgarians and even the Soviets were involved in the pope's shooting. And yet the remark went completely unreported; not even the local newspaper, the *Las Vegas Sun*, mentioned it.[65]

When I asked Clark about the line, he recalled that, because the event was a small one, no one in the administration had preapproved the speech, even though he was a Reagan cabinet member at the time. Had the speech run through the normal White House channels of approval, surely some pragmatist would have insisted that the line be removed.

Even more interesting were the pieces Clark filed away in the same box as that speech. One was a four-page typewritten copy of a story by investigative journalist Michael Ledeen, apparently a draft of a piece that Ledeen published in the December 1982/January 1983 newsletter of the Jewish Institute for National Security Affairs, titled "The Bulgarian Connection."[66] More than twenty years later, Clark told me he had discussed the issue with Ledeen and considered the article "a keeper."

Stapled to the article, as an addendum, was a transcript from the December 11, 1982, edition of the Milan-based *Il Giornale Nuovo*, which did some of the best reporting on this subject. It was an interview with Colonel Stefan Svredlev, former head of the Bulgarian secret services, who three years earlier had defected to West Germany. "I don't doubt the participation of the Bulgarian secret services in the attempt against the Pope," said Svredlev, "but [only] under instructions of the KGB, whose leader at the time, Yuri Andropov, could only have approved the operation at the command of Brezhnev."

Svredlev emphasized a point that Oleg Kalugin and many others have made: that the Bulgarians were "the most servile" Communist Bloc cronies. Bulgarians, he said, strictly "follow the instructions of the KGB, which has its own officers in every sector of Bulgarian espionage, and also Bulgarian agents who clandestinely report to the KGB." During his years in Bulgaria's "services," Svredlev said, the KGB agents on the ground were the "true chiefs," reporting directly to Moscow. Their primary concern was to destroy "internal and external enemies."

John Paul II was a major external enemy. Svredlev said that the Soviets exerted so much control over the Bulgarian secret services that the operation to kill Pope John Paul II could have happened without knowledge of the Bulgarian spy chief or even of Todor Zhivkov himself.

Again, Bill Clark retained all this information well over two decades later, having moved the documents from his White House files to his personal papers on his California ranch. To say that he was suspicious of the Soviets was an understatement.[67]

THE TRIAL

The CIA's May 1985 report came just as the trial of Agca's Bulgarian and Turkish accomplices was starting in Rome. As the case went into the courtroom, the Kremlin went to work issuing furious denials from the pages of *Pravda*, *Izvestia*, and other communist organs.

Moscow elevated one of the accused, Sergei Antonov, to martyr-like status. On May 30, *Pravda* published a statement from the National Committee for the Defense of Antonov—the sudden existence of which *Pravda* had announced to Russians only on May 25. The statement called the trial the latest phase of "the political provocation that reactionary circles in the West have undertaken against people's Bulgaria and other socialist countries." The accusations against Antonov and his countrymen were nothing but Agca's "psychopathic fantasy," the statement continued, and yet the West was using the Turk's "fabrications" to unleash "a vile propaganda campaign against the socialist world." Antonov's Moscow defenders charged that the "imperialist" powers were using the trial "to step up the confrontation between the two social and political systems that exist in today's world and to replace the ideological struggle in the international arena with the actual psychological warfare that imperialism is unleashing as part of its heralded 'crusade' against socialism."[68]

The Soviets wasted no time declaring an "Unjust Trial," the title of an *Izvestia* piece published May 29. The article repeatedly referred to Agca as a "right-wing" "terrorist" and always placed his "charges" and "testimony" in quotation marks.[69]

Of course, if the situation demanded a different slant, the Kremlin was happy to portray Agca in sympathetic terms. A June 20 piece in *Izvestia* condemned the "intensive manipulation" that Agca "had been subjected to in his jail cell," and how "the judges had tried to block his testimony."[70]

On and on the propaganda wheel would turn. When the trial ended almost a year later, the Soviet totalitarian regime, the master of the show trial, would decry it as a giant miscarriage of justice. The court acquitted Antonov and his fellow defendants of conspiring to assassinate the pope, leading *Pravda* to crow, "So the false antisocialist and anti-Bulgarian version has collapsed."[71]

But had it? Once again, the redoubtable Claire Sterling cleared up the confusion. Referring to the acquittal of the Bulgarian and Turkish defendants, Sterling wrote: "Many took this to mean that the jury had found them innocent. It didn't. The verdict was simply 'not guilty for lack for sufficient proof,' known in Italy as the 'formula of doubt.' Evidently, the jury had a lot of doubts." Sterling pointed out that, "in keeping with Italian legal practice," the presiding judges wrote a formal explanation of the jury's decision. The report ran more than 1,200 pages and, in Sterling's words, "cited ample evidence to revive the Bulgarian connection, thought to be dead as a doornail."[72]

In a news story, the *New York Times* similarly reported: "The acquittal for lack of proof is a formula under Italian law implying that evidence exists to support both the guilt and innocence of a defendant and that the court is unable to decide. The verdict is therefore unlikely to end the debate over the case."[73]

Indeed it wouldn't. Despite Moscow's wishful thinking, the case against Bulgaria and the Soviets hadn't "collapsed." As we will see later in this book, new evidence would emerge two decades later to indicate their complicity in the plot to kill the pope.

Part 5

ENDING AN EVIL EMPIRE

30

NOVEMBER 1985–DECEMBER 1987

THE PRESIDENT AND THE "CLOSET CHRISTIAN"

Ronald Reagan and Pope John Paul II were under no illusions about the Soviets. The Soviets' record was clear; the president and the pope had spent decades warning of the dangers international communism posed and the crimes it had committed.

Now Reagan and John Paul II had their eyes on Mikhail Gorbachev. They would maintain a prudent skepticism, but they hoped and prayed that he was indeed a different kind of Soviet leader. They showed their willingness to work with the new general secretary.

Reagan, in particular, was eager to meet with Gorbachev. He had gone his whole first term without sitting down with a Soviet leader, but his goal all along had been to deal directly with his counterpart from the USSR. Reagan believed in personal diplomacy and was confident in his negotiating abilities, having honed his skills during many showdowns with Hollywood executives as head of the Screen Actors Guild. These were points the president's critics missed. Even some conservatives expressed alarm at Reagan's apparent change in attitude toward the Soviet Union after he began meeting with Gorbachev.[1]

And meet he did. Beginning in late 1985, Reagan would sit down with Gorbachev five times in just over three years: in Geneva (November 1985), Reykjavík (October 1986), Washington (December 1987), Moscow (May–June 1988), and New York (December 1988).

These meetings were of enormous significance in creating a path toward the end of the Cold War. This chapter cannot do justice to their many details, dialogues, and doings. I will give closest attention to the surprising spiritual dynamic underpinning the first three summits. At each meeting, religion was among Reagan's top priorities, and not just that of persecuted believers behind the Iron Curtain. Like John Paul II, Reagan began to wonder whether the leader of the atheistic Soviet empire was pro-Christian—and maybe even a closet Christian.

DISCUSSING THE BIBLE—AND ATHEISM—IN GENEVA

Reagan's first summit with Gorbachev, in Geneva, Switzerland, was scheduled for November 19, 1985. This would be the moment the president had pushed for since his first year in office, and especially after surviving John Hinckley's assassination attempt. He saw the chance to sit down and negotiate with the Soviet leader as part of the Divine Plan.

As the summit approached, Reagan prepared himself and his people. He and his speechwriters worked on the draft of an address to the nation that would make the case for the summit. Speaking from the Oval Office on November 14, he would tell the country: "I want to share with you my hopes and tell you why I am going to Geneva. My mission, stated simply, is a mission for peace.... It is to sit down across from Mr. Gorbachev and try to map out, together, a basis for peaceful discourse even though our disagreements on fundamentals will not change."[2] Working on the draft with his speechwriters two days earlier, Reagan decided he wanted God to be part of the speech. He penciled in a personal sentiment: that it was "most important" for everyone to understand, from Washington to Moscow, that "we're all God's children."[3] This meant that the atheist Soviets, too, were God's children, even if they denied it.

Reagan's chief speechwriter, drafter of the Evil Empire address two years earlier, was thinking of God as well. Prior to Geneva, Tony Dolan attempted to give the president two rosaries—one for Reagan and possibly one for Gorbachev—and a memo explaining Fátima. This was only a few months after Reagan's speech in Portugal mentioning Fátima. To Dolan's knowledge, these items never got to the president, even though Dolan was typically able to get things to Reagan. "I was told it was shortstopped," Dolan told me in July 2014, "which was unusual."[4] Of course, as I learned from archival research at the Reagan Library in August 2015, Dolan's memo on Fátima did reach Reagan (as seen in chapter 28).

Dolan and Reagan had a good relationship, including on spiritual matters and Catholic-Protestant differences. Dolan told me of a humorous moment that occurred when he, Reagan, and Ben Elliott were discussing a speech draft that included a biblical quotation. Elliott, one of Reagan's top speechwriters, was a devout evangelical. As Dolan recalls, Elliott and Reagan were gently arguing over the chapter and verse for a passage from Saint Paul. Dolan joked, "Mr. President, I'm sorry I can't help you with this, but, as you know, I'm Catholic." Not missing a beat, Reagan looked at the Bible and deadpanned, "Oh, they don't let you look at this, do they?"[5]

When Reagan got to Geneva, he discovered that Mikhail Gorbachev actually quoted Scripture.

First he noticed that the leader of the Evil Empire invoked God's name, typically in expressions like "only God knows" or "God help us," which seemed to be sincere and not in passing or in vain.[6] In their first plenary meeting at Geneva, Gorbachev said to Reagan: "We have never been at war with each other. Let us pray God that this never happens."[7] The Soviet leader also invoked God during his and Reagan's historic fireside chat at a lakeside cabin.[8]

Gorbachev's invocation of the Bible came during dinner later that evening. Toasting the president and the U.S. delegation, the Soviet leader quoted Ecclesiastes, which interpreter Pavel Palazchenko recorded this way: "For every thing there is a season, and a time for every purpose under the heavens. A time to be born, and a time to die... a time to break down, and a time to build up... a time to throw away the stones, and a time to gather the stones together." Palazchenko wrote of this moment years later, after the Cold War, when he could speak freely. The interpreter noted that when Gorbachev said this, religion was still officially "suspect" in the USSR. But Palazchenko said he was not surprised. "It sounded quite natural and sincere coming from Gorbachev," he wrote.[9] Of course, it was a safe quotation, not theologically loaded, more along the lines of a proverb.

In his reply toast, Reagan acknowledged Gorbachev's quotation and then quoted a passage from Acts 16.[10]

As the Gorbachevs and Reagans sat for dinner together, Gorbachev made an interesting statement that would explain why quoting the Bible came naturally to him. He told Reagan that although his wife, Raisa, was an atheist, his own Christian grandmother had read the Bible to him as a child.[11] "The president was convinced," Press Secretary Larry Speakes later wrote, "the childhood exposure to the Bible had had an influence."[12] Reagan surely found it curious that Gorbachev specified that his wife was an atheist but did not characterize his own belief.

In fact, Reagan informed one of his advisers that just such a thought occurred to him. The president told his cabinet secretary, Alfred Kingon, about a compelling moment with Gorbachev during a formal dinner at Geneva (presumably the same dinner). As Kingon recounted the story, Reagan and Gorbachev sat on opposite sides of the table, with Mrs. Gorbachev sitting with President Reagan and Mrs. Reagan sitting with General Secretary Gorbachev. The table was very wide, and all the food, drinks, flowers, and other decorations made it difficult to carry on conversation across the table. But at one point, said Kingon, Gorbachev got very excited and initiated a cross-table conversation. Specifically, Reagan saw Gorbachev point to his wife, Raisa, and heard him say loudly, "Ask *her*, she's the atheist."[13]

Reagan and Kingon pondered what this meant. Was Gorbachev saying that he was *not* an atheist? Said Kingon: "He [had] professed that he was [an atheist]. But from that moment on, Reagan felt that Gorbachev was a believer." Kingon asked Reagan point blank whether he had pushed Gorbachev on his religious beliefs. "Did you ask him?" Kingon said to the president. "Did you try to find out or probe?" Reagan told Kingon, with regret: "I couldn't. The conditions were never right to do so."

We do know that Gorbachev was not exaggerating about his wife. A Marxist-Leninist atheist to the bone, Mrs. Gorbachev was a scholar of Lenin who admired the Bolshevik godfather's atheism, and she was a proud, open nonbeliever. She even taught a course on atheism at Moscow State University, as the Gorbachevs informed the Reagans in Geneva.[14]

But Ronald Reagan was impressed by what he had learned about Raisa's husband, the Soviet general secretary. He could not get it off his mind after the summit, or for years to come. His close White House aide and friend Michael Deaver never forgot how Reagan called him in for a debriefing upon his return from Geneva. The president's attitude and tone were "festive" and "infectious." Deaver was expecting Reagan to confide some breakthrough in trade or missile negotiations. Instead, he whispered two words to Deaver: "He believes." An incredulous Deaver responded, "Are you saying the general secretary of the Soviet Union believes in God?" Reagan walked his statement back, but only a tiny bit: "I don't know, Mike, but I honestly think he believes in a higher power."[15]

Some observers raised the possibility that the general secretary was preying on Reagan's religious sympathies to benefit the USSR's negotiating position.[16] The skepticism was warranted, given the Soviet leadership's well-earned reputation for dishonesty. Before he became president, Reagan himself had warned that a Soviet leader's false piety could be an effective negotiating ploy with an American president.[17] Reagan was on guard for Soviet tricks. Again, he had been duped by communists in his past. As encouraged as he was by what he heard from Gorbachev, he would not suddenly roll over in negotiations—as he demonstrated by taking a forceful line at Geneva and in subsequent summits.

In any case, evidence has subsequently emerged to show that Gorbachev spoke this way even to hardened Soviet atheists. For instance, Anatoly Chernyaev shared in his published diary an exchange with Gorbachev in 1989 in which the general secretary told him: "One can become a politician. But there has to be a foundation...a vessel. The contents will come with experience, but the vessel comes from God." Gorbachev added: "Take me, for example. Have I changed much since childhood? Not really. In essence I am the same as I always was." He shared this thought with a Kremlin nonbeliever.[18]

After Geneva, President Reagan came to suspect, and privately remarked constantly, that the new Soviet leader might be a "closet Christian."[19] It became almost an obsession in his thinking about Gorbachev. Even if Gorbachev was not a devout Christian, Reagan discerned that the general secretary seemed to retain some basic Christian beliefs and values that he must have acquired from his upbringing.[20]

Nelle Reagan's son must have seen it as part of the DP, helping bring light into the Soviet darkness.

BALANCING PRIORITIES

Eleven months after Geneva, Reagan and Gorbachev met again in Reykjavík, Iceland. At this meeting, Reagan showed that he would continue to take a hard line in negotiations with the Soviet leader. Over the course of two days, the U.S. and Soviet sides came incredibly close to an agreement that would eliminate all nuclear weapons—but Gorbachev kept insisting on restricting the Strategic Defense Initiative (SDI) to the laboratory. Reagan concluded that Gorbachev "had brought me to Iceland" with one purpose: to "kill" SDI. The president recorded in his diary that "the price was high but I wouldn't sell." And "that's how the day ended," he added. They walked away without a deal. Reagan later described it as "one of the longest, most disappointing—and ultimately angriest—days of my presidency."[21]

Despite that frustrating conclusion at Reykjavík, Reagan and his advisers believed that the summit had provided hope. After all, both sides had agreed in principle to abolish nuclear weapons. And so the president recognized the next summit, scheduled for Washington in December 1987, as a grand opportunity.

Reagan would not, however, back off from his calls for religious freedom in the USSR. He raised the issue of religious persecution in the Soviet Union persistently and emphatically, to the point that it annoyed Gorbachev.[22] Reagan was right to needle Gorbachev. Although liberal journalists in the West had rushed to canonize Gorbachev, the fact was that religious persecution continued under his leadership, especially initially. For example, the USSR continued to jail Russian Jews for their faith and would not permit them to emigrate.

On November 30, 1987, just a week before Gorbachev arrived in Washington for the next summit, President Reagan delivered a speech at the Heritage Foundation in which he blasted Moscow for ongoing abuses of basic civil liberties, particularly religion. Reagan's tough language at that moment rattled many in his administration, because Gorbachev was coming to town to finalize the historic Intermediate-Range Nuclear Forces (INF) Treaty. The world badly needed this treaty, which would abolish an entire class of nuclear missiles. And no one wanted strong words from Reagan that might scuttle the agreement. The State Department was especially concerned, as were the ever-worried "pragmatists" in the Reagan White House.

Reagan did not want to jeopardize the treaty either. He badly wanted it, too. He had often spoken of his "dream" to abolish nuclear weapons. But he would not keep silent on these other matters, because he believed that human rights were equally important. Religious freedom was especially important: the soul was eternal; the state was not.

And so, in his November 30 speech, Reagan delivered some remarkable assessments. "Few moves on the part of the Soviet government could do more to convince the world of its sincerity for reform," Reagan began—

the audience was probably expecting words on missiles to follow—"than the legalization of the Ukrainian Catholic Church."

Yes, legalization of the Ukrainian Catholic Church. This was a high priority in Reagan's mind, no less important than the status of the INF Treaty. That was because the Ukrainian Catholic Church had long been one of the staunchest forces of organized opposition to the Kremlin. Whereas other Ukrainian faiths had been compromised by internal forces or by Moscow, the Ukrainian Catholic Church remained under the leadership of the Vatican. It was still harassed, beaten, and damaged, but it remained outside of Soviet control.

Reagan's words that day, which probably meant little to American ears, surely resonated with his friend at the Vatican. John Paul II lamented the mistreatment of Ukrainian Catholics and longed to go to Ukraine himself and try to make a difference.[23]

Reagan continued: "One of the truest measures of *glasnost* will be the degree of religious freedom the Soviet rulers allow their people—freedom of worship for all." Unless and until those reforms were initiated, Gorbachev's *glasnost*—good as it was—was merely "a promise as yet unfulfilled."[24]

Inside the Soviet Union, it was clear that the communist leadership did not embrace freedom of worship. Quite the contrary. A year earlier, in advance of the Reykjavík summit, *Pravda* had published a front-page editorial, "Fostering Committed Atheists." The editorial underscored the "urgent need" to foster those atheists as a vital part of "communist building." *Pravda* noted that "atheist education is an inalienable constituent part" of the "transforming force" of Marxist-Leninist ideology. The editorial commended the Twenty-Seventh Congress of the Communist Party of the Soviet Union (CPSU) for taking the lead in this atheist indoctrination. Gorbachev, of course, was general secretary of the CPSU.

But such work was not enough, *Pravda* said. "Ideological cadres must take care to improve the forms and methods of atheist work," the editorial stated. "What is needed is a clear, systematic approach, a well thought-out program of activity, and close interaction with other spheres of ideological educational work." Specifically, "labor collectives" should embrace every opportunity "to surround their comrade with concern and to prevent him from being drawn into a religious association or sect." *Pravda* invoked the highest authority—Lenin:

> V.I. Lenin repeatedly reminded people that the more scientifically the struggle against religious ideology is waged, the greater is the

> success achieved in it.... An acute need is arising to investigate, for example, the essence and nature, the specific causes, the degree of religiosity in various regions of the USSR, [and] the individual reasons why people turn to religion.... The struggle against religious ideology requires all conscious working people and communists, above all, to be drawn into the ranks of champions of atheist education.[25]

Reagan was right: Moscow's call to engage in the "struggle against religious ideology" did not conform with *glasnost*. And he would keep the pressure on Gorbachev as long as he felt the Soviets were not doing enough to fix the problem.

MAKING HISTORY IN WASHINGTON

The Washington Summit took place December 7–10, 1987. Here, too, Reagan would seize the opportunity to press issues of faith, and to share his faith.

In a White House dinner held in honor of Gorbachev on December 8, Reagan told the general secretary and his delegation, "Man's most fundamental beliefs about the relationship of the citizen to the state and of man to his Creator lie at the core of the competition between our two countries."[26] In his address to the nation before Geneva, Reagan had referred to U.S. and Soviet "disagreements on fundamentals." Now he was making plain to the Soviet leadership what he meant by those fundamental disagreements.

The next evening, Gorbachev hosted a dinner in Reagan's honor at the Soviet embassy in Washington. Both men gave toasts. When it was Reagan's turn, the president raised his glass and, without a hint of reluctance, invoked the Spirit of the season:

> General Secretary Gorbachev, you've declared that in your own country there is a need for greater *glasnost*, or openness, and the world watches expectantly and with great hopes to see this promise fulfilled.... Thomas Jefferson, one of our nation's great founders and philosophers, once said, "The God who gave us life, gave us liberty as well." He meant that we're born to freedom and that the need for liberty is as basic as the need for food. And he, as the great revolutionary he was, also knew that lasting peace would only

> come when individual souls have the freedom they crave. What better time than in this Christmas and Hanukkah season, a season of spirit you recently spoke to, Mr. General Secretary, when you noted the millennium of Christianity in your land and spoke of the hopes of your people for a better life in a world of peace. These are hopes shared by the people of every nation, hopes for an end to war; hopes, especially in this season, for the right to worship to the dictates of the conscience.[27]

Once again, Reagan was putting "the right to worship" alongside the need for abolishing weapons in terms of importance.

Despite the fears of some members of his administration, Reagan's demands for religious freedom in the Soviet Union did not ruin the negotiations on the INF Treaty. Gorbachev came to the conference ready to finalize the missile deal. He told Reagan, "I am convinced it's God's will that we should cooperate." He seems to have been sincere in this comment, as he repeated the phrase in his memoirs, published in 1995.[28]

At the summit, the United States and the USSR made major strides on arms control; nuclear weapons; nuclear testing; chemical weapons; conventional forces; exchanges of citizens, students, and scientists; trade; the environment; atomic energy; space; and more. The highlight came on December 8, with the signing of the INF Treaty. The treaty banned all nuclear weapons with a range of 300–3,400 miles. Each side, the Soviet Union and the United States, had a huge array of these missiles deployed in Europe. Back in the first year of his presidency, on November 18, 1981, Ronald Reagan had publicly proposed a plan for each side to reduce those arsenals to zero—what he called the "zero option."[29] The nuclear-freeze movement and certain liberal bishops had insisted this would never happen. But here at the Washington summit, it happened. Ultimately, the treaty would eliminate nearly 2,700 missiles.[30]

It was the greatest nuclear-arms treaty in history. It was the first and only agreement to abolish an entire class of nuclear weapons. No other treaty had been so comprehensive or done so much to reduce the threat of nuclear war.

Reagan and Gorbachev signed the agreement in the East Room of the White House. The American president said he hoped that this "history-making agreement" would be "not an end in itself but the beginning of a working relationship" that enabled the two sides to tackle other urgent issues. These issues included not just strategic offensive nuclear weapons but also the balance of conventional forces in Europe, the "destructive and tragic regional conflicts that beset so many parts of our globe," and "respect for the human and natural rights God has granted to all men."

The president asked Gorbachev whether he cared to share a few words. The general secretary responded: "I will venture to say that what we are going to do, the signing of the first-ever agreement eliminating nuclear weapons, has a universal significance for mankind, both from the standpoint of world politics and from the standpoint of humanism." Such public affirmation of "humanism" would become common for Gorbachev. He continued: "May December 8, 1987, become a date that will be inscribed in the history books."[31]

It certainly would.

31

DECEMBER 8, 1987

AN IMMACULATE PEACE

Ronald Reagan and Mikhail Gorbachev surely didn't it plan it this way, but the day they signed their historic INF Treaty—December 8, 1987—happened to be the Feast Day of the Immaculate Conception of the Blessed Virgin Mary.

In the Roman Catholic Church, every December 8 officially honors the Immaculate Conception of the Virgin Mary. The term *Immaculate Conception* refers to God's preserving Mary from the taint of original sin from conception, to prepare a full-of-grace vessel for a pure God to enter the world. (Many erroneously believe that the term relates to the birth of Jesus.) December 8 is a special day for the Church—a holy day of obligation, in which all practicing Catholics worldwide are asked to attend Mass and receive the sacrament of Holy Communion. It also happens to be the *patronal* feast day of a handful of countries—among them, Portugal and the United States.

Reagan and Gorbachev probably did not notice the connection to that special day of veneration of the Blessed Mother, but one who no doubt noticed was Pope John Paul II. This pope had, of course, consecrated his life and papacy to Mary, and just a few years earlier, not long before Gorbachev came to power, he had consecrated Russia to the Blessed Mother. More than that, at the start of the year he had proclaimed 1987 a "Marian Year," to begin on June 7, 1987, running between the solemnities of Pentecost and the Assumption of Mary in 1988.[1]

This was only the second Marian Year in all of Roman Catholic Church history; Pope Pius XII had proclaimed the first in 1954, on the centenary of the dogma of the Immaculate Conception. When Pope John Paul II made the announcement in his homily on New Year's Day 1987, it came as a complete surprise.[2] Now, as 1987 neared its end, signs of peace were emerging. Could Russia's coming "errors" and "persecutions," which Our Lady of Fátima had reportedly warned about seventy years earlier, be coming to an end?

MESSAGE FROM MEDJUGORJE

There were more Marian elements in this particular year of peace.

Most intriguing, America's Protestant president, who by this point clearly knew about Fátima, took an interest in another set of reported Marian apparitions: those in Medjugorje, in central Yugoslavia.

The Virgin Mary allegedly had appeared consistently in Medjugorje in the months and years since the first reported apparition, on June 24, 1981. Though the Catholic Church had not approved the apparitions, thousands if not millions of enraptured visitors had flocked to the communist village. Among them were not only priests of John Paul II's Church but also some people who worked for President Ronald Reagan. That is how, in 1987, Medjugorje drew the attention of Reagan himself.

The first reported appearance of Mary at Medjugorje came just a month after the shooting of John Paul II and just three months after the shooting of Reagan. It shortly followed Reagan's encounters with Cardinal Cooke, Mother Teresa, and others who affirmed what he had been sensing—that God had spared his life for a special purpose. John Paul II felt the same. Both men would share their mutual conviction that they had been spared for a higher purpose of reversing communism's errors and bringing peace.

Revisiting that context is helpful here, given that a message of peace and higher purpose was precisely what the lady in communist Yugoslavia was reportedly bringing. The six young people who reported witnessing the Virgin Mary said that peace, *world peace*, was her most consistent and important message. The visionaries quoted her saying: "Please pray to Jesus. I am His mother and I intercede for you with Him. But all prayer goes to Jesus. I will help. I will pray."[3]

As early as the fourth day of the reported sightings, the (mostly) teens had provoked a growing sensation that alarmed authorities.[4] Like the Fátima children, these devout youngsters were hauled to the police station and interrogated. They were examined by doctors and psychiatrists and priests alike. The medical professionals insisted they were medically and mentally fine. The communist authorities summoned a Franciscan priest, Father Jozo Zovko, pastor of Saint James Church in Medjugorje, and ordered him to stop the gatherings along the hillside.[5]

Father Jozo was initially skeptical of the children's claims. Eventually, however, he became convinced of the legitimacy of their reports. He became their foremost advocate. He protected them in his church, where they would convene and where the visits from the lady were said to continue. As he did, the communists did what came naturally to them: they persecuted him. On August 18, 1981, Father Jozo was consigned to eighteen months of hard labor, imprisoned for refusing to close the church and halt what he and others believed was a blessed miracle. The communists also smashed up the church, broke and scattered religious articles, and generally ransacked the parish.[6]

That first year at Medjugorje was a difficult one, but by the mid-1980s, things had eased up. Father Jozo was released from prison, and the alleged visitations had become a regular part of daily life. The communist authorities also seemed to cool, almost certainly because the influx of tourists brought infusions of currency that the communist state desperately needed. Even Communist Party members set up stands to sell religious artifacts that they otherwise would have destroyed.[7]

Then, in 1986, a commission led by Bishop Pavao Žanić, who oversaw the Medjugorje diocese, concluded its investigation into the reported apparitions. Bishop Žanić had doubted the appearances from the beginning and had reportedly denounced the sightings as "the greatest scam in the history of the Church." Some observers contended that he stacked the commission with members prejudiced against the apparitions.[8] Once Žanić's commission completed its investigation, the bishop traveled to Rome to present the findings. Here, accounts differ, but he reportedly met with the prefect for the Congregation of the Doctrine of the Faith, Cardinal Joseph Ratzinger—the future Pope Benedict XVI. According to some, Ratzinger expressed strong disappointment with Žanić and his methods. Not long thereafter, the Vatican dissolved Žanić's commission and initiated a separate investigation.[9] Though Medjugorje sources are notoriously sloppy, this account has credibility. In fact, once Ratzinger became pope, he ordered the creation of a special commission to investigate the Medjugorje apparitions.

The next year—the Marian Year of 1987—Ronald Reagan learned about this magical lady in Marshal Tito's former stomping grounds from two people with whom he worked closely. One was chief speechwriter Tony Dolan; the other was Ambassador Alfred Kingon. Ultimately, through Kingon, the visionaries themselves had a line of formal communication to Reagan.

AMBASSADOR

Born in Brooklyn in May 1931, Alfred Kingon had been a successful businessman, investor, and editor before joining the Reagan administration in 1982. He would fill several posts in the administration. In January 1985, Kingon was appointed deputy assistant to the president and cabinet secretary, a powerful position for which he was granted greater authority over more areas than his predecessor, owing to his close relationship with Reagan. In January 1987, the start of this significant year of peace and faith, Reagan appointed Kingon to be (as quoted in the official appointment announcement) "Representative of the United States of America to the European Communities," with the "rank and status of Ambassador Extraordinary and Plenipotentiary." The position is better known today as ambassador to the European Union (a group that did not yet formally exist).

Kingon was not Catholic, and to this day he has no formal religious affiliation, but he had long harbored what he characterized as a "profound interest in Marian apparitions." "I'm not a Catholic, but I deeply, deeply believe in God," he said in 1992. "I deeply believe in the Christ. And I deeply believe the apparitions in Medjugorje are real and important."[10]

Kingon and his wife, Jackie, first learned of Marian apparitions in the 1960s from friends who told them of certain appearances in Europe. Kingon visited apparition sites in Beauraing, Belgium; Garabandal, Spain; and even Zeitoun, Egypt. So when, in 1987, President Reagan posted him for assignment in Brussels and Kingon heard of apparitions in Medjugorje, the ambassador headed for Yugoslavia with Jackie.

In a 1992 talk at Notre Dame, during one of the university's annual conferences on Medjugorje, Kingon laid out his Medjugorje experiences. He put everything on the record to clarify exactly what happened during his 1987 visit, and what followed thereafter, because tidbits about a possible Reagan interest in Medjugorje had taken on a life of their own and led to lots of hyperbole and misreporting.[11] In 2014 I interviewed Kingon to confirm his account and learned additional details.[12]

As Kingon related in 1992, his connection to President Reagan and Medjugorje came through a Reagan speechwriter. "One of the speechwriters for Ronald Reagan knew about Medjugorje, found out that I knew about it," recalled Kingon. "He was a deep and devoted Catholic; he *is* a deep and devoted Catholic. And he told us if we ever wanted to go to call him. So when we got to Brussels, we did call him."

Kingon did not publicly name this speechwriter, but it was Tony Dolan. I confirmed that fact by e-mailing Dolan in July 2014, after watching video of Kingon's speech, a link to which I sent to Dolan. Dolan told me that he had traveled to Medjugorje in the fall of 1986. He did not go there on Reagan administration business; his trip was personal and spiritual, a pilgrimage in which he sought intercession for a very sick person who was close to him.[13]

Dolan never discussed Medjugorje with Reagan, but he did discuss it with Al Kingon, who began making arrangements to travel there. On his third day in Medjugorje, Kingon met one of the visionaries, Marija (also spelled and pronounced "Maria") Pavlovic, who was talking to a group of American tourists through Kathleen Parisod, a young American woman who lived with her and served as translator. Kingon was convinced that Pavlovic was genuine: "In her elegant simplicity, and her beautiful spiritual answers to the pilgrims, the way she lived, the way she carried herself, the way she talked, the way she prayed, it was very moving and convincing to us. After she finished with the tourists, we went into the house, Jackie and I, Kathleen, Marija... and we began talking. Then an interesting thing happened."

Father Svetozar Kraljevic, a leading Franciscan priest who served in Medjugorje, walked in and joined the conversation. He was particularly interested in U.S.-Soviet disarmament, the paramount issue on the table between Reagan and Gorbachev. As the conversation deepened, Pavlovic asked the Kingons to stay for lunch. Then, about three-quarters of the way through lunch, Pavlovic excused herself. She returned with a letter (which Parisod had helped her compose) and asked Kingon, "Can you give this to President Reagan?"

Kingon went back to Brussels. On November 13 he sent President Reagan a package that included Pavlovic's letter and an explanatory letter of his own, which ran about four pages.

Of course, this was an extraordinarily busy time for Ronald Reagan. His historic summit with the Soviet general secretary in Washington was less than a month away. His usual overwhelming pile of briefing papers was even more overwhelming. It took all his efforts to keep up with his reading. Nonetheless, Reagan did not ignore this Medjugorje message. It piqued his curiosity. On December 6, the day before the Washington summit, Kingon received a call from the White House. He was told that President Reagan had read the package and was "very, very moved" by the letter. More than that, Reagan wanted Kingon to provide him with the addresses of Marija Pavlovic and Kathleen Parisod so that he could write to them directly.[14]

Kingon told me that he later spoke to Reagan about the letter in the Oval Office, one-on-one. Reagan again said he had been "very moved" by the correspondence.[15] Since well before entering the White House, Reagan had spoken of his belief that the world needed a spiritual revival,[16] and the alleged miraculous appearances of the Virgin Mary in communist Europe was producing precisely that.

Remarkably, the message of Medjugorje had reached the most powerful political leader on the planet, who received it wholeheartedly. Ronald Reagan now knew about Mary and Medjugorje. He was briefed firsthand via a missive from one of the visionaries.

"YOUR PRESIDENT, HE CALL ME"

Several Medjugorje sources have reported that President Reagan even tried to call Marija Pavlovic but couldn't get through. "That's not accurate," Kingon said. "I was the one who was trying to call [Pavlovic] and couldn't get through the Yugoslavian phone system, it being what it is. And I did [get through]. What I tried to convey to them [Pavlovic and friends] was that the president would get in touch with them directly, knowing he was going to mail letters back, not on the telephone."

Journalist Wayne Weible, author of several popular books on Medjugorje, offers a slightly different account. Weible arrived in the village for one of his many pilgrimages in December 1987.[17] Weible, who also was not Catholic,[18] wrote that, while he stayed in Pavlovic's home, Pavlovic excitedly told him, "Your president, he call me—here at my house!"

Weible asked, "You mean—President Reagan of the United States?"

Pavlovic replied: "Yes! He call but—he cannot talk. I talk to his office, his secretary."

Taken aback, Weible asked why Ronald Reagan would call her. "I sent him a letter about Medjugorje," Pavlovic explained, "about Our Lady's coming and asking for peace. He is meeting with Gorbachev for treaty, and I wanted him to know about Our Lady."[19]

The next morning, Weible checked the details with Kathleen Parisod. Parisod informed Weible of the Kingon lunch and the letter exchanges. She said that President Reagan had been "deeply touched" by the letter and had "tried to reach Marija by telephone" but "was cut off twice," owing to the poor Yugoslavian phone system. Parisod continued, "Then, on December 8, his secretary called Marija and told her how much he had appreciated her letter."

I checked the White House phone logs at the Reagan Library for records of any telephone call from President Reagan or his personal secretary to Marija Pavlovic or anyone else in Medjugorje from mid-November through mid-December 1987. I saw nothing in the records. I also reviewed Reagan's schedule for December 8, 1987, which gave no indication of any Reagan phone call to anyone on that impossibly busy day.[20]

Weible's account goes further. With Pavlovic sitting next to her confirming the details, Parisod told Weible, "The best part is that as the president was entering the room to sign the treaty—which just happened to be December 8, the Feast of the Immaculate Conception—he turned to the ambassador and told him that he had been deeply affected by the message of Medjugorje and wanted 'Those two girls to know it.'"[21]

"The ambassador" that Weible presented here seems to be Ambassador Al Kingon. The identity is not absolutely clear, but Kingon is the only ambassador mentioned in the chapter, if not the entire Weible book. But Kingon was not present for the signing of the INF Treaty. When I asked Kingon about this report, he said, "That makes no sense whatsoever."[22] It is a charming story that sounds Reaganesque, but I cannot confirm it.

In general, however, Kingon and Weible offer similar accounts with similar timetables.

Reaching Out to Gorbachev

Kingon related another element of the story, also occurring on December 8. That day, he said, "I called Marija and conversed with Kathleen and she said that she and Marija were saying, 'Too bad we didn't know Russian because we could have sent a message to Gorbachev.'" Kingon said he "didn't think very much of it." But after he hung up the phone, he was inspired to spend the evening in prayer, and then, he later remembered, something "hit me with a tremendous force, and I wrote her a letter on December 9 saying, 'Don't worry about that, I can get it translated into Russian.'"

It struck Ambassador Kingon that he could perhaps get the Medjugorje message translated and into the hands of Mikhail Gorbachev via the U.S. ambassador to the Soviet Union, his friend Jack Matlock.

On December 11, President Reagan's secretary of state, George Shultz, called all American ambassadors to Oslo, Norway, for a two-day meeting to discuss the Washington summit. This was Kingon's chance to ask Matlock in person. Before the meeting, Kingon pulled his friend into a side room for a private talk. He wasn't sure how to broach the subject: he had no knowledge of Matlock's religious beliefs or those of his wife, Rebecca. He asked Matlock whether he was Catholic. Matlock replied, "No, I'm a Lutheran."

Kingon asked, "Jack, did you ever hear of Fátima?"

Matlock said, "Yes, it's a city in Portugal."

This suggested to Kingon that Matlock knew nothing about Fátima's renowned Lady. "I was in trouble," recalled Kingon.

He then asked, "Look, what do you know about Marian apparitions?"

Matlock responded, "Marian what?"

Kingon then gave a quick synopsis of Marian apparitions, starting with Fátima, and then said that "there was one taking place in Yugoslavia" and that one of the visionaries had given him a letter for President Reagan. The visionary was now hoping to send the message to Gorbachev. Could Matlock help?

According to Kingon, Matlock "hesitated for all of about two seconds and said, 'Yes.'"

He asked Matlock how they could get the message translated to Russian, and Matlock replied, "Don't worry about that, I'll have my staff translate it into Russian."

As soon as Kingon returned to Brussels, he wrote to Marija Pavlovic and Kathleen Parisod: "Let it [the message] come, don't worry about the translation. I'll take care of it and get it into the Kremlin."

Kingon did not hear anything for weeks. Then, in February 1988, not long before he and his wife were scheduled to visit Leningrad and Moscow, the Austrian ambassador to the European community, Wolfgang Wolte, requested a private meeting. The two ambassadors engaged in "pleasant chitchat" before Wolte got to his point. Kingon recalled:

> [Wolte] says, "Ambassador, I know you've been traveling around Europe." I said, "You know I have, Wolfgang. I've gone to the EFTA [European Free Trade Association] countries." That's the six countries that are surrounding... the [European] Community countries. He says, "I hear you've gone to Yugoslavia." And then I knew. And I said, "Yes." He said, "Did you visit a town called Medjugorje?" And I said, "Yes." Well, he then takes [out] this large envelope.

Wolte handed Kingon a package from one of his deputies in the Austrian foreign ministry. This deputy, said Kingon, "had gotten to know Marija, taken Marija's message, translated it into Russian, [and] wrote a five-page summary in Russian." Wolte then handed Kingon "thirty-nine pages of the Lady's messages translated into Russian."

Kingon was thrilled, but he also knew that he could not give a head of state thirty-nine pages of material. He exercised some editorial discretion. He took "Marija's message" (presumably the five-page summary) and "left the rest of it behind." When he traveled to the Soviet Union later that month, he gave Marija Pavlovic's letter to Jack Matlock. It was destined for the hands of Mikhail Gorbachev.

As Kingon recounted these details at Notre Dame in 1992, he did not divulge the name of the Soviet official to whom Ambassador Matlock handed the message. "I know that man swore he would give it to President Gorbachev," said Kingon. "Given the state of affairs in the Soviet Union then and now, I'm a little reluctant to tell you who it was. But he was a very, very prominent person in the Soviet hierarchy.... We are convinced that Gorbachev got the message."

When I talked to Kingon in 2014, I told him that I suspected the "very prominent" Soviet official was Ambassador Anatoly Dobrynin. Kingon confirmed that it was Dobrynin. By then, Dobrynin had passed away, and Kingon felt it was safe to share his name publicly.

Recall that when Pope John Paul II visited America in 1979, he had blessed Ambassador Dobrynin to wish the Soviet Union "success in striving for world peace."

In our interview, Kingon said: "Jack Matlock told me that Dobrynin got it [the letter] to Gorbachev. But Dobrynin didn't want us to talk about it." Kingon was warned not to expect a response from Gorbachev. And to Kingon's knowledge, no response ever came. Likewise, I have been unable to find any evidence of Gorbachev's reaction. Did Gorbachev read the message closely? Was he, like Reagan, "very moved"? Might it have touched him enough to become an item of discussion when he met with Pope John Paul II? Gorbachev has not been forthcoming, and Vatican records on John Paul II's discussions with Gorbachev remain sealed.

Kingon adds useful perspective on these events. "Through the grace of God, I was able to get messages to two presidents in a bad time," he said at Notre Dame. "The truth is remarkable enough. It doesn't need embellishment. It doesn't need stories of what the president or general secretary supposedly did. A lot of stuff has been added on that isn't so. There are no accidents in the universe. What happened was extraordinary enough."

Kingon—a non-Catholic—tried to make sense of these events and whether they were connected to the historic changes that soon followed:

> The Cold War ended. Communism began to manifest its inevitable decline. The Berlin Wall came down. What role did all of this play? Is it true that Mary defeated communism?... If I've learned anything in life, I've learned this: the only will of God is love; all the rest are the choices of men.... Our job is to surrender to God. And I think that's what happened. All of us who pray. All who prayed responding to Mary's call, and all who prayed in general allowed the inner calls, and the conditions changed, and men responded to the changed conditions.

That was precisely the Marian message of Medjugorje.

JOHN PAUL II AND MEDJUGORJE

What was John Paul II's take on the Marian message of Medjugorje? Pinning down his views has never been easy. Despite his Marian enthusiasm, the Holy Father, like the rest of the institutional Catholic Church, treated claims of apparitions with great care and vigilance. Whereas the miracle at Fátima had seventy thousand witnesses to attest to the supernatural experiences of the three children, no single gathering of witnesses has been able to corroborate the Medjugorje phenomenon, even as many have felt something quite special and had their lives changed there since 1981.

John Paul II never made any official statements on Medjugorje. Many comments about Medjugorje have been attributed to him, some apocryphal. His leading biographer, George Weigel, has shied away from the topic, never writing about it in his books or many articles on the late Holy Father.[23]

Overall, the statements that do exist portray John Paul II as sympathetic to Medjugorje. An article in *Inside the Vatican* says that the Holy Father "reportedly" told a bishop, "If I were not the Pope, I would probably have visited Medjugorje by now." (A visit by the head of the Roman Catholic Church might suggest the Church's approval of the reported apparitions.) The same article quotes him in another context, during the Balkans War in the mid-1990s: "All around Medjugorje bombs have been falling, and yet Medjugorje itself was never damaged. Is this not perhaps a miracle of God?"[24] Another alleged quotation from John Paul II on the subject is this: "If they are converting, praying, fasting, going to confession and doing penance, let them go to Medjugorje."[25] (For the record, similar statements are attributed to Mother Teresa, who some claim had positive feelings on Medjugorje.)[26]

Whatever his personal views, John Paul II was wary of publicly indicating his approval of a phenomenon that the Church continued to investigate (and still has not certified as a miracle).

But one thing the pope had no doubt about was the Immaculate Conception of the Blessed Mother, a miracle that his Church many years earlier had officially affirmed. On December 8, 1987, the Feast Day of the Immaculate Conception, John Paul II visited Rome's Piazza di Spagna (home of the famous Spanish Steps) and placed roses at the feet of the Column of the Immaculate Conception, a magnificent bronze statue of the Virgin Mary that sits atop a twelve-meter-high marble column. Popes visit the site every December 8. On this day in 1987, John Paul II issued a brief statement, released only in Italian. The Holy Father said that Mary was "redeemed by the sublime view of the merits of her Son" and was "of sublime grace." He declared that everyone from every city and every country who passed that column was on his or her own "pilgrimage of faith" with the Immaculate Virgin. "Are we not on a journey together with her?" he said. "This is the question that the Church makes for us all in this Marian Year."

On this day dedicated to Mary, in the year Pope John Paul II had dedicated to Mary, remarkable changes were occurring. The Church had long ago made December 8 a day of peace. Now, on December 8, 1987, the leaders of the world's two superpowers had likewise made it a day of peace.

32

JUNE–DECEMBER 1987

REAGAN'S FÁTIMA BRIEFING

Amid his unprecedented summits with Mikhail Gorbachev, President Reagan maintained his close connection with Pope John Paul II. The pope even influenced an important Reagan administration policy decision regarding John Paul II's native land.

On February 19, 1987, two months after returning from the Reykjavík summit, Reagan decided to lift the sanctions on Poland that his administration had put in place after the Polish communist regime declared martial law in December 1981. Reagan wrote in his diary: "I signed a measure lifting Polish sanctions in answer to pleas by Pope & Lech Wałęsa. They were beginning to hurt the Polish people & that was never our intention." Present for the signing were the former Polish ambassador Romuald Spasowski and his wife, Wanda, who had met with Reagan soon after defecting to the United States in December 1981.[1]

No doubt, the Polish pontiff was pleased by this move. It is true that John Paul II, in a letter that Archbishop Achille Silvestrini relayed to the president in January 1982, had taken pains to dispute reports "suggesting that the Holy See disapproved of the U.S. actions imposing sanctions against the Soviet Union and Poland." (This was the same letter in which the Vatican said that the Holy See and the United States operated on "complementary" planes—the former on the "moral plane" and the latter on the "political plane.") But by early 1987, the situation was changing. There was a new man in Moscow. Just as important, the situation on the ground in Poland had changed, as Reagan acknowledged in announcing the decision. "In 1983 martial law was lifted," he wrote in the official statement, "and thousands of political prisoners have been freed in a series of amnesties. Since the final amnesty last September, no one has been arrested on political charges in Poland."[2] And two prominent Poles, the pope and the Solidarity leader, had persuaded the president that sanctions had begun to "hurt the Polish people."

In the summer of 1987, Reagan and John Paul II would meet not once but twice—in Vatican City in June, and in Miami in September. These meetings came in between the Reagan-Gorbachev summits in Reykjavík and in Washington, giving the president and pope ample opportunity to discuss what was happening between the two superpowers.

Overshadowed by the U.S.-Soviet summits, the Reagan–John Paul II meetings in 1987 received scant attention at the time and have gone largely unacknowledged by history. For example, the Reagan Library has nothing on the June 6 meeting in Vatican City.[3] (The Vatican archives surely contain some notes on the meeting, but they will not be available for viewing until 2062.)

It is shocking how little documentation there is on these meetings. That has been history's loss.

REAGAN'S "AMBASSADOR TO FÁTIMA"

A presidential trip to Europe provided the occasion for Reagan and John Paul II's first meeting since Alaska in May 1984. On June 3, 1987, the president and first lady left Washington for an economic summit in Venice with the Group of Seven (G7) countries and their heads of state. The summit would not formally start for several days; it would convene mainly June 8–10. Reagan's only formal presummit activity was his meeting with the pope.

Hours before Reagan's meeting with Pope John Paul II, the president received an intriguing briefing that has never before been reported.

The person who briefed Reagan was Frank Shakespeare, whom the president had named U.S. ambassador to the Vatican several months earlier, replacing his friend Bill Wilson. Shakespeare had served as U.S. ambassador to Portugal from 1985 to 1986.

Born in New York City on April 9, 1925, Shakespeare had been a successful CBS TV executive, serving as president of the network from 1950 through 1969. In 1969, President Nixon tapped him to head the U.S. Information Agency. He returned to the private sector in 1973, becoming an executive vice president at Westinghouse and later president of RKO General. In 1981, Reagan brought him in as chairman of the Board for International Broadcasting, where he oversaw operations for Radio Free Europe. Reagan nominated Shakespeare to be ambassador to Portugal on July 24, 1985.

It was his work at both the Portugal post and the Vatican that compelled me to call Frank Shakespeare. I spoke to him for an hour on February 21, 2013, and had a follow-up conversation on March 5 of that year. Soon to turn eighty-eight years old, he was healthy and sharp as a tack, providing answers in his New York no-nonsense way—street-smart, tough, and sometimes a touch abrasive.

I began our first interview by noting Reagan's Catholic sympathies and "sensibilities," his relationship with the pope and so many Catholics on his staff and in his immediate family, and even his largely unknown appreciation for the Blessed Mother. Then I asked Shakespeare a question he had probably never heard from a historian: did Ronald Reagan ever express interest in or ask about Our Lady of Fátima, including in discussions with John Paul II?

Shakespeare paused. He seemed almost taken aback by the question. Then he began a lengthy response; he immediately focused on what Reagan would have discussed with the pope:

> Here's how it [Fátima] would have come up and did come up: First off, they [Reagan and John Paul II] felt the need to counsel each other very frequently. As the head of the world's leading spiritual power, and the head of the world's leading temporal power, both of them fairly new to the job, and with John Paul II being the first non-Italian pope in over four hundred years, they felt a need for one another's counsel.
>
> Now, at some point, the pope would have said to Reagan: "For anyone to talk to me in depth about foreign policy, about Russia, about the Cold War, they will need to understand my thinking and

relationship to Mary and also Mary's appearance at Fátima and the whole relationship between Mary and Russia and the Cold War." In turn, Ronald Reagan most certainly would have then said, "Well, what do you mean by Mary and Fátima?" And the pope would have said, "Well, over sixty years ago, Mary appeared to three small children in the village of Fátima, in Portugal...." He would have explained. Then he would have said: "So, if someone is going to talk to me about foreign policy, Mr. President, you will need to understand that. You will need to understand this and how it relates to my foreign policy."

Reagan surely would have said, "Okay, explain Fátima to me...."

Shakespeare's prefatory comments were similar to how I began this book: anyone who wants to understand John Paul II and this unique story of the twentieth century needs first to understand how Mary and Fátima relate to the picture, regardless of whether he or she is a believer. Reagan himself, Shakespeare noted, would have needed that understanding.

I said to Shakespeare: "Now, you can't say for sure where and when and whether they [Reagan and John Paul II] had that conversation, but you believe it would had to have happened at some point? That's what you're saying?"

Shakespeare answered, "Yes, that's exactly right." He added, "Very clearly, the pope would have said to Reagan that there can't be someone between us who can speak to us on Russia and foreign policy without understanding Mary and Fátima."

I asked Shakespeare, "And that someone between them turned out to be you?"

He answered, "Yes, it was me."

It was rather surprising that Shakespeare was in this position to begin with. He shared with me the story of how he had been picked as ambassador to Portugal. He had been walking along a street in Washington one afternoon when he bumped into President Reagan's deputy secretary of state, "who I didn't know at all," Shakespeare recalled.[4] He continued:

> And out of the blue, he asked me if I'd consider being ambassador to Portugal. It was an amazing thought, totally out of the blue. Given all I had done before, in industry and elsewhere, it would have been considered a step down. If I had been offered [the post of] ambassador to France, I would have shrugged and said, "Eh, I'll think about it."

> I must have stunned him because I said on the spot, "I would accept it immediately." And the reason was Fátima, which fascinated me from my childhood. I wasn't going to be ambassador to Portugal, in my mind; I was going to be ambassador to Fátima. I didn't tell him that, of course, but that was my thinking.

Shakespeare revealed that he had told Reagan all about Fátima during the June 1987 trip to Italy. As we have seen, Reagan already knew about Fátima by then; he had mentioned it in his May 1985 speech to Portugal's parliament, discussed it with Bill Clark, and perhaps even discussed it with the pope, who reportedly sent the president a book on Fátima. But Shakespeare, with his detailed knowledge of Fátima, provided a new depth of perspective.

Shakespeare recalled the context for his Fátima conversation with the president. He noted that he had not been ambassador to the Vatican for long when Reagan's office called him and said, "The president wants to meet with you at the G7 in northern Italy." The president would arrive in Venice on June 3 and wanted to meet with Shakespeare there. Then, on June 6, Reagan would fly down to Rome to meet with the pope. The White House told Shakespeare: "He wants you to fly with him from northern Italy to Rome. You'll be with him the whole time, in his private room on the plane and in the car."

Shakespeare recognized immediately that this meant a good deal of one-on-one time with the leader of the free world.

Sure enough, when the trip came along, the ambassador was afforded rare access to the president. Shakespeare recalled: "It was about an hour-and-a-half flight [from Venice to Rome], and then we drove for a while in the car.... I talked to Reagan about Fátima on this trip, in the plane and the car." He had Reagan's complete attention. Shakespeare could not recall, twenty-six years later, Reagan's exact words in response to his briefing on Fátima. But he remembered the Protestant president's being locked in, highly attentive and engaged: "He listened very, very carefully—very intently. He was *very* interested."

Reagan no doubt would have listened intently. This son of a Catholic father, who surrounded himself with Catholic aides, respected those who venerated the Virgin Mary. Remember, too, that Reagan always had a mystical side. Frank Shakespeare said in another context that both Reagan and John Paul II were "mystics" who shared "almost a mystical bond."[5]

I asked Shakespeare whether John Paul II ever talked to him personally about Fátima. He said, "Yes, but I'm not going to talk to you about that." For whatever reason, Shakespeare felt the need to protect this information and to continue to keep it secret, perhaps all the way to the grave. "But," he added, "I will tell you that Mary, in the eyes of the tippy-tippy top of the Catholic Church... there's a belief that that [Fátima] absolutely happened."

About that, there has never been any question.

THE PRESIDENT AND THE POPE MEET AGAIN

After the stimulating discussion with Frank Shakespeare on the trip from Venice, Ronald Reagan arrived at the Vatican in midmorning on June 6, 1987. He and John Paul II would sit down in the Vatican Library, where they had met five years earlier (almost to the day).

June 6 was a Saturday, not a normal diplomatic day. But as the first Saturday of the month, it was a fitting time for John Paul II to meet with Reagan: Our Lady of Fátima—subject of the recent Reagan-Shakespeare conversation—had asked the world to set aside the first Saturday of every month as a special day of devotion to pray and make reparation for blasphemies and offenses against her Immaculate Heart and against the Lord. She specifically requested prayer for world peace, the subject that would dominate the president's and pontiff's public statements that day.

At the Vatican, Reagan and John Paul II greeted each other warmly and enthusiastically. They grasped each other with both hands.[6]

"Wonderful to see you," said John Paul II in Polish-accented English.

"Wonderful to see *you* again," Reagan responded.

The two then sat in the library in straight-backed mahogany chairs, with no aides present. Media and photographers and staff left the two leaders alone.

They reemerged after a discussion that lasted about an hour.[7] It was one of the longest one-on-one conversations the president and the pope ever had, and yet the meeting received little press attention outside Italy.

Reagan and John Paul II did not reveal details of their private discussion. The president said that their conversation had been "just great," noting broadly: "We had a very interesting discussion on a number of subjects. The pope and I share the same views on many subjects." John Paul II likewise divulged little. His public statements stuck to broad principles, such as his hope that an end to the arms race might free "immense resources" that could be used to "alleviate misery and feed millions of hungry human beings."[8]

The only further insight on the private conversation came from brief comments that Vatican and White House officials gave to reporters. In its very short account of the meeting, the *New York Times* reported, "Vatican and American officials said the meeting had focused on disarmament, East-West relations, the Middle East, Central America and North-South cooperation."[9] In the words of the *Los Angeles Times* (which published one of the few worthwhile press accounts of the meeting), White House spokesman Marlin Fitzwater related that Reagan had updated the pope on "U.S.-Soviet relations" and the status of "arms control negotiations ... aimed at removing short- and intermediate-range missiles from Europe." Here, six months before the Washington summit, Reagan told the pope that he was (to quote the *Los Angeles Times*) "optimistic about reaching a nuclear arms control agreement with the Soviet Union."[10]

John Paul II was surely buoyed by this news, particularly given Reagan's earlier run-ins with American bishops over whether his peace-through-strength approach would yield genuine reductions in nuclear arms. Liberal Catholics had complained that "Reagan the nuclear warmonger" was building up an arsenal for the purpose of launching atomic Armageddon; now just the opposite was unfolding. What Bill Clark had four years earlier assured the bishops, Ronald Reagan now reassured their pope—and these assurances would find full vindication when the INF Treaty was signed in December.

Finally, Fitzwater quoted President Reagan as saying, "Most of our discussions were on U.S.-Soviet relations and on General Secretary Gorbachev."[11]

Based on that White House statement, one wonders whether Mikhail Gorbachev's faith was a matter of discussion. Reagan was intrigued by the possibility that they were dealing with a closet Christian in Moscow; so was John Paul II—as we shall see later in this book. Did it come up in their conversation?

For that matter, did the president and pope pray together about Gorbachev specifically or about other matters? I asked Frank Shakespeare whether he knew of Reagan and John Paul II's praying together on this occasion or others. He said, "I don't know precisely, but I overwhelmingly think they did so." When I replied, "It's hard to imagine that they wouldn't have prayed together," he unhesitatingly agreed.[12]

During their previous meeting at the Vatican, Reagan and John Paul II had discussed the assassination attempts against them and their belief that divine forces had intervened to spare their lives for a special purpose. Since then, Reagan had learned from Bill Casey that the Soviets were behind the shooting of John Paul II. Meanwhile, the pope himself suspected that the trail of responsibility led to Moscow. It would be surprising if in this private discussion the two men did not at least acknowledge the evidence of communist culpability on that intense Feast Day of Our Lady of Fátima in May 1981.

Here is where a comment by Owen Smith, Bill Casey's son-in-law and close aide, becomes especially interesting. Recall that Smith told me the pope had asked Casey and Reagan to keep quiet about a Soviet hand in the shooting, so as not to provoke World War III. Casey had died only four weeks before this Vatican meeting (more on that later). It is possible that the Holy Father asked Reagan here in this Vatican meeting to keep his suspicions quiet. Unfortunately, the lack of available historical documentation on the meeting makes it impossible to confirm such a dialogue.

"THE FREEDOM THAT GOD GAVE US ALL"

When the president and the pope came out of the library, they appeared before the cameras to issue public statements in the Pontifical Palace.

Reagan went first, right at noon. "Your Holiness," the president began, "I am truly grateful for the opportunity to visit with you again in this place of peace. You've always said that the power of love for our fellow man is stronger than the evils that befall mankind.... And one feels the power of that strong moral force here in this holy city of Saint Peter, just as we see it in your courageous and compassionate leadership."[13]

Peace was a central theme that day. When Pope John Paul II spoke after Reagan, he reiterated a point he had made after the president's first visit to the Vatican—that "world peace might be fostered" through, among other things, "constructive negotiations aimed at ending the arms race."[14]

In his public statement, Reagan brought up another subject close to the pontiff's heart: Poland. In just two days, John Paul II would leave for another trip to his native land. Reagan knew this and made sure to highlight the visit in his speech. In the process, he made an unexpected theological-philosophical reference regarding the matter of free will:

> As you embark on a pastoral visit to the land of your birth, Poland, be assured that the hearts of the American people are with you. Our prayers will go with you in profound hope that soon the hand of God will lighten the terrible burden of brave people everywhere who yearn for freedom, even as all men and women yearn for the

> freedom that God gave us all when he gave us a free will. We see the power of the spiritual force in that troubled land, uniting a people in hope, just as we see the powerful stirrings to the East of a belief that will not die despite generations of oppression. Perhaps it's not too much to hope that true change will come to all countries that now deny or hinder the freedom to worship God. And perhaps we'll see that change comes through the reemergence of faith, through the irresistible power of a religious renewal. For despite all the attempts to extinguish it, the people's faith burns with a passionate heat; once allowed to breathe free, that faith will burn so brightly it will light the world.[15]

This was a powerful passage in a brief public statement. And every word of it came from Reagan himself, I learned.

In a sense, of course, all the president's words were the president's words. Reagan reviewed, amended, and signed off on everything his speechwriters penned for him. And his speechwriters were adept at capturing the president's "voice," writing what they believed he would have written himself. In many cases, they took language directly from speeches Reagan had written long ago.[16]

But in the case of this passage on free will and religious renewal in Poland, every word came verbatim from Reagan's mouth. The two speechwriters responsible for crafting Reagan's speeches on this European trip, Josh Gilder and Peter Robinson, revealed how it happened.[17]

On May 18, 1987, Reagan met with Gilder and Robinson in the Oval Office to discuss his speeches for the upcoming Europe trip, including the Vatican visit. They knew that Pope John Paul II would leave for Poland right after Reagan visited the Vatican, and they wanted to make sure the president acknowledged the papal trip in his remarks.

Gilder knew that Reagan had expressed strong support for Poland throughout his second term.[18] In February, for example, Reagan had asserted that "the light of freedom continues to shine in Poland," adding, "The commitment and sacrifice of hundreds of thousands of Polish men and women have kept the flame alive, even amid the gloom." The American president invoked the slogan of the nineteenth-century Polish independence movement, which Karol Wojtyła would have known by heart: "For Your Freedom and Ours." "That," said Reagan, "is our slogan, too. And it is more than a slogan; it is a program of action." Reagan was insisting on freedom not merely as a lofty idea but as an actual goal resulting from a plan of action.[19]

Given such a sweeping vision, Gilder asked Reagan during their May 18 meeting whether he had something in particular he wanted to say to the pope, especially regarding Poland. Was there anything weighing on his heart? Yes, said the president. Reagan replied with those exact words on prayer, on Poland, on religious renewal, on the power and stirrings of the spiritual force, on the yearning "for the freedom that God gave us all when he gave us a free will"—thoughts that would have warmed the heart of the Polish pontiff.

Remembering that Oval Office meeting, Gilder told me that he carefully transcribed Reagan's extemporaneous comments, word for word. "I was writing really fast," he said, "and I managed to get down just about everything he said." After the meeting, he commented to Robinson on what the president had said: " 'The freedom that God gave us all when he gave us a free will.' Beautiful, right?"

The young speechwriter deployed the fresh content smack in the middle of the president's June 6 statement. Gilder had begun his initial draft with some bland statements the State Department had supplied. "Everything was, 'Hello, it's great to be here in the Vatican, how's everybody doing?' " he remembered. "The remarks didn't say anything."

Now, he had remarks that said something.

He needed to clear the text with various White House and State Department officials, the infamous process known as "staffing." When the remarks came back to Gilder, the entire section Gilder had transcribed from Reagan was crossed out.

Stunned, Gilder called the State Department official who had nixed that section. "Why did you take out the material?" he asked.

The Foggy Bottom establishmentarian answered, "I think it's inappropriate to have so much language about God."

"So much language about God?" Gilder responded. "The president will be talking to the pope!"

The State Department official relented only when Gilder informed him that Reagan himself had supplied the passage. It stayed.

"A YEAR OF PRAYER AND DEVOTION TO THE VIRGIN MARY"

In his public statement at the Vatican, Reagan made another fitting comment: he invoked the Virgin Mary. Addressing the pope, Reagan said: "I know that today marks the beginning of a very important time for you personally and for the people of your faith, for it's this day that you begin the observance of a year of prayer and devotion to the Virgin Mary with a worldwide prayer for peace. I wish you great joy, happiness, and fulfillment in the coming months. And I thank you, your Holiness, and may God bless you."[20]

Here, Reagan referred to the opening of the Marian Year that the pope had declared. That evening, on the Vigil of Pentecost, Pope John Paul II would give his Solemn Opening for the Marian Year.[21]

Twenty-seven years later, I asked Josh Gilder whether he or Reagan had included the acknowledgment of Mary. Reagan, as we have seen, constantly made handwritten edits and additions to speeches, sometimes at the last minute. Gilder could not recall for sure. "[I] wouldn't be surprised if I wrote it," he told me in an e-mail, "as Peter Robinson was very attuned to JPII's special reverence for the Virgin Mary and I remember discussing it with Peter often.... But it's possible RR inserted it at the last moment."[22]

For the record, the original draft of the speech held in the Presidential Handwriting File of the Reagan Library contains no handwritten insertions or remarks by Reagan, suggesting that Gilder, not the president, penned the line.[23]

TWO FREEDOM FIGHTERS—IN BERLIN AND POLAND

Ronald Reagan's second trip to the Vatican had been another unforgettable one, even as he and the Holy Father remained tight-lipped about what they said. "We talked for an hour—an interesting hour," confided Reagan to his diary. The president wrote in the clipped style that was typical of his diary entries: "I filled him [the pope] in as best I could on Nicaragua & General Secretary Gorbachev. Then Nancy arrived, press photographers, our entire team & his." Reagan noted that he and the pope shared their public remarks, exchanged gifts, and "then we left the Pope & went to the Sala Clementina room to meet & be greeted by the American Seminary students from No. Am. College."[24]

That was it. No specifics on what he and the pope talked about inside the Vatican Library.

In private letters to friends, Reagan shared only brief thoughts on his meeting with John Paul II. "Yes the pope speaks English and a half dozen other languages for that matter," he said in response to a question from his longtime pen pal Ruddy Lee-Hines. "We had a good visit."[25] In a letter that same day to his friend Phil Regan, he expressed stronger feelings, writing that John Paul II was "a truly great human being." The president added, "Our visit is something I'll long remember."[26]

Historians have not remembered the visit as well. That may be because other events on Reagan's European tour overshadowed the Vatican stop. Most notably, less than a week after leaving Rome, Reagan delivered one of the most important speeches of his presidency, and indeed of the twentieth century.

After his first meeting with the pope at the Vatican, Reagan had traveled to London to give his famous Westminster Address, in which he called for a "crusade" against communism that would leave Marxism-Leninism on the "ash-heap of history." Now, five years later, Reagan left the Vatican inspired to deliver his signature statement in his assault against the Soviet empire. This was his landmark "Tear down this wall!" speech in Berlin.

On June 12, 1987, the president stood before the Brandenburg Gate outside the Berlin Wall. "There is one sign the Soviets can make that would be unmistakable, that would advance dramatically the cause of freedom and peace," said Reagan. "General Secretary Gorbachev, if you seek peace, if you seek prosperity for the Soviet Union and Eastern Europe, if you seek liberalization: Come here to this gate. Mr. Gorbachev, open this gate. Mr. Gorbachev, tear down this wall!"[27]

The crowd erupted. All Germans, West and East, knew that Gorbachev alone held that power. The Soviet leader saw the Berlin Wall as a guarantee that Germany could not again invade the Soviet Union. He was not ready to budge in Berlin.[28] But now Reagan had challenged him to live up to his claims that he supported human rights and a new Soviet Union by taking down the ugliest symbol of repression in the communist world.

Not surprisingly, officials from the State Department, including Secretary of State George Shultz, and the NSC, including National Security Adviser Colin Powell, had repeatedly tried to cut the "Tear down this wall" line from Reagan's speech, saying it was too "provocative." The line stayed only because of the efforts of the speechwriter, Peter Robinson, and the president himself. "The boys at State are going to kill me [for saying the line]," Reagan told an aide, "but it's the right thing to do."[29]

The speech outraged the Kremlin, of course. Master Moscow agitator Georgi Arbatov, who had previously denounced Reagan as a man "completely divorced from reality,"[30] called the Berlin Wall demand "plain blackmail, blackmail by an American cowboy," and "political vulgarity!" On the same television program, Arbatov's fellow agitprop artist Valentin

Falin fulminated against Reagan's "frantic demagoguery." Falin declared righteously, "The Soviet leaders do not come into the house of someone else to either close or open gates"—the same Soviet leaders who had closed the gates of Berlin and ordered the construction of the wall.[31]

But one who was surely impressed with Reagan's statement was Pope John Paul II, who was behind the Iron Curtain, in his native Poland, when the president made his speech in Berlin. This was his third pilgrimage to Poland since becoming pope.

The trip started on June 8, just after the kickoff of the Marian Year. The itinerary had been a subject of intense negotiations between the Vatican and Warsaw. Poland's communist authorities would later express dismay that the pontiff behaved "more aggressively than we expected" during the trip.[32]

The communists found too "aggressive" the pope's traveling to Gdańsk, the home of Solidarity, and his meeting again with Lech Wałęsa. As historian Robert Service later put it, the Polish pope effectively gave his "ecclesiastical benediction to Solidarity." Service further argued that the pontiff's homilies on human rights, human dignity, and justice, paired with his "principled words of defiance" and his exhorting Poles to live their lives according to Christian beliefs, posed a direct challenge to the political legitimacy of atheistic communism.[33]

Perhaps the pope was expressing righteous anger in the face of unrestrained communist aggression toward the late Father Jerzy Popiełuszko, the chaplain to Solidarity who had been pummeled to death and dumped in the Vistula River since the last papal visit. Maybe he was unafraid to defy killers who always found a way to object to an apostle of freedom. And so the native Pole boosted Poland's freedom fighters in Gdańsk, while his American ally boosted freedom fighters in Berlin.

On June 12, the day Reagan visited the Berlin Wall, John Paul II issued a prayer appeal at Jasna Góra, before Our Lady of Częstochowa. He had come there, he said, as a "man of the consecration." By that he meant "the mystery of the Eucharist," the consecrated Eucharist, the Real Presence of Christ in which lives "the One who 'loved us to the end.'" In turn, he said, he wanted to bring the "great things" made possible by the consecrated Eucharist and further "consecrate them to the One who is our Mother, to her who is the Lady of Jasna Góra, Lady of our nation and Queen of Poland."[34]

It was the same Lady to whom he had consecrated communist Russia. It was the same Lady who had warned of Russia's long line of crimes and errors.

At the Brandenburg Gate that same day, the pope's Protestant brother in Christ was making his own appeal that good would prevail.

BACK TO AMERICA

In their brief public remarks at the Vatican in June, both the president and the pope talked enthusiastically about John Paul II's upcoming trip to America, scheduled for September. In Reagan's first visit to the Vatican, in June 1982, he had urged the pontiff "to carry your ministry" to the western and southern parts of the United States. He reaffirmed that in his June 1987 remarks.[35] Now, on September 10, 1987, it became a reality.

John Paul II landed in Miami at 2 P.M. on Thursday, September 10. It was the beginning of a ten-day, nine-city tour that would take the pope from Florida to South Carolina, Louisiana, Texas, Arizona, California, and Michigan.[36] He would deliver forty-four speeches, statements, and homilies. This kind of intense schedule was typical for the sixty-seven-year-old pontiff, who remained remarkably energetic even after being shot six years earlier.

Ronald Reagan was there to greet John Paul II when the pope disembarked his Alitalia 727 jetliner. For Reagan, it had already been a long day. After starting early in the morning with his usual NSC and intelligence briefings, the president met with staffers Kenneth Duberstein, Thomas Griscom, and Marlin Fitzwater, gave an interview to *USA Today*, did an event with students, briefly returned to the Oval Office, authorized an official ambassadorial nomination, and then headed for the South Grounds of the White House lawn to hop a Marine helicopter for Andrews Air Force Base to fly to Miami. That was all before 11:24 A.M.[37]

This kind of intense schedule was typical for the seventy-six-year-old president, who remained remarkably energetic even after being shot six years earlier.

After Reagan greeted John Paul II, the president and the pontiff gave short remarks, speaking under a canopy on the tarmac. Both men looked fit, pictures of health. It was a pleasant atmosphere. Each smiled and serenely listened as the other addressed the crowd. They acted as if they knew each other well. To some degree, they did. This was the fourth time they had met, and the second in about twelve weeks.

Reagan greeted the pontiff by quoting the Second Vatican Council and the distinguished Catholic philosopher Jacques Maritain, who had written, "The Founding Fathers were neither metaphysicians nor theologians, but their philosophy of life and their political philosophy, their notion of natural law and of human rights, were permeated with concepts worked out by Christian reason and backed up by an unshakeable religious feeling." These were concepts that most definitely appealed to John Paul II: natural law, human rights, reason, and the American Founding. Reagan added, "From the first, then, our nation embraced the belief that the individual is sacred and that as God himself respects human liberty, so, too, must the state."[38]

That particular month, noted Reagan, marked the two hundredth anniversary of the U.S. Constitution. John Paul II would make clear his admiration for that document throughout his visit.

The pope sounded that theme in his opening statement. Speaking in slow but steady English, he signaled his great respect for the Declaration of Independence, the Constitution, and America's triumph on behalf of "inalienable human rights" and "life, liberty, and the pursuit of happiness."[39]

September 10, 1987, is remembered with almost no notes in the Reagan Library. But Reagan and John Paul II spent roughly six hours with (or within close proximity of) each other that day, staying together for a string of afternoon and evening appointments.[40] That night they would have another private audience, just the pope and the president, at the Vizcaya Museum on Biscayne Bay.[41]

The pontiff gave a formal address at the Vizcaya Museum. They were very American comments, fully in keeping with the thinking of the American Founders—and of Ronald Reagan—on the vital reinforcing relationship between faith and freedom.[42]

Addressing Reagan, the Holy Father said that he wanted to express "my own deep respect for the constitutional structure of this democracy, which you are called to 'preserve, protect and defend.'" The American Constitution that he so admired, the pope said, grew out of "the original American political faith with its appeal to the sovereignty of God." John Paul II understood the "moral and spiritual principles" and "ethical concerns" in the Constitution "that influenced your Founding Fathers." He pointed to the corollary words of the Declaration, heralding its "inalienable rights given by the Creator."

The pontiff continued: "Among the many admirable values of this nation there is one that stands out in particular. It is freedom. The concept of freedom is part of the very fabric of this nation as a political community of free people."

Unlike many modern Americans, this pope, like the president he stood beside, grasped that freedom was "a great blessing of God." John

Paul II affirmed: "From the beginning of America, freedom was directed to forming a well-ordered society and to promoting its peaceful life. Freedom was channeled to the fullness of human life, to the preservation of human dignity and to the safeguarding of all human rights." The pontiff added that "this is the freedom that America is called to live and guard and to transmit." It was "ordered freedom."

This was music to Reagan's ears. From his reading of modern American political philosophers, the president understood that this "ordered liberty" (as Russell Kirk called it) was precisely what a conservative was called to conserve.[43]

The pontiff explicitly connected the proper exercise of freedom to God's guidelines on how freedom should be used. "The only true freedom, the only freedom that can truly satisfy, is the freedom to do what we ought as human beings created by God according to his plan," said the pope. "It is the freedom to live the truth of what we are and who we are before God, the truth of our identity as children of God, as brothers and sisters in common humanity."

Reagan, as we have seen, had a similar understanding of faith and freedom. A year later, to honor the bicentennial of Georgetown University, a Catholic college, the president would say: "At its full flowering, freedom is the first principle of society; this society, Western society. And yet freedom cannot exist alone. And that's why the theme for your bicentennial is so very apt: learning, faith, and freedom. Each reinforces the others, each makes the others possible. For what are they without each other?" He continued: "Tocqueville said it in 1835, and it's as true today as it was then: 'Despotism may govern without faith, but liberty cannot. Religion is more needed in democratic societies than in any other.'"[44]

Like so many other Reagan lines, this one was similar to a statement by Fulton Sheen. "A religion can live without democracy," wrote Sheen. "But democracy cannot live without religion."[45]

Ronald Reagan and John Paul II were in complete harmony on this fundamental issue.

The Vizcaya visit afforded the pope and the president opportunities to talk. Press photos showed the two leaders strolling through the Italianate villa's extensive gardens, engaged in conversation. And after John Paul II's formal address, they sat down one-on-one at the museum. The meeting lasted close to an hour.[46]

When they finished their discussion, the two men faced the media once more with prepared remarks. It was 7:15 P.M. Reagan told the press that it had been the second time that year that he had met "in private audience" with "His Holiness Pope John Paul II." Actually, it had been the second time in just three months. Reagan gave a broad overview of what he and the pope had discussed. He said that they had talked about the "practical aspects of ideals we share: peace, justice, and the expansion of freedom." He had assured the pontiff of his commitment to extend democracy throughout Latin America. Reagan also offered that they had discussed "the prospects for improved relations between the United States and the Soviet Union." The president added that the United States was "unshakeably committed to the establishment of an enduring world of peace and to the extension or expansion of human freedom around the globe. Indeed, without freedom, there can be no peace."[47]

Reagan's comments became more specific when he mentioned that he had briefed the pontiff on the INF negotiations, which would soon bear fruit: "On arms control, we discussed the nearness of an agreement that would eliminate all American and Soviet INF missiles for the first time in history, achieving not just a limitation but an actual reduction in nuclear weapons." The phrase *actual reduction* was key here; pre-Reagan arms-control agreements had limited the only growth in nuclear arsenals. "Of course," said Reagan, "all of this depends upon Soviet willingness to get down to the hard work of completing an agreement. We stand ready as well for another historic agreement—one that would reduce strategic arms on both sides by half."

Reagan made his remarks to the press while standing aside John Paul II. With that, he bade the pope farewell "with affection," noting that Mrs. Reagan would be greeting the pontiff in Los Angeles in a few days.

In his diary entry for the day, written late that evening, a surely tired Reagan confided even less than he had to the media. He noted briefly that he and Nancy had joined roughly five thousand other people at the Miami airport to greet the pontiff and then later in the afternoon joined him again at an art museum "where he & I had a one-on-one—joined later by Nancy for a 2 on 1.... We did our farewell speeches before the press & went our separate ways."

Amid these few sentences, Reagan succinctly summed up his thoughts on John Paul II: "He's truly a great man."[48]

COUNTERING A COMMUNIST SMEAR

From Miami, the pontiff began traveling around the United States. It would be a whirlwind tour, as he traversed more than ten thousand miles in ten days. He appeared in massive venues such as the Louisiana Superdome and Los Angeles's Dodger Stadium.

Among his most interesting meetings was one he held on September 11, before he left Miami. John Paul II met with representatives of American Jewish organizations in Dade County. The Pole, who had been close to many Jewish people throughout his life, had done much to reconcile hurt feelings with Jewish people throughout his papacy. This was another such occasion.

Here he again underscored the horrors of the Holocaust, especially those in Auschwitz, near his home. Those poor souls had been "exterminated only because they were Jews," the pontiff said. The "suffering of Israel's children" and the "dehumanizing outrages" they endured, he said, had strengthened "ever more deeply" the Church's "common bond with the Jewish people and with their treasure of spiritual riches in the past and in the present."[49]

In the next section of his remarks, the pontiff referred to another injustice involving the Jewish people. "It is also fitting to recall the strong, unequivocal efforts of the popes against anti-Semitism and Nazism at the height of the persecution against the Jews," John Paul II said. "Back in 1938, Pius XI declared that 'anti-Semitism cannot be admitted,' and he declared the total opposition between Christianity and Nazism by stating that the Nazi cross is an 'enemy of the Cross of Christ.'" But this was not the only Pius of the era to have repudiated Nazism. There was another, one much maligned and totally misunderstood: "And I am convinced that history will reveal ever more clearly and convincingly how deeply Pius XII felt the tragedy of the Jewish people, and how hard and effectively he worked to assist them during the Second World War."

There it was: a defense of Pius XII. It was short, but it was there, and surely as uncomfortable as it was unexpected. It was a controversial thing to say, because the communists' smear of Pius XII had proven so successful. Nonetheless, it was something that had to be said. And it had major credibility coming from the lips of this pope.

THE DEATH OF BILL CASEY

Five years earlier, Reagan and John Paul II had identified their shared mission: to end atheistic communism. In 1987 they lost one of their most important allies in this cause: Bill Casey, Reagan's CIA director, who on multiple occasions had secretly flown to Rome to brief the pope.

Casey died on May 6, 1987, just a month before Reagan and John Paul II reconnected at the Vatican. Casey had been in the hospital for some time after a brain tumor and other serious maladies. His death was not unexpected, but it was still hard to accept. Reagan called Casey's widow, Sophia, to personally express his condolences.[50] The president attended the funeral on Long Island.[51]

As Bill Clark told me, Ronald Reagan had the "highest regard" for Casey and his capabilities. He also knew that Casey's faith was integral to what he did. The day his CIA director died, Reagan issued a statement that remarked on Casey's "deep religious faith."[52] Like Reagan, Casey saw himself as doing God's will within a Divine Plan. That was an aspect of Casey that few knew. Surely John Paul II knew it, and saw it during his meetings with the CIA director. Herb Meyer, Casey's close aide, witnessed Casey's sense of a commitment to a divine calling amid the Cold War battle. Recall that Meyer said that when Casey was named CIA director, he believed that God had given him "one more shot." Meyer summed up:

> Casey [had been] a poor kid from Queens. He was one year older than Reagan. He made a lot of money in tax work, venture capital. He'd been in several high government positions along the way. He was from that World War II generation, serving in and out of government, very patriotic, deeply religious, seriously rich, self-made. And he was drifting into an affluent retirement when Ronald Reagan called. The next thing you knew, he was CIA director. And when he wound up running the CIA, Bill thought God had given him one more shot. He wasn't going to waste it.[53]

One more shot to do what? Meyer put it bluntly: "To take out the Soviet Union."[54]

For six years, Bill Casey took his shot. He seized every moment he believed that God had given him. He had done all he could to take out the Soviet Union. His work was finished. And now those efforts were beginning to pay off.

THE DUTY OF OUR TALENTS

As 1987 came to a close, Ronald Reagan and John Paul II—the heads of the world's temporal and spiritual powers—could look back on important achievements. The Marian Year was in bloom, and it would continue into 1988, the final full year of the Reagan presidency, when they could hope for and expect still more triumphs.

Pope John Paul II might have had some of these achievements in mind when he gave a blessing from Saint Peter's Square at the close of the year, December 30, 1987, and pointed to the New Testament parable of the talents. The pontiff said, "The story of the human race described by Sacred Scripture is, even after the fall into sin, a story of constant achievements, which, although always called into question and threatened by sin, are nonetheless repeated, increased, and extended in response to the divine vocation given from the beginning to man and to woman (cf. Gen. 1:26–28) and inscribed in the image which they received."[55]

This was a philosophical statement, but the pope applied it to current realities, and especially to men who sought to do God's will with the talents and gifts they had received. Such could be a challenging task, but it was a duty: "Anyone wishing to renounce the difficult yet noble task of improving the lot of man in his totality, and of all people, with the excuse that the struggle is difficult and that constant effort is required, or simply because of the experience of defeat and the need to begin again, that person would be betraying the will of God the Creator." The pope pointed to "the Lord Jesus himself, in the parable of the talents," who emphasized the severe treatment given to the man who dared to hide the gift received.

"It falls to us," said the Holy Father, "who receive the gifts of God in order to make them fruitful, to 'sow' and 'reap.'" He stated that a deeper pondering of this parable "will make us commit ourselves more resolutely to the duty, which is urgent for everyone today, to work together for the full development of others."

Both John Paul II and Ronald Reagan strongly professed to do the work of God with their talents—"whatever time I have left is for Him," Reagan had said after surviving the assassination attempt in March 1981. They were working on behalf of all people. It was a constant struggle, fraught with the experience of defeat and the need to begin all over again. It was, nonetheless, a commitment they needed to pursue resolutely. To do otherwise would be to betray the will of God.

33

MAY–JUNE 1988

REAGAN'S MISSION TO MOSCOW

On the afternoon of May 3, 1988, a White House press conference was held that was unlike any before it. At 2:44 P.M., in the East Room, the president of the United States appeared with four Russian dissidents: Iosif Begun, Reverend Stefan Matveiuk, Mykola Rudenko, and Father Vladimir Shibayev. They were religious leaders, Jew and Christian. President Reagan proclaimed that although the White House had welcomed many significant people over many decades, none was "more important, none of greater faith and moral courage, than these four men."[1]

They had suffered for their faith under communism in Russia. Reagan informed the White House press corps, "The presence of these four men here today is testimony to the fact that our witness here in the West can have an impact."

What sort of witness? A witness to faith and to freedom.

The president of the United States made a public vow to the four men:

> I promise that the witness of faith that you have brought here today will not be confined within these four walls, or forgotten when this meeting is ended. I will carry it in my heart when I travel to the Soviet Union at the end of this month. And I will say that the most fitting way to mark the millennium of Christianity in Kiev Rus would be granting the right of all the peoples and all the creeds of the Soviet Union to worship their God, in their own way.

It was an extraordinary pledge for a president to make, and not one that a liberal and secular press corps was accustomed to hearing. Reagan's vow surely raised eyebrows.

The president said that there were "encouraging signs" for religious freedom in the USSR, where the communists' atheistic revolution had been devoted "to reshaping man" and denying "one of the most basic teachings of the Judeo-Christian belief: that after God shaped Adam from dust, he breathed into him the divine principle of life."

Reagan then shared a story with the four dissidents:

> Recently, a woman wrote a letter and enclosed in the letter was a copy of what can only be called a prayer. But the story of that—it's in that single page—of a young Russian soldier in a shellhole in World War II, knowing that his unit was going to . . . advance the attack, looking up at the stars and revealing for the first time that he had been taught all his life that there was no God. But now he believed there was. And he looked up at the heavens and spoke so sincerely and said, "Maybe before the night is over I'll be coming to You. And I hope You will forgive what I believed for so long, the foolishness, because I know now there is a God." And that letter was found on the body of the young soldier who was killed in the coming engagement. I thought sometimes of taking it to Moscow with me—maybe the General Secretary might like to read it.

The president would, in fact, take that letter to Moscow and share it with Mikhail Gorbachev.[2]

ONWARD, CHRISTIAN SOLDIER

Over the next three and a half weeks, as he prepared to go to Moscow for a summit with Gorbachev, Reagan repeatedly called attention to Soviet religious persecution and vowed to push for greater religious rights in the USSR.[3] For example, in Chicago the day after he welcomed the Russian dissidents, he underscored four freedoms that he intended to emphasize when he got to the Soviet Union. First and foremost among them was freedom of religion.[4]

Then, on May 27, while in Finland en route to the USSR, Reagan reminded Finns that atheistic Moscow, which, according to official Soviet statistics, was down to only about forty churches, had been once known as the "City of the Forty Forties," earned by its extraordinary 1,600 belfries. "The world welcomes the return of some churches to worship after many years," said Reagan, "but there are still relatively few functioning churches and almost no bells."

Reagan conceded that Gorbachev was changing things. He quoted the general secretary: "Believers are Soviet people…and they have the full right to express their conviction with dignity." He applauded Gorbachev's dedication to that principle but wanted more: "What a magnificent demonstration of good will it would be for the Soviet leadership for church bells to ring out again not only in Moscow but throughout the Soviet Union."[5]

Joseph Stalin was rolling over in his grave.

Once Reagan got to Moscow, he talked constantly about his faith. He was in the USSR for his fourth summit with Gorbachev, which occurred from May 29 to June 2, 1988. But the way he shared his faith during the trip, the president could have been confused for a missionary.[6]

Ben Elliott, an evangelical and one of Reagan's top speechwriters, later told me that Reagan's use of religious language was quite intentional: "On such a historic trip, Reagan wanted every word to have meaning. He wanted every word to be heard."[7] Official Reagan biographer Edmund Morris stated flatly, "He wants to see Christianity in Moscow, it's as simple as that."[8] Morris wrote that Reagan "became obsessed with the notion that an 'underground religion' was rising like a water table beneath the surface of Soviet society."[9] The British intellectual Malcolm Muggeridge had told Reagan that such a "resurgence" of Christianity was in fact occurring in the USSR. In a 1983 letter, the otherwise gloomy Brit informed Reagan that this Christian resurgence was the "most important happening" in the world, demonstrating that "the whole effort sustained over sixty years to brainwash the Russian people…has been a fiasco."[10]

Like John Paul II, Reagan had long seen religion as an ally in the effort to bring freedom to the Soviet Union. Reagan was circumspect about this goal when speaking publicly, but in private he was quite direct, as evidenced by letters he wrote during his presidency. In a July 1981 letter, for instance, Reagan stated, "I have had a feeling... that religion might well turn out to be the Soviets' Achilles' heel." He added, "I've had some reports that it is even going on in an underground way in Russia itself."[11]

In a February 1984 letter to an old friend, Reagan said he hoped that "the hunger for religion" in the USSR might be tapped as "a major factor in bringing about a change in the present situation."[12]

"Hunger for religion" was a phrase that the Reverend Billy Graham had used in giving Reagan an on-the-ground report about the Soviet Union. Graham told the president that this hunger underlay "everything." Reagan was certain that was accurate, even as the repressed Russian citizenry didn't "dare admit it."

In a December 1987 talk to students in Jacksonville, Florida, Reagan talked about the makeshift Bibles he had seen from the USSR. He told the students that when Russians "get their hands on a Bible—it is so difficult there, and they're not supposed to have them—they cut them up and make them into these little books so that everybody has just a few verses of their own of the Bible. And one of those was sent to me to show me what they do."[13]

This information probably came from Graham. Declassified documents show that a week earlier Reagan had received a letter from the legendary preacher updating him on Russia. Graham claimed that "under those babushkas of those little shuffling figures" going to church in the USSR were not old women but a few youthful faces, an indication (both men hoped) that Soviet youngsters were "hungry for God." Graham implored the president to keep that thought "in the back of your mind at all times in your dealings" with the Soviets.[14]

Reagan most certainly would. He promised the Jacksonville students that he and Gorbachev would "have a few words" about Soviet religious persecution.[15] And when he arrived in Moscow in late May 1988, he made clear that religious belief and freedom were his priorities.

It was supposed to be a summit, with all the expected talk of politics and missiles. It was that, but much more.

"GOD'S HEAVENLY WILL"

On Sunday, May 29, 1988, President Reagan's plane touched down in Moscow at Vnukovo-2 airport. He and the first lady descended the stairs and made contact with Soviet soil at 2:05 P.M. They were greeted with banners and perfect skies.

Soviet planners had done their best to put a smiley face on communism. They had repaved the streets around Spaso House, the U.S. ambassador's residence, where the first couple would be staying. Just around the block, two dilapidated structures on Sadovoye Koltso had been refinished with uncharacteristic speed, as had the ugly buildings across from the Kremlin. Grass and flowers had been planted.[16] The prostitutes had also been cleaned up, and cleared away.[17]

The Reagans were welcomed by Andrei Gromyko, the Soviet foreign ministry fixture whom Reagan had once described as "that frosty old Stalinist." The Reagans and Gromyko struggled through small talk.

Reagan would have much preferred the welcome of Patriarch Pimen of Moscow. That day, the patriarch of the Russian Orthodox Church had proclaimed that "God's heavenly will" was about to bring them all together: Reagan, Gorbachev, and their peoples.[18]

The Reagans headed to the Grand Kremlin Palace to meet the general secretary. They ascended the Grand State Staircase, at the top of which they found Lenin, in the form of a large canvas that captured the Bolshevik godfather instructing the Communist Youth League in 1920. "I sort of expected him to be there," the president later said mordantly.

As the Reagans strolled into Saint George's Hall, the magnificent ceremonial chamber in the Kremlin Palace, the Gorbachevs entered from the opposite end. The couples met in the center of the room.

Reagan made a few remarks and concluded by saying, as he looked up at the legion of Kremlin atheists, "Thank you and God bless you."

Igor Korchilov, Gorbachev's translator, immediately noticed that his comrades were horrified; in using the "G" word, their American guest had committed blasphemy in Lenin's house. "The heretofore impregnable edifice of Communist atheism was being assaulted before their very eyes," Korchilov later wrote.[19] It was something they needed to get accustomed to—quickly.

THE ONE-ON-ONE

At 3:26 P.M., the leaders of the two superpowers commenced their first one-on-one meeting of the summit. The conversation lasted a little over an hour. Gorbachev spoke first. When it was time for the president of the United States to speak, Reagan went to the issue foremost on his mind: religion in Russia. He did not let a believer go unaccounted for—Protestant, Ukrainian Catholic, Jew, Muslim. All, said the American president, had a right to their God and to the church, synagogue, or mosque of their choice. Reagan told the general secretary that if he enhanced religious freedoms in his country, he would be viewed as a "hero" around the world.[20]

Gorbachev conceded that there had been "excesses" against religion long ago in Bolshevik Russia but said there was no "serious problem" today. Reagan was not satisfied with that answer. He pressed the general secretary to protect religious liberty. The two leaders proceeded to debate the issue. During their back-and-forth, Reagan made good on the thought he had expressed to the four Russian religious dissidents at the White House: he read Gorbachev the letter about the young Russian soldier in the shell hole in World War II.

It is not clear whether Gorbachev or anyone in the Soviet delegation was particularly moved. Nonetheless, Reagan persisted. This issue was critical. The discussion of religious faith took up a quarter of the entire conversation.[21]

Consider that. With all of the issues at stake between the superpowers, from trade to treaties, from embargoes to nuclear weapons, the one that began and dominated the two leaders' first one-on-one at the 1988 Moscow summit was religious freedom. That was Reagan's doing. Nothing else concerned Reagan more.

DAY TWO

The next day, Monday, May 30, President Reagan delivered three sets of formal remarks, first at the Danilov Monastery, then at Spaso House, and then during toasts at dinner that evening.

Reagan seemed most inspired by his visit to the recently restored historic monastery. Founded in the year 1282, the Danilov Monastery stood as an oasis of orthodox Christianity in a spiritual desert. It was named for its founder, Prince Daniel of Moscow, who became a monk shortly before his death. The Russian Orthodox Church canonized Daniel.

The Danilov Monastery had endured many trials through seven centuries, none worse than what the rampaging Bolsheviks brought. In 1929 Stalin's government shut down the monastery, expelled the monks and their novices, and turned the facility into a prison managed by the Soviet secret police, the NKVD.

The Soviets also dispatched the glorious bells that hung in the monastery. The most impressive among them was the thirteen-ton Bolshoi bell. The Kremlin would have melted down these bells as it did so many others, but an American capitalist, Charles Crane, intervened to save them. Crane purchased the Danilov bells from the Soviets (who desperately needed the hard currency) and donated them to Harvard University.

The Soviets did not reopen the doors of the Danilov Monastery until the 1980s, and not until 1988 was the restoration of the monastery complete—just in time for Reagan's visit. It was a positive religious change under Gorbachev that Reagan appreciated.

On the afternoon of May 30, President Reagan arrived early at Danilov to examine icons that had been restored. He listened attentively as one of the Father Superior's aides tutored the president on the restoration techniques used.

Thus inspired, Reagan began his speech at 2:35 P.M. He expressed thanks for the opportunity to meet those who had helped make the monastery's "return to the Russian Orthodox Church a reality." He added, "I am also addressing in spirit the thirty-five million believers whose personal contributions made this magnificent restoration possible." Referring to the monastery's beautifully restored icons, Reagan said: "Like the saints and martyrs depicted in these icons, the faith of your people has been tested and tempered in the crucible of hardship. But in that suffering, it has grown strong, ready now to embrace with new hope the beginnings of a second Christian millennium."[22]

The American president made abundantly clear what he hoped to see: "a new age of religious freedom in the Soviet Union." Reagan said it was his and his fellow Americans' prayer "that the return of this monastery signals a willingness to return to believers the thousands of other houses of worship which are now closed, boarded up, or used for secular purposes."

Reagan went further. Explaining that Americans "feel it keenly when religious freedom is denied to anyone anywhere," he told his audience that he and his countrymen "hope with you that soon all the Soviet religious communities that are now prevented from registering, or are banned altogether, including the Ukrainian Catholic and Orthodox Churches, will soon be able to practice their religion freely and openly and instruct their children in and outside the home in the fundamentals of their faith." The president called for "a resurgent spring of religious liberty." He used Mikhail Gorbachev's own language to make the case, expressing his hope that "*perestroika* will be accompanied by a deeper restructuring, a deeper conversion, a *metanoia*, a change in the heart, and that *glasnost*, which means giving voice, will also let loose a new chorus of belief, singing praise to the God that gave us life."

Ronald Reagan wanted religious *glasnost*.

Addressing dissidents who had suffered in their native land, Reagan boldly cited a man who had long been persona non grata in the USSR: Aleksandr Solzhenitsyn, "one of this country's great writers and believers." The president quoted a "beautiful passage" that was "about the faith that is as elemental to this land as the dark and fertile soil." The passage read:

> When you travel the byroads of central Russia, you begin to understand the secret of the pacifying Russian countryside. It is in the churches. They lift their belltowers—graceful, shapely, all different—high over mundane timber and thatch. From villages that are cut off and invisible to each other, they soar to the same heaven. People who are always selfish and often unkind—but the evening chimes used to ring out, floating over the villages, fields, and woods, reminding men that they must abandon trivial concerns of this world and give time and thought to eternity.

Reagan was keenly aware of where he was speaking and its meaning. But he and his speechwriters probably were not aware of the particularly deep meaning of the chiming of bells at the Danilov Monastery, which the Stalin regime had so ruthlessly removed (and which would not be restored to the monastery until years after Reagan's death).

The president finished by asking the assembled, "In our prayers we may keep that image in mind: the thought that the bells may ring again, sounding through Moscow and across the countryside, clamoring for joy in their newfound freedom."

The president's words no doubt moved the Father Superior and his acolytes. Tears of joy were shed that afternoon.

But not at the Kremlin, where atheism was still the faith of choice.

In a typical response, an editorial in a government-controlled Soviet publication stated: "To put it mildly, we were amazed by what we heard from the president. The same old lament about 'freedom of worship in the Soviet Union.'"[23]

That was Moscow's take on Reagan's words at Danilov: Reagan was uttering a tired old lament. He was whining about religion.

SPASO HOUSE

From Danilov Monastery, Reagan set off for the U.S. ambassador's residence at Spaso House. Located one mile west of the Kremlin at No. 10 Spasopeskovskaya Square, Spaso House and the square on which it is located are named for the church that stands aside the diplomatic residence—the Church of Salvation on the Sands, erected in 1711. In Russian, "Spaso" means salvation.[24]

At 4:30 the president began his speech. His audience was filled with Soviet dissidents, including a number of persecuted believers.

Reagan told the assembled why he "so wanted this meeting to take place." "You see," he told the dissidents, "I wanted to convey to you that you have the prayers and support of the American people, indeed of people throughout the world." He wanted all of them to be "encouraged and take heart"; "I came here hoping to do what I could to give you strength."[25]

Reagan noted that from the outset of his administration, he had stressed that "an essential element in improving relations between the United States and the Soviet Union is human rights and Soviet compliance with international covenants on human rights." As he often did, he acknowledged some "hopeful signs" but said Moscow needed to do much more: "The basic standards that the Soviet Union agreed to almost thirteen years ago in the Helsinki accords, or a generation ago in the Universal Declaration of Human Rights, still need to be met." Specifically, he spoke of freedom of religion, freedom of speech, and freedom of travel—with religion the first of the freedoms. Once again, the president said he hoped the Soviet government would permit all the peoples of the Soviet Union to worship their creator as they saw fit.

Reagan ended his remarks with a deeply personal message: "Coming here, being with you, looking into your faces, I have to believe that the history of this troubled century will indeed be redeemed in the eyes of God and man, and that freedom will come to all. For what injustice can withstand your strength, and what can conquer your prayers?"

He then departed from his prepared text: "Could I play a little trick on you and say something that isn't written here? Sometimes when I'm faced with an unbeliever, an atheist, I am tempted to invite him to the greatest gourmet dinner one could ever serve and, when we finished eating that magnificent dinner, to ask him if he believes there's a cook. Thank you all and God bless you."[26]

Reagan did not articulate his point in detail, or arguably even well. But religious believers would recognize it. The president's point was that human beings, their planet, their universe, were here not by random chance but by design—by a Designer.

Mikhail Gorbachev would not have been surprised to hear this story from the president. Reagan had ended their first one-on-one in Moscow with the same story. What had been Gorbachev's response then? According to the American note taker, the general secretary told Reagan that the only possible answer to whether there was a cook had to be "yes."[27]

"A BETTER WAY OF SETTLING THINGS"

The second day of the Moscow summit finished with a dinner at the Grand Kremlin Palace. Gorbachev, the host, proposed the first toast. Speaking in Russian with an interpreter translating into English, Gorbachev gave a "toast" that was really a speech—at 1,442 words (in English), it was 400 words longer than Reagan's Spaso House speech. He covered everything from the Warsaw Pact and missiles to the Afghan war. Socialism got its usual vigorous plug: "We see ourselves even more convinced that our Socialist choice was correct, and we cannot conceive of our country developing without socialism—based on any other fundamental values. Our program is more democracy, more glasnost, more social justice with full prosperity and high moral standards."[28]

The general secretary made no mention of faith backing those moral standards, nor any mention of religion at all.

The president then raised his glass to speak, as the translator interpreted his words in Russian. Reagan's "toast" likewise took the form of a speech—1,253 words. But his remarks were more personal. After thanking Gorbachev and his staff for their hospitality and for "the opportunity to meet with so many divergent members of Soviet society," Reagan made another faith-centered gesture. He said he had brought a gift from his "former profession," one that had "something important to say to us about what is under way this week in Moscow." Reagan handed Gorbachev a videotape of a 1956 Gary Cooper movie *Friendly Persuasion*. It was "not as well known as some" movies, said Reagan, but he considered it "an American classic," a story of family and romantic love and of dedication to "higher principle."[29]

Reagan explained that the film was about an Indiana Quaker in the tumult of the American Civil War. As Quakers, the Quaker farmer and his family renounce violence, and each character must confront the moral dilemma the Civil War poses. "The film shows not just the tragedy of war," Reagan told Gorbachev, "but the problems of pacifism, the nobility of patriotism, as well as the love of peace."

The president recounted a key scene from the film, when Confederate raiders burn down the barn of a fellow Quaker, a neighbor of the Cooper character. That neighbor denounced violence earlier in the story, Reagan explained, "but now that the enemy has burned his barn, he's on his way to battle and criticizes his fellow Quaker [Cooper's character] for not joining him in renouncing his religious beliefs." But another neighbor is present: "It is this neighbor, although a nonbeliever, who says he's proud of the Quaker farmer's decision not to fight. In the face of the tragedy of war, he's grateful, as he says, that somebody's holding out for a better way of settling things."

Reagan got to the point of this latest parable: "It seems to me, Mr. General Secretary, that in pursuing these summit meetings we, too, have been holding out for a better way of settling things."

The president raised his glass to toast "the art of friendly persuasion, the hope of peace with freedom, the hope of holding out for a better way of settling things." And then Reagan mortified his atheistic hosts once again with his signature sign-off: "God bless you."[30]

GOD'S GIFT OF LIBERTY

The next day, the third day of the Moscow summit, Reagan arrived at the Kremlin at 10 A.M. for a negotiating session with Gorbachev. Their talks were fairly conventional, with no theatrics and no great breakthroughs. Then the two took a walk through Red Square. The general secretary tried to coax Reagan toward Lenin's tomb, the macabre site where the embalmed one lay for posterity. Reagan deftly avoided the corpse, conjuring up a polite reason not to enter the communist inner sanctum. He put his arm around Gorbachev, his friend whom he called "Mike," and headed in the opposite direction.

As the two men continued their stroll through Red Square, they paused with Saint Basil's Cathedral in the backdrop, its spires pointed toward heaven. The photos of that moment were a fitting encapsulation of this fourth Reagan-Gorbachev summit.

Perhaps the most striking moment of the tour through Red Square came when a reporter asked Reagan whether he still believed the USSR was an "Evil Empire." "No," the president replied. "That was another time, another era."

After that historic walk, the president addressed a group of Soviet writers, artists, and poets at the A. Fadeyev Central House of Men of Letters. These intellectuals understood the essentiality of freedom of speech and conscience. Reagan talked to them about his art, acting, which he connected to the soul: "In acting, even as you develop an appreciation for what we call the dramatic, you become in a more intimate way less taken with superficial pomp and circumstance, more attentive to the core of the soul—that part of each of us that God holds in the hollow of his hand and into which he breathes the breath of life."[31]

On this point, Reagan quoted a Russian poet, Nikolai Gumilev: "The eternal entrance to God's paradise is not closed with seven diamond seals. It is a doorway in a wall abandoned long ago—stones, moss, and nothing more."

It was another example of how Reagan would find a way to talk about God, the soul, and the person in every venue he could while in Moscow.

Reagan's grandest moment came a few hours later at Moscow State University, where he spoke to students. He shared the gospel of faith and freedom, the "twin beacons" he deemed indispensable and inseparable. Recall that in his 1981 Christmas address on martial law in Poland, Reagan had proclaimed that these twin beacons "brightened the American sky."[32] He hoped they might illuminate the Moscow sky as well.

For Reagan, this speech might have been the high point of the summit. Several times during his presidency, beginning with his June 1982 Westminster Address, Reagan had declared a "forward strategy of freedom." That strategy was on full display at Moscow State University. In his address, Reagan deployed the word *freedom* twenty-four times, often in the context of faith.

In perhaps the strongest passage of the speech, the president told the young people:

> Go to any American town, to take just an example, and you'll see dozens of churches, representing many different beliefs—in many places, synagogues and mosques—and you'll see families of every conceivable nationality worshiping together. Go into any schoolroom, and there you will see children being taught the Declaration of Independence, that they are endowed by their Creator with certain unalienable rights—among them life, liberty, and the pursuit of happiness—that no government can justly deny; the guarantees in their Constitution for freedom of speech, freedom of assembly, and freedom of religion. . . .

> But freedom is more even than this. . . . It is the right to dream—to follow your dream or stick to your conscience, even if you're the only one in a sea of doubters. Freedom is the recognition that no single person, no single authority or government has a monopoly on the truth, but that every individual life is infinitely precious, that every one of us put on this world has been put there for a reason and has something to offer.

Reagan wanted these Soviet students to know something that Americans knew about freedom: "that liberty, just as life itself, is not earned but a gift from God." Americans, Reagan added, "seek to share that gift with the world."[33]

These were words that the Russian students were not accustomed to hearing. To receive their diplomas, all graduates of Moscow State University had to recite a profession of faith to the state.[34] Atheism had long been a mandatory course at the school.

Reagan conveyed to the students the hope he had shared repeatedly in recent weeks: "Today the world looks expectantly to signs of change, steps toward greater freedom in the Soviet Union."

The president ended his speech with these words for the communist faithful: "We do not know what the conclusion will be of this journey, but we're hopeful that the promise of reform will be fulfilled. In this Moscow spring, this May 1988, we may be allowed that hope. . . . Thank you all very much, and *da blagoslovit vas gospod*—God bless you."

A "God bless you" in Russian.

John Paul II would have loved every moment of this speech, having never attained such a platform in Moscow.

Most satisfying, Reagan delivered this faith-and-freedom message in front of a giant marble bust of Lenin. The president later quipped that when the students gave him a standing ovation, he looked at the Lenin statue and saw it weeping.[35]

The students were impressed; so was Gorbachev's translator. "It was a real tour de force," Igor Korchilov said of Reagan's speech. "I think it may have been his finest oratorical hour. . . . It was one of the finest examples of oratory I had ever heard." He compared Reagan to "a real professor," lecturing Russians in what was essentially an American civics lesson.[36]

The civics lesson had ended, but the Sunday school lesson was about to begin.

GIVING VOICE

Reagan returned to Spaso House, where he would host a state dinner for Gorbachev in the Chandelier Room. This was a late night, with the seventy-seven-year-old president not giving his toast until 10 P.M.[37]

Speaking after Reagan, Gorbachev would deliver another long (1,210-word), conventional speech. Reagan's toast was altogether different. In his salute to Gorbachev, the president of the United States spoke mystically of what he called "the voice":

> Mr. General Secretary, . . . I believe . . . we both hear the same voice, the same overwhelming imperative. What that voice says can be expressed in many ways. But I have found it in vivid form in [Boris] Pasternak's poem "The Garden of Gethsemane." Listen, if you will, to Pasternak's account of that famous arrest:
>
> "There appeared—no one knew from where—a crowd of slaves and a rabble of knaves, with lights and swords and, leading them, Judas with a traitor's kiss on his lips.
>
> "Peter repulsed the ruffians with his sword and cut off the ear of one of them. But he heard: 'You cannot decide a dispute with weapons; put your sword in its place, O man.'"
>
> That's the voice. "Put your sword in its place, O man." That is the imperative, the command. And so we will work together that we might forever keep our swords at our sides.[38]

There's a good chance that Gorbachev did not fully comprehend what Reagan was talking about. Yes, Reagan had quoted a Soviet poet and novelist—one whose work the Stalin regime had kept from being published. Yes, Reagan's comment had something to do with Christianity. And yes, it involved putting weapons away for the sake of peace, a point that was germane to their discussions. But Reagan could have easily expressed the ambition for peace without sharing an account from the gospel of Jesus Christ.

"SOMETHING WE'RE NOT USED TO"

The final day of the five-day summit was June 2, a Thursday. It ended with a brief farewell ceremony, held at 10:07 A.M. in Saint George's Hall, the same room in the Grand Kremlin Palace where the Reagans and

Gorbachevs had met on the first day. Reagan would not leave Moscow without delivering another religious message.

Reagan invoked the spirit of Saint George. "Mr. General Secretary," he said to Gorbachev, "it is fitting that we are ending our visit as we began it, in this hall, named for the Order of Saint George. I would like to think that our efforts during these past few days have slayed a few dragons and advanced the struggle against the evils that threaten mankind—threats to peace and to liberty. And I would like to hope that, like Saint George, with God's help, peace and freedom can prevail."

Reagan reminded the Gorbachevs, both the possible "closet Christian" and his atheist wife, that he had arrived on a Sunday—in fact, Trinity Sunday, when Christians celebrate the Holy Trinity (Father, Son, and Holy Spirit). He thus quoted a Russian proverb: *Troitsa: ves' les raskroitsya*. The president spoke it in Russian. What did it mean? "On Trinity Sunday, the whole forest blossoms."

Gorbachev's translator conceded that the Russian saying was totally foreign to the atheist officials present, including Mikhail Gorbachev, who gazed at Reagan with a bemused stare. That was okay with the president. They could think about it. It was now part of the official closing transcript.

For his final benediction, Reagan opted for simpler language he had repeated throughout the trip: "Thank you and God bless you."[39]

Reagan's words had not fallen on deaf ears. Kremlin apparatchiks and common Russian residents alike caught his many religious references.

"I'm not religious," said one Moscow woman, "but I was delighted to hear him [Reagan] end his speeches by saying 'God bless you.' We never heard it said before on television."[40]

Daniil Granin, a Russian novelist whose *Bison* was one of the major books in Russia in 1987, said of Reagan: "One thing pleased me especially—his religiousness. Hearing religious vocabulary from a politician is something we're not used to."[41]

After his final "God bless you," following his affirmation of the Holy Trinity, the president strode away and boarded his airplane. Ronald Reagan's Moscow mission was complete.

34

JUNE 1988

ENDING THE SOVIET "WAR ON RELIGION"

When he returned to the White House, Ronald Reagan seemed pleased with his Moscow trip, even as his State Department preferred he would have shushed about the religion stuff.[1] Back in Washington, the president noted that he had been "dropped into a grand historical moment."[2] And he seized the moment.

Reagan's work in Moscow did not end with the summit. He remained there in spirit. He prayed for the Soviets and urged others to do so. A few weeks after he returned to Washington, Reagan addressed kindred spirits at a Student Congress on Evangelism, where he encouraged his younger Christian brothers and sisters to pray that Gorbachev and the Soviet Union "would soon grant" religious freedoms to the nation's many believers.[3]

That prayer was answered.

Religious faith in the USSR began to flourish. Some changes had already occurred under Gorbachev: the Soviets had released certain religious dissidents from jail or given them amnesty; they had returned a number of buildings to the Russian Orthodox Church; and they had eased restrictions on receiving Bibles from abroad. But now the reforms suddenly accelerated.

Mikhail Gorbachev, unique among Soviet leaders since 1917, called off the seventy-year war on faith.

A NEW ERA

Did Reagan's actions in Moscow and prodding in advance of the trip prompt those changes? Perhaps. They clearly did not hurt.

Many of Gorbachev's changes took place in the spring of 1988, beginning in April and going through June—exactly when Reagan turned up the heat on the religious freedom issue. The president spoke more forcefully, passionately—and publicly—during this period than at any other time. And he often told the Soviets that they could expect agreements with the United States based in part on advances in Soviet religious freedom. Those were agreements that Gorbachev wanted badly.

Consider the timing of the changes.

On April 29, 1988, as Reagan was pushing religious freedom in the lead-up to the Moscow summit, Gorbachev met with the top leaders of the Russian Orthodox Church, including Patriarch Pimen. The seventy-seven-year-old Pimen had headed the Orthodox Church since 1971, leading a flock that numbered as many as 50 million in a country of 280 million people. It was Pimen who would welcome Reagan by proclaiming that "God's heavenly will" brought the president to Moscow.

This Kremlin session marked the first meeting between the Communist Party leadership and Church leadership since World War II, when Stalin momentarily reembraced the Church for the purpose of trying to defeat Hitler. Gorbachev's meeting with Pimen and five members of the Holy Synod was not low-key; it was widely publicized in the Soviet Union, and widely considered historic. In a striking shift in state policy, Gorbachev said that the Church had a role to play in helping effect the changes in society that were top priorities of *perestroika*.[4]

After that meeting and through 1988, Gorbachev gave the green light to reopen hundreds of Orthodox churches, possibly as many as eight hundred that year alone. He also supported the opening of monasteries, including the Danilov Monastery. In a ceremony televised to 150 million viewers on *Vremya*, the main evening newscast, the Kremlin museum returned religious relics to the Church, sacred items that had been seized in the Moscow Church Trials in the 1920s.[5]

In June, while Reagan was still in Moscow, Soviet authorities announced that the state would return the Kiev Pechersk Monastery, one of Russia's oldest and most sacred shrines. The NKVD had closed the eleventh-century monastery in the 1920s; under Khrushchev, the Kremlin had reopened it as a museum. Pechersk was one of the centers from which Christianity spread throughout the region.[6] Now it was free again. Reagan was no doubt thrilled by that news, as were Russian believers.

Just as the Moscow summit was finishing, Gorbachev allowed two weeks of unprecedented commemorations marking the millennium of the Russian Orthodox Church: Prince Vladimir of Kiev had converted his pagan state of Rus' a thousand years earlier, in June 988. These events would kick off a yearlong series of commemorations. Celebrations occurred in three different Soviet cities, including Moscow. Although the general secretary was not present, Raisa Gorbachev participated in the pomp and pageantry that marked the opening ceremonies at Moscow's Bolshoi Theater.[7]

Gorbachev had asked the patriarch of the Russian Orthodox Church to invite representatives of all the world's religions to Moscow for the celebrations. Thus, Patriarch Pimen presided over a special service in the Epiphany Cathedral, where he was joined by hundreds of church leaders representing many different denominations and nations. The attendees included the archbishop of Canterbury, Robert Runcie, and Cardinal Johannes Willebrands, John Paul II's representative from the Vatican.

In a powerful moment, the Orthodox Church canonized nine new saints, the first since the revolution of 1917. The ceremonies included religious services, debates, symposia, press conferences, and exhibits showcasing relics, artifacts, icons, and treasures, drawing huge numbers of both believers and nonbelievers.[8]

This time, the state did not seize relics or melt down bells into more "useful things." To the contrary, the bells rang out across Russia. It was the sound of a new era.

"One of the Most Crucial Decisions at the End of the Cold War"

These celebrations were crucial in another respect: they enabled the Vatican to open a dialogue with Gorbachev.

When, at Gorbachev's behest, the patriarch of the Russian Orthodox Church invited Catholic representatives to Moscow, John Paul II sent not one delegation but two—a "religious delegation" and a "political delegation."[9]

The pope himself could not come, less because of the general secretary of the Soviet Communist Party than because of the steadfast refusal of Patriarch Pimen. The Russian Orthodox Church still jealously guarded its turf. (John Paul II would never get to visit Russia. It was one of his greatest frustrations.)

Heading the pope's political delegation was the Vatican secretary of state, Cardinal Agostino Casaroli. John Paul II also sent a Delegation of the Catholic Episcopate, comprising about a dozen cardinals and bishops from around the world, including the communist countries of Poland, Latvia, Vietnam, and Hungary. Recognizing the significance of this opportunity, representatives of the Holy See worked hard to ensure that Moscow did not rescind the invitation at the last moment.[10]

Vatican officials would later call John Paul II's move to send these delegations "one of the most crucial decisions at the end of the Cold War."[11] It is difficult to argue with that. Here is why.

At the last minute, Gorbachev and his foreign minister, Eduard Shevardnadze, received Cardinal Casaroli's delegation in the Kremlin. At the meeting, Casaroli handed Gorbachev a letter from the pontiff, as well as a memorandum the pope wrote laying out what he perceived as the major problems in Vatican-Soviet relations.[12] The Soviet leader read the letter and the accompanying memorandum on the spot.

The contents of the letter were not made public at the time, but George Weigel later published it in *Witness to Hope*. Dated June 7, 1988, the letter was addressed to "His Excellency, Mr. Mikhail Gorbachev." The pope adopted a personal tone, beginning nearly every paragraph with "I." After opening with a statement of the Catholic Church's "great respect and affection" for the "great spiritual patrimony" of the Eastern Slav peoples, the Holy Father expressed his "relief" and appreciation for the INF Treaty that Gorbachev and Reagan had signed several months earlier, on the Feast Day of the Immaculate Conception.[13]

The pope continued, "With great attention I have noticed the announcement you have made that a new law on freedom of conscience will soon be passed." This step would take some time—the Supreme Soviet did not pass the law for another two years—but it would be momentous: the measure pledged that the government would not "restrict the study, financing or propagandizing" of religion.[14]

John Paul II said he was convinced that "your work, Mr. General Secretary, has created great expectations and legitimate hope on the part of believers." He also expressed hope that the Holy See and the Soviet government could establish "direct contact" with each other.

The pope's June 7 letter to Gorbachev finished: "I wish peace and prosperity to you and to all the peoples of the Soviet Union, to whom go my esteem and very cordial thoughts. Please accept, Mr. General Secretary, the expression of my highest consideration."

Gorbachev was quite pleased with this "friendly message," as he later described it.[15] Weigel called it a "historic letter," one that began a conversation inconceivable three years earlier.[16] It begged—no *required*—a Soviet response, and a positive one. In all, the Vatican viewed the Soviet initiation (and subsequent response) as a "signal" that Moscow desired a dialogue.[17]

The Vatican officials discovered other interesting information during their Kremlin visit. Both Gorbachev and Shevardnadze emphasized that they had been baptized at birth.[18] Gorbachev went further. He told Casaroli that his mother, Maria, was a deaconess in the Russian Orthodox Church. When they were alone in their cottage in Privolnoye, he said, she would surreptitiously remove an icon from the wall or mantel and bless him with it.[19]

When Casaroli reported all this to the pontiff, John Paul II was impressed.[20]

The pope must have been even more impressed when Gorbachev, the next month, went to Poland for a four-day visit. The general secretary ventured to Kraków and met with Karol Wojtyła's spiritual children, the Polish youth, whom he implored not to "miss the *perestroika* train." The capstone of the trip—at least in the pontiff's eye—came when Gorbachev strolled into Saint Mary's Church, where auxiliary Bishop Jan Szkoden showed him the renowned large wooden triptych from the late Gothic period.[21] The pontiff must have been touched by this, or at the least interpreted it as a signal of goodwill.

AN "UNQUALIFIED RIGHT" TO WORSHIP

While Reagan was in Moscow, Soviet authorities provided an important concession on what had long been a vexing faith issue. They permitted the Russian Orthodox Church and Roman Catholic Church to open talks in Finland to clarify the status of the Ukrainian Catholic Church.

After World War II, Stalin had ordered Ukrainian Catholics to merge with the Russian Orthodox Church, which was a serious blow to the freedom of millions of Ukrainian Catholics.[22] This, too, had attracted Reagan's special concern.

Many more changes took place. Russian Orthodox parishes kept opening at a furious pace; the expansion was so rapid that there were not enough priests to fill the parishes. Church leaders could, for the first time, minister to hospitals, run publications, appear on radio and television, and even run for office.[23]

Things were not perfect. Many more churches remained shut or were monitored by the government—as were many officials in the Russian Orthodox Church, which the KGB had penetrated. Many laws restricting religious freedom were still on the books. Oxford's Keston Institute, which monitored religious freedom in Russia, argued that Ukrainian Catholics were receiving less freedom than Orthodox believers because they were not as nationalistic.

Ronald Reagan understood that the veil of repression had not completely lifted. Nonetheless, things were far better.

To return to the earlier question: did the American president's pressure play a role in the changes? Gorbachev has never told us whether Reagan was a motivation in his actions. His religious liberalization was at least partly an extension of the general improvement that *glasnost* ushered in.

Reagan later seemed to suggest that he believed his moves in Moscow had made a difference. In his memoirs, published nearly two years after his presidency ended (and after Gorbachev had been elected the first president of the Soviet Union), Reagan recalled how he had consistently linked U.S.-Soviet agreements to Soviet improvement in human rights, and particularly religious freedom. He said he was "ready" at the Moscow summit when Gorbachev mentioned "his desire for increased U.S.-Soviet trade." Reagan wrote, "I'd thought about what I was going to say when he brought up the issue: One reason we have trouble increasing trade with your country, I said, was that many members of Congress as well as many other Americans oppose it because of what they consider Soviet human rights abuses." He added that he "raised an issue that had been on my mind for a long time: religious freedom in the Soviet Union." Knowing that this was a subject that easily angered Gorbachev, Reagan handled it diplomatically, telling the general secretary: "This isn't something I'm suggesting we negotiate, just an idea. I'm not trying to tell you how to run your country, but I realize you are probably concerned that if you allow too many of the Jews who want to emigrate from the Soviet Union to leave, there'll be a 'brain drain,' a loss of skilled people from your economy." The president then asked Gorbachev, "Did it ever occur to you, on this whole question of human rights, that maybe if the Jews were permitted to worship as they want to and teach their children the Hebrew language, that maybe they wouldn't want to leave the Soviet Union?"[24]

Reagan wrote, "Whether my words had any impact or not, I don't know, but after that the Soviet government began allowing more churches and synagogues to reopen."[25]

It seems clear that Reagan's words and actions influenced religious change in the USSR. The president found a willing partner in Gorbachev, who had learned religious toleration early on from his atheist-communist grandfather.[26] In a memoir published in 2000, Gorbachev stated that under *glasnost* and *perestroika* he led the Soviet Union on "a firm course" toward "freedom of conscience," based on his "belief that religious people are worthy of respect." He added, "Religious faith is an intensely private matter, and each citizen should have the unqualified right to his or her own choice."[27]

FREEDOM GAINED

In the end, who gets credit for religious freedom in Russia is less important than the freedom so many gained. Ronald Reagan, from his governorship to his presidency, kept a sign on his desk that read, "There is no limit to what a man can do or where he can go if he doesn't mind who gets the credit." It was a philosophy that served Reagan well in his public life and his plans for a better world.

This much we know for certain: A seventy-year "war on religion" (in Mikhail Gorbachev's apt phrase), orchestrated by what had been an "Evil Empire" (in Ronald Reagan's apt phrase), ended peacefully under the leadership of Gorbachev and Reagan. The religious repression was finally over. The bells could ring once again.

35

1989–1991

THE COLLAPSE OF THE EVIL EMPIRE

Anyone who witnessed the events of November 9, 1989, will not soon forget them. That day, East Germans confidently ascended the Berlin Wall that had separated them from their brethren for three decades. To have done so on any previous day since August 13, 1961, would have been unthinkable: East German guards would have shot them on the spot. But this time, those who scaled the wall were safe. That was because communist authorities for the first time had permitted the free flow of people through East German border crossings. And the Berlin Wall came tumbling down.

November 9, 1989, did not simply mark the fall of the Berlin Wall. Given that the wall was a physical barrier closing off the communist world, it was a manifestation of the Iron Curtain—a concrete-and-barbed-wire curtain. Thus, its collapse that day symbolized the collapse of the Iron Curtain. Communist regimes throughout the Eastern Bloc would soon fall—as would, eventually, the Soviet Union itself.[1]

RONALD REAGAN'S "BEST FRIEND"

Ronald Reagan was simply thrilled with the events of November 9, 1989. He had been calling for the fall of the Berlin Wall for decades. His first public statement to that effect came in his high-profile 1967 debate with Robert F. Kennedy. Most famously, he had called on Gorbachev to "tear down this wall" two years earlier at the Brandenburg Gate.

Now, the wall had fallen, less than a year after Reagan left the presidency. He could kick back and watch the fall of the Berlin Wall, and of the wider Communist Bloc, with delight.

Just before he left the Oval Office, Reagan had met with Natan Sharansky, the Russian Jew who had first read Reagan's warnings of an "Evil Empire" from a Soviet prison camp. Sharansky was inspired that "the leader of the free world had spoken the truth"—and he spread news of Reagan's statement through Permanent Labor Camp 35 by tapping the message on the walls of his prison cell. Then, in 1986, Sharansky was among the political prisoners Mikhail Gorbachev released—after Reagan and his administration had applied intense pressure. By January 1989, Sharansky was a guest at the White House, where President Reagan presented him with a Congressional Gold Medal. During the ceremony, Sharansky told Reagan, who would leave office just nine days later, that if he was ever saddled by any "sad moments," he should think about Sharansky's "happy family" and of all the people "who are free today not because of some good will of Soviet leaders but because of their struggle and your struggle."[2]

By the spring of 1989, something astounding was unfolding in Karol Wojtyła's Poland. On April 4, after two months of negotiations with Solidarity and other opposition groups, Poland's Communist Party countenanced something that was once inconceivable: free and fair parliamentary elections. The agreement abolished the position of general secretary in favor of a president, officially recognized Solidarity as a political party, and created a new upper chamber of the legislature to which all one hundred seats would be put up for open election. The elections were scheduled for June 4, nearly a half century after Stalin had promised free and fair elections in Poland and FDR had put faith in the assurances of "Uncle Joe."

In effect, this Polish agreement marked the death of Warsaw's communist regime.

As Poland's June elections approached, Ronald Reagan, enjoying retirement in California, welcomed some Polish visitors at his Century

City office near Hollywood. Chris Zawitkowski, an ethnic Pole who, after the Cold War's end, became head of the Polish-American Foundation for Economic Research and Education, brought along another Polish American and two Solidarity members who had come a long distance to meet their presidential hero. They came to express their gratitude and to ask for some advice. Zawitkowski asked Reagan, the master campaigner, whether he had any words of wisdom for the two Solidarity members as they readied for the June elections.[3]

No doubt these gentlemen expected Reagan, who had won landslide political victories first in California as governor and then for the presidency of the United States, to give political advice. Reagan, however, looked higher in answering their question. In a John Paul II–like affirmation, Reagan counseled the Polish campaigners, "Listen to your conscience, because that is where the Holy Spirit speaks to you."

The men nodded in appreciation, if not surprise.

In another unexpected move, the former president pointed to a picture of Pope John Paul II that hung on his office wall. "He is my best friend," Reagan told the Poles. "Yes, you know I'm Protestant, but he's still my best friend."

Ronald Reagan's *best friend*—Pope John Paul II.

One of Reagan's guests, Solidarity member Antoni Macierewicz, offered the former president a gift. Like many of his Polish brothers, Macierewicz once had been thrown in jail by the communists. While there, he busied himself with carving a special Madonna. The persecuted Solidarity member wanted Reagan to have the image of the Mother of Christ that he had carved under duress imposed by evildoers.

Reagan accepted. He held the Madonna in his hands and said that he and Nancy would be proud to have her in their home.

Reagan was likewise proud of what the Solidarity men and their colleagues achieved once they got back to Poland. In the June 4 elections, Solidarity candidates claimed every one of the roughly one-third of seats in the lower chamber of the legislature that the communists opened to balloting. And in the newly created upper chamber, Solidarity claimed ninety-nine of the one hundred new seats.

In short, Solidarity won more than 99 percent of available legislative seats.[4] Communists did not claim a single seat.

In December 1990, Lech Wałęsa put a capstone on the victory over communism by emerging as Poland's freely elected president. Wałęsa refused to form a coalition government with the remaining Communist Party delegates in the old chamber. Eventually, parliament accepted a

Solidarity-led government. Macierewicz, the former prisoner, became Poland's minister of internal affairs.

Wałęsa led Poland's transition to a free society and free economy.

Those elections in June 1989 had repercussions far beyond Poland. Mikhail Gorbachev later said that once Poland held those elections, he knew the communist game was over. He had grasped that the emergence of Solidarity threatened not only "chaos in Poland" but also the "ensuing break-up of the entire Socialist camp."[5] Other members of the Soviet leadership became convinced that Solidarity's massive victories in Poland signaled that the Soviet system would break up.[6]

Both Ronald Reagan and John Paul II had seen Poland as "the linchpin in the dissolution of the Soviet empire" (in Bill Clark's words). They were right. The dissolution began in Karol Wojtyła's Poland, months before the Berlin Wall fell.

The Pope Meets Gorbachev

John Paul II was enjoying this as much as Ronald Reagan was. But for the pontiff, there was no retirement from his post, no term limits. The chair of Saint Peter was his until death. And he seemed to pick up the mantle from Reagan in directly dealing with Gorbachev. Reagan's summits with the Soviet leader were over, but for John Paul II, it was time for a first personal summit.

On December 1, 1989, three weeks after the Berlin Wall came down, the world witnessed a shocking sight: a Soviet leader at the Vatican smiling and shaking hands with a pope. Mikhail Gorbachev came to Rome to meet with Pope John Paul II. It was the first-ever encounter between a pope and a Soviet leader. Stalin or Lenin would have shaken hands with a pope only when hell froze over.

It had been a year and a half since John Paul II's political delegation to the Soviet Union handed Gorbachev a personal letter from the pope, which the general secretary read on the spot. That meeting had started a dialogue. In August 1989, a Soviet emissary came to Castel Gandolfo to hand the pope a letter from Gorbachev. This seven-page missive, not publicly released at the time, revealed Gorbachev's knowledge of John Paul II's writings. "I know what you have written," the Soviet general secretary stated. He praised the pontiff's "personal attitude and activities" and "positive contribution to international life." In a statement that surely affected the Polish pope, Gorbachev asserted, "I think that, for the first time since the great world tragedy which hit humanity a half-century ago—and of which your homeland, Poland, was the first victim—the world seems to have renewed hope." He also appealed to the pope by referencing the new Soviet law on freedom of conscience, "which is presently in the phase of preparation." He hinted at establishing diplomatic relations, "a new level in the relations between the Soviet Union and the Vatican." The general secretary concluded with this historic olive branch: "We must meet."[7]

In early September, two months before the fall of the Berlin Wall, the Soviet official in Rome announced that Gorbachev and John Paul II would meet when the Soviet leader headed to Malta for his first summit with the new American president, George H. W. Bush.[8]

The meeting came to pass on December 1. The *New York Times* captured the moment this way: "For the first time ever, the leader of atheistic Soviet Communism meets the Vicar of Christ."[9]

When Gorbachev met the pope at the Vatican's Apostolic Palace, he appeared uncomfortable. Many observers thought that he looked overwhelmed, in awe amid the majesty of the moment and the place. Years later he would describe it as a "beautiful atmosphere."[10]

The two men met in the library, taking opposite sides of a wooden desk. For the first five minutes they were alone and spoke in Russian. After that, interpreters entered, with the pontiff alternating between Polish and Italian, while Gorbachev continued speaking in Russian. The meeting would last about an hour and fifteen minutes.[11]

Twenty years later the Russian government released a transcript of what the two said with the translators present.[12] The transcript runs more than 3,600 words in length. The Soviet leader did most of the talking.

Gorbachev began by expressing his appreciation for this "meeting of two Slavic people," and by thanking the pontiff for his "peace-making efforts." The pope humbly replied, "We are trying." He thanked Gorbachev for his own efforts at peace.

John Paul II made many references to "fundamental human rights," including "freedom of conscience, from which stems religious freedom." He used the word *conscience* seven times in the dialogue. He also affirmed an individual's freedom of choice: "A person becomes a believer through free choice; it is impossible to make someone believe." He added, "Of course, freedom of conscience has to extend to Baptists, Protestants, Jews, as well as Muslims."

Gorbachev seemed to agree. He told the pope, "I have listened to your words very carefully and from my side would like to speak about three concerns: peace, our *perestroika*, and in connection to it the freedom of conscience and religion."

But Gorbachev veered off into a discourse on moral relativism, as he often had with Reagan. He instructed the pope that no one can make any claim to absolute truth, which the pontiff would have disagreed with heartily (as did Reagan). Gorbachev said, "One must not claim to have the absolute truth and to try to impose it on others." John Paul II would have agreed with the second part, that "to impose" was wrong.

Gorbachev referred to "the framework of our general understanding of universal human values," but he quickly added that "everything depends on the choice of the people," that "it is up to the person what philosophy and religion to practice." The pope had already made the point that religious belief is a matter of free choice. The Soviet leader was making a different point, however. "Let each side remain itself while respecting the traditions of the other side," Gorbachev said. "Universal human values should become the primary goal, while the choice of this or that political system should be left up to the people."

Gorbachev's moral philosophizing left much to be desired—as John Paul II, a former professor of moral philosophy, surely recognized. Consider the obvious question that Gorbachev's claim raised: what if one's side was the tradition of authoritarianism, or totalitarianism, or if "the people" chose a political system or certain policies that repressed other people or denied them their inherent dignity?

Gorbachev's meandering discourse in this area carried on at length. The pope got in merely a three-word interruption before the Soviet leader went on. The pontiff must have sensed that this was not the time for a tutorial.

Gorbachev finally changed the subject to something the pope would have appreciated much more: "I would also like to say that the problems of your homeland—Poland—are very close to me," the Soviet leader said. "In the recent years I have done and will continue to do everything I can to ensure good relations between Poland, Russia, and the Soviet Union." John Paul II responded, "I thank you on behalf of my homeland."

The Soviet leader moved to more practical matters—and took an important step forward—when he said, "I hope that after this meeting our relations will gain new momentum and I assume that at some point in the future you could visit the USSR."

This was a major offer. No pope had ever set foot in Moscow.

John Paul II did not miss a beat. "If this were allowed," he replied, "I would be very glad to."

Note his carefully stated response. Who needed to allow the visit? Not only the Kremlin but also the leadership of the Russian Orthodox Church. The latter would turn out to be the obstacle.

As the conversation came to a close, John Paul II once again thanked Gorbachev for the invitation to Moscow, saying, "I can well appreciate its weight and importance." Gorbachev responded by thanking the pope "for the atmosphere and content of today's conversation," then added, "I will count on this dialogue to continue."

At the end of their meeting, as they left the library, the two men connected with Raisa Gorbachev, the general secretary's hard-core Marxist-Leninist wife. Gorbachev, now much more relaxed, said to his wife with a grin, "Raisa, I introduce you to His Holiness Pope John Paul II, who is the highest moral authority on Earth, besides being a fellow Slav like us." The pontiff affably replied, "Yes, I'm the first Slav pope." He added, "I'm sure that Providence paved the way for this meeting."[13]

When the two men spoke to the press, John Paul II seemed to sense the great spiritual-political import at hand. George Weigel described the pope's hands as "trembling with emotion" when he came to the podium to speak.[14] Others noticed his shaky hands. This was not, one assumes, an early onset of Parkinson's disease. Rather, the Holy Father seemed overcome by this moment.

When Gorbachev spoke, the leader of the atheistic communist empire repeatedly referred to the pontiff as "Holy Father" and "Your Holiness."[15] As author John Koehler said, "It was an astonishing compliment, indeed, by a man who once had been one of the signers of an order to the KGB calling for the pope's 'physical elimination, if necessary.'"[16]

Gorbachev told the press, "A truly extraordinary event has taken place, made possible by the profound changes that are taking place in many countries and nations."[17] In his post–Cold War memoirs, he again called the meeting "an extraordinary event." Gorbachev wrote that after his visit to the Vatican, his contacts with the Holy Father "intensified," and his regime "repeatedly exchanged views with the Holy See." He added, "His Holiness sent me messages of support and understanding in my most difficult hours."[18]

Yes, Pope John Paul II and General Secretary Mikhail Gorbachev made history on December 1, 1989. One especially impressed with this meeting was Sister Lúcia, who seven decades earlier had reported Our Lady of Fátima's warning about the errors of atheistic communism. The hand of God, the aging Carmelite nun said, "has even moved one of the main leaders of atheistic communism to travel to Rome to meet with the Holy Father and...acknowledge him as God's highest representative...to receive the embrace of peace and ask forgiveness for the mistakes of his party."[19]

To say that Gorbachev had come asking for forgiveness for the Communist Party was probably overstating things, but as Weigel wrote, the December 1 meeting was "symbolically" a moment of surrender. The communist war against Karol Wojtyła and his people, waged for decades, was over.[20]

Perhaps this was why the pope's hands trembled.

EMBRACING THE INEVITABLE

In Warsaw, Berlin, and Rome, a series of inconceivable events had occurred in 1989. Then, on February 7, 1990, the unthinkable happened again, this time in Moscow: the Community Party's monopoly ended in the USSR.

That day, the Communist Party Central Committee agreed to Gorbachev's proposal to strike Article 6 from the Soviet constitution. That article had guaranteed the Communist Party's iron grip on power for more than seventy years. The party leadership also accepted the plan for a Western-style cabinet system and presidency. General Secretary Gorbachev would become President Gorbachev.[21]

Gorbachev and a key group of reformers were responsible for a political earthquake.

Of course, that earthquake may never have come about, and certainly not as early as it did, were it not for the efforts of Ronald Reagan and John Paul II, and the forces they had helped set in motion.

Reagan had been calling for political pluralism in the USSR long before Gorbachev made it happen. Eight years earlier, in May 1982, Reagan signed NSDD-32, the document Bill Clark's NSC had prepared that formally set the goal of "encourag[ing] long-term liberalizing and nationalist tendencies within the Soviet Union and allied countries." In the spirit of that directive, in June 1982, NSC member Tom Reed publicly expressed the Reagan administration's "fondest hope" to "one day convince the leadership of the USSR to...seek the legitimacy that comes only from the consent of the governed."[22] That same month, in his Westminster Address, President Reagan proposed to "foster the infrastructure of democracy." The Reagan administration went further with its crucial January 1983 NSDD-75, another directive written by Clark's

NSC. NSDD-75 advocated "the process of change in the Soviet Union [and Eastern Europe] toward a more pluralistic political and economic system." The Reagan administration issued these directives two to three years before Gorbachev even became general secretary.

Gorbachev faced other pressures as well. Inside the USSR, Boris Yeltsin (the future president of Russia) and other reformers prodded the Soviet leader to make changes. And freedom movements were spreading from Poland throughout Eastern Europe.

Alexander Yakovlev, the Politburo member and Gorbachev confidant who ultimately pushed the February 1990 reform, apparently proposed some form of political pluralism as early as 1985, Gorbachev's first year in office. Gorbachev at least contemplated the idea at the time. But Anatoly Chernyaev, Gorbachev's foreign-affairs assistant from 1986 to 1991, reports that not until 1990 did Gorbachev decide finally to eliminate the Communist Party's infallible status.[23]

Gorbachev biographer Archie Brown, an Oxford scholar, is perhaps the West's leading authority on the general secretary. Brown offers a highly favorable treatment of Gorbachev, but he concedes that "it was no part of Gorbachev's initial conception to introduce a fully-fledged political pluralism in which the Communist Party would become just one party competing with others."[24]

Brown also points to the potent influence of the democratic and independence movements that had swept through Eastern Europe—all of which Reagan and John Paul II had supported and even catalyzed, especially in Berlin and Poland. The Berlin Wall had fallen; in Czechoslovakia the Velvet Revolution had peacefully ended four decades of Communist Party rule; in Bulgaria the communist dictator Todor Zhivkov had fallen and the Communist Party had ceded its monopoly; in Romania the people had overthrown the longtime communist dictator Nicolae Ceaușescu; in Yugoslavia the Communist Party had effectively dissolved.

Was Gorbachev somehow going to buck these historical forces? As Brown notes, once those forces arose, and as Gorbachev began freeing up things in the USSR and making qualified statements on democracy, the concept of pluralism—like *glasnost* and the other freedoms it spawned—took on a life of its own. Gorbachev eventually embraced what was inevitable, what was natural, and what was right.[25]

He did so, he insists to this day, to try to preserve the Soviet Union. But by ending the Communist Party monopoly on power, Gorbachev was, whether he knew it or not, edging the Evil Empire closer to its tomb.

Ronald Reagan did know it. On December 5, 1990, a year after the Berlin Wall fell, Reagan spoke in Cambridge, England, where he demonstrated a shrewd understanding of what Gorbachev's taste of freedom would bring. "As is always the case," said Reagan, "once people who have been deprived of basic freedom taste a little of it, they want all of it. It was as if Gorbachev had uncorked a magic bottle and a genie floated out, never to be put back in again. *Glasnost* was that genie."[26] Reagan said this a full year before Gorbachev's resignation and the official dissolution of the Soviet Union.

Soon everything was collapsing around Gorbachev.[27] Gorbachev's chief of staff, Valery Boldin, later wrote of the Soviet leader, "Attempting to change society, he unintentionally destroyed [our] statehood."[28]

Of course, that unintended outcome was a beautiful outcome. We can debate the extent to which Mikhail Gorbachev deserves credit for the result, but it is undeniable that he was the leader who finally made political pluralism happen in the USSR. Ronald Reagan, for all he did to help create the conditions in which such pluralism could even be considered, did not hold the political power in Moscow to make the historic change to the Soviet constitution that Gorbachev pushed through.[29] Even Boris Yeltsin didn't. It was Gorbachev who ended the Communist Party's monopoly after so many decades, and he did so without a shot fired, without a purge or a show trial, without putting any dissenter in jail.

JOYOUS CHANGES

The Soviet action on February 7 must have thrilled Ronald Reagan and Pope John Paul II. It was no doubt an answer to a prayer. An awful apparatus that had so viciously persecuted millions of believers, from Cardinal Stepinac to Pope Pius XII to Cardinal Mindszenty to countless others unknown to history, was finally stripped of its enshrined power.

This change came as the Vatican and the communist world were building new bridges.

On February 6, the day before the Soviet leadership ended the Communist Party's monopoly, John Paul II made a significant move, appointing Ján Chryzostom Korec, a Jesuit, as bishop of Nitra in the Slovak portion of Czechoslovakia.[30] Named after Saint John Chrysostom, an early Church father, Korec had a story not unlike Mindszenty's or Stepinac's: persecuted by communists, Korec was shipped in and out of prison. Whereas Mindszenty was momentarily freed during Hungary's

1956 revolution, Korec was momentarily freed during the 1968 Prague Spring, another uprising that Moscow suppressed. Mindszenty at least was able to take refuge in the U.S. embassy. Korec was sent back to jail. After intense international protest, he was released, but still monitored by communist authorities. He worked underground, disobeying communists and clandestinely ordaining priests. Like Mindszenty, he was ultimately stopped not by communist persecution but by the cowardice of Pope Paul VI's *Ostpolitik*. The pope asked Korec to cease his underground work, and the priest loyally obeyed his pontiff. Just as in Hungary, silencing the brave priest did no good: the Church continued to be repressed.

When you handed the communists an olive branch, they snapped it in half.

Now, after the Velvet Revolution, Korec's suffering was over. Pope John Paul II understood the evil that Korec had faced down and rewarded him by elevating him to bishop.

Pope Paul VI would have shuddered at the possible Soviet backlash. John Paul II never did. And clearly, the situation had changed in Moscow. No slap-down came from the Kremlin. Quite the contrary, the very next day the Soviet general secretary undermined the Soviet Communist Party. John Paul II's willingness to proceed unafraid was again rewarded.

Then, on February 9, the Vatican formally reestablished diplomatic relations with Hungary. Hungary thus became the second Soviet Bloc nation to resume formal dealings with the Holy See, following Poland the previous summer. Immediately after the signing ceremony in Budapest, the Vatican secretary of state, Cardinal Casaroli, told the press that he envisioned no obstacles to restoring relations with other countries in the rapidly disintegrating Warsaw Pact.[31]

Casaroli and his pope were impressed with steps Hungarian officials had taken to restore the reputation of Cardinal Mindszenty, who died fifteen years earlier. Casaroli attended a ceremony in Budapest in which Hungary's acting president, Mátyás Szűrös, described Mindszenty as a victim of injustice and a patriot, stating that the late churchman "should now get his just place in the history of our nation."[32]

That included a physical place. Mindszenty's remains still were outside the country. It had been his dying wish that they be brought home. John Paul II wrote a letter to Hungarian cardinal László Paskai in which he made clear that he had not forgotten that Mindszenty "wore the crown of thorns."[33] Then the pope announced that he was planning a trip to Hungary the next year. In 1991, after Hungary held free elections, the democratically elected government would repatriate the cardinal's remains and rebury Mindszenty in Esztergom.[34]

More joyous changes came during that historic late winter and early spring of 1990. On March 14, John Paul II named twelve new bishops (seven for the Latin rite Church and five for the Greek Catholic Church) to Romania, the surest sign that Ceaușescu (executed the previous Christmas) was dead and buried.[35]

Then, on March 15, the Roman Catholic Church and the Soviet Union reestablished full diplomatic relations for the first time since 1923.[36]

Another stunning change occurred in Czechoslovakia. Václav Havel, the persecuted dissident playwright who did hard jail time under the communists, had been elected president of Czechoslovakia at the end of 1989. It was an amazing turnabout. On April 21, 1990, when he welcomed Pope John Paul II to his country, Havel did not hesitate to describe the turn of events as miraculous: "I am not sure that I know what a miracle is. In spite of this, I dare say that, at this moment, I am participating in a miracle: the man who six months ago was arrested as an enemy of the State stands here today as the President of the State, and bids welcome to the first Pontiff in the history of the Catholic Church to set foot in this land."[37]

The playwright continued the refrain as he honored John Paul II:

> I am not sure that I know what a miracle is. In spite of this, I dare say that at this moment I am participating in a miracle: in a country devastated by the ideology of hatred, the messenger of love has arrived; in a country devastated by the government of the ignorant, the living symbol of culture has arrived; in a country that, until a short time ago, was devastated by the idea of confrontation and division in the world, the messenger of peace, dialogue, mutual tolerance, esteem and calm understanding, the messenger of fraternal unity in diversity has arrived. During these long decades, the Spirit was banished from our country. I have the honor of witnessing the moment in which its soil is kissed by the apostle of spirituality.

It was a time of miracles.

THE FINAL MEETING

More than a decade earlier, Ronald Reagan had identified John Paul II as "the key." Eight years earlier, the two leaders had met in the Vatican and confided their belief that their lives had been spared for the purpose of ending Soviet communism. Now, as that atheistic communist empire collapsed, Reagan had the opportunity to reconvene with the pope.

Reporters at the time, and historians since, missed this meeting almost completely.

In September 1990 the former president made a victory lap of sorts, a trip to the former communist world to which he and Pope John Paul II had helped bring liberty.

Reagan embarked on a ten-day, four-country European tour. Fittingly, the trip started at the Berlin Wall. Cameras captured the former president with a hammer in hand, smashing the symbol of cold, dead atheistic communism. "It feels great," he told reporters. "It'll feel better when it's all down." He added: "I don't think you can overstate the importance of it. I was trying to do everything I could for such things as this."[38]

Most press coverage of Reagan's European trip was confined to his visit to the Berlin Wall. As a result, the cameras and microphones were absent for what was perhaps an even more powerful encounter: Reagan's visit with John Paul II at Castel Gandolfo.

This fifth meeting between Reagan and the pope was the first with Reagan out of power. It was a friendly and personal visit, not a state visit. Even the Italian media largely ignored the former president's appearance in Rome.[39] *USA Today* was one of the only Western sources to bother reporting on the meeting, and it ran only these three sentences about the session: "Former president Ronald Reagan and his wife, Nancy, finished up their European tour by visiting with Pope John Paul II at the papal summer palace outside Rome. The pope ended the 30-minute meeting with the words 'God bless America,' the Vatican said. No other details were released."[40] A UPI report added this: "Vatican sources said Reagan probably told the pope of his favorable impressions of changes in the Soviet Union."[41]

That was pretty much the extent of Western media coverage. But two decades later, in August 2012, I interviewed one of the people who went on the trip with the Reagans, Joanne Drake, the longtime personal aide to Mrs. Reagan. Via Drake, I also asked Mrs. Reagan about the visit with the pope. Drake and Mrs. Reagan remembered that the meeting, which only the Reagans and Pope John Paul II attended, took place at 11 A.M. on September 20, 1990, at Castel Gandolfo and lasted about an hour. Mrs. Reagan recalled it as "a warm and wonderful meeting."[42]

The Reagans had just come from Berlin, Warsaw, Gdańsk, Leningrad, and Moscow, conferring with Lech Wałęsa and the Gorbachevs, among others. I asked Mrs. Reagan whether her husband and the pontiff celebrated the collapse of communism and all that had transpired over the past year. She recalled that they "did discuss all of these people and places with the pope," but more than two decades later, she simply could not recollect significant details beyond the fact that this was a warm, personal, friendly conversation. She reiterated that she had only happy memories of all their meetings and relationship. Mrs. Reagan had actually met twice with John Paul II without her husband: in Rome in early May 1985 (she was touring Europe while President Reagan was back at the White House) and then in California in September 1987, during the pontiff's U.S. tour.[43]

This fifth meeting between Reagan and John Paul II would turn out to be their last. It is a shame that virtually nothing is known or recorded of this meeting, aside from Vatican notes that will remain sealed until 2065. We know from Mrs. Reagan that they did discuss the blessed events that had occurred in Europe over the past year. Surely these two men—Ronald Reagan and his "best friend"—acknowledged and thanked God for all that had happened since they took bullets more than nine years earlier.

This must have been a poignant moment. If only we knew more, and if only they knew it would be the last time they would see each other.

BACK TO FÁTIMA

Eight months after Reagan paid his respects to the death of communism at the Berlin Wall, John Paul II paid his at Fátima. As he prepared for this visit, scheduled for May 10–13, 1991, there was growing hope that the pontiff would reveal the Third Secret of Fátima, still sealed in a vault at the Vatican.

While in Fátima, John Paul II spent more time with the Blessed Mother and also with the little girl who had seen her there seventy-four years earlier, Sister Lúcia.[44] Lúcia, by this point, had spent more than forty years in a convent in Coimbra, Portugal. She would spend the remainder of her life there, though she did return to the Fátima site several times, including three occasions when she met with Pope John Paul II.

John Paul II's 1991 visit to Fátima came on the tenth anniversary of his shooting. On May 12, prior to a candlelight prayer vigil, the pope kneeled for nearly ten minutes in complete silence before a statue of Our Lady of Fátima, a move that left many of the assembled speechless (and left the TV commentators with no words to air). When the pontiff spoke, he paid homage to the "redemption of mankind through the intercession and with the help of her whose virginal feet have always and will continue to crush the head of the ancient serpent." He invoked the March 1984 Act of Consecration for the first time in Fátima and said: "Hail, Holy Mother! Hail, sure hope which never disappoints! *Totus tuus*, O Mother! Thank you, heavenly Mother, for having guided people to freedom with your motherly affection."[45]

The pontiff also looking forward, foreseeing new dangers. Pleading to the Blessed Mother on behalf of "new conditions of peoples and the Church," he said prophetically, "There is the danger of replacing Marxism with another form of atheism which, praising freedom, tends to destroy the roots of human and Christian morality." He urged Europe, from the free West to the recently freed East, that it could not reclaim its "true identity" without discovering and recovering its common Christian roots.[46] It was a battle he would wage until the end of his life, as the forces of secular progressivism did everything from committing millions of abortions in the name of "freedom" to banishing God from the new constitution of the European Union.[47]

When the pope returned to Rome from Fátima, he told a group of pilgrims in his May 15 general audience that he considered the past decade of his life to have been a *dono gratuito*, a "free gift," one granted in a "special way by Divine Providence."[48]

GORBACHEV'S LAST STAND

As Ronald Reagan and John Paul II celebrated the new freedoms coming to the former Soviet Bloc, Mikhail Gorbachev was fighting for his political survival as the last leader of a dying Soviet Union.

Throughout 1991, Gorbachev was a study in contradiction. One day he acted like a democrat, and the next day he would speak like a diehard Marxist-Leninist—or even order the use of lethal force (including chemical gas) against democracy seekers in Latvia or Lithuania.[49] He would hail communism and then denounce it. In January 1991 he declared: "I am not ashamed to say anywhere in public that I am a communist and believe in the socialist idea. I will die believing this and will pass into the next world believing this."[50] Such a blunt statement may have surprised his many admirers in the West. But Gorbachev was never the liberal, Western-style reformer some made him out to be. *Time* magazine was closer to the truth back in 1988: "When he [Gorbachev] speaks of 'democracy,' as he incessantly does, he does not mean anything Thomas Jefferson would have recognized; he promotes freer discussion within the Communist Party only as a substitute for the political opposition he makes clear he will not tolerate."[51]

And yet, toward the very end, Gorbachev seemed to understand that his final showdown was with the forces of stalwart communism. By the summer of 1991, he was calling out the disciples of Marx and Lenin. An example came at the July 25–26 plenary session of the Soviet Central Committee, where Gorbachev derided "communist fundamentalism" and said that in the Soviet Union the writings of Marxism-Leninism had been turned into "a collection of canonical texts."[52]

They had indeed. The writings of Karl Marx and Vladimir Lenin were accorded a sacred status. (Gorbachev himself had been guilty of Lenin veneration.)[53] Ronald Reagan had called Marxism-Leninism "that religion of theirs."[54]

Soviet hard-line communists were not pleased with what Gorbachev was doing. One of them, Oleg Baklanov, Central Committee secretary for the defense industry, compared Gorbachev's approach to foreign policy (meaning to the United States) with Stalin's appeasement of Hitler. Hard-liners hurled angry words at Gorbachev during the Twenty-Eighth Congress of the Communist Party of the Soviet Union and other events.[55] They began privately to plot a course of action.

Their discontentment culminated in a desperate coup attempt against Gorbachev. On August 19, 1991, Stalinist holdovers seized Gorbachev at his Crimean dacha and made one last bid to salvage atheistic communism. They failed: on August 21, coup leaders fled Moscow and Gorbachev was reinstalled in power. The hard-liners had lost. The hope for liberty was preserved.

The journalist Pavel Chichikov provided an emotional account of this unnerving moment for freedom-loving Russians. As the frightening possibility of a coup unfolded, he went immediately to the only Catholic church in Moscow at the time, just down the street from KGB headquarters. "I walked straight back to the sanctuary and fell on my knees before a statue of the Blessed Virgin," said Chichikov. "Then I burst into tears."[56]

As he poured out his heart and soul, his act of devotion elicited laughs from the KGB church watchers assigned to the pews.

Chichikov knew that there was good reason to be afraid. He was personally in mortal danger from thugs still clinging to the Stalinist state. The fear was pervasive. "There was a sense of impending doom everywhere," he recalled.

Chichikov escaped danger, and he later felt certain that it was the Blessed Mother who guided him to safety. The coup attempt ended on August 21, which happened to be the eve of the Feast of the Queenship of Mary, a day Pope Pius XII had proclaimed in 1954, his Marian Year. Pius XII was the first pope who had attempted to consecrate communist Russia to the Blessed Mother's Immaculate Heart. Before August 22 became the Feast Day of the Queenship of Mary, it had been the Feast Day of the Immaculate Heart of Mary.[57]

A FIRST (AND LAST) ANNIVERSARY FOR THE SOVIETS

The Marian pope, John Paul II, was relieved that Mikhail Gorbachev had survived the coup attempt. On August 23, just back in Rome from his visit to the late Cardinal Mindszenty's Hungary, the pope sent a telegram to the freed Gorbachev. He extended his "fervent good wishes" and thanked God for "the happy outcome of the dramatic trial which involved your person, your family and your country."

The pontiff expressed hope that Gorbachev would continue his "tremendous task for the material and spiritual renewal of the Soviet Union."[58]

Renewal was definitely afoot. In mere months, the USSR would no longer exist. Gorbachev had survived the assault from hard-line communists, but he couldn't withstand the other forces gathering against him. As Ronald Reagan had said the previous year, Gorbachev had let the freedom genie out of the bottle.

Perhaps a mystical sign of the coming renewal occurred on October 13, 1991. It would be the final anniversary of Fátima's Miracle of the Sun in the life of the USSR—and the first and only anniversary that Russians living under the Soviet Union were permitted to celebrate. The Miracle of the Sun had occurred just days before the outbreak of the Bolshevik Revolution.

"For the first time," writes Timothy Tindal-Robertson, "the ceremonies in Fátima were attended by pilgrims from Russia and, by permission of President Yeltsin, live television coverage of this event was shown in Moscow and all over the Soviet Union." An estimated thirty to forty million people in the former Evil Empire watched the seventy-five-minute broadcast of the Fátima ceremonies. As Tindal-Robertson notes, the first Russian pilgrimage to Fátima "aptly symbolized" the end of the religious persecution under Soviet communism. The broadcast was so popular that it ran again on November 7—ironically, the date of the Bolshevik Revolution as marked in the Gregorian calendar.[59]

On December 8, the leaders of Russia, Belarus, and Ukraine signed an agreement that established the Commonwealth of Independent States—effectively dissolving the USSR.[60] December 8 was, of course, the Solemnity of the Immaculate Conception of the Blessed Mother.

The only thing still holding the Soviet Union together was Mikhail Gorbachev, clinging to his dreams of a better USSR. Gorbachev would hang on for two more weeks. Then, on December 25, he called Reagan's successor, President Bush. He wished Bush a merry Christmas and told him that he was resigning his post as leader of the Soviet Union, giving way to Boris Yeltsin's Russian Federation.

With that, the Soviet Union was officially over. The end for a regime that had viciously persecuted religious believers came on Christmas Day in the West.[61]

Gorbachev had been sensing the need to step aside for some time, according to one of his close aides. "It was not accidental that during this year Gorbachev started thinking (and speaking about in his close circle) about leaving," Anatoly Chernyaev wrote in his diary in 1990. Chernyaev, a committed atheist, followed with this: "He [Gorbachev] sensed that the mission assigned to him by God and history had been fulfilled."[62]

Gorbachev had seen this as God's assignment to him? That is a revelation.

Ronald Reagan and John Paul II also believed that God had assigned them a mission. And by the close of 1991, they had seen it accomplished.

THE LAST LAUGH

Once the communist collapse came, Russian government officials were eager to talk openly about their erstwhile empire. Andrei Kozyrev, President Yeltsin's foreign minister, was quick to explain that it was a mistake to use the name "Union of Soviet Socialist Republics": "It was, rather, [an] evil empire, as it was put."[63]

Arkady Murashev, a young leader in Yeltsin's Russia, told reporter David Remnick: "He [Reagan] called us the 'Evil Empire.' So why did you in the West laugh at him? It's true!"[64]

Sergei Tarasenko, the chief assistant to Soviet foreign minister Eduard Shevardnadze, offered a similar take: "So the president said, 'It is an evil empire!' Okay. Well, we [were] an evil empire."[65]

Genrikh Trofimenko, the onetime director of the prestigious Institute for U.S. and Canada Studies of the Russian Academy of Sciences, added a slight adjustment to Reagan's description. What was his objection? Reagan's "Evil Empire" label, said Trofimenko, "was probably too mild."[66]

Many Western observers had laughed at Ronald Reagan for calling the Soviet Union an Evil Empire, or they had reprimanded him for his "primitive" analysis. But high-level Soviet officials confirmed exactly what he said.

People also laughed at Reagan when he said that "the march of freedom and democracy" would "leave Marxism-Leninism on the ash-heap of history." Just nine years later, he had been proven right.

Part 6

REVELATIONS AND GOODBYES

36

MAY 13, 2000

THE THIRD SECRET OF FÁTIMA—REVEALED

With communism smoldering on what Ronald Reagan called the "ash-heap of history," John Paul II was giving his attention to the prophecies of Fátima.

In October 1997, six years after the dissolution of the USSR, the pope from now-free Poland marked the eightieth anniversary of the Miracle of the Sun with a public letter to the bishop of Leiria-Fátima. He wrote, "On the threshold of the third millennium, as we observe the signs of the times in this 20th century, Fátima is certainly one of the greatest." The message of Fátima, the pope said, "announces many of the later events and conditions them on the response to its appeals: signs such as the two world wars, but also great gatherings of nations and peoples marked by dialogue and peace." He said that Fátima "stands out and helps us see the hand of God, our providential Guide and patient and compassionate Father also in the 20th century."[1]

And when the third millennium opened, the pope decided it was time at last to reveal the Third Secret of Fátima to the faithful around the world.

THE ANNOUNCEMENT

The pontiff had gone to Fátima on the first anniversary of the shooting, in May 1982, and again on the tenth anniversary, in May 1991. Now, for the new millennium, for his Great Jubilee, he went to Fátima once more, May 12–13, 2000. On this visit, the pope beatified two of the three visionaries, the late siblings Jacinta and Francisco Marto, who came nowhere near living out the long century as their cousin Lúcia had. They became the two youngest nonmartyrs the Church ever beatified.[2]

When the Mass ended on May 13, the Vatican secretary of state, Cardinal Angelo Sodano, made an announcement: the pope had decided to reveal the much-anticipated Third Secret. In the presence of the Holy Father, he read from a text that Pope John Paul II had preapproved:

> On this solemn occasion of his visit to Fátima, His Holiness has directed me to make an announcement to you. As you know, the purpose of his visit to Fátima has been to beatify the two "little shepherds." Nevertheless he also wishes his pilgrimage to be a renewed gesture of gratitude to Our Lady for her protection during these years of his papacy. This protection seems also to be linked to the so-called third part of the "secret" of Fátima.
>
> That text contains a prophetic vision similar to those found in Sacred Scripture, which do not describe photographically the details of future events, but synthesize and compress against a single background facts which extend through time in an unspecified succession and duration. As a result, the text must be interpreted *in a symbolic key* [emphasis in the original].
>
> The vision of Fátima concerns above all the war waged by atheistic systems against the Church and Christians, and it describes the immense suffering endured by the witnesses of the faith in the last century of the second millennium. It is an interminable *Way of the Cross* led by the Popes of the twentieth century.

Without explicitly stating that he was revealing the Third Secret, Sodano proceeded to do just that, speaking of a white-robed bishop who falls in a flurry of enemy fire:

> According to the interpretation of the "little shepherds," which was also confirmed recently by Sister Lúcia, "the Bishop clothed in white" who prays for all the faithful is the Pope. As he makes his way with great difficulty towards the Cross amid the corpses of those who were martyred (Bishops, priests, men and women Religious and many lay people), he too falls to the ground, apparently dead, under a hail of gunfire.[3]

Sodano linked this scenario directly to the events of May 13, 1981. "After the assassination attempt of 13 May 1981," he said, "it appeared evident that it was 'a mother's hand that guided the bullet's path' [John Paul II's words], enabling 'the Pope in his throes' to halt 'at the threshold of death.'"

Sodano—again, in the presence of the pontiff, reading a letter the pope had preapproved—also connected this discussion directly to the collapse of communism: "The successive events of 1989 led, both in the Soviet Union and in a number of countries of Eastern Europe, to the fall of the Communist regimes which promoted atheism. For this too His Holiness offers heartfelt thanks to the Most Holy Virgin."

Perhaps the Vatican anticipated the letdown that Fátima watchers would feel with the announcement: many had wondered whether the Third Secret might envision some calamity that heralded the second coming of Christ. For Sodano said, "Even if the events to which the third part of the 'secret' of Fátima refers now seem part of the past, Our Lady's call to conversion and penance, issued at the start of the twentieth century, remains timely and urgent today." He quoted the pope: "The Lady of the message seems to read the signs of the times—the signs of our time—with special insight.... The insistent invitation of Mary Most Holy to penance is nothing but the manifestation of her maternal concern for the fate of the human family, in need of conversion and forgiveness."

The secretary of state explained that more information on the Third Secret would be forthcoming. He closed his announcement by stating that, "in order that the faithful may better receive the message of Our Lady of Fátima," the pontiff had charged the Congregation for the Doctrine of the Faith—led by its prefect, Cardinal Joseph Ratzinger—with making public "the third part of the 'secret'" while offering an "appropriate commentary."

"THE FUTURE IS NOT IN FACT UNCHANGEABLY SET"

The Vatican released additional information the next month. On June 26, 2000, Cardinal Ratzinger and the secretary of the Congregation for the Doctrine of the Faith, Archbishop Tarcisio Bertone, held a historic press conference in the Vatican Press Room. Cardinal Ratzinger would later remember this period by saying that John Paul II (and Lúcia) realized "that the time had come to dispel the air of mystery that shrouded" the last secret.[4]

Archbishop Bertone had prepared a history of the written recording of the Third Secret, detailing its path from Lúcia's pen in the 1940s; to its being sealed in an envelope in the Secret Archives of the Holy Office on April 4, 1957; through Pope John XXIII's reading it but deciding not to act on it; through Pope Paul VI's reading it but deciding not to disclose it; through Pope John Paul II's asking for the envelope and reading it in the hospital while recovering from the shooting.[5]

Bertone's office publicly released four documents: Sister Lúcia's handwritten account of the First and Second Secrets, from 1941; her handwritten text of the Third Secret, from 1944; a letter Pope John Paul II wrote to Lúcia on April 19, 2000; and Bertone's written account of his interview with Lúcia on April 27, 2000.[6]

Archbishop Bertone had met with Lúcia to verify once more that the Third Secret document was genuine and to confirm that the Vatican's interpretation of the message was accurate. Pope John Paul II personally had tasked Bertone to meet with the nun before the Vatican publicly disclosed the Third Secret.

Bertone asked Lúcia whether the Third Secret referred to the shooting of Pope John Paul II. She said yes. He asked whether the "Bishop dressed in White" (the description in her original letter) was embodied in the person of Pope John Paul II, the bishop of Rome (the only bishop who wears white). She said yes.[7]

Cardinal Ratzinger presented the written "commentary" on the Third Secret that Cardinal Sodano had promised at Fátima. His lengthy "Theological Commentary" was classic Ratzinger, written in eloquent prose and reflecting his scholarly, reflective approach. Before he addressed the Third Secret in the commentary, Ratzinger carefully considered the theological status of public versus private revelations, their differences, their authority, their treatment by the Church and the flock.

As he reviewed the Third Secret, the future successor to Pope John Paul II emphasized God's respect for human freedom. After describing the Fátima vision's "angel with the flaming sword" as an image of destruction, Ratzinger wrote:

> The vision then shows the power which stands opposed to the force of destruction—the splendor of the Mother of God and, stemming from this in a certain way, the summons to penance. In this way, the importance of human freedom is underlined: the future is not in fact unchangeably set, and the image which the children saw is in no way a film preview of a future in which nothing can be changed. Indeed, the whole point of the vision is to bring freedom onto the scene and to steer freedom in a positive direction. The purpose of the vision is not to show a film of an irrevocably fixed future. Its meaning is exactly the opposite: it is meant to mobilize the forces of change in the right direction. Therefore we must totally discount fatalistic explanations of the "secret," such as, for example, the claim that the would-be assassin of 13 May 1981 was merely an instrument of the divine plan guided by Providence and could not therefore have acted freely, or other similar ideas in circulation. Rather, the vision speaks of dangers and how we might be saved from them.

Ratzinger's interpretation calls to mind Fulton Sheen's assessment decades earlier in *Peace of Soul*: "God refuses to be a totalitarian dictator in order to abolish evil by destroying human freedom."[8] Sheen referred to Mary's "*fiat*," the Latin word for her assent to the angel Gabriel to conceive and give birth to Jesus.[9] He called this assent the greatest example of the "character" of human freedom, of how human freedom can be the cause for the greatest glory to God. Discerning how God's creatures should harness freedom for good rather than evil became a significant theme of the papacies of John Paul II and Benedict XVI—the former Joseph Ratzinger. Benedict would argue that the modern West suffers from a "confused ideology of freedom," too often using freedom to hurt others.

Cardinal Ratzinger, in his commentary on the Third Secret, continued to emphasize human freedom and agency as he analyzed Lúcia's imagery:

> The place of the action is described in three symbols: a steep mountain, a great city reduced to ruins and finally a large rough-hewn cross. The mountain and city symbolize the arena of human history: history as an arduous ascent to the summit, history as the arena of human creativity and social harmony, but at the same time a place of

> destruction, where man actually destroys the fruits of his own work. The city can be the place of communion and progress, but also of danger and the most extreme menace. On the mountain stands the cross—the goal and guide of history. The cross transforms destruction into salvation; it stands as a sign of history's misery but also as a promise for history.

Lúcia and her fellow visionaries saw people step into this "arena of human history"—most notably, the "Bishop dressed in white." Avoiding ambiguity, Cardinal Ratzinger immediately quoted Lúcia's assessment of this white-robed figure: "We had the impression that it was the Holy Father." Ratzinger continued:

> The Pope seems to precede the others, trembling and suffering because of all the horrors around him. Not only do the houses of the city lie half in ruins, but he makes his way among the corpses of the dead. The Church's path is thus described as a *Via Crucis* [the Way of the Cross], as a journey through a time of violence, destruction and persecution. The history of an entire century can be seen represented in this image. Just as the places of the earth are synthetically described in the two images of the mountain and the city, and are directed towards the cross, so too time is presented in a compressed way. In the vision we can recognize the last century as a century of martyrs, a century of suffering and persecution for the Church, a century of World Wars and the many local wars which filled the last fifty years and have inflicted unprecedented forms of cruelty. In the "mirror" of this vision we see passing before us the witnesses of the faith decade by decade.

To pinpoint the source of that "suffering and persecution," Ratzinger quoted from Sister Lúcia's May 12, 1982, letter to Pope John Paul II: "The third part of the 'secret' refers to Our Lady's words: 'If not, [Russia] will spread her errors throughout the world, causing wars and persecutions of the Church. The good will be martyred; the Holy Father will have much to suffer; various nations will be annihilated.'"

Ratzinger turned to the shooting of Pope John Paul II and the pope's own assessment of the Third Secret:

> When, after the attempted assassination on 13 May 1981, the Holy Father had the text of the third part of the "secret" brought to him,

> was it not inevitable that he should see in it his own fate? He had been very close to death, and he himself explained his survival in the following words: "...it was a mother's hand that guided the bullet's path and in his throes the Pope halted at the threshold of death" (13 May 1994). That here "a mother's hand" had deflected the fateful bullet only shows once more that there is no immutable destiny, that faith and prayer are forces which can influence history and that in the end prayer is more powerful than bullets and faith more powerful than armies.

THE MESSAGE OF FÁTIMA

Ratzinger came to what he called the "final question"—namely, "What is the meaning of the 'secret' of Fátima as a whole (in its three parts)? What does it say to us?"

He stressed that the Third Secret no longer offered a preview of an event to come but instead referred to something that had taken place. On this point he quoted from Cardinal Sodano's statement at Fátima the previous month: "The events to which the third part of the 'secret' of Fátima refers now seem part of the past." Ratzinger went on:

> Those who expected exciting apocalyptic revelations about the end of the world or the future course of history are bound to be disappointed. Fátima does not satisfy our curiosity in this way, just as Christian faith in general cannot be reduced to an object of mere curiosity. What remains was already evident when we began our reflections on the text of the "secret": the exhortation to prayer as the path of "salvation for souls" and, likewise, the summons to penance and conversion.

Ratzinger finished his commentary by reiterating the crucial message that events are not fixed, and that human freedom must be employed as a force for good in the world:

> I would like finally to mention another key expression of the "secret" which has become justly famous: "my Immaculate Heart will triumph." What does this mean? The Heart open to God, purified by contemplation of God, is stronger than guns and weapons of every kind. The *fiat* of Mary, the word of her heart, has changed the

> history of the world, because it brought the Savior into the world—because, thanks to her *Yes*, God could become man in our world and remains so for all time. The Evil One has power in this world, as we see and experience continually; he has power because our freedom continually lets itself be led away from God. But since God himself took a human heart and has thus steered human freedom towards what is good, the freedom to choose evil no longer has the last word. From that time forth, the word that prevails is this: "In the world you will have tribulation, but take heart; I have overcome the world" (Jn 16:33). The message of Fátima invites us to trust in this promise.

It was a lesson on good and evil, on faith and freedom, that John Paul II understood, and that Ronald Reagan would have commended. Freedom is a good thing, but only if used for good. Freedom must be employed not to choose evil but to fight evil.

Cardinal Ratzinger, John Paul II's future successor, thus closed his analysis of the Third Secret not with visions of hell and damnation but with words of hope. And with that, the Third Secret of Fátima was, at long last, no longer a secret.[10]

37

JUNE 5, 2004

RONALD REAGAN'S SILENT GOODBYE

The transition into the twentieth century was a time for silence for Ronald Reagan. In November 1994, four years after his final meeting with John Paul II, Reagan composed a handwritten letter to his fellow Americans informing them that he had Alzheimer's disease, which would lead the old horseman "into the sunset of [his] life."

The cruel disease robbed him of memories of everything from Dixon to Washington, from World War II to the Cold War, from Hollywood to the Evil Empire, from the Rock River to the White House, from Nelle and Jack to Nancy and his children. But Nelle had so ingrained in him the thinking that everything, good and bad, was part of God's Divine Plan. Ronald Wilson Reagan had done his work in the century past, and now, with a new century arriving, it was time to go—serenely and quietly.

In the summer of 1997 the former president, attended by caretakers and security men, carefully kept from the media's cameras, was enjoying a stroll through Armand Hammer Park near his home in Bel Air, California. He was approached by a tourist named Yakob Ravin, who was with his twelve-year-old grandson. The two were Jewish Ukrainian émigrés, the kind of people Reagan had constantly pressed Gorbachev to set free. Grandfather and grandson now lived near Toledo, Ohio. They were thrilled to happen upon Reagan, a liberator to them and their people. They asked whether Reagan would pose for a photo with the boy. The former president, hobbled by a fading memory, perhaps even slightly perplexed by the request, nonetheless obliged with a grin. But Ravin wanted to say something more to the eighty-six-year-old freedom fighter.

"Mr. President," said Ravin, "thank you for everything you did for the Jewish people, for Soviet people, to destroy the communist empire."

Reagan had always been humble, never congratulating himself for taking down Soviet communism. But now he had a simple response for Ravin: "Yes, that is my job."[1]

REMEMBERING AND HONORING REAGAN

The next seven years for Ronald Reagan were a period of steadily increasing incognizance. He ebbed away, kept going only by a robust frame that had survived everything from seventy-seventy rescues in the Rock River to the bullets fired from John Hinckley's revolver.

Reagan died on June 5, 2004, at the age of ninety-three. His millions of admirers took the loss with a mix of sadness and relief. He had long ago vanished from the public eye and his own sense of self and reality.

Mikhail Gorbachev was dismayed, telling reporters, "I take very hard the death of Ronald Reagan."[2] The former leader of the Evil Empire sent Mrs. Reagan a letter: "Your husband has earned a place in history and in people's hearts."[3]

John Paul II had taken a special interest in Reagan's plight in his last years. Biographer George Weigel recorded that in his conversations with the pontiff, "John Paul II often asked how Reagan was doing and was saddened to hear that Alzheimer's disease had robbed him of" his memories.[4] Shortly before Christmas 2001, the Holy Father asked Weigel, "How is President Reagan?" The biographer told the pope a story he had just heard from Edwin Meese, Reagan's longtime adviser. Reagan, in a discussion with Meese, could not even remember that he had been president. John Paul II reacted to the tale with sorrow and asked Weigel to tell Mrs. Reagan that he was praying for her and her husband.[5]

By June 2004, John Paul II was himself ailing and failing. Advanced Parkinson's disease had hobbled him. For Reagan, the body was strong but the mind had gone; for John Paul II, the mind was strong but the body had gone. The world would watch the pope suffer in his final years.

Only one day before Reagan's death, in a gesture the former president would have loved, President George W. Bush traveled to Rome to award Pope John Paul II the Presidential Medal of Freedom, America's highest civilian honor. (Three years later the president of Poland, Lech Kaczyński, would posthumously confer upon Reagan the Order of the White Eagle, Poland's highest civilian honor.) This was one of the suffering pope's increasingly rare public appearances. He was hunched over in visible agony, hobbled not just bodily but also in the ability to articulate basic words. Still, in his halting delivery, the pontiff managed to thank Bush and to express his gratitude to President Reagan for extending diplomatic relations to the Holy See twenty years earlier. "I send my regards to President Reagan and to Mrs. Reagan, who is so attentive to him in his illness," said John Paul II.[6]

Reagan was, at that moment, nearing his final breaths.

The next day the pope issued a statement on the death of his old ally. He hailed Reagan's "contributions [to] the historical events that changed the lives of millions of people, especially in Europe."[7] He also sent a telegram of condolence to Mrs. Reagan. The pope, whose liberated countrymen were now building statues of Reagan, told the former first lady, "I recall with deep gratitude the late president's unwavering commitment to the service of the nation and to the cause of freedom, as well as his abiding faith in the human and spiritual values which ensure a future of solidarity, justice, and peace in our world."[8]

John Paul II could not attend Reagan's funeral; his infirmities made intercontinental travel impossible. But the pontiff displayed his high regard for Reagan by dispatching the Vatican's highest-ranking official (aside from himself) as a special papal envoy to the funeral in California. That official was Secretary of State Angelo Sodano.[9] Sodano had been the pope's special envoy to reveal the Third Secret of Fátima four years earlier in Portugal, and now the cardinal stood for John Paul II on another special occasion close to the pontiff's heart.

A week after Reagan's death, a letter to the editor in the *Washington Post* revealed still another fascinating parallel between the pope and the president. Dr. Roger Peele, who had been head of psychiatry at Saint Elizabeth's Hospital, the federally operated psychiatric facility in Washington, D.C., divulged a secret he had carried for decades. In 1983, the same year Pope John Paul II met with Mehmet Ali Agca to forgive his would-be assassin, Reagan tried to arrange a private meeting with John Hinckley at Saint Elizabeth's. He had forgiven Hinckley while lying in the hospital, fighting for his life; now he wanted to forgive his shooter in person. "He really wanted to do it," Dr. Peele said more than twenty years later. But the psychiatrist ultimately advised Reagan that his patient was not psychologically ready for such a meeting. Reagan deferred to the doctor's judgment. The president "said he only wanted to do what was in Mr. Hinckley's best interests." When Hinckley's lawyer learned of Reagan's actions, he remarked on "the magnanimity of the president, a man of grace, great grace."[10]

Millions of Eastern Europeans remembered this man of grace as well. The tributes poured forth from people who were now free from the bondage of international communism thanks in no small part to Reagan. A Romanian newspaper called Reagan "the political leader who contributed the most to the fall of the totalitarian communist system." In Estonia, a former Soviet republic, a writer called Reagan "the president of Eastern Europe." A Hungarian business journalist wrote, "Everyone doing business in the free markets of Central and Eastern Europe, or voting in their democratic elections, owes it all to Ronald Reagan."[11]

Joining the chorus of tributes was the Vatican's first official diplomatic representative in Washington, Cardinal Pio Laghi, with whom Reagan—and, more so, Bill Clark and Bill Casey—developed a very constructive relationship. "Reagan was really a great believer and I would say Christian," said Laghi. "I would also say a great president. He had vision." The cardinal recognized what Reagan and Pope John Paul II had ignited together: "I think President Reagan, with the direction of John Paul II, a Polish pope, understood that a kind of electric line with some dynamite extended beyond the Berlin Wall and sooner or later it would provoke the collapse of that wall. He realized that having a Polish pope and *Solidarność* would be for him a key to destroy what he'd often call the 'evil empire.'"[12]

Laghi's former cappuccino partner, and Reagan's spiritual partner, Bill Clark, was deeply grieved. From his law office in Paso Robles, the seventy-two-year-old Clark extolled Reagan's commitment to life, from defending the voiceless in the womb to the voiceless in communist dungeons of Eastern Europe and the USSR. Clark called Reagan "a defender of the innocent, young and old alike."[13]

HAIL MARY

Reagan's funeral services prompted an outpouring of emotion unseen by the American public since the tragic death of John F. Kennedy. People of all ages flocked to Washington and waited in line overnight for the opportunity simply to walk past Reagan's casket at the Capitol Rotunda. In California, cars stopped for miles along Route 101 to salute the black limousine that carried Reagan's body to its final resting place.

Reagan's son Michael, who shared his father's faith, thought of Nelle. "I remember with great clarity my father's emotion when Nelle Reagan, my grandmother, passed away," Michael said. "Until today I didn't understand the feeling of loss and pain which comes when a parent leaves you.... He played an important role in pointing me to God.... The greatest gift my father ever gave me was the simple knowledge that I would see him in heaven one day."[14]

Reagan's funeral service at Washington National Cathedral was captivating. The church bells—that sound that had once so enraged Soviet atheists—rang out forty times at noon in Reagan's honor. Former Republican senator John Danforth, an Episcopal priest, officiated the service. Befitting Reagan's personal faith, the men of the cloth who read from Scripture at the service were an ecumenical lot. Rabbi Harold Kushner repeated Reagan's favorite passage from Isaiah: "But they that wait upon the Lord shall renew their strength; they shall mount up with wings as eagles." Rabbi Kushner no doubt knew that this was one of Reagan's dearest passages, but he would not have known that it was also a favorite of Ben Cleaver, the pastor of Reagan's youth who had so influenced him. Cardinal Theodore McCarrick read Matthew 5:14–16, the New Testament passage Reagan most frequently invoked, in which Jesus Christ speaks of a "city on a hill" and letting one's "light shine before men, that they may praise your good deeds and praise your Father in heaven."

President George W. Bush and his father, Reagan's vice president, delivered remarks. The elder Bush's voice cracked as he told the gathered that he learned more from Reagan than from anyone he encountered in all his years in public life. Margaret Thatcher, weakened by a stroke, provided a tribute via videotape. Lech Wałęsa was there. So was Mikhail Gorbachev, who came to pay tribute to his old negotiating partner. He had attended many "Red funerals" in his lifetime, secular ceremonies where any mention of God was banished. This service was no such thing.

Bill Clark was there as well. Since arriving in Washington and encountering his old friend's body in a sealed casket at the Rotunda,

Clark had struggled to keep his emotions in check. That was the closest he had been to Reagan physically in several years. He had been preparing for his friend's death for quite some time. But he was still not fully prepared. The bottled-up emotions became wells of tears. And then, at the funeral, came something totally unexpected that prompted Clark's tears to flow more vigorously.

The great Irish tenor Ronan Tynan stepped to the altar and launched into a breathtaking rendition of Schubert's "Ave Maria."[15] Like many others in the cathedral, Clark listened, stunned, tears running. "Ave Maria" was a hymn that he had known since childhood, and that would one day play at his own funeral, as well as that of his wife, Joan. He had not, however, expected to hear it at the funeral of his Protestant friend, no matter Reagan's Catholic sympathies. The hymn's title is Latin for the most common of all Marian prayers, the "Hail Mary," which in English declares:

> Hail Mary, full of grace, the Lord is with thee.
> Blessed art thou among women, and blessed is the fruit of thy womb, Jesus.
> Holy Mary, Mother of God, pray for us sinners, now and at the hour of death.
> Amen.

The piece was powerful, rousing the heart, the mind, the soul. And yet it left many puzzled. Why "Ave Maria"? Who had chosen that quintessentially Catholic hymn at this Protestant funeral service for a non-Catholic president?

The answer was Ronald Reagan himself. Reagan had chosen the hymn years earlier, when planning his service, before Alzheimer's robbed him of his faculties.[16]

Why did Reagan pick it?

It was a question that Bill Clark and I discussed at the time and many times later. But we could not come up with a clear answer.

In October 2007 I posed the question to Nancy Reagan, via her longtime chief assistant, Joanne Drake. I e-mailed Drake: "Bill Clark and I have struggled to figure out why Reagan chose . . . this completely Catholic hymn. Can you tell us why Reagan picked this hymn? Maybe it was a favorite of his father? Was this a John Paul II influence? . . . If anyone would know, it would be you or Nancy."[17]

Drake responded for Mrs. Reagan: "I don't think it was anything more complicated than he absolutely loved this hymn . . . and the thought of an Irish tenor singing it was perfection in his eyes."[18] (Reagan was an Irish American who loved everything Irish.) She added: "He felt very close to Pope John Paul II.... There is no question that the Holy Father was an influence in the President's life (my guess is that the opposite is also true), but in the end I think the selection of 'Ave Maria' was based solely on the beauty of the music and the potential for a powerful performance by an Irish tenor."

No question, that was part of it. But was there something more?

I asked Mrs. Reagan the same question twice more—five years later and seven years later, in August 2012 and August 2014. On these occasions I tried to dig into her husband's feelings about the Blessed Mother. Again, Joanne Drake relayed the former first lady's response, saying that, unfortunately, Mrs. Reagan "just doesn't know."[19] Drake reiterated: "Mrs. Reagan said simply that it was one of her husband's favorite songs. She didn't know if there were any reasons other than that for choosing it to be part of the funeral service."[20]

Drake, however, shared her own insights, which were based on her long relationship with the Reagans. She traveled with both Reagans extensively, and was at Castel Gandolfo for Ronald Reagan's final visit with John Paul II in September 1990. A Catholic herself, Drake told me she believed that Reagan had a fondness for Mary in part because he "was really taken" with the impact of mothers. She noted Reagan's strong attachment to his own mother, whom "he regarded as his teacher in both a spiritual and practical sense." She recalled how Reagan often talked about Nelle's charity work "when he read a news story about a child or family down on their luck—homeless, jobless, ill, etc." This, said Drake, "would give him great pause for deep thought and often times cause him to ask if there was a way to help.... He wrote many checks throughout his life to both individuals and charities, and continued this practice as president, doing it anonymously." Reagan had "a small voice in his head that he told me was his mother," Drake added. Because of his mother, Reagan "had an extraordinary respect for all mothers," she told me, "and I believe he looked upon the Virgin Mary as a guiding light for these mothers and therefore held her up as a supreme example."

Drake offered another reason for Reagan's regard for Mary. She told me that Reagan had "great respect for the rituals of the church, not just the Catholic faith, but he loved the hymns and ceremony of a church service in general." She also noted, "I do think he was influenced by having Catholics in his family, and he wore this banner proudly when he met John Paul II."

Drake noticed the parallels between the Protestant president and the Catholic pope: "Those men were so similar in their approaches to people—they loved people from all walks of life, it didn't matter if they were the janitor or the queen of England, they enjoyed what each one brought to the relationship without judgment of any kind."

I also asked Michael Reagan why his father chose "Ave Maria" to be sung at his funeral. Michael did not have an answer, "other than [that] my father always showed great respect for other beliefs.... He was surrounded by Catholics."[21]

I even presented the question to Ronan Tynan, who sang the hymn at the funeral. Tynan told me: "I also was surprised about the Ave Maria, considering he was Protestant.... Mrs. Reagan said to me one of President Reagan's requests was that they would have an Irish tenor who would fill the walls of the Washington Cathedral. I was aware he had a devotion to the Blessed Mother. Mrs. Reagan used to keep in contact with me and wrote a beautiful letter after the funeral."[22]

Within Tynan's short e-mail response might be the answer: *Reagan had a devotion to the Blessed Mother*. Did he?

That is something that Tynan could not have known well, but someone close to Reagan could have made him "aware" of it in asking him to sing at the funeral. *Devotion* seems too strong a word, better suited to describing how John Paul II, the Marian pope, regarded the Blessed Mother.

But it does not seem too strong to say that Ronald Reagan had a high regard, respect, and fondness for the mother of Christ. She both intrigued him and appealed to him. Given all we have seen about Reagan—from the influence of his Catholic father to his devotion to his own mother, from the many Catholics on his staff to those in his family, from his ecumenical approach to faith to his pronounced mystical streak, from his keen interest in the Fátima apparitions to his being "very, very moved" by a letter from a Medjugorje visionary, and finally to his bond with the Marian pope, John Paul II—his choice of "Ave Maria" for his funeral no longer seems all that surprising.

DEPARTURES

One person who must have been especially gratified by Reagan's acknowledgment of the Virgin Mary at his death was his old friend at the Vatican. John Paul II might well have influenced that compelling public acknowledgment of the Blessed Mother. He no doubt said at least one "Hail Mary" for his departing partner.

The words of the "Hail Mary"/"Ave Maria" ask the Blessed Mother to pray for sinners at the hour of their death. Reagan's hour had come; John Paul II's was rapidly approaching. The two friends and partners would pass from this world less than a year apart.

38

APRIL 2, 2005

DIVINE MERCY FOR JOHN PAUL II

The twentieth century had ended, and the journey for many of its faithful pilgrims had as well. John Paul II, with his entrustment to Mary, placed in service to the greater glory of God, stated that "all men and women, pilgrims on the earth, are able to foresee in Mary the 'destiny of glory' that awaits them." She remained, he said in an August 2003 Angelus message, "a sign of sure hope," the fulfillment of God's promise that "evil and death will not have the last word." Like "a shining star from heaven," the pope said, Mary "directs our daily journey on earth." That is why "we must never lose trust and peace," no matter how "incomprehensible certain events may appear to be in human history."[1]

A year earlier, the Holy Father said that by looking to the Blessed Mother, "we understand better the meaning and value of our earthly pilgrimage." And now, for John Paul II, whose own earthly pilgrimage was nearing its end, it was time to look back to better understand the meaning of the last century.

LOSING LÚCIA

For another faithful child of Mary, another voice of the twentieth century, the hour of death was coming as well.

On February 13, 2005, Lúcia dos Santos, the only survivor of the three Fátima children, passed away at the age of ninety-seven. The child of Fátima died on yet another thirteenth, and had far outlived Jacinta and Francisco, just as the Lady at the Cova da Iria had foretold. Her last words amid a period of extended suffering were directed to the bishop of Rome: "I offer this suffering for the Holy Father."[2]

Lúcia's last decades had been rich ones of ongoing service. Caravans would flock to Fátima to see her, so much so that she had to be relocated with a new identity for protection.[3]

She was there on May 13, 2000, when Pope John Paul II beatified Francisco and Jacinta during what turned out to be his last visit to Fátima. There he remembered the hands that had saved him in Saint Peter's Square nineteen years earlier: "And once again I would like to celebrate the Lord's goodness to me when I was saved from death after being gravely wounded on 13 May 1981.... Father, to you I offer praise for all your children, from the Virgin Mary, your humble Servant, to the little shepherds, Francisco and Jacinta."

During that Fátima pilgrimage, Lúcia handed the pontiff an envelope. To this day we do not know what was in the envelope. Cardinal Bertone believes that Lúcia wrote John Paul II several letters during his papacy but, to his frustration, does not know where those letters are now.[4]

Bertone had met with Lúcia less than a month earlier to confirm the Vatican's understanding of the Third Secret before it was divulged at the Beatification Mass for Jacinta and Francisco. He met with her a second time, on November 17, 2001, to confirm that everything related to Fátima had been revealed. "Everything has been published," she affirmed. "There are no more secrets." The two met for a third time on December 9, 2003. This time, the visionary from Fátima offered a prophecy of her own, telling Bertone she would not see him again until her funeral. That turned out to be accurate. And when she died, Cardinal Bertone officiated her funeral.[5]

An ailing John Paul II, fast approaching his own final gasps, was in no condition to attend Lúcia's funeral, let alone leave the Vatican. But he did issue a statement on behalf of his Fátima friend. "Sister Lúcia bequeaths to us an example of great fidelity to the Lord and joyous attachment to his divine will," wrote the Holy Father. "I have always felt supported by the daily gift of her prayers, especially during the most difficult moments of trial and suffering. May the Lord reward her for her great and hidden service to the Church."[6]

THE EARTHLY DEPARTURE OF JOHN PAUL II

John Paul II was experiencing his own difficult moments of trial and suffering, for all the world to witness. People everywhere could see the agony he endured in his end stages of Parkinson's disease. The man suffered terribly in his final months, if not years.

The end of his suffering came on April 2, 2005. He was eighty-four. It had been a long life and papacy. On May 25, 1998, just after his seventy-eighth birthday, John Paul II became the longest-serving pope of the twentieth century, surpassing Pope Pius XII.[7] Even then, he had seven more years to go.

The pope was buried in a simple wooden casket. Many were struck at the contrast between the majesty of Saint Peter's Square and this simple encasement. It was a throwback to the simplicity of his native Poland. The only decoration on the casket was a Marian cross, a symbol of Karol Wojtyła's life of dedication to the mother of his Savior.

The pope's death occurred on the vigil and eve of Divine Mercy Sunday, which he had instituted in 2000 at the canonization Mass of a little-known, uneducated Polish nun, Faustina Kowalska, the first saint of the new millennium. Christ had told Faustina that the world would need an Ocean of Mercy in the period ahead; the nun died a year before Hitler and Stalin jointly invaded and annihilated Poland, her (and Karol Wojtyła's) homeland. In canonizing his native sister, the Polish pontiff paid divine homage to Faustina by instituting an international Feast of the Divine Mercy on the Sunday after Easter. Faustina reported that in her visions Christ had called for the Church to institute this day to grant atonement for humanity's sins, an eternal source of mercy and grace in the face of evil.[8] It was John Paul II who followed through, decades later. Now he died after the Mass for Divine Mercy was celebrated in his room.

The pope's death also occurred on a First Saturday, a Fátima devotional day.[9]

From the moment of the pope's death, the faithful were demanding his elevation to sainthood. Cries of "*Santo, subito!*" (meaning "Saint, right now!") could be heard from the faithful in Saint Peter's Square. One of the first official acts of John Paul II's successor, Pope Benedict XVI—

who as Cardinal Joseph Ratzinger had connected so many Fátima dots to John Paul II in his June 2000 "Theological Commentary"—was to announce the opening of canonization proceedings for the Fátima pope.

MIKHAIL GORBACHEV ON AN "EXTRAORDINARY MAN"

When John Paul II died, Mikhail Gorbachev, former leader of the empire that had repressed the pope's native Poland, called the pontiff "an extraordinary man" and "a devoted servant of the Church of Christ." Gorbachev said that John Paul II "did a lot to prepare for the end of the Cold War, for the coming together of peoples," and "did a lot to remove people from the danger of a nuclear conflict." The pope, said Gorbachev, had used his "high position" in the "best possible way." The former Soviet leader concluded by offering his highest compliment: "He was a humanist. Really. A Humanist with a capital H, maybe the first humanist in world history."[10]

These sentiments were nothing new for Gorbachev. Thirteen years earlier he had written a *New York Times* piece in which he credited the pontiff as a major contributor in liberating the communist world: "Everything that happened in Eastern Europe in recent years would have been impossible without the pope's presence and the enormous role, including the political one, he played in the world arena." Gorbachev said that the pope's actions were of "immense significance." He summed up, "In a word, he is great man." The article was titled "My Partner, the Pope."[11]

In that *New York Times* article, Gorbachev described their relationship as one of "mutual affection and understanding." After their historic December 1989 meeting, the two leaders met whenever Gorbachev came to Rome. In a March 1992 column for the Italian publication *La Stampa*, Gorbachev said that he and the pope also carried on an "intense exchange of letters." This correspondence would have encompassed the terminal phase of the Soviet Union. The former general secretary characterized their relationship as "instinctive, perhaps intuitive, and certainly personal," one that went beyond their shared Slavic heritage.[12]

At Gorbachev's request, *La Stampa*'s editors personally delivered the text to the pope as a token of the former Soviet leader's esteem and friendship.

The pontiff read the text slowly, first in Russian and then the Italian translation. After a while, he looked up at the editors from *La Stampa* and said: "These words are sincere. And they confirm what I have always thought about Gorbachev: he is a man of integrity."

The pope told the editors: "It's true, there was something instinctive between us, as if we had already known each other. And I know why that was: our meeting had been prepared by Providence." John Paul II went further: "He [Gorbachev] does not profess to be a believer, but with me I recall he spoke of the great importance of prayer and of the inner side of man's life. I truly believe that our meeting was prepared by Providence."[13] According to George Weigel, the pope on many occasions described Gorbachev to colleagues and friends as a "providential man."

As Weigel noted, it seems more likely that Gorbachev was "the instrument of a Providence he never understood" than "the conscious servant of a higher design."[14] But the key point is that John Paul II saw Gorbachev as performing the will of Providence (knowingly or not) in peacefully ending the Cold War and the communists' seventy-year war on religion.

Ronald Reagan would have agreed: it was part of the DP.[15]

After John Paul II died, Gorbachev divulged that his contacts with the pope had "continued practically right up to the very end." The two had "quite recently" exchanged messages on "several topics," Gorbachev said. He suggested that the Slavic pope again had expressed his desire for better dialogue and cooperation between the Catholic Church and the Russian Orthodox Church.[16] That was an unfulfilled wish that, like his desire to visit Moscow, the pontiff unfortunately would take to the grave.

CONFIRMED AT LAST: THE SOVIET ROLE IN THE SHOOTING OF JOHN PAUL II

It is no surprise that Mikhail Gorbachev's statements at the time of the pope's death included no mention of his Soviet state's role in the near-death of John Paul II twenty-four years earlier.

But right around the time of the pope's death, crucial information began to emerge about the 1981 assassination attempt. The first piece of information came in February 2005 with the release of a short memoir by John Paul II, *Memory and Identity*. The book grew out of a series of interviews the pope gave back in the early 1990s, but it wasn't published until shortly before his death. This was the book in which (as we saw in chapter 23) the pope noted that gunman Mehmet Ali Agca "was a professional assassin" and added: "This means that the attack was not his own initiative, it was someone else's idea; someone else had commissioned him to carry it out."[17] The pope didn't say whom he suspected of commissioning the hit, but this published statement confirmed that the pope had long ago concluded that Agca had not acted alone.[18]

Dramatic new evidence about the assassination attempt emerged only days before John Paul II died. Two Italian newspapers, *Corriere della Sera* and *Il Giornale*, caused an international media sensation when they reported that new documents found in the files of former East German intelligence services confirmed that the Soviet KGB had ordered the assassination attempt and assigned it to Bulgarian agents, who enlisted the help of Turkish extremists, including Agca. The East German secret police, the vicious Stasi, was tasked to coordinate the operation and cover it up.[19]

These files showed that in August 1982 Markus Wolf, East Germany's chief of espionage, had initiated Operation *Papst* (Pope) in response to requests from his Bulgarian pals to help cover any Agca tracks that might point their way. This would involve several sophisticated layers of disinformation, attempts to blame the papal shooting on innocents in the West. Very little is known about the details of this operation, though, as George Weigel has stated, it is inconceivable that it would have been mounted without Soviet approval or even supervision.[20]

A year later, in March 2006, came the most important revelation to date. In a report that made headlines around the world, a special investigative commission of the Italian parliament concluded that the Soviet Union was in fact behind the shooting of Pope John Paul II. The Italian investigation determined that the order to carry out the attack came from the very top of the communist regime, from General Secretary Leonid Brezhnev. The commission also implicated Yuri Andropov, the KGB leader who would succeed Brezhnev as general secretary the next year. According to the Italian report, Brezhnev asked the USSR's super-secret Main Intelligence Directorate, known as the GRU (a group independent of the KGB, the press noted), to eliminate the Polish pope because of the threat he posed to communism's hold on Eastern Europe.[21]

"This commission believes, beyond any reasonable doubt, that the leadership of the Soviet Union took the initiative to eliminate Pope John Paul II," the report concluded. "They relayed this decision to the military secret services for them to take on all necessary operations to commit a crime of unique gravity." The report also confirmed the Bulgarian connection that had long been suspected, though it pinned most of the blame on Moscow. The commission said that although "some elements" of the Bulgarian secret services were involved, the Bulgarian role was mainly intended to divert attention from the locus of responsibility: the Soviet Union. The Italian senator who headed the commission said the evidence confirmed the Soviet link without doubt.[22]

The Italian parliament's report also implicated Sergei Antonov as unquestionably having had contacts with the GRU. The report concluded that Antonov's work for the Bulgarian airline office in Rome was crucial, given that airlines fell under the military-intelligence jurisdiction of the GRU. The commission had incontrovertible photographic evidence that Antonov was standing near Agca at the time of the shooting.[23] Recall that the Soviet press had steadfastly defended Antonov as an innocent framed and persecuted by the Western press, which was covering for the true perpetrators: the CIA.

This bombshell report was released several months after a veteran CIA source "categorically" told me that "neither the KGB nor the Bulgarian service was involved in the attempt on the pope's life." This source, a longtime official of the agency, stated that he had looked "very carefully" into the assassination attempt and determined that "the conspiracy theory, favored by [Bill] Casey as well, was wrong."[24] Once again, it was the voice of the establishment.

I shared these words with Bill Clark at the time. He was incredulous. He emphasized a point that he (and many others) had made previously: "Just about everything Bulgaria did was at the behest of the KGB.... The Bulgarians had no incentive, no motive to do this on their own. And this was the pattern of the Soviets. They *always* got someone else to do the dirty work. Always." Clark added, "Bill Casey was convinced, primarily through Italian friends, that Bulgarians, doing the work for the KGB, did the dirty work on this."[25]

If anything was slightly off in Clark's words, it was the acronym *KGB*. Casey learned that the GRU did the dirty work on this one.

In 2006, Clark's suspicions, as well as those of his president, his CIA director, and his pope, seemed to have been confirmed. Of the four—Clark, Reagan, Casey, and John Paul II—only Clark lived to hear the verdict from the Italians.

Other investigators reached the same conclusion. Michael Ledeen—whose December 1982 article "The Bulgarian Connection" I discovered in Clark's files right around this time—had been on this trail for years. Like the Italian commission, he ultimately discerned that the Kremlin was involved via the GRU, not the KGB. His information came from Italian and German sources and from a "friend in the Vatican," he told me. Ledeen, too, had heard of the CIA's internal investigative group under Casey, and that that group had identified the GRU, though he said he had "never seen their documentation."[26]

Ion Mihai Pacepa, the highest-ranking defector from the Soviet Bloc, also pointed to Bulgaria and the GRU. In *Disinformation*, the book he cowrote with the scholar Ronald J. Rychlak, the former Romanian spy chief reported that it was Soviet "military intelligence"—the GRU—that had tried to eradicate the pope. The book did not give details but stated, "An operation was eventually mounted [against John Paul II] by Soviet military intelligence... through its friends in Bulgaria." Pacepa and Rychlak's account suggested why the GRU, not the KGB, would have been tapped: "defending the Soviet bloc was a military assignment."[27]

These reports, of course, confirmed what many observers had long suspected. Zbigniew Brzezinski, President Jimmy Carter's Polish-born, anticommunist national security adviser, had said in 1983, "It takes an act of faith *not* to believe the Bulgarians did it."[28] Twenty years after the shooting, he was just as firm: "I do still suspect that the KGB was behind it," he said, adding that the Soviet communist leadership obviously considered the new Polish pope a "menace."[29]

George Weigel told me, "If you can find a Pole who didn't think the Lubyanka [KGB headquarters] was at the end of the causal chain that ended up with Agca, I'd like to meet him or her." Weigel noted that "no sane Pole" of John Paul II's generation "doubts that the skein of responsibility eventually wound its way back to Moscow."[30]

One such Pole is the journalist Tomasz Pompowski, cited several times earlier in this book. By the time of the pope's death, Pompowski had been researching the shooting of John Paul II for years, and he, too, had concluded that the GRU planned the attack. In March 2006 he told Bill Clark and me via e-mail that the GRU had launched its attack against the pontiff from the outset of the papacy, first with what he described as "character killing"—that is, disinformation. When that was insufficient, said Pompowski, the GRU decided to kill the pope and then "blow up" Lech Wałęsa in a second grisly murder. Pompowski added that Brezhnev "wanted to invade Poland and attack Western countries in Europe," even if the Soviet leader ultimately judged that his Red Army could not pull it off.[31] Much of this is consistent with what I have reported in this book.

Pompowski even implicated Mikhail Gorbachev. He pointed to a 1979 order signed by top Soviet leaders—including Gorbachev—that authorized measures "beyond disinformation" to stop the pope. Citing Italian intelligence sources, Pompowski called this a plan for the "physical elimination" of John Paul II.

Of course, Pompowski was referring to the November 13, 1979, document by the Secretariat of the Central Committee of the Soviet Union calling for "additional measures" against Pope John Paul II, measures going "beyond disinformation and discreditation"—the major finding that John Koehler would later report in his book *Spies in the Vatican*. Koehler quoted the interpretation of the Italian security services, which judged that the Soviet document had called for the "physical elimination of JP II."[32] "I was shocked when I had found this order," Koehler told the Polish press in 2008. "The means 'beyond disinformation and discreditation' meant only one thing: an approval to kill the pope."[33]

Not everyone agrees with that assessment. George Weigel, in his book *The End and the Beginning*, argued, "Contrary to some reports, the Central Committee decree did not order the assassination of John Paul II, for the Central Committee Secretariat was an administrative body that lacked the competence to order such measures." But Weigel cited the Polish historian Andrzej Grajewski to make the point that "the very existence of the decree, as well as what seems to have been a parallel set of secret operational instructions to the KGB on active measures, strongly suggests that, within a year after John Paul II's election, Soviet intelligence considered the Pope the single greatest threat to their position."[34]

In other words, even an observer who doubts that the 1979 Soviet order authorized the "physical elimination" of the pope debunks the ludicrous idea that Moscow saw John Paul II as a "stabilizing element" in Poland—which, as Robert Gates reported, was the "dominant" view among CIA "experts." And if Soviet intelligence officials considered the pope to be the "single greatest threat to their position," one can only imagine what they might want to do to him. The KGB and GRU murdered far lesser threats.

Mikhail Gorbachev has also denied that the 1979 decree, which he signed (along with eight other Soviet leaders), signaled an approval to kill the pope. In an interview with the Italian publication *Il Tempo*, he insisted that the document referred to "political actions" and that "nothing was ordered against the pope as a person."

Interestingly, even Gorbachev revealed how misguided the CIA establishment's assessment was at the time: he said that "the Cold War was at its peak," and as a result "the activity of the pope, geared toward fighting totalitarian regimes, could only be perceived as dangerous and hostile by the Soviet government."[35]

In explaining that the Soviet leadership could not have ordered any violent actions against the pope, Gorbachev said, "At that time, similar action had been eliminated and forbidden from the KGB's arsenal." Note that he referred to the KGB, not the GRU. (It is also possible that the GRU acted without Gorbachev's knowledge.)

Another sensational report came in February 2009. Father Zdzisław Król, the chancellor of the Warsaw Metropolitan Curia, claimed that the Soviets had also tried to kill the pope during John Paul II's 1987 return visit to Poland. According to the Polish priest, Soviet intelligence had (again) hired a Bulgarian assassin to take out the pope. The act of evil was allegedly planned for the city of Częstochowa, home of the most revered Marian shrine in Poland. Father Król said that the hit man's wife, a Catholic, confessed to the priest that her husband had secret details of the pope's itinerary and was plotting to shoot John Paul II. The Church took the claim seriously and alerted Polish authorities, who arrested the would-be assassin, according to Father Król's account.[36]

Still other reports have surfaced on the communist role in attacking the pope, all of them pointing back to Moscow. Back in 1999 the Italian parliament's terrorism commission obtained files from the Stasi and from the communist-era Czech secret service suggesting two KGB plots against the pope, code-named "Pagoda" and "Infection." According to these files, mere hours after John Paul II was elected pope in October 1978, the KGB put out the call to Warsaw Pact intelligence services to run disinformation campaigns to discredit the new pontiff, to spy on the Vatican by (among other cloak-and-dagger dramatics) planting a bug inside a statue of the Virgin Mary, and to run "provocations that do not exclude his [the pope's] physical elimination."[37]

WHAT THE POPE KNEW

A few years after John Paul II's death, two new books shed light on what the pope thought about the 1981 plot to kill him. In 2008 Stanisław Dziwisz, by then elevated to cardinal, published an account of his decades of friendship with Karol Wojtyła, including his service as the pope's personal secretary. It was here that Dziwisz disclosed the pope's suspicion "that the KGB was behind" the attempt on his life.[38]

John Koehler reinforced this point, and provided more detail, when he published *Spies in the Vatican*. For the book, Koehler interviewed Paul Henze, who, along with Claire Sterling, had done the best early work unraveling Soviet complicity in the shooting of the pope. Henze had been a CIA station chief in Turkey (among other assignments) and had worked for the NSC under Zbigniew Brzezinski before devoting his time to researching the papal assassination attempt, which resulted in the book *The Plot to Kill the Pope*. He told Koehler that his chief link to the Holy See and the Holy Father was Jan Nowak-Jeziorański, director of Radio Free Europe's Voice of Free Poland. Henze said, "Nowak assured me that the Holy Father had no doubt about the fact that the KGB had mounted the plot."

That aligned with Cardinal Dziwisz's account. But Henze went further. He told Koehler that the pope had concluded he could not level any allegation against the Soviets:

> If he [John Paul II] accused the Soviets directly of trying to eliminate him, they would merely deny that they had done so and would generate a barrage of pseudo-evidence that they were innocent. The pope felt that no matter how strong the accusations he might make would be, they would not necessarily be accepted in the West.... On the other hand, he concluded he would be in a stronger position vis-à-vis the old men in the Kremlin if he refrained from making open accusations—or letting such accusations be made by his closest associates—letting suspicion grow and evidence of Soviet complicity accumulate.

As Henze added, the pope's reasoning "was logical and proved accurate," showing him to be a wise statesman.[39]

This same logic may have kept the Reagan administration from publicly mentioning a Soviet hand in the May 1981 shooting. Recall that Bill Casey's aide and son-in-law, Owen Smith, told me that John Paul II had asked Reagan and his advisers to keep quiet about the Soviets' role in the assassination plot.

Corroborating evidence for Casey's claim emerged shortly after the pope died. Thomas Melady recalled his first meeting with John Paul II after President George H.W. Bush appointed him ambassador to the Vatican. It was October 1, 1989, nine months after Reagan left the White House. "In his very calm voice," Melady remembered, "Pope John Paul II told me that he did not want the United States government to make an issue of the 1981 plot to assassinate him." When the new ambassador said that he wanted the U.S. government to dig deeper into the plot, the Holy Father responded, "No, not now." Melady noted that the pope probably did not want to do anything to interfere with the dialogue the Vatican had opened with Mikhail Gorbachev. Keep in mind that just two months later the pope would have his first meeting with the Soviet leader.[40] It could be, too, that John Paul II wanted the new Bush administration to continue a policy of silence that he and Reagan had previously agreed on.

THE TWENTIETH CENTURY ENDS

The historian John Lukacs argued that the twentieth century ended, symbolically, in 1989, when communism, the scourge that defined the century, collapsed.[41] It is an insightful observation. One might say, however, that the twentieth century ended not early but late, with the death of Pope John Paul II in April 2005, on the heels of the death of Ronald Reagan in June 2004. They were the two leaders who, more than any others, brought about the fall of communism.

And if the century terminated in 2005, I would argue that it began in 1917. That was the year of the Bolshevik Revolution, when Lenin and his fellow Marxists seized power in Russia and began exporting communism internationally. The ruthless atheistic-communist empire they built was precisely the "Evil Empire" Reagan and John Paul II faced down.

John Paul II, the Marian pope, would have pointed to that other important set of events in 1917: the reported apparitions of the Virgin Mary in Fátima, Portugal, from May through October. The Lady of Fátima predicted that another, more deadly war would soon follow the Great War then being waged; that Russia would "spread its errors throughout the world, raising up wars and persecutions of the Church," and become an "instrument of chastisement"; and that a pope—a "Bishop dressed in white"—would be shot and killed. On May 13, 1981, sixty-four years to the day after the first reported apparition, Pope John Paul II would be shot and nearly killed. He read the third and last "secret of Fátima," which had been sealed in a Vatican vault for decades, as he lay recuperating in the hospital. John Paul II became convinced that the protective hand of Mary had kept Mehmet Ali Agca's bullet from killing him. This was a pope who had long before dedicated his life, priesthood, and papacy to Mary.

It was fitting that new evidence of Soviet complicity in the 1981 assassination attempt emerged just before the pope's death, right at this symbolic end of the twentieth century. Had John Paul II seen all the evidence—including the reports that emerged in the months and years after he died—he would have found confirmation that the Second and Third Secrets of Fátima were closely linked. As he had long suspected, the attempt to kill him was among atheistic-communist Russia's many "errors" and "persecutions" and crimes over a long and bloody century.

The Soviets wanted to assassinate this pope because they understood, as did Reagan and the team he assembled in Washington—including Bill Clark and Bill Casey—that Poland was the linchpin of the Soviet Bloc. Moreover, it was the only nation within the Soviet empire that managed to survive the atheistic-communist assault on religion. It endured because of its staunch Catholicism. Thus, the election of a Polish pope—a shock, considering that Italians had held the papacy for 455 years—was an affront to the USSR. More than that, it frightened Moscow. Those fears became more pronounced after John Paul II's triumphant visit home in 1979, which inspired and emboldened the Solidarity movement that would so unnerve the communist leadership.

Ultimately, John Paul II survived the assassination attempt to join forces with Ronald Reagan—who also had survived a bullet, only six weeks earlier, and who would precede him in death by less than a year—to undermine Soviet communism in Poland and then all of Eastern Europe. As Reagan had told the pontiff, they shared the "dubious distinction" of surviving assassination attempts. When the two sat down for the first time, in the Vatican in June 1982, they confided that they felt it was nothing short of "miraculous" that they had survived. They both felt their lives had been spared for a special purpose: to end atheistic communism. Together, they dedicated themselves to achieving that goal.

According to the conventional wisdom of the time, seeking to bring down the Soviet empire was quixotic at best, dangerously delusional at worst. But a pope and a president achieved just that.

Epilogue

JUNE 27, 2011

KINDRED SPIRITS, KINDRED SOULS

On June 27, 2011, in a special event that the U.S. media ignored, a "Thanksgiving Mass for the Blessed John Paul II and for the Life of President Ronald Reagan" commenced at Saint Mary's Basilica in Kraków, Poland, Karol Wojtyła's beloved city. A contingent from the Reagan Presidential Foundation was in attendance.[1]

Saint Mary's Basilica is a towering thirteenth-century structure dedicated to the Assumption of the Blessed Virgin. The magnificent church has more than a dozen special altars, from the ornate central high altar to smaller ones dedicated to Saint Anne, Saint Mary Magdalene, Saint Jerome, Saint Augustine, Saint Joseph, Saint Stanisław, and other figures. In August 1939, just before the Nazi invasion, the Poles disassembled the church's centuries-old, beautifully carved main altarpiece and hid the sculptures. The Germans soon found the altarpiece, however, and seized it. After the war, Polish authorities recovered the sacred treasure in Nuremberg. After an extensive renovation, the high altar returned to its rightful place at Saint Mary's in 1957—when a young priest named Karol Wojtyła was serving his sixth of seven years of priestly duties at the church. Three decades later, on June 9, 1979, Pope John Paul II stood in front of the altar in all its glory as he presided at Mass during his first visit home as history's first Polish pontiff.[2]

And so, on June 27, 2011, it was at this church, dedicated to Poland's and the universal Church's Blessed Mother, that Poles held a memorial Mass of thanksgiving for two leaders who had united to bring down the great atheistic-communist menace of the previous century.

So many milestones in the lives of Ronald Reagan and Karol Wojtyła occurred at very nearly the same time. This distinctive confluence continued in death, as the thanksgiving Mass demonstrated. Saint Mary's chose this occasion because 2011 marked both the centenary of Reagan's birth (February 6) and the beatification of Pope John Paul II (May 1—Divine Mercy Sunday). Beatification was a crucial marker on the path to the Polish pope's eventual canonization.

The welcome statement in the Mass program highlighted the bonds these two men had shared:

> Pope John Paul II and President Ronald Reagan were united by a singular bond of friendship. They were united in their concern for the world's future. And their efforts helped to bring about a restoration of freedom, justice, and peace in the world. We trust that the great achievements of Blessed John Paul II and President Ronald Reagan will not only find their place in the history books of Poland and the United States but will continue to strengthen the bonds of friendship that exist between the two nations.

Officiating the Mass was Cardinal Stanisław Dziwisz, longtime aide to the late Polish pontiff, who had held a wounded pope in his arms on May 13, 1981. Dziwisz gave a powerful homily on the meaning of Reagan and John Paul II. This world, Cardinal Dziwisz noted, is "a battlefield of good and evil, love and hatred, truth and falsehood, solidarity and egotism." Each of us faces a choice as to which side we wish to stand on, he said; "today we recall two great men who stood before this very choice, and how their decision influenced the course of history and shaped the world in which we live today."

Cardinal Dziwisz focused on what united these two men, even as they operated in different spheres and came equipped with a unique set of experiences. Both John Paul II and Reagan, he said, "set their eyes on the same goal, and that is why they were united in so many matters." That goal was to bring down what Reagan "so aptly named 'the evil empire.'" The two leaders were "instrumental in bringing about the collapse of Communism in Poland and in the countries of Central and Eastern Europe."

The Polish cardinal closed by thanking God for the life, teaching, guidance, and pastoral leadership of John Paul II, and for the life and work of Ronald Reagan and "all the good" he brought about.

"A SINGULAR BOND"

"Pope John Paul II and President Ronald Reagan were united by a singular bond of friendship."

This line from the program of the Saint Mary's thanksgiving Mass may seem like embellishment. After all, Reagan biographers typically pay little heed to this friendship. To cite only a couple of examples, Lou Cannon, the first authoritative Reagan biographer, included only five references to John Paul II in his 883-page biography, and Edmund Morris, the official Reagan biographer, managed merely one passing reference to the pontiff in his 874-page tome.[3]

But look again. Recall that in the spring of 1989 Reagan told visitors from the Polish Solidarity movement that the pope was his "best friend." The Poles were not the only ones to hear Reagan say that about John Paul II. Mrs. Reagan herself heard her husband express his special regard for the pontiff. The late Martin Anderson, who was a close adviser to the president and later one of the most prolific researchers and writers on Reagan, said that Nancy Reagan told him John Paul II was her husband's "closest friend."[4]

Reagan's use of these terms to describe Pope John Paul II surely reflected a certain genial overstatement on the president's part.[5] It's not as if the two leaders were buddies, getting together for barbecues and telephoning each other to catch up about their lives. But the "best friend" designation should not be dismissed either. It speaks to the remarkable bond Reagan and John Paul II formed.

Bill Clark, who was one of Reagan's closest confidants and advisers, more than once described Reagan and John Paul II to me as "kindred spirits, kindred souls." I used that phrase when I interviewed Frank Shakespeare, Reagan's second ambassador to the Vatican (and self-identified first and only "ambassador to Fátima"). Shakespeare had a unique view as someone who knew and briefed both the president and the pope. In our interview, he seized on the description immediately: "Yes! That's exactly what they were—kindred spirits and kindred souls."[6]

The dissimilarities between Reagan and John Paul II—American and Pole, Protestant and Catholic, political leader and spiritual leader—are so obvious that they can obscure the many important areas of kinship. Throughout this book we have seen the intriguing parallels between their lives: the health crises their mothers experienced when they were eight years old, the deaths of their fathers in 1941, their shared experiences in acting and athletics, the unconventional paths they took to their positions, their mystical sides, and so much more.

Ultimately, the bond they formed did not hinge on such similarities or even on their mutual affection, real as those things were. Their partnership and friendship went deeper than that. Philosophically, the two leaders shared an understanding of the reinforcing relationship of faith and freedom, the importance of ordered liberty, and the evil of atheistic, totalitarian communism. They seemed to sense this philosophical kinship before they ever met; they began a rich correspondence in the first year of Reagan's presidency that set the tone for their later meetings. Reagan recognized the importance of a partnership with the pope even before he became president: footage of the pope's 1979 trip to Poland moved him to tears and convinced him that John Paul II "would help change the world." The pope was "the key," and Reagan was intent on making him and the Vatican an ally.

No other single factor brought them closer together than the attempts on their lives. When Reagan was shot, a shocked pope prayed for his recovery; just six weeks later, it was the president's turn to be shocked and to pray. Reagan felt so concerned about the pope that he asked National Security Adviser Dick Allen for updates every day for weeks. In each case, recovery was no sure thing: insider accounts of their (strikingly similar) near-death experiences show that Reagan and John Paul II were not exaggerating when they later said it was "miraculous" that they both survived.

History often turns on such fascinating confluences or coincidences. Here two towering world leaders were shot only six weeks apart early in their tenures (Reagan had been president just two months; John Paul II had been pope only two and a half years). What is perhaps most striking about the twin assassination attempts is the effect they had on the victims, and thus on twentieth-century history. Before the shootings, Moscow had worried about the effects of having these two outspoken anticommunists in the world's most prominent positions of political and spiritual leadership. What the Soviets couldn't have anticipated was how much the pope's and president's shared "dubious distinction" drove John Paul II and Reagan together, creating precisely the partnership the Kremlin feared most.

Of course, neither John Paul II nor Ronald Reagan saw any of this as a "confluence" or a "coincidence." The Marian pope was convinced not merely that Our Lady of Fátima had predicted the attempt on his life but also that the Blessed Mother had intervened to cause gunman Mehmet Ali Agca to miss his precise target. John Paul II believed in Divine Providence—that "the destiny of all nations lies in the hands of a merciful Providence." Reagan, always his mother's son, believed that "all things were part of God's Plan." The assassination attempts were most certainly part of that plan, in Reagan's eyes. When he and the pope met for the first time a year after the shootings, he said, "Look how the evil forces were put in our way and how Providence intervened." Reagan also saw his and the pope's efforts to defeat an "Evil Empire" as part of a providential plan. That is why he and Bill Clark so often referred to the DP—the Divine Plan.

Reagan and John Paul II believed that God had spared their lives for a reason. And during that pivotal June 1982 meeting at the Vatican, they privately, but quite explicitly, joined forces to fulfill what they saw as their special mission: to hasten the demise of the atheistic-communist empire and free the millions living in subjugation.

The bonds between John Paul II and Ronald Reagan ran far deeper than most observers have ever realized. No, they were not pals or buddies, despite their obvious affection for each other. They were united in their pursuit of an overriding objective, a world-changing one. That objective flowed from their staunch anticommunism and from their spiritual bond. They shared the conviction that totalitarian communism was an affront to human freedom and human dignity. And they both believed that they were part of a providential plan.

Frank Shakespeare saw the Reagan–John Paul II relationship as profoundly providential as well; the timing of their rise to power "was extremely significant," he told me.[7] Shakespeare saw something else that linked the president and the pope: "Through it all is the extraordinary weaving of Fátima."[8]

The Fátima connection is perhaps the most surprising link between John Paul II and Ronald Reagan. But it is clear from aides who briefed Reagan that the Protestant president, who always had a fondness for the Virgin Mary, was intensely interested in accounts of the Fátima apparitions and the Blessed Mother's reported prophecies in 1917.[9] There is even evidence to suggest that Reagan may have discussed Fátima with John Paul II himself.

Pope Benedict XVI may have best summed up how Fátima connects to the special partnership between John Paul II and Reagan. John Paul II's successor, who as Cardinal Joseph Ratzinger had written the "Theological Commentary" on Fátima's Third Secret, traveled to the Portuguese village on May 13, 2010. Benedict said, "In sacred Scripture we often find that God seeks righteous men and women in order to save the city of man and he does the same here, in Fátima."[10]

Pope John Paul II and President Ronald Reagan answered the call. As Cardinal Dziwisz said, they chose the side of good against evil, and in coming together to do so, they "influenced the course of history." They rewrote the ending of the story of the twentieth century.

Acknowledgments

As I write these acknowledgments, I glance at an old note I found only a few weeks ago, a note telling myself that I needed to write this book. More than ten years old, it records that my commitment came on Divine Mercy Sunday, April 23, 2006. I was inspired by a documentary on Saint Faustina that good friend Kathy Whittaker gave my wife, Susan. I had just finished my book *The Crusader: Ronald Reagan and the Fall of Communism* and was juggling two other book projects. I laid it all out in the note, including this time line: "I can aim for a 2017 release on the 100th anniversary of Fátima and the Bolshevik Revolution." Lest I pat myself on the back for my foresight and managerial skills, I also wrote this laughable directive to myself: "This book needs to be short: no more than 100–200 pages." My editor, Jed Donahue, will get a chuckle out of that. I handed him a manuscript well over a thousand pages.

Thus, this book has been years in the making, so long that some of those I want to acknowledge may be surprised to realize they contributed to it. Most have been students of mine at Grove City College in Grove City, Pennsylvania. In no particular order, I thank Shannon McDade, Allison Bimber, Alex Welch, Hannah Lutz, Annabelle Rutledge, Matt Costlow, Thomas Whittaker, Sharon Koss, Natalie Nagel, David Kirk, Andrew Kloes, Allan Edwards, Drew Brackbill, Jennifer Moyer, Nick Clinton, Brittany Pizor, Alex Brown, Claire Healey, and Melissa Borza. Among them, David Kirk was our go-to guy in the final stretch; right up to the end he went with research questions to the Reagan Library, where he has served as a docent during the summers. I also thank Julie Fox, who was especially helpful in her research on Claire Sterling's findings, and Rachel Bovard, who collected material on Ronald Reagan's public responses to questions on a suspected Soviet role in the shooting of John Paul II. Finally, Daniel Hanson, a student who speaks and reads Russian, was indispensable in digging through Soviet press archives. My daughters Abigail and Amanda helped pick the wonderful cover photo for this book.

Special thanks to my friend Fred Kingery, a terrific guy. Fred served as my connection to Jack, whose story of the events in West Berlin on March 29–30, 1981, I tell in chapter 17. I also thank Ann Lewis of the Reagan Centennial Commission; Kirby Hanson and John Heubusch of the Reagan Presidential Foundation; John Morris of Eureka College; Mike Murtagh of Eureka College; Andrew Coffin, Kimberly Begg, Ron Robinson, and the rest of the staff at Young America's Foundation and the Reagan Ranch Center; the late Herb Romerstein; and Reagan biographer Craig Shirley. I am especially grateful to Joanne Drake, longtime right hand to the late Nancy Reagan, who was extremely helpful in getting answers to my questions directly from the former first lady, and to Michael Reagan, truly his father's son. I also appreciate the many former Reagan staffers and aides to Bill Clark and Bill Casey who helped in my research. I am indebted to all the many sources, both named and unnamed, who consented to interviews.

I also want to express my thanks to the whole team at the Intercollegiate Studies Institute and its publishing imprint, ISI Books. Jed Donahue, Anthony Sacramone, and Tom Cusmano have all been a pleasure to work with. Jed is an extraordinary, gifted editor, a master of his craft. I was very concerned about finding the right editor for this book, which is so special to me. There was never any doubt in my mind that Jed was the guy. He does absolutely everything in the editing process, from finessing minor details and fact checking and copyediting to overhauling the content with major structural changes and deletions of text that (even when intriguing) simply had to go. He is amazing. Jed was clearly part of the DP. I am grateful as well to the generous ISI supporters who helped make it possible to publish and promote this book, including Carole Beecher Brown, Bill and Anne Burleigh, Phil Gasiewicz, George O. Pfaff, Thomas J. Posatko, and C.J. Queenan Jr.

* * * *

Finally, I would like to express special gratitude to the person to whom I dedicate this book, who became not only the subject of one of my biographies but also a friend and mentor: William P. Clark. I want to thank Clark and also take a moment to close out his story, which relates to many of the themes of this book.

It was through Clark that I set off on an investigation into a possible Soviet role in the attempted assassination of Pope John Paul II. When Bill and I worked on his biography (*The Judge: William P. Clark, Ronald Reagan's Top Hand*, which Ignatius Press published in 2007), we spent months together as he recounted his past and we excavated material from the dusty shelves and boxes of his home office, his town office, his barn, and his tack room. When I was not staying at his ranch, or sitting with him in his living room or car, we were chatting by phone at least weekly and often daily (sometimes multiple times per day).

A pivotal moment came when I asked him this question one day in the summer of 2005: "Bill, did Reagan ever suspect a Soviet role in the shooting of Pope John Paul II?" He responded slowly: "Well, Paul, . . ." I found myself so engrossed in what he told me that I neglected to push the button on my handheld audio recorder. And there it began.

The original manuscript of my Clark biography included three thousand words on Reagan, Clark, and the attempted assassination of Pope John Paul II. (At the time I did not know about Casey's secret CIA investigation.) To my great consternation, Clark asked that I remove this material from the manuscript before I submitted it to the editor. I tried to persuade Clark to change his mind, explaining that I merely wanted to note Reagan's, Bill Casey's, and his own reasonable suspicions of a Soviet role in the shooting. I suggested that the account cast Reagan as a responsible president who kept his conjecture to himself out of fear of upsetting the world. I also noted that suspicions of a Soviet role had been a news story at the time; major newspapers had even reported Clark's meeting with Casey to discuss the CIA's investigation. In other words, this was part of the historical record and thus merited inclusion.

Clark understood my points but still advised against incorporating the episode in his biography. He said he did not know for sure whether the Soviets had ordered the shooting and did not want to go on the record with speculation. Having run Reagan's foreign policy and been a judge, Clark had learned to be prudent and avoid speculation in his on-the-record statements. "I don't want the focus of attention to be on a part of the book for which we are not absolutely sure and clear," he told me.

I was disappointed, but I honored Clark's request to leave the material out. In agreeing to be his biographer, I had promised him that I would honor his wishes to exclude information he preferred not to disclose. We made the final decision on July 6, 2006. The published version of *The Judge* retained only a few words on the assassination attempt.

Clark understood that he was depriving a historian of a significant story. As we resolved our final course of action that July day at his ranch, he looked at me with a wry smile and, with a wink, said, "Of course, this might be something you could use one day in another of your books." He repeated the thought later: "This will eventually come out. And you have enough here for another book."

The wise judge was right. The patient approach he counseled led me to investigate the story much more thoroughly, conducting many interviews, filing repeated FOIA requests, and burrowing into the archives. More than a decade after our initial conversations on the subject, the material in this book is the result.

* * * *

At that point Clark was planning a final trip to Europe with his beloved wife, Joan, as the two raced against time, Bill with Parkinson's and Joan with the loss of memory. He envisioned a visit to Rome to reconnect with his old friend Pio Laghi and intended to ask Laghi some questions on the shooting of John Paul II. He told me that the answers would be too late for our biography but not for a subsequent work of mine.

That trip never happened. Joan contracted an aggressive form of pancreatic cancer that took her long before dementia could become too debilitating. She died in April 2009.

Joan, too, had been a victim of the communist errors that Our Lady of Fátima had warned against. She was born in Czechoslovakia on July 23, 1931. The nation was captured by Nazis and then communists. Joan escaped via West Berlin in 1952, where she met a twenty-something GI named Bill Clark.

Joan Brauner Clark despised communism even more than did Bill Clark and Ronald Reagan—because she, like John Paul II, had lived it. But it would be Bill's and Reagan's and John Paul II's task to undermine it.

When she passed, I got the news of her death in a somber voicemail from Bill, which to this day I have not erased. He seemed to handle the death stoically, but he told me it was much harder than he had expected. He had always expected to go first. They would have no final trip to Europe. And likewise Bill would not reunite with Pio Laghi, who had died on January 11, 2009, in Rome, a few months before Joan passed.

After Joan's death, Bill Clark became a Franciscan friar. I got confirmation of that development in the "DP" from Bill via a phone message on Sunday, October 17, 2010. I was unable to return the call before he telephoned again on Monday; he also had his faithful assistant, Liana, e-mail me asking me to call him right away. Liana sent a PDF of the letter accepting him into the Franciscan order. When I called him, he said, "Boy, I'm so glad it's you." He told me he was now officially a Franciscan friar, Third Order (the Third Order is composed of laymen and laywomen who live in marriage and in families). "Paul, I've been thinking about this since 1949," he said. "The Holy Spirit sort of guided me in." Clark joined more than sixty years after he left an Augustinian novitiate to go into public service and fight the Cold War.

As Clark took this final step, he paused to consider his late wife's role in this special grace. "Maybe [it was] that extra intercession of Joan in heaven," he told me. "She's smiling, I'm sure."

Bill Clark decided he was going to reach out to Mikhail Gorbachev. We recalled Gorbachev's praying at the tomb of Saint Francis in Assisi. "Now," said Clark, "he'll be told he has an actual Franciscan friar and order praying for him."

Unfortunately, Clark's condition steadily and then precipitously worsened. The meeting with Gorbachev never transpired.

Clark died on August 10, 2013, at age eighty-one. He had been ailing for a long time, suffering terribly for months. He quipped, "The good Lord gave Parkinson's to saints like John Paul II and my father, and now he has gotten around to giving it to sinners like myself." Like Saint Francis, he accepted the trial as part of what one endures in this world on behalf of God's kingdom.

Clark had called me one day in tears, choked up by the news that the Franciscan order had given him permission to be buried in the habit. In the end, he considered himself unworthy of such a burial. His son Paul told me in an e-mail: "He wore the habit once when they made him a friar, Third Order. That was when he spent a lot of time at the mission—actually living there for a few months and receiving religious instruction. He never wore it again and he was buried in civilian clothes."

Bill Clark's funeral Mass was held on August 14, 2013. It was the eve of the Assumption of Mary. He was carried out of his chapel in a plain pine coffin, just like Pope John Paul II's. The hymn sung during Holy Communion at the Mass was "Be Not Afraid." Those words of Christ in Scripture always reminded Clark of John Paul II's exhortation.

Bill Clark's life, like the lives of Ronald Reagan and John Paul II, bears witness to the president's and pope's affirmation that there is purpose and worth to each and every life, and that every human being is unique and unrepeatable within the Divine Plan.

Paul Kengor
March 7, 2017

Notes

PROLOGUE: MAY 13, 1981: MOSCOW TAKES ITS SHOT

1 Estimates on the crowd size generally ranged from ten thousand to thirty thousand.
2 On this quotation, see Brian Crozier, *The Rise and Fall of the Soviet Empire* (Rocklin, CA: Forum, 1999), 358.
3 Here are two occasions when Reagan quoted these words from Wałęsa: Reagan, "Remarks at the Centennial Meeting of the Supreme Council of the Knights of Columbus," Hartford, Connecticut, August 3, 1982; and Reagan, "Address Before a Joint Session of the Irish National Parliament," June 4, 1984.
4 Published in the Soviet literary journal *Polimya*, March 1981. Translated by Alex Alexiev, "The Kremlin and the Pope," *The Rand Paper Series* (The Rand Corporation, Santa Monica, CA), April 1983, 13.
5 See Paul Kengor, *The Crusader: Ronald Reagan and the Fall of Communism* (New York: HarperPerennial, 2007).
6 The one who struck the blow was Mehmet Ali Agca. He would name Todor Aivazov, Sergei Antonov, Omer Bagci, Musa Cerdar Celebi, Bekir Celenk, Oral Çelik, and Zelio Vasilev. On this, see Claire Sterling, *The Time of the Assassins* (New York: Holt, Rinehart, and Winston, 1985), 263. Throughout this book, I have incorporated material from Sterling's tireless investigation and also from (among others) the superb work of the Italian judge Ilario Martella, who produced an exceptional 1,243-page report in late

1984, implicating all of these men (three Bulgarians and five Turks) in a conspiracy to assassinate John Paul II.

7 Sterling, *The Time of the Assassins*, 251; and Judge Martella's report, titled *Ordinanza di rinvio a giudizio* (Ruling for indictment and trial), October 26, 1984 (hereafter referred to as "Judge Martella report").

8 Some sources report the gun used as a 9-millimeter Browning, whereas others report it as a 9-millimeter Walther.

9 Judge Martella report.

10 Thomas J. Craughwell, *St. Peter's Bones* (New York: Image Books, 2013), 11.

11 Some reports claim that Çelik fired the third shot, which hit the pontiff. Most accounts claim that the first shot was fired around 5:13 P.M. Rome time. Among the more popular sources on the shooting, see Tad Szulc, *Pope John Paul II: The Biography* (New York: Scribner, 1995), 389; and Carl Bernstein and Marco Politi, *His Holiness: John Paul II and the Hidden History of Our Time* (New York: Doubleday, 1996), 304.

12 I do not know of other writers who have made an explicit Fátima connection to the 5:13 time. I noticed the irony on my own, though I'm sure I'm not the first. That said, others have reported the time as 5:17 and even 5:19. The *New York Times* the next day reported the time as 5:19 P.M. (see Henry Tanner, "Pope Is Shot in Car in Vatican Square…2 Bullets Hit Pontiff," *New York Times*, May 14, 1981). Cardinal Stanisław Dziwisz, in his book, *A Life with Karol* (New York: Doubleday, 2007), also says that the time was 5:19 (page 130), as do Andrew Apostoli, *Fátima for Today* (San Francisco: Ignatius Press, 2010) (see page 187), and Cardinal Tarcisio Bertone, *The Last Secret of Fátima* (New York: Doubleday, 2008) (see page 161), both of which are extremely reliable. To the contrary, George Weigel, in his authoritative biography, *Witness to Hope: The Biography of Pope John Paul II* (New York: Harper, 1999), reports the time as 5:13 (see page 412), as does John O'Sullivan in *The President, the Pope, and the Prime Minister: Three Who Changed the World* (Washington, DC: Regnery Publishing, 2006) (see page 66); O'Sullivan draws his account from several on-hand witnesses and authoritative biographies.

13 Sources vary on the exact role of the nun. All agree that she was the first to grab Agca, though some say she held his arm firmly and long enough for others to subdue him whereas others claim she subdued him by knocking him down. Some sources even claim that the nun grabbed Acga's arm while he was shooting and thus redirected the bullet just enough to spare the Holy Father's life, a claim I believe is apocryphal. In *Vicars of Christ: Popes, Power, and Politics in the Modern World* (New York: Crossroad, 1998), Michael P. Riccards writes, "A nun from Bergamo, Sister Letizia, had deflected the aim of the professional assassin by pulling on his jacket, and thus probably saved John Paul's life" (page 287). In *The Book of Assassins: A Biographical Dictionary from Ancient Times to the Present* (New York: Wiley, 2012), George Fetherling writes: "Agca dropped his pistol and turned to escape when he was knocked to the ground and subdued by Suor [Sister] Letizia, a large and robust nun. Letizia shouted, 'Why did you do it?' To which Agca responded, 'Not me, not me.' Agca was held until police arrived." As these details suggest, Sister Letizia's physical makeup has been reported differently as well. Fetherling calls her "large and robust." Other sources, such as Claire Sterling, have described her as a "sturdy little nun." Sterling, *The Time of the Assassins*, 4.

14 Sterling, *The Time of the Assassins*, 4, 206.

15 Tanner, "Pope Is Shot in Car in Vatican Square."

16 Quoted in Tanner, "Pope Is Shot in Car in Vatican Square."

17 Dziwisz, *A Life with Karol*, 133–34.

18 See, e.g., O'Sullivan, *The President, the Pope, and the Prime Minister*; Weigel, *Witness to Hope*; George Weigel, *The End and the Beginning: Pope John Paul II—The Victory of Freedom, the Last Years, the Legacy* (New York: Doubleday, 2010); Robert Conquest, "The Historical Failings of CNN," in Arnold Beichman, ed., *CNN's Cold War Documentary* (Stanford, CA: Hoover Institution Press, 2000); Richard V. Allen, "Pope John Paul II,

Ronald Reagan, and the Collapse of Communism: An Historic Confluence," in Douglas E. Streusand, Norman A. Bailey, and Francis H. Marlo, eds., *The Grand Strategy That Won the Cold War: Architecture of Triumph* (Lanham, MD: Lexington Books, 2016); Carl Bernstein, "The Holy Alliance," *Time*, February 24, 1992; and Bernstein and Politi, *His Holiness*.

19 Allen, "Pope John Paul II, Ronald Reagan, and the Collapse of Communism: An Historic Confluence"; Richard V. Allen, interviewed in the PBS documentary *Liberating a Continent: John Paul II and the Fall of Communism* (2016); O'Sullivan, *The President, the Pope, and the Prime Minister*, 92.

20 Bernstein, "The Holy Alliance," 31.

CHAPTER 1: MAY 13, 1917: AN ECHO

1 Pope John Paul II, *Redemptoris Mater*, March 25, 1987.

2 Pope John Paul II, Angelus message on the Solemnity of the Assumption of the Blessed Virgin Mary, Castel Gandolfo, August 15, 2003.

3 An excellent resource that tracks these claims is the Marian Library/International Marian Research Institute at the University of Dayton (Ohio). It reports: "A statistical analysis of the Marian apparition directory reveals the following results. During the twentieth century, there have been 386 cases of Marian apparitions. The Church has made 'no decision' about the supernatural character regarding 299 of the 386 cases. The Church has made a 'negative decision' about the supernatural character in seventy-nine of the 386 cases. Out of the 386 apparitions, the Church has decided that 'yes' there is a supernatural character only in eight cases: Fátima (Portugal), Beauraing (Belgium), Banneux (Belgium), Akita (Japan), Syracuse (Italy), Zeitoun (Egypt), Manila (Philippines) (according to some sources), and Betania (Venezuela)." In sum, this source points to eight cases. Another source, Cardinal Tarcisio Bertone, in his authoritative *The Last Secret of Fátima* (New York: Doubleday, 2008), says that the Church has recognized eleven Marian apparitions (page 10). There are serious claims of Marian apparitions dating back to the third century, with an alleged appearance recorded by Saint Gregory of Nyssa. The major apparitions approved by the Church, however, really begin in the sixteenth century, with Our Lady of Guadalupe in Mexico, followed by famous appearances in places like Lourdes, France, in 1858.

4 As just one example, countless thousands if not millions of Catholics are convinced that the Virgin Mary has been for decades appearing (with regularity) in an area of the former Yugoslavia called Medjugorje. Many Church leaders are convinced that the apparitions are genuine, or at least are open to the possibility that they are. Pope Benedict XVI was, at the least, sympathetic, as was John Paul II, and as is (reportedly) Pope Francis. Still, the institutional Church has not certified the appearances and the many supernatural claims that the faithful insist have transpired there. The Church does not rush into these decisions.

5 Bertone, *The Last Secret of Fátima*, 97–98.

6 Apostoli, *Fátima for Today*, 43–44.

7 Ibid., 44–45.

8 See the June 26, 2000, official Vatican statement, "The Message of Fátima," published by the Holy See's Congregation for the Doctrine of the Faith. It is also summarized by Apostoli, *Fátima for Today*, 53–56, and Bertone, *The Last Secret of Fátima*, 44–48.

9 What happened at Fátima has been retold in countless articles, books, pamphlets, Web postings, and every other form of recording imaginable. Some of these are reliable; others are not. In my account that follows, I relied in particular on two recent books that I strongly recommend to readers: Father Andrew Apostoli, *Fátima for Today*, and Cardinal Tarcisio Bertone, *The Last Secret of Fátima*. The latter includes a foreword from the

then-sitting pope, Pope Benedict XVI, and is probably unmatched as the most official contemporary source on the subject. I also relied on official Vatican documents. In addition, particularly good on the subject of John Paul II, Mikhail Gorbachev's Russia, and Fátima is an unheralded work by Timothy Tindal-Robertson, *Fátima, Russia, and Pope John Paul II* (Still River, MA: The Ravengate Press, 1992). I have tried consistently to cite these three gentlemen when relying specifically on their unique works or insights.

10 Apostoli, *Fátima for Today*, 123–25.

11 Dr. Almeida Garrett's full account is published in a lengthy (396-page) collection of Fátima eyewitness accounts compiled by Antonio Maria Martins, *Novos Documentos de Fátima* (San Paulo: Edicoes Loyola [Loyola Editions], 1984). Garrett's account has been translated and republished by many Fátima sources. It can be found online at the Fátima website, www.fatima.org.

12 This account has been excerpted and republished in many sources. The text used here appears in Bertone, *The Last Secret of Fátima*, 18–19.

13 Bertone, *The Last Secret of Fátima*, 18.

14 The numbers on the crowd size vary, but most estimate the total present at seventy thousand. The Bertone book claims that seventy thousand assembled in the Cova da Iria alone (Bertone, *The Last Secret of Fátima*, 18). The Apostoli book says seventy-five thousand total—roughly fifty-five thousand "in the area of the Cova da Iria" and an additional twenty thousand who observed the miracle "from as far as 25 miles away" (Apostoli, *Fátima for Today*, 128).

15 For more testimonies, see Apostoli, *Fátima for Today*, 129–34, and also the website of EWTN: http://www.ewtn.com/fatima/apparitions/October.htm.

16 Quoted by David Gress, "The Second Fall," *National Review*, July 12, 1999.

17 Michael D. Hull, review of John Keegan's *The First World War*, published in *Military History*, February 2000, 66.

18 Quoted in George Nash, "Slouching Toward Catastrophe," *Imprimis* 21, no. 4 (April 1992).

19 Afonso Costa, Declaration to the Congress of Free Thought, March 26, 1911, quoted in Brother Michel de la Sainte Trinité, *The Whole Truth about Fátima: The Secret and the Church* (Buffalo: Immaculate Heart Publications, 1989), vol. 2.

20 Pope Pius X, *On the Law of Separation in Portugal*, May 24, 1911.

21 Giancarlo Finazzo, "The Virgin Mary in the Koran," *L'Osservatore Romano*, April 13, 1978.

22 Fulton J. Sheen, *The World's First Love: Mary, Mother of God* (New York: McGraw-Hill, 1952), 204–7.

23 Angelo Stagnaro, "Pilgrimage to Where the Sun Danced," *National Catholic Register*, May 9, 2010.

24 Sheen, *The World's First Love*, 207.

25 Apostoli, *Fátima for Today*, 12.

CHAPTER 2: OCTOBER 26, 1917: THE DEVILS TAKE OVER

1 This passage is adapted from Aleksandr Solzhenitsyn, *The Gulag Archipelago, 1918–1956* (New York: Harper and Row, 1974), 346–49.

2 Dmitri Volkogonov, *Lenin: A New Biography* (New York: The Free Press, 1994), 374.

3 Ibid., 374, 380.

4 Ibid., 376.

5 Lenin's biographer records, "Usually able to control himself, now he stormed and cursed." Ibid., 376.

6 Ibid., 376–78.

7 Ibid., 383.

8 Solzhenitsyn, *The Gulag Archipelago*, 346–49; and Volkogonov, *Lenin*, 382.
9 J.M. Bochenski, "Marxism-Leninism and Religion," in B.R. Bociurkiw et al., eds., *Religion and Atheism in the USSR and Eastern Europe* (London: Macmillan, 1975), 11.
10 See Alexander N. Yakovlev, *A Century of Violence in Soviet Russia* (New Haven and London: Yale University Press, 2002), 157.
11 This is per the Julian, or Old Style, calendar that Russia then observed; this calendar was thirteen days behind the Western calendar.
12 Lenin wrote this in a November 13 or 14, 1913, letter to Maxim Gorky. See James Thrower, *God's Commissar: Marxism-Leninism as the Civil Religion of Soviet Society* (Lewiston, NY: Edwin Mellen Press, 1992), 39.
13 Wurmbrand's testimony occurred in May 1966 and is excerpted in his book *Tortured for Christ* (Bartlesville, OK: Living Sacrifice Book Company, 2013).
14 The repression was pursued in varying degrees among the Soviet Bloc nations. Romania, Albania, East Germany, and Czechoslovakia were especially repressive.
15 For an extended discussion, see Paul Kengor, "The Communist War on Religion," posted at www.globalmuseumoncommunism.org.
16 The "opiate of the masses" remark is well known. The source for the quotation "communism begins where atheism begins" is Fulton J. Sheen, *Communism and the Conscience of the West* (Indianapolis and NY: Bobbs-Merrill, 1948). Sheen, who spoke and read several languages, translated the quote into English from an untranslated Marx work.
17 Marx and Engels, *The Communist Manifesto* (New York: Penguin Signet Classics, 1998), 74.
18 See Bochenski, "Marxism-Leninism and Religion," 11.
19 Quoted in Thrower, *God's Commissar*, 39. Another translation of this quotation comes from Robert Conquest, in his "The Historical Failings of CNN," in Beichman, ed., *CNN's Cold War Documentary*, 57.
20 See Daniel Peris, *Storming the Heavens: The Soviet League of the Militant Godless* (Ithaca, NY: Cornell University Press, 1998).
21 Soviet officials substituted secular civil ceremonies infused with communist ideology, known as "red weddings," "red baptisms," and "red funerals." In red baptisms, infants were given social "godparents" who undertook to ensure that the child was brought up to become a worthy "builder of communism." The parents of newborn children would promise to raise their children "not as slaves for the bourgeoisie, but as fighters against it." Young mothers would declare: "The child belongs to me only physically. For his spiritual upbringing, I entrust him to society." See Thrower, *God's Commissar*, 64; Jennifer McDowell, "Soviet Civil Ceremonies," *Journal for the Scientific Study of Religion* 13, no. 3 (1974): 265–79; and David E. Powell, "Rearing the New Soviet Man," in Bociurkiw et al., *Religion and Atheism in the USSR and Eastern Europe*, 160–65.
22 W. Bruce Lincoln, *Red Victory: A History of the Russian Civil War* (New York: Simon and Schuster, 1989), 476–77.
23 Vladimir Lenin stated this in *Pravda*, June 16, 1913, republished according to the original *Pravda* text in *Lenin, Collected Works* (Moscow: Progress Publishers, 1977), 19:235–37.
24 See my discussion in Paul Kengor, *Takedown: From Communists to Progressives, How the Left Has Sabotaged Family and Marriage* (Washington, DC: WND Books, 2015).
25 On the antireligious museums, see "A Restored Look for the Long-Ignored Churches of Russia," Associated Press, July 23, 1976.
26 Hedrick Smith, *The Russians* (London: Sphere Books, 1976), 396.
27 Ibid., 396.
28 Lincoln, *Red Victory*, 474.
29 Volkogonov, *Lenin*, 379.
30 On this, see Solzhenitsyn, *The Gulag Archipelago*, 37–38.
31 Volkogonov, *Lenin*, 381.

32 Gerhard Simon, "The Catholic Church and the Communist State in the Soviet Union and Eastern Europe," in Bociurkiw et al., *Religion and Atheism in the USSR and Eastern Europe*, 212–13.
33 The American "socialists" were Boris Reinstein and S.J. Rutgers.
34 John Riddell, ed., *Founding the Communist International: Proceedings and Documents of the First Congress, March 1919* (New York: Pathfinder Press, 1987), 41–43.
35 V.I. Lenin, "Welcoming Remarks at the First Congress of the Communist International," March 2, 1919, *Collected Works*, 28:455–77.
36 See Richard Pipes, *Communism: A History* (New York: A Modern Library Chronicles Book, 2001), 93.
37 Among other sources, see Crozier, *The Rise and Fall of the Soviet Empire*, 38–40, and Stephane Courtois et al., *The Black Book of Communism* (Cambridge: Harvard University Press, 1999), 275–76.
38 Richard Pipes, "The Cold War: CNN's Version," in Beichman, ed., *CNN's Cold War Documentary*, 45–46. These guidelines are consistent with the goals of Leninism, outlined in Lenin's 1920 work, *"Left-Wing" Communism: An Infantile Disorder.*
39 See Jane Degras, ed., *The Communist International, 1919–1943: Documents* (London: Oxford University Press, 1956), 1:166–72.
40 The party flag unfurled in America in the fall of 1919, when two communist parties took form, the Communist Labor Party (CLP) and the Communist Party of America (CPA). They were organized at a convention in Chicago during the first week of September. The CLP and a faction of the CPA merged in 1920 to form the United Communist Party. Later, the CPA and UCP merged under the name of the former—CPA. In 1921 this group changed its name to the Workers Party of America; the name changed again in 1925, to Workers (Communist) Party of America. In 1929 the communists formed a single Communist Party USA (CPUSA). This sequence of name changes and mergers is described by Harvey Klehr in his opening to the Library of Congress reference book *Files of the Communist Party of the United States of America in the Comintern Archives.*
41 E-mail correspondence with Herbert Romerstein, April 16, 2007.
42 Printed in "The Communist Party of the United States of America: What It Is, How It Works," Committee on the Judiciary, U.S. Senate, 84th Congress, 2nd Session, April 23, 1956 (Washington, DC: GPO, 1956), 2.
43 This is published in the English translation of *The Capitalist World and the Communist International Manifesto of the Second Congress of the Third Communist International* (Moscow: Publishing Office of the Third Communist International, 1920), 23. This is the "American edition" published by the United Communist Party of America.
44 "The Communist Party of the United States of America: What It Is, How It Works," 2.
45 Lenin, "Welcoming Remarks at the First Congress of the Communist International."
46 Ronald J. Rychlak, *Hitler, the War, and the Pope* (Huntington, IN: Our Sunday Visitor, 2000), 6.
47 Alden Hatch and Seamus Walshe, *Crown of Glory: The Life of Pope Pius XII* (New York: Hawthorn Books, 1957), 81.
48 Ibid., 81–83.
49 See Lenin, *Collected Works*, 31:291. See also Lenin's 1901 essay, "Where to Begin?"
50 For daring to do so, Reagan was excoriated not only by Soviet communists but also by American liberals. For a lengthy examination, see Paul Kengor, *Dupes: How America's Adversaries Have Manipulated Progressives for a Century* (Wilmington, DE: ISI Books, 2010), 371–76.
51 Rychlak, *Hitler, the War, and the Pope*, 13–14.
52 For the details in this section on Pacelli, I am indebted to Hatch and Walshe's biography. See Hatch and Walshe, *Crown of Glory*, 83–85.
53 Ibid., 84–85.

CHAPTER 3: MAY 1920–JUNE 1922: A BIRTH IN POLAND AND A REBIRTH IN THE MIDWEST

1 "Il beato Giovanni Paolo II ha rischiato di non nascere," *Vatican Insider*, October 16, 2013; and Steven Ertelt, "Book: Pope John Paul II's Mother Rejected Doctor's Abortion Suggestion," LifeNews.com, October 16, 2013. This report, if accurate, is somewhat of a revelation. I e-mailed the story to George Weigel, the preeminent biographer of John Paul II, asking whether he had any knowledge of the late pope's mother's being advised to have an abortion. He did not, stating, "I certainly never heard any such thing from him." Correspondence with George Weigel, October 22, 2013.
2 Weigel, *Witness to Hope*, 27–28.
3 See, among others, Timothy Snyder, *Bloodlands: Europe Between Hitler and Stalin* (New York: Basic Books, 2012), 137; M.D. Aeschliman, "How the Poles Saved Civilization, Part II," *Crisis Magazine*, May 29, 2012; and Peter Hetherington, "Miracle on the Vistula," *International Business Times*, July 18, 2012.
4 E-mail correspondence with Robert Clemm, June 10, 2016.
5 See, for example, the website of "Inside Poland": http://inside-poland.com/t/august-15-the-anniversary-of-the-miracle-on-the-wisla/.
6 Edward Stourton, *John Paul II: Man of History* (London: Hodder & Stoughton, 2006), 11; and Weigel, *Witness to Hope*, 27–32.
7 Pope John Paul II, *Gift and Mystery: On the Fiftieth Anniversary of My Priestly Ordination* (New York: Image, 1996), 20.
8 The prayer was this: "Holy Spirit, I ask you for the gift of Wisdom to better know You and Your divine perfections, for the gift of Understanding to clearly discern the spirit of the mysteries of the holy faith, for the gift of Counsel that I may live according to the principles of this faith, for the gift of Knowledge that I may look for counsel in You and that I may always find it in You, for the gift of Fortitude that no fear or earthly preoccupations would ever separate me from You, for the gift of Piety that I may always serve Your Majesty with a filial love, for the gift of the Fear of the Lord that I may dread sin, which offends You, O my God." See, among others: Jason Evert, "John Paul II and the Blessed Sacrament," *Catholic World Report*, April 18, 2014; Francis Phillips, "Saint John Paul II's Father Is a Role Model for All Men," *Catholic Herald*, June 16, 2014; and the appendix (page 132) of the book *John Paul II, Man of Prayer: The Spiritual Life of a Saint* (Leominster, UK: Gracewing, 2014), by Clare Anderson and Joanna Bogle, confirmed via an e-mail from Joanna Bogle, August 13, 2016.
9 John Paul II, *Gift and Mystery*, 9–22.
10 Peggy Noonan, *John Paul the Great* (New York: Viking, 2005), 129.
11 Gian Franco Svidercoschi, "The Jewish 'Roots' of Karol Wojtyła," posted at the Vatican website, http://www.vatican.va/jubilee_2000/magazine/documents/ju_mag_01111997_p-46_en.html.
12 Weigel, *Witness to Hope*, 31.
13 Edmund Morris, *Dutch: A Memoir of Ronald Reagan* (New York: Random House, 1999), 11.
14 Neil Reagan interviewed by Barbara Walters on ABC's *20/20*, special episode titled "Ronald Reagan: At Home on the Ranch," November 25, 1981.
15 I personally tabulated the number of residences via information at the Reagan Library.
16 Source: "Genealogical Information on Ronald Wilson Reagan," Office of the Press Secretary, The White House, provided by the Ronald Reagan Library. Another source lists the couple as married at Saint Emanuel's Catholic Church in Fulton, Illinois. One source lists the marriage date as November 18, 1904, whereas another says November 8, 1904, and still another local source that I consulted reports the date as November 4. Most sources I have seen in Reagan biographies list the Church of the Immaculate Conception in Fulton, Illinois, as the church where Jack and Nelle were married. A Reagan

Library information sheet on Ronald Reagan's family states that Jack's name is listed as "Jack" on his marriage application but as "John" on his marriage certificate.

17 Morris, *Dutch*, 11.

18 E-mail from Ann Lewis, chair of the Reagan Centennial Commission of Dixon, Illinois, March 3, 2011. For this particular e-mail, Ann consulted (among others) Dixon historian Greg Langdon, who attends First Christian Church, and whose parents knew the Reagans.

19 Biographer Anne Edwards says that Reagan's father was so lacking in outward faith that Neil claimed he did not know that his father was Catholic until he was almost eighteen years old. I find this extremely difficult to believe, even as Anne Edwards is generally reliable. If Neil said this, he must have said it half-jokingly. See Anne Edwards, *Early Reagan: The Rise to Power* (New York: Morrow, 1987), 33–39, 58.

20 One surviving piece of confirming evidence is an events box printed on the front page of the *Dixon Telegraph* newspaper from September 7, 1928, which noted Neil's role in an upcoming play at the Dixon Theater by the "Dixon Council of the Knights of Columbus."

21 One clip from the *Tampico Tornado* newspaper of April 26, 1906, affirmed that Jack Reagan had attended "a large meeting of the Knights of Columbus" in the nearby town of Clinton the previous Sunday.

22 E-mail from Ken Mendel, chancellor of Dixon Council #690, Dixon, Illinois, Knights of Columbus, September 23, 2005.

23 E-mail from Ann Marie Fiondella, Department of Membership Records, File Maintenance, Knights of Columbus, September 26, 2005.

24 Nelle's church retains the original registers that list attendees of all the Sunday school classes she taught.

25 Ronald Reagan, *An American Life* (New York: Simon and Schuster, 1990), 22.

26 It was said (including by Ronald Reagan himself) that Jack left the religious rearing to Nelle, who happily accepted. See Reagan letter to Kenneth J. Bialkin, published in Kiron Skinner, Annelise Anderson, and Martin Anderson, eds., *Reagan: A Life in Letters* (New York: Free Press, 2003), 2.

27 See Paul Kengor, *God and Ronald Reagan: A Spiritual Life* (New York: Harper, 2004).

28 Reagan, *An American Life*, 20–21. Reagan added on Nelle, "If something went wrong, she said, you didn't let it get you down: You stepped away from it, stepped over it, and moved on." Later on, "something good will happen and you'll find yourself thinking—'If I hadn't had that problem back then, then this better thing that *did* happen wouldn't have happened to me.'"

29 Source: "Enrollment Directory for the Year 1922," First Christian Church, Dixon, Illinois.

30 On this, see Ronald Reagan with Richard Hubler, *Where's the Rest of Me?* (New York: Duell, Sloan & Pearce, 1965), 10; Peggy Noonan, *When Character Was King: A Story of Ronald Reagan* (New York: Viking-Penguin, 2001), 153; Edwards, *Early Reagan*, 59–60; and Fran Swarbrick, ed., *Remembering Ronald Reagan* (Dixon, IL: Creative Printing, 2001), 17.

31 Sources: "Christian Church Notes," *Dixon Telegraph*, August 3, 1925; "Most Interesting Discussion on Prayer," *Dixon Telegraph*, January 8, 1926; and "Christian Church Notes," *Dixon Telegraph*, October 26, 1925.

32 Source: "Christian Church Notes," *Dixon Telegraph*, February 22 and March 19, 1928.

33 See Swarbrick, *Remembering Ronald Reagan*, 3–4; Gordon P. Gardiner, "Nelle Reagan: Mother of Ronald Reagan, President of the United States," *Bread of Life* 30, no. 5 (May 1981): 6; and Morris, *Dutch*, 12.

34 Edwards, *Early Reagan*, 59, 105.

35 See the examples in Kengor, *God and Ronald Reagan*.

36 Morris, *Dutch*, 12.

37 Reagan, *Where's the Rest of Me?*, 13.

38 On Wojtyła's seeking swimming as a form of recuperation and exercise in the 1980s, see Noonan, *John Paul the Great*, 52.
39 Reagan, *Where's the Rest of Me?*, 23; and Reagan letter to Mrs. John B. White, Peoria, Illinois, October 5, 1982, published in Skinner, Anderson, and Anderson, *Reagan: A Life in Letters*, 11.
40 Reagan, *Where's the Rest of Me?*, 23.
41 Reagan speaking on *Ronald Reagan: A Legacy Remembered*, History Channel productions, 2002.
42 See Kengor, *The Crusader*, 305–15.
43 Interview with Bill Clark, July 17, 2003.

CHAPTER 4: 1924–1939: THE "SATANIC SCOURGE" OF COMMUNISM

1 Hatch and Walshe, *Crown of Glory*, 118.
2 George Seldes, *The Catholic Crisis* (New York: Julian Messner, 1939), 4–5, 345–46.
3 Hatch and Walshe, *Crown of Glory*, 117.
4 President Franklin Delano Roosevelt, "Letter to the Pope on Peace and Relieving Suffering," December 23, 1939.
5 "Pacelli Lunches with Roosevelt," *New York Times*, November 6, 1936.
6 See Kengor, *Dupes*.
7 See Charles R. Gallagher, *Vatican Secret Diplomacy: Joseph P. Hurley and Pope Pius XII* (New Haven: Yale University Press, 2008), 87–88.
8 I detail this at length in Kengor, *Dupes*.
9 FDR said this to his former ambassador to the USSR, William C. Bullitt. See Orville H. Bullitt, ed., *For the President—Personal and Secret: Correspondence Between Franklin Delano Roosevelt and William C. Bullitt* (Boston: Houghton Mifflin, 1972), 595–99; and William C. Bullitt, "How We Won the War and Lost the Peace," *Life*, August 30, 1948, 94.
10 "Cardinal Pacelli Now Pope Pius XII visits President Roosevelt," Rose Kennedy Personal Papers collection, box 6, John F. Kennedy Presidential Library.
11 My thanks to the diligent staff at the John F. Kennedy Library for digging for this information and supplying photocopies from Rose Kennedy's diary. One of the researchers at the library looked through the John F. Kennedy Personal Papers, Joseph P. Kennedy Personal Papers, and the Rose Kennedy Personal Papers, and did not come across any specific mention that JFK was present at the meeting.
12 "The Kennedy Family—Their Ties to Bronxville," posted at www.myhometownbronxville.com, retrieved December 20, 2013.
13 Kudos to Nigel Hamilton for reporting the Pacelli visit. Hamilton does not note whether JFK was present. See Nigel Hamilton, *JFK: Reckless Youth* (New York: Random House, 1992), 175.
14 Details on Pacelli's American tour come from Hatch and Walshe, *Crown of Glory*, 118.
15 The Catholic Church stated these things in the influential 1937 encyclical *Divini Redemptoris*.
16 These are all cited in section 1 of *Divini Redemptoris*.
17 Whittaker Chambers, "Peace and the Papacy," *Time*, August 16, 1943.
18 Thomas C. Reeves, *America's Bishop: The Life and Times of Fulton J. Sheen* (San Francisco: Encounter Books, 2001).
19 Kathleen L. Riley, *Fulton J. Sheen: An American Catholic Response to the Twentieth Century* (Staten Island, NY: Alba House, 2004), 225.
20 Ibid., ix.
21 Catholics who love Sheen and Reagan alike have asked me this question. I was once asked by the director of the official Sheen museum/birthplace in Illinois.

22 Mrs. Reagan answered my question in April 2013 via her longtime personal secretary, Joanne Drake, who asked her directly on my behalf. Source: E-mail correspondence with Joanne Drake, April 1, 11, and 22, 2013.
23 Reeves, *America's Bishop*, 85.
24 Biographers Thomas Reeves and Kathleen Riley differ on the date of Sheen's audience with Pope Pius XI. I have opted for the more specific date Reeves gives: July 23, 1934. Riley says simply that Sheen met with Pius "in 1935." I see no indication that Sheen met with the pope in consecutive years. See Reeves, *America's Bishop*, 85–87; Riley, *Fulton J. Sheen*, 106, 135.
25 See, among others: Fulton J. Sheen, *Communism and the Conscience of the West* (Indianapolis and New York: Bobbs-Merrill, 1948); Fulton J. Sheen, *The Church, Communism, and Democracy* (New York: Dell, 1954), 138–39.
26 Sheen, *The Church, Communism, and Democracy*, 138.
27 Ibid., 61.
28 Ibid., 69.
29 Ibid., 122; Riley, *Fulton J. Sheen*, 138–39, 168.
30 Reeves, *America's Bishop*, 87.
31 Ibid., 87–88.
32 Ibid., 88.
33 Riley, *Fulton J. Sheen*, 149.
34 Fulton J. Sheen, *Treasure in Clay: The Autobiography of Fulton J. Sheen* (1980; repr., New York: Image Books, 2008), 46, 231–32.
35 Reeves, *America's Bishop*, 145.
36 Sheen, *Communism and the Conscience of the West*, 78–79.
37 Sheen, *Treasure in Clay*, 232; Reeves, *America's Bishop*, 131, 219.
38 Riley, *Fulton J. Sheen*, 95; Reeves, *America's Bishop*, 112, 128, 139.

CHAPTER 5: 1939–1945: "BLOOD, BLOOD, BLOOD, AND AGAIN BLOOD"

1 Saint Maria Faustina Kowalska, *Diary of Saint Maria Faustina Kowalska: Divine Mercy in My Soul* (Stockbridge, MA: Marian Press, 2005), xv.
2 "The Apostle of Divine Mercy: Saint Maria Faustina of the Congregation of Sisters of Our Lady of Mercy (1905–1938)," published by the Congregation of Marians of the Immaculate Conception (Stockbridge, MA, 1993).
3 For a good online source, provided by the Congregation of Marians of the Immaculate Conception, the group that has become the leading American source on Faustina's concept of Divine Mercy, see http://www.divinemercysunday.com/vision.htm.
4 Laurence Rees, *World War II Behind Closed Doors: Stalin, the Nazis, and the West* (New York: Pantheon, 2008), 19.
5 Rees, *World War II Behind Closed Doors*, 19.
6 The quotations and description from Tokarev come mainly from Rees, *World War II Behind Closed Doors*, 56–57, though most of the descriptive details are my own.
7 See Rees, *World War II Behind Closed Doors*, 56–57.
8 Interviewed a half century later, Dmitri Tokarev recalled what happened to his NKVD men responsible for this "horrible business": one officer "went mad," and "my first deputy shot himself dead,... my driver shot himself dead, and even Blokhin shot himself dead." See the BBC documentary based on Rees's book, *World War II Behind Closed Doors*, part 1 (2008).
9 Reeves, *America's Bishop*, 131–32.
10 Ibid., 132.
11 Riley, *Fulton J. Sheen*, 109.
12 Reeves, *America's Bishop*, 145.

13 Riley, *Fulton J. Sheen*, 114.
14 Reeves, *America's Bishop*, 134.
15 Riley, *Fulton J. Sheen*, 114.
16 Chambers, "Peace and the Papacy."
17 Reeves, *America's Bishop*, 133.
18 Weigel, *Witness to Hope*, 45–46.
19 Noonan, *John Paul the Great*, 52.
20 Francois Grosjean, *Life with Two Languages* (Cambridge, MA: Harvard University Press, 1982), 286.
21 See Arthur F. McClure, C. David Rice, and William T. Stewart, eds., *Ronald Reagan: His First Career, A Bibliography of the Movie Years* (Lewiston, NY: Edwin Mellen Press, 1988), 12–17.
22 Reagan was on the cover of *Modern Screen* for the October 1944 issue.
23 Doug McClelland, *Hollywood on Ronald Reagan: Friends and Enemies Discuss Our President, the Actor* (Winchester, MA: Faber and Faber, 1983), 178.
24 John Meroney, "Night Unto Reagan," *National Review Online*, August 4, 2005.
25 See Joseph Shattan, *Architects of Victory: Six Heroes of the Cold War* (Washington, DC: Heritage Press, 1999), 236; John Meroney, "Rehearsals for a Lead Role," *Washington Post*, February 4, 2001; and Reagan, *Where's the Rest of Me?*, 6–7.
26 See, among others, Edward M. Yager, *Ronald Reagan's Journey: Democrat to Republican* (Lanham, MD: Rowman and Littlefield, 2006), 19–21.
27 Father Peter John Cameron, "Pope John Paul II, Playwright Saint," *National Catholic Register*, April 20, 2014.
28 Ibid.
29 Ibid.
30 Szulc, *Pope John Paul II*, 117; Noonan, *John Paul the Great*, 130; Weigel, *Witness to Hope*, 68.
31 Morris, *Dutch*, 177.
32 Ibid.
33 Reagan, *Where's the Rest of Me?*, 99; Maureen Reagan, *First Father, First Daughter* (Boston: Little, Brown and Company, 1989), 61; and Morris, *Dutch*, 12.
34 Reeves, *America's Bishop*, 138–39.
35 The full text of Stalin's August 19, 1939, speech to the Central Committee is published in Crozier, *The Rise and Fall of the Soviet Empire*, 519–21.
36 There are differing accounts of precisely where Kolbe had this vision and exactly what kind of form the vision took. There is no doubt, however, that the year was 1906, in the town of Pabianice, and that the vision was the Blessed Mother in some form.
37 See, among others, Patricia Treece, *A Man for Others: Maximilian Kolbe, Saint of Auschwitz* (Huntington, IN: Our Sunday Visitor, 1982), 1.
38 See Father Michael E. Gaitley, *33 Days to Morning Glory* (Stockbridge, MA: Marian Press, 2014), 57.
39 Ibid., 111.
40 Quoted ibid., 111.
41 Some accounts claim that three prisoners escaped.
42 Quoted in Mary Craig, *Blessed Maximilian Kolbe: Priest Hero of a Death Camp* (London: The Catholic Truth Society, 1973).
43 Riley, *Fulton J. Sheen*, 115; and Reeves, *America's Bishop*, 145.
44 Fulton J. Sheen, *Liberty, Equality, and Fraternity* (New York: Macmillan, 1938), 118.
45 Riley, *Fulton J. Sheen*, 121.
46 Reeves, *America's Bishop*, 132.
47 Richard Pipes, *Vixi: Memoirs of a Non-Belonger* (New Haven: Yale University Press, 2003), 55–56.
48 On this, see George Weigel, *The Cube and the Cathedral: Europe, America, and Politics Without God* (New York: Basic Books, 2005).

49 Reeves, *America's Bishop*, 155.
50 Ibid., 156–57.

CHAPTER 6: 1945–1952: THE IRON CURTAIN DESCENDS

1 Conrad Black, *Franklin Delano Roosevelt: Champion of Freedom* (New York: Public Affairs, 2003), 1081.
2 Black, *Franklin Delano Roosevelt*, 1081.
3 Quoted by Arnold Beichman, "FDR's Failure Not Forgotten," *Human Events*, May 13, 2005.
4 Frances Perkins, *The Roosevelt I Knew* (New York: Penguin, 2011), 83–85.
5 Robert Dallek, *Franklin D. Roosevelt and American Foreign Policy: 1932–1945* (New York: Oxford University Press, 1995), 521; Black, *Franklin Delano Roosevelt*, 1080.
6 Reeves, *America's Bishop*, 158.
7 Pope Pius XII, "Wisdom—Not Weapons of War," *Collier's Weekly*, January 5, 1946, 11–13.
8 "The Refugees Still Wait," *New York Times*, October 5, 1947, E8.
9 The camps were also located in Britain, Canada, Belgium, and Latin America. See "Marshall Says DP Exit Would Ease U.S.-Russian Friction in Europe," *New York Times*, July 17, 1947, A6.
10 "Rosenwald Urges U.S. to Take DP's," *New York Times*, May 13, 1947, A8.
11 "Reagan Backs Bill for DP's," *New York Times*, May 8, 1947, A5.
12 President Harry Truman, "Remarks Before a Joint Session of Congress Announcing Aid to Greece and Turkey," March 12, 1947.
13 Gerhard Simon, "The Catholic Church and the Communist State," in Bociurkiw et al., eds., *Religion and Atheism in the USSR and Eastern Europe*, 218.
14 A relaxation of tensions came in the 1950s and also in an agreement between Tito and the Vatican in June 1966, though relations between the dictator and the Holy See were never good.
15 Anthony Henry O'Brien, *Archbishop Stepinac: The Man and His Case* (Ann Arbor: University of Michigan Press, 1947), 37.
16 Hatch and Walshe, *Crown of Glory*, 195.
17 Douglas Hyde, "Utterly Ruthless 'Man of Steel,'" *Catholic Herald*, November 26, 1954.
18 "Archbishop Behind Bars," *Time*, September 30, 1946.
19 Ronald J. Rychlak, "Cardinal Stepinac and the Roman Catholic Church in Croatia During World War II," *New Oxford Review*, November 2009.
20 Hatch and Walshe, *Crown of Glory*, 195.
21 O'Brien, *Archbishop Stepinac*, 71.
22 Hatch and Walshe, *Crown of Glory*, 195.
23 "Archbishop Behind Bars."
24 "Religion: Deal Rejected," *Time*, July 23, 1951.
25 Ion Mihai Pacepa and Ronald J. Rychlak, *Disinformation: Former Spy Chief Reveals Secret Strategies for Undermining Freedom, Attacking Religion, and Promoting Terrorism* (Washington, DC: WND Books, 2013), 76.
26 Ibid., 77.
27 Ibid.
28 Ibid.
29 Ibid., 79.
30 On this, see my foreword to Pacepa and Rychlak, *Disinformation*, iv–viii.

CHAPTER 7: 1956–1963: CRUSHING HUNGARY AND SMEARING PIUS XII

1 David Weinstein, *The Forgotten Network: DuMont and the Birth of American Television* (Philadelphia: Temple University Press, 2004), 157.
2 Reeves, *America's Bishop.*
3 Sheen, *Life Is Worth Living* (New York: McGraw-Hill, 1953), 62. This book published material used in Sheen's TV broadcast by the same name.
4 Sheen, *Communism and the Conscience of the West*, 78–79.
5 Ibid., 204.
6 Fulton Sheen was one of the few who grasped the historical-spiritual parallel. "On October 23 of the year 1956," he wrote, "Hungarians throughout the world and particularly in Hungary celebrated the five-hundredth anniversary of the death of their great national hero, St. John Capistrano. He freed Hungary. On the five-hundredth anniversary of that liberation on October 23, 1956, a group of students and workers marched.... The peaceful demonstration broke into an open declaration of freedom.... John Capistrano looked down on Hungary from heaven." See Sheen, *The Church, Communism, and Democracy*, 153–54.
7 Beverly Ann James, *Imagining Postcommunism: Visual Narratives of Hungary's 1956 Revolution* (College Station, TX: Texas A&M Press, 2005), 57.
8 Ibid., 55.
9 This episode of *GE Theater* was titled "No Skin Off Me." It aired February 3, 1957. A copy of the video is located at the Ronald Reagan Library.
10 McClure, Rice, and Stewart, eds., *Ronald Reagan: His First Career*, 188–93. See also Peter Schweizer, *Reagan's War: The Epic Story of His Forty-Year Struggle and Final Triumph over Communism* (New York: Doubleday, 2002), 33.
11 See Kiron K. Skinner, Annelise Anderson, and Martin Anderson, eds., *Reagan's Path to Victory: The Shaping of Ronald Reagan's Vision: Selected Writings* (New York: Free Press, 2004), 228.
12 Governor Ronald Reagan, "Veterans Day Address at North Albany Junior High School," Albany, Oregon, November 11, 1967.
13 H. W. Crocker III, *Triumph: The Power and Glory of the Catholic Church* (New York: Three Rivers Press, 2001), 407–8.
14 This associate was Bill Clark, whom I will discuss later.
15 Sheen, *The Church, Communism, and Democracy*, 143–44.
16 In 1992, when communism was finally defeated in Hungary, Budapest officials placed a crucifix at the site, with a sign that read: "Here stood the Regnum Marianum. Mátyás Rákosi destroyed it in 1951." James, *Imagining Postcommunism*, 58.
17 Sheen, *The Church, Communism, and Democracy*, 146–47.
18 Ibid., 148.
19 Ibid., 144.
20 Quoted in the literature provided by the Cardinal Mindszenty Foundation.
21 Pacepa and Rychlak, *Disinformation*, 83.
22 Hatch and Walshe, *Crown of Glory*, 195.
23 Pacepa and Rychlak, *Disinformation*, 83.
24 Hatch and Walshe, *Crown of Glory*, 195; Sheen, *The Church, Communism, and Democracy*, 144.
25 Sheen, *The Church, Communism, and Democracy*, 144.
26 Pacepa and Rychlak, *Disinformation*, 85.
27 This description is published in Sheen, *The Church, Communism, and Democracy*, 152.
28 Riley, *Fulton J. Sheen*, 161.
29 Dates vary on the exact year of Stephen's crowning.
30 See the brief official history at the website of the U.S. embassy in Hungary: http://hungary.usembassy.gov/holy_crown.html.
31 Sheen, *The Church, Communism, and Democracy*, 155.

32 Ibid., 149–50; Sheen, *Treasure in Clay*, 121, 125.
33 Pacepa and Rychlak, *Disinformation*, 80.
34 Ibid., 83.
35 Ibid., 80.
36 Crocker, *Triumph*, 403.
37 For a summary of these authors and more, see Pacepa and Rychlak, *Disinformation*, 197–99.
38 Pacepa and Rychlak, *Disinformation*, 59.
39 See "Radio Moscow Linked to Rumors Against Pius XII," Zenit.org, June 13, 2005. The *Zenit* piece refers to a 2005 article published by the Italian periodical *La Civitta Cattolica* dealing with this important broadcast by Radio Moscow. According to *Zenit*, the writer of the Italian article, Father Giovanni Sale, analyzed "the Communist radio's role in defaming Pius XII, specifically its reaction to the Pope's address of June 2, 1945, the feast of St. Eugene." Sale wrote that Radio Moscow broadcast a program that "assumed... a paradigmatic value, as it summarized very well the point of view of the radical left about the Holy See's activity during the time of war." Sale went on: "So began the 'Black Legend'—which in the main has come down to our days—of a Pius XII friend and ally of the Nazis."
40 Pius's anticommunist work was so pervasive that it requires no documentation here, but an early contemporaneous biography (worthy of consultation) was 1957's *Crown of Glory: The Life of Pope Pius XII* by Alden Hatch and Seamus Walshe.
41 "Pravda Alleges Hitler-Pius Pact," *New York Times*, March 1, 1946, 11.
42 See the encyclical *Orientales Omnes Ecclesia*, December 23, 1945, posted at the Vatican website, http://w2.vatican.va/content/pius-xii/en/encyclicals/documents/hf_p-xii_enc_23121945_orientales-omnes-ecclesias.html.
43 Pacepa and Rychlak, *Disinformation*, 59.
44 E-mail from Pacepa and Rychlak, August 22, 2012.
45 For a short article, see Edward Pentin, "The Plot to Kidnap Pius," *National Catholic Register*, July 12–25, 2009.
46 Ion Mihai Pacepa, "A Plan to Assassinate Pope Pius XII?" *World Net Daily*, October 8, 2013.
47 Lapin states this in an endorsement published in the opening pages of Dalin's book.
48 Rabbi David G. Dalin, *The Myth of Hitler's Pope: How Pope Pius XII Rescued Jews from the Nazis* (Washington, DC: Regnery, 2005), 48.
49 Ibid., 63–73.
50 Ibid., 10–11, 63.
51 Ibid., 14, 100–101.
52 Lapide reported this in his 1967 book, *Three Popes and the Jews*. This number is higher than Ron Rychlak's more recent estimate of a half million Jews saved. See Pinchas Lapide, *Three Popes and the Jews* (New York: Hawthorn Books, 1967), 215; Dalin, *The Myth of Hitler's Pope*, 10–11; and Ronald J. Rychlak, *Righteous Gentiles: How Pius XII and the Catholic Church Saved Half a Million Jews from the Nazis* (Dallas: Spence Publishing, 2005).
53 See, among others, Tindal-Robertson, *Fátima, Russia, and Pope John Paul II*, xiv–xv, 23–24, 192, 195.

CHAPTER 8: NOVEMBER 22, 1963: COMMUNISM'S ERRORS REACH DALLAS

1 For details in this section, I'm indebted to former Grove City College president Richard Jewell, who shared this information in a gripping two-hour lecture on the Kennedy assassination at Grove City College on November 21, 2013. The details are from my notes. If there are any errors, they are mine entirely.

2 Doris O'Donnell, *Front-Page Girl* (Kent, OH: Kent State University Press, 2006), 138–39.
3 Simon Usborne, "The LBJ Missal: Why a Prayer Book Given to John F. Kennedy Was Used to Swear in the 36th US President," *The Independent*, November 16, 2013.
4 Gary Scott Smith, *Faith and the Presidency* (New York: Oxford University Press, 2006), 260–61.
5 See Hamilton, *JFK: Reckless Youth*, 183.
6 Joan Blair and Clay Blair Jr., *The Search for JFK* (New York: Berkley, 1976), 58.
7 Hamilton, *JFK: Reckless Youth*, 188–89; and Deirdre Henderson, *Prelude to Leadership: The European Diary of John F. Kennedy* (Washington, DC: Regnery, 1995), 121–23.
8 Hamilton, *JFK: Reckless Youth*, 188–89.
9 See Hamilton, *JFK: Reckless Youth*, 255; Henderson, *Prelude to Leadership*, 124.
10 Rychlak, *Hitler, the War, and the Pope*, 112.
11 Hamilton, *JFK: Reckless Youth*, 256–57. According to Joan and Clay Blair, the only Kennedy not to attend was Joe Jr., who was in Spain. Blair and Blair, *The Search for JFK*, 58.
12 Material provided by Ron Rychlak via e-mail correspondence, November 18, 2013.
13 Hamilton, *JFK: Reckless Youth*, 257.
14 Ron Rychlak also confirmed for me that Ted Kennedy received his First Communion from Pope Pius XII.
15 Herbert S. Parmet, *Jack: The Struggles of John F. Kennedy* (New York: The Dial Press, 1980), 218; Henderson, *Prelude to Leadership*, 127.
16 Parmet, *Jack: The Struggles of John F. Kennedy*, 261, 317–18.
17 Ibid., 317–18.
18 Oswald and his mother initially stayed with Lee's brother and brother's wife and baby, in an apartment at 325 East 92nd Street in Manhattan. It was a volatile situation. Lee and his mom soon moved to 1455 Sheridan Avenue in the Bronx. Source: Warren Commission Report, 675–76.
19 Warren Commission Report, 695.
20 "Who Was Lee Harvey Oswald?" *Frontline*, PBS, November 19, 2013. Transcript posted at http://www.pbs.org/wgbh/pages/frontline/biographies/oswald/transcript-52/. See also Edward Jay Epstein, "Who Was Lee Harvey Oswald?" *Wall Street Journal*, November 22, 1983.
21 "8 Things You May Not Know About Lee Harvey Oswald," *Frontline*, PBS, November 19, 2013, http://www.pbs.org/wgbh/pages/frontline/biographies/oswald/8-things-you-may-not-know-about-lee-harvey-oswald/.
22 There are numerous sources on this information. One article that confirms details in this paragraph is Peter Savodnik, "Lee Harvey Oswald, Disappointed Revolutionary," *Wall Street Journal*, October 5, 2013.
23 Vincent Bugliosi, *Reclaiming History: The Assassination of President John F. Kennedy* (New York: W.W. Norton, 2007), 938–40.
24 The best source for this (which quotes all the Soviet participants) is the seminal biography of Nikita Khrushchev by Sergei Khrushchev: Sergei N. Khrushchev, *Nikita Khrushchev and the Creation of a Superpower*, trans. Shirley Benson (University Park, PA: Penn State University Press, 2001), 627–42. According to Robert McNamara, JFK's defense secretary, Castro told him thirty years later, "Bob, I did recommend to Khrushchev that they [the nuclear missiles] be used." See McNamara interviewed in Errol Morris's documentary *The Fog of War: Eleven Lessons from the Life of Robert S. McNamara* (2003). McNamara also shared this account on PBS's *NewsHour with Jim Lehrer*, February 22, 2001. I quote these sources and more in a piece I wrote titled "Death by Fidel," published in the *American Spectator*, November 27, 2016.
25 See Ira Stoll, "JFK, Conservative," *American Spectator*, October 2013, 22–23.
26 Henderson, *Prelude to Leadership*, 9–10.
27 Senator John F. Kennedy, "Commencement Address at Assumption College," Worcester, MA, June 3, 1955.

28 These words are taken from Kennedy's *Public Presidential Papers*, specifically the volumes for the years 1961 (page 341) and 1962 (page 723n). See also Martin Walker, *The Cold War and the Making of the Modern World* (London: Fourth Estate, 1993), 132; Eric Hobsbawm, *The Age of Extremes: A History of the World, 1914–1991* (New York: Pantheon Books, 1994), 231n.
29 See, among others, William Murchison, "Dallas, 1963," *American Spectator*, October 2013, 26–32.
30 James Piereson, "JFK—Casualty of the Cold War," *Wall Street Journal*, November 15, 2013.
31 Jim Newton, *Justice for All: Earl Warren and the Nation He Made* (New York: Penguin, 2006), 410.
32 See, among others, M. Stanton Evans and Herbert Romerstein, *Stalin's Secret Agents: The Subversion of Roosevelt's Government* (New York: Threshold Editions, 2012), 138–39.
33 Piereson, "JFK—Casualty of the Cold War."
34 James Reston, "Why America Weeps: Kennedy Victim of Violent Streak He Sought to Curb in the Nation," *New York Times*, November 23, 1963.
35 Credit to George Will for noticing the juxtaposition: George F. Will, "When Liberals Became Scolds," *Washington Post*, October 9, 2013.
36 Gladwin Hill, "Leftist Accused," *New York Times*, November 23, 1963, 1.
37 Editorial, "Spiral of Hate," *New York Times*, November 25, 1963.
38 "A Popular Russian: Oleg Danilovich Kalugin," *New York Times*, May 11, 1959, 7. See my profile of this episode in my book *All the Dupes Fit to Print: Journalists Who Served as Tools of Communist Propaganda* (Owings, MD: America's Survival, 2013), 2–3.
39 Oleg Kalugin, *The First Directorate: My 32 Years in Intelligence and Espionage Against the West* (New York: St. Martin's Press, 1994), 42, 45, 75.
40 Ibid., 58.
41 Pacepa and Rychlak, *Disinformation*, 231–32.
42 Ibid., 234.
43 Ibid., 241–42.
44 Ibid., 242–43.
45 Ibid., 241–44.
46 I document this connection in Kengor, *Dupes*.
47 Pacepa and Rychlak, *Disinformation*, 244–45.
48 Ibid., 245.
49 See Ion Mihai Pacepa, *Programmed to Kill: Lee Harvey Oswald, the Soviet KGB, and the Kennedy Assassination* (Chicago: Ivan R. Dee, 2007). Pacepa and Rychlak summarize this in *Disinformation* on pages 235–40. See also Ion Mihai Pacepa, "Lucky Stars," *National Review*, October 25, 2007.
50 Pacepa himself cites that Warren Commission line but rejects it categorically. Pacepa and Rychlak, *Disinformation*, 209.
51 Savodnik, "Lee Harvey Oswald, Disappointed Revolutionary."
52 James Piereson, *Camelot and the Cultural Revolution: How the Assassination of John F. Kennedy Shattered American Liberalism* (New York: Encounter Books, 2007), 142.
53 Will, "When Liberals Became Scolds."
54 Bugliosi, *Reclaiming History*, xxvii.
55 Ronald Reagan, "Remarks at a Fundraising Reception for the John F. Kennedy Library Foundation," June 24, 1985.

CHAPTER 9: 1946–1959: BATTLING COMMUNISTS IN POLAND AND HOLLYWOOD

1 See John Paul II, *Gift and Mystery*, 45–46; Weigel, *Witness to Hope*, 79.
2 Weigel, *Witness to Hope*, 80–81.

3 Ibid., 82.
4 On this, see Reagan, *An American Life*, 106–7.
5 My research suggests that this incident occurred in 1946, but I have not been able to pinpoint a month or exact date.
6 See Kengor, *God and Ronald Reagan*, where I first reported this information.
7 See my detailed discussion of this in Kengor, *Dupes*, 37–38. Foster's major book on the subject was titled *Toward Soviet America* (1932).
8 Riley, *Fulton J. Sheen*, 158; Reeves, *America's Bishop*, 132.
9 Reagan, *Where's the Rest of Me?*, 162.
10 Ibid.
11 For a more detailed discussion, see Kengor, *Dupes*, chs. 10–11.
12 Peter Hanson, *Dalton Trumbo, Hollywood Rebel: A Critical Survey and Filmography* (Jefferson, NC: McFarland, 2001), 79.
13 See John Howard Lawson, *Film in the Battle of Ideas* (New York: Masses & Mainstream, 1953).
14 See Gladwin Hill, "Reagan Weighing a New Role in Gubernatorial Race on Coast," *New York Times*, January 23, 1965.
15 See Schweizer, *Reagan's War*, 25–27, 33.
16 Written at the end of 1950, the article was published in the January 22, 1951, issue. Ronald Reagan, "How Do You Fight Communism?" *Fortnight*, January 22, 1951, 13.
17 Michael Reagan, Jane's adopted son, told me this. I asked whether his father knew Fulton Sheen. Michael said that he was not aware of a relationship and that he would have heard about one if it existed. I also asked whether Ronald Reagan and Fulton Sheen ever met. Michael knew of no such occasion. I put the same question to Nancy Reagan (through her secretary, Joanne Drake). Nancy knew of no such occasion.
18 E-mail from Michael Reagan, April 8, 2014.
19 Some sources date the conversion as December 8, 1953, though there are very few sources on this. Michael Reagan has shared the December 8, 1954, date with me on many occasions, in conversation and in e-mails.
20 E-mail and conversation with Michael Reagan, April 8, 2014.
21 Author conversations with Michael Reagan.
22 Quoted in Joseph Lewis, *What Makes Reagan Run? A Political Profile* (New York: McGraw-Hill, 1968), 46; Lou Cannon, *Reagan* (New York: Putnam, 1982), 141.
23 Reagan, "America the Beautiful," commencement address, William Woods College, June 1952. See also Kate Link, "When Reagan Came to Fulton," *Kingdom Daily News*, March 22, 1981.
24 Here are merely three examples among many, one from each decade ahead: On July 4, 1968, Reagan said: "Call it mysticism if you will. I have always believed there was some divine plan that placed this nation between the oceans to be sought out and found by those with a special kind of courage and an overabundant love of freedom." (Quoted in Lou Cannon, *Ronnie and Jesse: A Political Odyssey* [Garden City, NY: Doubleday, 1969], 259.) On January 25, 1974, speaking before the Conservative Political Action Conference (CPAC) in Washington, DC, Reagan said, "I have always believed that there was some divine plan that placed this great continent between two oceans." (Text in James C. Roberts, ed., *A City Upon a Hill: Speeches by Ronald Reagan Before the Conservative Political Action Conference, 1974–1988* [Washington, DC: American Studies Center, 1989], 3.) On January 31, 1983, as president, Reagan said, "I've always believed that this blessed land was set apart in a special way, that some divine plan placed this great continent here between the two oceans to be found by people from every corner of the Earth—people who had a special love for freedom." ("Remarks at the Annual Convention of the National Religious Broadcasters," January 31, 1983.)
25 Reagan performed at the Last Frontier in February 1954. The hotel, now named the New Frontier, provided the information about Reagan's time at the Last Frontier.

26 Nancy Reagan interviewed in "Reagan," *The American Experience.* She gave a number of other examples in her 1980 autobiography. See Nancy Reagan with Bill Libby, *Nancy* (New York: Morrow, 1980), 143.
27 Before giving Reagan the *GE Theater* role, CBS reportedly considered putting him in as host of the weekly educational series *Omnibus*, looking to the "unmistakably American" Reagan to replace the British-born journalist Alistair Cooke. Cooke stayed on, and *Omnibus* ran from 1952 to 1959. On this, see John Carman, "Geographic's 'Adventures' in Pointlessness," *San Francisco Chronicle*, December 22, 1999; *"Omnibus": Television's Golden Age*, PBS, 1999; William Hawes, *Filmed Television Drama, 1952–1958* (Jefferson, NC: McFarland, 2002), 17.
28 *GE Theater* began on September 12, 1954, and ran in thirty-to-sixty-minute installments. In all, two hundred episodes were made during the show's eight-year run. See McClure, Rice, and Stewart, eds., *Ronald Reagan: His First Career*, 188; Morris, *Dutch*, 304.
29 "General Electric Theater—1954–57," directory of show episodes on file at the Ronald Reagan Library; McClure, Rice, and Stewart, eds., *Ronald Reagan: His First Career*, 188–93.
30 "Investigation of Un-American Propaganda Activities in the United States," Special Committee on Un-American Activities, House of Representatives, 78th Congress, Second Session, on H. Res. 282, App. Part IX, Vol. 1 (Washington, DC: GPO, 1944), 340–55.
31 Marion Freed Miller, *I Was a Spy: The Story of a Brave Housewife* (Indianapolis: Bobbs-Merrill, 1960). See McClure, Rice, and Stewart, eds., *Ronald Reagan: His First Career*, 193–94; Skinner, Anderson, and Anderson, *Reagan: A Life in Letters*, 145n.
32 Matthews said it gave him his first "sense of Reagan the politician." Source: Chris Matthews speaking at "The Reagan Legacy" conference, Ronald Reagan Library, Simi Valley, CA, May 20, 1996.
33 Reagan letter to Lorraine and Elwood Wagner, June 3, 1962, YAF collection.
34 Weigel, *Witness to Hope*, 146–47.

CHAPTER 10: THE 1960S: A TIME FOR CHOOSING

1 Cannon, *Ronnie and Jesse: A Political Odyssey*, 69.
2 Ibid.
3 UPI, "Red Threat Is Cited," *New York Times*, May 9, 1961.
4 See, e.g., UPI, "Reagan Spreads Warning About Reds in Hollywood," *The Independent* (Wilkes-Barre, PA), July 23, 1961.
5 Ronald Reagan, "Encroaching Government Controls," *Human Events*, July 21, 1961.
6 Ibid.
7 Ibid.
8 Reagan, "A Foot in the Door," Address to the Illinois Manufacturers' Costs Association, May 9, 1961. Text on file at the Ronald Reagan Library.
9 Cited by Schweizer, *Reagan's War*, 35. Schweizer cites: "Warns of Red Menace: Film Star Ronald Reagan to Speak," *Bakersfield Californian*, September 16, 1961, 19–20; Ronald Reagan, "Encroaching Control," *Vital Speeches of the Day*, September 1961.
10 The letter is dated October 19, 1961. Reagan mailed the letter from his office in Palisades, California. It is now owned by a private collector, Steven S. Raab.
11 Reagan, "Speech Given to Fargo Chamber of Commerce," Fargo, ND, January 26, 1962. Quoted in Matthew Dallek, *The Right Moment: Ronald Reagan's First Victory and the Decisive Turning Point in American Politics* (New York: Free Press, 2000), 27.
12 "Reagan Warns U.S. Is in War," *Bartlesville Examiner Enterprise*, March 1, 1962.
13 See "Reagan Says Free World, Reds at War," *Dallas Times Herald*, February 27, 1962;

Editorial, "In Our Opinion—'Losing Our Freedom...By Installments,'" *Angleton Times*, February 29, 1962. (The date on the paper seems inaccurate, since that year was not a leap year.)

14 "Reagan Warns U.S. Is in War." See also "Encroachment of Government Hit in CC Talk," "Rose City Rambler," and "Reagan Thrashes Federal Control," all published in the *Tyler Morning Telegraph*, February 27, 1962.
15 Michael Reagan with Jim Denney, *The New Reagan Revolution* (New York: St. Martin's Press, 2010), 110–11.
16 Ibid.
17 Michael Reagan shares this account. His father told it to him at the dinner table. See Reagan, *The New Reagan Revolution*, 102–3.
18 Reagan, "Remarks and Question-and-Answer Session with Women Leaders of Christian Religious Organizations," October 13, 1983.
19 See Reagan weekly radio address, May 7, 1983, published in Fred Israel, ed., *Ronald Reagan's Weekly Radio Addresses* (Wilmington, DE: Scholarly Resources Inc., 1987), 1:101.
20 William Rose, "The Reagans and Their Pastor," *Christian Life*, May 1968, 46.
21 Reagan wrote this in a January 9, 1985, letter to Mrs. Hugh Harris of Sierra Madre, California. The letter is published in Skinner, Anderson, and Anderson, *Reagan: A Life in Letters*, 47.
22 Reagan, *The New Reagan Revolution*, 110–11; and phone conversation with Michael Reagan, October 17, 2013.
23 The speech was taped earlier that day in front of an audience of about two hundred people. Reagan did it in one take. The speech was broadcast on the West Coast at 9:30 P.M. that evening. For an excellent article on the speech and facts surrounding it, see Craig Shirley, "How Reagan's Speech Changed History," *Newsmax*, October 8, 2014, 28–33. See also Kengor, *God and Ronald Reagan*, 109–11.
24 For the official Reagan Library posting of the speech, see https://reaganlibrary.gov/sreference/a-time-for-choosing-speech.
25 Churchill made these remarks in a radio speech broadcast from London to America on June 16, 1941, when he received an honorary doctorate from the University of Rochester, in the New York town where Churchill's mother had been born. It was Churchill's first honorary degree from an American university. A version posted at www.winstonchurchill.org reads: "The destiny of man is not decided by material computation. When great causes are on the move in the world, stirring all men's souls, drawing them from their firesides, casting aside comforts, wealth and the pursuit of happiness in response to impulses at once awe-striking and irresistible, we learn that we are spirits, not animals, and that something is going on in space and time, and beyond space and time, which, whether we like it or not, spells duty." Reagan would quote these Churchill lines again as president.
26 Weigel, *Witness to Hope*, 166–69.
27 E-mail from Tomasz Pompowski, November 12, 2014.
28 Dziwisz, *A Life with Karol*, 26.
29 Pompowski, November 12, 2014.
30 Ibid.
31 Ibid.
32 Ibid.
33 Dziwisz, *A Life with Karol*, 26.
34 Ibid., 33–35.
35 Weigel, *Witness to Hope*, 189–90.
36 Dziwisz, *A Life with Karol*, 33–35.

CHAPTER 11: MAY 6, 1975: THE DRY MARTYRDOM OF CARDINAL MINDSZENTY

1 Ronald Reagan, "Remarks to the Conservative Political Action Conference," Washington, DC, March 1, 1975.
2 Located in "Ronald Reagan: Pre-Presidential Papers: Selected Radio Broadcasts, 1975–1979," January 1975 to March 1977, Box 1, Ronald Reagan Library. See also Kiron Skinner, Martin Anderson, and Annelise Anderson, *Reagan, In His Own Hand* (New York: Free Press, 2001), 10–12.
3 Discussion with Andrea Di Stefano, Trevignano Romano, Italy, June 11, 2014.
4 Weigel, *Witness to Hope*, 233.
5 On John Paul II and Yalta, see Weigel, *Witness to Hope*, 232–33.
6 József Cardinal Mindszenty, *Memoirs* (New York: Macmillan Publishing, 1974).
7 See Paul Kengor and Patricia Clark Doerner, *The Judge: William P. Clark, Ronald Reagan's Top Hand* (San Francisco, CA: Ignatius Press, 2007).
8 See "Cardinal Refuses Honorary Degree from Santa Clara U.," *Catholic Herald*, June 7, 1974.
9 Kengor and Doerner, *The Judge.*
10 Sheen, *Communism and the Conscience of the West*, 49–52.
11 See Courtois et al., *The Black Book of Communism.*
12 Located in "Ronald Reagan: Pre-Presidential Papers: Selected Radio Broadcasts, 1975–1979," January 1975 to March 1977, Box 1, Ronald Reagan Library. See also Skinner, Anderson, and Anderson, *Reagan, In His Own Hand*, 10–12.
13 Christopher Andrew and Vasili Mitrokhin, *The Sword and the Shield: The Mitrokhin Archive and the Secret History of the KGB* (New York: Basic Books, 1999), 298.
14 "Bulgaria Talks Help Ostpolitik," *Catholic Herald*, November 26, 1976.
15 Agostino Casaroli, *The Martyrdom of Patience: The Holy See and the Communist Countries (1963–1989)* (Toronto: Ave Maria Centre for Peace, 2007), 353. This book was originally published in Italian in 2000.

CHAPTER 12: SUMMER OF 1976: TWO FREEDOM FIGHTERS IN AMERICA

1 Dziwisz, *A Life with Karol*, 40–41.
2 Weigel, *Witness to Hope*, 223.
3 Dziwisz, *A Life with Karol*, 39.
4 Weigel, *Witness to Hope*, 225.
5 Dziwisz, *A Life with Karol*, 39.
6 "Today in Philadelphia History: 41st International Eucharistic Congress begins," Philly.com, August 1, 2013.
7 Weigel, *Witness to Hope*, 225.
8 The text of the speech appeared originally in the November 18, 1976, issue of *L'Osservatore Romano*, the newspaper of the Holy See. It was republished in the newspaper on October 26, 1978. It is posted at the website of EWTN.com, http://www.ewtn.com/library/Doctrine/EUCHCONG.HTM.
9 "Notable & Quotable," *Wall Street Journal*, November 9, 1978, 30.
10 Weigel, *Witness to Hope*, 226.
11 Douglas Brinkley, *Gerald R. Ford: The 38th President, 1974–1977* (New York: Times Books, 2007), 109.
12 See Lee Edwards, *William F. Buckley Jr.: The Maker of a Movement* (Wilmington, DE: ISI Books, 2010).
13 See my documentation of this in Kengor, *11 Principles of a Reagan Conservative*, 38–42.
14 From the prepresidential period, see, among others, Reagan, "Speech to Members of Platform Committee," Republican National Convention, July 31, 1968, filed in "RWR—

Speeches and Articles (1968)" folder, vertical files, Ronald Reagan Library; Reagan speaking before CPAC, January 25, 1974, Washington, DC, text appears in Roberts, ed., *A City Upon a Hill*, 11–12; and Reagan, "Commencement Remarks at Marlborough College Prep School for Girls," Los Angeles, June 6, 1974, filed in, "RWR—Speeches and Articles (1974–76)" folder, vertical files, Ronald Reagan Library. See also Reagan, "Letters to the Editor," radio broadcast, June 1975, located in "Ronald Reagan: Pre-Presidential Papers: Selected Radio Broadcasts, 1975–1979," January 1975 to March 1977, Box 1, Ronald Reagan Library; and Skinner, Anderson, and Anderson, *Reagan, In His Own Hand*, 15–16.

15 Reagan, "Nationally Televised Address," ABC-TV, July 6, 1976. Speech filed in "RWR—Speeches and Articles (1974–76)" folder, vertical files, Ronald Reagan Library.
16 Quoted by Martin Anderson, *Revolution* (San Diego: Harcourt Brace Jovanovich, 1988), 43.
17 Reagan speaking on "Reagan," *The American Experience*, PBS.
18 Morris, *Dutch*, 402.
19 Nancy Reagan recalled these words in an interview on "Reagan," *The American Experience*, PBS.
20 For a handwritten copy of that broadcast, see Skinner, Anderson, and Anderson, *Reagan, In His Own Hand*, 4, 9–10, and inside cover of book.
21 Edmund Morris speaking on "Reagan," *The American Experience*, PBS.
22 Maureen Reagan, "A President and a Father," *Washington Times*, June 16, 2000, A23.
23 "The Church in the World," *The Tablet*, November 13, 1976.
24 Casaroli, *The Martyrdom of Patience*, 345.
25 "Bulgaria Talks Help Ostpolitik," *Catholic Herald*, November 26, 1976.
26 Casaroli, *The Martyrdom of Patience*, 351.
27 Ibid.

CHAPTER 13: 1977–1978: "WE WIN AND THEY LOSE"

1 Allen states in "Pope John Paul II, Ronald Reagan, and the Collapse of Communism: An Historic Confluence" that the date was "in February 1977, ten days after Jimmy Carter's inauguration." Ten days after the inauguration would have been January 30, 1977, which is consistent with the late January date that Allen has given in the past, including to me.
2 E-mail from Richard V. Allen, November 9, 2015.
3 Interview with Richard V. Allen, November 12, 2001. See also Allen, "Pope John Paul II, Ronald Reagan, and the Collapse of Communism: An Historic Confluence." The chapter (in Streusand, Bailey, and Marlo's *The Grand Strategy That Won the Cold War*) is a product of an address that Allen gave to a gathering of American bishops at the Pope John Paul II Cultural Center at the Catholic University of America on November 14, 2004. The full title, as reflected in a contemporary Catholic News Agency item the next day, was "Pope John Paul II, Ronald Reagan, and the Collapse of Communism." Source: E-mail from Richard V. Allen, November 9, 2015.
4 Allen, "Pope John Paul II, Ronald Reagan, and the Collapse of Communism: An Historic Confluence."
5 Ibid.
6 Interview with Richard V. Allen, November 12, 2001; Richard Allen, "An Extraordinary Man in Extraordinary Times: Ronald Reagan's Leadership and the Decision to End the Cold War," Address to the Hoover Institution and the William J. Casey Institute of the Center for Security Policy, Washington, DC, February 22, 1999, text printed in Peter Schweizer, ed., *The Fall of the Berlin Wall: Reassessing the Causes and Consequences of the End of the Cold War* (Stanford, CA: Hoover Institution Press, 2000), 52.

7 Reagan said "that the history of this troubled century will indeed be redeemed in the eyes of God and man." Reagan, "Remarks to Soviet Dissidents at Spaso House in Moscow," May 30, 1988.
8 Fulton J. Sheen, *Life of Christ* (New York: Doubleday, 1977), 21.
9 See my book *Dupes*, among others.
10 President Jimmy Carter, "The President's Overseas Trip Question-and-Answer Session with Reporters on Board Air Force One en Route to the United States," January 6, 1978.
11 "Hungary Restrained as Crown Is Returned," UPI, January 6, 1978.
12 President Jimmy Carter, "Remarks of the President and First Secretary Edward Gierek at the Welcoming Ceremony," Warsaw, Poland, December 29, 1977.
13 Carter, "The President's Overseas Trip Question-and-Answer Session with Reporters on Board Air Force One en Route to the United States."
14 Curtis Wilkie, a liberal journalist for the *Boston Globe*, filed a revealing December 31, 1977, report on a Polish woman who was among those who had wanted to meet with Carter and Western journalists but were denied. Carter's routine was carefully controlled.
15 President Jimmy Carter, "The President's News Conference," December 30, 1977.
16 This was reported by news sources at the time, including the Associated Press and the December 31, 1977, edition of the *New York Times*.
17 President Jimmy Carter, "Visit of President Josip Broz Tito of Yugoslavia Remarks at the Welcoming Ceremony," March 7, 1978.
18 President Jimmy Carter, "Visit of President Tito of Yugoslavia Toasts at the State Dinner," March 7, 1978.
19 President Jimmy Carter, "Visit of President Tito of Yugoslavia Joint Statement," March 9, 1978.
20 Carter, "Visit of President Josip Broz Tito of Yugoslavia Remarks at the Welcoming Ceremony."
21 A handwritten draft of the text is on file at the Reagan Library. Located in "Ronald Reagan: Pre-Presidential Papers: Selected Radio Broadcasts, 1975–1979," April 1977 to September 1977, Box 2, Ronald Reagan Library.
22 See Thrower, *God's Commissar*, 61. On Soviet secular holidays that replaced religious holidays like Christmas and Easter, see Powell, "Rearing the New Soviet Man," in Bociurkiw and Strong, *Religion and Atheism in the USSR and Eastern Europe*, 157–65.
23 Reagan, "Religious Freedom," radio broadcast, July 31, 1978.
24 Riley, *Fulton J. Sheen*, 138–39.
25 For this account I have drawn on several sources, all of them from Richard V. Allen, and all consistent: Allen, "Pope John Paul II, Ronald Reagan, and the Collapse of Communism: An Historic Confluence," Allen in Schweizer, ed., *The Fall of the Berlin Wall*, 55–56; Allen in Peter Hannaford, ed., *Recollections of Reagan* (New York: William Morrow, 1997), 6–8. Also, Allen spoke of the incident and noted that it occurred specifically in the month of November, in an interview for the documentary *In the Face of Evil: Reagan's War in Word and Deed* (American Vantage Films and Capital Films I, LLC, 2005).
26 See Schweizer, *Reagan's War*, 108.
27 Debate between Ronald Reagan and Robert F. Kennedy, "The Image of America and the Youth of the World," CBS News, "Town Meeting of the World," internationally televised, May 15, 1967. A video of the debate is located at the Reagan Library. I have a transcript of the debate, which I obtained from Bill Clark, who held a copy in his personal files for almost forty years. See also "The Ronnie-Bobby Show," *Newsweek*, May 29, 1967, 26–27.
28 Allen, in Schweizer, ed., *The Fall of the Berlin Wall*, 55–56.

CHAPTER 14: 1978–1979: "BE NOT AFRAID"

1 Dziwisz, *A Life with Karol*, 57.
2 See Noonan, *John Paul the Great*, 16–17. Noonan cites (among others) Bernstein and Politi, *His Holiness*.
3 Noonan, *John Paul the Great*, 17.
4 Bernstein and Politi, *His Holiness*, 169.
5 Dziwisz, *A Life with Karol*, 60–61.
6 See Simon, "The Catholic Church and the Communist State in the Soviet Union and Eastern Europe," 212–13.
7 Szulc, *Pope John Paul II*, 264.
8 Andrew and Mitrokhin, *The Sword and the Shield*, 511, 663n.
9 Ibid., 508–10.
10 Dziwisz, *A Life with Karol*, 42.
11 Ibid., 42–43.
12 Ibid., 43.
13 Roger Boyes and John Moody, *Messenger of the Truth* (Warsaw: Drukarnia Loretanska, 2013), 48–49. This book was originally published by Boyes and Moody as *The Priest and the Policeman* (New York: Summit Books, 1987). Boyes updated the 2013 version.
14 Dziwisz, *A Life with Karol*, 64–65.
15 "New Head of the Catholic Church," *Current Digest of the Soviet Press* 30, no. 42 (November 15, 1978): 20.
16 Ibid.
17 Andrew and Mitrokhin, *The Sword and the Shield*, 509.
18 Ibid., 508–9.
19 Bernstein and Politi, *His Holiness*, 175.
20 Weigel, *Witness to Hope*, 279.
21 Boyes and Moody, *Messenger of the Truth*, 48.
22 Andrew and Mitrokhin, *The Sword and the Shield*, 512.
23 George Weigel, "And the Wall Came Tumbling Down: John Paul II and the Communist Crack-up," Address at Grove City College, February 15, 2001.
24 Hejmo has denied this charge, but no less than Cardinal Józef Glemp, hardly a reckless anticommunist, said of Hejmo: "Certainly he was a spy. The documents and papers that were made public last year prove it." Glemp was referring to documents released in 2005 by the Polish National Remembrance Institute. See "Vatican Informers Spied on Pope John Paul II," *National Catholic Register*, September 17–23, 2006.
25 Dziwisz, *A Life with Karol*, 64.
26 Ibid., 69–71.
27 Weigel, *Witness to Hope*, 372, 431.
28 Ibid., 372.
29 See Alexiev, "The Kremlin and the Pope," 9.
30 Ibid., 6.
31 Ibid., 10.
32 Bernstein and Politi, *His Holiness*, 174–75.
33 Andrew and Mitrokhin, *The Sword and the Shield*, 512.
34 Ibid.; Dziwisz, *A Life with Karol*, 115.
35 Andrew and Mitrokhin, *The Sword and the Shield*, 512.
36 Boyes and Moody, *Messenger of the Truth*, 51.
37 George Weigel, *The End and the Beginning: Pope John Paul II—The Victory of Freedom, the Last Years, the Legacy* (New York: Doubleday, 2010), 109–10.
38 Weigel, *Witness to Hope*, 305.
39 "Homilies 1979," available at https://w2.vatican.va/content/john-paul-ii/en/homilies/1979.index.5.html. Retrieved November 4, 2015.

40 "Homily of His Holiness John Paul II," Holy Mass, Victory Square, Warsaw, Poland, June 2, 1979. Transcript taken from official Vatican website: https://w2.vatican.va/content/john-paul-ii/en/homilies/1979/documents/hf_jp-ii_hom_19790602_polonia-varsavia.html. Retrieved November 4, 2015.
41 Dziwisz, *A Life with Karol*, 116–18.
42 See "Narrator's Preface," Dziwisz, *A Life with Karol.*
43 Noonan, *John Paul the Great*, 29.
44 Ibid., 25.
45 Dziwisz, *A Life with Karol*, 116.
46 Noonan, *John Paul the Great*, 30.
47 "Farewell Ceremony at Jasna Góra," Address of His Holiness John Paul II, Częstochowa, Poland, June 6, 1979, http://w2.vatican.va/content/john-paul-ii/en/speeches/1979/june/documents/hf_jp-ii_spe_19790606_polonia-jasna-gora-congedo.html. Retrieved November 4, 2015.
48 Weigel, *Witness to Hope*, 312.
49 "Meeting with University Students of Kraków," Address of His Holiness John Paul II, Kraków, Poland, June 8, 1979, http://w2.vatican.va/content/john-paul-ii/en/speeches/1979/june/documents/hf_jp-ii_spe_19790608_polonia-cracovia-universitari.html. Retrieved November 4, 2015.
50 Dziwisz, *A Life with Karol*, 119; Weigel, *Witness to Hope*, 315.
51 Weigel, *Witness to Hope*, 318.
52 Ibid., 320.
53 "Farewell Ceremony at Balice Airport," Address of His Holiness John Paul II, Kraków, Poland, June 10, 1979, http://w2.vatican.va/content/john-paul-ii/en/speeches/1979/june/documents/hf_jp-ii_spe_19790610_polonia-balice-congedo.html. Retrieved November 5, 2015.
54 Quoted by Alexiev, "The Kremlin and the Pope," 11.
55 Weigel, *The End and the Beginning*, 110–11; Dziwisz, *A Life with Karol*, 118.
56 See Kengor, *The Crusader.*
57 Weigel, *The End and the Beginning*, 111.
58 Weigel states that the import of those nine days in Poland was not lost on one key Slavic observer: Aleksandr Solzhenitsyn. Solzhenitsyn witnessed the pope's reception in Poland from his exiled home in Vermont. He was elated: "This is the greatest thing to happen to the world since World War I," he declared. "It's the first real sign of hope since the Bolshevik revolution." Quoted by Weigel, "And the Wall Came Tumbling Down."
59 Editorial, "The Polish Pope in Poland," *New York Times*, June 5, 1979, A20.
60 Allen, "Pope John Paul II, Ronald Reagan, and the Collapse of Communism: An Historic Confluence."
61 Ibid.
62 Quoted in Schweizer, *Victory*, 35–36, 59, 69, 159–61; Bernstein and Politi, *His Holiness*, 270.
63 Allen, "Pope John Paul II, Ronald Reagan, and the Collapse of Communism: An Historic Confluence."
64 Ibid.
65 Among them was a compelling November 2, 1976, piece about the Katyn Forest massacre.
66 This particular broadcast was titled "The Pope in Poland." Located in "Ronald Reagan: Pre-Presidential Papers: Selected Radio Broadcasts, 1975–1979," October 31, 1978, to October 1979, Box 4, Ronald Reagan Library. For a full transcript, see Skinner, Anderson, and Anderson, *Reagan, In His Own Hand*, 174–75.
67 Located in "Ronald Reagan: Pre-Presidential Papers: Selected Radio Broadcasts, 1975–1979," October 31, 1978, to October 1979, Box 4, Ronald Reagan Library. For a full transcript, see Skinner, Anderson, and Anderson, *Reagan, In His Own Hand*, 176–77.

68 See Reagan, "Address to the Roundtable National Affairs Briefing," Dallas, TX, August 22, 1980, speech text located at Reagan Library, "Reagan 1980 Campaign Speeches, August 1980," vertical files.
69 See Reagan, "Address to the Roundtable National Affairs Briefing"; Reagan, "Address to the International Brotherhood of Teamsters," Columbus, OH, August 27, 1980, speech text located at Reagan Library, "Reagan 1980 Campaign Speeches, August 1980," vertical files; and Reagan, "Remarks in New Haven," New Haven, CT, October 6, 1980, speech text located at Reagan Library, "Reagan 1980 Campaign Speeches, October 1980," vertical files.
70 Bill Clark, "President Reagan and the Wall," Address to the Council of National Policy, San Francisco, CA, March 2000, 7–8.
71 Interview with Bill Clark, August 24, 2001.
72 Ibid.
73 On U.S. territory, Pope John Paul II met with Presidents Carter (1979), Reagan (1984 and 1987), and Clinton (1993, 1995, and 1999).
74 President Jimmy Carter, "Remarks at the Welcoming Ceremony for Pope John Paul II," October 6, 1979.
75 President Jimmy Carter, "Visit of Pope John Paul II, Remarks at White House Reception," October 6, 1979.
76 Weigel, *Witness to Hope*, 352.
77 See ibid., 350–52.
78 "The Popes Who Came to America," *National Catholic Register*, April 20, 2008.
79 Pope John Paul II, "Address of His Holiness John Paul During His Visit to the Cathedral of Philadelphia." October 3, 1979, http://w2.vatican.va/content/john-paul-ii/en/speeches/1979/october/documents/hf_jp-ii_spe_19791003_philadelphia-cathedral.html.
80 Anatoly Dobrynin, *In Confidence* (New York: Random House, 1995), 500–501.
81 See transcript posted at official Vatican archive/website: http://w2.vatican.va/content/john-paul-ii/en/speeches/1979/october/documents/hf_jp-ii_spe_19791002_general-assembly-onu.html.
82 See Weigel, *The End and the Beginning*, 114.
83 Weigel, *Witness to Hope*, 327–28; Weigel, *The End and the Beginning*, 114.
84 John Koehler, *Spies in the Vatican* (New York: Pegasus Books, 2009), 87–88.
85 Ibid.
86 Ibid., 62–64.
87 Michael Wines, "Upheaval in the East: 1980 Soviet Defector Emerges with Account of KGB Plots," *New York Times*, March 3, 1990.
88 Koehler, *Spies in the Vatican*, 63; Wines, "Upheaval in the East."

Chapter 15: 1980–1981: An Era of Renewal

1 See Crozier, *The Rise and Fall of the Soviet Empire*, 358.
2 Among examples of Reagan using this line, see Reagan, "Remarks at the Centennial Meeting of the Supreme Council of the Knights of Columbus," Hartford, CT, August 3, 1982; Reagan, "Address Before a Joint Session of the Irish National Parliament," June 4, 1984.
3 Arthur R. Rachwald, *In Search of Poland* (Stanford, CA: Hoover Institution Press, 1990), 3.
4 Cited by Crozier, *The Rise and Fall of the Soviet Empire*, 359.
5 See Andrew and Mitrokhin, *The Sword and the Shield*, 516; Weigel, *Witness to Hope*, 323.
6 See, among others, Reagan, "Proclamation 4891—Solidarity Day," January 20, 1982.
7 Schweizer, *Victory*, 29, 31.

8 Reagan, "Address to the International Brotherhood of Teamsters," Columbus, OH, August 27, 1980, speech text located at Reagan Library, "Reagan 1980 Campaign Speeches, August 1980," vertical files.
9 Schweizer, *Victory*, 29, 31.
10 Acknowledging this spiritual link, Russia expert James Billington notes that as a "bottom-up mass movement rooted in religion," Solidarity was not the typical movement that apparatchiks could domesticate by decapitation or by offering carrots and sticks to its members. James H. Billington, "The Foreign Policy of President Ronald Reagan," Address to the International Republican Institute Freedom Dinner, Washington, DC, September 25, 1997, 2.
11 Quoted in Rowland Evans and Robert Novak, *The Reagan Revolution* (New York: Dutton, 1981), 11–12.
12 These details were published in the Italian newspaper *Il Messaggero* (The Messenger) in the January 16 and 18, 1981, editions.
13 Sterling, *The Time of the Assassins*, 143, 209–10, 236; Claire Sterling, "Agca's Other Story: The Plot to Kill Wałęsa," *New York Times*, October 27, 1984.
14 See Kengor and Doerner, *The Judge*.
15 See Kengor, *Dupes*, 86.
16 Eric Pace, "William Casey, Ex-CIA Head, Is Dead at 74," *New York Times*, May 7, 1987.
17 Kengor and Doerner, *The Judge*, 102–3.
18 "Untouchable Crook: Political Profile of CIA Director W. Casey," *Sovetskaya Rossiya*, December 17, 1986, printed as "Sovetskaya Rossiya Profiles CIA Director Casey," in *Foreign Broadcast Information Service*, FBIS-SOV-31-Dec-86, December 31, 1986, A2–A5.
19 Casey said this in his October 1986 speech at Ashland College. A *Pravda* article said he made the claim in San Antonio, Texas, as well.
20 Interview with Herb Meyer, February 5, 2009.
21 See *Wolf Blitzer Reports*, CNN, April 7, 2005, transcript at http://www.cnn.com/TRANSCRIPTS/0504/07/wbr.01.html.
22 Interview with Herb Meyer, February 5, 2009.
23 On this and more from Meyer, see Kengor, *The Crusader*, 199.
24 The meeting took place in Fulda, Germany, in November 1980, but it was not reported until October 1981, when the German publication *Stimme des Glaubens* gave what it reported to be a verbatim account of the pope's meeting with a select group of German Catholics. In the interim, John Paul II was shot.
25 As to what the pope's comments meant, the fatima.org website maintains: "When Pope John Paul II spoke at Fulda, he had not yet been the victim of the 1981 assassination attempt. Speaking of the Third Secret of Fátima, he did not allude to anything resembling a future assassination attempt (which in 2000 the Vatican announced to be the subject of the final part of the Secret that Our Lady revealed at Fátima in 1917), but rather to imminent chastisement and worldwide tribulation." Retrieved from www.fatima.org, October 24, 2013.

Chapter 16: March 30, 1981: A Bullet for a President

1 One of the best sources on Reagan's shooting and the immediate aftermath is Michael K. Deaver, *A Different Drummer: My Thirty Years with Ronald Reagan* (New York: Harper, 2001), 127–54.
2 Douglas Brinkley, ed., *The Reagan Diaries* (New York: HarperCollins, 2007), 12.
3 Quoted in Morris, *Dutch*, 429. See also Reagan, *An American Life*, 261–62; Brinkley, *The Reagan Diaries*, 12. The original quotation circulated in *Dutch* and *An American Life* seems to have been taken from Reagan's diary entry.
4 Brinkley, *The Reagan Diaries*, 12.

5 I spoke to Evans twice about this, in interviews (by phone) on March 8, 2005, and February 22, 2006.
6 Evans remembered the gathering place as a kind of "reception room" with a couch and some chairs. He was not sure of the name of the room but believed it was not part of the White House living quarters.
7 Brinkley, *The Reagan Diaries*, 12.
8 See Kengor and Doerner, *The Judge*, 75, for details on the closeness of Clark and Nancy in Sacramento.
9 Patti Davis, *Angels Don't Die: My Father's Gift of Faith* (New York: HarperCollins, 1995), 26–27.
10 Maureen Reagan, *First Father, First Daughter*, 279. Many Reagan staffers and family members have spoken of how Ronald Reagan believed that he was spared for a special purpose. Among many others, see Michael Reagan with Joe Hyams, *On the Outside Looking In* (New York: Kensington Publishing, 1988), 198; Davis, *Angels Don't Die*, 38; Bob Slosser, *Reagan Inside Out* (Waco, TX: Word Books, 1984); Kenneth Duberstein, interviewed for CNN documentary *The Reagan Years: Inside the White House*, part 2, aired February 18, 2001; Lyn Nofziger, quoted in "Reagan Officials on the March 30, 1981, Assassination Attempt," Reagan Oral History Project, http://millercenter.org/oralhistory/news/reagan-assassination-attempt.
11 Brinkley, *The Reagan Diaries*, 12; Reagan, *An American Life*, 263; Morris, *Dutch*, 432.
12 Reagan, "Remarks to the Annual National Prayer Breakfast," February 4, 1982.
13 Reagan, *An American Life*, 269.
14 Michael Deaver, interviewed for CNN's *The Reagan Years: Inside the White House*, part 2. See also Deaver, *A Different Drummer*, 151–53.
15 The letter was sent on April 24, 1981. Many Reagan letters followed after this, including more than one to each of the subsequent Soviet general secretaries.
16 This quotation is rendered with very slight variations in wording in different sources, though the meaning is always precisely the same. This is the most commonly quoted version, including by Edmund Morris in *Dutch*. The only witness was apparently Mike Deaver, who arranged for Cooke to meet with the president. He remembered Reagan saying, "I have decided that whatever time I may have left is for Him." Deaver, *A Different Drummer*, 145–47.
17 Brinkley, *The Reagan Diaries*, 13.
18 Interview with Louis H. Evans, February 22, 2006.
19 Interview with Colleen Townsend Evans, April 10, 2016.
20 Brinkley, *The Reagan Diaries*, 13.
21 Morris, *Dutch*, 434–35.
22 Reagan, "Address Before a Joint Session of the Congress on the Program for Economic Recovery," April 28, 1981.
23 Robert P. Mooney, "Reagan Disputes U.S. 'Sickness,'" June 14, 1968, *Indianapolis Star*, 1; and "Reagan Asks Bold U.S. Stand in Viet," *Indianapolis News*, June 14, 1968.
24 Pages from Sirhan's diaries have been published but are difficult to find. They are also hard to find online. Here are two recent sources that have published images from the diaries, from which I quote in this section: Robert Blair Kaiser, *RFK Must Die!* (New York: Overlook Press, 2008), 383–84, 394–96; Mel Ayton, *The Forgotten Terrorist: Sirhan Sirhan and the Assassination of Robert F. Kennedy* (Washington, DC: Potomac Books, 2007), 292–94.
25 Reagan, "Remarks at the First Annual Commemoration of the Days of Remembrance of Victims of the Holocaust," April 30, 1981; Reagan, "Address at Commencement Exercises at the United States Military Academy," May 27, 1981. See also Reagan, "Remarks at Eureka College," February 6, 1984. He quoted Pius's remark in his private correspondence as well, such as in a December 19, 1984, letter to the Reverend Edward Davis of Spokane, Washington, located in Presidential Handwriting File, Presidential Records, Ronald Reagan Library, Box 11, Folder 155.

26 Viktor Levin speaking on the weekly Moscow TV news program *International Observers Roundtable*, carried by the Moscow Domestic Service, June 3, 1984, transcript printed in *Foreign Broadcast Information Service*, FBIS-SOV-4-JUN-84, June 4, 1984, CC8.

CHAPTER 17: MARCH 29–30, 1981: THE SOVIET INVASION THAT WASN'T

1 This suggests that Casey himself, and not just the CIA and NSA, received the troop-status intel that Jack had passed along on March 29, 1981.
2 See Richard V. Allen, "The Day Reagan Was Shot," *Atlantic Monthly*, April 2001. Allen, the national security adviser, tape-recorded the crisis management discussions in the White House Situation Room immediately after Reagan was shot. His *Atlantic Monthly* article remains the definitive account of precisely what was said in the White House that day and is highly recommended to students of the subject. In the article, Allen writes, "The first assessments by the Pentagon revealed that more Soviet submarines than usual were off the East Coast." Allen's transcript shows Secretary of Defense Caspar Weinberger saying, "The nearest submarine is [redacted] minutes, forty-seven seconds off, which is about two minutes closer than normal."
3 See Allen, "The Day Reagan Was Shot." Allen's transcript shows that Defense Secretary Weinberger and others in the Situation Room said they had raised the alert status without specifically changing the DEFCON ("defense condition") status. The transcript shows, and Haig also wrote in his memoir, that the secretary of state argued with Weinberger about the change to the alert status, and whether such a change could be undertaken without altering the DEFCON. (Haig wrote, "I began to suspect that Weinberger did not know whether he had raised the DEFCON or, if he had raised it, to what level." See Alexander M. Haig Jr., *Caveat: Realism, Reagan, and Foreign Policy* [New York: Macmillan, 1984], 157.) Regardless, Reagan officials took security measures and sent alerts to the Strategic Air Command. Clearly, the U.S. military was at some form of heightened alert.
4 On the 2:25 time, see "Statement by Assistant to the President David R. Gergen About the Attempted Assassination of the President," *Public Papers of the Presidents of the United States: Ronald Reagan*, March 30, 1981.
5 "Statement by Assistant to the President David R. Gergen About the Attempted Assassination of the President."
6 Allen, "The Day Reagan Was Shot."
7 "Remarks by Secretary of State Alexander M. Haig, Jr., About the Attempted Assassination of the President," *Public Papers of the Presidents of the United States: Ronald Reagan*, March 30, 1981.
8 In his memoir, Haig said that he was "shocked" when, in the Situation Room, Weinberger said he had raised the alert status. "Depending on the nature of the instructions issued by Weinberger, any such change would be detected promptly by the Soviet Union," Haig wrote. "In response, the Russians might raise their own alert status, and that could cause a further escalation of our side. That fact that this was happening would be reported on television and radio, and the news would let loose more emotion, exacerbating the existing climate of anxiety and anger and fear. Moreover, the Soviet leaders might very well conclude that the United States, in a flight of paranoia, believed that the USSR was involved in the attempt to assassinate the President. Why would we alert our military forces if a lone psychotic had been responsible? The consequences were incalculable." See Haig, *Caveat*, 156.
9 Quoted in Alan Peppard, "Command and Control: Tested Under Fire," *Dallas Morning News*, May 13, 2015.
10 At 3:30 that afternoon, Attorney General Edwin Meese called from the hospital and said that with the vice president absent, "the national command authority" rested with

Secretary of Defense Weinberger. Meese added that "Al [Haig] is to calm other governments." See Allen, "The Day Reagan Was Shot."

11 Bill Clark initially shared this material with me for Kengor and Doerner, *The Judge*.
12 Kengor and Doerner, *The Judge*, 125–26.
13 This is not to excuse all of Haig's behavior. The military man was mercurial and hotheaded. Dick Allen's transcript of the discussions in the White House Situation Room on March 30, 1981, reveals the palpable tension in the room, much of which Haig brought on. Haig's tendency to ruffle feathers would ultimately prompt Ronald Reagan and just about every member of the administration to want the secretary of state out of office. Haig resigned in July 1982.
14 Phone conversation with Bill Clark, August 22, 2011.
15 See, e.g., Mark Kramer, "Poland, 1980–81: Soviet Policy During the Polish Crisis," *Cold War International History Project Bulletin* no. 5 (Spring 1995); Mark Kramer, "Jaruzelski, the Soviet Union, and the Imposition of Martial Law in Poland: New Light on the Mystery of December 1981," *Cold War International History Project Bulletin* no. 11 (Winter 1998); Mark Kramer, "Colonel Kukliński and the Polish Crisis, 1980–81," *Cold War International History Project Bulletin* no. 11 (Winter 1998); "'In Case Military Assistance Is Provided to Poland': Soviet Preparations for Military Contingencies, August 1980," introduced and translated by Mark Kramer, *Cold War International History Project Bulletin* no. 11 (Winter 1998).
16 Timothy Garton Ash, *The Polish Revolution: Solidarity*, 3rd ed. (New Haven, CT: Yale University Press, 2002), 88–89.
17 Rachwald, *In Search of Poland*, 9–10.
18 Ibid.
19 Andrew and Mitrokhin, *The Sword and the Shield*, 520.
20 E-mail exchanges with Tomasz Pompowski, March 3, 2006.
21 Andrew and Mitrokhin, *The Sword and the Shield*, 520.
22 Eduard Shevardnadze, *The Future Belongs to Freedom* (New York: Free Press, 1991), 121.
23 E-mail correspondence from Marek Jan Chodakiewicz, October 12, 2011.
24 On the other hand, a common counterargument, noted by Shevardnadze, is that the "quick solution" (i.e., force) had not worked well in Afghanistan, which was already creating major problems for Moscow. So why repeat the mistake, at an even more chaotic level, in Poland?
25 Benjamin Weiser, *A Secret Life: The Polish Officer, His Covert Mission, and the Price He Paid to Save His Country* (New York: PublicAffairs, 2004), 3. I also learned of Kukliński's importance from Gus Weiss, who told me only vaguely that Kukliński "earned his salary during the crisis." Interview with Weiss, November 26, 2002.
26 See the official Kukliński website in English, specifically this page: http://www.kuklinski.us/page11.htm.
27 Jerrold and Leona Schecter, *Sacred Secrets: How Soviet Intelligence Operations Changed American History* (Dulles, VA: Brassey's, 2002), 305.
28 Allen, "Pope John Paul II, Ronald Reagan, and the Collapse of Communism: An Historic Confluence."
29 The December 16, 1980, letter is published in Weigel, *Witness to Hope*, 406–7. See also Weigel, *The End and the Beginning*, 123–24.
30 See Kengor, *The Crusader*, 94–95.
31 Interview with Caspar Weinberger, October 10, 2002.
32 Pipes, *Vixi*, 168–69; e-mail from Richard Pipes, August 20, 2011.
33 See Kengor, *The Crusader*, 93–94.
34 E-mail from Richard Pipes, August 20, 2011.
35 See Andrew and Mitrokhin, *The Sword and the Shield*, 521.
36 Weigel, *The End and the Beginning*, 129.
37 Sterling, *The Time of the Assassins*, 129.

38 "U.S. Warns Russians and Poles on Force Against the Unions," *New York Times*, March 27, 1981.
39 John Darnton, "Millions in Poland Go on 4-Hour Strike to Protest Violence," *New York Times*, March 28, 1981, 1.
40 Sterling, *The Time of the Assassins*, 129.
41 John Darnton, "Polish Ruling Body Reaches an Impasse on Averting Strike," *New York Times*, March 30, 1981; John Darnton, "Polish Strike in Abeyance as Pact Is Signed," *New York Times*, March 31, 1981.
42 Douglas J. MacEachin, *U.S. Intelligence and the Confrontation in Poland, 1980–1981* (University Park, PA: Pennsylvania State University Press, 2002).
43 Ibid., 117–35.
44 Ibid., 119–121.
45 Ibid., 122.
46 Ibid., 125–26.
47 Ibid., 128–30.
48 Bernard Gwertzman, "U.S. Expects Tensions in Poland to Ease," *New York Times*, March 31, 1981.
49 MacEachin, *U.S. Intelligence and the Confrontation in Poland, 1980–1981*, 134–35.
50 MacEachin includes information on an April 3 intelligence memo: "Just as the U.S. administration was conveying its perception that the crisis appeared to be receding," recorded MacEachin, U.S. intelligence "suddenly escalated its warning of a Soviet military intervention" in an April 3 Alert Memorandum, which stated that Soviet leaders had become "convinced" that "military intervention is necessary." But then, at the end of his chapter, MacEachin notes the cooldown by April 7–8. In all likelihood, the April 3 memo had been devised amid the escalation over the previous weeks in March. Of course, even then, the situation would remain tense throughout 1981. Ibid., 131.
51 This is evident because the original copies (which also typically have coloring, not just black-and-white text) contained their original staples, which had not been removed (as is required) by archivists in the research room before the copies were made and then the originals restapled.

Chapter 18: May 13, 1981: A (Soviet) Bullet for a Pope

1 Alexiev, "The Kremlin and the Pope," 12–13.
2 Ibid., 13.
3 André Frossard and Pope John Paul II, *"Be Not Afraid!": Pope John Paul II Speaks Out on His Life, His Beliefs, and His Inspiring Vision for Humanity* (New York: St. Martin's Press, 1984), 251.
4 Pope John Paul II, *Memory and Identity: Conversations at the Dawn of a Millennium* (New York: Rizzoli, 2005), 160.
5 Dziwisz, *A Life with Karol*, 131–32.
6 John Paul II, *Memory and Identity*, 160.
7 Frossard and John Paul II, *"Be Not Afraid!"* 227.
8 Dziwisz, *A Life with Karol*, 133.
9 John Paul II, *Memory and Identity*, 161.
10 Frossard and John Paul II, *"Be Not Afraid!"* 236–37; Weigel, *Witness to Hope*, 413.
11 John Paul II, *Memory and Identity*, 160–62.
12 Lawrence K. Altman, "The Doctor's World: After Assassination Attempts, Those Unreliable Early Reports," *New York Times*, June 2, 1981.
13 Altman, "The Doctor's World: After Assassination Attempts, Those Unreliable Early Reports"; and John Paul II, *Memory and Identity*, 161.
14 Frossard and John Paul II, *"Be Not Afraid!"* 225.

15 Weigel, *The End and the Beginning*, 132.
16 John Paul II, *Memory and Identity*, 160.
17 Dziwisz, *A Life with Karol*, 135.
18 Ibid., 134–35.
19 Rychlak, *Hitler, the War, and the Pope*, 14–15; Hatch and Walshe, *Crown of Glory*, 82–83.
20 R. W. Apple Jr., "Police Trace the Path of the Suspect from Turkey to St. Peter's Square," *New York Times*, May 15, 1981.
21 Quoted in Sterling, *The Time of the Assassins*, 3.
22 Quoted ibid.
23 Quoted ibid., 9.
24 To cite just one of innumerable examples of suspicions of Bulgaria, see this early account: "A Murky but Intriguing Trail," *Time*, December 27, 1982, 25.
25 Dziwisz, *A Life with Karol*, 139–40.
26 "A Murky but Intriguing Trail."
27 Dziwisz, *A Life with Karol*, 135.
28 On August 11 the two envelopes were returned to the archives of the Vatican's Holy Office. Bertone, *The Last Secret of Fátima*, 161; Dziwisz, *A Life with Karol*, 135.
29 Dziwisz, *A Life with Karol*, 136.
30 Ibid.
31 Weigel, *Witness to Hope*, 413.
32 Dziwisz, *A Life with Karol*, 136; Weigel, *The End and the Beginning*, 235. The pope would say in a separate context, "I came to understand that true devotion to the Mother of God is... very profoundly rooted in the Mystery of the Blessed Trinity, and the mysteries of the Incarnation and the Redemption." See Pope John Paul II, *Crossing the Threshold of Hope*, ed. Vittorio Messori (New York: Knopf, 2005), 213.
33 Note that the pope said the shooting had occurred not only on the exact date when Mary appeared but also the exact *hour*. This is a very intriguing claim that I was not able to confirm. Sources agree that the May 13, 1917, apparition occurred sometime in the afternoon, after the children ate their lunches and played. See Apostoli, *Fátima for Today*, 43.
34 John Paul II, *Memory and Identity*, 163.
35 Wikipedia entries are not reliable sources, but they are valuable reflectors of popular perception.
36 Sterling, *The Time of the Assassins*, 39–46.
37 See Sterling, *The Time of the Assassins*, 17–20.
38 See Pacepa and Rychlak, *Disinformation*.
39 Sterling, *The Time of the Assassins*, 21, 31.
40 Ibid., 31.
41 He eventually changed his mind, or was advised to change his mind, and wore different shoes and clothes.
42 The paper trail for this exchange is interesting. Reagan's words are printed on a White House Situation Room cable, today housed at the Reagan Library. Titled "Reply to Get-Well Message from Pope to President," it is printed on a document with the date "05/25/81" on top, but it seems to have been sent to the Vatican from the White House sometime earlier in May 1981. Interestingly, the cable states that the "White House has no record of actual receipt" of a get-well message from the pope, even though such a message had been printed in the Vatican newspaper, *L'Osservatore Romano*. There must have been a failure in direct delivery to the White House. Nonetheless, the published text of the message in *L'Osservatore Romano* meant that the Vatican had prepared a message. That being the case, the Reagan team made sure that the president responded with his appreciation.
43 The text of this message is likewise printed in a "05/25/81" White House Situation Room cable held at the Reagan Library. The official Reagan Library file citation is: Executive

Secretariat (ES), National Security Council (NSC), Head of State File (HSF): Records, Vatican: Pope John Paul II, Ronald Reagan Library, Box 41, Folder "Cables 1 of 2."

44 Allen, "Pope John Paul II, Ronald Reagan, and the Collapse of Communism: An Historic Confluence."

45 The letter, prefaced by a May 22, 1981, White House memo from Mort Allin to Larry Speakes (both of the White House press office), is held at the Reagan Library.

46 Thomas Alvarez, ed., *The Prayers of Teresa of Avila* (Hyde Park, NY: New City Press, 1990), 41–42.

47 Bob Woodward, *Veil: The Secret Wars of the CIA, 1981–1987* (New York: Simon and Schuster, 1987), 102.

CHAPTER 19: MAY–SEPTEMBER 1981: COMMENCEMENT

1 Though Reagan otherwise did not seem to suffer from a significant spelling disability, he wrote "Cardinal Crowell" here, which appears to be his spur-of-the-moment (pre-Google) phonetic spelling of Cardinal John Krol, the Philadelphia prelate with whom Reagan had a good relationship. Brinkley, *The Reagan Diaries*, 18.

2 See my discussion of this in two pieces: Paul Kengor, "Reagan at Notre Dame," *National Review Online*, May 16, 2011; Paul Kengor, "A Welcome Correction," *National Review Online*, May 18, 2011.

3 I reviewed these drafts personally at the Reagan Library in August 2015. My assistant David Kirk reviewed them in January 2015.

4 Another possible explanation is, in my view, less likely: that the archives are missing a final draft of the speech that included such a passage.

5 Reagan, "The President's News Conference," June 16, 1981.

6 See Laurence I. Barrett, *Gambling with History: Reagan in the White House* (New York: Doubleday, 1983), 124; Deaver, *A Different Drummer*, 114.

7 The records at the Reagan Library tell us only of a White House luncheon in the Family Dining Room that included twelve people: President Reagan, Nancy Reagan, Mother Teresa, a Sister Priscilla (described as a "traveling aide to Mother Teresa"), a Mrs. Vi Collins (the U.S. sponsor to Mother Teresa), Michael Deaver, Senator Mark Hatfield and his wife, Thomas Getman (chief legislative aide to Hatfield), Patricia Bye (described as secretary to the "Office of the Deputy Chief of Staff"), a John Billings, and a Mercedes Wilson. The President's Daily Diary for that June 4, held today in the Reagan Library, records that from 12:28 P.M. to 1:34 P.M. the president and first lady had lunch with Mother Teresa and then escorted her to her motorcade on the South Grounds and bid her farewell. The diary then notes that from 1:34 P.M. to 1:39 P.M. the president "participated in a question and answer session with members of the press" and quickly returned to the Oval Office.

8 Reagan, "Exchange with Reporters Following a Luncheon with Mother Teresa of Calcutta," June 4, 1981.

9 In May 1985, Reagan would award Mother Teresa the Presidential Medal of Freedom, the highest civilian honor. Over the years, Mother Teresa wrote and called President Reagan asking for his and his country's assistance in helping her feed the world's poor, and always telling the president, "I will pray for you." On October 19, 1984, for example, she sent Reagan a two-page handwritten letter that closed with the words "I will pray for you." Reagan responded with a telephone call, as recommended in an October 26, 1984, memo on White House letterhead by staff member Michael A. McManus Jr. Another memo on White House letterhead (no author listed) from September 17, 1987, noted Mother Teresa was expected to call the president. These documents are on file at the Reagan Library.

10 Other pronunciations include "Med-jew-gore-yay" and "Med-jew-gore-ee-uh." A friend

who has studied the pronunciation and has visited the village several times tells me that native speakers typically pronounce it "Med-jew-gore-yah."

11 See narrative details in Wayne Weible, *Medjugorje: The Message* (Brewster, MA: Paraclete Press, 1989), xi–xii.
12 Differing accounts provide varying dates of birth for the visionaries.
13 Weible, *Medjugorje*, 9–13.
14 Ibid., 64.
15 Medjugorje sources report the date as June 24, 1981. The websites www.medjugorje.org and www.medjugorje.com are not run by the Catholic Church and are not official websites, but they are the go-to sites on the subject. Both list the date of the first apparition as June 24, 1981. Likewise, the page on Medjugorje at the very reliable EWTN website lists June 24, 1981.
16 TASS statement, May 14, 1981, republished in *Current Digest of the Soviet Press* 33, no. 20 (June 17, 1981): 18.
17 A. Filippov, "Concerning the Attempt on the Life of John Paul II," *Pravda*, May 15, 1981, republished in *Current Digest of the Soviet Press* 33, no. 20 (June 17, 1981): 18.
18 M. Mikhailov, "Red Herring," *Izvestia*, September 8, 1981, republished in *Current Digest of the Soviet Press* 33, no. 36 (October 7, 1981): 16.
19 Sterling, *The Time of the Assassins*, 134–35, 151–52, 164, 167–69, 183.

Chapter 20: December 13, 1981: Martial Law

1 David Cross, "Shooting Reported in Poland as Troops Break Wave of Strikes," *The Times* (London), December 16, 1981; Dziwisz, *A Life with Karol*, 144.
2 Boyes and Moody, *Messenger of the Truth*, 76.
3 Boyes and Moody, *Messenger of the Truth*, 83–95; Dziwisz, *A Life with Karol*, 144.
4 "Ex-Prime Minister Among Those Held," *The Times* (London), December 14, 1981; Cross, "Shooting Reported in Poland."
5 Ibid.
6 Ibid.
7 Dziwisz, *A Life with Karol*, 143–44.
8 Ibid.; Weigel, *The End and the Beginning*, 138.
9 Brinkley, *The Reagan Diaries*, 55.
10 Richard Owen, "How Army Has Filled Vacuum Left by Party," *The Times* (London), December 14, 1981.
11 Rachwald, *In Search of Poland*, 18–19.
12 See the official Kukliński website in English, specifically this page: http://www.kuklinski.us/page11.htm. See also Rachwald, *In Search of Poland*, 21.
13 E-mail correspondence from Marek Jan Chodakiewicz, October 12, 2011.
14 See Shevardnadze, *The Future Belongs to Freedom*, 121; Pipes, *Vixi*, 169.
15 Shevardnadze, *The Future Belongs to Freedom*, 121.
16 Mark Kramer of Harvard contends that as the decisive moment approached for martial law in December 1981, Jaruzelski "lost his nerve" and began urging Moscow to send Soviet troops to Poland to help him introduce martial law. By that point, Moscow was firmly against sending troops and, writes Kramer, "tersely brushed aside [Jaruzelski's] repeated pleas." Kramer's findings strongly challenge the view of Jaruzelski as peacemaker.
17 The transcript was published in major newspapers around the world on December 14 and 15, 1981.
18 Official Soviet TASS statement, published in *The Times* of London, December 14, 1981, 6.
19 Cross, "Shooting Reported in Poland."
20 Schweizer, *Victory*, 29, 31.

21 Agostino Bono, "Officials Say Pope, Reagan Shared Cold War Data, but Lacked Alliance," *Catholic News Service*, November 17, 2004.
22 Reagan, "Excerpts from a Telephone Conversation with Pope John Paul II About the Situation in Poland," December 14, 1981. See also Weigel, *The End and the Beginning*, 138.
23 Several documents in the Reagan Library relate to the agenda items for the original December 15 Casaroli visit to the White House, including a December 3, 1981, State Department memo titled "Request for Appointment with the President: Vatican Secretary of State Casaroli," written by L. Paul Bremer to James W. Nance of the White House.
24 The plans for this meeting are sketched out in four documents housed at the Reagan Library: a May 6, 1981, State Department memo by L. Paul Bremer, a May 7 White House memo written by Elizabeth Dole, and two May 11 White House memos, one by Richard V. Allen and the other by Charles P. Tyson.
25 "President's Working Lunch with Agostino Cardinal Casaroli," Memorandum of Conversation, White House, December 21, 1981, prepared by James W. Nance, held at Reagan Library.
26 Martin and Annelise Anderson, *Reagan's Secret War: The Untold Story of His Fight to Save the World from Nuclear Disaster* (New York: Crown, 2009), 80–82.
27 Weigel, *The End and the Beginning*, 138–39.
28 Brinkley, *The Reagan Diaries*, 55–56.
29 "President's Working Lunch with Agostino Cardinal Casaroli," Memorandum of Conversation, 4.
30 Weigel, *The End and the Beginning*, 139–42.
31 Ibid., 140.
32 "President's Working Lunch with Agostino Cardinal Casaroli," Memorandum of Conversation, 4. Not until around this point in the conversation had the men started to discuss the subject of nuclear confrontation. Most of the discussion was on martial law in Poland.
33 Documents located in ES, NSC, HSF: Records, Vatican: Pope John Paul II, Ronald Reagan Library, Box 41, Folders "Cables 1 of 2" and 8107378–8200051.
34 December 29, 1981, letter from Ronald Reagan to Pope John Paul II. Document is located in ES, NSC, HSF: Records, Vatican: Pope John Paul II, Ronald Reagan Library, Box 41, Folder 8107378–820051. The document was declassified on July 18, 2000.
35 I was unable to locate via the Reagan Library or the National Archives a single list of all phone calls between President Reagan and Pope John Paul II and thus am unable to quantify their phone communications.
36 Anderson and Anderson, *Reagan's Secret War*, 90.
37 This exchange is on file at the Reagan Library.
38 Reagan Library archivist Shelly Williams examined the letter, and neither she nor I was able to confirm whether the handwriting was Reagan's. I also showed the letter to Bill Clark's son, Paul, and his cousin, Pat Clark Doerner, who coauthored Clark's biography with me. They were unable to make a match. (I found the letter after Bill Clark had passed away.) The most distinctive marking in the penciled handwriting is the unusual shape of the writer's "G" in the word *God's*. The odd "G" style does not seem to match Reagan's or Clark's typical scribbling of the letter "G."
39 See Pipes, *Vixi*, 170–72.
40 These December 21, 1981, minutes from the NSC meeting are filed in the "Executive Secretariat NSC: NSC Meeting Files" at the Ronald Reagan Library. I have quoted from these minutes in other books and writings. They are also quoted and presented by Martin and Annelise Anderson in *Reagan's Secret War*, 83–86.
41 This section is from page 7 of the NSC meeting minutes of December 21, 1981. Parentheses in original document.
42 Brinkley, *The Reagan Diaries*, 57.

43 See Pipes, *Vixi*, 170–72.
44 Reagan, *An American Life*, 304; Brinkley, *The Reagan Diaries*, 58.
45 One source that captures the three previous instances is Anderson and Anderson, *Reagan's Secret War*, 83–87.
46 Letter from Ronald Reagan to Leonid Brezhnev, December 23, 1981, ES, NSC, HSF: Records, USSR: GSB (8190210), Box 38, Ronald Reagan Library. This document was declassified on October 22, 1999. I believe that the letter was a combination of two drafts, one by Richard Pipes (which formed the opening paragraphs) and the other by the State Department. See Pipes, *Vixi*, 172–73.
47 Dziwisz, *A Life with Karol*, 145.
48 Weigel, *The End and the Beginning*, 138; Dziwisz, *A Life with Karol*, 145–46.
49 Deaver, *Behind the Scenes*, 142–43.
50 That was how Reagan described the meeting in his December 22, 1981, diary entry. See Brinkley, *The Reagan Diaries*, 57–58.
51 Deaver, *Behind the Scenes*, 142–43.
52 Reagan, "Exchange with Reporters About Soviet Ambassador Romuald Spasowski," December 22, 1981.
53 Speechwriters Ben Elliott and Tony Dolan told me (via separate e-mails, both sent December 24, 2012) that the main speechwriter for this address was Aram Bakshian.
54 Among other examples, see Reagan, "Proclamation 4891—Solidarity Day," January 20, 1982.
55 Reagan, "Address to the Nation About Christmas and the Situation in Poland," December 23, 1981.
56 Y. Nilov, "No Scruples . . . ," *Novoye Vremya*, January 1, 1982, 8–9, published as "Weinberger's Remarks on Poland, Church Assailed," in *Foreign Broadcast Information Service*, FBIS-SOV-19-JAN-82, January 19, 1982, F1–3.
57 Valentin Zorin, "Moscow Viewpoint," December 27, 1981, published as "Zorin Commentary," in *Foreign Broadcast Information Service*, FBIS-SOV-30-DEC-81, December 30, 1981, F3–5.
58 "Imperialist Interference Rebuffed," TASS, December 29, 1981, published as "Zolnierz Wolnosci on Reagan Address," in *Foreign Broadcast Information Service*, FBIS-SOV-30-DEC-81, December 30, 1981, F2–3.
59 These contacts included Cardinal Terence Cooke and his replacement, Cardinal John O'Connor, and Archbishop Philip Hannan of New Orleans. Reagan's diary, his letters on file at the Reagan Library, and his phone calls listed at the Reagan Library include several exchanges with each of these men. At the Reagan Library, I found records of more than a dozen phone calls from Reagan to leading Catholics, including Mother Teresa. On May 23, 1988, Reagan called Cardinal O'Connor on behalf of Pope John Paul II concerning Cuba and the USSR.
60 Christie L. Chicoine, "Remembering Reagan's Presence in Philadelphia," *Catholic Standard and Times*, June 2004. The *Catholic Standard and Times* is the newspaper of the archdiocese of Philadelphia.
61 Reagan, "Remarks at a Polish Festival in Doylestown, Pennsylvania," September 9, 1984. On July 16, 1984, Reagan called Cardinal Krol to invite him to give the invocation at the Republican National Convention.
62 Interview with native Pole Barbara Dudek, conducted by Margie Dudek, November 2004.
63 Interview with Jan Pompowski, October 31, 2005, translated by Tomasz Pompowski.
64 Weigel, *The End and the Beginning*, 143; Dziwisz, *A Life with Karol*, 147.
65 Barrett, *Gambling with History*, 298.

CHAPTER 21: JANUARY–JUNE 1982: FACE TO FACE IN THE VATICAN

1 See Brinkley, *The Reagan Diaries*, 60. On November 16, 1981, as Allen came under fire, Reagan recorded his suspicion that "bureaucratic sabotage was at work": "In other words, our admin. not Dick Allen is the target." Ibid., 50.
2 For much more on the Soviet strategy put in place in those two pivotal years, see my biography of Clark: Kengor and Doerner, *The Judge*.
3 "How the Vatican Tried to Avert War," *National Catholic Register*, June 24, 2007.
4 Allen, "Pope John Paul II, Ronald Reagan, and the Collapse of Communism: An Historic Confluence."
5 Ibid.
6 In early February, James Rentschler and Richard Allen at the NSC and L. Paul Bremer at the State Department tracked Pope John Paul II's travel and alerted the White House to the opportunity for Reagan to welcome the pontiff to American territory, even if only briefly. Reagan happily obliged. The Reagan Library has on file a number of memos on the subject. They include February 5 and 19, 1981, NSC memos from James Rentschler to Richard Allen, an undated NSC memo from Allen to Mike Deaver at the White House, and February 6 and 10 memos from L. Paul Bremer to Allen.
7 Cable from John Paul II to President Ronald Reagan, February 26, 1981, time listed on cable as "11:30A AST," filed at Reagan Library.
8 Interview with Bill Clark, August 24, 2001. This was the first of many such conversations I had with Clark on this subject.
9 Reagan, "Remarks at the National Legislative Conference of the Building and Construction Trades Department, AFL-CIO," April 5, 1982.
10 Reagan, "Address at Commencement Exercises at Eureka College," Eureka, IL, May 9, 1982.
11 NSDD-32 was a summary of a report released in April 1982. The NSDD and the report are both on file at the Reagan Library. The NSDD was declassified in 1996. See also Christopher Simpson, *National Security Directives of the Reagan and Bush Administrations: The Declassified History of U.S. Political and Military Policy, 1981–1991* (Boulder, CO: Westview Press, 1995), 63–66; and my discussion of NSDD-32 in Kengor, *The Crusader*, 128–30.
12 Allen, "Pope John Paul II, Ronald Reagan, and the Collapse of Communism: An Historic Confluence."
13 Interview with Thomas C. Reed, March 14, 2005; and Thomas C. Reed, *At the Abyss* (New York: Ballantine Books, 2004), 235–37, 249.
14 See my discussion in *The Crusader*, 129–30.
15 See, among others, Apostoli, *Fátima for Today*, 90, 191–92; Gaitley, *33 Days to Morning Glory*, 102, 190.
16 Bertone, *The Last Secret of Fátima*, 49–50. Bertone says that Lúcia "wrote to the Holy Father on May 12, 1982." It is not clear to me whether the Holy Father received the May 12 letter before his May 13 homily at Fátima. Regardless, he, like her, was already convinced that Our Lady had intervened to save his life the year before. He, like her, had made the explicit connection to Fátima.
17 Roughly 3,600 words in length, the homily was published in the May 17, 1982, edition of *L'Osservatore Romano*, and is available at the EWTN online library: http://www.ewtn.com/library/PAPALDOC/JP820513.HTM.
18 Much of the remainder of the homily spoke of consecrating the world to the Immaculate Heart of Mary. Apparently Pope John Paul II intended this homily to offer the consecration of Russia that the Lady of Fátima had called for. There seems little dispute that the consecration was not successfully accomplished at this point; John Paul II would seek a much more deliberate consecration two years later, on March 25, 1984. That consecration will be discussed later in this book.
19 Gaitley, *33 Days to Morning Glory*, 190n.

20 Other speechwriters who came on the scene later were Catholic as well: for instance, Peggy Noonan, who wrote (among others) the Farewell Address and the beautiful *Challenger* speech ("they slipped the surly bonds of earth to touch the face of God"), and Peter Robinson, who wrote the Berlin Wall speech and who converted to Catholicism during the Reagan presidency.

21 Allen, "Pope John Paul II, Ronald Reagan, and the Collapse of Communism: An Historic Confluence." Bill Clark, who was close with the defense secretary, told me a number of times that he was impressed by Weinberger's commitment to a strict liturgical Episcopalianism.

22 On Reagan's ordeal, see Morris, *Dutch*, 250–51.

23 See Kengor and Doerner, *The Judge*, 13–18.

24 Weigel, *The End and the Beginning*, 127–28.

25 Father Timothy Radcliffe, "Called to Do and to Be," *Give Us This Day*, November 2011, 141.

26 Weigel, *The End and the Beginning*, 127–28.

27 See, among others, Weigel, *The End and the Beginning*, 435; Apostoli, *Fátima for Today*, 182.

28 "How Groups Voted in 1984," Roper Center for Public Opinion Research, Cornell University, https://ropercenter.cornell.edu/polls/us-elections/how-groups-voted/how-groups-voted-1984/.

29 The survey was conducted by Kelton Research for the National Geographic Channel. See Kenneth T. Walsh, "1980s Nostalgia: Poll Finds Reagan Beats Obama in a Landslide," *U.S. News and World Report*, April 10, 2013. See also Paul Kengor, "The End of the Reagan Era?" *American Spectator*, January 21, 2013.

30 See, among others, Apostoli, *Fátima for Today*, 182.

31 Source: E-mail correspondence with Joanne Drake, Mrs. Reagan's personal secretary, August 29, 2012, following conversations with her and her conversations with Mrs. Reagan, all held in August 2012. Mrs. Reagan pointed this out more than once.

32 Kirby Hanson, a longtime staff member at the Reagan Presidential Foundation and friend of the Reagans, recounted the moment when Mrs. Reagan reacted to the photo of the pontiff and commented on his similarities to her husband. Interview with Kirby Hanson at the Reagan Library, August 2012.

33 George Weigel, "Blessed John Paul II and His Times," *First Things*, June/July 2011.

34 Many sources could be cited on this, though it is now unnecessary given the widespread understanding (especially among scholars) that Reagan abhorred nuclear weapons and sought to reduce or even eliminate them rather than increase them. Two scholars who have published extensively on this are Beth Fischer and Paul Lettow. See Beth A. Fischer, *The Reagan Reversal* (Columbia: University of Missouri Press, 2000); and Paul Lettow, *Ronald Reagan and His Quest to Abolish Nuclear Weapons* (New York: Random House, 2005). Important secondary works include Melvyn Leffler, *For the Soul of Mankind* (New York: Macmillan, 2007); and David E. Hoffman, *The Dead Hand: The Untold Story of the Cold War Arms Race and Its Dangerous Legacy* (New York: Random House, 2010). See also my chapter "A World of Fewer Nuclear Weapons: Ronald Reagan's (Not-So-Surprising) Willingness to Negotiate," in Jeffrey L. Chidester and Paul Kengor, eds., *Reagan's Legacy in a World Transformed* (Cambridge, MA: Harvard University Press, 2015).

35 Weigel, *The End and the Beginning*, 127–28.

36 See "The Pope and the President: A Key Adviser Reflects on the Reagan Administration," interview with Bill Clark, *Catholic World Report*, November 1999. This interview was republished under the title "Pope John Paul II and President Reagan" in the April 11, 2005, edition of *Human Events*, which was a tribute issue to John Paul II.

37 Frank Shakespeare speaking to the Schoenstatt Heights community in Madison, WI, April 7, 2006.

38 I laid out a number of principles common to Reagan and John Paul II in a March 25,

2014, lecture at Franciscan University (Steubenville, Ohio), titled "Reagan Conservatism and Roman Catholicism." The speech is adapted from my book *11 Principles of a Reagan Conservative* (New York: Beaufort Books, 2014).

39 George Washington, First Inaugural Address, April 30, 1789, https://www.archives.gov/exhibits/american_originals/inaugtxt.html.

40 John Paul II articulated this relationship in his March 1995 encyclical *Evangelium Vitae* (Gospel of Life), sections 18–20.

41 Joseph Ratzinger, *Christianity and the Crisis of Cultures* (San Francisco: Ignatius Press, 2006).

42 Reagan, "Radio Address to the Nation on Family Values," December 20, 1986.

43 As president, Reagan supported a Human Life Amendment to the Constitution, which would have inserted into the Constitution these words: "the paramount right to life is vested in each human being from the moment of fertilization without regard to age, health, or condition of dependency." He favored providing every human being, at all stages of development, with protection as "persons" with the "right to life" under the Fourteenth Amendment. See William P. Clark, "For Reagan, All Life Was Sacred," *New York Times*, June 11, 2004. The Fourteenth Amendment (as well as the Fifth Amendment) declares a right to "life," but Reagan would have gone further by supporting and interpreting that right as a right to life for the unborn.

44 Reagan, "State of the Union Address," February 4, 1986.

45 Reagan, "Remarks at the Annual Meeting of the American Bar Association," Atlanta, GA, August 1, 1983.

46 Pope John Paul II, Homily at the Holy Mass on the Mall, Washington, DC, October 7, 1979.

47 Bernstein, "The Holy Alliance."

48 Ibid.

49 See Raymond Arroyo's interview with Bill Clark on EWTN's *The World Over*, recorded at the Clark ranch in Shandon, CA, September 4, 2009. The original interview has been rebroadcast several times, including in the weeks after Clark's death in August 2013.

50 Ibid.

51 "The Pope and the President," *Catholic World Report*.

52 Ibid.

53 See ibid.; Bernstein, "Holy Alliance," 30.

54 Clark interview with Arroyo, *The World Over*.

55 "The Pope and the President," *Catholic World Report*.

56 In *The Crusader* (page 139), I addressed the Bernstein-*Time* phrase "The Holy Alliance." The phrase provoked some hostile reactions that I never really understood. George Weigel bristled at the label, as did Richard V. Allena. (See, among others, Bono, "Officials Say Pope, Reagan Shared Cold War Data, but Lacked Alliance"; Weigel, *The End and the Beginning*, 127.) My sense from reading Weigel's and Allen's objections is that they think the phrase overdramatizes, and undeservedly seeks to formalize, the relationship between John Paul II and Reagan. Dick Allen calls the White House–Vatican alliance a "historic confluence," not a *formal* alliance. He speaks of the president and the pope as moving along "parallel tracks" with a common "convergence of interests." Allen states that the two shared a "prayerful vision" for the world, including a shared commitment to a "crusade for freedom" to bring liberty to Eastern Europe. That was what was solidified at the Vatican that day in June 1982. It was no small thing. See Allen, "Pope John Paul II, Ronald Reagan, and the Collapse of Communism: An Historic Confluence." Bill Clark told me: "The idea that this was some sort of 'Holy Conspiracy' is overreaching a bit. There was no plot or plan between the two sides.... We knew we were both going in the same direction and so we decided to collaborate, particularly on intelligence issues regarding the Eastern Bloc." Clark described the relationship that unfolded as a "natural convergence of interests," whereby Reagan, he, and other officials would "work

together with their counterparts at the Vatican." Clark said the collaboration was never "a formal alliance as such," but it was significant. Of course, few such relationships are ever "formal." Neither the Reagan-Thatcher nor Reagan-Gorbachev partnerships were "formal" either. Interview with Bill Clark, August 24, 2001.

57 Quoted in Schweizer, *Reagan's War*, 213.

58 Bernstein, "The Holy Alliance," 28–35.

59 Ibid., 29–31.

60 On June 28, 1982, James Rentschler of the NSC sent a memo to Bill Clark titled "Presidential Response to the Pope on Lebanon." Clark and Reagan discussed the matter and quickly formulated a response to the Holy Father, which was sent June 30.

61 Reagan, "Address to Members of the British Parliament," June 8, 1982.

62 Lou Cannon, "Reagan Radiated Happiness and Hope," *George*, August 2000, 58.

63 See my examples in Kengor, *The Crusader*, 143–44.

64 "Meeting in the Vatican," *Pravda*, June 19, 1982, and TASS, June 18, 1982, republished in *Current Digest of the Soviet Press* 34, no. 25 (July 21, 1982): 19. Similarly, a piece in the Czech communist publication *Tvorba* claimed: "It is known that the American president, during his June sojourn in Rome, enjoined John Paul II to assume a more resolute posture in connection with the situation in Poland, to interfere more into the internal affairs of that country. As a reward, Ronald Reagan has shown his readiness to raise financial support, which the Roman Catholic Church would distribute among the opposition in Poland." See Alexiev, "The Kremlin and the Pope," 14.

65 George Weigel in June 2004 wrote that there was not "very much discussion between the principals" who served Reagan and John Paul II. Weigel's view (to my knowledge) has changed since then, in large part because of information he now knows about Bill Clark and from Bill Clark. Weigel was able to talk to Clark about this before Clark's death. See George Weigel, "The President and the Pope," *National Review*, June 28, 2004.

66 In December 2015, a research assistant of mine, Annabelle Rutledge, searched for information on Casey's Rome trips and interactions with John Paul II in Casey's personal papers at the Hoover Institution but found nothing.

67 Interview with Owen Smith, December 30, 2005.

68 See Bernstein, "The Holy Alliance."

69 Shakespeare told this to Al Regnery, who, in turn, shared it with me.

70 Malachi Martin, *The Keys of This Blood: The Struggle for World Dominion Between Pope John Paul II, Mikhail Gorbachev, and the Capitalist West* (New York: Touchstone, 1990), 120.

71 See Bernstein, "The Holy Alliance."

72 Q&A with Cardinal Pio Laghi, "How the Vatican Tried to Avert War," *National Catholic Register*, June 24, 2007.

73 Clark's deputy, Bud McFarlane, said that these discussions were handled completely outside of normal State Department channels. McFarlane knew that Clark and Casey were meeting with Laghi, and that Laghi had seen the president, but says that he was personally unaware of the substance of the discussions. See Bernstein, "The Holy Alliance," 28–35.

74 Clark interview with Arroyo, *The World Over*.

75 Ibid.

76 Clark told me that he did occasionally jot down some "indecipherable" notes from the meetings, which he used to brief the president. But he said he always tossed them in the trash when he was finished informing Reagan. Consistent with this claim, I never found even one such note among all of Clark's large private holdings from this dynamic period.

77 Clark interview with Arroyo, *The World Over*.

Chapter 22: July–December 1982: Moscow Under Suspicion

1 Alexiev, "The Kremlin and the Pope," 13–14.
2 Ibid.
3 Ibid.
4 V. Makhin, "Religion in the Conceptual Arsenal of Anticommunism," *Politicheskoye Samoobrazovanie*, December 1982, 117–18, translated by Alexiev, "The Kremlin and the Pope," 15.
5 *Neue Zuercher Zeitung*, June 16, 1982, cited by Alexiev, "The Kremlin and the Pope," 15.
6 Alexiev, "The Kremlin and the Pope," 15–16.
7 Ibid.
8 Claire Sterling, "The Plot to Murder the Pope," *Reader's Digest*, September 1982. See also Reuters, "Soviet and Bulgarian Role Hinted in Shooting of the Pope by Turk," *New York Times*, August 17, 1982.
9 Sterling, *The Time of the Assassins*, 113.
10 I've written about this in Kengor and Doerner, *The Judge*, 194–95.
11 Testimony of Herbert Romerstein, published in "Soviet Active Measures," Hearings Before the Subcommittee on European Affairs of the Committee on Foreign Relations, U.S. Senate, 99th Congress, First Session, September 12 and 13, 1985, 89.
12 *The Man Who Shot the Pope*, NBC, September 21, 1982. See Eric Pace, "TV: Program on Shooting of Pope," *New York Times*, September 21, 1982. See also http://www.peabodyawards.com/award-profile/the-man-who-shot-the-pope-a-study-in-terrorism.
13 V. Barsov and L. Kruglov, "Falsifiers from NBC," *Izvestia*, October 4, 1982, republished in *Current Digest of the Soviet Press* 34, no. 40 (November 3, 1982): 16.
14 "Hostile Act," *Izvestia*, December 1, 1982, republished in *Current Digest of the Soviet Press* 34, no. 48 (December 29, 1982): 16.
15 "Absurd Claims," *Pravda*, December 14, 1982, republished in *Current Digest of the Soviet Press* 34, no. 50 (January 12, 1983): 16; "Slanderers Condemned," *Pravda*, December 22, 1982, republished in *Current Digest of the Soviet Press* 34, no. 51 (January 19, 1983), 22–23; and "Absurd Insinuations," *Pravda*, December 18, 1982, and *Izvestia*, December 19, 1982, republished in *Current Digest of the Soviet Press* 34, no. 51 (January 19, 1983), 14.
16 "Record for Slander," *Izvestia*, December 30, 1982, republished in *Current Digest of the Soviet Press* 34, no. 52 (January 26, 1983): 17–18.
17 To recount all the swipes in the Soviet press during this period would be repetitive and perhaps even depressing. Consider just a handful of examples among many: Vladimir Bolshakov, "The Tracks Lead to Langley," *Pravda*, January 5, 1983, republished in *Current Digest of the Soviet Press* 35, no. 1 (February 2, 1983): 17–18; "Report by Bulgarian Agency," *Pravda*, March 4, 1983, republished in *Current Digest of the Soviet Press* 35, no. 9 (March 30, 1983): 18; S. Potapov, "Behind the Scenes: Stepping Up Anti-Soviet Hysteria," *Izvestia*, April 13, 1983, republished in *Current Digest of the Soviet Press* 35, no. 11 (March 16, 1983): 19; "Vatican Chief's Anti-Socialist Attacks," *Pravda*, August 20, 1983; "Was He Kidnapped by the CIA?" *Literaturnaya Gazeta*, October 12, 1983; N. Paklin, "Ali Agca's Flood of Lies," *Izvestia*, December 21, 1983; and "Provocateurs Fail," *Pravda*, December 22, 1983.
18 Romerstein, "Soviet Active Measures," 61; Joshua Muravchik, "'Glasnost,' the KGB, and the 'Nation,'" *Commentary*, June 1988.
19 Romerstein, "Soviet Active Measures," 61.
20 See ibid., 90–92; Pacepa and Rychlak, *Disinformation*.
21 Romerstein, "Soviet Active Measures," 59–60.
22 See ibid., 81–88, 212–13. These pages reprint several of these articles, including the July 1983 piece from *Pace e Guerra*.
23 Koehler, *Spies in the Vatican*, 9, 15, 169.

24 This was the January 6, 1983, edition of the newspaper. Cited in Claire Sterling, *The Time of the Assassins*, 184–85.
25 Interview with Richard Pipes, via e-mail, April 7, 2014. When I asked Pipes whether he discussed this matter with Reagan or Casey, he answered, "I never spoke either to Reagan or Casey about this matter."
26 The full transcripts of these press conferences are available in the *Public Papers of the Presidents of the United States: Ronald Reagan* (Washington, DC: GPO, 1983 and 1984). Those bound hard-copy volumes are today available online. A Google search of Reagan's name along with the quotations should take the researcher directly to the site.
27 Flora Lewis, "Sarajevo and St. Peter's," *New York Times*, February 4, 1983,
28 Discussion with Bill Clark, July 5, 2005.
29 Ibid.
30 Discussion with Bill Clark at his ranch near Paso Robles, CA, July 11, 2005.
31 Interview with Roger Robinson, February 21, 2006.
32 Interview with John Lenczowski, April 3, 2015.
33 Interviews with Kenneth deGraffenreid, April 7, 8, and 9, 2015.
34 Interview with Owen Smith, December 30, 2005.
35 Interview with Bernadette Casey Smith, November 15, 2005.
36 Smith believed that Ambassador Vernon Walters shared this information with him. Also, Smith was told that the Vatican is holding it back and likely will continue to do so for a long time. It could be decades, maybe generations, before we see the evidence. Rest assured, however, John Paul II saw something compelling, as did Casey. Interview with Owen Smith, December 30, 2005.
37 I asked Frank Shakespeare, who was very close with Bill Casey and who later served as U.S. ambassador to the Vatican, whether Casey ever talked to him about possible Soviet involvement in the shooting of the pope. He answered: "No, he did not. But anything at the very highest level, like this—Casey would know. He would know about it. He was absolutely in on it. You could be 100 percent certain that if it was known, Casey would have known." I asked Shakespeare whether President Reagan had ever talked to him about a Soviet role in the shooting. He quickly said, "No, he didn't." I also asked whether John Paul II or anyone at the Vatican ever talked to him about possible Soviet involvement in the shooting. He answered: "No. No one said *anything* to me on that." Interview with Frank Shakespeare, March 5, 2013.
38 William P. Clark, Memorandum for the President, "Summitry," August 5, 1983. Memo in Clark's files.
39 See Jack F. Matlock Jr., *Reagan and Gorbachev: How the Cold War Ended* (New York: Random House, 2004), 66.

CHAPTER 23: 1983: DEALING WITH AN "EVIL EMPIRE"

1 Boyles had also mocked Stalin's line in a sermon he delivered October 22, 1978, in response to the elevation of a Polish cardinal as pope of the universal Roman Catholic Church. "Perhaps God chose to breech the Iron Curtain," Boyles declared to his congregation. "A psychological spear has been thrust into the flesh of communism, deep, almost to the heart of the Soviet system itself." He asked his fellow Presbyterians: "What would Khrushchev say now that the Catholic Church has penetrated to the heart of the Soviet system itself?" Reagan was not yet a parishioner and thus did not know of the sermon. When I pointed out to Boyles that Reagan had cited the Stalin line not long after, he was impressed. He told me in an e-mail: "In 1978 I had no real awareness of RR, and certainly not of his radio broadcasts, or of his quoting of 'how many divisions has the Pope?'" E-mail from John Boyles, February 22, 2013.
2 E-mail from John Boyles, February 22, 2013.

3 Reverend John Boyles, "Seventh Annual Ronald Reagan Lecture," Grove City College, Grove City, PA, February 5, 2013.
4 See my lengthy discussion in Kengor, *God and Ronald Reagan*, 161–64.
5 Reagan, "Remarks at the Annual Convention of the National Religious Broadcasters," January 31, 1983.
6 On Muggeridge and Reagan, see Kengor, *God and Ronald Reagan*, 253, 292.
7 Reagan, *An American Life*, 558.
8 Bob Morrison (who joined John Boyles), "Seventh Annual Ronald Reagan Lecture."
9 Boyles, "Seventh Annual Ronald Reagan Lecture."
10 Ibid.
11 Interview with George P. Shultz, July 15, 2003.
12 Reagan, *An American Life*, 558.
13 On this, see Shultz private letter to Reagan, July 18, 1983, located in PHF, PR, RRL, Box 7, Folder 90; George P. Shultz, *Turmoil and Triumph* (New York: Charles Scribner's Sons, 1993), 164–65; Shultz speaking on "Reagan," *The American Experience*; Reagan, *An American Life*, 558; interview with Shultz; Dobrynin, *In Confidence*, 517–21.
14 Interview with Shultz.
15 Reagan, *An American Life*, 572.
16 Professor Kiron Skinner, the excellent Reagan biographer, underscores that Ronald Reagan's first major achievement with the Soviet Union was a human rights issue; it was "the Christians," as she put it. Kiron Skinner, "Sixth Annual Ronald Reagan Lecture," Grove City College, Grove City, PA, February 16, 2012.
17 Interview with Frank Carlucci, "The Reagan Presidency," *Miller Center Journal* 2 (Spring 1995): 43. See also Fred Barnes, "In the Evil Empire," *New Republic*, June 20, 1988, 8–9.
18 Reagan, "Remarks at the Conservative Political Action Conference Dinner," Washington, DC, February 18, 1983.
19 E-mail correspondence with Tony Dolan, October 21, 2014.
20 E-mail correspondence with Tomasz Pompowski, October 23, 2005.
21 Weigel, *The End and the Beginning*, 152–53.
22 Ibid.
23 On this, see Kengor, *God and Ronald Reagan*, 245–49.
24 The press conference was held January 29, 1981.
25 Reagan's expressed this sentiment, about praying for those who live in "totalitarian darkness," on many other occasions. It was as basic as the Gospel words he had learned from his mother and the church of his youth, as well as from books like *That Printer of Udell's*. It was about loving thy neighbor as thyself. Through his life and through the final days of his presidency, he would tell audiences that "God's gift... is for all mankind," and would tell both American and Soviet audiences—and even groups of American and Soviet students together—to realize that "we're all God's children." Reagan made many such statements as president, with sincere concern for the souls of Soviet people. "The clerk and the king and the Communist were made in His image," he said. "We all have souls." Thus, he said, "I'm convinced, more than ever, that man finds liberation only when he binds himself to God and commits himself to his fellow man." Reagan repeatedly stressed that his complaints were with the Soviet system, not the Soviet people. Quite the contrary, he insisted that the Soviet people were "the warmest, friendliest, nicest people you could ever meet," and said, "I pray that the hand of the Lord will be on the Soviet people." Similarly, way back in 1937, the Catholic Church in *Divini Redemptoris* had stated clearly, "It is no part of Our intention to condemn en masse the peoples of the Soviet Union. For them We cherish the warmest personal affection." See Reagan, "Remarks at the Annual National Prayer Breakfast," February 4, 1988; Reagan, "Remarks to Participants in the Yale University–Moscow State University Exchange Project," October 3, 1988; Reagan, "Remarks Following Discussions with Pope John Paul II," Vatican City, June 6, 1987; Reagan, *An American Life*, 709; Reagan,

National Association of Evangelicals meetings, March 8, 1983, and March 6, 1984; Reagan, "Remarks at the Annual Convention of the National Religious Broadcasters," January 31, 1985.

26 Anthony Lewis, "Onward Christian Soldiers," *New York Times*, March 10, 1983.

27 Richard Cohen, "Convictions," *Washington Post*, May 26, 1983.

28 The Commager quote has been widely quoted. Among recent sources, see Charles Krauthammer, "Reluctant Cold Warriors," *Washington Post*, November 12, 1999, A35; and Morris, *Dutch*, 475.

29 Editorial, "Reverend Reagan," *New Republic*, April 4, 1983. Not all reactions were negative. British intellectual Malcolm Muggeridge fired off a letter of support, telling Reagan that his history was right on target. Muggeridge told the president that when he was a young journalist in Moscow in 1932, he encountered "anti-God museums, the total suppression of the scriptures and related literature, the ridiculing of the person of Christ and his followers, the whole force of the most powerful and comprehensive propaganda machine ever to exist, including the schools and universities, geared to promote Marxist materialism and abolish Christianity forever." In his crusty British candor, Muggeridge proclaimed to Reagan the fundamental difference between Christianity and Marxism: "Christianity happens to be true, and Marxism... 'unresisting imbecility.'" Letter is located in Ronald Reagan Library, PHF, PR, Box 6, Folder 78.

30 Reagan, *An American Life*, 569–70.

31 Ronald Reagan, *Speaking My Mind: Selected Speeches* (New York: Simon and Schuster, 1989), 168–69.

32 Ibid., 108.

33 Natan Sharansky tribute to Ronald Reagan, published in the *Jerusalem Post*, June 7, 2004.

34 Among examples not quoted in this chapter, see Reagan, "Remarks at the Annual Washington Conference of the American Legion," February 22, 1983; Reagan, "Remarks and a Question-and-Answer Session at a World Affairs Council Luncheon," Los Angeles, CA, October 28, 1988.

35 This April 27, 1981, NSC memo from Pipes to Allen, along with other related follow-up documents, including the presidential proclamation that resulted from Pipes's suggestion, are housed at the Reagan Library.

36 Reagan, "Remarks to Polish Americans," Chicago, IL, June 23, 1983.

37 Reagan, "Remarks at a Ceremony Marking the Annual Observance of Captive Nations Week," July 19, 1983.

38 In August 1984 he found himself celebrating the annual Polish festival in Doylestown, Pennsylvania, where he quoted John Paul II: "Freedom is given to man by God as a measure of his dignity.... As children of God, we cannot be slaves"—a quote he repeated at a White House luncheon marking the fortieth anniversary of the Warsaw Uprising. Reagan, "Remarks at a White House Luncheon Marking the Fortieth Anniversary of the Warsaw Uprising," August 17, 1984; Reagan, "Remarks at a Polish Festival," Doylestown, PA, September 9, 1984.

39 Aleksandr Bovin, "A Face Not a Policy," *Izvestia*, January 10, 1982, 5, published as "Bovin on U.S. Poland Policy," in *Foreign Broadcast Information Service*, FBIS-SOV-10-JAN-82, January 10, 1982, F5. See also Vitaly Korionov, "Production Line of Crimes and Hypocrisy," *Pravda*, January 10, 1984, published as "'Unprecedented Wave' of Lies Seen in U.S.," in *FBIS*, FBIS-SOV-13-JAN-84, January 13, 1984, A4.

40 See Jared McBrady, "The Challenge of Peace: Ronald Reagan, John Paul II, and the American Bishops," *Journal of Cold War Studies* 17, no. 1 (Winter 2015): 129–52, and my review of McBrady's excellent article in the June 2015 online academic journal *H-Diplo* (*History and Diplomacy*).

41 Quoted in McBrady, "The Challenge of Peace," 129.

42 Estimates on crowd size vary from 500,000 to a million on June 12, 1982.

43 For a recent treatment, see Robert Service, *The End of the Cold War: 1985–1991* (New York: Public Affairs, 2015), 93–101.
44 See my detailed analysis of this in my chapter "A World of Fewer Nuclear Weapons: Ronald Reagan's Willingness to Negotiate," in Chidester and Kengor, eds., *Reagan's Legacy in a World Transformed*, 139–64.
45 Marjorie Hyer, "U.S. Bishops Firm on Pastoral Letter," *Washington Post*, November 18, 1982.
46 McBrady, "The Challenge of Peace," 142.
47 Ibid., 137.
48 For example, another was Reverend Stephen Majoros of Toledo, Ohio, who wrote a letter on February 4, 1983.
49 On this, see Kengor and Doerner, *The Judge*, ch. 9.
50 McBrady, "The Challenge of Peace," 144.
51 Ibid., 144.
52 Ibid., 145.
53 Ibid., 146.
54 Ibid., 146.
55 Kenneth A. Briggs, "Bishops' Letter on Nuclear Arms Is Revised to 'More Flexible' View," *New York Times*, April 6, 1983.
56 "Bishops Rethink the Unthinkable," *New York Times*, April 10, 1983.
57 McBrady, "The Challenge of Peace," 152.
58 Ibid.
59 Andrew and Mitrokhin, *The Sword and the Shield*, 508, 521, 538–39.
60 Ibid., 538.
61 Ibid., 538–39.
62 Szulc, *Pope John Paul II*, 388–89.
63 Dziwisz, *A Life with Karol*, 150.
64 Ibid., 152.
65 Homily of the Holy Father, "Eucharistic Celebration at Jasna Góra," June 19, 1983, http://w2.vatican.va/content/john-paul-ii/pt/homilies/1983/documents/hf_jp-ii_hom_19830619_jasna-gora.html.
66 Dziwisz, *A Life with Karol*, 152–53.
67 Ibid., 153.
68 Ibid., 120, 153–54.
69 Ibid., 154.
70 Ibid., 150.
71 Ibid., 151.
72 Ibid., 152–53.
73 Ibid., 153.
74 Ibid.
75 Ibid., 156.
76 Section 409 of the *Catechism of the Catholic Church*.
77 John R. Barletta with Rochelle Schweizer, *Riding with Reagan: From the White House to the Ranch* (New York: Citadel Press, 2005), 52.
78 See Kengor and Doerner, *The Judge*, 246, 253.
79 Reagan, "Remarks to Reporters on the Soviet Attack on a Korean Civilian Airliner," September 2, 1983.
80 Reagan, "Address to the Nation on the Soviet Attack on a Korean Civilian Airliner," September 5, 1983.
81 The last quotation is cited in Hedrick Smith, "Reagan's Crucial Year," *New York Times*, October 16, 1983.
82 Andropov said this on September 28, 1983. See Strobe Talbott, *The Russians and Reagan* (New York: Vintage, 1984), 122.

83 Reagan, "Remarks at the Annual Pulaski Day Banquet," New York, NY, September 25, 1983.
84 Reagan, "Question-and-Answer Session with Reporters on the Cease-Fire in Lebanon," New York, NY, September 25, 1983.
85 Brinkley, *The Reagan Diaries*, 182.
86 I heard the late Father Benedict Groeschel, who knew Bill Clark very well, share this story more than once. Groeschel did not give the date of this encounter, but it must have been on September 25, 1983, the day Reagan visited Cooke during his Pulaski Day speech in New York. Reagan's diary (the excerpts selected and published by editor Douglas Brinkley) document that Reagan met with Cooke on the cardinal's deathbed on that date. If there was another encounter between that day and October 6, the day Cooke died, I am unaware of it.
87 Records at the Reagan Library register phone calls from Reagan to Cooke on February 23, 1982, and September 15, 1983. The second of these obviously concerned Cooke's health, and it prompted a nice, full-page typed letter from Cooke in response the same day. The cardinal stated: "I am very grateful to you and your wife Nancy for your thoughtful telephone call following the announcement of my illness. Your prayers, your good wishes and your loving concern are a source of great comfort to me." This was a warm note, with the cardinal adding: "I want you to know that I am offering my prayers and my sufferings for the gift of God's peace among all the members of His human family. In doing so, I am united with millions of our fellow citizens in beseeching the Lord to assist you and your collaborators as you seek every possible road to true justice and lasting peace at home and in every part of the world." The good cardinal was "offering up" (as Catholics say) his suffering. Reagan was especially moved by one particular note he had received from Cooke, encouraging the president in his statements on behalf of unborn human life. The president shared the note with a group of pro-life leaders gathered at the White House, whom he encouraged to keep fighting against what John Paul II called the "Culture of Death." Reagan said: "I'd like to leave with you a quotation that means a great deal to me. These are the words of my friend, the late Terence Cardinal Cooke, of New York. 'The gift of life, God's special gift, is no less beautiful when it is accompanied by illness or weakness, hunger or poverty, mental or physical handicaps, loneliness or old age. Indeed, at these times, human life gains extra splendor as it requires our special care, concern, and reverence. It is in and through the weakest of human vessels that the Lord continues to reveal the power of His love.'" Reagan, "Remarks at a White House Briefing for Right to Life Activists," July 30, 1987.
88 John Paul II, *Memory and Identity*, 163.
89 Dziwisz, *A Life with Karol*, 138.
90 John Paul II, *Memory and Identity*, 163.
91 Ibid., 163–64.
92 Dziwisz, *A Life with Karol*, 137.
93 Ibid., 137–38.
94 Ibid., 138.
95 Ibid., 142.

CHAPTER 24: MARCH 25, 1984: THE CONSECRATION OF RUSSIA

1 Brinkley, *The Reagan Diaries*, 228.
2 Ibid.
3 Bertone, *The Last Secret of Fátima*, 82.
4 Apostoli, *Fátima for Today*, 251.
5 Tindal-Robertson, *Fátima, Russia, and Pope John Paul II*, 23–25; Apostoli, *Fátima for Today*, 193.

6 Apostoli, *Fátima for Today*, 193.
7 Dziwisz, *A Life with Karol*, 180; Apostoli, *Fátima for Today*, 193. See the photo of the act of consecration in Apostoli's book and Tindal-Robertson's book.
8 Bertone, *The Last Secret of Fátima*, 83–84.
9 The account provided here is drawn from two sources: Leo Maasburg, *Mother Teresa of Calcutta: A Personal Portrait* (San Francisco: Ignatius, 2011), 111–16; and an interview with Maasburg as part of the 2013 documentary series *Mother Teresa: All for Jesus*, Episode 4, "All for Jesus Through Mary," hosted by Sean Brown and broadcast by EWTN television network.
10 The text I use here was originally published in *L'Osservatore Romano*, the weekly English edition, April 2, 1984, 8–10. It is available online at http://www.ewtn.com/library/papaldoc/consecra.htm.
11 Apostoli, *Fátima for Today*, 195; Tindal-Robertson, *Fátima, Russia, and Pope John Paul II*, 25–27.
12 These words are taken from a videotaped interview with Amorth posted at http://www.youtube.com/watch?v=vG3Bw3Z_gbM. It was recorded and posted in 2012 by Fátima TV.
13 Edward Pentin, "Pope Francis' Consecrating the World to Mary Culminates Fátima Celebration," *National Catholic Register*, October 15, 2013.
14 Apostoli, *Fátima for Today*, 249–61.
15 Tindal-Robertson, *Fátima, Russia, and Pope John Paul II*, 26–41.
16 Tuy was the Spanish city that housed the novitiate where Lúcia would stay after her initial years in the convent in Pontevedra. It was there, in another apparition in June 1929, that the Blessed Mother told Lúcia that the "moment" had come for the Holy Father to make the consecration to Russia.
17 Apostoli, *Fátima for Today*, 197–99; also printed online at EWTN.com as "Letters from Sr. Lúcia Santos, OCD on the Consecration," at https://www.ewtn.com/expert/answers/Fatima1984.htm.
18 Bertone, *The Last Secret of Fátima*, 56, 82, 161.
19 Ibid., 83.
20 Ibid., 82–83.
21 Dziwisz, *A Life with Karol*, 180.

Chapter 25: May 1984: Together Again

1 The exact time is registered in official White House documents on file at the Reagan Library.
2 Bernstein, "The Holy Alliance," 31.
3 Letter from Joseph P. Folds to President Ronald Reagan, July 29, 1981, on file at the Ronald Reagan Library.
4 Letters to President Ronald Reagan on file at the Ronald Reagan Library: Robert P. Dugan Jr. (May 28, 1986); B.E. Pitts Jr. (June 9, 1986); Robert L. Maddox (May 22, 1986); and John V. Stevens (May 28, 1986).
5 During this same month of February 1984, Vice President Bush met with John Paul II at the Vatican, prompting a February 22 follow-up letter from Reagan to the pontiff.
6 Kris Capps, "President, Pope Will Meet Here," *Daily News-Miner*, March 20, 1984.
7 Henry Kamm, "Pope Starts Trip Today to Asia and the Pacific," *New York Times*, May 2, 1984.
8 Steven R. Weisman, "Reagan and Pope Confer in Alaska on World Issues," *New York Times*, May 3, 1984.
9 Benjamin Taylor, "Reagan, Pope Talk of Peace, Hunger," *Boston Globe*, May 3, 1984.
10 Stan Jones, "Thirty-Nine Hours of History in Fairbanks," *Daily News-Miner*, May 3, 1984.

11 Skinner, Anderson, and Anderson, *Reagan: A Life in Letters*, 773.
12 Taylor, "Reagan, Pope Talk of Peace, Hunger."
13 Jones, "Thirty-Nine Hours of History in Fairbanks."
14 Reagan, "Remarks at a Luncheon with Community Leaders in Fairbanks, Alaska," May 1, 1984.
15 Reagan, "Remarks at the Welcoming Ceremony for Pope John Paul II in Fairbanks, Alaska," May 2, 1984.
16 The pope's words are included in the official transcript published in the *Public Papers of the Presidents of the United States: Ronald Reagan*, just after Reagan's words. See Reagan, "Remarks at the Welcoming Ceremony for Pope John Paul II in Fairbanks, Alaska."
17 Weisman, "Reagan and Pope Confer in Alaska on World Issues."
18 "Statement by Principal Deputy Press Secretary Speakes on the President's Meeting with Pope John Paul II," May 2, 1984.
19 Conversation between Reagan Library archivist and my research assistant David Kirk, January 16, 2015, at the Ronald Reagan Library.
20 In *Witness to Hope* (two paragraphs on pages 394–95), Weigel very briefly mentions the papal visit to Alaska but says nothing of the meeting with Reagan there.
21 See interview with Jerry Olsavsky on the radio show *Blessed to Play*, hosted by Ron Meyer, carried on EWTN Radio, produced February 14, 2014.
22 John Paul II said, "I am deeply honored by the presence of President Reagan who, himself, is just returning from an important trip to China." See Reagan, "Remarks at the Welcoming Ceremony for Pope John Paul II in Fairbanks, Alaska."
23 In October 1983, President Reagan nominated Clark to replace the politically problematic James Watt as secretary of the interior. Reagan had actually rejected Clark's resignation as national security adviser in December 1982, saying he was too valuable in that post. When the Interior Department top spot opened up, the president granted his close adviser's request for a change. Not everyone in the administration was happy with the move. UN ambassador Jeane Kirkpatrick called it a "disastrous mistake." See Kengor and Doerner, *The Judge*, 246–63.
24 Reagan, "Remarks at the Welcoming Ceremony for Pope John Paul II in Fairbanks, Alaska."

CHAPTER 26: OCTOBER 19, 1984: THE MARTYRDOM OF FATHER JERZY POPIEŁUSZKO

1 Boyes and Moody, *Messenger of the Truth*, 20. I am indebted to the work of Roger Boyes and John Moody for this chapter. Boyes and Moody reported from on the ground in Poland in the 1980s, working for such respected news organizations as *Time*, UPI, Reuters, and *The Times* of London. As noted, their book, *Messenger of the Truth*, was originally published in 1987 under the title *The Priest and the Policeman* by Summit Books, an imprint of Simon and Schuster. The book was the basis for a 2014 documentary, *Messenger of the Truth*, written and produced by Paul Hensler. See http://www.messengerofthetruth.com/. E-mail correspondence with coauthor John Moody, November 12 and 17, 2014.
2 Ibid., 25.
3 Ibid., 37–38.
4 Ibid., 68–70.
5 Ibid., 83.
6 Ibid., 91.
7 Father Jerzy Popiełuszko, translated by Ewa Hermacinski, *His Sermons, 1982–1984, From the Masses for the Fatherland at Saint Stanislaus Kostki Church* (Warsaw: Wydawnictwo Sióstr Loretanek, 2014), 7.

8 Ibid., 17.
9 Ibid., 22–23.
10 Ibid., 24–25.
11 Ibid., 27–30.
12 Ibid., 41–45.
13 Weigel, *The End and the Beginning*, 165; Popiełuszko, *His Sermons*, 48–50.
14 Popiełuszko, *His Sermons*, 9.
15 Boyes and Moody, *Messenger of the Truth*, 98–100.
16 Ibid., 105–6.
17 Ibid., 24.
18 Ibid., 107.
19 Ibid., 109.
20 Ibid., 23.
21 Ibid., 157.
22 Ibid., 133.
23 Boyes and Moody actually attended Father Jerzy's Fatherland Masses. Ibid., 159 and 171.
24 Ibid., 159–60.
25 Popiełuszko, *His Sermons,* 147–49.
26 Boyes and Moody, *Messenger of the Truth*, 169.
27 Ibid., 176–77.
28 Ibid., 177.
29 For the details in this section, I have relied on the excellent reporting of Boyes and Moody in *Messenger of the Truth* (pages 185–231 and 249).
30 Interview with Piotr Litka, *wPolityce Forum*, October 21, 2016, available in English translation as "What Facts Were Concealed in the Murder of Blessed Jerzy Popiełuszko?" CurrentEventsPoland.com, October 29, 2016.
31 See, e.g., Matthew Day, "KGB 'Involved' in Murder of Polish Priest," *The Telegraph* (London), October 21, 2008; Sherry Tyree, "Fr. Jerzy Popiełuszko and the KGB," *St. Louis Post-Dispatch*, October 24, 2008.
32 E-mail exchanges with Tomasz Pompowski, October 17, 20, and 22, 2014.
33 Weigel, *The End and the Beginning*, 166.
34 Statements by Pope John Paul II, October 24 and 28, 1984, available (in Italian) at the Vatican website, www.vatican.va.
35 Weigel, *The End and the Beginning*, 172–73.
36 Reagan, "Statement on the Death of Father Jerzy Popiełuszko of Poland," October 31, 1984.
37 Reagan, "Proclamation 5840—Captive Nations Week, 1988," July 13, 1988.
38 Popiełuszko, *His Sermons*, 11–14.

Chapter 27: March 1985: A New Kind of Soviet Leader

1 Reagan, "Remarks and a Question-and-Answer Session at a Luncheon with Radio and Television Journalists," June 8, 1988. Even at the time, in 1984 and 1985, Reagan was saying, "They keep dying on me."
2 Lawrence K. Altman, "U.S. Doctors Believe Andropov Had Failing Kidney When He Took Office," *New York Times*, February 11, 1984.
3 Martin McCauley, *Russia, America, and the Cold War, 1949–1991*, rev. 2nd ed. (London and New York: Routledge, 2013), xxxvii.
4 Reagan, *An American Life*, 14–15, 641.
5 Reagan, "The President's News Conference," December 8, 1988.
6 Mikhail Gorbachev, *Memoirs* (New York: Doubleday, 1996), 23, 328; Mikhail Gor-

bachev, Keynote Address at Annual Ronald Reagan Day Dinner, hosted by Eureka College, held at the Peoria Civic Center, Peoria, IL, March 27, 2009.

7 Gorbachev, Keynote Address at Annual Ronald Reagan Day Dinner.

8 Archie Brown, *The Gorbachev Factor* (New York: Oxford University Press, 1996), 27.

9 My thanks to Soviet/KGB expert Jack Dziak for his assistance with this information. E-mail correspondence with Jack Dziak, July 17–18, 2015.

10 This is a well-known statement attributed to Gromyko. Among others, see the obituary "Andrei A. Gromyko: Flinty Face of Postwar Soviet Diplomacy," *New York Times*, July 4, 1989.

11 See my discussion in Kengor, *The Crusader*, 223–27, 297–99.

12 Gorbachev invoked Lenin again and again, expressing a "thirst to know him." He called Lenin "an inexhaustible source of dialectical creative thought, theoretical wealth and political sagacity." He said: "We draw inspiration from Lenin. Turning to him, and 'reading' his works each time in a new way, Lenin could see further." He also proclaimed, "We have always learned, and continue to learn, from Lenin's creative approach." Mikhail S. Gorbachev, *Perestroika: New Thinking for Our Country and the World* (New York: HarperCollins, 1987), 25, 45, and 145.

13 By October 1980, noted Archie Brown, Gorbachev already showed signs of being a "serious reformer." Now it looked like the reformer was on his way to becoming a general secretary. Brown, *The Gorbachev Factor*, ix–x.

14 Dobrynin, *In Confidence*, 485.

15 Anatoly Chernyaev, *My Six Years with Gorbachev* (University Park: Pennsylvania State University Press, 2000), 10.

16 Chernyaev, *My Six Years with Gorbachev*, 46.

17 Gorbachev, *Memoirs*, 328.

18 Ibid.

19 Mikhail Gorbachev, *On My Country and the World* (New York: Columbia University Press, 2000), 20–21.

CHAPTER 28: MAY 1985: A PRESIDENT IN PORTUGAL

1 "Reagan Cheered, Jeered in Talk to Europe Parliament: U.S. Policies Draws Fire of Hecklers," Associated Press, May 8, 1985.

2 Specifically, Reagan's decision to visit the Bitburg military cemetery generated controversy because many Nazi SS officers were buried there.

3 Reagan, "Remarks to Citizens in Hambach, Federal Republic of Germany," May 6, 1985.

4 Reagan, "Address to a Special Session of the European Parliament in Strasbourg, France," May 8, 1985.

5 "Reagan Cheered, Jeered in Talk to Europe Parliament."

6 Reagan, "Address to a Special Session of the European Parliament in Strasbourg, France."

7 "Reagan Cheered, Jeered in Talk to Europe Parliament."

8 Edward Schumacher, "Reagan, in Lisbon, Says Communism Is on the Decline," *New York Times*, May 10, 1985.

9 Ibid.

10 Service, *The End of the Cold War*, 95–98.

11 Ibid., 95–100.

12 Discussion with Tony Dolan by phone, July 24, 2014, and e-mail exchanges, July 8, 2014.

13 In 1952, while Reagan was president of the Screen Actors Guild, Warner Brothers released *The Miracle of Our Lady of Fátima*, which Reagan surely knew about.

14 I pressed Pompowski on this point in two separate exchanges: e-mail exchanges with Tomasz Pompowski, October 14, 2014, and July 23, 2015. Pompowski has further details

on those Clark-Reagan Fátima conversations that he asked me not to share because he plans to publish them in his own work.

15 The March 7, 1983, letter from Pio Laghi and the March 18, 1983, letter from President Reagan are on file at the Ronald Reagan Library.

16 Discussion with Dolan, July 24, 2014.

17 For a telling example of this, see Peter Robinson's description, provided at Grove City College on February 3, 2010, Fourth Annual Ronald Reagan Lecture, posted at the website of the Center for Vision and Values.

18 Discussion with Dolan, July 24, 2014, and e-mail exchanges, July 8, 2014. Dolan was informed of this reaction by Reagan officials who attended the speech, including Ambassador Frank Shakespeare.

19 Discussion with Dolan, July 24, 2014, and e-mail exchanges, July 8, 2014. In July 2015 I reviewed the original draft of this speech in the Presidential Handwriting File of the Reagan Library (Series III: Presidential Speeches, 4/3/85–5/30/85, Box 19). The text shows no handwritten remarks from Reagan on the page that refers to Fátima. Reagan often wrote comments such as "Do you think it's okay if I mention this?" or "This will really shake them up." In this case, however, Reagan made no comments on the draft.

20 Schumacher, "Reagan, in Lisbon, Says Communism Is on the Decline."

21 Ibid.

22 TASS, "What the U.S. President's Visit to Europe Showed," *Pravda*, May 11, 1985.

CHAPTER 29: MAY 1985: "THE RUSSIANS DID IT"

1 Examination of the President's Daily Schedule, Reagan Library, July 2015.

2 I submitted my first FOIA request on this material (via e-mail) on May 15, 2009.

3 Brinkley, *The Reagan Diaries*, 327, xiii. Brinkley also notes that "Nancy Reagan requested that a few entries be edited out for personal reasons." Given the context of the Reagan-Casey meeting, it is hard to imagine how "personal reasons" would have come into play in this redaction.

4 "Lies to Order," *Pravda*, May 10, 1984, and TASS, May 9, 1984, republished in *Current Digest of the Soviet Press* 36, no. 19 (June 6, 1984): 24.

5 E. Kovalev, "Outrage Against Truth," *Izvestia*, October 28, 1984, republished in *Current Digest of the Soviet Press* 36, no. 43 (November 21, 1984): 22.

6 Interview with Bernadette Casey Smith, November 15, 2005.

7 Claire Sterling, "Bulgaria Hired Agca to Kill Pope, Report of Italian Prosecutor Says," *New York Times*, June 10, 1984.

8 Sterling, *The Time of the Assassins*, 3.

9 Ibid., 5.

10 Ibid., 8.

11 "A Murky but Intriguing Trail," *Time*, December 27, 1982.

12 Ibid.

13 Ibid.

14 See Alexandre de Marenches, *The Evil Empire: The Third World War* (London: Sidgwick and Jackson, 1988), 188; Morris, *Dutch*, 472.

15 See Sterling, *The Time of the Assassins*, 8, 265.

16 Philip Taubman, "CIA Inept on Pope Plot, D'Amato Says," *New York Times*, February 8, 1983.

17 Sterling, *The Time of the Assassins*, 8.

18 William Safire, "You Have No Proof," *New York Times*, December 27, 1982.

19 Henry Kamm, "Plot on Pope: Bulgaria Tie?" *New York Times*, December 29, 1982.

20 Sterling, *The Time of the Assassins*, 11.

21 Taubman, "CIA Inept on Pope Plot, D'Amato Says."

22 Among others who took action was Senator Jesse Helms, North Carolina Republican, who proposed a bill in the summer of 1984 officially declaring Bulgaria a terrorist-supporting nation, cutting off funds intended to promote trade between the United States and Bulgaria, and applying certain sanctions to the country. The Reagan administration's response to this is an intriguing topic for further research. I came across that response unexpectedly in unclassified files from the White House Office of Records and Management at the Reagan Library in the summer of 2012. The original documents that I viewed and photocopied had not been photocopied at the library before, evidenced by the fact they still had staples in them. (It is Reagan Library/National Archives policy to remove any staples before documents can be copied.) This particular group of documents was among Bulgaria materials contained in one of the library's Country "CO" folders. Beginning in 1984, the Departments of State and Treasury responded to the proposed bills on behalf of the Reagan administration, with the NSC's Robert McFarlane (Bill Clark's successor) in the loop and analyzing the various responses. The process went on through at least the spring of 1985, as shown by (among other documents) an April 9, 1985, NSC memo written by Paula Dobriansky. Some of these documents speak for President Reagan, though all seem several steps removed from him. For example, a document by the State Department's Richard E. Combs, dated August 15, 1984, is written "on behalf of the President." The memo states: "The Congress and the Administration agreed that any action at this time condemning the Bulgarians, even a symbolic one, could be viewed unhelpfully by the international community as an attempt to interfere with the on-going Italian investigation into the attempted assassination of Pope John Paul II." I cannot speak to Ronald Reagan's personal thinking or role in this. I have no other documents or information.

23 Taubman, "CIA Inept on Pope Plot, D'Amato Says."

24 Sterling, *The Time of the Assassins*, 192, 195.

25 Ibid., 195.

26 Philip Taubman, "CIA Reports to Senate Panel on Shooting of Pope," *New York Times*, February 19, 1983.

27 Nicholas Gage, New York Times News Service, "Pope Plot Data Points to Bulgaria," *Chicago Tribune*, March 23, 1983. See also "Gray Smoke Over the Vatican," *New York Times*, March 25, 1983; and Sterling, *The Time of the Assassins*, 195.

28 Sterling, *The Time of the Assassins*, 196.

29 Ibid., 185.

30 Ibid., 192–93.

31 The reporters on the scene were mostly Italian. An Associated Press report was picked up and published in the July 9, 1983, *New York Times* under the headline "Agca Asserts KGB Aided in Pope Plot," from which these quotations are pulled. See also Claire Sterling's account in *The Time of the Assassins*, 140–41.

32 Quoted in Woodward, *Veil*, 99–100.

33 Sterling, *The Time of the Assassins*, 191–92, 195, 197.

34 Paul B. Henze, *The Plot to Kill the Pope* (New York: Scribner, 1983).

35 Sterling, "Bulgaria Hired Agca to Kill Pope, Report of Italian Prosecutor Says."

36 Associated Press, "Soviet Criticizes Report," *New York Times*, June 19, 1984.

37 Claire Sterling, "Behind Agca's Gun," *New York Times*, November 21, 1986.

38 Sterling would nicely distill the essential facts of the judge's report in her updated 1985 version of *The Time of the Assassins*. See Sterling, *The Time of the Assassins*, 245–63.

39 See, among others, Warren H. Carroll, *The Rise and Fall of the Communist Revolution* (Front Royal, VA: Christendom Press, 1995), 688.

40 Kalugin, *The First Directorate*, 176–77.

41 Ibid., 202.

42 See Kengor, *The Crusader*, 119–20.

43 Andrew and Mitrokhin, *The Sword and the Shield*, 522.

44 My thanks to Dr. John J. Dziak for his insights on post–Cold War Russian intelligence. Dziak told me that only "the GRU (Military Intelligence) never changed names or subordination [after the Soviet collapse]. It belongs to the [Russian] General Staff." In 1991 the KGB was "split into several stand-alone agencies with different names in an effort by Yeltsin to break its power. The breakup did not last." E-mail from John Dziak, November 10, 2010.
45 I am referring to Tomasz Pompowski (Polish) and Ion Mihai Pacepa (Romanian), both of whom I will cite later in this book, in the chapter on John Paul II's death.
46 Robert M. Gates, *From the Shadows: The Ultimate Insider's Story of Five Presidents and How They Won the Cold War* (New York: Simon and Schuster, 1996).
47 Ibid., 239–40.
48 Ibid., 240–1.
49 Ibid., 241.
50 Ibid., 356.
51 Ibid., 355.
52 Ibid., 355–56.
53 Ibid., 356.
54 For the record, long after this, some newspapers indirectly reported on the CIA investigation. The reporting occurred in the context of Bob Gates's nomination as secretary of defense in December 2006. On December 4, 2006, the *Los Angeles Times* published an article filled with mistakes, written as perhaps a hit piece against the Gates appointment. The article went so far as to claim that the contention of a Soviet role in the pope shooting was "proved false." The article offered no evidence or sources. See Peter Spiegel and Julian E. Barnes, "Hints of a Rumsfeld-ian style," *Los Angeles Times*, December 4, 2006.
55 "The Gates Hearings: Excerpts from CIA Documents Released in Gates Hearings," *New York Times*, October 2, 1991.
56 Anthony Lewis, "Onward, Christian Soldiers," *New York Times*, March 10, 1983.
57 Anthony Lewis, "Too Clever by Half," *New York Times*, October 7, 1991.
58 I have inserted punctuation to make the note easier to read and understand.
59 See Kengor, *The Crusader*, 210–11. In 1984 Secretary of Defense Caspar Weinberger and his Pentagon staged a "successful" test of the Strategic Defense Initiative. In reality, the Pentagon placed a beacon on the target missile and a receiver on the interceptor to demonstrate that the missile-defense system worked. The *New York Times* reported on the rigged test nine years later. The *Times* asked Weinberger about the incident; the former secretary of defense said only: "You always work on deception. You're always trying to practice deception. You are obviously trying to mislead your opponents." See Tim Weiner, "Lies and Rigged 'Star Wars' Test Fooled the Kremlin, and Congress," *New York Times*, August 18, 1993. I personally asked Weinberger about the staged test in September 2005, near the end of his life. He would not confirm the speculation—though Peter Schweizer, a longtime confidant and coauthor of Weinberger, confirmed the SDI incident to me. He specifically pointed to a 2001 conversation in which Weinberger told him that the "disinformation" had, in fact, been carried out. Interview with Peter Schweizer, September 19, 2005. In an e-mail exchange, Schweizer gave me the go-ahead to use this material and cite him as the source.
60 On the State Department, for instance, the veteran ambassador Jack Matlock wrote on page 66 of his book *Reagan and Gorbachev*, "We asked the CIA to examine what was known and make a judgment."
61 Examination of President's Daily Schedule, Reagan Library, July 2015. President Reagan was in Europe May 1–10. My research assistant and I also checked the Reagan phone logs prior to May 16, going back to mid-April. They show only two brief phone calls between Reagan and Casey, the first on April 19 (taking place from 4:55 to 5:10 P.M.) and the second on April 22 (taking place from 9:48 to 9:49 A.M.). The logs offer

no notes or information on what the two men discussed. The calls were recorded in "The Daily Diary of President Ronald Reagan," on file at the Reagan Library.

62 The preschedule for May 16, 1985, includes the typed words "Meeting with William Casey"; below that, the name "McFarlane" appears in parentheses. The latter refers to National Security Adviser Robert McFarlane. But McFarlane's name is not handwritten on the final schedule, which suggests that the national security adviser did not attend the meeting. When I interviewed McFarlane, his response indicated that he was not present at Casey's briefing of the president. "I don't recall Bill Casey giving the president such a report," McFarlane told me, "although I expect that Bill did direct such a report to be done." The president's final schedule for May 16 includes the following handwritten comment next to the entry for this meeting: "Regan-Casey." That notation apparently refers to Donald Regan, who had become White House chief of staff only three months earlier. Regan came into the role seeking to limit staffers' access to the president. (See, e.g., Norman D. Sandler, "Regan Draws a Smaller White House Inner Circle," UPI, March 26, 1985.) In his role as "gatekeeper," Regan may well have sat in on Casey's meeting with Reagan. Did the chief of staff stay for the whole meeting? Did he leave after the initial discussion of the Beirut bombing, before Casey discussed the highly sensitive CIA investigation? The official White House records do not say. Reagan, in his diary, mentioned only Casey. My sources told me that Casey briefed Reagan with no one else in the Oval Office. Since neither Bob Gates nor Richard Kerr mentioned Donald Regan among the top Reagan officials who received "Agca's Attempt to Kill the Pope: The Case for Soviet Involvement," it seems unlikely that Regan would have been part of the briefing on Casey's highly confidential investigation. Both Robert McFarlane and his successor as national security adviser, Admiral John Poindexter (who took over in December 1985), told me that they had no knowledge of Casey's report. Poindexter told me, "I don't remember such a report." But both also agreed that suspicions centered on Moscow. McFarlane said, "It has always seemed likely to me that the Soviets bear responsibility at least indirectly for the attack since Agca trained [at] a Soviet terrorist training camp (and was probably carried as a sleeper after that)." Poindexter told me, "There was a suspicion that the Soviets were behind the attempted assassination." Interview with Robert McFarlane, April 12, 2015; interview with John Poindexter, April 12, 2015.

63 My personal thanks to David Kirk, my research assistant, for his persistence in helping me dig out this material at the Reagan Library. It was not until the summer of 2015 that we finally confirmed the Reagan-Casey meeting on May 16, 1985.

64 Both David Kirk and I searched at the Reagan Library, in July and August 2015.

65 A number of searches, from Google to Yahoo to Lexis-Nexis and more, yielded no examples of the speech being covered by the press. A volunteer on the library staff at the University of Nevada–Las Vegas searched *Las Vegas Sun* microfiche archives.

66 Michael Ledeen, "The Bulgarian Connection," newsletter of the Jewish Institute for National Security Affairs, 3, no. 17 (December 1982/January 1983): 1.

67 Clark was not the only close Reagan adviser to harbor these suspicions. Defense Secretary Caspar Weinberger also suspected Soviet involvement, as Peter Schweizer related to me. Schweizer wrote several books with Weinberger and spent countless hours with him on the phone, in person, on speaking and book tours, and more. They worked together throughout the 1990s and right up until Weinberger's death in March 2006. I personally interviewed Weinberger several times. Given my different research interests at those times, I regrettably did not ask about the Soviet role in the attempted assassination. About a year and a half after Weinberger's death, however, I posed the question to Schweizer. "Did Cap ever tell you anything about the Soviets being behind the shooting of the pope in 1981?" I asked Schweizer in an e-mail. "Nope," replied Schweizer, "but he assumed they were." E-mail exchange with Peter Schweizer, September 30–October 1, 2007.

68 "Statement by the Soviet National Committee for the Defense of Antonov," *Pravda*, May 30, 1985, published in *Current Digest of the Soviet Press* 37, no. 22 (June 26, 1985): 20.

69 N. Paklin, "Unjust Trial," *Izvestia*, May 29, 1985, published in *Current Digest of the Soviet Press* 37, no. 22 (June 26, 1985): 20.
70 N. Paklin, "Notes from the Trial in Rome: Giovanni Pandico's 'Bombshell,'" *Izvestia*, June 20, 1985, published in *Current Digest of the Soviet Press* 37, no. 25 (July 17, 1985): 15–16.
71 G. Zafesov, "Trial in Rome Ends," *Pravda*, March 30, 1986, published in *Current Digest of the Soviet Press* 38, no. 13 (April 30, 1986): 18.
72 Sterling, "Behind Agca's Gun."
73 John Tagliabue, "6 Are Acquitted in Plot on Pope: Ruling Ambiguous," *New York Times*, March 30, 1986.

Chapter 30: November 1985–December 1987: The President and the "Closet Christian"

1 Dinesh D'Souza in his biography of Reagan cites a few prominent examples from Reagan's second term: William F. Buckley Jr. said, "To greet it [the Soviet regime under Gorbachev] as if it were no longer evil is on the order of changing our entire position toward Adolf Hitler." George F. Will wrote, "Reagan has accelerated the moral disarmament of the West…by elevating wishful thinking to the status of political philosophy." And Charles Krauthammer called Reagan's reasons for changing his assessment of the Soviet Union "ignorant and pathetic." All quoted in Dinesh D'Souza, *Ronald Reagan: How an Ordinary Man Became an Extraordinary Leader* (New York: Touchstone, 1997), 185.
2 Reagan, "Address to the Nation on the Upcoming Soviet–United States Summit Meeting in Geneva," November 14, 1985.
3 Reagan inserted this into the draft on November 12. Draft located in PHF, PS, RRL, Box 21, Folders 404 and 405.
4 Discussion with Tony Dolan, July 24, 2014, and e-mail exchange, July 8, 2014.
5 Discussion with Dolan, July 24, 2014.
6 Dinesh D'Souza says that Gorbachev also invoked the name of Jesus, saying things like "Only Jesus Christ knows the answer to that." D'Souza doesn't cite a source for this reference, and he is the only source I have read that claims that Gorbachev invoked the "J" word. D'Souza, *Ronald Reagan*, 187.
7 See "Geneva Meeting: Memcons of Plenary Sessions and Tête-à-Tête," November 19–21, 1985, declassified May 2000, RRL, Box 92137, Folders 1 and 2; Morris, *Dutch*, 561.
8 See "Geneva Meeting: Memcons," November 19–21, 1985.
9 Pavel Palazchenko, *My Years with Gorbachev and Shevardnadze: The Memoir of a Soviet Interpreter* (University Park, PA: Pennsylvania State University Press, 1997), 44.
10 Reagan quoted the passage as: "We are all of one blood regardless of where we live on Earth." Reagan told the guests, "We should never forget that." Palazchenko, *My Years with Gorbachev and Shevardnadze.*
11 See Palazchenko, *My Years with Gorbachev and Shevardnadze*; "Geneva Meeting: Memcons," November 19–21, 1985.
12 Larry Speakes, *Speaking Out: The Reagan Presidency from Inside the White House* (New York: Scribner, 1988), 134–35.
13 Alfred Kingon, speaking at the 1992 National Conference on Medjugorje, University of Notre Dame.
14 The official "Memcons" (Memoranda of Conversation) of the Geneva Summit, declassified in May 2000, show that the Gorbachevs relayed this fact about Raisa to the Reagans in a dinner conversation on November 20, 1985. These details are found in "Geneva Meeting: Memcons," November 19–21, 1985.
15 Deaver, *A Different Drummer*, 118.

16 The point has been raised by D'Souza, Morris, and Cannon. In particular, see D'Souza, *Ronald Reagan*, 187; Morris, *Dutch*, 561, 569.

17 In a September 1978 radio broadcast, Reagan commented on Brezhnev's invoking God's name with born-again Baptist Jimmy Carter at their summit. "I'm sorry that I can't believe in his sincerity," Reagan said of Brezhnev. "Indeed I think he was hypocritical and deliberately using the Lord's name to curry favor or soften up the President, who does believe in God as Brezhnev does not." Quoted by Ronnie Dugger, *On Reagan: The Man and His Presidency* (New York: McGraw-Hill, 1983), 516.

18 Source: "The Diary of Anatoly Chernyaev: 1989," published online in six yearly installments by the National Security Archive housed electronically by George Washington University, retrieved by the author, May 26, 2011. Chernyaev wrote in his 1990 diary, speaking of Russian Orthodox Christians, "I cannot believe that they believe, unless of course they are not well in the head, their psyche is unbalanced." And yet he immediately countered: "Of course, it is possible that God exists.... But not the kind of god worshipped by the church. Rather, a real Creator. There is something up There (!) that no science can explain."

19 See, among others, Morris, *Dutch*, 519.

20 Interview with Edwin Meese, November 23, 2001.

21 See Paul Lettow's excellent account of the Reykjavík summit, from which I have taken these Reagan quotations (from Reagan's diary and his memoirs). Lettow, *Ronald Reagan and His Quest to Abolish Nuclear Weapons*, 218–29.

22 See the discussion in Kengor, *God and Ronald Reagan*, 288–92.

23 The Polish pontiff would finally visit Ukraine in June 2001, on a meaningful four-day trip (June 23–27).

24 Reagan, "Remarks at a Luncheon Hosted by the Heritage Foundation, November 30, 1987," *Presidential Papers*, 1987, 2:1389–92.

25 Editorial, "Fostering Committed Atheists," *Pravda*, September 28, 1986, 1, printed as "Pravda Editorial on 'Struggle' Against Religion," in *Foreign Broadcast Information Service*, FBIS-SOV-17-OCT-86, October 17, 1986, R4–5.

26 Reagan, "Dinner in Honor of Mikhail Gorbachev at the White House," December 8, 1987.

27 Reagan, "Toast at a Dinner Hosted by Soviet General Secretary Mikhail Gorbachev at the Soviet Embassy," December 9, 1987.

28 Gorbachev wrote, "'I am convinced it's God's will that we should cooperate,' I added." Gorbachev, *Memoirs*, 457.

29 Reagan, "Remarks to Members of the National Press Club on Arms Reduction and Nuclear Weapons," November 18, 1981.

30 See the official numbers from the U.S. Department of State, which lists 2,692 missiles removed: https://www.state.gov/t/avc/trty/102360.htm, retrieved February 17, 2017.

31 Reagan, "Remarks on Signing the Intermediate-Range Nuclear Forces Treaty," December 8, 1987.

CHAPTER 31: DECEMBER 8, 1987: AN IMMACULATE PEACE

1 See, among others, Pope John Paul II, *Redemptoris Mater*, section 49. In this encyclical the pope stated, "This Marian Year will begin on the Solemnity of Pentecost, on June 7." See also the official Vatican website for the 1987 time line: http://www.vatican.va/news_services/press/documentazione/documents/santopadre_biografie/giovanni_paolo_ii_biografia_pontificato_en.html#1987; Weigel, *Witness to Hope*, 576; and Robert Suro, "Pope Proclaims a Year Dedicated to Virgin Mary," *New York Times*, January 2, 1987.

2 Suro, "Pope Proclaims a Year Dedicated to Virgin Mary."

3 Quoted in Wayne Weible, *Medjugorje: The Message* (Brewster, MA: Paraclete Press, 1989), 52–53.
4 All but one of the youngsters were teenagers. The youngest was ten years old at the first sightings. Of the six visionaries, four were girls and two were boys.
5 Weible, *Medjugorje: The Message*, 13.
6 Ibid., 20.
7 Ibid., 160–61.
8 Ibid., 275–81.
9 There are numerous sources on this. Weible reports the same ibid., 276–77.
10 Kingon, 1992 National Conference on Medjugorje. In an August 2014 interview, Kingon told me that he believes in God but has no formal religious affiliation. He was not raised according to a Christian tradition; his mother was a nonpracticing Jew and his father converted to Christian Science. During our interview, Kingon told me that he continued to believe that something significant was happening at Medjugorje and that he hoped the apparitions and messages were genuine, but he noted that he could not be sure. He awaited some form of authentication from the Catholic Church before committing his heart too deeply. "Hopefully we will eventually learn and see," he said.
11 The material from Kingon that follows in this chapter is taken from that public speech. Kingon's speech, which runs roughly thirty-six minutes in length, is available on several Medjugorje websites. I found it at http://en.gloria.tv/?media=375122, retrieved July 2014.
12 Interview with Alfred Kingon, August 11, 2014. Kingon told me that he has never written down his experiences. His talk at Notre Dame was the one occasion in which he decided to go on the record—and, even then, only verbally. My interview with him in August 2014 might be the only formal follow-up to his 1992 appearance at Notre Dame. Reporters were not interested in his story.
13 Discussion with Tony Dolan by phone, July 24, 2014, and several e-mail exchanges in July 2014.
14 Kingon told me that Reagan's reaction to getting the news and messages of Medjugorje has been the subject of great embellishment, with exaggerated claims that Reagan had fallen to his knees in reverence and exaltation. "That absolutely never happened," said Kingon. "Presidents don't do that—and Ronald Reagan never did.... There's crazy stuff out there about RR falling to the floor on his knees when he heard. He didn't fall to the floor. I assure you of that."
15 I asked Kingon (August 11, 2014) whether he and Reagan said anything more about Medjugorje at that moment. He said they did not. At that time, Kingon was still ambassador, and they were meeting to discuss business related to the European Union. "When I came home [to the United States] for briefings etc.," Kingon told me in an e-mail dated August 18, 2014, "I always stopped in to see RR. He always wanted it. At one of those meetings we discussed Medjugorje and it was there that he told me how moved he was."
16 See Kengor, *God and Ronald Reagan*, 125–26.
17 Weible's dating for this period is not precise in his book. He seems to say that he arrived in Medjugorje in October 1987 but a few paragraphs later quotes his Medjugorje hosts (Marija Pavlovic and Kathleen Parisod) referring in the past tense to events that occurred in the first week or so of December 1987. See Weible, *Medjugorje: The Message*, 306–7. Still, the general structure of his account conforms to the broader late 1987 time line. And in a June 10, 2014, e-mail, Weible clarified for me that he had arrived in Medjugorje "late at night in the latter part of December."
18 Weible later converted to the Catholic Church, but he was not Catholic at this time.
19 Weible, *Medjugorje: The Message*, 306–7.
20 Research assistant David Kirk and I looked in the Reagan Library for any record of phone calls from President Reagan to Yugoslavia during this time period—specifically, between the dates of November 13, 1987, and December 10, 1987. We examined presi-

dential call logs, President Reagan's daily diary, and his available personal notes. We also consulted (the public) *Reagan Diaries*. We found no record of any contact. If there was a phone call from one of President Reagan's secretaries or aides to Yugoslavia during this time, on behalf of the president, the Reagan Library archives would not have that information, according to library archivists. Records of the secretary's phone logs might be kept at the National Archives in Washington, DC, the Reagan Library staffers told us. But when we contacted the National Archives, staff told us that they do not have those secretarial records.

21 Weible, *Medjugorje: The Message*, 308.
22 Interview with Kingon, August 11, 2014.
23 In a July 22, 2014, e-mail, Weigel told me, "I've never written on the subject." He acknowledged his own doubts about the apparitions; he said, "Many good things have happened to individuals at Medjugorje but the Church has never pronounced on the veracity of the visions or the visionaries."
24 Antonio Gaspari, "Medjugorje: Deception or Miracle?" *Inside the Vatican*, November 1996.
25 This alleged quotation appears on most Medjugorje websites and in most books.
26 Weible, *Medjugorje: The Message*, 331–33.

CHAPTER 32: JUNE–DECEMBER 1987: REAGAN'S FÁTIMA BRIEFING

1 Brinkley, *The Reagan Diaries*, 476.
2 Reagan, "Statement on the Lifting of Economic Sanctions Against Poland," February 19, 1987.
3 I checked for materials during a two-day research trip to the Reagan Library on August 5–6, 2015. Neither I nor two of the archivists I worked with were able to come up with anything.
4 At this point in 1985, that person would have been either Kenneth Dam or John Whitehead. Whitehead replaced Dam in July 1985. Frank Shakespeare agreed (in our follow-up conversation) that it was one of the two, but he couldn't remember which. Interestingly, he said he had been "carefully told by the White House [he didn't specify by whom or why] not to be in conversation with the State Department. So I didn't know them well at all."
5 Frank Shakespeare speaking to the Schoenstatt Heights community in Madison, WI, April 7, 2006.
6 Jack Nelson and James Gerstenzang, "Reagan Tells Pope of Arms Pact Hope: Rome Talks Focus on U.S.-Soviet Ties and Removing Missiles From Europe," *Los Angeles Times*, June 7, 1987.
7 The account by the *New York Times* and by Reagan himself as published in the *Reagan Diaries* estimated that the meeting lasted an hour. The *Chicago Tribune* specified fifty-three minutes. Frank Shakespeare (who was there and served as the president's escort) estimated two hours, but he may have been including all the time the pope and president spent together, including with the media.
8 Gerald M. Boyd, "Pope, with Reagan, Urges an End to Arms Race," *New York Times*, June 7, 1987.
9 Boyd, "Pope, with Reagan, Urges an End to Arms Race."
10 Nelson and Gerstenzang, "Reagan Tells Pope of Arms Pact Hope."
11 Ibid.
12 Interview with Frank Shakespeare, March 5, 2013.
13 Reagan, "Remarks Following Discussion with Pope John Paul II in Vatican City," June 6, 1987.
14 Pope John Paul II, "Address of the Holy Father John Paul II to Mr. Ronald Reagan, President of the United States of America," June 6, 1987.
15 Reagan, "Remarks Following Discussion with Pope John Paul II in Vatican City."

16 Chief Reagan speechwriter Tony Dolan has told me this countless times, as has Peter Robinson. It is also obvious from even a cursory glance at the speech drafts on file at the Reagan Library, which, in addition to having countless marks from Reagan's own pen, include many anecdotes and verbatim passages from speeches Reagan wrote well before he became president.

17 The following information comes from several personal discussions I had with Josh Gilder and Peter Robinson, including (respectively) in Washington, DC, in May 2014 and in Grove City, PA, in February 2010. It is also taken from e-mail exchanges with both men, including a series of e-mails with Josh Gilder, May 9–12, 2014. Robinson provided the fullest original account in his book *How Ronald Reagan Changed My Life* (New York: ReganBooks, 2003), 191–93.

18 Reagan, "Statement on the Fifth Anniversary of the Founding of the Solidarity Movement in Poland," August 31, 1985.

19 See Reagan, "Statement on the Lifting of Economic Sanctions Against Poland."

20 Reagan, "Remarks Following Discussion with Pope John Paul II in Vatican City."

21 See the official time line at the Vatican website: http://www.vatican.va/news_services/press/documentazione/documents/santopadre_biografie/giovanni_paolo_ii_biografia_pontificato_en.html#1987.

22 E-mail correspondence with Josh Gilder, May 15, 2014.

23 My research assistant David Kirk inspected the draft at the Reagan Library in January 2015.

24 Brinkley, *The Reagan Diaries*, 504.

25 Reagan letter to Ruddy Lee-Hines, June 25, 1987, published in Skinner, Anderson, and Anderson, *Reagan: A Life in Letters*, 808.

26 Reagan letter to Phil Regan, June 25, 1987, published in Skinner, Anderson, and Anderson, *Reagan: A Life in Letters*, 735.

27 Reagan, "Remarks on East-West Relations at the Brandenburg Gate in West Berlin," June 12, 1987.

28 See my discussion in *The Crusader*, 266.

29 See Robinson, *How Ronald Reagan Changed My Life*, 101–10.

30 Arbatov speaking on Moscow TV's Studio 9 program, November 2, 1985, transcript in *Foreign Broadcast Information Service*, FBIS-SOV-4-NOV-85, November 4, 1985, CC4–5.

31 *Studio 9* (television program), June 18, 1987, transcript printed as "Studio 9 Participants Discuss Reagan's Recent Speeches," in *Foreign Broadcast Information Service*, FBIS-SOV-19-JUN-87, June 19, 1987, A1–10.

32 See Service, *The End of the Cold War*, 302.

33 See ibid.

34 Pope John Paul II, "Words of John Paul II to the Faithful Before the Meeting of Prayer," Częstochowa, Poland, June 12, 1987. Posted at the Vatican website: http://w2.vatican.va/content/john-paul-ii/it/speeches/1987/june/documents/hf_jp-ii_spe_19870612_incontro-czestochowa.html.

35 Nelson and Gerstenzang, "Reagan Tells Pope of Arms Pact Hope."

36 Roberto Suro, "The Papal Visit: Pontiff Embraces Welcome in Miami," *New York Times*, September 11, 1987; Bruce Buursma, "Pope Welcomed by Reagan: Bernardin in Miami as Tour Starts," *Chicago Tribune*, September 11, 1987.

37 Official Presidential Daily Schedule for Thursday, September 10, 1987, on file at the Reagan Library. I checked with the Reagan Library for a list of Reagan's activities the remainder of the day, but we found no such list. I checked in person while doing research there in August 2015 and then checked with archivists on two other occasions via my research assistant David Kirk, in November 2015, and then shortly before this book went to press, in March 2017. Again we found nothing.

38 Reagan, "Remarks at the Welcoming Ceremony for Pope John Paul II in Miami, Florida," September 10, 1987.

39 Pope John Paul II, "Welcome Ceremony: Address of His Holiness John Paul II," International Miami Airport, Miami, FL, September 10, 1987. See http://w2.vatican.va/content/john-paul-ii/en/speeches/1987/september/documents/hf_jp-ii_spe_19870910_aeroporto-miami.html.
40 I have not been able to find a record of Reagan's schedule for that day, which would make clear exactly how much time he spent with John Paul II. My research assistant and I checked repeatedly with the Reagan Library, including as recently as March 1, 2017, just before this book went to press.
41 Suro, "The Papal Visit."
42 Pope John Paul II, "Address of His Holiness John Paul II," Vizcaya Museum, Miami, FL, September 10, 1987. See http://w2.vatican.va/content/john-paul-ii/en/speeches/1987/september/documents/hf_jp-ii_spe_19870910_reagan-museo.html.
43 See my discussion in Kengor, *11 Principles of a Reagan Conservative*, 10–19.
44 Reagan, "Remarks at Georgetown University's Bicentennial Convocation," October 1, 1988.
45 Fulton Sheen, *Whence Come Wars* (New York: Sheed and Ward, 1940), 60–61.
46 See Norman D. Sandler, "President Reagan Assured Pope John Paul II Thursday of...," UPI, September 10, 1987; *The Papal Visit: John Paul II in Miami* (Miami: Miami Herald Publishing Company, 1987), 10. Without access to the president's schedule for that day, it is impossible to determine exactly how long this one-on-one lasted.
47 Reagan, "Remarks Following Discussions with Pope John Paul II in Miami, Florida," September 10, 1987.
48 Brinkley, *The Reagan Diaries*, 529.
49 Pope John Paul II, "Meeting with the Representatives of the Jewish Organizations of the United States of America: Address of His Holiness John Paul II," Dade County, Miami, FL, September 11, 1987. See http://w2.vatican.va/content/john-paul-ii/en/speeches/1987/september/documents/hf_jp-ii_spe_19870911_organizzaz-ebraiche.html.
50 Reagan, "Call to Mrs. Sophia Casey," May 6, 1987, Presidential Handwriting File: Phone Calls, Folder 181, Ronald Reagan Library.
51 The funeral proved controversial. With President Reagan sitting in the front pew, Bishop John McGann delivered a homily that took the form of a left-wing political statement. He denounced Reagan administration policies, and especially policies he believed the dead Casey had played a special role in advancing. One of the mourners, *American Spectator* editor R. Emmett Tyrrell Jr., accused McGann of "ethics [that] might astonish a pagan." See R. Emmett Tyrrell Jr., "William J. Casey, RIP," *American Spectator*, July 1987. Bill Casey's daughter, Bernadette, later told me: "Everyone was appalled. I have a box full of nasty letters from angry people. But, you know, the Church is filled with humans." Interview with Bernadette Smith, November 15, 2005. Another attendee, Richard Ramos, told me that he noticed Jeane Kirkpatrick amending her eulogy in her pew as the bishop fired away at the dead Casey. Ramos looked over at Reagan and was impressed by the president's unflinching demeanor in the face of the bishop's crudeness. Discussion with Richard Ramos, Washington, DC, March 4, 2016.
52 Reagan, "Statement on the Death of William J. Casey," May 6, 1987.
53 Herb Meyer speaking at the Third Annual Ronald Reagan Lecture, Grove City College, Grove City, PA, February 5, 2009. Meyer reaffirmed this to me in an August 28, 2015, e-mail: "As I said, he figured that God had given him one last shot and he wasn't going to waste it. And he didn't."
54 Meyer made this point both in his Reagan Lecture at Grove City College and in his e-mail to me.
55 Blessing of Pope John Paul II, Saint Peter's Square, Vatican City, December 30, 1987.

CHAPTER 33: MAY–JUNE 1988: REAGAN'S MISSION TO MOSCOW

1 Reagan, "Remarks at a White House Briefing on Religious Freedom in the Soviet Union," May 3, 1988.
2 "1988 U.S.-Soviet Summit Memcons," May 26–June 3, 1988, Ronald Reagan Library, Box 92084, Folder 2. These "memoranda of conversation" are the notes transcribed by the official note taker.
3 Reagan, "Remarks on Departure for the Soviet–United States Summit in Moscow," May 25, 1988.
4 Reagan, "Remarks and a Question-and-Answer Session with Members of the National Strategy Forum," Chicago, IL, May 4, 1988.
5 Reagan, "Remarks to the Paasikivi Society and the League of Finnish-American Societies," Helsinki, Finland, May 27, 1988.
6 For an extended analysis, see my book *God and Ronald Reagan*, 281–320.
7 Interview with Ben Elliott, September 20, 2001.
8 Morris speaking in an interview on "Reagan," *The American Experience*.
9 Morris, *Dutch*, 519.
10 Malcolm Muggeridge, March 1983 letter, located in PHF, PR, RRL, Box 6, Folder 78. Reagan quoted this in the first term of his presidency but remembered it throughout. See Reagan, "Remarks at the Annual Convention of the National Religious Broadcasters," January 31, 1983.
11 This was a July 9, 1981, letter to John O. Koehler, published in Skinner, Anderson, and Anderson, *Reagan: A Life in Letters*, 375.
12 Reagan said this in a February 15, 1984, letter to Suzanne Massie of Irvington, NY, published in Skinner, Anderson, and Anderson, *Reagan: A Life in Letters*, 379.
13 Reagan, "Remarks and a Question-and-Answer Session with Area High School Seniors," Jacksonville, FL, December 1, 1987.
14 Graham wrote other letters to Reagan on religion in the USSR, including on April 29, 1988, and April 26, 1982. Letters are located in PHF, PR, RRL, Boxes 2, 19, and 20, Folders 35, 312, and 327A.
15 Reagan, "Remarks and a Question-and-Answer Session with Area High School Seniors."
16 For details in this section, I'm deeply grateful to the record keeping of Igor Korchilov, who was there. See Igor Korchilov, *Translating History: Thirty Years on the Front Lines of Diplomacy with a Top Russian Interpreter* (New York: Scribner, 1997), 145–55.
17 The details from this section (including the paragraphs that follow) were drawn from a number of sources, from James Billington to Igor Korchilov to records at the Reagan Library, as well as reports in the *New York Times* and *Washington Post*. Among them, Korchilov's book was most helpful. Also especially helpful was *Public Papers of the Presidents of the United States: Ronald Reagan*, 1988, 672–715.
18 Statement of Moscow news agency TASS in English, May 29, 1988, printed as "Patriarch Prays for 'Success' of Summit," in *Foreign Broadcast Information Service*, FBIS-SOV-88-104, May 31, 1988, 20.
19 Korchilov, *Translating History*, 155.
20 "1988 U.S.-Soviet Summit Memcons," May 26–June 3, 1988.
21 The discussion of religious rights take up two and a half pages of the nine pages of the meeting transcript. "1988 U.S.-Soviet Summit Memcons," May 26–June 3, 1988.
22 Reagan, "Remarks to Religious Leaders at the Danilov Monastery in Moscow," May 30, 1988.
23 "Filaret Regrets Reagan Remarks," *Argumenty I Fakty* no. 23 (June 4–10, 1988): 3, translated text from Soviet media printed in *Foreign Broadcast Information Service*, FBIS-SOV-88-108, June 6, 1988, 16–19, and FBIS-SOV-88-111, June 9, 1988, 23–24.
24 I thank Bob Morrison for informing me of this very meaningful translation.

25 Reagan, "Remarks to Soviet Dissidents at Spaso House in Moscow," May 30, 1988.
26 Reagan would tell the same story to a student evangelical group in Washington two months later, on July 28. Reagan, "Remarks to the Student Congress on Evangelism," July 28, 1988.
27 "1988 U.S.-Soviet Summit Memcons," May 26–June 3, 1988.
28 Mikhail Gorbachev, "Toast of General Secretary Gorbachev of the Soviet Union at the State Dinner in Moscow," May 30, 1988.
29 Reagan, "Toast of the President at the State Dinner in Moscow," May 30, 1988.
30 "1988 U.S.-Soviet Summit Memcons," May 26–June 3, 1988; Korchilov, *Translating History*, 165.
31 Reagan, "Remarks at a Luncheon Hosted by Artists and Cultural Leaders in Moscow," May 31, 1988.
32 Reagan, "Address to the Nation on Christmas and the Situation in Poland," December 23, 1981.
33 Reagan, "Remarks and a Question-and-Answer Session with the Students and Faculty at Moscow State University," May 31, 1988.
34 A number of missionaries to Russia have independently informed me of this fact.
35 Reagan later recounted this detail in a September 1990 conversation with Gorbachev. See Korchilov, *Translating History*, 355.
36 On this, see especially Korchilov, *Translating History*, 172.
37 Reagan and Gorbachev, "Toasts at a State Dinner Hosted by the President at Spaso House in Moscow," May 31, 1988.
38 Reagan, "Toasts at a State Dinner Hosted by the President at Spaso House in Moscow."
39 Reagan, "Statement at Closing Ceremony for Moscow Summit," June 2, 1988.
40 Quoted by Dusko Doder and Louise Branson, *Gorbachev: Heretic in the Kremlin* (New York: Viking, 1990), 320.
41 Terry Muck, "Still the Evil Empire?" *Christianity Today*, July 15, 1988, 15.

CHAPTER 34: JUNE 1988: ENDING THE SOVIET "WAR ON RELIGION"

1 See Barnes, "In the Evil Empire," 9.
2 Quoted by Lou Cannon and Don Oberdorfer, "The Scripting of the Moscow Summit," *Washington Post*, June 9, 1988.
3 Reagan, "Remarks to the Student Congress on Evangelism," July 28, 1988.
4 John-Thor Dahlburg, "Russian Orthodox Patriarch Pimen Dies at 79," *Los Angeles Times*, May 4, 1990.
5 Hedrick Smith, *The New Russians* (New York: Random House, 1990), 395–96.
6 Thom Shanker, "1,000-Year-Old Church Pins Hopes on New Era of Soviet Openness," *Chicago Tribune*, June 6, 1988; Michael Parks, "Talks Set on Ukraine Church Status: Catholics, Russian Orthodox to Take Up Sensitive Issue," *Los Angeles Times*, June 5, 1988.
7 Smith, *The New Russians*, 395–96.
8 Wallace L. Daniel, *The Orthodox Church and Civil Society in Russia* (College Station, TX: Texas A&M University Press, 2006), 36–37.
9 Tad Szulc, "Principled Allies: Gorbachev and the Pope," *Newsweek*, April 10, 1995.
10 Weigel, *Witness to Hope*, 572.
11 Szulc, "Principled Allies."
12 Szulc, "Principled Allies"; Weigel, *Witness to Hope*, 572–73.
13 Weigel, *Witness to Hope*, 573–74.
14 "Soviets Back Law on Religious Freedom," *New York Times*, September 27, 1990.
15 Gorbachev, *Memoirs*, 508; Szulc, "Principled Allies."
16 Weigel, *Witness to Hope*, 575.

17 Szulc, "Principled Allies."
18 Gorbachev, *Memoirs*, 508; Szulc, "Principled Allies."
19 Casaroli told this to Thomas Melady, U.S. ambassador to the Holy See from 1989 to 1993 under President George H.W. Bush. See Thomas P. Melady, "John Paul II Rejected Assassination Inquiry," *National Catholic Reporter*, April 29, 2005.
20 Gorbachev, *Memoirs*, 508; Szulc, "Principled Allies."
21 Bogdan Turek, "Soviet Leader Mikhail Gorbachev Implored Thousands...," United Press International, July 12, 1988.
22 Shanker, "1,000-Year-Old Church Pins Hopes on New Era of Soviet Openness."
23 See Smith, *The New Russians*, 395–96.
24 Reagan, *An American Life*, 705–6. Reagan's intentions were sincere with this comment, but it turned out he was wrong. Russia's Jews fled the country in hordes the moment the Soviet Union dissolved and they were free to do so. Enormous numbers of them went to Israel—some 769,000 people from 1989 to 1998. Seven decades of an Evil Empire had been enough for them. See "Israel's Population at 6 Million," Associated Press, December 31, 1998.
25 Reagan, *An American Life*, 706.
26 Aside from Gorbachev's earlier cited memoirs, see also Gorbachev, *On My Country and the World*, 20–21, 93, 106, 193, 268.
27 Ibid., 21.

CHAPTER 35: 1989–1991: THE COLLAPSE OF THE EVIL EMPIRE

1 Anyone in the Roman Catholic Church who thought about it carefully might have noticed a certain spiritual parallel: November 9 happens to be the only date on the liturgical calendar when the Church holds a feast day for an edifice. Specifically, every November 9 honors the dedication of the Saint John Lateran Church in Rome, the official home church of the pope and the diocese of Rome. The Saint John Lateran Basilica is the official "mother church" of Rome, of the world, of Christendom. It is the visible symbol of the universal Church. Originally erected by the Emperor Constantine and dedicated in the year 324, Saint John Lateran is the oldest and highest ranking of the Catholic Church's basilicas, exceeding even Saint Peter's Basilica, which, contrary to public perception, is not the pope's or diocese's official church. The Catholic Church has held a feast day to honor the Lateran Basilica every November 9 since the twelfth century. As the Jesuit priest Mitch Pacwa observes, this feast day is a "major celebration" in the Latin rite because (among other reasons) the construction of Saint John Lateran was a major victory after Christians had suffered centuries of persecution. Now, on this November 9, the Berlin Wall, the most visible symbol of communist persecution of Christianity, fell. And the Saint John Lateran Basilica still stood, having withstood the communists' relentless attacks. See Father Mitch Pacwa's homily, daily Mass, Our Lady of the Angels Monastery, Irondale, AL, November 9, 2010, broadcast on EWTN television.
2 Reagan, "Remarks on Presenting Congressional Gold Medals to Natan and Avital Shcharansky and an Informal Exchange with Reporters," January 11, 1989.
3 Interview with Chris M. Zawitkowski, November 9, 2005.
4 The operative word here is *available*, given that communists did their best to limit the number of contested seats. Still, this was progress.
5 Gorbachev, *Memoirs*, 478–79.
6 During a 1993 conference at Princeton, Sergei Tarasenko, who had been the top aide to Soviet foreign minister Eduard Shevardnadze, said that the overwhelming results of Poland's 1989 elections convinced him and the Soviet leadership, particularly in the foreign ministry, that the Soviet system could not endure. Tarasenko transcript is published in Wohlforth, ed., *Witnesses to the End of the Cold War*, 112–13.

7 Szulc, "Principled Allies"; Clyde Haberman, "What Gorbachev Wants from the Pope," *New York Times*, November 26, 1989; Weigel, *Witness to Hope*, 575.
8 Alan Riding, "Pope and Gorbachev to Meet," *New York Times*, September 11, 1989.
9 Haberman, "What Gorbachev Wants from the Pope."
10 "Gorbachev Remembers Pope John Paul II," Radio Free Europe/Radio Liberty, interview with Gorbachev conducted on April 3, 2005, posted at http://www.rferl.org/content/article/1058353.html.
11 Clyde Haberman, "The Kremlin and the Vatican: Gorbachev Visits Pope at Vatican; Ties Are Forged," *New York Times*, December 2, 1989.
12 The transcript was published by (among other sources) the Catholic News Service (CNS). The State Archive of the Russian Federation released the document as part of its Yakovlev Collection. The translation that CNS and other sources published was done by Anna Melyakova of the Washington-based group the National Security Archive. See https://cnsblog.wordpress.com/2009/12/11/inside-the-john-paul-ii-gorbachev-meeting/.
13 William D. Montalbano, "Gorbachev Visits Pope, Vows Church Freedom," *Los Angeles Times*, December 2, 1989; Haberman, "The Kremlin and the Vatican."
14 Weigel, *Witness to Hope*, 602.
15 Joseph A. Reaves, "Gorbachev Pledges New Religious Liberty," *Chicago Tribune*, December 2, 1989.
16 Koehler, *Spies in the Vatican*, 263. Recall that the phrase *physical elimination* reflected the interpretation of the Italian security services. The Soviet document itself did not use those words; the document instead called for "additional measures beyond disinformation and discreditation" to be used against the pope "if necessary." As we will see later in this book, Gorbachev in a January 2000 interview denied this interpretation. See Koehler, *Spies in the Vatican*, 128–29.
17 Haberman, "The Kremlin and the Vatican."
18 Gorbachev, *Memoirs*, 508–9.
19 Bertone, *The Last Secret of Fátima*, 86.
20 Weigel, *The End and the Beginning*, 177.
21 Francis X. Clines, "Soviet Leaders Agree to Surrender Communist Party Monopoly on Power," *New York Times*, February 8, 1990. The main architect of the proposal was Alexander Yakovlev, a Politburo member and Gorbachev confidant who was part of a group of Soviet reformers.
22 Thomas Reed, Address to the National Convention of the Armed Forces Communications and Electronics Association, June 16, 1982, quoted in Thomas C. Reed, *At the Abyss: An Insider's History of the Cold War* (New York: Presidio Press, 2004), 237.
23 Brown, *The Gorbachev Factor*, 105–6, 193–94.
24 Ibid., 96.
25 Ibid.
26 Reagan, "Address to the Cambridge Union Society," Cambridge, England, December 5, 1990, quoted in Frederick J. Ryan Jr., ed., *Ronald Reagan: The Wisdom and Humor of the Great Communicator* (San Francisco: Collins, 1995).
27 See the detailed chronology of Soviet events in Jack F. Matlock Jr., *Autopsy of an Empire: The American Ambassador's Account of the Collapse of the Soviet Union* (New York: Random House, 1995), 749–59.
28 Valery Boldin, *Ten Years That Shook the World* (New York: Basic Books, 1994), 336. Ambassador Jack Matlock, a keen observer as close to the scene as anyone, put it well when he summarized: "When he came to power, Gorbachev still believed in the Soviet system.... He was convinced that the instrument to achieve...changes would be the Communist Party itself.... Gorbachev's policies eventually...destroy[ed] the system they were intended to save." See Matlock, *Reagan and Gorbachev*, 110.
29 Jack Matlock agrees on these points. See Matlock, *Reagan and Gorbachev*, 317–18.
30 Weigel, *Witness to Hope*, 609.

31 Clyde Haberman, "Upheaval in the East: Hungary; Hungarians and Vatican Restore Diplomatic Ties," *New York Times*, February 10, 1990.
32 Ibid.
33 Weigel, *Witness to Hope*, 609.
34 Haberman, "Upheaval in the East: Hungary."
35 Weigel, *Witness to Hope*, 609.
36 "Vatican Resuming Ties with Moscow," *New York Times*, March 16, 1990; Weigel, *Witness to Hope*, 609.
37 "Havel: Sharing a Miracle," *L'Osservatore Romano*, April 30, 1990.
38 Marc Fisher, "The Old Warrior at the Wall," *Washington Post*, September 13, 1990, D1–2.
39 "Reagan Has Private Audience with the Pope," UPI, September 20, 1990.
40 "Reagan: Ended European Trip by Meeting with Pope," *USA Today*, September 21, 1990, A5.
41 "Reagan Has Private Audience with the Pope."
42 E-mail correspondence with Joanne Drake, August 29, 2012, following conversations with her and her conversations with Mrs. Reagan, all done in August 2012.
43 Mrs. Reagan usually traveled with her husband. I do not know whether she was present with President Reagan in Fairbanks in May 1984 during that meeting with the pope. As for her May 1985 visit with John Paul II, Ronald Reagan wrote in his diary on May 2, 1985, "Nancy left us for her trip to Rome—an audience with the Pope & schedule that will keep her away 'til May 4." Reagan mentions nothing else in the diary, and I have seen no material on what Mrs. Reagan discussed with the pope. Brinkley, *The Reagan Diaries*, 321.
44 Bertone, *The Last Secret of Fátima*, 161.
45 Tindal-Robertson, *Fátima, Russia, and Pope John Paul II*, 79–80, 173–74, 178.
46 Ibid., 219–20.
47 For a lengthy discussion on the constitution battle, see Weigel, *The Cube and the Cathedral*.
48 As posted in Italian at the Vatican website: "Tutto questo decennio lo considero come dono gratuito fatto a me in modo speciale dalla Divina Provvidenza," http://w2.vatican.va/content/john-paul-ii/it/audiences/1991/documents/hf_jp-ii_aud_19910515.html.
49 On Gorbachev's deadly use of force in the Baltics in early 1991, one of the best contemporary analyses was the editorial "Gorbachev's Tanks," *New Republic*, February 4, 1991, 9–10.
50 Gorbachev speaking on the documentary *Yeltsin*, produced by Pacem Productions and First Circle Films, and broadcast nationally on PBS in August 2000.
51 George J. Church, "The Education of Mikhail Sergeyevich Gorbachev," *Time*, January 4, 1988.
52 Quoted in Brown, *The Gorbachev Factor*, 291–92.
53 See Kengor, *The Crusader*, 224–25.
54 Reagan, "The President's News Conference," January 21, 1982.
55 See Russell Bova in Michael Ellman and Vladimir Kontorovich, eds., *The Destruction of the Soviet Economic System: An Insiders' History* (Armonk, NY: M.E. Sharpe, 1998), 49–51.
56 Pavel Chichikov, "The Answer," *National Catholic Register*, January 15–21, 2006.
57 See Tindal-Robertson, *Fátima, Russia, and Pope John Paul II*, 83–89, 187. More than any source I know, Tindal-Robertson has recognized these fascinating parallels.
58 Weigel, *Witness to Hope*, 651.
59 Tindal-Robertson, *Fátima, Russia, and Pope John Paul II*, 183–86.
60 The official encyclopedia website of Russia, Russiapedia, states, "The document stated that the USSR ceased to exist as a subject of international law and geopolitical reality." See http://russiapedia.rt.com/on-this-day/december-8.
61 Christmas Day for the Russian Orthodox Church that season was January 7, 1992.

Francis X. Clines, "Gorbachev, Last Soviet Leader, Resigns: U.S. Recognizes Republics' Independence," *New York Times*, December 26, 1991.

62 "The Diary of Anatoly Chernyaev: 1990," retrieved by the author, May 26, 2011.

63 Kozyrev on ABC News, *This Week with David Brinkley*, August 25, 1991, transcript #513, 7.

64 David Remnick, "Dead Souls," *New York Review of Books*, December 19, 1991, 79.

65 Tarasenko said this during a February 25–27, 1993, conference at Princeton. Tarasenko transcript is published in William C. Wohlforth, ed., *Witnesses to the End of the Cold War* (Baltimore and London: Johns Hopkins University, 1996), 20.

66 Genrikh Aleksandrovich (Henry) Trofimenko, presentation at 1993 Hofstra University Conference on the Reagan Presidency, published in Eric J. Schmertz et al., eds., *President Reagan and the World* (Westport, CT: Greenwood Press, 1997), 136.

CHAPTER 36: MAY 13, 2000: THE THIRD SECRET OF FÁTIMA—REVEALED

1 "Message of Pope John Paul II to the Bishop of Leiria-Fátima for the 80th Anniversary of the Fátima Apparitions," letter sent from the Vatican, October 1, 1997, posted at the Vatican website, http://w2.vatican.va/content/john-paul-ii/en/speeches/1997/october/documents/hf_jp-ii_spe_19971001_fatima.html.

2 Bertone, *The Last Secret of Fátima*, 32.

3 "Address of Cardinal Angelo Sodano Regarding the 'Third Part' of the Secret of Fátima at the Conclusion of the Solemn Mass of John Paul II," Fátima, Portugal, May 13, 2000, posted at the Vatican website, http://www.vatican.va/roman_curia/congregations/cfaith/documents/rc_con_cfaith_doc_20000626_message-fatima_en.html. See also Weigel, *The End and the Beginning*, 235–37.

4 Bertone, *The Last Secret of Fátima*, ix.

5 Ibid., 27–30, 46–48. Another good source on the history from John XXIII to Paul VI to John Paul II is Apostoli, *Fátima for Today*, 210–14.

6 These documents are all published at the Vatican website as "The Message of Fátima," from the Congregation for the Doctrine of the Faith, with the full package dated June 26, 2000. See http://www.vatican.va/roman_curia/congregations/cfaith/documents/rc_con_cfaith_doc_20000626_message-fatima_en.html.

7 Bertone, *The Last Secret of Fátima*, xiii, 36–39, 162–63.

8 Fulton J. Sheen, *Peace of Soul* (New York: Whittlesey House, 1949), 40.

9 See Luke 1:38: "Then Mary said, 'Here am I, the servant of the Lord; let it be with me according to your word.' Then the angel departed from her."

10 Some Fátima watchers still question whether what the Church revealed as the Third Secret of Fátima was truly the secret, or at least whether it was the whole secret. The Church says that the Third Secret we know is the one and only Third Secret, and that nothing is being hidden—a fact backed by the two sources I've cited throughout this book, the works of Cardinal Bertone and Father Apostoli. Lúcia herself told Bertone, on November 17, 2001, that "everything" had been revealed and published and that "there are no more secrets." (See Bertone, *The Last Secret of Fátima*, 55, 63–66, 162; Apostoli, *Fátima for Today*, 263–68.) Another authoritative source is Archbishop Loris Francesco Capovilla, who as personal secretary to Pope John XXIII in 1959 watched the pontiff open the Third Secret and even read the secret himself. "There are not two truths from Fátima and nor is there any fourth secret," Copevilla said in September 2007. "The text which I read in 1959 is the same that was distributed by the Vatican." He added, apparently with some annoyance: "I have had enough of these conspiracy theories. It just isn't true. I read it, I presented it to the Pope and we resealed the envelope." (See "Last Surviving Witness Says Third Fátima Secret Is Fully Revealed," Catholic News Agency, September 12, 2007.)

Chapter 37: June 5, 2004: Ronald Reagan's Silent Goodbye

1 Lawrence K. Altman, "Reagan's Twilight: A Special Report," *New York Times*, October 5, 1997.
2 Vladimir Isachenkov and Jim Heintz, "Reagan Mourned in Former 'Evil Empire,'" *Moscow Times*, June 7, 2004.
3 The Reagan Library and Museum posted Gorbachev's letter on its website.
4 George Weigel, "An Extraordinary Pair," *Arlington Catholic Herald*, June 25–July 1, 2009.
5 George Weigel, "The Reagan Centenary," *Catholic Difference*, January 12, 2011.
6 "Address of Pope John Paul II to the Honorable George W. Bush, President of the United States of America," official Vatican statement, June 4, 2004.
7 The statement came from Vatican spokesman Joaquín Navarro-Valls.
8 Weigel, *The End and the Beginning*, 361. Weigel reported that this language probably came from the Vatican's Secretariat of State but hastened to add that the sentiments of "deep gratitude" were "wholly those" of John Paul II.
9 Weigel, *The End and the Beginning*, 381.
10 Henri E. Cauvin, "President Offered in '83 to Meet with Hinckley," *Washington Post*, June 12, 2004. See also Craig Shirley, *Last Act: The Final Years and Emerging Legacy of Ronald Reagan* (Nashville: Thomas Nelson, 2015), 233.
11 See the tributes in the afterword of the revised edition of Kengor, *God and Ronald Reagan* (2005 edition), 340–42.
12 Q&A with Cardinal Pio Laghi, "How the Vatican Tried to Avert War," *National Catholic Register*, June 24, 2007; "Cardinal Pio Laghi (1922–2009)," *National Catholic Register*, January 25–31, 2009.
13 "Statement from Judge William Clark Regarding Ronald Reagan's Passing," issued by the Young America's Foundation, June 5, 2004.
14 Statement from Michael Reagan Regarding His Father's Passing, June 5, 2004.
15 David Von Drehle, "Reagan Hailed as Leader for 'the Ages,'" *Washington Post*, June 12, 2004.
16 Joanne Drake and several other Reagan Foundation/Library staff confirmed to me that Reagan himself chose the hymn.
17 E-mail exchange with Joanne Drake, October 1, 2007.
18 The official *Public Papers* of the Reagan presidency record one Reagan reference to the hymn "Ave Maria." In an April 10, 1988, speech to the National Association of Religious Broadcasters, Reagan told a funny story about his days as a radio announcer in Iowa in the early 1930s. The evangelist Aimee Semple McPherson was in Des Moines and Reagan was asked to interview her. Near the end of the interview, Reagan motioned to the control room to play a record. He said he expected "nothing less than the 'Ave Maria,'" and yet the technician chose "Minnie the Moocher's Wedding Day" by the Mills Brothers. It is a humorous story, but it is interesting that for a special religious hymn, even one selected for a Protestant evangelist, Reagan expected "Ave Maria."
19 E-mail exchanges with Joanne Drake, August 18, 19, and 21, 2014.
20 E-mail from Joanne Drake, August 29, 2012.
21 E-mail from Michael Reagan, July 20, 2007.
22 E-mail exchange with Ronan Tynan, March 18, 2013.

Chapter 38: April 2, 2005: Divine Mercy for John Paul II

1 Pope John Paul II, Angelus message on the Solemnity of the Assumption of the Blessed Virgin Mary, Castel Gandolfo, August 15, 2003.
2 Bertone, *The Last Secret of Fátima*, 20.
3 Ibid., 19.

4 Bertone wonders whether these letters are "among the documents... now jealously guarded by his [John Paul II's] personal secretary, Cardinal Stanisław Dziwisz." Bertone, *The Last Secret of Fátima*, 83.

5 Ibid., 27–28, 162–63.

6 Weigel, *The End and the Beginning*, 381.

7 Weigel, *Witness to Hope*, 834.

8 Faustina also claimed such visions of mercy from the Blessed Mother. "As for you," Mary reportedly told her, "you have to speak to the world about His great mercy and prepare the world for the Second Coming of Him who will come." The world would need mercy. Jesus, she maintained, gave her the same message: "Speak to the world about My mercy; let all mankind recognize My unfathomable mercy. It is a sign for the end times." See Kowalska, *Diary of Saint Maria Faustina Kowalska*, 260–61, 264, and 332.

9 John Paul II did not die on the thirteenth of the month, as Lúcia had. But Fátima watchers and even high-level Vatican officials noticed that the number thirteen, as Cardinal Bertone put it, "seems to have been fated to play a role" in the pope's life. The pope was shot on the thirteenth; he beatified Jacinta and Francisco on the thirteenth; the numbers in the date of his death, 4-2-2005, added up to thirteen; even the numbers in his *time* of death, 21:37 (9:37 P.M.), added up to thirteen. See Bertone, *The Last Secret of Fátima*, 12.

10 "Gorbachev Remembers Pope John Paul II," Radio Free Europe/Radio Liberty, interview with Gorbachev conducted on April 3, 2005, posted at http://www.rferl.org/content/article/1058353.html.

11 Mikhail S. Gorbachev, "My Partner, the Pope," *New York Times*, March 9, 1992.

12 The piece in the Turin-based *La Stampa* was published and then quoted and republished by many Western sources between March 3 and 9, 1992. The *New York Times* piece "My Partner, the Pope" was very similar and seems to be largely republished from Gorbachev's original *La Stampa* column.

13 Enzio Mauro and Paolo Mieli, "'He Is a Man of Integrity,' Pontiff Says of Gorbachev," *La Stampa*, March 9, 1992.

14 Weigel, *Witness to Hope*, 604–5.

15 As we have seen, Reagan thought Gorbachev might be a "closet Christian," which would have made the Soviet leader more than an unconscious instrument of a Providence he didn't understand. Some of Gorbachev's words and actions over the past two decades have caused others to wonder whether Reagan's suspicions were right. In a book published in 2000, Gorbachev referred to *homo sapiens* as "God's highest creation." That did not seem to be the assessment of an atheist, even if in that book he outlined a philosophy that was extremely humanistic and only vaguely spiritual. (See Gorbachev, *On My Country and the World*, 20–21, 93, 106, 193, 268.) In October 2003, Michael Reagan, a popular syndicated talk-radio host at the time, interviewed Gorbachev on stage for a live event hosted by the University of North Florida in Jacksonville. Reagan repeatedly pressed Gorbachev on whether he was a believer. Gorbachev repeatedly dodged the question—but he did say he was not a "doubter or atheist." (Michael Reagan shared this account in a conversation with me on February 11, 2004, and has discussed it with me many times since. The local Florida press ran a few stories on Reagan's interview with Gorbachev, but none mentioned Gorbachev's statements regarding his religious belief.) Then, in mid-March 2008, Gorbachev visited the Basilica of Saint Francis in Assisi, Italy. He was seen kneeling for a half hour before the tomb of Saint Francis, apparently in silent prayer. Gorbachev told reporters: "I feel very emotional to be here at such an important place not only for the Catholic faith, but for all humanity. It was through Saint Francis that I arrived at the Church, so it was important that I came to visit his tomb." The reporter from London's *Telegraph* capitalized "Church." Which "Church" did this refer to? Gorbachev also told the press, "Saint Francis is, for me, the alter Christus, the other Christ." This was enough for *The Telegraph* to declare in a headline, "MIKHAIL GORBACHEV ADMITS HE IS A CHRISTIAN." (Malcolm Moore, "Mikhail Gorbachev Admits He Is a Christian," *The Telegraph*

[London], March 19, 2008.) But Gorbachev quickly denied the reports, dismissing them as "fantasies." He said, "To sum up and avoid any misunderstandings, let me say that I have been and remain an atheist." (Ethan Cole, "Gorbachev Dispels 'Closet Christian' Rumors; Says He Is Atheist," *Christian Post*, March 24, 2008. See also Paul Kengor, "Red Herring: Mikhail Gorbachev's Not-Quite Conversion," *Christianity Today*, April 4, 2008.)

Despite Gorbachev's denials, Bill Clark took special notice of the events at Assisi. The former Soviet leader's statements at the tomb seemed too strong to dismiss. The Gorbachev connection to Francis was especially poignant to Clark because of Clark's longtime connection with Saint Francis, whose "Peace Prayer" he often recited with Reagan and had inscribed over the entrance to the chapel he built in California. Clark began working all his diplomatic contacts to reach Gorbachev. On April 9, 2008, he told me that he had heard from informed "religious friends" who knew Gorbachev that "the jury is still out" on whether Gorbachev was a Christian, and, in fact, "the word is that he has converted but doesn't quite know how to talk about it or deal with it publicly." Clark arranged to have a rare Russian translation of the works of Saint Francis hand-delivered to Gorbachev. That package also included a copy of *The Judge*, my book about Clark, which was largely a spiritual biography. Two weeks later, on April 24, Clark called and told me, off the record, that Gorbachev wanted to meet with him to talk about Saint Francis and the Christian faith generally; the meeting, said Clark, "is in the process of being arranged." The seventy-six-year-old Clark saw this as an opportunity to fulfill a duty to Ronald Reagan, who had died four years earlier. Reagan had always wondered whether Gorbachev was a believer, and now Clark saw an opening to discuss Christianity with the former Soviet leader.

Clark's meeting with Gorbachev was not to be. Their vast geographic differences made a meeting difficult. Just as important, Clark was suffering from advancing Parkinson's, the same disease that had afflicted the pope. His physical abilities were declining, and he suffered from diminishing confidence; he felt (unjustifiably) that the Parkinson's severely limited his mental effectiveness. Clark told me that on the rare occasions when Gorbachev was visiting California, he (Clark) did not feel "up to" a meeting, healthwise.

16 "Gorbachev Remembers Pope John Paul II."

17 John Paul II, *Memory and Identity*, 163.

18 In 2002, reports emerged that the pontiff had "absolved Bulgaria" and dismissed a "Bulgarian connection" in the shooting. I have always interpreted the pope's statement as absolving the Bulgarian *people*, or avoiding placing too much blame on Bulgaria specifically when other forces (chiefly in Moscow) had organized and directed Agca. Vatican spokesman Joaquín Navarro-Valls clarified, "The Holy Father... literally said, 'I never believed in the so-called Bulgarian connection because of my great esteem and respect for the Bulgarian people.'" See "Pope Clears Bulgaria over Shooting," CNN.com, March 24, 2002. Moreover, Cardinal Stanisław Dziwisz made a series of comments in his book *A Life with Karol* in which he dismissed a "so-called Bulgarian connection" while seeming to point to Moscow, suspecting, "at least hypothetically, that the KGB was behind whoever made the immediate decision." Dziwisz, *A Life with Karol*, 139–42.

19 These reports appeared in the international press, in sources ranging from Agence France-Presse to Catholic World News, mainly on March 30, 2005.

20 See Weigel, *The End and the Beginning*, 132; "Stasi Files Implicate KGB in Pope Shooting," *Deutsche Welle*, April 1, 2005.

21 See, among others, Philip Pullella, "Soviet Union Ordered Pope Shooting: Italy Commission," Reuters, March 2, 2006; Edward Pentin, "Bombshell Claim: Soviets Wanted Pope Killed," *National Catholic Register*, March 12–18, 2006, A1.

22 Pullella, "Soviet Union Ordered Pope Shooting: Italy Commission"; Pentin, "Bombshell Claim: Soviets Wanted Pope Killed."

23 Koehler, *Spies in the Vatican*, 129–30.

24 This is the language in correspondence from July 18, 2005. The source's words were provided to me via another CIA source who acted as an intermediary.

25 Discussion with Bill Clark, July 5, 2005.
26 E-mail exchanges with Michael Ledeen, April 13, 2015.
27 Pacepa and Rychlak, *Disinformation*, 187.
28 Brzezinski said this to Claire Sterling. Sterling, *The Time of the Assassins*, 198.
29 Zbigniew Brzezinski interviewed for the 2001 documentary *Witness to Hope*, on the life of Pope John Paul II, produced by W/R Productions, and based on the biography by George Weigel.
30 E-mails from George Weigel, April 17, 2014, and May 27, 2014.
31 E-mail exchanges with Tomasz Pompowski, March 3, 2006.
32 Koehler, *Spies in the Vatican*, 88–89.
33 "Did Gorby Order Hit on Pope John Paul II?" *World Net Daily*, May 6, 2008.
34 Weigel, *The End and the Beginning*, 115.
35 Quoted in Koehler, *Spies in the Vatican*, 88–89. According to Koehler, this interview of Gorbachev in *Il Tempo* appeared in the January 20, 2000, edition, which was long before Koehler reported on the document in his 2009 book.
36 "Reported: Another attempt to assassinate John Paul II," *Catholic World Report*, April 2009; and "Priest: 2 Others Plotted to Kill JP II," *National Catholic Register*, March 1–7, 2009.
37 "Report: KGB Wanted Pope Eliminated," Associated Press, November 3, 1999; Rory Carroll, "KGB Plotted to Kill Pope and Bug Vatican," *The Guardian* (London), November 3, 1999.
38 Dziwisz, *A Life with Karol*, 139–40.
39 Koehler, *Spies in the Vatican*, 130–34.
40 Thomas P. Melady, "John Paul II rejected assassination inquiry," *National Catholic Reporter*, April 29, 2005.
41 John Lukacs, *A Short History of the Twentieth Century* (Cambridge, MA: Belknap Press, 2013), 2.

EPILOGUE: JUNE 27, 2011: KINDRED SPIRITS, KINDRED SOULS

1 Mrs. Reagan, frail of health, did not attend, nor did any members of the Reagan family. Joanne Drake, Mrs. Reagan's longtime personal assistant, did attend. My profound gratitude to her for making me aware of this occasion and sharing program materials from the Mass. All information that I am quoting in this section comes from the materials handed out at the Mass, most of which had English translations aside the Polish. I first interviewed Joanne Drake about the thanksgiving Mass in August and September 2012 and did so again in August 2015, via direct conversation at the Reagan Library and also via e-mail correspondence.
2 "St. Mary's Basilica, Cracow," official guidebook (Wrocław, Poland: Wydawnictwo Zet, 2009), provided by Joanne Drake.
3 Lou Cannon, *President Reagan: The Role of a Lifetime* (New York: Simon and Schuster, 1991); Morris, *Dutch*, 531. No offense intended to Cannon and Morris, who are *far* from alone in giving short shrift to Reagan's relationship with John Paul II.
4 Mary Claire Kendall heard this from Martin Anderson in June 2009 when Anderson was speaking at the Heritage Foundation regarding his book *Reagan's Secret War*. Kendall reported on it at the time in an article for *The Wanderer*, "Reagan Revisited," August 6, 2009. She also wrote about it in "Seeing the Duke in a Whole New Light," Breitbart.com, June 11, 2009. I confirmed this with Kendall in e-mail exchanges on November 24–25, 2015. I followed up by e-mailing Annelise Anderson, Martin's spouse and coauthor, for confirmation on November 27, 2015. (Martin Anderson had since passed away.) Annelise responded with an e-mail on December 9, 2015, in which she confirmed: "I remember the event—Martin and I were both there. And we talked to Mary Claire afterward, as well. I think Mary Claire's article is an accurate reflection

of her (Mary's) conversation, or interview, with Martin." Annelise did, however, add a caveat: "I think 'close friends' is not a good description of the relationship.... RR and JPII were not 'pals' in the sense of friends who get together and talk about 'stuff.' My guess is that neither one of them had friends of that type. They were both too busy." I make the same observation in this epilogue. Annelise made another point similar to one I make in this book: she listed some of the many commonalities between the two men and added, "There's enough here of interest without getting into the question of what it means to be a 'friend' and what 'closest' means." Precisely. The key point is that they shared unique bonds and were united in a pursuit of an objective of supreme importance, politically, historically, and spiritually.

5 In his long life, Reagan considered many people to be good friends, and surely he called more than one of these his "best friend" at one time or another. His close friends included Charlie Wick, Bill Clark, Bill Wilson, and A. C. Lyles, among others. Mary Claire Kendall quotes Lyles as referring to the legendary John Wayne as an "extremely close friend" of Reagan. (Kendall, "Seeing the Duke in a Whole New Light.") Some Reagan biographers have insisted that Reagan was a "distant" person who had no best friend, and perhaps not even any close friends. This assertion is unfounded. A full book could be written on Reagan's many close friends, with whom he exchanged countless letters. Did he have a single "best friend"? Probably not, even though he referred to John Paul II as just that. Not all men, however, can identify a single best friend. I would hazard that most men cannot.

6 Interview with Frank Shakespeare, February 21, 2013.

7 Interview with Shakespeare.

8 Frank Shakespeare speaking to the Schoenstatt Heights community.

9 Ronald Reagan was not Catholic, but as we have seen, he was surrounded by Catholics in his family and on his staff. He understood the Church well and respected the Catholic faith. Robert Reilly, who served as President Reagan's liaison to the Catholic community, quipped to me, "We considered Reagan an honorary Catholic." (E-mail correspondence with Robert Reilly, September 3, 2015.)

Few realize how devout Reagan's first wife, Jane Wyman, became. In fact, at the time of this writing, the only mention of Wyman's being a Catholic on her Wikipedia page is a single line that cites my book *God and Ronald Reagan* as the source. Wyman was known as an Academy Award–winning film actress who also had a lead role in the hit 1980s TV series *Falcon Crest*. After her fourth and final divorce, in her forties, she chose to remain single the rest of her life; the Church became her closest companion. She attended daily Mass for more than fifty years, according to her son, Michael. So pious was Wyman that when she starred on *Falcon Crest*, she had it written into her contract that she would have her own priest on staff for daily Mass and the Eucharist. Unbeknownst to Hollywood and the wider world, Wyman quietly became a Third Order Dominican nun, living according to the order's rules and guidelines. She took vows with the sisters and joined their community. When she died on September 10, 2007, at age ninety, she was buried in habit and full regalia according to her sisterly order.

Reagan and Wyman's son, Michael, returned to the Catholic Church in 2010, when his wife, Colleen, and daughter, Ashley, were received into the Church.

Ronald Reagan's brother, Neil Reagan, and Neil's wife, Bess, were daily communicants. Neil picked up and relit the torch that Jack Reagan, his father, had let go out. Robert Reilly remembers a remarkable statement Neil Reagan made about his brother: asked whether there was anything else he could wish for his brother, given that Ronald had been a movie and TV star, governor, and president, Neil responded, "Yes, I wish he would become a Catholic." (E-mail correspondence with Reilly, September 2–4, 2015.)

10 "Homily of His Holiness Pope Benedict XVI," Holy Mass, Esplanade of the Shrine of Our Lady of Fátima, May 13, 2010, http://w2.vatican.va/content/benedict-xvi/en/homilies/2010/documents/hf_ben-xvi_hom_20100513_fatima.html.

Index

INTERCOLLEGIATE
STUDIES INSTITUTE
Educating for Liberty